Computer Graphics and Virtual Environments

From Realism to Real-time

We work with leading authors to develop the
strongest educational materials in computer science,
bringing cutting-edge thinking and best
learning practice to a global market.

Under a range of well-known imprints, including
Addison-Wesley, we craft high quality print and
electronic publications which help readers to understand
and apply their content, whether studying or at work.

To find out more about the complete range of our
publishing, please visit us on the World Wide Web at:

www.pearsoneduc.com

Computer Graphics and Virtual Environments

From Realism to Real-time

MEL SLATER, ANTHONY STEED AND YIORGOS CHRYSANTHOU

University College London

Addison-Wesley

An imprint of **Pearson Education**

Harlow, England · London · New York · Reading, Massachusetts · San Francisco · Toronto · Don Mills, Ontario · Sydney
Tokyo · Singapore · Hong Kong · Seoul · Taipei · Cape Town · Madrid · Mexico City · Amsterdam · Munich · Paris · Milan

Pearson Education Limited
Edinburgh Gate
Harlow
Essex CM20 2JE

and Associated Companies throughout the world

Visit us on the World Wide Web at:
www.pearsoneduc.com

First published 2002

ISBN 0 201 62420 6

British Library Cataloguing-in-Publication Data
A catalogue record for this book is available from the British Library

Library of Congress Cataloging-in-Publication Data
Slater, Mel.
  Computer graphics and virtual environments: from realism to real-time / Mel Slater, Anthony Steed, and Yiorgos Chrysanthou.
      p. cm.
  Includes bibliographical references and index.
  ISBN 0-201-62420-6
    1. Computer graphics. 2. Virtual reality. I. Steed, Anthony. II. Chrysanthou, Yiorgos.
  III. Title

  T385 .S59 2001
  006–dc21
                                                                2001034338

10 9 8 7 6 5 4 3 2 1
06 05 04 03 02

Typeset in 9/12 Stone Serif by 35
Printed and bound in the United States of America

- To Yvonne, Laurence and Freda – Mel
- To Rachel and my parents – Anthony
- To Isabelle, Melina and Athena – Yiorgos

Contents

Part 6 From realism to real-time II

Preface

Real-time virtual environments are a fundamental part of the revolution in communications that has taken place at an ever-increasing pace over the past decade. We can watch news presented by virtual newscasters, play first-person 3D graphically based games with other players distributed over the world, soon we are likely to be arguing for loans with virtual bank managers. Computer graphics is both a driving technology for virtual environments and also driven by the real-time demands of such systems. In conflict with the need for real-time there is also a quest for greater and greater realism in what may be displayed. This book addresses the science of computer graphics in the context of real-time virtual environments. We aim to show, at an introductory level, how a real-time graphics system may be built, and what has to be sacrificed from the point of view of realism in order to achieve this. We also pay attention to the perceptual, dynamic and interaction aspects of virtual environments, together with associated display and interaction devices.

As a textbook in the field of 3D computer graphics and virtual environments, our presentation is unusual in a number of ways. We adopt the philosophy of presenting material on a "need to know" basis. We start the book with very high level descriptions of perceptual issues related to virtual environments, lighting, and color perception, as well as the necessary mathematics needed to understand the book. We then immediately turn to a more practical approach and show how one of the most popular methods for producing high quality globally illuminated, "photo-realistic" images may be easily implemented, using ray tracing. We then gradually move towards a real-time system by relaxing the assumptions of ray tracing, chapter after chapter, until we have presented a system that can generate images of 3D scenes in real-time. In other words, we describe the typical rendering pipeline of a graphics system. Traditional computer graphics is based on point-light sources which (at best) may be used to generate "hard" looking shadows. In the quest towards greater illumination realism, while still staying within the ambit of a real-time system, we show how "softer" more realistic looking shadows may be generated. We then return to the issue of generating globally illuminated photo-realistic images using the radiosity algorithm, which by the way uses real-time methods for rendering (under certain conditions). Then we return again to ray tracing, and introduce a number of techniques that speed this up (although it would still certainly not be real-time).

This book is genuinely "top down" in its approach. For example, we motivate the clipping and rendering of 2D lines in the context of methods necessary for speeding up ray tracing (how to trace a line through a uniformly subdivided space is similar to how a line is rendered on a 2D display device). We believe that this approach is pedagogically sound – the problem of clipping or rendering lines in 2D is not, in itself, too interesting, but motivated by the needs of higher level operations (such as ray tracing or radiosity) these fundamental algorithms are brought to life, and also crucially illustrate a way of thinking that goes beyond their particular application. Really a computer graphics course should be teaching this "way of thinking" rather than just a set of techniques.

The book has an "interlude" from rendering by discussing two approaches to modeling, based on constructive solid geometry and curves and surfaces. We then turn to issues directly concerned with virtual environments: dynamics and interaction within virtual worlds.

The final two chapters retrace the steps from realism to real-time but at a higher level. One chapter presents a survey of modern techniques for global illumination, such as path tracing and photon tracing. The final chapter reviews a number of methods for increasing the frame-rate for real-time graphics systems: based on visibility, level of detail techniques, and image-based rendering. The final part of this chapter introduces a new "light field" paradigm for computer graphics.

The book includes examples from two very popular and important systems: VRML as a scene description language, and OpenGL as a real-time rendering system. Examples are given in a C-like notation, as we believe C to be a common denominator for readers who know C, C++, or Java.

Unlike many textbooks we have not relegated the mathematics to an appendix. A reasonable grounding in mathematics, with knowledge and experience such as might be available to an undergraduate computer science student, is essential to the understanding of this book, and we have been up-front about this and put it in Chapter 2, with various other pieces of mathematics distributed throughout the book. However, no matter what it looks like at first glance *there is no hard mathematics in this book.* If $\int_B \int_A f(x, y)dxdy$ scares you then it shouldn't! All it means is that a function is evaluated at a point (x, y) and multiplied by a small area $(dx \times dy)$ around that point. The small "volume" that results is summed over an area of the XY plane given by x in the region A and y in the region B. You do not have to understand how to actually evaluate integrals analytically in order to understand this book. However, you will need to understand (at least sometimes) what expressions such as the above mean at a general level.

This book is aimed at senior year undergraduates (typically final year BSc Computer Science students) or postgraduates studying computer graphics or the visual aspects of virtual environments. It can be used for an approximately full semester (30–45 hours) course. The aim of the book is to give students practical knowledge of the fundamentals of the graphics rendering pipeline, modern techniques to maximize the frame rate, and also some in-depth information about rendering photo-realistic images. The major focus of the book, in terms of motivation, is virtual environments. We therefore take care not simply to present algorithms for computer graphics, but to put these in the context of VEs and some of the basic underlying perceptual issues in these areas.

One path through the book for an undergraduate course might be as follows: start the lectures with Chapter 5, which introduces ray casting in the context of a simple scene made of spheres. The purpose of this is that from day one the students are involved in the actual process of building a system that will (very soon) allow them to generate globally illuminated scenes with ray tracing. Meanwhile devote discussion sessions and tutorials to Chapters 1 through 4, which cover perceptual issues (do the simple perceptual experiments described in that chapter; they can be a great deal of fun as well as being educational), check over the mathematics in Chapter 2 (not everyone will be familiar with all the concepts described in that chapter), then crucially devote resources to Chapter 3 on the general problem of lighting and the radiance equation. Almost certainly one or two lectures as well as discussion groups should be devoted to this, since the radiance equation is essentially what computer graphics rendering is all about, and the radiance equation acts as a unifying principle for all the chapters on rendering. Then continue to discuss color perception (Chapter 4). Meanwhile the lectures can move on to ray tracing, and the students given ray tracing programming assignments to carry out (just for simple scenes containing spheres). Within about three weeks the students will be generating ray traced images (a great boost to confidence) and know something about the central equation of graphics rendering – the radiance equation.

Chapters 7 through 13, which show how to build a real-time system; can be motivated by asking a few questions. Why is ray tracing so slow? How can we represent scenes with objects other than spheres? How can we render from an arbitrary virtual camera position? If we lose the global illumination characteristics of ray tracing, how can we shade anything? If each point within each object has to be shaded, how is it possible to have real-time rendering? If we lose the automatic visibility computations of ray tracing, how can we compute visibility in general scenes? By the end of Chapter 13 the readers should have a very good idea of how to build a complete 3D graphics system, starting from one single primitive function: how to set a pixel to a specific color. So although our approach is "top down," in the last instance it is also "bottom up," since that is the ultimate point of Chapters 7 through 13 – how to build such a system from the bottom up.

A certain type of undergraduate course can then move straight to Chapter 15, and sample how radiosity solutions are achieved. Then round things out with a return to ray tracing in Chapter 16 – how to speed this up. Finally complete the course by studying Chapter 17 – the most basic of graphics algorithms, how to clip and render lines (remember that the motivation for these operations would have been given in the faster ray tracing chapter, Chapter 16).

Now a more in-depth course would have followed Chapters 7 through 13 with a close look at how shadows can be generated in real-time (Chapter 14) before studying radiosity and then faster ray tracing. The chapters on constructive solid geometry and curves and surfaces for computer aided geometric design are stand-alone. Such a more in-depth course could then move to Chapters 22 and 23 which discuss more advanced issues in global illumination and real-time rendering.

If the reader is also interested in interaction within virtual environments, and common problems within real-time interaction systems such as collision detection, then it is a good idea to take a break from rendering and study Chapters 20 and 21 at this point.

The earliest version of this book was written in 1991 when one of the authors (MS) was teaching the CS184 (Foundations of Computer Graphics) course at University of California Berkeley. Since those early days the book has grown enormously, being used at Queen Mary, University of London for the Interactive Computer Graphics course during 1992–95, and for Computer Graphics at University College London, since 1995. Versions of it have also been used at the University of Lancaster, and at the University of Cape Town in South Africa. It has also been used on Masters courses at UC Berkeley in 1992, Queen Mary 1992–95 and at UCL on both computer graphics and virtual environments courses. MS moved from Queen Mary to UCL in 1995, and was soon accompanied by former PhD students YC and AJS, who have since joined the faculty at UCL. The three of us collaborated on the computer graphics teaching, and this book is the product of that collaboration.

Mel Slater, Anthony Steed and Yiorgos Chrysanthou
London, April 2001

Acknowledgements

This book would not have been possible without the assistance of many people. We would especially like to thank Martin Usoh, Tony Tsung-Yueh Lin, and Edwin Blake all of whom have been associated with earlier stages in the development of this book. Jesper Mortensen, Joao Oliveira, David-Paul Pertaub, and Franco Tecchia helped in the production of some of the figures. We would like to thank Christian Babski, Mireille Clavien, Ioannis Douros, George Drettakis, Neil Gatenby, David Hedley, Marc Levoy, Alf Linney, Céline Loscos, David Luebke, Alan Penn, Claudio Privitera, Bernard Spanlang, Lawrence Stark, Daniel Thalman, Tzvetomir Vassilev, Greg Ward, Mary Whitton, Peter Wonka and Hansong Zhang for making material for figures available, and to Amy Goldstein for modeling. We would also like to thank the following for their assistance in various ways: Alan Chalmers, Daniel Cohen-Or, Rabin Ezra, Patrick M. Hanrahan, Phil Huxley, David Mizell, Jan-Peter Muller, Gareth Smith, and Shankar N. Swamy.

We would like to thank the following companies and organizations: Center for Parallel Computers (PDC) Royal Institute of Technology Stockholm, Lightworks, SGI, and Virtual Research Systems Inc.

A special thanks to the staff at Pearson Education, in particular to Keith Mansfield who has helped and encouraged us over the years, and Senior Editor Mary Lince who has guided us through the final stages to the preparation of this book.

Finally we would like to thank our graphics students over the years at University College London, Queen Mary London, and University of California Berkeley who were the fundamental inspiration for this work.

A Companion Website accompanies *Computer Graphics and Virtual Environments* by Mel Slater, Anthony Steed and Yiorgos Chrysanthou.

Visit the *Computer Graphics and Virtual Environments* Companion Website at www.booksites.net/slater

Here you will find valuable teaching and learning material including:

For Students:
• End of chapter exercises.

For Lecturers:
• Powerpoint slides for teaching.

For Students and Lecturers:
• Class libraries to accompany the book in C and Java to run on Windows, Irix and Linux systems

1

Introduction: a phantom world of projections

"What is a real world, don Juan?"

"A world that generates energy; the opposite of a phantom world of projections, where nothing generates energy, like most of our dreams, where nothing has an energetic effect."

Carlos Casteneda, *The Art of Dreaming*,
HarperCollins Publishers, New York, 1993, p. 164

1.1   Introduction

Computer graphics is concerned with the modeling, lighting, and dynamics of virtual worlds and the means by which people act within them. It creates the "phantom world of projections." The "phantom world" today is called a "virtual environment" or a "virtual reality." It is in a very literal sense a "world of projections" – *three-dimensional representations* of objects are *projected* to *two-dimensional displays*. People see and interact with the phantom objects formed by the images on these displays and experience an illusory alternate reality. People may act as if they were in that alternate reality, the real world around them becoming distant and dim. Their activity within the alternate reality in itself reinforces and informs their internal mental models which are at the heart of the illusion of reality.

The computer that stores the abstract representations and runs the programs and hardware that eventually creates the 2D displayed images may be linked by a network to other computers displaying different views of this same phantom world to other people. The people engaged in this may themselves be represented in the virtual reality as three dimensional entities projected to the 2D displays – and thus be able to see and interact with one another – independently of the real physical distance between them. Hence the virtual reality becomes a shared and social reality.

Such networked virtual environments exist today – with the capability of creating wide area virtual social realities with thousands of simultaneous participants (Singhal and Zyda, 1999). They are created with technology from many fields, since they must maintain a wide area heterogeneous network supporting visual, auditory, and ideally touch and force-feedback displays and interactive input devices.

1.2 Scope

This book is concerned with the *visual* aspects of virtual environments – creating, lighting, and visually displaying the three-dimensional virtual environment, and allowing people to interact with it.

We adopt a novel "top down" approach. We begin in this chapter to consider the perceptual reasons, rooted in the human visual system, as to why virtual environments work at all. The next chapter is devoted to the highest and most abstract level – some of the fundamental mathematics required for computer graphics. In Chapter 3 we consider, still at a very abstract level, the problem of illumination, that is, lighting of environments that consist of graphical objects and show that 3D graphics rendering is fundamentally concerned with the solution of an equation that describes light energy at any point in an environment. In the subsequent chapter (Chapter 4) we consider the response of the human visual system to that lighting in the perception of color.

We then start on a path from a particular method of rendering scenes with a relatively realistic method of illumination rendering called "ray tracing" which simulates some of the global characteristics of lighting in an environment. In chapter after chapter we relax the assumptions of ray tracing and show how a system capable of real-time rendering, but at the cost of illumination simplicity, can be achieved.

We then turn to an alternative method for a certain kind of illumination realism called "radiosity," and then again turn back to ray tracing to examine methods for achieving this at faster speeds. This discussion of ray tracing motivates the most primitive of graphics operations such as drawing a straight line in 2D on a display.

This approach is "back to front" compared with the usual approaches to computer graphics, which often starts with low-level primitive operations such as drawing lines and polygons, moving on through 2D graphics architecture, and finally to 3D. The philosophy of this book, however, is to start from the highest level and introduce concepts and methods as they are needed. So primitive operations such as 2D line and polygon rendering and clipping are left to the last instance.

The treatment up to that point in the book is almost entirely based on considering the world as if it were made of flat polygons or triangles. We relax this assumption and show how to generate solid models of curved objects in Chapter 18 and curved surfaces in Chapter 19.

This completes the first part of the book – a path from a certain kind of realism to graphics systems that support real-time rendering. Having shown how such a rendering system is constructed we discuss the issues of dynamics (Chapter 20) and interaction (Chapter 21) within virtual worlds.

Finally, we briefly trace the path again from realism to real-time. We include a survey chapter on more sophisticated rendering methods for photo-realism (Chapter 22), and a survey chapter on some of the latest techniques for real-time performance (Chapter 23).

The remainder of this introductory chapter will discuss some aspects of the modeling components of computer graphics and virtual environments. We will introduce some basic ideas and terminology, and continue with a discussion of the issue as to why virtual reality "works" at all.

1.3 Modeling and virtual environments

Objects

The origin of computer graphics is generally agreed as being marked by publication of the seminal paper by Ivan Sutherland, describing the Sketchpad System (Sutherland, 1963). Sutherland's system (Figure 1.1) allowed users to interactively draw on a screen, using a pointing device called a "light pen." Many of the concepts that we take for granted today were invented for this system: for example, the idea of a "rubber band line" – that is, stretching out a line across the display as if it were a rubber band, with it staying in place in the position in which it was released. The ideas behind two-dimensional viewing ("windows," "viewports," and "clipping") were also invented for this system. Most importantly – and this is the issue that separates computer graphics from just being a medium for the presentation of pictures – the concept of a *graphical object* was invented, that is, an entity with its own semantics and interactive behavior – albeit in a primitive form, but nevertheless the starting point for a new science.

For the time being we can think of an object as an encapsulated, self-contained "thing" – that has structure and behavior – typically embodied in software: an instance of a data structure and a set of functions. A simple example is the marking of a single point in some space. The object has a visual representation (or many possible visual representations), and has a behavior in

Figure 1.1
Ivan Sutherland at work
on the Sketchpad System

response to the "messages" that form part of its own semantics (e.g., move the marker to another point). Another simple example is everything that goes into making a "button" which is part of an interactive program. The button exists as a piece of software, it has a visual representation, and it has behavior that responds to certain events (typically mouse events).

Once we have the capability to define a set of independent (but possibly mutually interacting) objects, there is the possibility of defining a new "world" – a set of entities following laws and behaviors built into them by the computer program that brings the stuff of the world into being. In an application the illusion of a world is maintained by the interactions between this basic stuff of the world, which people perceive as things, the graphical objects, and the high-level internal cognitive models of the group of people interacting within it. Their behaviors are themselves embodied in that world through objects that represent them – typically each person is represented by a virtual character, or *avatar*, whose dynamics corresponds in some fashion to the activities, behavior, and movements of their physical human counterparts. Computer graphics gives us the ability to visually depict this world with an infinite variety of possible representations.

Such worlds are commonly called "Virtual Environments" (VEs). Ellis (1991) has provided a useful analytic framework for the discussion of such VEs. He classifies a virtual environment as having three major components: content, geometry, and dynamics. The content consists of the "objects" that make up the environment, the geometry consists of dimension, metric and the extent or boundaries of the environment, and the dynamics consists of the rules of interaction between the objects (for example, how a button responds to a mouse event, or in physical simulations, how objects respond to collisions with other objects). In the next section we consider the content and in Chapter 2 the geometry.

Content of a VE

The content of an environment is to do with how it is modeled. An environment contains a set of objects, as discussed above. At any moment in time any object has a *description* and a *state*. The description includes information about its geometry, substance, and potential behaviors. The geometric description is relative to some coordinate frame (we will discuss this more thoroughly in Chapter 2). It determines unambiguously the location and orientation of the object at that point of time, and its relation to other objects, within the environment. The *state* determines unambiguously the state of the object – which depends on the semantics of that object in relation to the rest of the environment.

A special subset of the objects are called actors. An *actor* is an object that can initiate an interaction with another object or actor. It can do this through information exchange. There is a special actor, a human operator, or *participant* in the environment. The participant has a visual representation within the environment (e.g., a cursor in the simplest possible graphical application, a full humanoid representation, an avatar, in more sophisticated applications). A more complex example was provided by Neal Stephenson in his 1993 novel *Snow Crash* (Bantam Books, paperback). The *Metaverse* is a three-dimensional virtual world that humans can enter into embodied as "Avatars" – typically 3D graphical representations of the human body (or something approximating this). But some objects, supposedly Avatars, were really system Daemons representing processes carried out by the computer systems maintaining the Metaverse in human form. In William Gibson's novels (e.g., *Neuromancer*, Ace Books) such non-human entities are called AIs.

In Figure 1.2 we show a schematic representation of a shared VE system. We suppose that the computer stores a database representing the set of all objects in the scene. Each object has a geometric description, for example a collection of primitive shapes out of which it is constructed. This may be at a relatively high level (such as a description in terms of objects that are defined by equations, such as spheres or cylinders) or more typically relatively low level, in terms of a set of triangles that tessellate the surface of the object. Each object will have information regarding its material and physical properties, and in particular how it reflects light (its radiant properties). Other information may also be provided, such as its acoustic properties (e.g., is it a sound source?) and behavioral properties (e.g., how does it respond if prodded or probed?). The scene

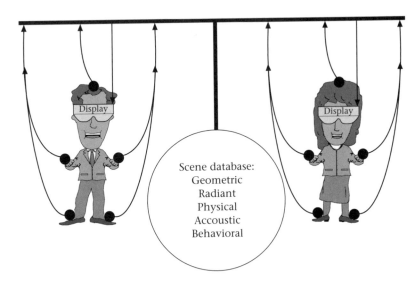

Figure 1.2
Schematic for a shared
virtual environment system

database is the total description of all the objects and any other information required to give an unambiguous specification of the entire scene.

This database must be stored somewhere on the computer network that maintains the shared virtual environment. For example, it might be copied to every machine, or there might be one master copy, segments of which are distributed as needed to each machine. There are many different strategies for distributing and updating a VE and the interested reader is referred to Singhal and Zyda (1999). Each computer on the network typically supports one human participant. Each participant is the recipient of display information, such as the visual, auditory, and any other information such as tactile or force feedback data, forming the sensory input from the VE to that person. In the ideal situation, this virtual sensory data provides sensory input on all sensory systems and fully encloses the participant in those displays. This is an ideal that is never achieved – more typically only the visual and auditory systems are included, and there is always information from the real world, so that the participant is never entirely fully enclosed.

The small circular blobs in Figure 1.2 represent tracking devices. The participants have their sense data determined by the VE system, and also their own movements are tracked, and fed back into the system. The tracking system in particular therefore determines the sensory displays as a function of head and body tracking. For example, a participant looking in one direction will see and hear different aspects of the VE compared to another direction. The participant can bend down, for example, and see underneath a virtual table. The tracking data determines where the head and body of the participant is, and therefore displays sensory information appropriate to that viewpoint and bodily orientation. Typically in a VE system only the position and orientation of the head and one hand are tracked (see Chapters 20 and 21).

What happens when in a VE the participant looks down at his or her own body? There are two alternative situations. In the first, and most common situation, the participant wears a head-mounted display (see below) which displays the environment as a function of head-tracking. One of the objects in the scene database will be a representation of the participant's body, a virtual body, which will change according to the actions of person: when he puts out his hand, the corresponding virtual hand will be put out. The scene database description of this avatar is therefore updated according to the tracking information of the person that it represents. If a participant on another node in the shared VE looks at a moving person, they will see the avatar representing that person move. Changes to the scene database must somehow be distributed to all nodes in the environment, so that – of course subject to network delays – they are all experiencing the same (virtual) reality.

There is another possibility: the participant might be in a "CAVE" (Figures 1.3 (color plate) and 20.2). "CAVE" stands for CAVE Automatic Virtual Environment (Cruz-Neira *et al.*, 1993). The CAVE concept and first implementation was at the University of Illinois at Chicago in 1992. Ideally a "CAVE" is a room that has all six walls as projection screens, on which a virtual environment (VE) is projected. A participant wears lightweight stereo glasses with a head-tracking device mounted. The displays show alternate left- and right-eye images and the stereo glasses are in sync with them, allowing only a left-eye image to enter the left eye, and similarly for the right eye (see the discussion of stereo below). The head-tracker is used to compute the eye-position of the wearer, and from a computation based on inter-ocular distance, the distance between the two eyes, stereo projections are computed (for each of the six walls). The glasses are based on a shutter technology used to present the alternate left/right eye frames to the viewer, who is then immersed in a completely surrounding VE. In practice "CAVE"s are commonly four-walled, consisting of front, left and right wall displays, and the floor. The projection system and software is organized so that participants are typically not aware of the corners of the physical room. Several people can be situated in the "CAVE" at the same time, though the display is completely correct for only one participant. The "CAVE" can also be multi-participant in the sense that avatars of people at physically remote sites can be present in the "CAVE," and therefore people at several locations can simultaneously inhabit the same shared space. Unlike a head-mounted display, a person in a "CAVE" will see his or her own real body, as in Figure 1.3. However, a person at a remote site will see an avatar representing that person.

1.4   Realism and real-time

Virtual environments must be displayed and the participants tracked in real-time in order for these to work at all. At the same time, what they display must be sufficiently realistic in order for people to be able to maintain the illusion of being in an alternate reality. However, there is a tension between these two

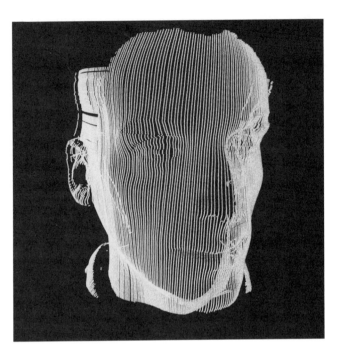

Figure 1.4
Laser scan of a human face
produces a 3D point-cloud
Courtesy of Joao Oliveira,
Department of Computer
Science, UCL

requirements. Before considering that, let's consider the several different meanings of the term "realism" in computer graphics.

Geometric realism

By "geometric realism" we mean that a graphical object has a close geometric resemblance to the real-world object being depicted. For example, there might be a complete and detailed architectural plan for a building, irrespective of whether or not the building exists physically. Although such plans are often represented as two-dimensional drawings, it is possible to construct 3D representations from the complete 2D information. Thus the dimensions of each wall, window, partition, and each interior object such as lights, tables, chairs, have exactly the same dimensional measurements as their real counterpart. Typically the 3D geometric representation is in terms of planar polygons (usually triangles), which cover the surface shape of the object as a patchwork. The more curved the object is in some region, the greater the number of triangles that are needed in order to preserve the close correspondence between the physical and virtual reality.

Figure 1.4 shows an image of a human face obtained from an optical surface scanner developed at UCL[1] (Figure 1.5). The particular face shown consists of

---

1. http://www.gene.ucl.ac.uk/face/

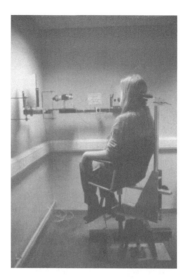

Figure 1.5
Face scanner
Courtesy of Alf Linney,
Department of Medical
Physics, UCL

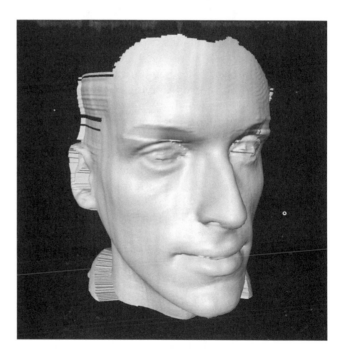

Figure 1.6
A rendering of the
laser scanned face
Courtesy of Joao Oliveira,
Department of Computer
Science, UCL

64028 (x, y, z) points (also referred to as *vertices*). The scanning process took approximately 10 seconds. In order to be usable for 3D graphics display, the points are organized into triangles. In this case 126108 triangles were obtained. The surface can be shaded and images can be produced such as that shown in Figure 1.6. This can be rotated in three dimensions, and thus displayable in different orientations.

A practical reason for geometric realism is in *virtual prototyping*. An object, installation, aircraft, building, or whatever the case may be is constructed virtually as part of the process of planning to build the real physical version. This may be part of the design process, or to examine the impact of the object on placement in its location, or to prototype its possible usage in situ.

Figure 1.7 (color plate) shows a virtual model of the London Millennium Eye. This model was constructed as part of the process of design of the usage of the space behind the Eye itself. Note that the model is geometrically accurate but still does not look real because the lighting and shading are not realistic.

Figure 1.8 (color plate) shows a very interesting application of virtual prototyping. The Maitreya Project aims to construct a 500 ft (152.4 m) statue of the Maitreya Buddha in Bodhgaya India. This statue is to last 1,000 years, set in a landscaped park including monasteries, meditation pavilions, a school, hospital, and study centres. Figure 1.8(a) shows a physical scale model of the statue made by artists which was used to produce a virtual prototype by laser scanning. The resulting virtual model can be used to get some idea of the enormous scale of the eventual real statue, in situ in Bodhgaya (Figure 1.8(b)). By locating the model in virtual reality people can virtually walk through the park and have some idea of what it will eventually be like to be in the actual park with the real statue, still many years away from actual construction. The virtual model is also being used by the artists to refine the design of the statue itself, for example by trying out different facial structures. The statue is seated on a throne, which has also been modeled virtually.

Virtual prototyping applications create geometrically real representations for an essential reason: often the geometry is used as the blueprint for the real physical object to be constructed. Another reason for geometrical accuracy is where the virtual model is to be used for a kind of rehearsal of events that are to take place in a real-life setting. For example, a model of fire pump outlet valves may be used by maintenance engineers in order to practice and to teach maintenance (Figure 1.9, color plate). If the geometry is not accurate then "negative skill transfer" may take place – the trainee may learn a skill in the virtual world which actually worsens performance in the real world.

Illumination realism

The virtual statue in Figure 1.8(b) looks real not only in a geometric sense, but also with respect to its illumination (although the surroundings are not correct in this regard). In fact the illumination is computed corresponding to how the statue would reflect sunlight on a particular day in the year, taking into account the time of day and therefore the angle of the sun. Part of virtual prototyping in this application also involves considerations of lighting – how the statue looks in situ does not depend simply on its physical surroundings, but on its relationship to sunlight.

Such illumination realism is of great importance in many applications of computer graphics, the most prominent example being architectural design. It is critical for architects to understand how their constructions will look under different lighting conditions, both natural and artificial, for lighting often has a bearing not just on aesthetics but also on functionality – for example, poorly lit areas of a city may be avoided because of anticipated crime.

As we shall see in Chapter 3, the computation of correct lighting is an extremely complex and computationally intensive aspect of computer graphics. The Buddha picture is relatively simple in terms of lighting – for only one object is lit, and interreflections between objects are not taken into account at all. Correct lighting of an interior architectural scene, however, must take into account the interreflections between all surfaces in the scene, not just the impact of the lights on each object individually.

The latter approach is called *local illumination* – each object is lit as if it were the only object in the scene apart from the light sources. *Global illumination* refers to a correct computation of the distribution of light in an environment, where inter-object reflections are taken into account. The images produced by such a method are sometimes referred to as *photo-realistic*, meaning that in principle such images should be indistinguishable from those taken by a real camera of the corresponding real scene under appropriate real lighting conditions (Figure 1.10, color plate).

Behavioral realism

A graphical object might not be the geometric representation of anything real at all, or perhaps an enormous simplification of something real, and also its lighting may be completely incorrect in comparison to physics. Nevertheless, such an object may seem to be completely "real" in some sense to an observer: for example, it may be a crude depiction of a human being, which nevertheless arouses an emotional state in observers.

Figure 1.11 (color plate) shows a snapshot from a virtual reality application that is concerned with developing a therapeutic treatment program for people who have a phobia of speaking in public (Pertaub *et al.*, 2001). Looking at this image it is clear that the characters depicted are not real, and the seminar room is likewise not real. People enter into a virtual reality and give a talk in front of the virtual audience. When the audience behaves in a hostile or bored manner, the human speakers exhibit signs of anxiety, and report a much higher level of anxiety compared to when the audience behaves in a way that is interested and friendly. Yet the human speakers know for sure that there is no "audience" there. This reaction cannot be caused by geometric realism in the virtual characters, because clearly they are not geometrically real. The response is caused by a degree of behavioral realism – the audience members have dynamic facial expressions, blink, make eye contact with the speaker, fidget and shuffle in their chairs, and generally give an exaggerated kind of behavioral

Figure 1.12
Cartoon of President
Clinton
Courtesy of Billy O'Keefe

realism – a characterization of audience friendliness or hostility. It appears that the human speakers in front of such virtual audiences can't but help respond to such behavior, even though intellectually they know full well that the audience behaviors are entirely the result of a pre-scripted computer animation program.

Generally cartoons work precisely because of their behavioral realism. Imagine a famous cartoon character, such as Donald Duck. It looks like nothing real on earth. Yet we recognize and respond to the emotional expressions depicted by the character, and indeed happily watch whole movies of its adventures. The stories are then told by people to one another just as if they were describing real events. The art of creating believable cartoon characters has been studied by animators such as Disney's, and are of great value in understanding what is important about the characterization of emotional expression (Thomas and Johnston, 1981).

Caricatures, impressionism, and iconic representation

Figure 1.12 shows a cartoon drawing of a famous person. We all immediately recognize the caricature of President Clinton – yet from the point of view of realism it looks in fact nothing like the "real" President. We recognize the President because the cartoon relies on our existing internal visual cognitive model of the President. It exaggerates certain key features which provide a match to our internal representations. Most of the work involved in the depiction is in fact going on inside the minds of the perceivers. The image "lies in the beholder," to paraphrase a famous saying. It is the skill of the artist to

Figure 1.14
A child's drawing
Courtesy of Amy Goldstein,
aged 6

understand those features that are essential, and which can be exaggerated in order to present an illusion that works.

In the world of art there have always been movements offering alternative representational approaches. Various schools of Realism believe that the purpose of art is to represent "reality." This was taken to an extreme in the Soviet Union under Stalin, where the style of "Socialist Realism" came to mean that art was supposed to present a true characterization of "reality" and anything else was considered "decadent."

Realism essentially results in a kind of static visual snapshot, a frozen moment of time. By abandoning the attempt to be visually accurate, *impressionism* instead provides an effect of movement, aliveness; such paintings seem to stimulate many senses, not just the visual sense. If we examine the Vincent Van Gogh painting reproduced in Figure 1.13 (color plate), it clearly is not a visually "realistic" picture of a river scene at night. Yet it gives a strong impression of movement: the shimmering of the water, the swaying of the boats, the old couple walking along by the water front, the sound of the rippling water. The richness of the painting, one that is clearly not photo-realistic, depicts a live scene, one where it is easily possible to imagine being there.

Figure 1.14 shows a child's drawing of a person. Look at it – of course it looks nothing like a person yet we immediately recognize it as such. Here the unwitting technique is an iconic representation. Somehow the drawing is transformed into a picture of a person by stimulating our internal cognitive visual model of a "person" (what is a person? – a head, a body, two arms, two legs). Such iconic representation is so powerful that it actually prevents most of us from being good at drawing. When we draw an object, even when we try to study it and draw what we believe that we see, we tend to draw what is in our heads rather than what we are really looking at. In other words, we *look* at an object, but we don't *see* it. We draw our internal models rather than constructing a drawing based on the sensory information from the external world.

In her remarkable book on drawing, Betty Edwards (1999) shows how we can become excellent at drawing by interfering with our iconic representations. For example, try to reproduce the President Clinton cartoon above. At your first attempt (unless you are already good at drawing) the results will not be too good. Now turn the cartoon upside down, and copy it again, concentrating on the strokes that you see, especially those that you see now because upside down they have lost their meaning, and therefore fail to trigger your internal cognitive model. When drawing from real life, try to concentrate on the spaces between surfaces, which are inherently meaningless, rather than on the (meaningful) surfaces themselves. It is a training on how to see, breaking down the tendency to look and let the sensory information activate your internal representation causing you to see your own iconic representation of the object.

We opened this chapter with a quote from Carlos Casteneda. It is part of the "Sorcerer's interpretation of the world" that we see what's in our heads, we see what we expect to see, relying most of our lives on one interpretation of the stuff that is the external world, filtered through our own perceptual, cultural, and ideological systems. Part of the sorcerer's training is to break down this fixed iconic interpretation and *see* the world.

The tension between realism and real-time

This tendency of human beings to iconicize the world is very fortunate indeed for the program of virtual reality. Why? Because it is extremely difficult to create "reality" on a computer display. Virtual environments rely on our inherent tendency to generalize from tiny samples of reality to form our experience of reality. We look at some line strokes supposed to be a "head," a "body," "two legs," and "two arms," and we *see* a human being! It is almost impossible to look at the set of lines in the plane of Figure 1.15 and not see a 3D cube (in fact two alternative cubes). Computer graphics often aims at realism, but in fact the results are often highly impressionistic, especially in animation. The picture of the audience in Figure 1.11 is very much an impressionistic one, as far removed from visual realism as any cartoon. Yet the application that it illustrates invokes the same range of anxiety and emotional responses in humans as when facing an audience in real life.

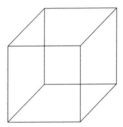

Figure 1.15
The Necker cube

The ideal "realism" in computer graphics means all of the above: geometric visual realism, behavioral realism, and illumination realism – these given in increasing order of difficulty. The fundamental tension in computer graphics is that these can be achieved only at the sacrifice of real-time performance. Yet real-time performance is essential for virtual reality to work at all.

There are several meanings to "real-time" in this context. First we note that the computer generates the illusion of movement and change on a display in exactly the same way as animated cartoons or movies. The computer generates and displays in correct sequence many images per second. Each image is called a *frame*. The *frame rate* is the number of different images per second actually displayed. This is usually measured in *Hertz* (Hz). A frame rate of 30 Hz means 30 images per second. If the frame rate is fast enough then human observers will see one continuously changing scene rather than the individual frames. In other words, the individual frames are integrated over time to produce a believable continuity of experience. The difference compared to animated cartoons and movies generally is that the sequence of images forming a cartoon always plays the same; there is no human intervention once the animation has started. In virtual environments, however, what is displayed depends on human intervention, so there is no fixed sequence of images, but rather the next image to be displayed depends on what the person in the VE does. There are several ways in which this can occur.

Real-time walkthrough. The human participant in a VE is able to move through it and look around it such that there is no noticeable delay between the intent and the result. For example, the participant forms the intent to turn his or her head around to the right-hand side. There is about 100 ms delay while this intent is transformed into the physical action of head turning. We suppose that the head rotation is tracked and known by the computer which must then continuously and smoothly update the display in order to display views of images that would be seen as the head turning. If a person is standing in front of a virtual building (Figure 1.16, color plate), then some parts of the building appear to move to their left and others come into view from the right as they turn their head to the right. There will be a delay in computing and rendering the next image frame on the display. This is called the display *lag*. The lag actually may change with time – for example, when a person is looking down the street more houses may be in view and therefore more rendering must be done, which takes a longer time, than when the participant is staring straight ahead at a brick wall which obscures most other things in the scene, and thus significantly less rendering is required. There is, of course, another component to the overall lag, which is the time that it takes for their head turns to be transmitted to the computer program by the tracking devices and the processing of the corresponding data. Ideally the frame rate should be around 60 frames per second. At 10 frames per second the world will appear very jerky, and immersion in such a world may lead to simulator sickness, a feeling akin to sea- or car-sickness. Movies operate at 24 frames per second. Most modern workstation displays operate at least at 60 Hz.

Real-time object interaction. In this case the participant has a means to change the environment by manipulation of objects within it – for example, picking something up and placing it somewhere else (Figure 1.17, color plate). Typically at least one hand of the participant is tracked and may be represented by a virtual hand in the VE. The computer program has a record throughout time as to where the virtual hand is located within the VE. When the hand intersects an object, and an appropriate trigger mechanism is fired, then the hand can grab hold of the object, and move it in various ways. As far as the underlying computer graphics rendering is concerned, this is no different from walkthrough, since each frame renders the scene according to the current state of each object within it. When the virtual hand moves, its position in the virtual world is updated in the database representing the scene, and so at the next rendering it will be shown in its new position. Of course, if there is lag, then the participant may have a feeling of moving their hand, but actually see their virtual hand move at a significantly later time (more than 100 ms would be noticeable). This lag can make the process of object selection and manipulation very difficult within a VE.

Interaction within a shared VE. The above examples have supposed an application running on one computer with its associated displays and tracking devices, servicing one human participant. However, it is not uncommon for one VE to be shared by several participants who are geographically situated around the world (Steed *et al.*, 1999). Each person of course has a local machine and displays, but the program and data describing events that occur within the VE are distributed across a network (such as the Internet). For example, participant A in London moves to pick up and move a virtual object. The data indicating that this has occurred is sent to all the other participants across the network, and their local copies of the scene database must be updated and their displays changed in order to reflect this change. Imagine participant A trying to "shake hands" or pass an object to participant B who may physically be thousands of miles away (in San Francisco, for example). A picks up the object, but it may be even seconds later that B sees the object being picked up, so A is seeing no reaction from B, and therefore decides to put the object down again; meanwhile B is reaching for the object . . . Clearly this introduces another delay into the system. No matter how fast (how small the lag) at each local site in this shared VE, the time involved in data transfer introduces a *latency* into the system. Each site individually may be running at 60 frames a second (60 Hz) but a latency of as small as 500 ms might completely kill any chance of meaningful interaction between the participants. (Latency has been studied extensively by Ellis and colleagues, see for example, Ellis *et al.*, 1999; Ellis *et al.*, 2000.)

A real-time requirement therefore makes enormous demands on computational, device, display, and network performance. Intentions should be experienced as being realized "instantaneously." In fact, as we shall see in the next section, even in the real world intentions are not realized instantaneously – there is a delay in the human perceptual and physiological system itself. So provided that virtual events occur within the margins allowed by human response times, events can be experienced as instantaneous, but this is far from being realized on today's systems.

Compromises are therefore inevitably made: it is impossible today even to walk through a realistically lit virtual environment in real-time – some aspect of the illumination realism *must* be sacrificed. In a complex scene it is often impossible to display each object with its full geometric realism. It may require tens of thousands of polygons to represent one human body accurately – imagine an application where there are thousands of human bodies, such as in virtual crowds. This is impossible to realize in real-time on today's hardware, so various simplification methods are employed instead; in the extreme, a human body can be represented by just one polygon, which itself has an image of a human body painted on it (for example, Tecchia and Chrysanthou, 2000)! Displaying the full complexity of the motions and movements of an object may require more computational power than rendering it with global illumination. A good example here is cloth (Figure 1.18, color plate). The physical equations are so complex in this case that real-time cloth animation with correct physical models is again impossible. Instead some compromise with and simplification of the physical laws governing cloth must be employed.

Finally, in the case of networks supporting shared virtual environments, there will always be significant and varying networking delays. It is certainly unreasonable to expect that at each moment each local site will have the correct state of all objects. Instead prediction algorithms are often employed, to take into account the state of the network and make best guesses as to the state of the world.

As we have said, there is an inherent conflict between the demands of realism, and the requirement for real-time. Computer graphics and its use within VEs is a compromise, but one that works extremely well, because of the peculiar properties of the human visual and perceptual system. Such low sampling of reality is required in order to maintain an illusion of reality, that compromises with reality generally work. We turn to this in more detail in the next section.

1.5 Presence and immersion

In the summer of 1999 we carried out one of an ongoing series of experiments at UCL concerned with the notion of *presence* in virtual environments. Presence is the usually unremarked sense of being in and reacting to events in a place. It is unremarked because for most of our waking conscious lives there is no doubt about where we are located, no mystery. We are where we are.

But where are we?

Human beings may uniquely have the ability to imagine – in an evolutionary sense imagination gives the advantage of being able to think ahead, plan out various strategies for survival, clearly an advantage in terms of natural selection. But imagination encompasses the invention of scenarios that never have nor will exist, and we can somehow locate ourselves in those scenarios. When reading a novel, although we are not "in" the novel, in a strong interpretation of presence we nevertheless do react in a physical sense to the narrative. For example, our heart may be set racing by a particularly dramatic episode, tears may involuntary come to our eyes as a result of a particularly sad passage – even though we know full well that in fact no events are actually taking place, or that they are taking place at a totally different level to that of the story, the act of reading. We react to the story, but if a character in the novel screams the warning "Fire!" we are absolutely not going to be in fear of our lives and run out into the street. At most we might flee the scene of the fire in our imagination, or *will* the characters of the novel to flee the fire, anxiously turning the pages to see the outcome of such a dramatic "event."

Transport yourself to a movie theater. In fact you are sitting down among many other people, perhaps not far from your home. After a while you are further transported in time and space to the far distant future on board a starship. Every so often someone in the theater will cough, or scrunch their bag of popcorn, or you will feel too cold, or too hot, or perhaps something too ridiculous to believe happens in the movie, and you are momentarily back in your seat among the other movie-goers. But the very fact that you "come back" to the theater means that in a certain sense you were temporarily and virtually somewhere else. Events will happen in the movie that will make your heart race, make you jump in your seat, or look away in horror, or bring involuntary tears to your eyes. But once again, if there is a fire aboard the starship, you're not going to rush out of the theater. You may will the heroes to survive with every ounce of your being, but still it isn't personal. On one level you have a sense of presence in a place other than your real physical surroundings, but at the fundamental level of the location and well-being of your own physical body, you are clearly present in the movie theater. The movie has engaged your senses, but the bodily reaction is very limited – some autonomic responses such as increased heart rate, perhaps sweating, perhaps involuntary jumps or gasps, but your whole body remains firmly sitting there along with all the others in the theater.

The other interesting feature about the movie experience is that although it is a shared experience in one sense, lots of people experiencing the same events at the same time, it is not shared in the sense that the other movie-goers are not up there with you "in" the movie. Even if you attend the movie with your closest friend, in the best movie they will become oblivious to you until it is over, when you walk out together exchanging experiences and commentaries.

Now suppose that it is one of those 3D movies, where you put on special glasses that integrate a left- and right-eye view into one overall stereo 3D visual experience. A missile comes flying toward you, up close to your face – there is a strong probability that you will physically duck your head, and try to avoid the impact. Even though intellectually you know that there is no missile, there's still some part of your brain that doesn't really know that it is virtual, and will react as if it were real. It is still very unlikely that if someone in the 3D movie shouts "Fire!" you will actually run out of your seat and leave the theater. In fact you are only rooted in the world of the film while you are sitting in your seat. Leaving your seat would be breaking the unspoken contract that you have with the movie director to stay in that world for the duration. You are only present in the movie while you stay in your seat, but being rooted to the seat is also a sign of not being present in the movie scenario. Your attention switches between the movie scenario and the real theater, you have some bodily reactions that belong to the movie scenario for sure, but your overall state is rooted in the theater.

Now you are at home playing the computer game based on the movie. You are totally involved in the events of the game, which is an online one shared by thousands of people throughout the world. Once again, a character in the game shouts "Fire!" Your heart races as you manipulate your avatar out of danger – in the world of the game. Of course, you have many physical reactions, perhaps you sway from side to side in your seat as the escape vehicle is buffeted by the explosion of the mother ship, but your physical body has to remain rooted in the physical chair of this world, in order for your attention to stay in that virtual world. There is some crossover, that is, events in the virtual world are crossing over to the real world to a limited extent, causing you to move and act in the real world, but those movements are quite different from what you would be doing if you were in the real scenario.

Now you are in bed; it was a particularly powerful movie and game, which have together sparked a dream, one of your more memorable realistic dreams. You are fully there in the scenario of the movie, on board the starship, engaging the Romulans in battle. Now if someone shouts "Fire!" you surely do your utmost to escape the devastation . . . only you don't, you're in bed, asleep. During a dream your capacity for motor movements is entirely shut down, you are essentially paralyzed; your autonomic nervous system is of course functioning to keep you breathing, some of your senses are still alert to help you avoid danger (e.g., a smell of burning will likely wake you up), but you are unable to physically move any of your limbs. Your eyes move rapidly from side to side during dreaming, in so-called REM (rapid eye movement) sleep. The discovery of REM sleep (Aserinsky and Kleitman, 1953) was an important breakthrough both in understanding the cycles of sleep and in understanding dreaming. The chances are that if you are awoken during REM sleep you will be interrupted from a dream, but not if you are awoken in non-REM sleep (LaBerg, 1985). So dreaming gives a very strong sense of presence in an alternate reality, only once again your real physical body is firmly grounded in the real world of the bedroom. However, dreams often contain an important overlap between the two locales of presence (the dream locale and the physical locale). Sigmund

Figure 1.19
Engraving of the prophet
Jacob having a dream
George Bernard/Science Photo
Library

Freud (Freud, 1983) reported the occurrence of *incorporation* – that is, where an event in the physical world of the dreamer becomes part of the mental world of the dream. Maury's famous dream about the French Revolution is documented where a piece of paper fell on his neck during sleep, which in the dream was interpreted as the fall of the guillotine.

In dreams the fantastic may happen (Figure 1.19) but our dreaming mind does not question these events. Returning to Carlos Casteneda's sorcerer Don Juan, a person of power can learn to become conscious during dreaming. One way to do this is to be critical in everyday life: where am I? Is this happening? How did I get here? This more critical attitude can spill over into our dreaming self, and through such introspection we can become aware that we are dreaming. Don Juan suggested setting up an instruction to look at your hands, and then away into the dream scene, and then at your hands again, as a way of helping to stabilize the dream scenario. Now in this dream state, you are fully conscious that it is a dream, you become very conscious of the seeming physicality of your dream body, and can, with practice, change the dream scenario at will – like you become the movie director and you're very much also in the movie. You can put the fire out with an act of your dreaming intent. Your conscious presence is in the scenario of the dream, but your physical presence remains once again in the physical place of your sleeping body. Stephen LaBerg of the Dream Research Laboratory of Stanford University has studied such lucid dreaming extensively (LaBerg, 1985). He utilized the eye movements of REM sleep so that lucid dreamers could signal the onset of a dream (while staying in the dream) to experimenters, thus for the first time opening up a simple communications channel between dreamer and external observer.

In The Graphics and Imaging Laboratory at the University of North Carolina at Chapel Hill there is a wide area tracking system mounted over an entire ceiling of 4.5 by 8.5 metres, with more than 2 m of height variation, with about 2,000 samples per second, and no more than 0.5 mm of error (Welch *et al.*, 2001). It tracks the head position and movements of a participant in a VE who wears a head-mounted display (HMD). The HMD delivers separate left- and right-eye images leading to a full 3D stereo view. Wherever the participant turns his or her head they will still be looking at visual streams entirely from the VE – the real world is completely shut out. The HMD can also deliver surround-sound audio. Since the head is tracked over a wide area, the participant can also really walk around and still be completely inside the VE (Usoh *et al.*, 1999). In some experiments the VE has consisted of a kitchen scenario, where simple plasterboard replicas have been placed in the real world in registration with their location in the virtual world. Thus the VE becomes a kind of superimposition of virtual over real. The space is the same in each, and there is some correspondence between physical objects in the laboratory and their virtual counterparts in the VE. If a participant reaches out to touch a kitchen table top, he or she will feel the plasterboard in the real world – thus superimposing the physical sensation of touch over the visual sensations from the HMD.

Now imagine that you are inside this scenario, the virtual kitchen, that you have been walking around exploring for a while. You have walked the length of the kitchen and adjoining rooms, and reached out and touched some objects. You are in the virtual kitchen, and suddenly you see that something on the stove has caught fire. You smell the burning, you feel some heat coming from that direction. You hear someone shout "Fire, get out of the kitchen!" You know that in reality you are standing in a laboratory, wearing a helmet. Every impulse in your body makes you want to get out of the kitchen. You know that it is ridiculous behavior, because "really" there is no fire, and even before the experiment started the experimenters told you that this would happen, but nevertheless you feel much safer walking out of the kitchen, and putting some distance between yourself and the sight, smell, and feeling of the burning stove. Not only is your heart racing but you really have walked, your whole body has been engaged.

The above experiment has not been actually carried out. However, a simpler one with startling results, that supports the hypothesis that you would move out of the virtual kitchen, has been carried out in a collaboration between UNC and UCL. The subjects of this experiment started off in a VE depicting a small room, and an adjoining room. In the small room they learned how to pick up and hold a box. They were then instructed to take the box into the second room, and place it on a chair at the far side of the room. This seems a simple enough task.

Figure 1.20 (color plate) shows the second room. From the outside it looks normal, but as soon as you enter it you see that the whole center of the floor is missing, and you are looking down into a pit of about 8 meters in depth. So to get to the chair on the other side you either have to walk around the edge of the room, precariously close to the edge of the pit, or else of course you can walk right across the empty space and quickly reach the chair. Now you know that there is no pit, and that if you step into the void nothing will happen. Nevertheless, the vast majority of subjects took the awkward route of walking around the edge, many of them with a very strong sense of vertigo. Visitors to the laboratory report a high degree of anxiety about getting close to the edge of the pit, with reactions much like those they would experience in a similar room in the real world. Intellectually they know for sure that no harm can come to them, yet there is some fundamental part of their perceptual system that does not understand this, that reacts to what it sees: there is a pit, it is dangerous, I must avoid it. The fact that this sense of presence is generated has been exploited for psychotherapy for fear of heights (Rothbaum *et al.*, 1995). The responses are the same as those of the public speaking application of Figure 1.11. There is no audience, but the reaction is as if there is one.

In the case of an *immersive virtual environment*, the *crossover* is very high. Participants react to events in the virtual world with their whole bodies. Our examples of the fire and the pit are rather dramatic, but this crossover also occurs in very mundane ways. In an immersive virtual environment, to look underneath a table, for example, the participant has to bend down; to reach to an object that is high – such as placing a virtual book on a virtual shelf – the participant has to stretch upwards. The participant can look behind by a whole body turn of 180 degrees. The participant can jump up and down. A strong notion of presence may therefore be defined as the extent of crossover from virtual environment to the real world: the greater the extent to which the participant uses his or her whole body, reacting to and initiating events in the virtual world much as he or she would to similar events in the real world, the greater the degree of presence. This is also a feedback loop, because the greater the sense of presence, the more that participants will use their bodies in natural ways.

We have used the term immersive virtual environment, and talked about immersion. Some authors have used the terms immersion and presence interchangeably, but we prefer to distinguish between them. Presence is a state of consciousness, a state of being in the location of the virtual world, and there are behavioral signs of presence as discussed above. It really only makes sense to talk about "presence" when there are signals from at least two competing environments: for example, the real world of the laboratory and the virtual world being experienced through the HMD and other devices. Imagine that the virtual world is supposed to be a hot desert, but the real world of the laboratory is freezing cold: to which set of signals will the participant respond at any moment? If there are signals from only one environment, then there is no issue of presence: the participant is present in that one environment, though knowing this is useless information.

Now *immersion* in an environment is related to the quantity and quality of sensory data that is from that environment. It is the extent to which the computer system delivers a surrounding stereo 3D environment, one that shuts out sensations from the "real world," accommodates many sensory modalities, and has rich representational capability (described, for example, in Slater and

Wilbur, 1997). These are measurable aspects of a VE system. For example, given two VE systems, and other things being equal, if one allows the participant to turn their head in any direction at all and still receive visual information only from within the VE then this is in our definition a more "immersive" system than one where the participant can only see VE visual signals along one fixed direction (as when looking at a small screen). Given two systems, if one has a larger *field of view* (FOV) than the other, then the first is more immersive than the second. The field of view is the angle subtended by the visual system. With our normal vision we have a field of view of approximately 180 degrees horizontally and about 120 degrees vertically. Typical HMDs only deliver FOVs of about 60 and 40 degrees respectively. As another example, if one system generates shadows in real-time and the other does not, then again, the first is more immersive. This is an example of the quality of the display. Finally, if two systems are the same in all respects but one includes sound and the other does not, the one with sound is more immersive. These are examples of what is meant by more or less "immersion." Clearly metrics can be established for each of these attributes which are descriptions of the system, rather than of participants' responses to the system. Presence is a human response; immersion is a description of the system itself.

Immersion as described is only part of the equation: it is to do with the display of sensory data: visual, auditory, and *haptic*, where haptic refers to sensations of touch and force feedback. It should ideally also include sensations of heat, and olfaction (smell), though these are rarely tackled in VEs. The other part of the equation is the extent and efficiency of *tracking*. A typical VE system tracks the participant's head and one hand. The orientation and absolute position of each is continually sampled by the tracking system, and this information is relayed to the computer, which adjusts the state of objects in its database accordingly, and carries out appropriate actions depending on collision events. At least as the participant's body moves, the corresponding avatar representation is updated. When a collision occurs between some tracked part of the body and some other object, an action might be generated depending on the properties and behaviors of that object. We have already mentioned lag and latency in tracking and world updates. The overall accuracy of the tracking depends on the geometrical accuracy (i.e., the degree of error involved in locating an object and its orientation in space), the sampling rate (number of samples per second), and the speed at which the data can be delivered to the computer and interpreted for use in displaying the state of the ongoing application.

The final piece in the presence equation is the participant's proprioceptive sense. *Proprioception* refers to the internal (unconscious) mental model that a person has regarding the current state and disposition of their body. It is as if we have a real physical body and a corresponding mental body. In order to know where your left foot is right now, you shouldn't need to look – your proprioceptive sense (together with other corresponding tactile information) will inform you. Sometimes the proprioceptive sense can be out of synch with the real body disposition (for example, a person can be hunched over and yet feel that they are standing up straight – see Sacks (1998), for various examples of such behavior), but normally it is an accurate representation of the state of the body. It works together with the sense of balance and the two together provide an internal mental model of the overall disposition of the body, the limbs, and their current movement.

Now a necessary condition for presence is that sensory data and proprioception match one another. A participant feels the sensation of moving his or her arm, and correspondingly sees the virtual arm of the avatar move. If the arm is moved towards a flame then ideally there should be a felt sensation of heat. The higher the degree of immersion, and the greater the overall match between sensory data and proprioception, the greater the degree of presence.

Walking in a VE is a very good example of this. Moving through a VE may be accomplished by really walking (as in the example of the UNC ceiling tracker) or by some artificial means, such as pressing a button on a mouse. In the first the participant has all the proprioceptive sensation of walking, and the accompanying sensory data of visual flow. In the case of the mouse button, the visual flow indicates movement, but the proprioceptive system reports that the participant is standing still pressing a mouse button. Sometimes the imperative to match visual and proprioceptive information is so great that participants will start to really walk once they have pressed the mouse button and experienced the visual flow. A discussion of the issue of walking can be found in Usoh et al. (1999).

Now let's return to the 1999 experiment at UCL mentioned at the start of this section. Twenty people were randomly selected and arbitrarily split into two groups of 10. Both groups were instructed to find a red box hidden in a laboratory area. One group carried out the task in the real lab, the other group carried out the task in a virtual copy of the lab. At the end of their search each subject was asked to fill out two completely different questionnaires that attempted to elicit their sense of presence during their search experience (Usoh et al., 2000). One questionnaire attempted to elicit presence based on six questions on the following themes: the sense of being in the laboratory, the extent to which it became the dominant reality, and the extent to which the laboratory space was remembered as a place, rather than just as images. The second questionnaire (Witmer and Singer, 1998) consisted of 32 questions based on themes concerned with factors thought to correlate with presence, such as the extent to which the person felt in control, the sense of involvement in the visual environment, and so on. The remarkable result of this experiment was that the scores for the degree of presence exhibited by the two groups were almost identical – that is, both those who had only experienced the real lab, and those who had only experienced the virtual lab, on the average reported the same overall degree of presence.

Figure 1.21 (color plate) shows images of the real and virtual labs. The real lab is far more – well, "realistic" – it is full of detail and clutter, there is no way that the virtual lab in which half the participants were immersed could be mistaken for reality! Now the conclusion reached by the experimenters was that the questionnaires themselves could not distinguish between real and virtual experiences – in other words, that each experience was considered by the subjects as self-contained, and their degree of presence in the virtual world was not in comparison to the degree of presence in the real world, but rather relativized to that particular experience judged against some ideal. Another conclusion was that subjects in an experiment will usually try to find meaning in the questions asked of them by the experimenters. If while obviously receiving sense data only from the real world they are asked questions relating to their sense of presence in that world, since they are obviously actually present, they may reinterpret the question to be something meaningful to them – such as their degree of interest, comfort or involvement. However, it is still remarkable that given the extreme simplicity of the virtual environment depicting the lab, the overall presence scores were as high as those for the real lab, for a randomly selected group of people.

Throughout the whole human existence it has been the case that what we see is where we are. More precisely, as we turn our heads and bodies around, and as we move around, there is no doubt that the sensory information that we receive depicts our location, where we are. Immersive virtual reality breaks that paradigm – what we see is not where we are, but has been generated by a computer on displays. Where we are is hidden from us by those displays. Although while in such an experience we know for sure that we are really where we really are (i.e., typically in a laboratory wearing a helmet that is attached to a computer), our sensory systems process the visual and other sense data from the virtual world in exactly the same way as any other "normal" sense data. Our perceptual systems do not know at a fundamental level that the environment we are seeing is illusory – therefore it cannot help but respond in just the same way that it would do given similar scenes in the real world. A virtual pit stimulates the same response in the autonomic nervous system as a real pit – no matter how much we repeat to ourselves "I know that it isn't real."

What we see is where we are, but where we are is in our heads! The readers of a novel automatically and unthinkingly translate the text into an internal scenario in their head, and respond to events in that scenario. The movie-goer and game player also transform the external visual and auditory data into an internal mental scenario – only the cues are richer, closer to what would be experienced as sensory data in reality. In immersive virtual environments, the same is true again – only here the sensory data is almost as overwhelming as it is in reality. The cues are more immediately related to the internal scenario that we create in our heads, only in this case, compared to text or a movie, the amount of transformation from the form of the media to our internal model is significantly less, and also we can change the ongoing flow of events through actions involving our whole body. Additionally in this case we see many of the same visual phenomena based on our movement that we see in reality. As we move our heads, objects that were not in view come into view, and objects that were in view disappear from view. The visibility relationships between objects change – an object that fully covered another object, now only partially covers it. There is full perspective foreshortening, that changes appropriately as our view changes. Most importantly, there is a *parallax* effect – as we move our heads from side to side it appears that objects closer to us move faster across our field of view than objects that are further away, and also the nearer objects seem to slide against the background of the objects further away.

In reality sensory cues from the external world coalesce with our internal mental representations of reality, and we operate from our internal representations, rather than being wholly driven and determined by sensory data from the real world. People become present in the virtual lab because in spite of the representational simplicity, they see tables, chairs, lights, and walls, and move through a spatial arrangement of these things as in everyday life. They interact with a model of the environment in their heads which has been sparked by visually sampling the virtual environment, by glimpsing the abstractly portrayed virtual objects. In much the same way as we look at a picture of some lines and see a 3D cube, or look at a "head," "body," "two arms," and "two legs" and see a "person," so in the VE we perceive recognizable objects that form a space in which we are immersed, and in which we can have a sense of presence. But we do exactly the same in reality too! Hence from this point of view it is not surprising that presence scores for the real world and the virtual world can be the same.

The above discussion may appear to be speculative, but very strong scientific evidence supports this view: that virtual reality works (induces presence) because it triggers exactly the same perceptive mechanisms as reality. We turn to this in the next section, inspired by the ideas of Professor L. Stark, University of California at Berkeley (Stark, 1995; Stark and Choi, 1996; Stark, Privitera, Yang, Azzariti, Ho, Blackmon and Chernyak, 2001), and also by Professor Richard Gregory (Gregory, 1998b).

1.6 How virtual environments work

"Virtual reality works because reality is virtual"

Professor Lawrence Stark, University of California, Berkeley

Reality is virtual

When we look around we experience a spatial and temporal continuum forming a very high resolution visual flow which sees a world in 3D. Wherever we look we see with high clarity, that is, each point in our vision is fully in focus, there are no spatial gaps in our visual flow, and there is temporal continuity, no gaps in time. This is, however, an illusion (Stark, 1995). Let's consider some of the reasons why.

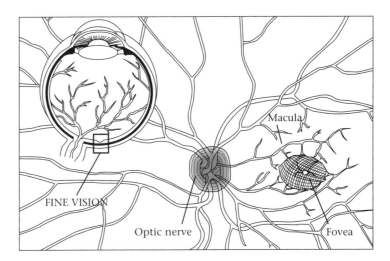

Macula

FINE VISION

Optic nerve

Fovea

Figure 1.22
The fovea as a region of high vision

Fixate your vision on some point in your present environment. Notice that the point on which your gaze is fixed and a small area around it has (for normal vision) the highest degree of clarity, not simply with respect to acuity, but also with respect to color. While maintaining your gaze on this one spot, become aware of regions that are further and further into the periphery of your field of vision. Notice that what is seen in these regions is not in focus, and that colors, if perceived at all, are more washed out. Examine Figure 4.4 on page 93 which shows a diagram of the human eye, and read the associated text, in particular the first paragraph (see "A Simple Model for the Visual System" on page 93). Note that the *retina*, onto which images are projected, contains millions of photo-sensitive receptor cells (rods and cones) which transform light energy into electrical signals transmitted to the visual cortex of the brain via the *optic nerve*. There is only one tiny region of the retina that is responsible for between 0.5 and 2 degrees of high resolution vision (the *macula* which contains the *fovea*). The retinal image is in focus only in this small region. The macula is a minute shallow depression on the retina (approximately 6 mm by 7 mm) which contains only the types of photo-sensitive receptor cells responsible for high acuity and color vision (the cones). The fovea (approximately 1.5 mm by 1.5 mm) is that region just behind the macula which has the highest concentration of the cone photoreceptors. This is shown in Figure 1.22. Light is focused by the optical properties of the eye onto the part of the retina which is the fovea for direct ahead vision, which results in fine detail and high color sensitivity.

So we only have high acuity vision at one small area of the visual field but we seem to see with high acuity everywhere. This is because our eyes are continually moving, and wherever we look, of course, is brought into the fovea, and therefore has great clarity. Vision is a sampling process, consisting of a sequence of alternate eye movements (often called *saccades*) and *fixations*.

The fixations bring information into the fovea (and of course also to the whole retina). The saccades move the eye from point to point as the environment is sampled. There are about three such fixations (or *foveations*) per second.

Now when you walk into a room (for example) the sampled information from such a process is actually relatively low. A few glances around the room and you already have a sense of seeing the whole room. First establish (or more commonly you already know) what kind of room: bedroom, kitchen, lounge, classroom, laboratory, and so on. Every room has a four walls, a floor and a ceiling, a door, and usually some windows. You see them, you see the other typical things associated with that kind of room, and you already have "seen the whole room."

It is easy to verify that you have not "seen the whole room." Try the following simple experiment, perhaps when you are next in a place which is not overly familiar to you. Look around as you would normally to get an idea of that place, let's suppose that it is a room, a library room, an office, or whatever. Now set up a mental filter, by saying to yourself "I want to see red." Look around the room again, without *trying* to see red things, but just have the intention in your mind to see red things. There is a high probability that your eyes will seemingly magically be drawn to red objects that beforehand you had not noticed were there at all, or that you had not noticed were red. Now repeat the same experiment again, but with a different filter: "I want to see green" – once again, you will probably become aware of green objects in your environment that were not seen before. You can repeat the same command to yourself even with more abstract intentions: "I want to see round shapes," "I want to see rectangles," "I want to see horizontal stripes," and so on. The latter may be particularly interesting: for example, you might suddenly see alignments between surfaces or edges that you had never seen before, even if you are in a relatively familiar place. Suddenly edges seem to line up, or you notice a horizontal grid or pattern on some appliance that you've never noticed before. There are many many ways of seeing an environment. You can change the way that you see by setting up specific commands to change perceptual filters. You can even vary this experiment by setting up very unusual filters: for example, suppose you are indoors or on an underground train; you might say: "I want to see trees" – and suddenly aspects of the environment will coalesce into tree-like shapes in quite unexpected ways.

The *scanpath* is the sequence of alternating saccades and fixations repeated over and over again when looking at an environment or picture (Stark and Choi, 1996). About 90 percent of the time is spent in fixations, revisiting the same points of interest in the scene, as if repeatedly verifying the notion, for example, that "yes, this is a room" and checking and rechecking various points of interest in the room. However, it is an illusion that you have seen the whole room – many, many details and even some gross features would have entirely escaped you. What you will notice is difference, however. If in some way this is not a normal room then it is likely that you will be puzzled, and be generating and testing many alternative explanations for whatever it is that is puzzling. Since we know that a room has four walls, a floor and a ceiling, arranged almost always as a cuboid, it is extremely hard to overcome this very strong presupposition.

Figure 1.23 (color plate) shows two young children standing in a room known as the Ames Room, named after a famous ophthalmologist, Adelbert Ames, Jnr, who first assembled this structure in 1946. (It can be experienced, for example, in the San Francisco Exploratorium.) The first illusion associated with this is that it looks like a normal room. The second illusion is the massive difference in size of the children. How is this possible? In all our experience we never encounter rooms with slanted floors, with non-cuboid shapes, and with walls not joining at right-angles. This room is constructed in such a way (Gregory, 1998a, pp. 32–36) so as to give the appearance of being "normal" from this viewpoint, but in fact it is not at all. The floor is sloping, the walls are not at right-angles. The larger twin is much nearer to our viewpoint than the smaller one. However, our visual system, because it *knows* about rooms, seems to insist on seeing the impossibility of the two different sized children rather than see the more likely hypothesis of a distorted spatial structure.[2]

So the first point is that our visual systems sample an environment by scanpath sequences, repeatedly returning again and again to the same regions of interest, verifying our internal mental models about what it is we are supposed to be seeing. In fact, what we see can be said to be already in our heads, we are seeing in our mind's eye, and what is being actively scanned from the environment is used more as evidence, hypothesis verification, rather than being the direct "cause" of what we see. We see what is in our mind's eye, and use sampled visual information to verify this. We verify it by continually checking and rechecking our environment, looking for confirmation or contradiction. The scanpath itself is driven by our internal mental model of where we are more than by what is "out there" – since our model itself determines what are the regions of interest that form part of the verification. Change the model and the scanpath itself changes.

Look at Figure 1.24 – what do you see first of all, a duck or a rabbit? Whatever you see, try to see the other interpretation now. Become aware of your differing automatic eye movements in response to which of the two interpretations you see. Your eye movements are governed by your model of what it is you are looking at – and they change depending on what you decide. There is a different way to look at the image depending on whether it is a duck or a rabbit. The "external world" – that is, the marks on the page – are of course invariant, so cannot in themselves be a cause of the different patterns of your eye movements.

Figure 1.25 shows another very famous example of such ambiguous figures. At first glance you might see an old woman with a prominent chin, or the head

---

2. For a true feast of such anomalies visit the Mystery Spot in Santa Cruz, California, http://www.mysteryspot.com

Figure 1.24
A duck or a rabbit?

Figure 1.25
Young or old woman?

of a young woman looking away. Can you change your interpretation of the figure? If so, notice again how the pattern of your eye movements changes.

Figure 1.26 shows another famous example: you may see a vase, or you may see the side view of two faces looking at one another. Stark *et al.* (2001) used a variant of this figure and recorded the scanpaths for subjects, who were given cues that reinforced the notion that it was a vase, or cues that reinforced the notion that it was two faces. Figure 1.27(a) shows the scanpath for a subject who was cued to see the image as two faces. The scanpath for the same subject seeing the image as a vase is shown in Figure 1.27(b). Notice that the scanpaths are quite different (there is a way to look at two faces which is different from the way to look at a vase), and the difference in such scanpaths for the subjects in the experiment as a whole was statistically significant. This is evidence that the scanpath is driven by our top-down cognitive model of what we are look-

Figure 1.26
A vase or two faces?

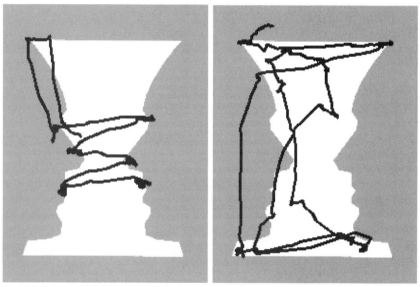

Figure 1.27
Scanpaths for two-faces
and vase interpretations
Courtesy of Professor Lawrence
Stark, University of California,
Berkeley

(a) Scanpath for two faces   (b) Scanpath for vase

ing at rather than only by what it is that we are observing – for obviously the latter is invariant in these examples of ambiguous figures.

Figure 1.28 shows an example from another experiment carried out by Stark and colleagues (Stark *et al.*, 2001). Subjects looked at a target set of letters shown on a grid for 20 seconds and their scanpath was recorded. An example target is shown in Figure 1.28(a) and the corresponding scanpath in Figure 1.28(b). They repeated this twice, the second time looking for 7 seconds. Then they were asked to look at a blank grid (Figure 1.28(c)) and to visualize the target. Again their scanpaths were recorded (for example, Figure 1.28(d)). The figure illustrates the similarity of the two scanpaths. Analysis of the data for the whole experiment showed that there was no significant difference between the

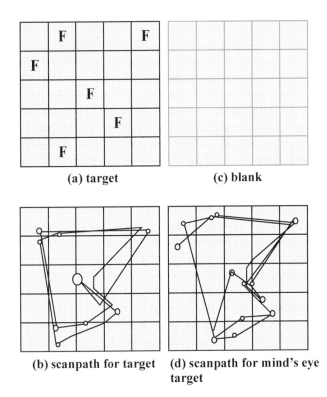

Figure 1.28
Scanpath for a target
in the mind's eye
Courtesy of Professor Lawrence
Stark, University of California,
Berkeley

scanpaths while looking at the target, and the corresponding scanpaths that were generated without any actual physical stimulus – in other words these scanpaths were generated by *seeing in the mind's eye*. Therefore, the evidence suggests that what we see in the external world, as indicated by the scanpath, is controlled not simply by the "stuff" of the external world, but by our internal cognitive models.

Our internal cognitive models are so strong that they can override what is actually "out there" and insist on seeing something for which there is no actual sensory data. Consider Figure 1.29 which shows a famous example of this. You will most likely see a triangle on top of three disks, with the triangle a brighter white than the surrounding page. You will probably even see the edges of the

Figure 1.29
Kanizsa's triangle

triangle in the empty space between the disks. Your perceptual system insists that there is a triangle there, because it has formed the hypothesis that what you are looking at is a white triangle placed over the three black disks. This is a much more likely explanation of what is seen rather than the true explanation that it is simply three disks with triangular portions cut out. Our perceptual system has filled in triangular edges, even in the empty space, which we cannot help but see, even though intellectually we know that they are not there, so strong is our internal model of what we are looking at.

This is a relatively "high level" example of this dominance of the cognitive model. There is another lower-level example, which clearly illustrates how the perceptual system literally fills in information that seems to be missing. Take another look at Figures 1.22 and 4.4 depicting the human eye. You will notice that signals are sent from the retina through to the visual cortex via the optic nerve. Where the optic nerve intersects with the retina there are no photo-sensitive receptor cells (no rods or cones). So there must be gaps in our visual field corresponding to these regions in both eyes. However, you are not aware of these gaps. It is possible to become aware of them, however, with a simple experiment. Hold out your left hand at arm's length, but with your hand and forefinger pointing to the right. Close your left eye, and align the tip of your forefinger with the bridge of your nose. Now similarly hold out your right hand at arm's length with your right-hand forefinger pointing towards the left. Your right arm should initially make approximately a 45 degree angle with the left. Now with your left eye closed, fixate your gaze on the tip of the forefinger of your left hand, and slowly bring the forefinger of your right hand towards the left (Figure 1.30). At some moment the tip of the forefinger of your right hand

Figure 1.30
How to see the gap left
by the optic nerve

Figure 1.31
The disk-shaped gap disappears when you fixate on the blob

will disappear! As you keep moving your right hand towards the left, the tip of the forefinger of your right hand will come back into vision again. The gap in vision corresponds to the area on the retina of your right eye where the optic nerve is.

Now why are we not usually aware of the discontinuity in vision caused by the optic nerve? It is because the visual system (probably at the level of processing in the retina itself) does some basic image processing based on inferences about what the visual experience ought to be by integrating information across neighboring areas. This is illustrated in Figure 1.31, due to R.L. Gregory. Fixate your gaze on the black circular blob towards the bottom right-hand corner of the figure. You will become aware that the circular gap in the horizontal lines soon disappears, and you may even see the horizontal lines slowly spread

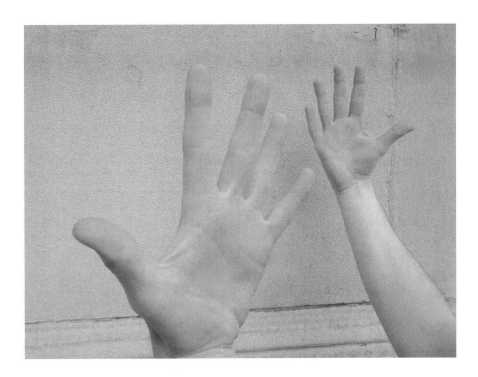

Figure 1.32
The size of hands

themselves across the gap to eliminate it. Our visual system forms the hypothesis that "really" it is much more likely for there to be a continuum of horizontal lines everywhere rather than this unexpected gap – so it eliminates the gap.

There is another very important example of how the visual system overrides sensory data with higher-level cognitive information; this is called *size constancy scaling* (Gregory, 1998b). Again this can be illustrated with another simple experiment suggested by R.L. Gregory. Hold out both hands, one at arm's length and the other at approximately half arm's length, with each hand facing you. Make a large separation between your hands. Close one eye and compare the sizes of your two hands – they look about the same – they are the size of hands! Now bring them close together, now one looks like the hand of a child in comparison to the other one (Figure 1.32). Our visual system compensates for the smaller area of the projection of objects on the size of the retina for objects that are known to be further away, or as directly induced by perspective cues in the image. Look at people near you and people in the distance. They look about the same size – the size of people! – yet the areas occupied on the retina are very different. If you look at a house or building in a typical street, it looks large (even though the proportion of retinal image it occupies will be relatively small). However, if you fly above a set of houses and look down on them, they look unreal, like a toytown village. We are used to seeing such buildings from ground level – our perceptual systems have little experience in seeing such objects from above. Size constancy scaling therefore makes things appear to be of different size than the actual sensory information which forms their images on the retina. However, a picture taken by a camera does not include constancy scaling, so that when we examine such a picture as in Figure 1.32 we see immediately that the images are actually of different sizes.

In another experiment suggested by R.L. Gregory (Gregory, 1998b) we can experience constancy scaling at work directly. Stare at a bright light for a few seconds, in order to form a good after-image. Then look at a wall in a room and notice the size of the after-image as if it were projected on the wall. Now as you move closer to the wall the after-image will become smaller. As you move away from the wall it will become larger. This is direct evidence that the apparent size of the image is changing with distance, even though the retinal image remains constant in size. Depth is one cue that constancy scaling is based on, the other is perspective. We consider this in the next section.

Seeing in 3D

With our two eyes we see the world in three dimensions. Each eye receives a slightly different view of the world and the visual system fuses these into one three-dimensional stereo view. The difference in the two images is called *binocular disparity*. Of course the simplest way to see this is to look somewhere in the environment where you are located now, and alternately switch between your two eyes, with at any moment one open and the other closed. Notice how the image shifts horizontally from left to right and back again, demonstrating the disparity. Notice also that the disparity is much greater for nearer objects than it is for objects further away.

Another way to experience this is to use Figure 1.33(a) (color plate). Get a stiff piece of paper, say A4 or US-letter sized, and hold one of the shorter edges lined up with the vertical dividing line between the two images, and the paper coming out at right angles from the book page. Now position your nose so that it is touching and lined up with the other shorter edge. Check that with your left eye you can see only the left image (by closing your right eye) and similarly with your right eye you can see only the right image. Now open both eyes and allow the two images to fuse into one. It will seem as if there are two sheets of paper, and between them a full stereo 3D image, with the man running towards you and the tunnel receding into the distance. This should be a very powerful effect.

This same figure can be used to illustrate two other very important aspects of seeing: accommodation and convergence. First, look again at Figure 4.4 on page 93, and notice the lens. By far the greatest optical power in the eye comes from the cornea, filled with a liquid called the aqueous humor. The lens is used for fine adjustments in order to bring a point of interest into full focus on the fovea. The lens is controlled by the ciliary muscles, which act to control its thickness, and thus its optical properties. *Accommodation* is that process of

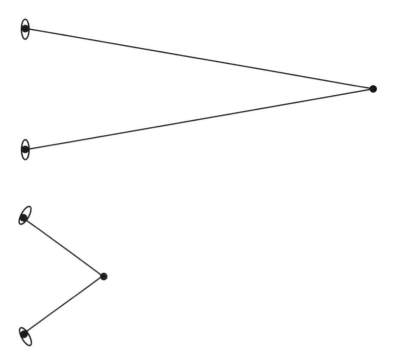

Figure 1.34
Convergence: for near objects the eyes rotate inwards

adjusting the lens to bring points in the scene into focus. *Convergence* on the other hand is that process whereby the eyes rotate inwards in order to focus on objects that are nearby, and rotate outwards, becoming parallel, for objects that are far away (Figure 1.34). Convergence is a very powerful cue for 3D vision, for the experience of depth in a scene.

In normal vision accommodation and convergence work together. This is not, however, a physiological necessity, but something that is learned. It is easy to illustrate that in virtual reality, where an entirely illusory 3D view is generated, the connection between accommodation and convergence breaks down. Look again at Figure 1.33, and this time gaze successively at the running man, and then at successive points down the tunnel. You should have the experience of changes in convergence as you fixate your gaze on each of these different parts of the scene at different virtual distances. How about accommodation? This of course is *fixed*, since in order to see the image at all in high clarity you must be focused on the sheet of paper containing the images. So convergence changes, but accommodation is fixed. This is believed by some practitioners to cause a degree of eye strain when using virtual reality equipment such as head-mounted displays, but no long-term effects on vision have been found.

Now close one eye and look around you (so many experiments!). What a surprise, the world is *still* seen in 3D! How is this possible, because we have shown above that the experience of 3D is premised on binocular disparity? How is it that TV and movies give such a strong impression of 3D that we do not even think about the fact that really we are obviously seeing entirely 2D

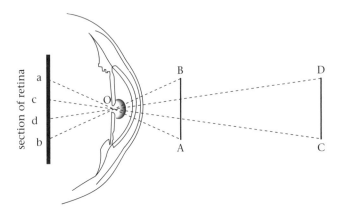

Figure 1.35
Linear perspective

images? How come we are afraid of 2D monsters, and why is it that 2D thrillers thrill us, and 2D comedy makes us laugh? This is because there are many other cues to the 3Dness of a scene other than binocular disparity. As we have noted, with one eye shut looking out to the real world, convergence still operates, which in itself is a powerful indication of depth. Second, in this circumstance there is still *head-movement parallax*, mentioned earlier – as we move our head, nearer points move faster than further points, another cue to depth in the scene. In movies and on TV there is not convergence nor head-movement parallax, but there is *motion parallax*. Objects moving across the camera appear to move faster if they are nearer than if they are further way. This is still a strong parallax depth cue. Now 2D images of 3D scenes have additional compelling depth cues, and we consider these in turn (Hodges and McAllister, 1993).

Linear Perspective. We have noted that the size of the image formed on the retina is inversely proportional to the distance of the object from the viewer. This is illustrated in Figure 1.35. We abstract away from the complexities of the eye; in particular, we assume that instead of the light passing through the pupil and through the cornea and lens, there is a single point (O) that admits light, which then forms an image on a (flat) retina. In computer graphics O is usually called the centre of projection, and the retina is called the *image plane* or *view plane*. We show an abstracted "side view" of the projection of two vertical bars AB and CD. AB projects to ba, and CD projects to dc. AB and CD are the same size, but the size of their projections are clearly inversely related to their distance from O. Note also that the images are upside down compared to the original objects.

Perspective provides a very significant depth cue. This is illustrated in Figure 1.36. The two vertical lighter shaded lines are the same height, but one looks much bigger than the other. Perspective gives the illusion of depth in this case, so that looks further away and, recalling constancy scaling, the visual system compensates for that by making its apparent size larger (see Gregory, 1998b, Chapter 10 for a full explanation).

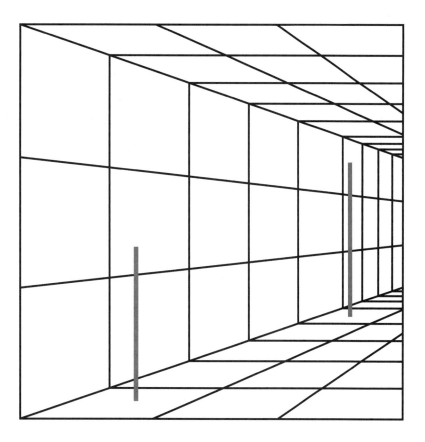

Figure 1.36
An illusion of linear perspective – thicker lines are the same height

The same effect can be seen in Figure 1.37. In this remarkably simple figure we have the impression of looking along some railway lines, or perhaps the edges of a road receding into the distance. Hence the top horizontal line looks much larger than the bottom one, because perspective gives us the impression that the top one is further away, and therefore must actually be bigger than it seems.

Figure 1.38 shows the famous Muller–Lyer illusion. Although both vertical lines are the same size, it looks as though the left-hand one is much smaller than the right-hand one. R.L. Gregory (Gregory, 1998b) has suggested that this can be accounted for by perspective inducing size constancy scaling. The left-hand figure gives the impression of a corner (e.g., between two walls) that is pointing towards us (looking at the corner of a building from the outside). The right-hand figure gives an impression of a corner but pointing away from us (looking at the corner of a room from the inside). Since the retinal images of the two vertical bars are the same size, but the perspective induces apparent depth, size constancy scaling results in an apparent difference in length of the vertical lines. The one pointing towards us is therefore "nearer" than the one pointing away, and so the right-hand vertical line is perceptually magnified.

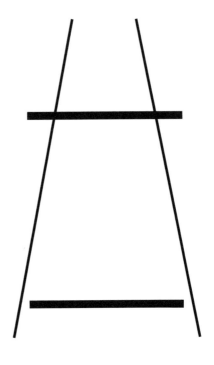

Figure 1.37
A variant of the Ponzo illusion

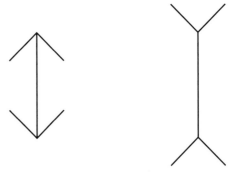

Figure 1.38
Muller–Lyer illusion

Texture gradient.   Examine Figure 1.13, in particular look at the water. The texture of the water is coarser the closer it is to the viewpoint, and finer as it recedes into the distance. Figure 1.39 shows a more abstract example. There are no perspective lines as such in this figure, just arrangements of blobs that get closer together and smaller the higher up in the figure that they are located. Nevertheless, the whole gives an impression of some kind of landscape receding into the distance. The perceptual psychologist J.J. Gibson carried out several studies of such texture gradients and how they are crucial in allowing us to

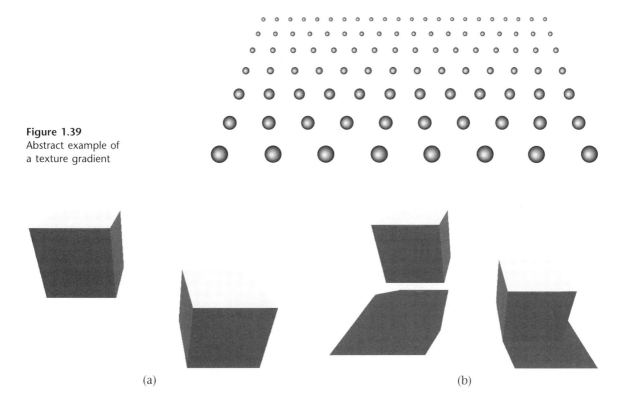

Figure 1.39
Abstract example of
a texture gradient

(a) (b)

Figure 1.40
Shadow depth cues
(a) shows two boxes
without shadows and
(b) shows the same
boxes with shadows.
The shadows help in
understanding the
relationship between
the boxes

make judgments about size and distances in real-world settings (which almost
always are replete with multitudes of textures) (Gibson, 1986).

Shadows and shading. Shadows can significantly enhance depth perception
in everyday reality (Puerta, 1989; Gregory, 1998b). A shadow conveys information both about the shape of an object, and about depth relationships within
the scene. A shadow of an object can be thought of as another view of the
object – one generated by a light source. Therefore crucial additional information is made available about the location of the object in space, since not only
is there a referent with respect to the observer, but the observer can see information with respect to another referent – the light source. Shadows also provide
direct information about spatial relationships of each object with its surrounding surfaces. Figure 1.40 provides a simple example. The cube on the left is
clearly at ground level. The cube on the right is not at ground level, and may
be further away from the viewpoint than the left-hand cube.

Occlusions. We have mentioned occlusions in the context of parallax effects
– that as you turn your head, or as objects move, the relationships between
them seem to change, that objects come into and out of view, with respect to

the field of view and with respect to one another. When an object partially obscures another, that is a clear indication that it is closer to the observer. Recall that this effect is so strong that it was the basis of the Kanizsa triangle illusion of Figure 1.29.

Lighting.   As we shall see in Chapter 3, light energy falls off inversely proportional to the square of the distance. Hence more distant objects become washed out with respect to their color and less sharp compared to close objects. Moreover, although computer graphics makes the simplifying assumption that light travels in a vacuum, of course for real-world scenes it does not, and the atmosphere influences the appearance of colour, increasingly so with distance: light from distant sources tends to appear more blue. Nearer objects are usually brighter in color (other things being equal). Objects further away are often fogged out by atmospheric effects. We learn from the earliest age to associate such effects with distance. Where relevant they provide strong depth cues, in particular, as in this picture, combined with each one of the other depth cues that we have considered in this section.

Time and space constancy

Do we see continuously in time, or are you aware of interruptions in your normal vision? Of course you are almost certainly not aware of such interruptions. But this is yet another illusion. Look at someone else for a while; is their vision very frequently interrupted? The answer is very definitely "yes" – every time someone blinks, of course, during that instant of the blink nothing is seen. Now that you recall the fact that you blink you are probably aware that indeed your vision is frequently interrupted. We blank this out; we typically do not notice the fact that we blink; our vision seems to be continuous and uninterrupted through time. There is also another way in which vision is frequently interrupted – each time that we move our eyes there is a big discontinuous jump in our visual field. Moreover, our eyes are moving almost all the time. It is difference that stimulates vision; if it were possible to hold the gaze totally fixed, then shortly we would see nothing, since the photoreceptor cells adapt. It is similar when there is a continuous background noise, such as the ticking of a clock; after a while you no longer hear it at all. Our senses on the whole adapt, and are continually stimulated by difference. We do not notice our eye movements because of *saccadic suppression*, which reduces visual sensitivity during such saccadic eye movements.

   Does the world continually move for you? The answer again is "no" – our visual field seems to be spatially stable. Another experiment: shut one eye and with your forefinger gently move the eyeball of your open eye. What happens? – your entire visual field moves in the direction of your prodding. But why does it not move when your eyes move naturally rather than being pushed externally by your finger?

As our continual eye movements jump our foveas from point to point in the visual scene, that visual scene must jump from locus to locus on the retina. A discharge "corollary" to the command the eye movement muscles receive, is sent before each eye movement to the Helmholtzian comparator, likely located in the paretal lobe. This precomputation provides for the illusion of space constancy. If retinal image motion is congruent with the commanded eye movement, the illusion exists. (Stark, 1995, pp. 7–8)

In other words, the visual system carries out a prediction pre-computation – if the eye movement command is to move the eyes by "x" then compensate the apparent image by "–x" in order to maintain a constant spatial field. So constancy through time is achieved by suppression of the effects of blinks and saccadic eye movements, and in space by look-ahead prediction of the expected amount of translation of the retinal image due to a command to move the eyes.

Hypotheses of the visual mind

What we see obviously depends on where and how we look. The scanpath theory provides evidence that what we see depends strongly on our internal cognitive models, in other words that we see in our mind's eye. The evidence suggests that scanpaths for an imagined object are similar to scanpaths generated by actually looking at that object. It also shows how scanpaths change depending on differing interpretations of what we are looking at: for example, the ambiguous figures such as Figure 1.26. Hence what we see is not a simple function of the light energy that comes into our eyes, but a matter also of what we expect to see. Further evidence for this is that the scanpaths are idiosyncratic both to individuals and to what is being looked at, and that they are repetitive. The fact that they are idiosyncratic to different people supports the notion that how we look is not only a function of what we are looking at: it also depends on our personal cognitive models. Moreover, if seeing were a function mainly of what is "out there" then we would expect scanpaths to attempt comprehensively to cover the entire scene. Instead there are typically a few key points that are visited over and over again, roughly in the same order. These are key features involved in seeing that kind of object, and the repetitions involve repeated confirmation that it really is this type of object that we are seeing and not another.

There are always multiple interpretations for any given pure sensory experience. Our visual mind seems to home quickly in on one with the highest probability, based on many factors such as prior knowledge, suggestion, experience, and surrounding context. Of course we rarely see isolated objects; they are almost always in a context which gives cues as to how they should be interpreted. The same object located in a kitchen or in a living room might be seen, in the absence of other knowledge, either as a microwave oven or as a computer screen. Where the objects remain ambiguous the visual mind seems to repeatedly switch between alternating hypotheses, so that we see first

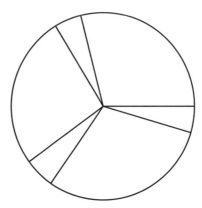

Figure 1.41
Ambiguous figure:
interpretations switch
spontaneously

one, and then the other, as if it goes into a loop, each interpretation with its own corresponding type of scanpath sequence. Look at the centre of the circle in Figure 1.41 and you will see an arrangement of triangles. Stare at the centre of the circle and the arrangement of triangles will change into another arrangement. Keep staring at the circle and it is likely that the arrangements will swap with increasing frequency. The visual mind is switching between two alternative hypotheses.

When someone is "in" a virtual environment, they are inevitably processing sense data from two different and contradictory sources. Typically visual information is generated exclusively from the virtual world, if a head-mounted display is being used. Let's suppose that auditory information is also coming only from the virtual world through ear phones attached to the HMD. However, of course the person is in a real laboratory standing on a real floor, typically in uncontrolled temperature, with real air currents, and real cables attached to the HMD, and the HMD itself has a significant weight. The totality of sensory data available to the participant in the VE is a mixture of that corresponding to the VE itself and that from the physical real-world setting of the whole experience. This is analogous to the ambiguous figures situation – where the same sensory data may be interpreted and seen in alternative ways. We have argued (Slater and Steed, 2000) that *presence* in an environment involves a selection between competing hypotheses, different ways of "seeing" (in its broadest sense) the totality of sensory data as supporting the hypothesis that the participant is in *this* world (virtual) rather than *that* world (real). Presence in the VE means that the sensory signals are organized in such a way that the participant temporarily experiences reality as that of the VE world, and responds to and initiates events in that world. Occasionally the interpretation will flip, and the sensory signals will correspond to "I am standing in a lab wearing a helmet."

Look at Figure 1.25 again. When you see the older woman you pay attention to quite different features of the drawing than when you see the younger woman: just another way of saying that the scanpaths are different for the two cases. Similarly, when you are present in the VE you pay attention to quite a

Figure 1.42
Randomly generated polygons consisting of 100 vertices – what do you see?

different set of signals than when you are not present in the VE but in the real-world setting of the experience. For example, in the latter case you might have shifted attention to tactile sensations of which you had been oblivious during moments of presence in the VE. Such flips of presence between VE and real-world interpretations are typical of many people's experience of virtual environments. An important issue for research is to discover the factors that influence the probability of one interpretation (presence in the VE) rather than the other (presence in the real-world setting).

We have argued in this section that a necessary condition for a sense of presence in the VE is that virtual sensory input stimulates the same top-down, cognitively dominated visual experience as sensory input from the real world. Gregory notes (Gregory, 1998b, p. 254) that "perceptions are but tenuously related to reality; being predictive hypotheses, having major contributions from top-down knowledge and sideways rules derived from the past." Stark's work indicates that we see in our mind's eye, the bottom-up sensory signals from the real-world being the basic data that provokes our visual minds to select between alternative hypotheses. The scanpath is a kind of read-out of the internal cognitive model that a person is applying to make sense of a particular pattern of visual sensory input signals.

Now what properties should (visual) sensory signals from virtual environments have in order to provoke this process, that leads the visual mind to operate essentially as it does with real-world signals? Of course *any* pattern of input signals, especially if they are inclusive, i.e., blocking out all other signals of the same sensory type, will force the visual system to try to make sense of it. People see meaningful structures in essentially random images such as in arrangements of tea leaves, clouds, and of course in the famous Rorschach ink blot images used in personality testing. For example, Figure 1.42 shows randomly generated polygons in which you may see some meaning. But what particular features does sensory data need to have in order to portray intended meaningful images?

We have discussed some possibilities in this chapter: figures portrayed with linear perspective, head-movement and motion parallax, texture gradients, depth suggested by visibility relationships and shadows. Object representations require a level of realism just sufficient to suggest the objects that are being simulated. Caricature is important, emphasis of certain key features, whatever the key features are that spark the visual mind into immediately forming the hypothesis that it is *that* kind of object (and no other). In the case of a human face, very simple representations of eyes, nose, and a mouth are sufficient to suggest this. In general we do not know what the key features are and attempt to produce a realistic model that captures the object in its entirety. In some applications, for example engineering assembly training, it is of course important that the virtual objects resemble their real counterparts as closely as possible in order to maximize the chance of a positive training effect.

However, virtual environments require not just the recognition of objects – that can happen with a few marks on a piece of paper. It is that the objects form a participant's environment, and that he or she is in that world. In this case we have emphasized the importance of the match between sensory data and proprioception. Perhaps a paradigmatic example of this is head-movement parallax – I turn my head or move it from side to side as part of a movement of the whole top half of my body, and the visual signals should change according to the everyday experience of parallax. If this happens then it is a very strong cue that my location is indeed amongst these objects. But there is still another crucial point: I am in an environment if I can reach out and touch it, if I can move through it and position my body in such a way that it can touch various of the objects. For example, I am standing by this table and I can move over to that chair and bend down and reach out to it with my hand. Now it may not really be "my" hand but a virtual hand with movements tracked from my real hand, but nevertheless there is this same matching of proprioception with sensory data laid over the illusion that I am amongst these objects. There is no other technological means of generating the illusion that I am surrounded by and can reach out to virtual objects than immersive VEs.

This ties up with our final point about perception too – Gregory puts great emphasis on exploration, on the very close connection between perceptual understanding through vision and understanding through active participation and manipulation of the world. A fundamental feature of immersive virtual environments is that they offer this possibility – not just seeing the world around you, but using your body to explore and understand it. This is like the difference between being driven somewhere in an automobile in a strange city, and driving there yourself. In the latter case you will have a much better understanding and memory of the route than in the former – or at least when you drive yourself the way that you see the environment will be quite different than if someone else drives you. A very famous experiment carried out by Held and Hein (Gregory, 1998b, p. 143) illustrates this: two kittens were brought up in darkness except for times when one actively explored the visual environment, and the other was carried along behind without itself being active. Both had the same chance for visual learning, but only one was active. The experiment suggested that only the one that actively explored the environment actually learned to see. Our own repeated experiments have shown that those given the chance to use their whole bodies in exploring a VE will generally achieve a higher sense of presence than those who just look at it (Slater and Steed, 2000). Immersive systems provide this unique capability to allow people to actively explore and understand an environment.

We return to the quote by Professor Stark at the head of this section: "Virtual reality works because reality is virtual." Since so much of our visual understanding of the world is tied up with our already existing cognitive knowledge, we do not have to attempt a faithful reproduction of reality in VEs for a sense of presence to be attained. This is good news, since as we will find in the subsequent chapters of this book, it is extremely hard to produce visual "reality," in real-time, with current-day computer graphics techniques.

1.7 Summary

This chapter has introduced the motivation, scope, and approach of this book. We go from the abstract to the concrete, and from realism to real-time. We have introduced the notion of the content of a virtual environment in this chapter, and described briefly how a VE consists of graphical objects. Typically the virtual scene is represented as a database of such objects, including their geometric, material, reflective, and behavioral properties.

We have paid considerable attention to perceptual issues, discussing the question as to how it is that virtual reality works at all. We see primarily in our mind's eye. It turns out that the "phantom world" is also the world of everyday life, not just the world of dreams and virtual environments.

Since we see in our mind's eye, virtual environments need to create the necessary signals for our visual minds to choose the interpretation that designers of the virtual world intended. There has been little study of the key points of interest in an environment necessary to give the illusion of virtual objects; we are flagging this here as an important aspect of VE research. The application area in which this subject has seen considerable attention is in way-finding in large environments – to which key features in an environment do people pay attention in order to learn to find their way around (Darken *et al.*, 1999)? We have touched on this, in our discussions of the sense of presence, but much needs to be discovered in the general field of key features of interest for environments.

In the next chapter we discuss some fundamental mathematics, and then in the subsequent chapter, still at a very abstract level, the issue of illumination. We then immediately follow this with a discussion of the human response to light – specifically the issue of color. These chapters may be thought of as concluding the introductory part of the book.

2 Mathematics for virtual environments

2.1 Introduction

In this chapter we introduce some of the essential mathematics used to describe and reason about virtual environments. Fundamentally this mathematics is used to describe objects, to manipulate objects, and also for the representation of illumination.

This discussion is certainly not meant to be mathematically rigorous, but rather relies on intuition, and is sufficient for our purposes.

2.2 Dimension

First, the concept of *dimension* of a space. This refers to the amount of freedom of movement that objects within the space have, while remaining totally within the confines of that space. It also refers to the minimum number of independent values that are required in order to specify unambiguously a location within the space.

If it were possible to think of "objects" contained within an environment specified with a 0 dimension, they would be unable to move at all. Moreover, no information is required in order to specify the position of an object within

0-dimensional space: it is just "there". A 0-dimensional space is just a single point (and from the point of view of objects within such a space, of course, there is nothing outside of it). Recall that a mathematical point has no "thickness," it has no area, it is "infinitesimally small," it is as close as it is possible to get to nothing while still being something.

Objects within a space of dimension 1 can move "left" or "right": that is, they can move in a direction, and then perhaps move in the opposite direction retracing the previous path, and that is all. The words "left" and "right" are in quotes, since the labelling of the direction is quite arbitrary. Actually these words can be misleading, since they imply a notion of horizontalness. However, in a 1D space it is impossible to think about the notion of "being horizontal" since that depends on a frame of reference that is more than one dimensional. A 1D space can be thought of as an infinitely long and continuous line (for beings within such a space there is nothing except this line!). In order to describe such a space we can construct a coordinate frame. Choose an arbitrary point and label it as 0, the origin. One direction from the origin is called *positive*, and the other is called *negative*. The entire part of the line in the positive direction is called the positive half-space, and similarly there is the negative half-space. The position of any point in the space is then specified by a single number representing the distance from the origin according to some agreed metric, and with a + or − sign according to whether it is in the positive or negative half-space on the line.

There can be infinitely many "objects" represented in 1D. Objects might be 0-dimensional (i.e., be single points) or be 1-dimensional, for example, intervals of the form: the object represented by all points greater than or equal to 1.0 but less than or equal to 2.0 also denoted as $\{x | 1 \leq x \leq 2\}$ or more simply as [1.0, 2.0]. In general such objects can be represented as any set of points in the 1D space.

Such a space could be used, for example, to provide a very simple representation of traffic flow on a highway. Here the highway is itself the "line" and the vehicles are represented as intervals of the form $[a, b]$. As a vehicle moves along the highway, so the values represented by $[a, b]$ would change (although the length $b - a$ would remain constant). Even in this simple space there are some computational problems that are certainly non-trivial. For example, given a collection of objects $[a_1, b_1], [a_2, b_2], \ldots, [a_n, b_n]$ quickly find the set of objects with overlapping intervals. Or suppose that in an interactive setting a human operator wishes to select an object with a (1D) cursor, the program would have to solve the following problem: given any point x on the line find as quickly as possible the (set of) objects being pointed at (if any), that is, the set of intervals $[a_i, b_i]$ containing x.

Objects within a space of two dimensions can move "left" and "right", or "up" or "down" (again these words are chosen as arbitrary labels). Moreover, any point that an object can reach by moving through sequences of moves from this set can also be reached directly by a straight line. In order to describe such a space we require two infinite lines that are orthogonal (perpendicular)

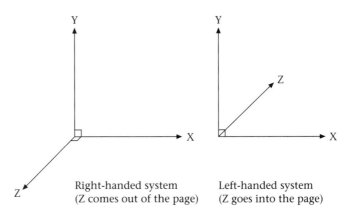

Figure 2.1
Right- and left-handed
coordinate systems

Right-handed system
(Z comes out of the page)

Left-handed system
(Z goes into the page)

to one another, and intersecting at a point labeled as the origin. This intersection point is the origin of a 2D coordinate system. By convention, one axis is "horizontal," and is called the X axis, and the other is "vertical" and called the Y axis. The origin is the point (0, 0). Any point in the 2D space can be referenced as a coordinate pair (x, y), where x represents the distance along the X axis from the origin, and y along the Y axis. Again, in such a coordinate system (usually called Cartesian) a metric is required to specify distance. Let $p_1 = (x_1, y_1)$ and $p_2 = (x_2, y_2)$ be two distinct points, then the distance p_1 to p_2 is given by:

$$|p_1 - p_2| = \sqrt{(x_2 - x_1)^2 + (y_2 - y_1)^2}$$
(EQ 2.1)

A similar description can be given for a 3D space. We use a Cartesian coordinate system, so that for a 3D space, we choose some convenient (but arbitrary) point as origin, and three orthogonal directions labeled as X, Y, and Z axes, the *principal axes*. All points are specified as offsets from the origin, along directions parallel to the principal axes. Note that the origin is (0, 0, 0), and the coordinate system is continuous. In general a point is represented by (x, y, z). In 3D we have a choice about the configuration of positive and negative conventions. Figure 2.1 shows so-called left- and right-hand 3D coordinate frames. In each case identify your first finger as the Y axis, and thumb as the X axis. The Z axis is specified as your second finger.

<hr />

2.3

Positions and directions: points and vectors

Relationship between points and vectors

Representing positions by points in this way is arbitrary up to the choice of origin and principal axes. A *vector* specifies a direction, and the magnitude of the direction, and is *the difference of two points*. In 3D, we will represent a vector also by (x, y, z), where it will be clear from context whether a point or a vector is required.

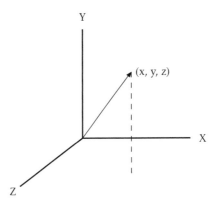

Figure 2.2
A vector in 3D

So suppose (4, 5, 6) and (3, 4, 5) are points, then (1, 1, 1) = (4, 5, 6) − (3, 4, 5) is a vector, representing the direction (1, 1, 1). A vector (x, y, z) may be visualized as a line with one end tied to the origin, and the other at the point (x, y, z) with an arrow at this point. This is shown in Figure 2.2.

A vector, then, is a difference of two points:

$$vector = point_2 - point_1 \qquad\qquad \text{(EQ 2.2)}$$

from which it follows that a point may be specified as the addition of a point and a vector:

$$point_2 = point_1 + vector \qquad\qquad \text{(EQ 2.3)}$$

Addition of vectors

Vectors may be summed, using the familiar parallelogram rule (EQ 2.4). An example is shown in Figure 2.3.

$$v_1 = (x_1, y_1, z_1)$$
$$v_2 = (x_2, y_2, z_2) \qquad\qquad \text{(EQ 2.4)}$$
$$v_1 + v_2 = (x_1 + y_1, x_2 + y_2, z_1 + z_2)$$

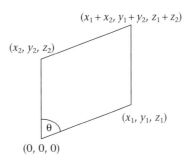

Figure 2.3
Addition of vectors

Notice that although it is meaningful to add vectors together, this is not the case for points (question to the reader: why not?).

Scaling of vectors

Suppose $v = (x, y, z)$ is any vector, then this can be scaled (for example, stretched) by multiplying throughout by a constant real number, say λ. Then,

$$\lambda v = (\lambda x, \lambda y, \lambda z) \tag{EQ 2.5}$$

is a new vector (and the new vector has the same *direction* as the old one if $\lambda > 0$). The new length can easily be found from the result:

$$|\lambda v| = |\lambda||v| \text{ where } |\lambda| = \lambda \text{ if } \lambda \geq 0 \text{ and } -\lambda \text{ if } \lambda < 0 \tag{EQ 2.6}$$

So note then, that given any two vectors v_1 and v_2 and any two real numbers λ_1 and λ_2, $\lambda_1 v_1 + \lambda_2 v_2$ is also a vector.

Norm of a vector

There are three noteworthy vectors that are said to form a *basis* for the entire space:

$$e_1 = (1, 0, 0)$$
$$e_2 = (0, 1, 0) \tag{EQ 2.7}$$
$$e_3 = (0, 0, 1)$$

This means that any (x, y, z) can be expressed as a linear combination of these three, since:

$$(x, y, z) = xe_1 + ye_2 + ze_3 \tag{EQ 2.8}$$

Note that an alternative notation is often used for the principal vectors e_1, e_2 and e_3, i, j, and k respectively.

The *norm* of a vector gives its length (in fact this provides the metric of the 3D space). Suppose $v = (x, y, z)$ is a vector, then its norm is denoted $|v|$, and is defined as:

$$|v| = \sqrt{x^2 + y^2 + z^2} \tag{EQ 2.9}$$

This is the distance from the origin to the point (x, y, z). So if p_1 and p_2 are two points, then $p_1 - p_2$ is a vector, and the distance between the points is the norm $|p_2 - p_1|$.

Given any vector $v = (x, y, z)$, suppose we are only interested in its direction and not at all in its length. Then for many purposes it is convenient to use another vector that has the same direction, but length 1. We can find such a vector by *normalizing* the original one. This is achieved as follows:

$$\text{norm}(v) = \frac{v}{|v|} \qquad \qquad \text{(EQ 2.10)}$$

It is very easy to show that $|\text{norm}(v)| = 1$. (Show this.)

Inner (dot) product of two vectors

Suppose we again have two vectors v_1 and v_2. The *dot product* of these two vectors, denoted by $v_1 \cdot v_2$, gives us important information about the angular relationship between them. This is defined by:

$$v_1 \cdot v_2 = x_1 x_2 + y_1 y_2 + z_1 z_2 \qquad \qquad \text{(EQ 2.11)}$$

Normalize each of the vectors v_1 and v_2 and then take the dot product of the normalized vectors. This gives us an important result:

$$\cos\theta = \frac{v_1 \cdot v_2}{|v_1| \times |v_2|} \qquad \qquad \text{(EQ 2.12)}$$

where θ is the angle between the two vectors.

Hence the dot product is proportional to the cosine of the angle between two vectors. Recall that $\cos 0 = 1$ and $\cos\frac{\pi}{2} = 0$.

The implication of the first result is that the dot product of a unit length vector with itself is 1. The implication of the second result is that vectors that are perpendicular to one another (we call such vectors *orthogonal*) have a zero dot product. This is a result of great use for later chapters.

Vector cross product

There is another binary operation on vectors that is geometrically significant – the *cross product* of two vectors, denoted $v_1 \times v_2$. This results in a *new vector* as follows:

$$v_1 \times v_2 = (y_1 z_2 - y_2 z_1,\ x_2 z_1 - x_1 z_2,\ x_1 y_2 - x_2 y_1) \qquad \text{(EQ 2.13)}$$

The properties of the cross product are as follows: First,

$$|v_1 \times v_2| = |v_1||v_2|\sin\theta \qquad \qquad \text{(EQ 2.14)}$$

where θ is the angle between the two vectors. Second, and of significant use in computer graphics, $v_1 \times v_2$ is orthogonal to both v_1 and v_2. Another way of saying this (though jumping ahead a little) is that v_1 and v_2 form a plane. Their cross product is *normal* to that plane (that is, it is perpendicular to it). Now an important question concerns the direction of the new vector – for example, if v_1 and v_2 were inscribed on the page in front of you (as in Figure 2.4), then would the new vector point out towards you or behind the plane away from you? The answer is that v_1, v_2 and $v_1 \times v_2$ form a right-handed system: if you identify v_1 with your thumb, and v_2 with your first finger, then $v_1 \times v_2$ will

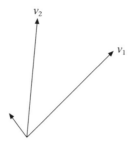

Figure 2.4
Forming the cross product

correspond to your second finger. In Figure 2.4, the cross product $v_1 \times v_2$ points out of the page, and $v_2 \times v_1$ points behind the page. In general it is easy to see that $v_1 \times v_2 = -v_2 \times v_1$ (such a property is called anti-symmetric. The dot product is, of course, symmetric).

The formula in (EQ 2.13) is not always easy to remember. There are two ways of "deriving" it. The first is to consider the following pseudo determinant:

$$D = \begin{vmatrix} i & j & k \\ x_1 & y_1 & z_1 \\ x_2 & y_2 & z_2 \end{vmatrix} \qquad \text{(EQ 2.15)}$$

where i, j and k are the principle unit vectors of (EQ 2.7).

Now expanding out the determinant:

$$\begin{aligned} D &= (iy_1z_2 + jz_1x_2 + kx_1y_2) - (kx_2y_1 + iy_2z_1 + jz_2x_1) \\ &= i(y_1z_2 - y_2z_1) - j(z_2x_1 - z_1x_2) + k(x_1y_2 - x_2y_1) \\ &= (y_1z_2 - y_2z_1, \; x_2z_1 - x_1z_2, \; x_1y_2 - x_2y_1) \\ &= v_1 \times v_2 \end{aligned} \qquad \text{(EQ 2.16)}$$

There is another still simpler way. Consider:

$$\begin{bmatrix} x_1 & x_2 \\ y_1 & y_2 \\ z_1 & z_2 \end{bmatrix} \qquad \text{(EQ 2.17)}$$

Now "hide" the first row, and evaluate the determinant (cross product) of the remaining two rows. This gives the x-coordinate of the cross product $y_1z_2 - y_2z_1$. Similarly "hide" the second row, and find the determinant of the remaining two rows. This gives $z_2x_1 - z_1x_2$ which is *minus* the y-coordinate of the cross product. Finally, hide the third row and take the determinant, to give $x_1y_2 - x_2y_1$ which is the required z-coordinate. Of course, some people find it easier to remember the formula, and others find it easier to remember ways of deriving the formula.

Of use later are the following relationships between the principal unit vectors, i, j and k. If we write $a \times b$ as ab, and aa as a^2, then it is easy to show the following:

$$i^2 = j^2 = k^2 = (0, 0, 0)$$
$$ij = k = -ji$$
$$jk = i = -kj \qquad \text{(EQ 2.18)}$$
$$ki = j = -ik$$
$$(ij)k = i(jk) = ijk = (0, 0, 0)$$

The last line of (EQ 2.18) shows that whichever order the cross product is carried out, i.e., whether first ij is found and then post-multiplied by k, or first jk is found and then pre-multiplied by i, the result is the same, so that ijk is well defined.

2.4 Directions and angles

Directions over the unit sphere

A vector represents a magnitude (the norm or length of the vector) and a direction. In computer graphics we are mostly interested in the directional properties of vectors. It is interesting and important to note that there is redundancy in representing a vector with three quantities x, y and z. It should be clear from (EQ 2.10) that in fact only two quantities are needed: the space of all possible directions in 3D is in fact a 2D space! The reason is that to specify a direction we only need to consider normalized vectors (since the length doesn't matter). For any normalized vector (x, y, z), it is obviously the case that:

$$x^2 + y^2 + z^2 = 1 \qquad \text{(EQ 2.19)}$$

Hence, if we know the values of x and y (say) then we can compute the value of z (except for its sign) using (EQ 2.19). More intuitively, any direction can be thought of as a line from the origin to a point on a unit sphere centered at the origin (the sphere represented by (EQ 2.19)). So all possible directions correspond to all possible points on the unit sphere. But the surface of a sphere is a two-dimensional entity – hence the space of all possible directions is two-dimensional.

Spherical coordinate representation

The spherical coordinate representation of a point in 3D space is often useful, and will be specifically used in the next section. In Figure 2.5, P is some point (x, y, z) and the distance from the origin O to P is $r = \sqrt{x^2 + y^2 + z^2}$. Q is the perpendicular projection of P to the XY plane. Angle β is the angle between the X axis and OQ, and angle α is the angle between the Z axis and OP.

By construction, the angle $\Delta OPQ = \alpha$, and so $OQ = r\sin\alpha$. From this it follows that:

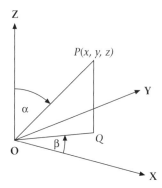

Figure 2.5
Spherical coordinates

$$x = r\sin\alpha\cos\beta$$
$$y = r\sin\alpha\sin\beta \qquad \text{(EQ 2.20)}$$
$$z = r\cos\alpha$$

Therefore, from the spherical coordinates (r, α, β), it is easy using these formulae to find the Cartesian coordinates (x, y, z). The inverse relationships can also be found from:

$$\alpha = \text{acos}\frac{z}{r}$$
$$\beta = \text{atan}\frac{y}{x} \qquad \text{(EQ 2.21)}$$

Solid angles

This motivates another representation of a direction vector: using angles to specify a point on a unit sphere. Figure 2.6 shows a unit sphere and vector v intersecting the sphere at P. A perpendicular is dropped from P to meet the XY plane at Q. The direction corresponding to v is completely specified by the two angles $\phi = X0Q$, and $\theta = Z0P$. The important result to note here is that the set of all direction vectors can be represented by the 2D space:

$$\Omega = \left\{ (\theta, \phi) | 0 \le \phi < 2\pi, -\frac{\pi}{2} \le \theta \le \frac{\pi}{2} \right\} \qquad \text{(EQ 2.22)}$$

In Figure 2.6 we have deliberately shown a small area on the sphere around the point P. Suppose this area is A. The *solid angle* corresponding to A is defined by:

$$\Gamma = \frac{A}{r^2} \qquad \text{(EQ 2.23)}$$

where r is the radius of a sphere. The unit of measurement is called a *steradian*. An entire sphere comprises $4\pi r^2/r^2 = 4\pi$ steradians. The solid angle may be thought of by analogy with an ordinary angle, which is determined by the

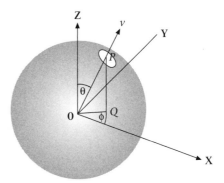

Figure 2.6
Direction vector based on spherical angles

length of the circumference of a circle that it circumvents, divided by the radius of the circle.

A *differential solid angle* is the solid angle subtended by a "differential area" – i.e., a patch "tending to area zero" on the surface of a sphere. This is usually denoted by $d\omega$. We can tie things together here by showing that an explicit formula for $d\omega$ can be found in terms of the angles θ and ϕ specifying a direction, i.e., a point on a sphere.

Figure 2.7 shows a point $p = (x, y, z)$ on a sphere of radius r, and a differential solid angle around p. We suppose that p has spherical coordinates (θ, ϕ). The point p lies on a circle at height z on the sphere with center C. The radius of this circle is $r\sin\theta$. Since the angle subtended by the small horizontal sweep along the circumference of this circle must be $d\phi$, we have:

$$d\phi = \frac{dh}{r\sin\theta}$$

(EQ 2.24)

$$\therefore dh = rd\phi\sin\theta$$

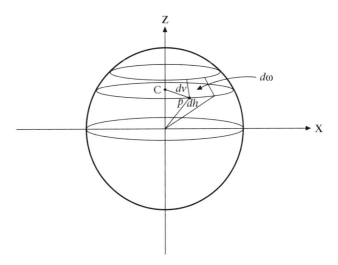

Figure 2.7
A differential solid angle

Similarly, if we consider the vertical sweep through angle $d\theta$ on the great circle containing p:

$$d\theta = \frac{dv}{r}$$

(EQ 2.25)

$$\therefore dv = rd\theta$$

Since a solid angle is area divided by the square of the radius, it follows from (EQ 2.24) and (EQ 2.25) that the required differential solid angle is:

$$d\omega = \frac{dh \times dv}{r^2}$$

(EQ 2.26)

$$= \sin\theta d\phi d\theta$$

Projected area

The final idea we wish to present here is that of *projected area*. In Figure 2.8(a) we show an area A and a plane P. Consider the projection of A onto P – that is, the image formed on P when each point of A follows a ray in direction v intersecting with P. If A and P are parallel, and the direction of projection is perpendicular to A (shown as n in the figure, usually called the *normal* to A) then the projected area is the same as the original area. If the direction of projection is not perpendicular (such as v in the figure), or equivalently if the area and plane are not parallel (as in Figure 2.8(b)) then the projected area is smaller than the original area. What matters only is the *cosine of the angle* between the direction of projection and the normal (perpendicular) to the area. The smaller the angle the closer the cosine is to 1, the projected area tending to be the same as the original area. The larger the angle the smaller the projected area, until in the limit when the angle is $\pi/2$ the projected area vanishes. Note that the cosine is the dot product of the normal and the direction of projection: $\cos\theta = n \cdot v$ assuming that the vectors are normalized.

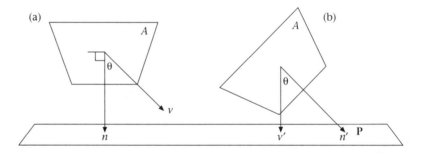

Figure 2.8
Projected area

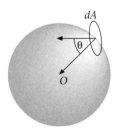

Figure 2.9
Solid angle of a
differential area

The *definition* of projected area is:

$A^v = A \cos \theta$

where v is the direction of projection

n is the normal to A

(EQ 2.27)

$\cos \theta = n \cdot v$

To avoid confusion, by A we do not mean the numerical area – rather we are using the word "area" here to mean "region." Hence A is the original region and $A^v = A \cos \theta$ is sometimes used as a notation for the projected region. If the actual area of A is written $|A|$, then $|A^v| = |A| \cos \theta$. However, we will usually not use the $| \ldots |$ symbol for notational convenience. It should be clear from context when a numerical area is meant rather than the region which has that area.

Projected areas can also be used to find solid angles of *differential areas* (areas "tending to zero"). Figure 2.9 shows an arbitrary but small area denoted dA and we wish to find the solid angle from point O, distance r from dA. Construct a sphere of radius r around O. The projected area towards O is $dA \cos \theta$ – i.e., this is its projected area onto the sphere. Then the differential solid angle subtended by the area is:

$$d\omega = \frac{dA \cos \theta}{r^2}$$

(EQ 2.28)

2.5

Flatness-preserving transformations

Barycentric combinations: flatness

In this section we study transformations that preserve "flatness." This is of great importance in 3D computer graphics, where the fundamental primitive is the planar polygon. When we transform an object that is constructed from polygons, we wish to be sure that the transformations leave the flatness (or planarity) of the polygons invariant. Also, such transformations are very useful

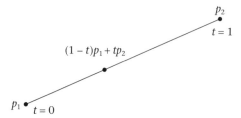

Figure 2.10
Parametric representation
of a line segment

for computational reasons – since we can simply transform the vertices of a polygon, and be sure that the transformed vertices correctly describe the new polygon. If this were not the case we would have to transform "every point" belonging to the original polygon (vertices, boundary, and inside) in order to get the shape of the transformed object. First we define our notion of "flatness," and then we specify the property of such a flatness-preserving transformation, usually called an *affine* transformation.

Line segments

A fundamental form in computer graphics is a straight line joining two points. This can be best represented in *parametric form*: given two points p_1 and p_2 in 3D space (actually in a space of any dimension), then the straight line that passes through them can be represented as all points $p(t)$ satisfying:

$$p(t) = (1-t)p_1 + tp_2 \qquad \text{(EQ 2.29)}$$

for any real number t (Figure 2.10).

If we want the *line segment* that connects p_1 to p_2, then t is restricted to the range [0, 1]. This result will be used again and again throughout this book. (Other forms of line representation will be discussed in Chapter 17.) Notice that this equation can be rewritten as:

$$p(t) = p_1 + t(p_2 - p_1) \qquad \text{(EQ 2.30)}$$

This form shows that the line segment can be considered as an origin point p_1 plus a vector $p_2 - p_1$ scaled by $t \in [0, 1]$.

Barycentric combinations

The parametric line representation is a special case of what is called a *barycentric combination*, which is a weighted sum of points, where the weights sum to 1. Let $p_1, p_2, \ldots, p_n$ be a sequence of points, and $\alpha_1, \alpha_2, \ldots, \alpha_n$ be any sequence of real numbers summing to 1, then

$$p = \sum_{i=1}^{n} \alpha_i p_i$$

with

$$= \sum_{i=1}^{n} \alpha_i = 1$$

(EQ 2.31)

defines a barycentric combination. Obviously, the special case $n = 2$ gives the straight line as in (EQ 2.29).

Assume for the moment that the points $p_1, p_2, \ldots, p_n$ all lie on the same plane (P) (Section 8.2).

Suppose we let the α_i values vary arbitrarily subject to the constraint that they always sum to 1. Each set of values $(\alpha_1, \alpha_2, \ldots, \alpha_n)$ corresponds to a point p in space. If we consider the collection of all such points (of course there are infinitely many) then it can be shown that the resulting surface will be the *plane P that passes through each of the points $p_1, p_2, \ldots, p_n$*. Intuitively, this is quite easy to see. If we select any two of the points, say p_a and p_b, we can set all $\alpha_i = 0$ except for α_a and α_b. Then the constraint requires that $\alpha_a + \alpha_b = 1$, which therefore means that all points on the straight line joining p_a and p_b are on P. Again now take any arbitrary point on this straight line, and call this point p_{ab}. Now choose another one of the original points, say p_c. Then repeating the same argument implies that all points on the line joining p_{ab} to p_c must also be on P. It follows from this that all points on the plane formed by p_a, p_b, and p_c must belong to P. Repeating this argument with each point from the original set shows that all such points must lie on the same plane, which must be P.

A *convex polygon* is such that all of its interior angles are less than 180 degrees. Another property is that any straight line segment between two points on the boundary of the polygon is contained inside the polygon. Now, if we further restrict the weights to be non-negative, $\alpha_i \geq 0$, $i = 1, \ldots, n$ then it is also easy to see that P becomes the smallest convex polygon (including the interior) that encloses all of the vertices $p_1, p_2, \ldots, p_n$. Should these vertices in fact describe a convex polygon, then P itself will be this polygon.

More generally, suppose that the p_i do not all lie on the same plane (which will usually be the case for $n = 4$). Then if we restrict the α_i to be non-negative, the shape P that is mapped out as p varies with varying α_i is called the *convex hull* of the points. The convex hull is the smallest convex polyhedron that encloses all of the points p_i. Mathematically, the convex hull is such that the straight line segment joining any two points on its boundary will always be inside (or on the boundary) of the convex hull. In particular, note that the centroid of the points (or "average") point will be inside the convex hull, and the average is:

$$\bar{p} = \frac{1}{n} \sum_{i=1}^{n} p_i$$

(EQ 2.32)

Affine transformations

An *affine transformation* is one that preserves barycentric combinations – and therefore preserves flatness. This property can be specified exactly as follows. Let p be a point in 3D space that is a barycentric combination as in (EQ 2.31).

Suppose f is a mapping from 3D space to 3D space, so that $f(p)$ is a point in this space. Then f is affine if and only if:

$$f(p) = \sum_{i=1}^{n} \alpha_i f(p_i) \qquad \text{(EQ 2.33)}$$

In other words, we get the same transformed point whether we first find the barycentric combination p and then compute $f(p)$ or alternatively whether we first find all the $f(p_i)$ and then find the barycentric combination of all the transformed points. Computationally it is always more efficient to do the latter when transforming the entire object formed from such barycentric combinations. In view of our discussion of flatness, it should be clear that an affine transformation of a planar polygon can be found by transforming each of its vertices, and then constructing the new polygon from these.

Matrix representation of affine transformations

The formulation (EQ 2.33) gives the property that defines an affine transformation, but does not give us a constructive formulation, i.e., what form does such a transformation take? We will derive the form of such a transformation in this section.

Since p is a point in 3D space, it is expressible as a coordinate (x_1, x_2, x_3). Moreover, let

$e_1 = (1, 0, 0)$

$e_2 = (0, 1, 0)$

$e_3 = (0, 0, 1)$

be the principal unit vectors. Also define $e_4 = (0, 0, 0)$. Then,

$$p = x_1 e_1 + x_2 e_2 + x_3 e_3 + x_4 e_4$$
$$= \sum_{i=1}^{4} x_i e_i \qquad \text{(EQ 2.34)}$$

where x_4 is anything. Since x_4 can be whatever we like without affecting (EQ 2.34), we shall choose

$$x_4 = 1 - x_1 - x_2 - x_3$$

and so

$$\sum_{i=1}^{4} x_i = 1 \qquad \text{(EQ 2.35)}$$

Consider now the principal unit vectors e_i. Let f be an affine transformation as before, then $f(e_i)$ is in 3D space, and therefore there must be coordinates λ_{ij} with

$$f(e_i) = (\lambda_{i1}, \lambda_{i2}, \lambda_{i3})$$

$$= \sum_{j=1}^{3} \lambda_{ij} e_j \tag{EQ 2.36}$$

Now from (EQ 2.34) and (EQ 2.35)

$$f(p) = \sum_{i=1}^{4} x_i f(e_i) \tag{EQ 2.37}$$

Substituting (EQ 2.36) into (EQ 2.37):

$$f(p) = \sum_{i=1}^{4} x_i \sum_{j=1}^{3} \lambda_{ij} e_j \tag{EQ 2.38}$$

Rearrange the order of summation in (EQ 2.38) to give:

$$f(p) = \sum_{j=1}^{3} e_j \sum_{i=1}^{4} x_i \lambda_{ij} \tag{EQ 2.39}$$

Recalling that $x_4 = 1 - x_1 - x_2 - x_3$, we can write $\mu_{ij} = \lambda_{ij} - \lambda_{4j}$ to obtain:

$$f(p) = \sum_{j=1}^{3} e_j \left(\sum_{i=1}^{3} x_i \mu_{ij} + \lambda_{4j} \right) \tag{EQ 2.40}$$

Expanding out using the meaning of the e_j, we get $f(p)$ in coordinate form:

$$f(p) = \left(\sum_{i=1}^{3} x_i \mu_{i1} + \lambda_{41}, \sum_{i=1}^{3} x_i \mu_{i2} + \lambda_{42}, \sum_{i=1}^{3} x_i \mu_{i3} + \lambda_{43} \right) \tag{EQ 2.41}$$

Putting this in perhaps more familiar notation, we now suppose that $p = (x, y, z)$ and $f(p) = (x', y', z')$. Then if f is an affine transformation, each new coordinate may be represented as a simple affine combination of each of the original coordinates, in other words:

$$\begin{aligned}
x' &= a_{11}x + a_{21}y + a_{31}z + a_{41} \\
y' &= a_{12}x + a_{22}y + a_{32}z + a_{42} \\
z' &= a_{13}x + a_{23}y + a_{33}z + a_{43}
\end{aligned} \tag{EQ 2.42}$$

for some constants a_{ij}.

Matrix representation

Expression (EQ 2.42) gives the general form of an affine transformation of a point (x, y, z) to the point (x', y', z'). It is convenient to express (EQ 2.42) in matrix form. As before, suppose $p = (x, y, z)$ and $f(p) = (x', y', z')$ where f is an affine, flatness-preserving transformation. There are three possibilities for representing this in matrix form. The first way is:

$$f(x, y, z) = (x', y', z') = (x, y, z) \begin{bmatrix} a_{11} & a_{12} & a_{13} \\ a_{21} & a_{22} & a_{23} \\ a_{31} & a_{32} & a_{33} \end{bmatrix} + \begin{bmatrix} a_{41} \\ a_{42} \\ a_{43} \end{bmatrix} \qquad \text{(EQ 2.43)}$$

Alternatively, we could get rid of the translation vector, and use:

$$(x', y', z') = (x, y, z, 1) \begin{bmatrix} a_{11} & a_{12} & a_{13} \\ a_{21} & a_{22} & a_{23} \\ a_{31} & a_{32} & a_{33} \\ a_{41} & a_{42} & a_{43} \end{bmatrix} \qquad \text{(EQ 2.44)}$$

We wish to make use of matrix multiplication in order to compute a sequence of such transformations. This is impossible using the forms of (EQ 2.43) and (EQ 2.44), since the successive matrices would not be suitable for multiplication. Instead, we introduce the *homogeneous* representation of a 3D point as $(x, y, z) \equiv (x, y, z, 1)$, to write:

$$(x', y', z', 1) = (x, y, z, 1) \begin{bmatrix} a_{11} & a_{12} & a_{13} & 0 \\ a_{21} & a_{22} & a_{23} & 0 \\ a_{31} & a_{32} & a_{33} & 0 \\ a_{41} & a_{42} & a_{43} & 1 \end{bmatrix} \qquad \text{(EQ 2.45)}$$

as the general matrix form of an affine transformation. Now all representative matrices are 4×4, and can therefore be multiplied together.

In general for any 3D point (x, y, z) there are an infinite number of equivalent homogenous representations of this point as (wx, wy, wz, w) (for any $w \neq 0$). This can be thought of as the parametric representation of a line in 4D space that passes through the origin and the point $(x, y, z, 1)$, with w as the parameter. For any homogeneous point, the equivalent point in 3D space is obtained by dividing the homogeneous representation through by w. In fact, the whole of 3D space may be thought of as the 3-dimensional subspace of 4D space defined by the hyper-plane $w = 1$. Hence given any homogeneous point (X, Y, Z, W) $(W \neq 0)$ the equivalent 3D point is $(X/W, Y/W, Z/W)$. The conventional representation of the 3D point (x, y, z) in homogeneous space is as $(x, y, z, 1)$ (i.e., with $w = 1$).

Standard transformations

In this section we study the standard transformations, for translation, scaling and rotation about the principal axes.

Translation matrix.   To translate by a vector (a, b, c) we use:

$$T(a, b, c) = \begin{bmatrix} 1 & 0 & 0 & 0 \\ 0 & 1 & 0 & 0 \\ 0 & 0 & 1 & 0 \\ a & b & c & 1 \end{bmatrix}$$ (EQ 2.46)

since $(x, y, z, 1) \, T(a, b, c) = (x + a, y + b, z + c)$.

Scaling matrix. To scale relative to the origin by a, b and c applied to x, y and z respectively:

$$S(a, b, c) = \begin{bmatrix} a & 0 & 0 & 0 \\ 0 & b & 0 & 0 \\ 0 & 0 & c & 0 \\ 0 & 0 & 0 & 1 \end{bmatrix}$$ (EQ 2.47)

since $(x, y, z, 1) \, S(a, b, c) = (ax, by, cz)$.

Rotation matrices. Rotation can only be relative to an axis – rotation with respect to a point is undefined since there are an infinite number of possible paths corresponding to a rotation by angle θ about a point. With respect to a single axis there are only two possible paths, depending on the direction taken. We will define the *positive direction as anticlockwise* when looking down the axis of rotation towards the origin (recalling that we are assuming a right-handed coordinate system, Chapter 1). Here we consider rotation about the principal X, Y, and Z axes.

Rotation about the Z axis. When we rotate a point (x, y, z) about the Z axis, the z-coordinate remains unchanged, since the path of the rotation is with respect to a circle at constant distance z, along the Z axis, from the origin. Therefore, we can ignore the z-coordinate, and consider only what happens to x and y. Here we rotate the point (x, y, z) around the Z axis, by angle θ in a positive (anticlockwise) direction (Figure 2.11). The transformation is $(x, y, z, 1) \, R_z(\theta) = (x', y', z)$.

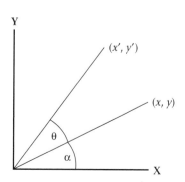

Figure 2.11
Polar coordinates –
rotation of a point

The following result is then obvious:

$$x' = r\cos(\alpha + \theta) = r\cos\alpha\cos\theta - r\sin\alpha\sin\theta = x\cos\theta - y\sin\theta$$
$$y' = r\sin(\alpha + \theta) = r\sin\alpha\cos\theta + r\sin\theta\sin\alpha = x\sin\theta + y\cos\theta \qquad \text{(EQ 2.48)}$$
$$z' = z$$

where r is the distance from the origin to (x, y).

This can be expressed in matrix form:

$$R_z(\theta) = \begin{bmatrix} \cos\theta & \sin\theta & 0 & 0 \\ -\sin\theta & \cos\theta & 0 & 0 \\ 0 & 0 & 1 & 0 \\ 0 & 0 & 0 & 1 \end{bmatrix} \qquad \text{(EQ 2.49)}$$

Rotation about the Y axis. An argument by symmetry (replacing x by z and y by x) shows that the Y axis rotation is:

$$R_y(\theta) = \begin{bmatrix} \cos\theta & 0 & -\sin\theta & 0 \\ 0 & 1 & 0 & 0 \\ \sin\theta & 0 & \cos\theta & 0 \\ 0 & 0 & 0 & 1 \end{bmatrix} \qquad \text{(EQ 2.50)}$$

Rotation about the X axis. A similar argument results in:

$$R_x(\theta) = \begin{bmatrix} 1 & 0 & 0 & 0 \\ 0 & \cos\theta & \sin\theta & 0 \\ 0 & -\sin\theta & \cos\theta & 0 \\ 0 & 0 & 0 & 1 \end{bmatrix} \qquad \text{(EQ 2.51)}$$

Inverse transformations. Each of the transformations has an inverse:

$$T^{-1}(a, b, c) = T(-a, -b, -c)$$
$$S^{-1}(a, b, c) = S\left(\frac{1}{a}, \frac{1}{b}, \frac{1}{c}\right) \text{ for } a \neq 0, b \neq 0, c \neq 0 \qquad \text{(EQ 2.52)}$$
$$R_s^{-1}(\theta) = R_s(-\theta) \text{ for all } s = x, y, z$$

Composition of transformations. Suppose we start with point $p = (x, y, z) \equiv (x, y, z, 1)$. If we apply a transformation M_0 to this point, we obtain $p_1 = pM_0$. If we apply a transformation M_1 to the new point we obtain $p_2 = p_1M_1 = pM_0M_1$. If we continue in this way applying transformations $M_3, M_4, \ldots$ it is easy to see that in general $p_i = pM_0M_1 \ldots M_i$. Hence a sequence of transformations applied to a point composes to a multiplication of all the matrices involved, in the same order as the transformations. From the point of view of efficiency, especially as the sequence of transformations is likely to be applied to many points, we would find $M = M_0M_1 \ldots M_i$ and then apply the single matrix M to all of the points.

It should be clear that such transformations, since they are matrix multiplications, are non-commutative. That is, $M_iM_j \neq M_jM_i$ in general. The order matters: scaling an object and then translating it does not result in the same new object as first translating it and then scaling.

In order to scale an object with respect to a point $q = (x, y, z) \neq (0, 0, 0)$ we would first apply a translation so that (x, y, z) is shifted to the origin, then apply the scaling, and finally translate back. Hence scaling with respect to an arbitrary point (x, y, z) would be obtained by:

$$T(-x, -y, -z)\,S(a, b, c)\,T(x, y, z) \tag{EQ 2.53}$$

Rotation about an arbitrary axis is more complicated and is discussed below.

Rotation about an arbitrary axis.   The rotation matrices R_x, R_y and R_z allow for rotation about the principal axes. These rotations in themselves are not sufficient – for example, unless an object happens to be centered on one of the principal axes, we would not be able to spin an object around an axis that intersects it. This kind of rotation is important – often in order to get a good understanding of the shape of an object we need to spin it around an axis that passes through it, or is at least near to it.

In this section we construct a composite transformation matrix (R) for rotation by angle α around an axis specified by two points $p_1 = (x_1, y_1, z_1)$ and $p_2 = (x_2, y_2, z_2)$. R can be constructed as follows:

(1) Translate so that p_1 is at the origin: $T(-p_1)$.

(2) Let $(x, y, z) = p_2 - p_1$ be the other end of the line segment, and write this in spherical form as (r, ϕ, θ). (Where $\alpha = \phi$ and $\beta = \theta$ with respect to Figure 2.5.)

(3) Apply the rotation $-\theta$ about the Z axis to bring Q on the ZX plane: $R_z(-\theta)$.

(4) Apply the rotation $-\phi$ about the Y axis, so that OP is now coincident with the Z axis: $R_y(-\phi)$.

Combining these we define the matrix $M = T(-p_1)R_z(-\theta)R_y(-\phi)$ that transforms the axis of rotation to be the Z axis. Now we can rotate by $R_z(\alpha)$, and then apply the inverse transformation M^{-1}. Hence the complete transformation is:

$$R = MR_z(\alpha)M^{-1} \tag{EQ 2.54}$$

where:

$$M = T(-p_1)R_z(-\theta)R_y(-\phi)$$
$$M^{-1} = R_y(\phi)R_z(\theta)T(p_1) \tag{EQ 2.55}$$

2.6   Quaternians

Definition

A quaternian is a generalization of the idea of complex numbers, especially useful in computer graphics for the specification of rotations, and also useful for creating key-frame animation sequences that interpolate rotations. Here we will outline the definition and simple use of quaternians without going into fine or rigorous mathematical detail. First we will define quaternians and some of the operations over them, and then we will give the geometric interpretation regarding rotations.

Suppose u_0 is a scalar value, and $\boldsymbol{u} = (u_1, u_2, u_3)$ is a vector. Then the 4-tuple (u_0, u_1, u_2, u_3) represents a quaternian, defined as:

$$u = u_0 + \boldsymbol{u}$$

or   (EQ 2.56)

$$u = u_0 + \boldsymbol{i}u_1 + \boldsymbol{j}u_2 + \boldsymbol{k}u_3$$

where $\boldsymbol{i}$, $\boldsymbol{j}$ and $\boldsymbol{k}$ are defined by:

$$\boldsymbol{i}^2 = \boldsymbol{j}^2 = \boldsymbol{k}^2 = \boldsymbol{ijk} = -1$$
$$\boldsymbol{ij} = \boldsymbol{k} = -\boldsymbol{ji}$$
$$\boldsymbol{jk} = \boldsymbol{i} = -\boldsymbol{kj}$$ (EQ 2.57)
$$\boldsymbol{ki} = \boldsymbol{j} = -\boldsymbol{ik}$$

The first line of (EQ 2.57) is the same as the definition of the "imaginary" number i ($i^2 = -1$). The remaining lines are the same as (EQ 2.18), the definitions for cross products for the principal unit vectors. Both of these interpretations are valid for quaternians.

The conjugate of a quaternian u is:

$$u^* = u_0 - \boldsymbol{u}$$ (EQ 2.58)

A *pure quaternian* has its scalar part $u_0 = 0$. Clearly there is an equivalence between the set of pure quaternians and the set of vectors in 3D space.

We use these definitions in order to motivate definitions of operations over quaternians.

Quaternian addition

Suppose $v = (v_0, v_1, v_2, v_3)$ is a quaternian, then

$$u + v = (u_0 + v_0) + \boldsymbol{i}(u_1 + v_1) + \boldsymbol{j}(u_2 + v_2) + \boldsymbol{k}(u_3 + v_3)$$
$$= (u_0 + v_0, u_1 + v_1, u_2 + v_2, u_3 + v_3)$$ (EQ 2.59)

Note that addition is commutative ($u + v = v + u$) and that the zero quaternian 0 (with all elements 0) is such that $u + 0 = 0 + u$ for any u.

Scalar multiplication

If u is a quaternian, and c a scalar, then

$$c \cdot u = c(u_0 + iu_1 + ju_2 + ku_3)$$
$$= (cu_0, cu_1, cu_2, cu_3)$$

(EQ 2.60)

Quaternian multiplication

Carry out the multiplicative expansion of

$$(u_0 + iu_1 + ju_2 + ku_3) \times (v_0 + iv_1 + jv_2 + kv_3)$$

in the usual way, but interpreting $a \times b$ as ordinary multiplication when both a, b are scalars, as vector cross product when both are different vectors, and as scalar times vector multiplication when one is a vector and the other is a scalar. However, in the expansion make sure that the order of vector cross product is always preserved.

Then

$$
\begin{aligned}
u \times v = \; & u_0 v_0 + iu_0 v_1 + ju_0 v_2 + ku_0 v_3 + \\
& iu_1 v_0 + i^2 u_1 v_1 + iju_1 v_2 + iku_1 v_3 + \\
& ju_2 v_0 + jiu_2 v_1 + j^2 u_2 v_2 + jku_2 v_3 + \\
& ku_3 v_0 + kiu_3 v_1 + kju_3 v_2 + k^2 u_3 v_3
\end{aligned}
$$

(EQ 2.61)

Now collect like terms together and use (EQ 2.57):

$$
\begin{aligned}
u \times v = \; & u_0 v_0 - u_1 v_1 - u_2 v_2 - u_3 v_3 + \\
& i(u_0 v_1 + u_1 v_0 + u_2 v_3 - u_3 v_2) + \\
& j(u_0 v_2 - u_1 v_3 + u_2 v_0 + u_3 v_1) + \\
& k(u_0 v_3 + u_1 v_2 - u_2 v_1 + u_3 v_0)
\end{aligned}
$$

(EQ 2.62)

Now using (EQ 2.8), (EQ 2.11) and (EQ 2.13):

$$u \times v = [u_0 v_0 - (\boldsymbol{u} \cdot \boldsymbol{v})] + (\boldsymbol{u} \times \boldsymbol{v}) + u_0 \boldsymbol{v} + v_0 \boldsymbol{u}$$

(EQ 2.63)

The term in the square bracket is a scalar, and the remainder of the expression is a vector. Hence this operation has resulted in the same form as (EQ 2.56) which is the definition of a quaternian. (EQ 2.63) is taken as the definition of quaternian multiplication, and clearly quaternian multiplication always results in a new quaternian. Note that the operation is not commutative $u \times v \neq v \times u$, but it is associative $u \times (v \times w) = (u \times v) \times w = u \times v \times w$.

Suppose u is a pure quaternian, $u = iu_1 + ju_2 + ku_3$, then

$$u^2 = -(\boldsymbol{u} \cdot \boldsymbol{u})$$

(EQ 2.64)

Quaternian inverse

Consider the multiplication of a quaternian and its conjugate:

$$u \times u^\star = u_0^2 + u_1^2 + u_2^2 + u_3^2$$

(EQ 2.65)

Similarly to the case of vectors, the norm $|u|$ of a quaternian is defined by:

$$|u|^2 = u \times u^* = u_0^2 + u_1^2 + u_2^2 + u_3^2 \qquad \text{(EQ 2.66)}$$

A unit quaternian has the property that $|u| = 1$. From (EQ 2.64) it follows that any pure unit quaternian (I) has the property:

$$I^2 = -1 \qquad \text{(EQ 2.67)}$$

To normalize any quaternian, we divide by its norm. Hence if u is any quaternian, we can define:

$$\text{norm}(u) = \frac{u}{|u|} \qquad \text{(EQ 2.68)}$$

Now consider

$$u \times \text{norm}(u^*) = \frac{u \times u^*}{|u|} \qquad \text{(EQ 2.69)}$$
$$= |u|$$

It follows that we can define the *inverse of a quaternian* as:

$$u^{-1} = \frac{u^*}{|u|^2} \qquad \text{(EQ 2.70)}$$

since $u \times u^{-1} = u^{-1} \times u = 1$.

Polar representation of quaternians

Let u be a unit quaternian, $u = u_0 + \boldsymbol{u}$. Since u is unit, we have:

$$|u|^2 = u_0^2 + |\boldsymbol{u}|^2 = 1 \qquad \text{(EQ 2.71)}$$
$$= \cos^2\theta + \sin^2\theta$$

for some $-\pi < \theta \le \pi$. Now we can always write:

$$s = \frac{\boldsymbol{u}}{|\boldsymbol{u}|} \qquad \text{(EQ 2.72)}$$
$$\therefore \boldsymbol{u} = |\boldsymbol{u}|s$$

where s is a unit vector. Hence, we can write:

$$u = \cos\theta + s\sin\theta \qquad \text{(EQ 2.73)}$$

as an alternative form for the representation of a quaternian.
    There is another way to look at this. From (EQ 2.72):

$$s = \frac{1}{|\boldsymbol{u}|}(iu_1 + ju_2 + ku_3) \qquad \text{(EQ 2.74)}$$

Then:

$$s \times s = s^2 = -1 \qquad\qquad \text{(EQ 2.75)}$$

Therefore:

$$\begin{aligned} u &= u_0 + \boldsymbol{u} \\ &= u_0 + |\boldsymbol{u}|s \end{aligned} \qquad\qquad \text{(EQ 2.76)}$$

where $s^2 = -1$, and since u is assumed to be a unit quaternian $u_0^2 + |\boldsymbol{u}|^2 = 1$. This is structurally identical to the usual form of a complex number $x + iy$, where $i^2 = -1$ is the so-called "imaginary" number. From complex number theory we know that $x + iy = \cos\theta + i\sin\theta$ (in the case where $x^2 + y^2 = 1$).

Any unit quaternian therefore can be decomposed into an expression given by (EQ 2.73), which means that quaternians have associated with them an angle (θ) and a unit vector (s). This is now used in showing how quaternians can be used to compute a rotation.

Quaternian rotation

We saw earlier that there is an equivalence between the set of pure quaternians and the set of vectors in 3D space. Suppose $\boldsymbol{p}$ is a vector, and p the corresponding quaternian. To make this absolutely clear, $p = 0 + \boldsymbol{p}$ in terms of the definition (EQ 2.56). Let u be any unit quaternian, such that $u = \cos\theta + s\sin\theta$. Then the multiplication upu^* results in a pure quaternian $q = 0 + \boldsymbol{q}$, and $\boldsymbol{q}$ is the rotation of $\boldsymbol{p}$ about the axis s by an angle of 2θ. Recall that in (EQ 2.54) we showed how to rotate a point about an arbitrary axis with the use of matrix transformations. With quaternians we can therefore accomplish exactly the same result with greater simplicity.

To illustrate this result we first consider a simple example – to rotate $\boldsymbol{p} = (x, y, z)$ about the Z axis (so $s = (0, 0, 1)$). First we find up.

$$up = -(\boldsymbol{u} \cdot \boldsymbol{p}) + \boldsymbol{u} \times \boldsymbol{p} \qquad\qquad \text{(EQ 2.77)}$$

using (EQ 2.63). But $\boldsymbol{u} = s\sin\theta = (0, 0, \sin\theta)$,

$$\begin{aligned} up &= -z\sin\theta + (-y\sin\theta, x\sin\theta, 0) + \cos\theta(x, y, z) \\ &= -z\sin\theta + (x\cos\theta - y\sin\theta, x\sin\theta + y\cos\theta, z\cos\theta) \end{aligned} \qquad\qquad \text{(EQ 2.78)}$$

Now we post-multiply up by $u^* = 0 - (0, 0, \sin\theta)$.

$$upu^* = (x\cos 2\theta - y\sin 2\theta, x\sin 2\theta + y\cos 2\theta, z) \qquad\qquad \text{(EQ 2.79)}$$

which reproduces the result of (EQ 2.48). In this example we have made use of the identities:

$$\begin{aligned} \cos 2\theta &= \cos^2\theta - \sin^2\theta \\ \sin 2\theta &= 2\sin\theta\cos\theta \end{aligned} \qquad\qquad \text{(EQ 2.80)}$$

Suppose that there are a sequence of rotations, angle $2\theta_i$ about axis s_i, for $i = 1, \ldots, n$. Then the result can be achieved by applying the quaternian rotation operator in sequence:

$$u_n u_{n-1} \ldots u_1 p u_1^* \ldots u_{n-1}^* u_{n^*} \qquad \text{(EQ 2.81)}$$

where $u_i = \cos\theta_i + s_i \sin\theta$. This is equivalent to finding the quaternian:

$$u = u_n u_{n-1} \ldots u_1 \qquad \text{(EQ 2.82)}$$

and using this as the single rotation operator upu^*. Typically there are many points that need to be transformed. It is immensely more efficient to compute the quaternian u once, and then repeatedly apply this to the points than to repeatedly find all the intermediate rotations (unless of course these are needed for an animation). The result also shows that any sequence of such rotations can always be represented as one single rotation.

2.7 Summary

This chapter started with the notion of dimension and how orthogonal coordinate frames can be used to characterize a space. We represent positions by points, and directions by vectors. We introduced the notions of solid angle and projected areas, and the relationship between these. Finally we examined the notion of affine transformation based on matrices, and an alternative representation for rotations based on quaternians.

For further reading on the mathematics underlying computer graphics, the following texts are recommended. Andrew Glassner's landmark reference work (Glassner, 1995) contains an extensive Appendix that covers linear algebra, the mathematics typically used in computer graphics. Hoggar (1992) covers a wide range of mathematics, including patterns and tilings, linear algebra, quaternians, fractals and chaotic systems. Finally a thorough review of rotation matrices and quaternians can be found in Kuipers (1999).

We have spent some time reminding readers of the very basics of points and vectors since these ideas and operations are fundamental to computer graphics. For the majority of this book, reflecting the vast amount of computer graphics practice, the type of geometry used to represent objects is that of simple polygons (often just triangles) inscribed on planes. Such planar polygons are mathematically and computationally easy to deal with. They have the advantage that most shapes can be approximated by collections of polygons or triangles, even curved shapes, provided that a relatively large number of triangles are used in the approximation. The "phantoms" that comprise virtual worlds are usually made of polygons.

3 Lighting – the radiance equation

3.1 Lighting: the fundamental problem for computer graphics

The idea of a scene being represented as a collection of graphical objects was introduced in Chapter 1. In computing terms this would be a data structure representing a collection of objects. Each object, for example, might be itself a collection of polygons. Each polygon is a sequence of points on a plane. This issue is taken up in detail in Chapter 8.

The "real world," however, is "one that generates energy." Our scene so far is truly a phantom one, since it simply is a description of a set of forms with no substance. Energy must be generated: the scene must be lit; albeit, lit with virtual light.

Computer graphics is concerned with the construction of virtual models of scenes. Modeling a scene is a relatively straightforward, if time-consuming, problem to solve. In comparison, the problem of *lighting* scenes is *the* major and central conceptual and practical problem of computer graphics. The problem is one of simulating lighting in scenes, in such a way that the computation does not take forever. Also, the resulting 2D projected images should look as if they are real. In fact, let's make the problem even more interesting and challenging: we do not just want the computation to be fast, we want it in *real-time*. Image frames, in other words, virtual photographs taken within the scene must be produced fast enough to keep up with the changing gaze (head and eye moves) of people looking and moving around the scene – so that they experience the same visual sensations as if they were moving through a corresponding real scene. Ideally, the simulation of lighting would be so accurate, and the speed of computation so great, that they would be unable to distinguish between the real and the virtual. Even more: objects in the scene could be moving, the light could be changing (e.g., a sunset), and the effect of the representations of the people immersed in the scene should also be taken into account as part of the lighting computation. In other words, I should see a reflection of my virtual self in the eyes of your virtual self.

Yes, well, this problem awaits a satisfactory solution.

3.2   Light

Why is the problem so hard to solve? It is because of the complexity of the interaction between light and objects in a scene. A full description of this is beyond the scope of this book. A very full treatment can be found in Glassner (1989), on which the current chapter is partially based. In this section we present some of the problems.

Visible light is electromagnetic radiation with wavelengths approximately in the range from 400 nm to 700 nm. Wavelength gives rise to the sensation of color (more about this in Chapter 4). It is well known that light has properties compatible with it being a wave phenomenon and also a particle phenomenon. In other words, if a wave model of light is adopted, and experiments carried out on this basis, then results are obtained which are compatible with the wave theory. On the other hand, the same is true if a particle model of light is adopted – results are compatible with this view of light too.

The particles are called *photons*, packets of energy which travel in a straight line in vacuum with velocity c (the usual symbol for the speed of light, approximately 300,000 m per second). Each photon carries energy E which is proportional to the frequency of its corresponding wave:

$$E = hf \qquad\qquad\qquad \text{(EQ 3.1)}$$

where h is called Planck's constant, and f is the frequency. The associated wavelength is inversely proportional to the frequency (the greater the frequency per unit time shorter the wavelength). In fact:

$$\lambda f = c \qquad\qquad\qquad \text{(EQ 3.2)}$$

since length of the wave (λ) times the number of waves per second must be the velocity.

Photons have another unusual property that they do not interfere with one another – two rays of light crossing one another do not interact. For example, photons along paths that reach into my eyes are not affected by other rays of photons crossing in front of my eyes.

The problem of how light interacts with surfaces in a volume of space is an example of a *transport* problem. In general this is concerned with the distribution of moving particles in a space – for example, the distribution of vehicles on a road system can be studied with equations similar to those that occur in light transport (though the study of most transport problems, including – unfortunately – vehicles, must take into account the effect of collisions amongst the particles).

We denote by Φ the *radiant energy* or *flux* in a volume V. The flux is the rate of energy flowing through a surface per unit time (it is measured in watts). The energy is proportional to the particle flow, since each photon carries energy. The flux may therefore be thought of as the flow of photons per unit time.

In fact the energy is proportional to the wavelength, so that to fully specify radiant energy in a volume we should use the notation Φ_λ, i.e., the radiant energy at wavelength λ (more precisely, in the range $[\lambda, \lambda + d\lambda]$). For the time being we shall drop the λ, and consider Φ as representing a specific wavelength. In perceptual terms λ produces the sensation of color, whereas flux is related to the sensation of brightness.

Now consider the total flux in a volume. First, this must be in dynamic equilibrium – that is, although of course particles are flowing through the volume, the overall distribution remains constant (for example, parts of a scene do not spontaneously become brighter or darker over time, other things being equal). It seems to an observer that immediately a light emitter is "switched on" in a scene, the light energy is instantaneously distributed through the scene, and the illumination remains constant. Of course it is not instantaneous, but appears so because of the speed of light.

Second, the law of conservation of energy applies. The total light energy input into the volume must be equal to the total energy that is output by or absorbed by matter within the volume. Light may be input into the volume in two ways: it flows in from outside (*in-scattering*) or it is emitted from within the volume itself (*emission*). Light may be output from the volume by *streaming* through it without interacting with any matter within the volume, or by interacting with matter in the volume and then being reflected out (*out-scattering*) or by being absorbed by that matter (*absorption*).

Hence we have the equation:

emission + in-scattering = streaming + out-scattering + absorption   (EQ 3.3)

Let's tie this down a bit further. Let $\Phi(p, \omega)$ be the flux at point p in direction ω, where $p \in V$ the volume, and $\omega \in \Gamma$ a set of directions of interest (hence ω is of the form (θ, ϕ)). Now each of the events, other than emission, in (EQ 3.3) is expressed in probabilitistic terms. For example, absorption is expressed as the probability density per unit time of a particle at point p travelling in direction ω being absorbed: $a(p, \omega)$. Hence the total absorbed density at this point and direction is $a(p, \omega)\Phi(p, \omega)$. If this is now integrated over the volume and directions, the total absorption in the volume is:

$$\Phi_a = \int_\Gamma \int_V a(p, \omega)\Phi(p, \omega)dpd\omega \qquad (EQ\ 3.4)$$

Similarly, let $k(p, \omega, \omega')$ be the probability that a photon travelling in direction ω at point p will be deflected into direction ω'. Then the total out-scattering is:

$$\Phi_o = \int_\Gamma \int_V \int_\Omega k(p, \omega, \omega')\Phi(p, \omega)d\omega'dpd\omega \qquad (EQ\ 3.5)$$

(Recall that Ω is the set of all directions on the unit sphere.)

There is a similar expression for in-scattering, Φ_i, but with the roles of ω and ω' reversed.

The streaming is the total flux over the whole surface, S, the boundary of V, in all directions. This is easy to write down as the integral:

$$\Phi_s = \int_\Gamma \int_S \Phi(p, \omega)dpd\omega \qquad (EQ\ 3.6)$$

Finally the emission density function is specified as $\varepsilon(p, \omega)$, the flux density emitted (photon energy per unit time) at point p in direction ω. Hence total emission in the volume is:

$$\Phi_e = \int_\Gamma \int_V \varepsilon(p, \omega)dpd\omega \qquad (EQ\ 3.7)$$

Now (EQ 3.3) may be written as:

$$\Phi_e + \Phi_i = \Phi_s + \Phi_o + \Phi_a \qquad (EQ\ 3.8)$$

Why do we care about all this? What has it got to do with computer graphics? The answer is surprising: if we knew $\Phi(p, \omega)$ then we would have a complete solution to the problem of lighting in computer graphics. It tells us the light energy flowing in every direction in which we might be interested (Γ) at every point throughout a volume of space (V). For example, suppose we had a virtual eye or camera in the scene, and wished to use that to make an image ("the phantom world of projections"). Then we would find all the rays of light that enter the lens (i.e., a set of $\omega \in \Omega$) and reach the retina of the eye or photographic film. This lens would correspond to a set of points p. Each ray that hits the surface of the lens therefore carries energy $\Phi(p, \omega)$ which determines the response of the eye or camera. An image would be formed, on the virtual retina or "film" plane, which when viewed by a person generates the sensations associated with seeing the virtual scene. (Of course, how this can be done is the subject of the rest of this book!)

Now how can we find $\Phi(p, \omega)$? We could try to solve the integral equation (EQ 3.8) for $\Phi(p, \omega)$. This is extremely hard and in practice cannot be achieved. Computer graphics is essentially about a series of different approximations and approaches to the solution of (EQ 3.8). The types of solution adopted depend on the requirements: a solution that delivers real-time performance is totally different to one that produces illumination realism, and there are compromises between these two extremes.

3.3   Simplifying assumptions

In order to get anywhere at all with the solution of (EQ 3.8) a number of simplifying assumptions are made which are usually applied across almost the whole realm of computer graphics.

Wavelength independence.   It is customary to assume that there is no inter-action between wavelengths. Therefore (EQ 3.8) can be solved at a sample of different wavelengths, and then these solutions combined together to estimate the wavelength distribution at a point along a ray. This rules out *fluorescence*. This is the process by which material absorbs light at one wavelength to reflect it out at a different wavelength within a short period of time.

Time invariance.   It is assumed that any solution of the equation for the distribution of energy remains valid over time unless something changes in the scene itself (e.g., an object moves position). This rules out *phosphorescence* which occurs when energy absorbed at one moment is emitted later after a (relatively) large time delay.

Light transports in a vacuum.   A very important simplifying assumption is that the volume of space through which light transports is a *vacuum*, though one dotted with the graphical objects of interest in a scene. In other words, the medium through which light travels is a *non-participating* medium rather than a *participating* medium. In this case a number of elements of the equation become simpler: absorption and out-scattering only occur at the boundaries of surfaces. There is no emission except from objects. There is no scattering or absorption, again except at the surfaces of objects. What this means is that a light ray that is unobstructed (i.e., a ray between two objects – sometimes called "free-space") has none of its energy absorbed, or scattered along that ray, and there are no particles of matter along the ray which them-selves generate additional light energy. This is a reasonable assumption for scenes representing building interiors – though even in this case the effects of dust cannot be taken into account. It is a less reasonable assumption for out-door scenes – it rules out rain and fog or any kind of lighting effects caused by the atmosphere.

Objects are isotropic. When photons strike a surface their energy may be partially absorbed and partially reflected. In an *isotropic* material, if we consider the incoming (or incident) direction of light, and an outgoing (reflected) direction, the relationship between these is the same over the whole surface of the object. This simplifies the types of expression involved in the $k(p, \omega, \omega')$ term, since now k is independent of p on the surface of such an object. An *anisotropic* material does not have this property.

3.4 Radiance

We have used flux in the discussion above because it is something that is easy to visualize – particles travelling through a volume, the number and rate of flow of such particles, and the effects of their collisions with matter in the volume. However, the real quantity of interest in computer graphics is not the flux itself, but a derivative of this quantity called the *radiance*. Radiance (L) is the flux that leaves a surface, per unit projected area of the surface, per unit solid angle of direction.

Let dA be the surface area from which the energy is leaving in direction θ relative to the normal (n) to dA, through a differential solid angle $d\omega$. This is shown in Figure 3.1. Then if the radiance leaving the "differential area" dA is L the corresponding flux is:

$$d^2\Phi = L dA \cos\theta d\omega \qquad \text{(EQ 3.9)}$$

As we let dA and $d\omega$ become vanishingly small $d^2\Phi$ represents the *flux along a ray* in direction θ. Another way to think about radiance then is that $L(p, \omega)$ is the function that is integrated over the solid angle and projected area in order to obtain the radiant power (flux) from that area.

In Figure 3.2 we show two small patches, dA and dB. Suppose r is the distance between them, and the radiance from dA to dB is L. Let's write $\Phi(dA, dB)$ as the radiant power transferred. Then:

$$\Phi(dA, dB) = L dA \cos\theta_A d\omega_B \qquad \text{(EQ 3.10)}$$

However, using (EQ 2.23) on page 56,

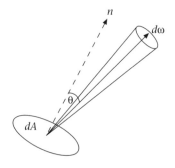

Figure 3.1
Radiance is flux per unit projected area per unit solid angle

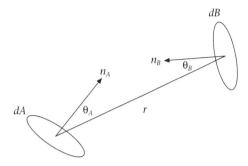

Figure 3.2
Flux between two
infinitesimal patches

$$d\omega_B = \frac{dB\cos\theta_B}{r^2}$$

(EQ 3.11)

$$\therefore \ \Phi(d(A,\ dB)) = \frac{LdA\cos\theta_A dB\cos\theta_B}{r^2}$$

This is called the fundamental law of photometry. Note also that by rearranging and again making use of (EQ 2.23), we obtain:

$$\Phi(dA,\ dB) = LdB\cos\theta_B\left(\frac{dA\cos\theta_A}{r^2}\right)$$

$$= LdB\cos\theta_B d\omega_B$$

$$= \Phi(dB,\ dA)$$

(EQ 3.12)

(EQ 3.12) shows that reversing the direction of the flow of light makes no difference to the flux – following the general principle that equations involving light energy are invariant when the direction is reversed.

(EQ 3.11) shows that flux diminishes by an amount equal to the inverse square of the distance – so that when the two areas are moved further apart the flux is diminished accordingly. However, this is not the case for radiance: radiance along a ray is constant – it is independent of the distance from the source.

This leads to a fundamental principle in computer graphics: we tend to forget about photons flowing through a volume of space, and instead abstract away from this underlying physics to think just about rays carrying light energy represented as radiance. *For computer graphics the basic particle is not the photon and the energy it carries but the ray and its associated radiance.*

There are three other characterizations of light energy that are important in computer graphics. The first is called *radiant intensity*. It is the radiant power (or flux) per unit solid angle (steradians). Hence, if I is the radiant intensity, then the associated radiant power is given in (EQ 3.13):

$$d\Phi = Id\omega$$

(EQ 3.13)

Hence, comparing with (EQ 3.10):

$$I = LdA\cos\theta$$

(EQ 3.14)

where L is the corresponding radiance.

The second is called *radiosity*. It is the flux per unit area that radiates from a surface, and is usually denoted by B. Hence, if B is the radiosity associated with the energy leaving area dA, the flux can be recovered as:

$$d\Phi = B dA \qquad\qquad\qquad\qquad \text{(EQ 3.15)}$$

Irradiance is the flux per unit area that arrives at a surface. It is usually denoted by E, and if the irradiance arriving at dA is E then the flux is:

$$d\Phi = E dA \qquad\qquad\qquad\qquad \text{(EQ 3.16)}$$

Suppose $L(p, \omega)$ is radiance arriving at point p along direction ω, then it follows from (EQ 3.9) that:

$$E(p, \omega) = \frac{d\Phi}{dA} = L(p, \omega)\cos\theta d\omega \qquad\qquad \text{(EQ 3.17)}$$

3.5   Reflectance

Up to now we have talked about the distribution of light energy in a scene, and made oblique references to light being absorbed and reflected from surfaces. Here we outline how this is taken into account in the computer graphics model for lighting. Suppose a ray of light energy hits a surface at p, with incident direction ω_i. The volume over which that energy may be reflected is the hemisphere whose base is the tangent plane at p. The reason for this should be clear: the hemisphere contains the entire set of directions visible from p which are not obscured by the surface of which p is a part (Figure 3.3).

The next question to ask is how much energy leaves the surface as a result in a reflected direction ω_r? We introduce the term $f(p, \omega_i, \omega_r)$ called the *bidirectional reflectance distribution function* (BRDF) which relates the reflected *radiance* at point p in direction ω_r to the incoming *irradiance* to point p in incident direction ω_i. Then:

$$L(p, \omega_r) = f(p, \omega_i, \omega_r) E(p, \omega_i) \qquad\qquad \text{(EQ 3.18)}$$

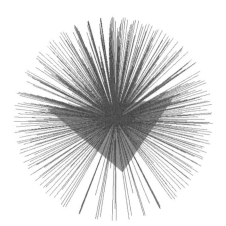

Figure 3.3
Light is radiated in a hemisphere about a point on a surface

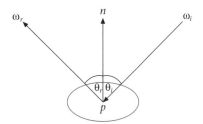

Figure 3.4
A specularly reflecting
surface

Exact specification of $f(p, \omega_i, \omega_r)$ for real surfaces in the world is an extremely complex task, especially if the surface is anisotropic (in which case f does vary with p). Computer graphics practice abstracts away from the complexity of the real world and mainly uses two idealizations of material properties called *specular* reflectors and *diffuse* reflectors, and mixtures of these. A specular reflector is a mirror-like surface, which reflects the incident ray as one outgoing ray such that the angle of incidence is equal to the angle of reflection (Figure 3.4). These angles are measured relative to the normal to the surface at p. Also, the vectors corresponding to ω_i and ω_r lie on the same plane as the normal. A very interesting proof of this can be found in Richard Feynman's lectures on physics (Feynman *et al.*, 1977, pp. 26-1 to 26-4). A diffuse reflector is a "rough" surface, which scatters the radiance of the incoming ray equally in all directions over the hemisphere above p. In this case it possible to show that:

$$f(p, \omega_i, \omega_r) \propto \frac{1}{\pi} \qquad\qquad \text{(EQ 3.19)}$$

where the constant of proportionality is the reflectivity of the material (i.e., the proportion of incoming flux which is reflected out across all directions).

More complex BRDFs can also be constructed. For example, with *glossy* reflection, an incident ray would have its energy dispersed in a cone about the ideal specularly reflected ray ω_r. A BRDF is typically constructed as a mixture of diffuse, specular and glossy components.

We have tacitly assumed that surfaces are opaque. However, transparent surfaces must also be taken into account. The approach is much the same, except that the light rays now would pass through different media (for example, from air to inside a block of ice) and the direction of transmission depends on the density – specifically the refraction index – of the material. This is discussed in more detail in Chapter 6. (See "Perfect specular transmission" on page 149. Also see Feynman *et al.*, 1977, pp. 26-3 to 26-4.)

3.6　The radiance equation

We said that the lighting problem would be completely solved if we could find $\Phi(p, \omega)$ for all points and directions, and that there is an equation for this function (EQ 3.8). We then introduced a number of restrictive assumptions on the road to making this equation more palatable, and also stated that the function really of interest is that for radiance rather than radiant power, $L(p, \omega)$ rather than $\Phi(p, \omega)$. With all the simplifying assumptions that have been suggested (and additional ones, beyond the scope of this book), and using the various terms that have been introduced, it is possible to derive a new equation from (EQ 3.8) that is much simpler to understand, expressed in terms of radiance rather than flux. This is called the *radiance equation*, and provides an equation for radiance at point p on a surface along the ray given by direction ω.

This equation expresses the fact that this radiance must be the sum of two quantities. The first is the amount of radiance directly *emitted* at this point (if any). For example, the point may itself be on a surface which is a light source. The second quantity is the amount of radiance *reflected* at this point. The amount reflected can be computed as the sum over all rays coming into p (the total irradiance) multiplied by the BRDF for this surface. Hence,

$$\text{radiance} = \text{emitted radiance} + \text{total reflected radiance} \qquad \text{(EQ 3.20)}$$

For any incoming direction ω_i the reflected radiance in direction ω is the irradiance multiplied by the BRDF. Using (EQ 3.17) and (EQ 3.18) this is:

$$f(p, \omega_i, \omega)L(p, \omega_i)\cos\theta_i d\omega_i \qquad \text{(EQ 3.21)}$$

If we integrate (i.e., "sum") this over the hemisphere of all incoming directions at p, we obtain:

$$\text{total reflection} = \int_\Omega f(p, \omega_i, \omega)L(p, \omega_i)\cos\theta_i d\omega_i \qquad \text{(EQ 3.22)}$$

The radiance equation for outgoing radiance $L(p, \omega)$ is therefore:

$$L(p, \omega) = L_e(p, \omega) + \int_\Omega f(p, \omega_i, \omega)L(p, \omega_i)\cos\theta_i d\omega_i$$

$$= L_e(p, \omega) + \int_0^{2\pi}\int_0^{\pi/2} f(p, \omega_i, \omega)L(p, \omega_i)\cos\theta_i \sin\theta_i d\theta d\phi \qquad \text{(EQ 3.23)}$$

where $L_e(p, \omega)$ is the emitted radiance.

This is an integral equation for the radiance function L, and much of the rest of this book is about how to solve it and hence find $L(p, w)$.

We have restricted p to lie on surfaces but in fact this restriction is unnecessary. Suppose p is not on a surface, then since radiance does not change along a ray in free space, we can trace the ray *backwards* in direction ω starting from p until we encounter a surface at p'. Then $L(p, \omega) = L(p', w)$.

Figure 3.5 shows a schematic representation of the radiance equation. Consider any incoming ray at p. According to the equation we need to compute the radiance along this ray. So we trace backwards along the incoming direction ω_i until we hit another surface at (say) p', and find the radiance $L(p', \omega_i)$. But in order to find this we need to invoke the radiance equation again. In other words, corresponding to each of the (uncountably infinite) number of

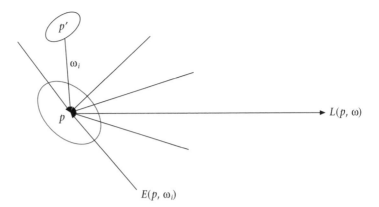

Figure 3.5
Illustrating the radiance
equation

incoming rays suggested in Figure 3.5 there is another copy of the same diagram, showing how the radiance along that ray was generated.

Putting this in everyday terms, the radiance equation highlights the fact
that illumination is *globally determined*. The light you see reflected from this
page of the book depends on the incoming light to the page, and on the
material properties of the surface of the page (the BRDF – how it reflects light).
The incoming light to the page depends on the direct light sources where you
are located, but also all the indirect light from other surfaces in your environment. The light reflected from those surfaces in turn depends on the direct
light reaching them, and all the indirect light from other surfaces in the environment, and so on.

3.7　Solutions of the radiance equation

In this section we consider various approaches to the solution of the radiance
equation, and in a real sense this section is an abstract guide to much of the
rest of this book.

In computer graphics applications the main interest in the radiance equation
is that it implicitly embodies the totality of all possible 2D views, i.e., images,
of the scene that it represents. The problem then becomes how to extract the
information needed to construct such images. The process of extracting 2D
projected images from the radiance equation is called *rendering*.

There are two approaches to this: the *view-independent* and the *view-dependent*
solutions. *View-dependence* means that the radiance equation is solved only for
that set of rays that are needed to form an image. We will study the mechanics
of specifying such a set of rays in Chapter 5 and onwards – for the time being,
as we mentioned earlier, it is the set of rays that are entering an "eye" or the lens
of a camera. These are the only rays that are visible to such an eye, the only
rays that cause the sensation of vision. Such a solution is called "view-dependent"
because if the viewing situation changes, for example if the eye looks in a
different direction, then the entire process of computing the radiance along the

eye-visible rays must be carried out again. So a view-dependent solution specializes in computing $L(p, \omega)$ for the set of (p, ω) such that p is on the surface representing the lens, and ω corresponds to the directions of rays through that lens.

A *view-independent* solution concentrates on pre-computing values for $L(p, \omega)$ across all surfaces of a scene and for as many directions as possible. Now when a particular image is required, the set of (p, ω) corresponding to the surface and directions through the lens are computed and the corresponding values of $L(p, \omega)$ are "looked up" rather than computed. This approach is called "view-independent" because a solution for $L(p, \omega)$ is found without regard to any particular viewing directions. View-independence has the advantage that producing an image of the scene is a constant time operation that is independent of the scene complexity and the particular view: it is just the time to compute the ray directions and intersections with the lens, and look up the corresponding L values.

Approaches to the solution of the radiance equation can be independently classified in two further ways – depending on whether the solution is local or global. A *local* solution at most takes into account only the direct effect of light sources on objects, and does not take into account inter-object reflection. This completely eliminates the recursion in (EQ 3.23). The integral is effectively replaced by a sum over those incident directions corresponding to rays coming from light sources (whose radiance values are known and therefore do not have to be computed recursively). To simplify things further, it is usually the case that such light sources are single points, so that for each point on the surface of an object there will be *one ray only* that represents an incoming radiance from a specific light source.

A *global* solution is one that takes into account the recursive nature of the radiance equation – in other words, at least some type of object interreflection is accounted for. The method called "ray tracing" only takes into account object interreflection for specular surfaces. The method called "radiosity" only takes into account object interreflection between diffuse surfaces. Other methods, usually called "Monte Carlo" methods statistically sample large sets of ray directions and find an approximate global solution based on these.

Table 3.1 classifies a number of approaches to computer graphics according to the type of solution of the radiance equation (local or global) and the

Table 3.1 Types of solution of the radiance equation

	Local	Global
View dependent	"real-time" graphics	ray tracing Monte Carlo path tracing
View independent	"flat-shaded" graphics	radiosity Monte Carlo photon tracing

phase-space of the solution (view dependent, or view independent). We briefly consider each in turn.

Flat-shaded graphics. The solution adopted for the radiance equation (EQ 3.23) is extremely simple: it is to ignore the integral completely so that $L(p, \omega) = L_e(p, \omega)$. In practice this means that each object has a preassigned radiance (think of this as a color). For any viewpoint the objects are simply projected to 2D and displayed in their color. We use this model in Chapter 5. It is view-independent because clearly the "solution" is obtained without taking any viewpoint into account. It is "local" because obviously there is no recursion in the solution, no impact even of primary light sources – except in the sense that each object is treated as a primary source.

Ray tracing. The radiance equation is simplified by only allowing point light sources and with BRDFs that only account properly for specular reflection. Suppose for example that there is only one (point) light source in a scene. Then each $f(p, \omega_i, \omega)$ will be non-zero for only one combination of ω and ω_i – that is, where the angle of incidence equals the angle of reflection. Hence there will be (at most) one incoming ray and one outgoing ray for each surface point. Now consider an "eye-visible ray," that is, a ray that is passing in an appropriate direction through the lens of the eye. Find the surface point (p) in the scene that is the origin for that ray. Trace a ray from p to the point light source and thereby compute the quantity $L_e(p, \omega)$ (which will be easily computable given the known radiance-emitting properties of the light). This quantity also includes a fudge called "ambient light" which is supposed to represent a total background illumination due to indirect lighting, and another fix called "diffuse light" which adds in a term to represent any diffuse characteristics of the surface (which is not globally accounted for in ray tracing). Now the remainder of the radiance equation is taken care of by recursively tracing the ray in the reflected direction from p until it hits another surface, and the radiance along that ray again computed recursively. The recursion continues until the amount of radiance added by a ray falls below some pre-assigned threshold. So each primary (eye-visible) ray spawns a whole tree of recursively followed reflected rays, each of which carries their radiance back up the tree towards the primary. Note that the light paths are being followed *backwards* – from the eye out to the scene! Ray tracing is view-dependent because solutions are found only for the specific set of rays entering the eye. It is global because the solution includes a special form of the recursive integral term. Ray tracing is considered in detail in Chapter 6, and revisited in Chapter 16.

Monte Carlo path tracing. This is similar to ray tracing – but can produce an estimated solution to the radiance equation that includes both specular and diffuse reflection. It follows the same general principle in that primary rays are traced into the scene from the eye. However, instead of the recursive rays following specific paths determined by the direction for specular reflection, rays are generated that follow a randomly selected direction. Thus given an intersection point p on a surface, the BRDF is sampled to randomly choose a ray to follow. This is continued from intersection point to intersection point until successive contributions are negligible. The whole process is repeated many times for each primary ray, and the results averaged together. Hence the space of all solutions for the particular eye is sampled. This is a view-dependent method because it starts from the primary eye-visible rays, and the solution is only valid for a particular view. It is clearly a global illumination method since it is a stochastic solution to the full radiance equation. This method is discussed in more detail in Chapter 22.

Real-time graphics.   The radiance equation is simplified further – the recursive element is completely removed. Light sources are again points. Only direct lighting is included – which means that the integral is replaced by a sum over light sources only, and only the local contribution of each light to p on a surface is computed. This is clearly a local solution. This approach differs from ray tracing in another sense: in ray tracing the primary eye-visible rays are traced out through the scene. In real-time graphics whole objects are "projected" to the lens surface – thus becoming 2D entities (rays are not explicitly used at all). In this 2D projected space pre-computed radiance values on the boundaries of the objects are interpolated to fill in the 2D visible solid areas of the objects. Ray tracing involves searching along the path of rays for objects that intersect the rays. Real-time graphics avoids this by directly projecting the objects to the lens surface – thus there are no computationally intensive ray–object intersection calculations. It is a view-dependent solution because the illumination on objects is, of course, only valid for a particular viewpoint and direction of view of an eye. The fundamental ideas of real-time graphics are presented in Chapters 9 through 13, and revisited in Chapter 23.

Radiosity.   The solution adopted for the radiance equation is to reduce the BRDF $f(p, \omega_i, \omega)$ to a constant with respect to direction, and entirely eliminate all directional aspects of the equation. As the name implies, the method also transforms the equation to be re-expressed in terms of radiosity rather than radiance. Now how is it possible to get away with eliminating all directional considerations? The answer is to assume that all surfaces are diffuse reflectors only. Recall that ideal diffuse reflectors scatter the energy of an incoming ray equally in all directions – hence direction is irrelevant. The surfaces of the scene are divided into small surface elements. The radiance equation reduces to a system of linear equations (one equation for each small surface element in the scene) where the unknowns are the radiosities associated with the surface elements. The solution to this equation therefore results in a radiosity being associated with each small surface element in the scene, or alternatively to points on the boundaries of those surface elements. It is a view-independent solution because it is in terms of the scene itself rather than for any particular set of rays for a specific eye. It is clearly a global solution, since it does take into account interreflection between the diffuse surfaces. Once the radiosity computation has been carried out it is then possible to use the approach of real-time graphics to produce specific views. Radiosity is discussed in Chapter 15.

Monte Carlo photon tracing. This attempts a general statistical solution of the radiance equation, though taking quite a different approach to path tracing. A large number of randomly distributed rays are traced from the light sources out into the scene. Each ray is traced to the nearest object that it intersects, and further rays are spawned based on the object's BRDF. Essentially this is a direct simulation of how light transports through an environment. However, this is a discrete representation of light transport. Of course each object will be hit by rays at a relatively small number of places, yet the radiance distribution over each entire object must be available for rendering purposes. In order to overcome this difficulty objects are partitioned into small surface elements, and these may be used, for example, to estimate a continuous density function over the surface of the object, so that the radiance in any direction and from any position on the surface can be estimated. This is clearly a global illumination solution. Like radiosity, there is a large up-front computation to perform, which estimates the distribution of radiance in the environment. Once this computation is finished, however, the scene may be quickly rendered from any viewpoint. This method is discussed in more detail in Chapter 22.

3.8 Visibility

There is an implicit but highly computationally intensive aspect of the radiance equation which is not obvious – this is the problem of *visibility*. Consider an incident ray to a surface point p. Where did that ray come from? Clearly from another surface. Which one? Ray tracing has to search explicitly for intersections of the ray potentially with all objects in the scene (though there are ways of speeding up this search, discussed in Chapter 16). This is one example of the visibility problem: we are only interested in incident rays from surfaces that are visible to the point p. (Even here there are complications, because rays through transparent objects are bent, and so even though a surface may not have straight-line visibility to p, it may still contribute radiance.)

The problem of visibility also occurs in real-time graphics, even though there is no explicit ray tracing. We said that all objects are projected to the surface of the lens. But of course not all objects will be visible to the eye – and of course objects may partially or fully obscure one another with respect to a particular viewpoint. So it is clearly not a matter of straightforward projection of objects – visibility relationships between objects with respect to a particular eye have to be taken into account. The solution that real-time graphics adopts is discussed in Chapter 13. The general problem of visibility is discussed in detail in Chapter 11.

3.9 Summary

This chapter has covered several issues:

- We have shown that efficient computation of scene lighting may be regarded as the central problem of computer graphics – it gives substance to the geometric form of scene description.

- We have introduced basic radiometric terms such as flux or radiant power, radiance, radiant intensity, irradiance, and radiosity.

- We have shown how the distribution of light in a scene may be described as a field of radiant power or more appropriately of radiance. A field is a function over points in a multi-dimensional space. The space here is 5-dimensional: each point of the form (p, ω). All information about the scene is encapsulated in the function $L(p, \omega)$.

- We introduced the radiance equation – an equation that $L(p, \omega)$ has to obey to satisfy the requirements of radiance distribution through a scene. This is the central equation of computer graphics, and all 3D display methods used in computer graphics are attempts at solving this equation – or (sometimes gross) simplifications of the equation.

- The process of rendering (2D projected) images of a scene is that of extracting the relevant information from the radiance field. This is equivalent to finding a way to solve the radiance equation – and we have briefly touched on several different methods used in computer graphics.

This has been a long chapter. It should be read again at the end of studying the rest of this book. This is because at the moment, if you have absorbed this material you will have a lot of understanding about lighting, but you still will have little idea about how to actually *do* anything. Revisit this chapter later – it both illuminates the remainder of the book, and is an abstract summary looking forward to the rest of the book.

So far we have introduced the description (or modeling) of a scene, and the fundamental problem of lighting it. People were only present implicitly – their "eye" is needed for rendering. In the next chapter we bring the human visual system into the equation.

4 Color and the human response to light

4.1   Introduction: color as spectral distributions

The previous chapter used quantities such as radiant flux, radiance, and so on that are from the field of *radiometry* – that is, the measurement of light energy. In this chapter we deal with *photometry* – that is, measurements appropriate to the response of the human visual system. Although it is a necessary condition for vision that light energy enters into our eyes, this does not determine what we *see*, as was discussed in Chapter 1. In this chapter we consider aspects of the human visual system in relation to color perception. This is vital for a good understanding of computer graphics. For example, rendering raw radiance values computed for a scene is often not only impossible because of the enormous range of values in a typical lit scene, but would anyway not usually give the desired results in the way that the image looks to an observer. The approach taken in this chapter is partially based on the work of Gomes and Velho (1997) with other material from Glassner (1995), and sources for specific data referenced in the text.

The photon stream emitted from a source flowing through a surface will normally consist of photons of different energies. Let λ represent wavelength, and $n(\lambda)$ be the density function for the wavelength distribution, meaning that in a small interval around λ there will be $n(\lambda)d\lambda$ photons flowing through the surface per unit time. From (EQ 3.2) on page 74 the energy associated with a photon is inversely proportional to its wavelength, hence the energy per unit time through the surface for a small interval of wavelength around λ will be

$$\frac{Kn(\lambda)}{\lambda}d\lambda \qquad\qquad (EQ\ 4.1)$$

for a constant K.

If we let

$$\Phi(\lambda) = \frac{Kn(\lambda)}{\lambda} \qquad\qquad (EQ\ 4.2)$$

then $\Phi(\lambda)$ is the *spectral radiant power distribution*.

It is this spectral distribution over wavelengths that is the *physical basis* for the sensation of color.

Imagine that a *spectrophotometer* were used to sample a particular source (whether emitter or reflecting surface) in the visible range of approximately 400 nm to 700 nm, and the radiant power were measured at each wavelength. Then we would have a spectral distribution of this radiometric quantity such as the one shown in Figure 4.1. This is represented by the function:

$$\Phi(\lambda)\ (\lambda_a < \lambda < \lambda_b) \qquad\qquad (EQ\ 4.3)$$

where $\Phi(\lambda)d\lambda$ gives the energy (in watts) for each wavelength and λ_a and λ_b are the upper and lower bounds of the visible spectrum. The integral of this function over the visible spectrum gives the total radiant power of the source (per unit time). Since all the other radiometric quantities, such as radiosity or radiance,

Figure 4.1
Spectral energy
distribution

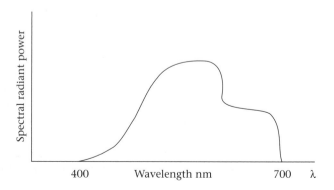

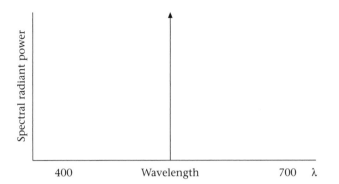

Figure 4.2
Spectral distribution for a
monochromatic source

are essentially derivatives of the radiant power, we can obtain such a spectral distribution for any of the other quantities.

When a surface emits or reflects light with a certain spectral distribution it gives rise to the *sensation* that we refer to as color. We will use the notation $C(\lambda)$ to refer to a general spectral distribution where it does not matter which of the specific radiometric terms is being considered. We may say that the color we perceive depends on $C(\lambda)$ as *filtered through the operations of the visual system*. Different types of animals with differing visual apparatus will "see" $C(\lambda)$ in quite different ways. Moreover, two $C(\lambda)$s will often be experienced by a visual system as producing the *same* color sensation even though they are quite different distributions. Such distinct distributions which are equivalent with respect to their perception by the same visual system are called *metamers* and play a highly significant role in the reproduction of color for computer graphics.

An energy source which emits light in one specific wavelength only is called *monochromatic*. Its corresponding $C(\lambda)$ function has its entire distribution located at a single point on the visible spectrum, so that the function may be thought of as an infinite vertical straight line located at this point but such that the "area under the curve" representing the energy is nevertheless finite (Figure 4.2). Mathematically this is represented by the *Dirac delta function*:

$$\delta(\lambda) = \begin{cases} \infty, & \lambda = 0 \\ 0, & \lambda \neq 0 \end{cases}$$

(EQ 4.4)

$$\int_{-\infty}^{\infty} \delta(\lambda)\,d\lambda = 1$$

where $[-\infty, \infty]$ is the real-line denoted by R. This function also has the useful property that:

$$\int_R f(t)\delta(x - t)\,dt = f(x)$$

(EQ 4.5)

A spectral distribution for the pure or monochrome color with wavelength λ_0 can therefore be represented as:

$$C(\lambda) = \delta(\lambda - \lambda_0) \tag{EQ 4.6}$$

In order to get a better understanding of monochromatic light we recall that Sir Isaac Newton discovered in 1666 that sunlight, which is perceived as white, consists of the whole visible spectrum. When this is decomposed by passing light through a prism, or more spectacularly through a rainbow, it is seen that it is made up of the entire visible spectrum – though specifically the colors that seem to stand out are (from low to high wavelength) violet, indigo, blue, green, yellow, orange and red. This is illustrated in Figure 4.3 (color plate).

Just as what we perceive as white light consists of a mixture of light at all wavelengths, so colored light is such a mixture – but rather than the spectral distribution being flat across all wavelengths there is typically a non-uniform distribution.

In this discussion so far we have mainly referred to energy being emitted from a source. The same argument applies to energy reflected from a surface. The light will be reflected according to the BRDF of the surface which should now be thought of as wavelength dependent. Hence energy of differing wavelengths will be diversely reflected by the surface material. It follows that energy reflected from a surface will also of course have a spectral distribution – i.e., the surface will appear colored. For example, a surface will look more reddish when photons from a white source with higher wavelengths have a greater probability of reflection according to the BRDF than photons of lower wavelength.

In this mathematical representation of color, the space of all visible colors is equivalent to the set of all such spectral distributions $C(\lambda)$ where $\lambda \in [\lambda_a, \lambda_b]$ and where $C(\lambda) \geq 0$, and for at least one λ, $C(\lambda) > 0$.[1] Any real physical system that is able to interpret (visualize) or generate colored (*chromatic*) light must somehow do this within the finite constraints of the physical world. One explanatory model is that the visual system does this by filtering the energy distribution through a finite number of channels and then using this to construct a finite signal to higher-order processing units in the brain – ultimately transformed into visual perceptions. Perceptions depend not only on the purely physical aspects of this processing, but also on many other psychological factors – such as expectations, memory, prior experience, and so on as part of the process of forming these perceptions. A physical emitter on the other hand constructs chromatic light by mixing together intensities of a finite number of sources. This finite set of sources provides a *basis* for the emitter system. It should be clear from this that a visualizer cannot "see" all possible colors, and an emitter cannot emit all possible colors, since the first is discretely sampling the infinite dimensional color space, and the second is attempting to reconstruct it on the basis of a finite number of basis functions. In the next sections we discuss visual systems, emitter systems, and the applications of these ideas to generating colors in computer graphics.

---

1. Some readers may be interested to note that the cardinality of this set is 2^c where c is the cardinality of the set of real numbers.

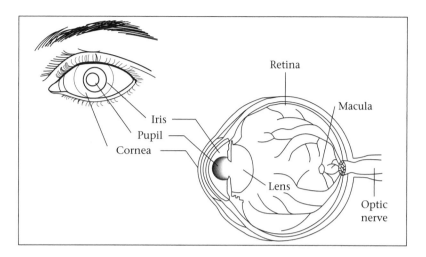

Figure 4.4
The human eye

4.2 A simple model for the visual system

Figure 4.4 shows a schematic of the human eye. Rays of light enter the eye via the pupil, and the size of the aperture is controlled by the iris – it is wider for dark environments, and narrower for bright ones. The rays of light are focused primarily by the eye as an optical system, consisting of the cornea which is filled with a transparent liquid called the vitreous humor, and with fine-grain focusing carried out by the lens. The thickness of the lens is controlled by the ciliary muscles. The back of the eye, the *retina*, consists of an array of many millions of photosensitive cells. There is a vast concentration of certain types of these cells in the *macula*, which is the area of highest clarity. Wherever we look there is only that particular spot which is completely in focus, representing the light that is focused on the macula. The entire image only seems to be in focus because our eyes are constantly moving and thus bringing different regions of the scene into focus. But if you hold your gaze on one particular spot and become aware of the clarity of the surrounding regions you will notice that the further out from the center the more blurred is the image. The results of processing carried out at the retinal level is passed through the optic nerve and finally through the cerebral cortex responsible ultimately for our sensation of vision.

There are two types of photosensitive cell coating the retina – called *rods* and *cones*. There are about 130,000,000 rods and between 5,000,000 and 7,000,000 cones. The rods are distributed over the retina and are responsible for night (*scotopic*) vision, and are also highly sensitive to movement – especially in the periphery. Cones are almost completely concentrated in and around the macula; they are responsible for visual acuity and color vision, and only operate in daylight (*photopic* vision).

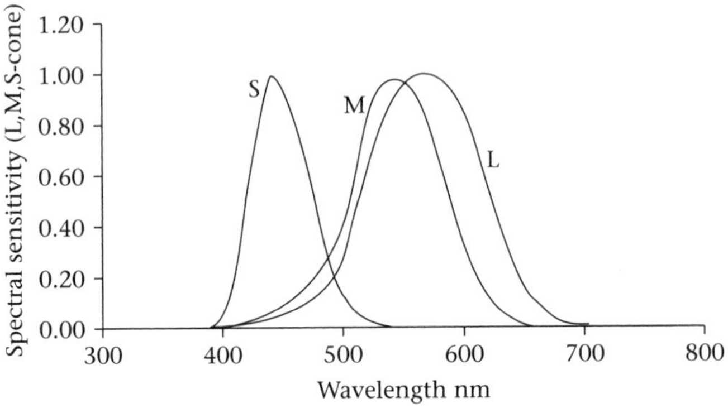

Figure 4.5
2-degree cone L, M, and S cone normalized response curves
Data from http://cvision.ucsd.edu/ based on Stockman and Sharpe (2000)

There are three types of cones regarding their response to light of different wavelengths. Some respond more in the long (reddish) wavelengths (L-cones), others in the medium (greenish) wavelengths (M-cones), and the third short (bluish) wavelengths (S-cones). The response functions are shown in Figure 4.5. In that figure 2-degree refers to the angle of view subtended by the eye by the observers looking at color samples in the experiments used to define these curves.

Let the three response functions be $L(\lambda)$, $M(\lambda)$ and $S(\lambda)$ respectively. Then a color represented by the spectral distribution $C(\lambda)$ is filtered through these response functions, resulting in three values:

$$l = \int_\Lambda C(\lambda)L(\lambda)d\lambda$$

$$m = \int_\Lambda C(\lambda)M(\lambda)d\lambda \qquad \text{(EQ 4.7)}$$

$$s = \int_\Lambda C(\lambda)S(\lambda)d\lambda$$

where $\Lambda = [\lambda_a, \lambda_b]$.

The LMS spectral response functions therefore map the infinite dimensional color space into a three-dimensional color space specified by triples of the form (l, m, s).

From (EQ 4.7) it is clear that completely different colors can nevertheless be mapped to the same triple – although their spectral distributions are distinct they are nonetheless *perceived* as the same color. As mentioned earlier, such colors are called metamers. If we let the mapping represented by (EQ 4.7) be represented as $LMS(C) = (l, m, s)$, then C_a and C_b are metamers if:

$$LMS(C_a) = LMS(C_b) = (l, m, s) \qquad \text{(EQ 4.8)}$$

A simple model for an emitter system

An emitter system generates chromatic light by additively mixing streams of energy which consist of lights with different spectral distributions. Physically this is equivalent to having a number of lights whose photon streams are mixed together. Each light emits energy with a known spectral distribution, and such that the *intensity* of the light can be varied. Just as the visual system uses three channels, so we will assume an emitter with three basis lights, which have spectral energy distributions $E_i(\lambda)$, $i = 1, 2, 3$. Then the spectral distribution of the emitter is:

$$C_E(\lambda) = \alpha_1 E_1(\lambda) + \alpha_2 E_2(\lambda) + \alpha_3 E_3(\lambda) \tag{EQ 4.9}$$

The α_i are the *intensities* and the E_i form the basis (and mathematically they are *basis functions*). It should be clear from (EQ 4.9) that the space of all possible colors of the form $C_E(\lambda)$ is a proper subset of the set of all visible colors. Putting this another way – there will be visible colors (i.e., spectral distributions) which cannot be generated by such a physical system. (Note that strictly speaking a color is a *sensation* produced by observing a spectral distribution, rather than the spectral distribution itself.)

A choice of basis functions which represent monochromatic light is of particular mathematical significance (and physical simplicity). The CIE (Commission Internationale de L'Eclairage[2]) defined the so-called CIE-RGB (Red, Green, Blue) basis in 1931 as follows:

$$E_R(\lambda) = \delta(\lambda - \lambda_R), \lambda_R = 700 \text{ nm}$$
$$E_G(\lambda) = \delta(\lambda - \lambda_G), \lambda_G = 546 \text{ nm} \tag{EQ 4.10}$$
$$E_B(\lambda) = \delta(\lambda - \lambda_B), \lambda_B = 436 \text{ nm}$$

These are called the CIE-RGB *primary colors*. The three spectral distributions clearly represent reddish, greenish, and bluish pure colors respectively. In this case the set of all reproducible colors are obtained by mixing together these red, green and blue primaries, hence the term RGB space, which is defined in (EQ 4.11).

$$C_{RGB}(\lambda) = \alpha_R E_R(\lambda) + \alpha_G E_G(\lambda) + \alpha_B E_B(\lambda) \tag{EQ 4.11}$$

In a physical sense what this means is that a color produced by such an emitter consists of a stream of photons each with one of these pure red, green, and blue wavelengths. Different colors are produced by the intensities (i.e., the "numbers") of photons of each type. It is therefore remarkable at first sight that such a system can be used to generate a large enough useful subset of perceivable colors to be useful.

---

2. http://cvision.ucsd.edu/

4.4 Generating perceivable colors

Suppose a surface in a real scene generates a color with spectral distribution $C(\lambda)$. This scene is simulated on a computer display, and the color represented by $C(\lambda)$ has therefore to be reproduced on the display. As we have seen from (EQ 4.9) a physical emitter will be unable to exactly reproduce a color with an arbitrary spectral distribution. However, it may be possible for it to produce a color with spectral distribution $C_E(\lambda)$ which is a *metamer* for $C(\lambda)$ with respect to the human visual system. Since a human observer would not be able to distinguish between the colors represented by $C(\lambda)$ and $C_E(\lambda)$, this solution would be sufficient.

Using (EQ 4.8) we require:

$$LMS(C) = LMS(C_E) = (l, m, s) \qquad \text{(EQ 4.12)}$$

When two colors are metameric in this way we will write:

$$C \approx C_E \qquad \text{(EQ 4.13)}$$

Note that in derived, perceptually based mathematical expressions, the $\approx$ symbol can be validly turned into the equality symbol. For example, given (EQ 4.13) it must be the case that $\int C(\lambda)L(\lambda)d\lambda = \int C_E(\lambda)L(\lambda)d\lambda$, otherwise they would not be metamers.

From (EQ 4.7):

$$l = \int_\Lambda C(\lambda)L(\lambda)d\lambda = \int_\Lambda C_E(\lambda)L(\lambda)d\lambda$$

$$m = \int_\Lambda C(\lambda)M(\lambda)d\lambda = \int_\Lambda C_E(\lambda)M(\lambda)d\lambda \qquad \text{(EQ 4.14)}$$

$$s = \int_\Lambda C(\lambda)S(\lambda)d\lambda = \int_\Lambda C_E(\lambda)S(\lambda)d\lambda$$

Let's consider just the L-cone equation, and make use of (EQ 4.9):

$$\int_\Lambda C(\lambda)L(\lambda)d\lambda = \int_\Lambda (\alpha_1 E_1(\lambda) + \alpha_2 E_2(\lambda) + \alpha_3 E_3(\lambda))L(\lambda)d\lambda$$

$$= \alpha_1 \int_\Lambda E_1(\lambda)L(\lambda)d\lambda + \alpha_2 \int_\Lambda E_2(\lambda)L(\lambda)d\lambda + \alpha_3 \int_\Lambda E_3(\lambda)L(\lambda)d\lambda \qquad \text{(EQ 4.15)}$$

Now $C(\lambda)$, $L(\lambda)$ and the $E_i(\lambda)$ will be known. Write:

$$\int_\Lambda C(\lambda)L(\lambda)d\lambda = c_L$$

$$\int_\Lambda E_i(\lambda)L(\lambda)d\lambda = e_{iL} \qquad \text{(EQ 4.16)}$$

and substitute this into (EQ 4.15), and apply the same notation for each of the three equations in (EQ 4.14):

$$\alpha_1 e_{1L} + \alpha_2 e_{2L} + \alpha_3 e_{3L} = c_L$$
$$\alpha_1 e_{1M} + \alpha_2 e_{2M} + \alpha_3 e_{3M} = c_M \qquad \text{(EQ 1.17)}$$
$$\alpha_1 e_{1S} + \alpha_2 e_{2S} + e_{3S} = c_S$$

or

$$\begin{bmatrix} e_{1L} & e_{2L} & e_{3L} \\ e_{1M} & e_{2M} & e_{3M} \\ e_{1S} & e_{2S} & e_{3S} \end{bmatrix} \begin{bmatrix} \alpha_1 \\ \alpha_2 \\ \alpha_3 \end{bmatrix} = \begin{bmatrix} c_L \\ c_M \\ c_S \end{bmatrix} \qquad \text{(EQ 4.18)}$$

This gives three linear equations in the three unknowns α_1, α_2, α_3. So since we would in principle know the three L, M, and S response functions and the basis functions for the emitter, we can find the intensities necessary to generate the required metameric color. In particular, if the RGB primaries are used as given in (EQ 4.10) the solution to the equation gives the appropriate "red," "green," and "blue" intensities for the required color with respect to the visual system. Moreover, in this case we can make use of the definitions of the RGB primaries in (EQ 4.10) and (EQ 4.5) so that:

$$\int_\Lambda E_R(\lambda)L(\lambda)d\lambda = e_{1L} = L(\lambda_R)$$

$$\int_\Lambda E_G(\lambda)L(\lambda)d\lambda = e_{2L} = L(\lambda_G) \qquad \text{(EQ 4.19)}$$

$$\int_\Lambda E_B(\lambda)L(\lambda)d\lambda = e_{3L} = L(\lambda_B)$$

and similarly for the medium and short response curves M and S. An examination of Figure 4.5 suggests that many of the coefficients in the matrix of (EQ 4.18) would be close to zero, which would further simplify the calculations.

To summarize so far: suppose our computer graphics solution permits the computation of a spectral distribution for a surface (or indeed for an individual ray) by repeated solutions of the radiance equation for different wavelengths thus constructing an estimate of the spectral distribution $C(\lambda)$. Suppose also that we knew the RGB primary basis for a particular display, and the L, M, and S cone response curves, then we could solve (EQ 4.18) in order to obtain the intensities at which the display primaries should be set to give us a color which looks the same as that represented by $C(\lambda)$. However, the situation is more complex than this.

4.5   The CIE-RGB color matching functions

A problem with using (EQ 4.18) is that it requires accurate knowledge of the L, M, and S cone response functions. These cannot be directly estimated but can only be found from other information. There is an alternative approach which relies on functions that can be estimated from relatively straightforward experiments. These are called the *color matching functions*, and are of vital importance in color theory.

Consider a monochrome color with wavelength λ_0 and therefore spectral distribution $\delta(\lambda - \lambda_0)$. Let $\gamma_i(\lambda_0)$ be the intensities for the generation of this color with respect to an emitter with basis functions $E_i(\lambda)$ as before. Then:

$$\delta(\lambda - \lambda_0) \approx \sum_{i=1}^{3} \gamma_i(\lambda_0)E_i(\lambda) \qquad \text{(EQ 4.20)}$$

Suppose we somehow found the values of $\gamma_i(\lambda_0)$ for each of a large number of wavelengths λ_0, this would give for every wavelength the intensities at which to set the primary basis colors in order to generate a metamer for a pure color of that wavelength. Note here that we are therefore treating the γ_i as functions of wavelength. We will return to the physical interpretation of these functions soon, but first we show their utility.

First we find the visual system responses for such a pure color of wavelength λ_0 making use of (EQ 4.5), (EQ 4.7):

$$\int_\Lambda \delta(\lambda - \lambda_0)L(\lambda)d\lambda = L(\lambda_0)$$

$$\int_\Lambda \delta(\lambda - \lambda_0)M(\lambda)d\lambda = M(\lambda_0) \qquad \text{(EQ 4.21)}$$

$$\int_\Lambda \delta(\lambda - \lambda_0)S(\lambda)d\lambda = S(\lambda_0)$$

Now substitute (EQ 4.20) into (EQ 4.21) and use (EQ 4.16) (we show the first row only, for L):

$$\int_\Lambda \left(\sum_{i=1}^{3} \gamma_i(\lambda_0)E_i(\lambda) \right) L(\lambda)d\lambda = L(\lambda_0)$$

$$\qquad \text{(EQ 4.22)}$$

$$= \sum_{i=1}^{3} \gamma_i(\lambda_0) \int_\Lambda E_i(\lambda)L(\lambda)d\lambda = \sum_{i=1}^{3} \gamma_i(\lambda_0)e_{iL}$$

Since λ_0 is arbitrary we replace it by λ, multiply through by $C(\lambda)$ and integrate out λ:

$$\sum_{i=1}^{3} e_{iL} \int_\Lambda \gamma_i(\lambda)C(\lambda)d\lambda = \int_\Lambda C(\lambda)L(\lambda)d\lambda \qquad \text{(EQ 4.23)}$$

Now use (EQ 4.15) and (EQ 4.16) on the right-hand side of (EQ 4.23) to give:

$$\sum_{i=1}^{3} e_{iL} \int_\Lambda \gamma_i(\lambda)C(\lambda)d\lambda = \sum_{i=1}^{3} e_{iL}\alpha_i \qquad \text{(EQ 4.24)}$$

Collecting similar terms:

$$\sum_{i=1}^{3} e_{iL}\left(\int_{\Lambda} \gamma_i(\lambda)C(\lambda)d\lambda - \alpha_i \right) = 0 \qquad \text{(EQ 4.25)}$$

Now if we carry out the identical construction for the M and S response curves, we obtain:

$$\begin{bmatrix} e_{1L} & e_{2L} & e_{3L} \\ e_{1M} & e_{2M} & e_{3M} \\ e_{1S} & e_{2S} & e_{3S} \end{bmatrix} \begin{bmatrix} \int_{\Lambda} \gamma_1(\lambda)C(\lambda)d\lambda - \alpha_1 \\ \int_{\Lambda} \gamma_2(\lambda)C(\lambda)d\lambda - \alpha_2 \\ \int_{\Lambda} \gamma_3(\lambda)C(\lambda)d\lambda - \alpha_3 \end{bmatrix} = \begin{bmatrix} 0 \\ 0 \\ 0 \end{bmatrix} \qquad \text{(EQ 4.26)}$$

Now assuming that the matrix on the left-hand side is of full rank and therefore invertible (we do not prove this here), we achieve the result:

$$\alpha_i = \int_{\Lambda} \gamma_i(\lambda)C(\lambda)d\lambda \qquad \text{(EQ 4.27)}$$

In other words, we can find the intensity levels (α_i) for the basis colors $E_i(\lambda)$ by forming the integral of the spectral distribution multiplied by the γ_i functions. These functions are called the *color matching functions* because they give for any pure color of wavelength λ the intensities of the basis colors to match that color.

The color matching functions can be estimated with a simple experiment. Generate a beam of the required pure reference color which has wavelength λ_0. Overlap three other beams which generate light with the three basis spectra, and adjust the intensities of those beams until a match is found for the reference color. Record the values of these intensities $\gamma_1(\lambda_0)$, $\gamma_2(\lambda_0)$, $\gamma_3(\lambda_0)$. Now repeat the same experiment for $\lambda_1, \lambda_2, \ldots, \lambda_n$ covering the range of the visible spectrum. This will result in estimates for the three functions.

Figure 4.6 shows the CIE-RGB color matching functions. These are obtained using the RGB primary colors given in (EQ 4.10) sampled at 5 nm intervals between 390 nm and 830 nm. These are called the "2 degree" color matching functions because the observer only sees a field of view of 2 degrees. There are 10 degree matching functions but the 2 degree ones are used in computer graphics because of the relatively narrow field of view when looking at a display.

It will be seen that some of the values are negative – how is this possible? Recall that this is color matching, and that we are relying on metamers in order to achieve these results. Now suppose we are trying to match the color at some

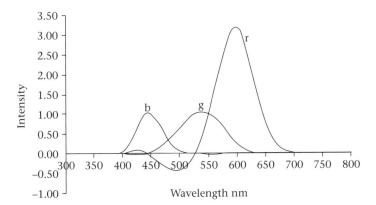

Figure 4.6
Stiles and Burch (1955)
2-deg RGB color
matching functions

wavelength γ_0. Then we are trying to find values $\gamma_1(\lambda_0)$, $\gamma_2(\lambda_0)$, $\gamma_3(\lambda_0)$ such that $\delta(\lambda - \lambda_0)$ is perceptually equivalent (metameric) to what can be produced by the three beams. In other words, we require:

$$\delta(\lambda - \lambda_0) \approx \gamma_1(\lambda_0)E_R(\lambda) + \gamma_2(\lambda_0)E_G(\lambda) + \gamma_3(\lambda_0)E_B(\lambda) \qquad \text{(EQ 4.28)}$$

Now it may be the case that such a match isn't possible. However, suppose that we add the red beam at the appropriate intensity to the reference beam, and then try to carry out a match with the remaining two colors. If there is a match then:

$$\delta(\lambda - \lambda_0) + \gamma_1(\lambda_0)E_R(\lambda) \approx \gamma_2(\lambda_0)E_G(\lambda) + \gamma_3(\lambda_0)E_B(\lambda) \qquad \text{(EQ 4.29)}$$

Hence the coefficient for the red primary would be negative. Similarly, if a match cannot be achieved by mixing the red primary with the reference light the green is used instead, and the match is attempted with the red and blue beams. Finally we would try the blue, and achieve a match with the red and green beams. In this way every pure color across the visible spectrum can be matched with an appropriate mix of red, green and blue primaries.

In practice the values used are in comparison to a "white point" – the beams are first adjusted to give a desired "white" color for that physical system. Then the intensities to match a particular pure color are calculated by dividing by the white point intensities. If the white point occurs with all three beams at their maximum intensity, then the intensities to match any pure color will be fractions (between 0 and 1) representing the proportion of maximum intensity for each beam.

To summarize – suppose we have the spectral distribution for the color from a surface $C(\lambda)$ (for example, we have computed this as a solution to the radiance equation for some surface in a virtual scene). Now we wish to generate a color on a display which gives the same sensation as if the observer were looking at $C(\lambda)$ in real life. Let's assume that the display works with the CIE-RGB primaries. Then we use (EQ 4.27) to compute the beam intensities (α_i)

where the γ_i are the RGB color matching functions. We pass these intensities to the display, and this can be thought of as acting according to (EQ 4.11) to produce a color which is a metamer for $C(\lambda)$. Let the CIE-RGB color matching functions be:

$$\bar{r}(\lambda) = \gamma_1(\lambda)$$
$$\bar{g}(\lambda) = \gamma_2(\lambda) \qquad \text{(EQ 4.30)}$$
$$\bar{b}(\lambda) = \gamma_3(\lambda)$$

Then

$$C(\lambda) \approx \alpha_R E_R(\lambda) + \alpha_G E_G(\lambda) + \alpha_B E_B(\lambda), \text{ where}$$

$$\alpha_R = \int_\Lambda \bar{r}(\lambda) C(\lambda) d\lambda$$

$$\alpha_G = \int_\Lambda \bar{g}(\lambda) C(\lambda) d\lambda \qquad \text{(EQ 4.31)}$$

$$\alpha_B = \int_\Lambda \bar{b}(\lambda) C(\lambda) d\lambda$$

We can find the RGB intensities $(\alpha_R, \alpha_G, \alpha_B)$ by numerical integration.

4.6 CIE-RGB chromaticity space

From the discussion in the previous section it should be clear that corresponding to each color $C(\lambda)$ there is a metamer $(\alpha_R, \alpha_G, \alpha_B)$ in CIE-RGB space. This mapping from the infinite dimensional space of spectral functions to a 3-dimensional space is obviously many–one (otherwise there would be no metamers). In this section we will examine what this 3-dimensional color space "looks" like in the following sense. Imagine that each visible color is transformed into its equivalent 3D point, and that the point is colored according to the intensities represented by the corresponding $(\alpha_R, \alpha_G, \alpha_B)$. Then as we move continuously through this space we would "see" continually changing colors. In other words, there is a volume of 3D space that corresponds to the set of all possible visible colors, and we could in principle create a volume of 3D space colored accordingly and then "fly" through it (e.g., in virtual reality). But it is very hard to visualize such a volume, and as it turns out it is unnecessary – we can get away with considering only 2D slices of that 3D volume.

First consider the pure wavelength monochromatic colors. For any such color with wavelength λ_0 we have $C(\lambda) = \delta(\lambda - \lambda_0)$. Using this in (EQ 4.31):

$$(\alpha_R(\lambda_0), \alpha_G(\lambda_0), \alpha_B(\lambda_0)) = (\bar{r}(\lambda_0), \bar{g}(\lambda_0), \bar{b}(\lambda_0)) \qquad \text{(EQ 4.32)}$$

for any $\lambda_0 \in [\lambda_a, \lambda_b]$.

Now as λ_0 ranges over all visible wavelengths, (EQ 4.32) sweeps out a curve in 3-dimensional space representing the metamers for the pure colors. Rather than try to draw such a curve in 3D space we will instead project the curve through the origin onto a plane, and render the projected curve. The conventional plane onto which the curve is projected is

$$\alpha_R + \alpha_G + \alpha_B = 1 \qquad\qquad \text{(EQ 4.33)}$$

where the α are the x, y and z coordinates of the 3D space.

Suppose $(\alpha_R, \alpha_G, \alpha_B)$ is a point on this curve. Then the parametric equation of the *line* from the origin through this point is:

$$(t\alpha_R, t\alpha_G, t\alpha_B), \text{ for all } t > 0 \qquad\qquad \text{(EQ 4.34)}$$

Where this line intersects the plane (EQ 4.33) we must have:

$$t\alpha_R + t\alpha_G + t\alpha_B = 1 \qquad\qquad \text{(EQ 4.35)}$$

and therefore:

$$t = \frac{1}{\alpha_R + \alpha_G + \alpha_B} \qquad\qquad \text{(EQ 4.36)}$$

Therefore the projection of any point $(\alpha_R(\lambda_0),\ \alpha_G(\lambda_0)\ \alpha_B(\lambda_0))$ onto the plane will be:

$$\left(\frac{\alpha_R(\lambda_0)}{\alpha_R(\lambda_0) + \alpha_G(\lambda_0) + \alpha_B(\lambda_0)},\ \frac{\alpha_G(\lambda_0)}{\alpha_R(\lambda_0) + \alpha_G(\lambda_0) + \alpha_B(\lambda_0)},\ \frac{\alpha_B(\lambda_0)}{\alpha_R(\lambda_0) + \alpha_G(\lambda_0) + \alpha_B(\lambda_0)} \right)$$

We carry out an *orthographic* projection to 2D by ignoring the third (blue) coordinate in this expression, and the result is shown in Figure 4.7. This is leading to what is called CIE-RGB "chromaticity space," as we shall see. Every point on this curve is based on the combination of RGB intensities required to produce the pure color of corresponding wavelength. Three such wavelengths are indicated on the curve.

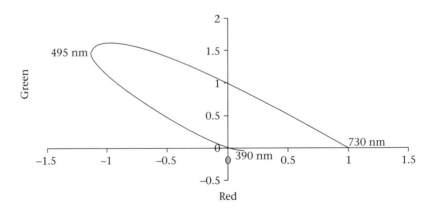

Figure 4.7
CIE-RGB chromaticity
space (not scaled for
white point)

Let's explore this space a little further. Suppose now that $C_1(\lambda)$ and $C_2(\lambda)$ are the spectral distributions for two distinct visible colors, and let the corresponding points in the RGB color space be:

$$\alpha_1 = (\alpha_{R1}, \alpha_{G1}, \alpha_{B1})$$
$$\alpha_2 = (\alpha_{R2}, \alpha_{G2}, \alpha_{B2})$$

(EQ 4.37)

Then

$$\alpha_1 = \left(\int_\Lambda \bar{r}(\lambda)C_1(\lambda)d\lambda, \int_\Lambda \bar{g}(\lambda)C_1(\lambda)d\lambda, \int_\Lambda \bar{b}(\lambda)C_1(\lambda)d\lambda \right)$$

$$\alpha_2 = \left(\int_\Lambda \bar{r}(\lambda)C_2(\lambda)d\lambda, \int_\Lambda \bar{g}(\lambda)C_2(\lambda)d\lambda, \int_\Lambda \bar{b}(\lambda)C_2(\lambda)d\lambda \right)$$

(EQ 4.38)

Now all points on the straight line joining α_1 and α_2 can be represented by the parametric form

$$(1-t)\alpha_1 + t\alpha_2 \text{ for all } t \in [0, 1]$$

(EQ 4.39)

From (EQ 4.38) this is a color metameric to $(1-t)C_1(\lambda) + tC_2(\lambda)$. Provided that t is between 0 and 1 (inclusive) this corresponds to a visible color (if $t < 0$ or $t > 1$ then the spectral distribution becomes negative and so cannot represent a visible color). Now when we project the straight line segment given by (EQ 4.39) onto the plane $\alpha_R + \alpha_G + \alpha_B = 1$ the projection is a straight line joining the projections of the two points α_1 and α_2. The implication of this is that all visible colors are projected onto this plane such that their projections are within (or on the boundaries of) the curve shown in Figure 4.7. Putting this another way, given any two points on the curve boundary, all points on the straight line between those points represent visible colors. Since any point inside the curve is on an infinite number of such possible straight lines, all points in the interior of the curve correspond to visible colors. Hence the set of all visible colors maps to the interior (and boundary) of the curve.

We now turn to a perceptual interpretation of the projection plane. Recall the L, M, and S cone response functions for the visual system. These define the responses of the three types of photosensitive cone cells to light of different wavelengths in the visible band. The total response of the visual system as a whole can be considered as a certain weighted average of these three response curves:

$$V(\lambda) = \beta_1 L(\lambda) + \beta_2 M(\lambda) + \beta_3 S(\lambda)$$

(EQ 4.40)

Specific values of the β_i results in the *spectral luminous efficiency* curve for the visual system denoted by $V(\lambda)$ and defined by the CIE standard. The graph of this function is shown in Figure 4.8.

Now given any spectral distribution $C(\lambda)$ the overall response of the visual system to this color can be computed by modulating the spectral distribution by the luminous efficiency function:

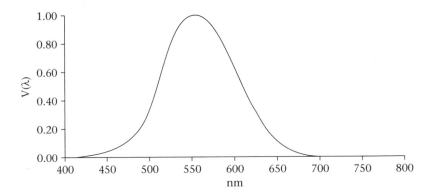

Figure 4.8
Spectral luminous
efficiency function

$$L(C) = K \int_\Lambda C(\lambda) V(\lambda) d\lambda \qquad \text{(EQ 4.41)}$$

where K is a specified constant to achieve the correct units of measurement for the quantity of interest (we will usually not write K below). In particular, if $C(\lambda)$ is a *radiance* spectral distribution, then L is called the *luminance* of the response, and $K = 680$ lumens/watt, with luminance is measured in "candelas per square meter." We said earlier that the visual system responds to radiance; in fact its response is radiance as modulated by the luminous efficiency function. This function when applied to any type of spectral energy distribution (for example the flux distribution rather than the radiance) transforms the radiometric quantity into an equivalent *photometric* quantity. The former types of quantity are physical energy measures, the latter are concerned with the corresponding response of the visual system.

Let's return to (EQ 4.11) which showed how a spectral distribution can be generated from the primary basis colors, and find the corresponding luminance:

$$C(\lambda) \approx \alpha_R E_R(\lambda) + \alpha_G E_G(\lambda) + \alpha_B E_B(\lambda)$$

$$\therefore L(C) = \alpha_R \int_\Lambda E_R(\lambda) V(\lambda) d\lambda + \alpha_G \int_\Lambda E_G(\lambda) V(\lambda) d\lambda + \alpha_B \int_\Lambda E_B(\lambda) V(\lambda) d\lambda \qquad \text{(EQ 4.42)}$$

which can be rewritten as:

$$L(C) = \alpha_R l_R + \alpha_G l_G + \alpha_B l_B$$

Now l_R, l_G and l_B are *constants* determined wholly by the primary basis and the luminous efficiency function. The set of all possible $(\alpha_R, \alpha_G, \alpha_B)$ satisfying (EQ 4.42) forms a plane in the 3D color space. But every point on this plane within the volume of visible colors has the same luminance $L(C)$. There is only one point that corresponds to the color $C(\lambda)$ though. So what is varying across this plane of constant luminocity? It must be what we normally perceive as *color* itself (i.e., "color" but abstracting away the luminance). However, in order to avoid terminological confusion we call this aspect of color the *chrominance*. So a color consists of two distinct and independent attributes: the scalar quantity that we call luminance, and the 2-dimensional quantity that we call *chrominance*.

Let's rewrite (EQ 4.42) slightly differently as:

$$\alpha_R l_R + \alpha_G l_G + \alpha_B l_B = L \qquad \text{(EQ 4.43)}$$

Remember that l_R, l_G and l_B are constants and (α_R, α_G, α_B) are variables representing the coordinate axes. If we multiply throughout by some constant $t > 0$ the equation is of course still satisfied, but now represents a plane with constant luminance tL. Let (α_R', α_G', α_B') be a specific point in the color space that satisfies (EQ 4.43). As we let t vary, the locus of ($t\alpha_R'$, $t\alpha_G'$, $t\alpha_B'$) is a straight line from the origin through the point (α_R', α_G', α_B'). The luminance is changing along this line (increasing with t) but the chrominance is invariant along the line. Hence the intersection of the line with the plane $\alpha_R + \alpha_G + \alpha_B = 1$ is simply a way of providing a 2-dimensional coordinate system characterizing the chrominance, thus leading to the chromaticity diagram discussed above.

4.7   CIE-XYZ chromaticity space

The CIE-RGB chromaticity diagram of Figure 4.7 is rather strange. It shows that a large proportion of visible colors are actually not physically achievable by an emitter based on the CIE-RGB primaries. No color with chromaticity outside of the first quadrant of this diagram (or equivalently in the first octant of the full 3D color space) can actually be realized with this basis – for these correspond to negative intensities.

The question arises as to whether there is an alternative set of primaries that give a more satisfactory result – in particular such that all visible colors are contained within the first quadrant of the diagram, and the corresponding matching functions are everywhere non-negative. The particular chromaticity diagram that arises is dependent on the choice of primary basis functions. First, we consider the relationship between systems with different basis functions, and then introduce the CIE-XYZ system which does have the desired property that all chromaticities are in the first quadrant.

Suppose E and F are two different sets of primary basis functions, so that for a given color $C(\lambda)$, we have (from (EQ 4.9)):

$$C(\lambda) \approx \alpha_1 E_1(\lambda) + \alpha_2 E_2(\lambda) + \alpha_3 E_3(\lambda)$$
$$C(\lambda) \approx \beta_1 F_1(\lambda) + \beta_2 F_2(\lambda) + \beta_3 F_3(\lambda) \qquad \text{(EQ 4.44)}$$

Now we should be able to write the basis functions in one system as expressed in the other system. For example:

$$F_1(\lambda) = \sum_{j=1}^{3} \alpha_{1j} E_j(\lambda)$$

$$F_2(\lambda) = \sum_{j=1}^{3} \alpha_{2j} E_j(\lambda) \qquad \text{(EQ 4.45)}$$

$$F_3(\lambda) = \sum_{j=1}^{3} \alpha_{3j} E_j(\lambda)$$

Writing this in matrix form:

$$\begin{bmatrix} F_1(\lambda) \\ F_2(\lambda) \\ F_3(\lambda) \end{bmatrix} = \begin{bmatrix} \alpha_{11} & \alpha_{12} & \alpha_{13} \\ \alpha_{21} & \alpha_{22} & \alpha_{23} \\ \alpha_{31} & \alpha_{32} & \alpha_{33} \end{bmatrix} \begin{bmatrix} E_1(\lambda) \\ E_2(\lambda) \\ E_3(\lambda) \end{bmatrix} \qquad \text{(EQ 4.46)}$$

or

$$F(\lambda) = AE(\lambda)$$

Now

$\alpha E(\lambda) = \beta F(\lambda)$, where $\alpha = (\alpha_1, \alpha_2, \alpha_3)$ and $\beta = (\beta_1, \beta_2, \beta_3)$

$\therefore \ \alpha E(\lambda) = \beta A E(\lambda)$, from which $\qquad \text{(EQ 4.47)}$

$\alpha = \beta A$

Also, from (EQ 4.47)

$$\alpha_j = \sum_{i=1}^{3} \beta_i \alpha_{ij}$$

$$\therefore \int \gamma_{Ej}(\lambda) C(\lambda) d\lambda = \sum_{i=1}^{3} \int \gamma_{Fi}(\lambda) C(\lambda) d\lambda \alpha_{ij} \qquad \text{(EQ 4.48)}$$

$$= \int \sum_{i=1}^{3} \gamma_{Fi}(\lambda) \alpha_{ij} C(\lambda) d\lambda$$

where $\gamma_{Ej}(\lambda)$ and $\gamma_{Fj}(\lambda)$ are the color matching functions for the two bases.
It follows that:

$$\gamma_{Ej}(\lambda) = \sum_{i=1}^{3} \gamma_{Fi}(\lambda) \alpha_{ij} \qquad \text{(EQ 4.49)}$$

From (EQ 4.46), (EQ 4.47) and (EQ 4.49) it can be seen that if we know the matching functions for one basis, and the transformation matrix from one basis to a second, we can easily find the matching functions for the second basis. Moreover, these are linear transformations.

The CIE defined a primary basis called the XYZ color system. The name is based on three primary basis functions $X(\lambda)$, $Y(\lambda)$, $Z(\lambda)$. These are defined such that X and Z have zero luminance, and the color matching function for Y is equal to the spectral luminous efficiency curve V. It follows that the XYZ primaries are not real colors (in order for X and Z to have zero luminance it follows that they must be negative over some of their range).

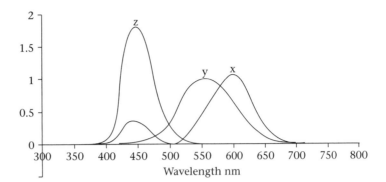

Figure 4.10
2-deg XYZ color
matching functions

In (EQ 4.45) consider E to be the RGB system, and F the new XYZ system. Then it can be shown that the conversion is defined by:

$$A = \begin{bmatrix} 0.489989 & 0.310008 & 0.2 \\ 0.176962 & 0.81240 & 0.010 \\ 0.0 & 0.01 & 0.99 \end{bmatrix} \quad \text{(EQ 4.50)}$$

In other words, given a CIE-RGB color the equivalent CIE-XYZ specification can by found by pre-multiplying by A as in (EQ 4.45). The inverse matrix will take a CIE-XYZ color into the equivalent CIE-RGB color:

$$A^{-1} = \begin{bmatrix} 2.3647 & -0.89658 & -0.468083 \\ -0.515155 & 1.426409 & 0.088746 \\ 0.005203 & -0.014407 & 1.0092 \end{bmatrix} \quad \text{(EQ 4.51)}$$

The functions $X(\lambda)$, $Y(\lambda)$, $Z(\lambda)$ define a color space in exactly the same way as before (in fact it is the *same space*, but represented with a transformed coordinate system). Hence any spectral distribution $C(\lambda)$ can be expressed as (in fact more correctly is metameric with):

$$C(\lambda) \approx X \cdot X(\lambda) + Y \cdot Y(\lambda) + Z \cdot Z(\lambda) \quad \text{(EQ 4.52)}$$

for constants X, Y, and Z.

The resulting chromaticity diagram is shown in Figure 4.9 (color plate).

The color matching functions $\bar{x}(\lambda)$, $\bar{y}(\lambda)$, $\bar{z}(\lambda)$ are shown in Figure 4.10. Note that they are non-negative everywhere, and the $\bar{y}(\lambda)$ function is identical to the spectral luminous efficiency curve V. These functions are tabulated.[3] Hence given a spectral distribution $C(\lambda)$ we can find the coefficients (X, Y, Z) from (EQ 4.53):

---

3. See for example http://cvision.ucsd.edu/

$$X = \int \bar{x}(\lambda) C(\lambda) d\lambda$$

$$Y = \int \bar{y}(\lambda) C(\lambda) d\lambda \qquad \text{(EQ 4.53)}$$

$$Z = \int \bar{z}(\lambda) C(\lambda) d\lambda$$

Note that the Y value will be the luminocity. The corresponding chromaticity values are found from:

$$x = \frac{X}{X + Y + Z}$$

$$y = \frac{Y}{X + Y + Z} \qquad \text{(EQ 4.54)}$$

$$z = 1 - x - y$$

4.8   Some characteristics of CRT displays

The CIE-XYZ color space is a standard, device-independent color space, constructed to show how all visible colors can be produced by an additive mixture of three primary colors. However, the primary colors for the XYZ space are imaginary, so that this space is not physically realizable by an emitter system based on generating color by additive combinations of a finite set of primaries. Nevertheless the XYZ space, precisely because it is device independent, and can represent all visible colors (up to metameric equivalence for the human visual system), is the correct one to use in computer graphics. Since an XYZ color cannot be displayed as such, the question arises as to how to convert it to a color that can be displayed on a real display monitor.

Before looking at this problem, we briefly describe in this section the characteristics of typical cathode ray tube (CRT) display systems that are current today. A very full treatment can be found in Glassner (1995) volume 1, Chapter 2.

A CRT display may be thought of as a 2-dimensional array of elements called *pixels* (condensed from "picture elements"). A pixel is the smallest unit of the display whose color can be independently set – the color of any pixel can be determined without affecting the color of any other pixel. The inside of the display is coated with light-emitting phosphors. Typically for each pixel there will be a pattern of three phosphor dots. When excited by an electron beam a phosphor will emit light. One phosphor in the pattern of three will emit "red" light, another "green," and the third "blue." The three phosphors per pixel are so close that their emitted light combines, to produce an additive color mixture. The CRT has three electron guns, which are carefully arranged so that the beam from each gun will only strike a phosphor of a particular color within each pixel area. The voltage of the beams determines the intensities of the emitted light from the three phosphors, thus allowing different additive combinations of RGB to be emitted.

A phosphor will have a *persistence*. This is the length of time before which the light energy emitted as a result of an electron hit will start to decay. Typically each phosphor is refreshed at least 60 times per second (60 Hz). This is achieved by the electron beams sweeping horizontally from left to right across the pixel array, and then vertically from bottom to top to begin the refresh cycle over again. This refresh is carried out in a pattern often called *raster scanning* – a horizontal array of pixels is refreshed, then the beams move to the start of the next row down, and the next row is refreshed, and when the last pixel on the bottom row is refreshed the beams return to the top left-hand corner and start over again. The time that it takes for the beams to return to the start of the next row down is called the "horizontal retrace time" and to get back from the bottom right-hand corner to the top left is called the "vertical retrace time." If the time for a complete screen refresh is longer than the persistence of the phosphors then the image will begin to decay. A refresh rate of at least 24 Hz is required for the human visual system to integrate across the refresh boundaries to maintain the illusion of a continuous image. In practice, today's display systems have much higher refresh rates.

The number of pixels of the display is usually called the *resolution*. Clearly the greater the resolution (typically today of the order of 1280×1024 where the first term is the number of pixels horizontally and the second the number of vertical pixels) the faster must the refresh cycle be in order to avoid flicker. A pixel is addressed by its coordinates on the display. Usually the origin (0, 0) is at the top left-hand corner and (x, y) counts the number of pixels from the left and top respectively. Note that this display space is "upside down" compared to the normal mathematical convention. However, if the number of vertical pixels is N, and if (x, y') is the pixel corresponding to (x, y) but represented with the normal mathematical convention of the Y-axis running from bottom to top in the positive direction, then

$$(x, y') = (x, N - 1 - y) \qquad \text{(EQ 4.55)}$$

Throughout this book *we will always assume that the coordinate system follows the normal mathematical convention* with positive Y going from bottom to top (don't be surprised if your first images appear upside down if you don't remember this, and you are using a graphics programming system that does not do the inversion for you).

Pixels are sometimes thought of as infinitesimal points. However, it should be clear from the above that pixels are finite in size, and have a light emission distribution that potentially spreads over neighboring pixels. Treating pixels as "points" leads to serious problems for image display – called *aliases*. For example, except for the horizontal, vertical, and 45 degree case, there is no such thing as a "straight line between two pixels." The pixels most closely approximating a line have to be carefully chosen, and their intensities adjusted to try to perceptually remove some of the jaggedness that results from this quantization. Generally a pixel display is a sampling of a continuous image, and ideally filtering techniques should be applied to try to get the best sampled approximation to the underlying true image.

What information determines the voltages of the electron beams for each pixel? The CRT monitor is of course controlled by a CPU. This has an associated special area of memory called the *frame-buffer*, which can be thought of as a 2-dimensional array of memory elements. We will assume for the moment that there is a one-to-one map between each memory element in the frame-buffer and each pixel. Now the size of each element in the frame-buffer crucially determines the color resolution of the display. The frame-buffer element must reserve a number of bits for red, a number of bits for green and a number of bits for blue. The value of, say, the "red" bits for a specific pixel determines the voltage of the electron beam when it strikes the red phosphor of that pixel. The greater the number of bits, the greater the range of colors that can be produced. There is a quantization process involved here. Typically today there are 8 bits reserved for each of the red, green, and blue primaries. So across the range of beam voltages only 256 different intensities will actually be generated by each beam. So (for the moment) we can think of a pixel corresponding to a memory element in the frame-buffer consisting of 24 bits, divided into three bytes. Each byte determines the voltage of the corresponding electron beam when it strikes that pixel. There are therefore $2^8 \times 2^8 \times 2^8 = 2^{24} = 16,777,216$ colors that can be displayed on such a device. Such a system is sometimes called *true color*.

In practice, the frame-buffer array may be larger than the number of pixels physically on the display, which means that at any moment the display may be thought of as a "window" onto the frame-buffer. Also, the number of bits per pixel may be considerably more than 24 since other information is also stored in pixels (more of which in later chapters). As an example, there may be a "mask" bit for each primary color, which when 1 allows this part of the stored pixel to be written to or changed, and when 0 does not allow this.

There is a different, memory efficient, arrangement for the representation of colors called *color-indexing* or *color lookup tables* (*CLUTs*). Each pixel is a fixed number of bits in the frame-buffer (let's say 8). There is a separate color lookup table with (in this case) $2^8 = 256$ entries. Each entry will consist of (say) three bytes, one for red, one for green, and one for blue. When a pixel is scanned for display its value in the frame-buffer (often called the *index*) is looked up in the color lookup table and then the intensities for red, green, and blue are determined by the red, green, and blue bytes in the lookup table. The advantage of this scheme is that clearly the overall memory requirement for the frame-buffer and color lookup table is significantly less than for true color. The disadvantage is that only 256 different colors can be simultaneously on the display. One advantage is that the CLUT can be used for simple animation (left as an exercise for the reader). It is possible for one system to be arranged so that the programmer can use it either as a true color system or as a CLUT, or indeed different windows on the same display used in different ways. We will only be using the true color system in this book.

From the point of view of the graphics programmer the interface to the color will be a group of functions that allow pixels to be set to have specific combinations of red, green, and blue. This can operate in a number of different ways. The most primitive function is of the following type:

```
SetPixel(x, y, red, green, blue)
```

where (x, y) determines which pixel is being referred to (these are non-negative integer coordinates in the range from $(0, 0)$ to $(M{-}1, N{-}1)$ where the resolution of the display is $M \times N$. The three color values are each in the range 0.0 to 1.0, where 0.0 determines that the beam is off, and 1.0 determines that the beam is at its maximum voltage. The interpretation of the values between 0.0 and 1.0 depends precisely on the color resolution (i.e., on how many bits per pixel are reserved for the RGB primaries).

It is important to note that typically the RGB values specified for a pixel control the beam voltages, and that there is *not* a linear relationship between the voltage and the intensity of emitted light from the corresponding phosphor. In fact the relationship is of the form:

$$\text{intensity } I = V^{\gamma} \qquad\qquad\qquad \text{(EQ 4.56)}$$

where γ is dependent on the specific display monitor (and is usually in the range from about 1.5 to 3.0). In order to correctly set the RGB values to get the desired intensity the inverse of this equation must be used:

$$V = I^{\frac{1}{\gamma}} \qquad\qquad\qquad \text{(EQ 4.57)}$$

and the resulting V used in the SetPixel function. This process is usually called *gamma correction*. Some display systems today perform this operation directly.

The RGB space of a monitor of course represents a color space in the way described in previous sections. Since each of the red, green, and blue components varies independently between 0.0 and 1.0, a schematic representation is often given, as shown in Figure 4.11. The line joining the black point $(0, 0, 0)$ with the white point $(1, 1, 1)$ is called the "gray line." This diagram is often called the "color cube." However, it can be misleading. Since all CRT displays are different, what is achieved with, say, $(0.5, 0.8, 1.0)$ on one display will not necessarily look the same on another. It is therefore important to return to the question of working with XYZ space and then converting the results to the system of a specific monitor.

4.9　Converting between RGB and XYZ color spaces

Consider a display RGB system with the primary basis $R(\lambda)$, $G(\lambda)$, $B(\lambda)$. Since these are physical colors they will have a representation in the XYZ chromaticity space. In particular, suppose that the relationship is as follows:

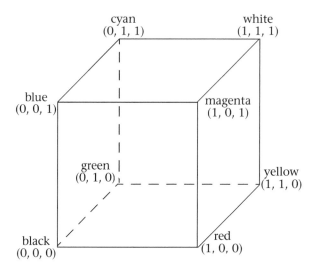

Figure 4.11
RGB color cube:
representation of an RGB
color system

$$R(\lambda) = X_R X(\lambda) + Y_R Y(\lambda) + Z_R Z(\lambda)$$
$$G(\lambda) = X_G X(\lambda) + Y_G Y(\lambda) + Z_G Z(\lambda) \qquad \text{(EQ 4.58)}$$
$$B(\lambda) = X_B X(\lambda) + Y_B Y(\lambda) + Z_B Z(\lambda)$$

Hence the 2-dimensional XYZ chromaticity coordinates corresponding to these colors are:

$$\left(\frac{X_R}{X_R + Y_R + Z_R}, \frac{Y_R}{X_R + Y_R + Z_R} \right) = (x_R, y_R)$$

$$\left(\frac{X_G}{X_G + Y_G + Z_G}, \frac{Y_G}{X_G + Y_G + Z_G} \right) = (x_G, y_G) \qquad \text{(EQ 4.59)}$$

$$\left(\frac{X_B}{X_B + Y_B + Z_B}, \frac{Y_B}{X_B + Y_B + Z_B} \right) = (x_B, y_B)$$

In practice, display manufacturers publish the 2-dimensional chromaticities, hence the right-hand sides of equation (EQ 4.59) would be known. Since the denominators in (EQ 4.59) are unknown, the XYZ colors corresponding to RGB can therefore be written as:

$$C_R = \alpha_R(x_R, y_R, z_R)$$
$$C_G = \alpha_G(x_G, y_G, z_G) \qquad \text{(EQ 4.60)}$$
$$C_B = \alpha_B(x_B, y_B, z_B)$$

Now we are after a matrix A that will convert from RGB to XYZ. In particular, the RGB color $(1, 0, 0)$ should map to C_R, $(0, 1, 0)$ to C_G, and $(0, 0, 1)$ to C_B (this is simply a change of basis). Hence:

$$C_R = (1, 0, 0)A$$
$$C_G = (0, 1, 0)A \hspace{4em} \text{(EQ 4.61)}$$
$$C_B = (0, 0, 1)A$$

So that:

$$A = \begin{bmatrix} \alpha_R x_R & \alpha_R y_R & \alpha_R z_R \\ \alpha_G x_G & \alpha_G y_G & \alpha_G z_G \\ \alpha_B x_B & \alpha_B y_B & \alpha_B z_B \end{bmatrix} \hspace{4em} \text{(EQ 4.62)}$$

It remains to determine $(\alpha_R, \alpha_G, \alpha_B)$. In the XYZ system the white point is $\left(\frac{1}{3}, \frac{1}{3}, \frac{1}{3}\right)$. The white point of the RGB system is typically $(1, 1, 1)$. Then:

$$(1, 1, 1) = \frac{1}{3}(1, 1, 1)A \hspace{4em} \text{(EQ 4.63)}$$

Rearranging:

$$\begin{bmatrix} x_R & x_G & x_B \\ y_R & y_G & y_B \\ z_R & z_G & z_B \end{bmatrix} \begin{bmatrix} \alpha_R \\ \alpha_G \\ \alpha_B \end{bmatrix} = 3 \begin{bmatrix} 1 \\ 1 \\ 1 \end{bmatrix} \hspace{4em} \text{(EQ 4.64)}$$

from which the unknowns can easily be determined. In practice, this matrix A serves two purposes:

- Given a color on a specific monitor that we wish to reproduce on another monitor, we can use A to convert to XYZ and then convert from this to the RGB of the second monitor using A^{-1} appropriate to that second monitor.

- Given a computed XYZ color we can use A^{-1} to convert to the RGB of a particular monitor.

This illustrates the utility of the device-independent nature of the XYZ system.

4.10   Color gamuts and undisplayable colors

The CIE-XYZ system can generate metamers for all visible colors – except that the primary colors are imaginary. Hence a physical system cannot be built on this basis. On the other hand, as we have seen, when the primaries are themselves visible colors, linear combinations of these cannot reproduce metamers for all visible colors. Suppose a display has three primaries R, G, and B with corresponding XYZ colors C_R, C_G, C_B. Then the chromaticity of these colors, c_R, c_G, c_B, will form a triangle on the CIE-XYZ chromaticity diagram. For example, such a triangle is shown in Figure 4.12. Now from our discussion around (EQ 4.39) we know that all points within this triangle correspond to visible colors for this system. The set of all such visible colors corresponding to a set of primaries is called the *color gamut* of the system. Clearly the color gamut varies

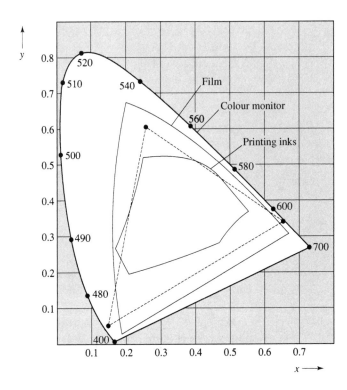

Figure 4.12
Color gamuts for several display systems
Watt: *3D Computer Graphics* 3rd edition, 2000, Addison-Wesley

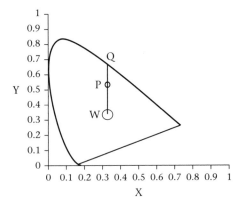

Figure 4.13
CIE-XYZ showing white point W and color at P

from display to display. Some examples are shown in Figure 4.12. So what happens when an XYZ color is converted to the equivalent RGB color and it is not displayable? Before we turn to this question, first some terminology.

Consider Figure 4.13. This shows the CIE-XYZ chromaticity diagram, and in particular the white point W at $(\frac{1}{3}, \frac{1}{3})$. It also shows another color P. Consider the line WP and where it intersects the boundary of the curve at Q. Q corresponds to a pure wavelength color, and is called the *dominant wavelength* of P.

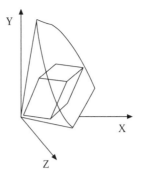

Figure 4.14
RGB cube mapped to the
CIE-XYZ color space

A color is called *saturated* the closer that it is to the color at its dominant wavelength. Specifically, the degree of saturation can be measured by *S*, where

$$S = \frac{WP}{WQ} \qquad\qquad (EQ\ 4.65)$$

Hence pure colors are 100% saturated. The more a color is "mixed" with white, the more *desaturated* it is said to be. Another way of thinking about a color is therefore as a combination of three values: its dominant wavelength (also called *hue*), which is the "color" itself, the degree of saturation (how "pure" the color is), and finally the degree of brightness or lightness (which cannot be shown on the chromaticity diagram since this is independent of luminance).

Now again suppose we have computed an XYZ color and we convert this to RGB coordinates using the results of (EQ 4.62). The converted color might not be displayable for two reasons (or both reasons):

- It might fall outside of the triangle on the chromaticity diagram, i.e., outside of the triangle defined by the primaries c_R, c_G, c_B. This will be indicated by at least one of the color intensities being negative. In other words, the chromaticity of this color is not displayable on the device in question.

- Another possibility is that its chromaticity may be displayable, but it corresponds to a color which has luminocity outside of the displayable range for this device. Putting this another way, suppose that we mapped the RGB cube of this device into the full 3D XYZ space, as illustrated in Figure 4.14. Any color outside of the mapped cube, even if its projection onto $X + Y + Z = 1$ falls inside the chromaticity diagram, cannot be displayed, because its luminocity does not fall in its range, and in this case at least one of the RGB values will exceed 1.

There is no agreed answer about what to do in these circumstances. This problem is known as *color clipping* or *clamping* – how to transform a non-displayable color into the displayable range (an in-depth discussion can be found in Hall, 1989, Chapter 5). If it falls outside of the color gamut, one strategy is to desaturate it by moving it along the line PW until it is just inside the gamut. This has the advantage of keeping the dominant wavelength of the color the same. If it is outside the RGB cube, a strategy might be to take the vector from the origin through the point corresponding to the color, and to intersect this with the RGB cube. If there is such an intersection the new color is then in range. This has the advantage of keeping the chromaticity of the color the same, but of course changing its luminocity. A detailed discussion of this issue is beyond the scope of this book; it becomes especially important in applications where color accuracy is important, such as in realistic illumination. Typically graphics systems clip a color simply by changing any negative values to 0, and any values greater than 1 to 1. Another strategy is to find the maximum coordinate (if greater than 1) and then scale the color coordinates so that the maximum is 1. (Question to the reader – what does this mean in terms of chromaticity?)

4.11 Summary: putting it all together

What usually happens in computer graphics rendering is that colors from the RGB space of the actual physical display are used throughout. In other words, light source emitters are specified as emitting light as an RGB triple (for example (1, 1, 1) for a white source), surface reflection functions reflect this type of representation of the light energy, and then these RGB values are used to set pixels. The problem of color clipping may still arise (for example, if there are several light sources then the colors are added together) but in general RGB values with negative entries cannot arise.

It should be clear from all of the previous discussion that this approach is quite incorrect. It is wrong for at least two reasons. The first is that the same computations on different displays will result in differently colored images. This is obviously because the RGB system is highly device specific, and an RGB value for one display may result in a different color on another display. However, the human visual system is remarkably "adaptable" so that the impact of the overall image may be the same. For example, in the simplest case where the entire image is darker, then this adaptation may lead to the observer essentially seeing the same image on two different displays (provided that the time gap between seeing each of them is sufficiently great!).

The second reason why this approach is incorrect is that of course RGB values are completely inappropriate measures of light energy. We have seen that we must distinguish between two different aspects of color: the energy that is produced by the physical world in terms of the distribution over wavelength, and then how the visual system responds to this distribution. The RGB system takes neither of these aspects into account. The RGB system is a means for describing colors on a display monitor, it is not a means for describing light energy in an environment. Now for much of computer graphics as it is experienced today it makes little difference – for the graphics is not meant to be portraying something that is "real" – i.e., it is not a simulation. For example, the question "Is this set of displayed colors correct for this computer game/ advertisement/logo physically correct?" has no meaning, since there is no right answer in physical or human-visual-system terms. The real question is – does it look right for the effect that is to be conveyed? – does it make the game, or advertisement, or logo more or less "attractive"? On the other hand, when the graphics is meant to be a simulation of lighting in an environment, to produce images that are realistic, then the RGB system is entirely inappropriate. It is used because of computational convenience, but this convenience is at the cost of visibly incorrect results for lighting simulation. Since the majority of this book is about graphics that "looks right" rather than correct lighting, this will not be an issue, but the reader must be aware of the pitfalls of using the RGB system. It is not a correct means for representing color.

So what is a more appropriate approach? The graphics rendering system should compute colors as $C(\lambda)$ spectral radiance distributions. This means that all illumination computations should be computed at a sufficient number of wavelengths for the spectral radiance distribution to be estimated, and then the CIE-XYZ color matching functions used to transform the spectral distribution into XYZ coordinates:

$$X = \int C(\lambda)\bar{x}(\lambda)d\lambda$$

$$Y = \int C(\lambda)\bar{y}(\lambda)d\lambda \qquad\qquad\qquad (EQ\ 4.66)$$

$$Z = \int C(\lambda)\bar{z}(\lambda)d\lambda$$

These can be transformed into CIE-XYZ chromaticity values, and a mapping such as defined in (EQ 4.62), but appropriate for the monitor RGB, used to map these into RGB values. The RGB values may need to be clipped, and finally gamma-correction applied to turn these into the correct values to send to the display using the `SetPixel` or whatever function is appropriate for determining the color of the group of pixels to be affected.

This is obviously far more complex and computationally intensive than just using RGB throughout, so no wonder that it is rarely done. Also, the discussion hides another important problem – how is $C(\lambda)$ to be obtained? This is a difficult and fundamental problem – not only must the distribution be sampled at a sufficient number of wavelengths, but they must be perceptually useful wavelengths that will make a contribution to the final image. We have seen that the visual system responds much less to light at wavelengths in the blue region compared to the green and red longer wavelengths, so a sensible sampling strategy should exploit this to advantage. This is beyond the scope of this book – see Hall (1999) for a recent survey.

In these recent chapters we have considered light and some aspects of the human response to light in a relatively abstract and high-level manner. This has provided us with understanding, but still we seem to be not one step closer to producing graphics on a real display. We turn to this in the subsequent chapters.

5   A painting metaphor for computer graphics

5.1   Introduction – the painting metaphor

5.2   Simulating the painting metaphor

5.3   Major concepts of graphics

5.4   Summary

5.1   Introduction – the painting metaphor

In this chapter we offer a first, very simplistic "solution" to the radiance equation (EQ 3.23). The approach is to ignore all but the first term on the right-hand side of the equation, and treat each object as if it were a light emitter in its own right, and not allow any interreflection between surfaces (i.e., the BRDF for each object in the scene is always 0). Moreover, each surface is completely homogeneous in the way that it emits light – it is the same for any point on the surface. There is a lot more to be said about this solution, but first we present a concrete discussion of this, and then return to the implications of the method in terms of the rendering equation. This first method is called the *painting metaphor*.

The artist shown in Figure 5.1 is looking through a frame, and transferring what he sees onto canvas. His skill lies in mixing the paints to derive the appropriate color, and accurate placement of the color brush strokes. For our purposes in this chapter we abstract away from artistic interpretation, and imagine that the painter is an automaton, perfectly reproducing onto the canvas what can be seen through the frame from a fixed observation point.

The task of the artist can be simplified by eliminating the problem of looking through a frame and then transferring what is seen onto a separate canvas. The painter can paint directly onto a transparent, acetate, material stretched across the frame. Let us further suppose that the acetate material is divided into a rectangular grid. The painter's task is now to successively look

Figure 5.1
The artist looks through a frame and paints onto a canvas
Still from *The Draughtsman's Contract* courtesy of the British Film Institute

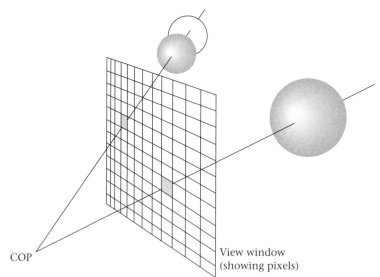

COP

View window
(showing pixels)

Figure 5.2
Rays converge at the "painter's eye" or "center of projection"

through each grid cell, choose an appropriate color, and then paint that cell with the color.

There are a number of fundamental assumptions in this process. The painter must look exactly through the center of each cell from exactly the same head position. In Figure 5.2 we show rays of light from the scene through the center of each cell, converging at a single image point. This image point is the "painter's eye." Compared with Chapter 4 this is an extremely simplified "eye" – in fact the eye may be thought of here as a combination of the acetate (analogous to the retina) and the single point of convergence (analogous to the pupil).

It is assumed that the cells are small enough so that there is just a single color to be seen through each cell. Alternatively, the color seen by looking through the center of each cell is representative of the color of the entire cell. These assumptions are equivalent to the idea that the cells may be thought of as infinitesimally small, with zero area – of course, an assumption that is incorrect when compared with the true situation. However small the cells, some are very likely to encompass edges, abrupt changes of color, in the scene. Nevertheless, we use the single color per cell assumption as a working method. The skill of the artist also lies in "blending" the many colors that might be seen through a single cell into one color suitable for the cell as a whole.

There is a further subtle assumption. The real artist, even if an automaton, will take time to complete the painting (especially if the cells are infinitesimally small, so that there is an infinite number of them). During that time the lighting conditions will change, and therefore the colors will change, unless the scene is located in a completely closed environment with only artificial light. Our artist is truly an automaton though – the entire painting is completed instantaneously.

In fact, why bother with an artist at all? Let's remove the "human element." Figure 5.3 shows how an image of a scene is produced with an old-fashioned "box camera." The box is almost completely light-secure – no light enters the box except through a tiny aperture. This is placed in the center of one side of the box so that the rays of light strike the opposite side. This opposite side is coated with a photosensitive material. Again we suppose that the photographic material is divided into a rectangular array of photosensitive cells. When the center of a cell is struck by a ray of light, the entire cell is "colored" according to the "color" of the corresponding light ray. We assume that the entire process is instantaneous. The aperture is the equivalent of the image point, the "painter's eye." The one major difference with our earlier artistic setup is that the image formed on the photographic material is upside down.

The acetate in the artistic metaphor, and the photographic material in the box-camera setup, each have an image formed upon them. This image is formed by the process of projection from three dimensions (the world) to two dimensions (the plane of the film or the acetate). The projection is linear – rays of light travel in straight lines, and intersect a planar surface. When the image

Figure 5.3
A box or "pin hole" camera. The light enters at C. Each point (P) is projected to the film

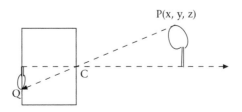

point is between the scene and the projection plane the image is upside down (as in the box camera case). When the image point is the other side the projection plane to the scene, the image is formed the right way up.

In the remainder of this chapter, we develop the mathematics for a simulation of the painting metaphor, and use this to lay the ground work for computer graphics.

5.2 Simulating the painting metaphor

Terminology

The artist renders the scene onto the acetate stretched across the frame. In computer graphics, the plane formed by the acetate is called the *view plane*, *image plane*, or *projection plane*. We will tend to use the term "view plane" in this book. The view plane, being a plane, is infinite in extent. However, the artist only looks through a particular rectangular portion of the view plane, as given by the frame. We call the frame the *view plane window*. The artist renders the world as seen through the view plane window. The view plane window is divided into a rectangular grid of cells. Each cell is called a *scene pixel*. A scene pixel has finite area. The color to be assigned to each scene pixel is determined by the color seen through its center (this assumption will be relaxed later). The painter's eye is the common meeting point of all rays of light from the scene through the centers of the scene pixels. This meeting point is variously called the *viewpoint*, *image point*, or *center of projection* (COP). The latter term is preferred in this book.

There are three major components of the painting metaphor to be developed: a scene, a view, and a rendering process. We consider each of these in turn.

A scene

A scene is a collection of objects. Each object has geometric and material properties. The shape of an object is determined by its geometric properties. For example, this might be a sphere, a cuboid, a tetrahedron, a polyhedron of some sort, even a single planar polygon such as a triangle. We will take a sphere as the major example to be used in this chapter, and make the very simplifying assumption that *the scene is composed entirely of spheres.*

Each object has material properties. In computer graphics we are mainly interested in those material properties that determine how an object reflects incident light, or indeed whether the object itself is a light emitter. Again here, we make an extremely simplifying assumption that each object (of course, a sphere) has a given fixed "color."

Each sphere is determined by its center and radius. The set of spheres forming the scene are located in a three-dimensional right-handed coordinate system, as shown in Figure 2.1. The coordinate system in which the scene as a whole is described is called *World Coordinates* (WC). For the time being this may be thought of as an arbitrary coordinate system chosen at the convenience of the scene designer.

A View: the Simple Camera

A *view* is a way of "looking" at the scene. In this chapter we take a very restricted form of view that we call the *Simple Virtual Camera* (or *Simple Camera*). The center of projection is a point somewhere along the positive side of the Z axis. The view plane distance is the distance of the COP from the origin. The view plane (plane of the acetate) is the XY plane. The view plane window is therefore a rectangle on the XY plane. A view plane and COP are not sufficient to determine the projection. As seen from the box camera analogy, the COP may be on either side of the view plane (if it is "behind" the view plane then the image will be the right way up, otherwise it will be upside down). Hence another parameter is needed to determine the primary direction of view. This is called the *view plane normal*. It is the normal to the view plane that will form an acute angle with any ray from the COP through a scene pixel. It is the "front" side of the view plane.

In this simulation, we take the view plane normal to be aligned with the negative Z axis. Since we have restricted the COP to the positive Z axis, and the direction of view is along the negative Z axis, the image will be formed right way up on the XY plane (in the rectangle demarcated by the view plane window), provided that all the scene objects are on the negative side of the Z axis.

Hence a view (in this case the restricted form of view called the Simple Camera) is described by the following parameters: the COP, the view plane window (VPW), and the view plane normal (VPN). These parameters are illustrated in Figure 5.4.

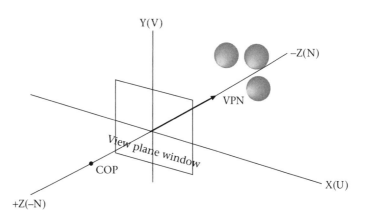

Figure 5.4
The simple camera
expressed in XYZ
world coordinates

Suppose we relabel the coordinate frame calling the positive X axis the positive U axis, the positive Y axis the positive V axis, and the negative Z axis the positive N axis. Then the UVN system is a left-handed coordinate system, often called the *viewing coordinate system* or the *eye coordinate system*. It describes the scene from the frame of the eye rather than with respect to a world frame. This is also shown in Figure 5.4. It will be noted that the viewing coordinate system has exactly the same scale, but different orientation, compared to WC. One of the processes that we will learn in a later chapter is how to redescribe the scene as described in WC to the scene described in viewing coordinates (VC). Obviously for the Simple Camera, this is a trivial task.

A way that might help in thinking about the Simple Camera is that we are designing a virtual world. In physical "other worlds" (for example, on the planet Mars) we can locate viewing devices, such as video cameras, and control those cameras from our "own world." Here we are constructing a virtual world, and the Simple Camera is our first (of course simple!) attempt to locate a camera into that world, and ultimately control it. Just as the results of a video camera are relayed to a monitor, so that we can use our own eyes to see through the monitor what the video camera is "seeing," so the results of the Simple Camera will be relayed through a monitor, or other display device, so that we can see into the virtual world. But how is this relay from what the virtual Simple Camera sees to the real world of the monitor display achieved?

A rendering process: ray casting

Given a scene and a view, we can set up a method for "rendering the scene." This is equivalent to simulating the artist's process of looking through the center of each cell, determining the color of the scene, and then painting the cell with that color.

The method we use is a simplistic realization of the Aristotelian understanding of human vision. In this theory energy is sent *out* from the eyes. Vision occurs when the energy strikes objects in the world. This causes sensations in the eyes and brain which are the basis of vision. This notion is "backwards" compared to our understanding today, as we have seen in Chapters 1 and 4.

There are some advantages, however, in following the Aristotelian notion – due to its algorithmic simplicity, and the fact that it leads directly to many of the major concepts employed in modern computer graphics. In fact it leads to a method, ray tracing, that can result in the generation of highly photo-realistic images. We will get onto that later. First we consider a simplified version of ray tracing called *ray casting*.

Ray casting involves following the paths of rays that start from the center of projection and pass through the center of the scene pixels. Each ray represents the "backwards" direction of light that is entering the "eye." Take any such ray, and find its intersection with the first object in the scene that it encounters (if any). Color the scene pixel according to the color of that object.

This is carried out for each ray that starts at the COP and passes through the center of a scene pixel. At the end of this process, the scene pixels will form an image on the view plane window. This is exactly analogous to the artist having painted an image on the acetate stretched across the frame. We now consider the mathematics of this process.

The view plane window is partitioned into $N \times M$ screen pixels. The pixel at position $(0, 0)$ is at the lower left corner of the view plane window, and the pixel $(M - 1, N - 1)$ is at the upper right. The lower left-hand corner of the view plane window is the point $(xmin, ymin)$ and the upper right-hand corner is $(xmax, ymax)$, each with z-coordinate 0, since the view plane is the XY plane.

Associated with each pixel (i, j) there is a corresponding rectangle. The width of each cell is $width = \dfrac{xmax - xmin}{M}$ and the height is $height = \dfrac{ymax - ymin}{N}$.

Hence the pixel (i, j) has its lower left corner at $(xmin + width \times i, ymin + height \times j)$, and its upper right corner at $(xmin + width \times (i + 1), ymin + height \times (j + 1))$ for $i = 0, 1, \ldots, M - 1$ and $j = 0, 1, \ldots, N - 1$. Therefore the center of the (i, j)th pixel is at $\left(xmin + width \times \left(i + \dfrac{1}{2}\right), ymin + height \times \left(j + \dfrac{1}{2}\right), 0 \right)$.

Given two points p_0 and p_1 the direction vector from p_0 to p_1 is $dp = p_1 - p_0$. The parametric equation of the ray starting from p_0 in direction dp is $p(t) = p_0 + t \cdot dp$, for $t \geq 0$. If we take p_0 as the COP, which is the point $(0, 0, d)$ where d is the *view plane distance*, and p_1 as the center of the (i, j)th pixel, then we have the parametric equation of the ray through this pixel.

The equation of a sphere centered at the origin with radius r is

$$x^2 + y^2 + z^2 = r^2 \qquad \text{(EQ 5.1)}$$

Where the sphere intersects the ray, both the equation of the sphere and the equation of the ray must be simultaneously satisfied. This occurs when

$$x(t)^2 + y(t)^2 + z(t)^2 = r^2$$

Here we are using the notation

$$p(t) = (x(t), y(t), z(t)) = (x_0 + tdx, y_0 + tdy, z_0 + tdz)$$

Substituting this into the equation for the sphere yields a quadratic equation in the unknown t:

$$t^2(dx^2 + dy^2 + dz^2) + 2t(x_0 dx + y_0 dy + z_0 dz) + (x^2 + y^2 + z^2 - r^2) = 0$$

This is an equation of the form:

$$At^2 + 2Bt + C = 0$$

with solution:

$$t = \frac{-B \pm \sqrt{B^2 - AC}}{A}$$

If the discriminator $B^2 - AC < 0$ then the ray does not intersect the sphere. If the discriminator is equal to 0, then the ray is tangent to the sphere, and otherwise it intersects it in two places. In this case it is the nearest point of intersection which is of interest, corresponding to the solution

$$t = \frac{-B - \sqrt{B^2 - AC}}{A}$$

Now this provides a solution to the problem of intersecting a ray with a sphere centered at the origin. If the sphere is not centered at the origin, the method may still be used. Of course we could directly repeat the above derivation, but starting with the general equation of a sphere with center at (a, b, c):

$$(x - a)^2 + (y - b)^2 + (z - c)^2 = r^2 \tag{EQ 5.2}$$

However, suppose that we have written the program that intersects a ray with a sphere centered at the origin. We can reuse this program to solve the more general problem. If we translate the sphere so that its new center is at the origin, and simultaneously translate the ray by the same amount, then the new ray will intersect the new sphere at exactly the same t-value as the original ray and sphere. The new ray will have its origin as $p_0 - (a, b, c)$, and its direction vector will be unchanged.

In this rendering process we need to find the t-value along the ray corresponding to the closest sphere. This requires intersecting the ray with all the spheres, keeping track of the smallest t-value (if any) that is found. The scene pixel is then set to the color of the corresponding sphere. If the ray strikes no sphere at all then the scene pixel should be left in its default "black" setting. Of course, this must be carried out for each ray that starts at the COP and goes through the center of a scene pixel.

Forming the displayed image

The rendering process described above is computationally very simple, although expensive. Let $r(i, j)$ be the ray starting from the center of projection, and through the (i, j)th scene pixel. Then for each $i = 0, \ldots, M - 1$, and $j = 0, \ldots, N - 1$, we must intersect $r(i, j)$ with each sphere in the scene, in order to find the minimum t-value. The color of the corresponding sphere (if any) is used to set the color of the (i, j)th scene pixel. There are ways to speed up this process, but we defer discussion of this to the context of ray tracing.

Imagine that all of the above had been implemented in a computer program. What would be seen on the display? The answer is "nothing!" – there would be no image formed on the display. Scene pixels are not pixels. We must establish a correspondence between scene pixels and real display pixels, so that the operation of setting the color of a scene pixel becomes that of setting the color of a real pixel.

First consider the more general problem. Suppose we have two rectangular windows [xmin, xmax] × [ymin, ymax] and [vxmin, vxmax] × [vymin, vymax]. The first of these areas will be referred to as a *window* and the second as a corresponding *viewport*. Concretely, the first represents the view plane window, and the second is an abstraction representing a rectangular region of the display on which we wish to map the window. (It is an abstraction because we are, for the moment, pretending that it is a continuous space, whereas in fact the display is, of course, discrete).

What properties should this mapping have? First, it should preserve linearity. In other words, straight lines should map to straight lines. Second, points in the window should map to corresponding points in the viewport – for example, the corners should map to the corresponding corners. Third, the *x* and *y* components of the mapping should be independent, so that, for example, lines that are parallel in the window are mapped to equivalent parallel lines in the viewport.

Taking into account these conditions, the mapping must be of the form:

$$x_v = A + Bx$$
$$y_v = C + Dy$$

where (x_v, y_v) is the point in the viewport corresponding to (x, y) in the window. Using the condition that corners must map to corners, the constants A, B, C, and D can be found, yielding the mapping:

$$x_v = vxmin + \frac{dv_x}{dw_x}(x - xmin)$$

$$y_v = vymin + \frac{dv_y}{dw_y}(y - ymin)$$

(EQ 5.3)

where dv_x and dw_x are the widths of the viewport and window respectively, and similarly for y.

This mapping can be used in the context of ray casting. However, we want the centers of the scene pixels to map to actual display pixels. Suppose on the display we have established a window with the same number of screen pixels as scene pixels. This display window will therefore have width M, and height N. The corresponding points in the mapping from view plane window to display window will therefore be:

Lower left corner:

$$\left(xmin + \frac{width}{2}, ymin + \frac{height}{2} \right) \rightarrow (0, 0)$$

and upper right corner:

$$\left(xmin + width \times \left(M - \frac{1}{2} \right), ymin + height \times \left(N - \frac{1}{2} \right) \right) \rightarrow (M - 1, N - 1)$$

5.3　Major concepts of graphics

With the basic metaphor followed in this chapter a number of fundamental concepts of computer graphics have been introduced.

Separation of scene specification, viewing and rendering. There are three major processes that have been considered. The first is the construction of the scene itself. In our example, this was very simple – just the placement of some spheres. A sphere is determined by only two parameters, the center and radius; it is relatively straightforward to place a set of spheres in 3D space in order to achieve the desired scene. In Chapter 8 we will consider the general process of scene modeling and construction.

Second, there is the specification of a view. Note that this is independent of the scene, in the sense that we do not take into account possible views when constructing the scene. An infinite number of possible views of the same scene are possible. Generally, a camera should permit views from any viewing point, in any direction and orientation. This is not possible with the simple camera; but even with the simple camera an infinite number of possible views may be selected – for example, by changing the view plane window and COP parameters.

Third, there is the rendering method. In this chapter we are considering only one rendering method, based on ray casting. Generally, given a scene and a way to specify a view, there are many possible rendering methods that could be used – ultimately dependent on the purposes of the application.

The view volume. The entire set of rays through the COP and the view plane window implicitly defines a pyramid-shaped volume in world space. Only objects that intersect this volume are potentially visible in the final image. Of course, even though an object might intersect this *view volume*, it might not be visible because it is obscured by other objects. Hence the view volume is implicitly defined by the COP and the view plane window. There are two other parameters that are often used in the specification of the view volume; these are the *near clipping plane* and *far clipping plane* as illustrated in Figure 5.5. These are planes parallel to the view plane, and with the near clipping plane nearer than the far clipping plane to the COP. Nothing beyond the far clipping plane, or in front of the near clipping plane, is projected into the view plane.

The process of restricting the final image only to that part of world space that is within the view volume is known as *clipping*. This view volume (or clipping volume) is specified by six planes – the top, left, right, and bottom plane, and the near and far planes. The first four of these are implicitly defined by the ray casting process (i.e., no ray outside of the top, left, right, and bottom planes can ever be generated, since only rays inside the view plane window are considered). The near and far planes can easily be incorporated by only considering the segment of each ray bounded by its intersection with the near and far plane.

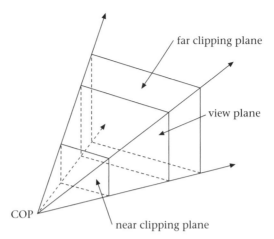

far clipping plane

view plane

COP

near clipping plane

Figure 5.5
The view volume

When later we examine different methods for rendering, we will be required to carry out a clipping process in order to eliminate parts of the scene outside the view volume before the process of rendering begins.

Aliasing. The quality of the final image depends on the resolution adopted for the view plane window (which should be the same as the final display resolution in pixels). Figure 5.6 (color plate) shows a sequence of images, each with increasing resolution. However, it is not just the resolution which determines the quality. The very nature of our rendering process involves discrete sampling of continuous phenomena. There is finite color resolution available. There is a finite number of scene (and display) pixels. There is a single color associated with each scene pixel, but the scene pixel itself has non-zero area so that many colors in the scene may be observed through it. This discretization produces "aliases" in the final image. These may be caused by low sampling of continuous entities in the scene (and hence the jagged appearance of smooth curves and lines) and the representation of many colors by one single color (for example, when a boundary between two colors in the scene is intersected by the volume associated with a scene pixel). In any situation where there is a discrete representation of a continuous entity, a potential way to reduce the aliasing is through greater sampling. We chose earlier to use one ray through the center of each scene pixel. An alternative would be to fire many rays through each scene pixel and then take the average of the colors found for each ray. Another way to think of this is to allow the scene pixel resolution to become greater than the display pixel resolution. Then several scene pixels could correspond to one display pixel. However, perhaps it is less restrictive to maintain the correspondence between scene and display pixels, since then we are free to choose any type of sampling pattern on the scene pixels. For example, we could pass rays through the corners and center of each scene pixel, sample each on a regular grid, an irregular grid (a jittered sampling scheme) or even use

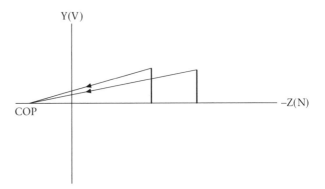

Figure 5.7
Image size depends on
distance from the COP

random sampling of points within each scene pixel. So each scene pixel would have many rays passing through it, and the final color for the pixel determined as an average of the color produced by each ray. Note that this average need not be a simple average, but an average weighted according to the position of the ray within each scene pixel – with a greater weighting towards the center than in the periphery.

Projection. The rendering process involves "projection" from 3D to 2D. The spheres are three-dimensional objects in a 3D world space. The image plane is two-dimensional. The ray casting method implicitly carries out the projection from 3D to 2D. The type of projection realized is called "perspective" projection, which operates something like (but not identical) to natural vision. In perspective projection objects of the same size are projected as larger or smaller depending on their distance from the COP if the COP is fixed, as illustrated in Figure 5.7. Nearer objects appear larger than further objects, even when they are the same size. In a later chapter we will see how to explicitly compute a perspective projection, and also some of its properties.

Lighting. A great simplification has been made that when a ray strikes an object a color is found. Where does this color come from? In the real counterpart to the painting metaphor the color is produced by the interaction between the material properties of the surfaces involved (i.e., how they emit, reflect and absorb light). Some objects are light emitters, some only reflect light and some do both. This lighting must itself be computed; ideally each ray would carry a spectral distribution. Obviously it is incorrect to associate a single color with each object – in effect treating each object as an emitter – as can be seen from the images produced by the program associated with this chapter. The images show flat disks (ellipses in fact). The projected spheres do not look like spheres, they do not look three-dimensional. A method for computing illumination, that is, allowing objects to reflect light, will be presented in the next chapter.

The radiance equation

How does this painting metaphor relate to a solution of the radiance equation? As mentioned in the introduction to this chapter, the solution is equivalent to taking each BRDF as 0, and therefore the equation reduces to:

$$L(p, \omega) = L_e(p, \omega) \qquad \text{(EQ 5.4)}$$

A second aspect of the solution is that the equation is solved only for a very restricted set of arguments. p is the COP, and the set of directions ω is limited to the ray directions into the COP through the centers of the scene pixels. The method is then exactly that described in the discussion immediately following (EQ 3.23) – each ray is traced backwards (that is, out into the scene) along these directions until it intersects an object (if any). Since each object has a constant light emission over its surface, a "color" corresponding to that emission is simply looked up, and the color transferred to the image pixel. Note that in this method we are working throughout in RGB monitor color space – a further enormously simplifying assumption, as we have seen in Chapter 4.

5.4 Summary

Figure 5.8 illustrates the various concepts introduced in this chapter. The idea is that a scene is made from objects. An object has a geometry and material properties. We made the simplifying assumption that the only type of geometry available is a sphere. Material properties consist solely of a given color for each object, represented in RGB form.

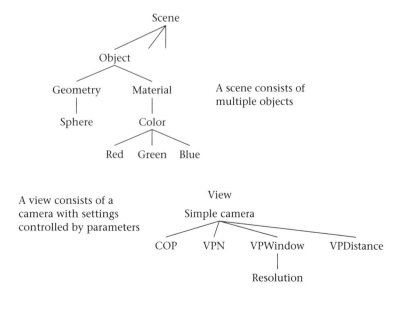

Figure 5.8
Structure of a scene and a view

A view of a scene is determined by the parameters of a simple camera. The center of projection (COP) is the point of convergence of all rays through the view plane window. In the simple camera this is restricted to lie on the positive Z axis, with the direction of view, the view plane normal, being in the direction of the negative Z axis. The view plane itself is the XY plane, and the view plane window is therefore a rectangular axis aligned rectangle on the XY plane.

Now each of these main components (scene, object, material, color, simple camera) can be represented as a programming "class" with a direct mapping from concept to class structure.

In the next chapter we improve the realism of the image by taking into account the material properties of objects, and by adding lights into the scene.

6 Local illumination and ray tracing

6.1   Introduction

The last chapter concentrated on the geometry of simple scene description and viewing. In this chapter we consider objects as material entities that reflect light and therefore are perceived as having color. In order to do this we concentrate on the *surfaces* of objects, rather than objects as volumes. The perceptual psychologist J.J. Gibson pointed out (Gibson, 1986, p. 16) that a surface is an *interface* between any two of the three states of matter – solid, liquid, and gas, for example, between a medium (the surrounding medium such as air) and a substance (such as metal) comprising the object.

In computer graphics we consider at the extremes that materials are of two abstract types with respect to the way that they reflect light: perfectly *diffuse* and perfectly *specular* surfaces. Given a single ray of light aimed at a point on

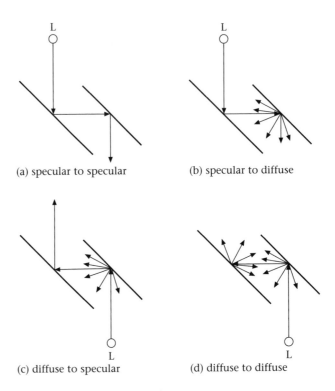

(a) specular to specular   (b) specular to diffuse

(c) diffuse to specular   (d) diffuse to diffuse

Figure 6.1
Four mechanisms of
light transport

a surface, a diffusely reflecting surface scatters light with equal radiance in all directions over an illumination hemisphere with the point at the center of its base. A specularly reflecting surface reflects and (in the case of transparent surfaces, transmits) light only in a narrow beam of small solid angle depending on the angle of incidence of the ray to the surface and the normal of the surface. A *perfectly specular* surface reflects and transmits light in a *single direction* instead of a narrow beam. It follows that there are at least four (ideal) mechanisms of light transport between surfaces in an environment (Wallace *et al.*, 1987) shown in Figure 6.1. This presents four situations, where there is a surface receiving a light ray and reflecting light that is received by another surface. Generally *ray tracing* successfully models the situation shown in (a) where all surfaces are perfect specular reflectors (and transmitters) of light. The model known as *radiosity* successfully models scenes where all surfaces are ideal diffuse reflectors, as shown in (d). Situations shown in (b) and (c) rely on probabilistic Monte Carlo methods, discussed in Chapter 22.

In this chapter we first consider the basic local illumination model that treats the interaction between a light source and a single surface. This model has been used in computer graphics since the early 1970s. It assumes that light sources are single points, or alternatively are specified as direction vectors to sources that are infinitely far away. It is a *local* model, in the sense that it only deals with interaction between light sources and surfaces, and does not take into account the reflection of light between surfaces illustrated in Figure 6.1 (except in an approximating manner). However, shading based on such local illumination models is simple to compute, gives acceptable results for simple scenes, and is fast enough for real-time 3D animation and interaction. Graphics workstations providing hardware support for 3D shading typically use a subset of the models presented here.

We continue the method of rendering introduced in the previous chapter, and extend this to become an elementary introduction to ray tracing, a global illumination method that attempts to deal with the situation shown in Figure 6.1(a) for multiple specular surfaces.

6.2 Diffuse reflection and Lambert's law

Diffuse reflection occurs for a perfectly matte surface, where reflected incident light "looks the same" from any viewing angle. More formally, such a surface obey's *Lambert's cosine law* which states that the reflected *radiant intensity* in any direction from a point on a perfectly diffuse surface varies as the cosine of the angle between that direction and the normal vector of the surface. As a consequence, the *radiance* from the surface at that point is the same regardless of the viewing angle.

If we let I be the radiant intensity, then

$$I \propto \cos\theta \qquad \text{(EQ 6.1)}$$

This is illustrated in Figure 6.2 where the vector V is towards the viewpoint. However, from (EQ 3.14) on page 79:

$$L \propto \frac{I}{\cos\theta} \qquad \text{(EQ 6.2)}$$

where L is the radiance, so that the radiance is independent of viewing angle for such a surface. The radiance (and therefore luminance) is the same for every ray emanating from a point on a perfectly diffuse (or Lambertian) reflector.

Now recall (EQ 3.18) on page 80 which states that the radiance associated with a reflected ray caused by an incident ray in a given direction is equal to the irradiance times the BRDF. Consider the situation shown in Figure 6.3, with a ray from a source patch (S) to a receiver (R) and then any reflected ray from R.

From (EQ 3.9) on page 78, the radiant power from source to receiver is:

$$\Phi = L_i \cdot dS \cdot \cos\theta_s \cdot d\omega \qquad \text{(EQ 6.3)}$$

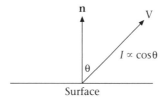

Figure 6.2
Lambert's cosine law

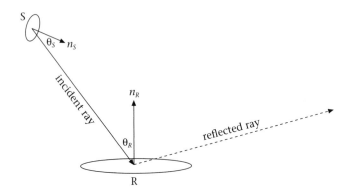

Figure 6.3
Radiant power (flux) from source S to receiver R

where L_i is the incident radiance along the ray, θ_S is the angle between the normal to the source patch and the direction of the ray. Expanding out the differential solid angle:

$$\Phi = L_i \cdot \cos\theta_S \cdot dS \cdot \frac{dR \cdot \cos\theta_R}{r^2} \qquad \text{(EQ 6.4)}$$

where r is the distance between the two patches. Irradiance (E) is radiant power per unit area of receiver, therefore:

$$E = I_i \cdot \frac{\cos\theta_R}{r^2} \qquad \text{(EQ 6.5)}$$

making use of (EQ 3.14) again, where I_i is the incident radiant intensity. Since the radiance is the same for every reflected ray from this point, the BRDF must also be a constant, given by (EQ 3.19) on page 81 and hence:

$$L_r = \frac{k_d}{\pi} \cdot I_i \cdot \frac{\cos\theta_R}{r^2} \qquad \text{(EQ 6.6)}$$

where L_r is the reflected radiance, k_d is the *coefficient of diffuse reflection*. This is a value between 0 and 1 which is the proportion of the light that is reflected by the surface rather than absorbed. Note that it is wavelength dependent. For the moment though, we notice that another form of Lambert's law for diffuse reflection is that the radiance of any reflected ray is proportional to the product of the intensity of the incident ray and the cosine of the angle between the normal to the surface at the point of reflection and the incident ray.

Now we consider how these relationships are generally treated in the computer graphics local lighting model. From (EQ 3.14):

$$I_i = L_i \cdot dS \cdot \cos\theta_S \qquad \text{(EQ 6.7)}$$

Other things being equal, this quantity will be maximized when $\theta_S = 0$. We write:

$$I_{i,max} = L_i \cdot dS \qquad \text{(EQ 6.8)}$$

Similarly, L_r will be maximized when $\theta_R = 0$, and $k_d = 1$. Using this together with (EQ 6.8):

$$L_{r,max} = \frac{1}{\pi} \cdot \frac{I_{i,max}}{r^2} \tag{EQ 6.9}$$

Using (EQ 6.6) and (EQ 6.9):

$$\frac{L_r}{L_{r,max}} = k_d \cdot \left(\frac{I_i}{I_{i,max}}\right) \cdot \cos\theta_R \tag{EQ 6.10}$$

Now the ratio of radiances will be equal to the ratio of radiant intensities, so we can write:

$$\frac{I_r}{I_{r,max}} = k_d \cdot \left(\frac{I_i}{I_{i,max}}\right) \cdot \cos\theta_R \tag{EQ 6.11}$$

Let's call the ratio of radiant intensity to its maximum the *normalized intensity*, and write

$$\bar{I} = \frac{I}{I_{max}} \tag{EQ 6.12}$$

Then:

$$\bar{I}_r = k_d \cdot \bar{I}_i \cdot \cos\theta_R \tag{EQ 6.13}$$

The normalized intensities are values between 0 and 1. What is usually done in computer graphics is to work *throughout* in these normalized intensities, and map these values to the RGB values of the display. Hence (EQ 6.13) is computed three times, for red, green, and blue intensities. From now on we will drop the bar on top of the I, and assume unless otherwise stated that the values are these normalized intensities. Hence the final form of this equation is:

$$I_r(\lambda) = k_d(\lambda) \cdot I_i(\lambda) \cdot \cos\theta_R$$
$$\text{for } \lambda = \lambda_{Red}, \lambda_{Green}, \lambda_{Blue} \tag{EQ 6.14}$$

where $\lambda_{Red}, \lambda_{Green}, \lambda_{Blue}$ are the monitor primary color intensities. For example, in the case of a white light source,

$$I_i(\lambda_{Red}) = I_i(\lambda_{Green}) = I_i(\lambda_{Blue}) = 1 \tag{EQ 6.15}$$

If the object is, say, more reddish, then the value of $k_d(\lambda_{Red}) = k_{d,red}$ would be chosen to be close to 1.0, whereas $k_d(\lambda_{Green}) = k_{d,green}$ and $k_d(\lambda_{Blue}) = k_{d,blue}$ would be closer to 0.0.

Objects may directly *emit* light (e.g., light bulbs when current is passed through them) and others only *reflect* light. The first are called light *sources* or *emitters*. It is assumed throughout the rest of this chapter that light sources are *point light sources*. A light is therefore characterized by a point denoting its position in space, and a normalized intensity that specifies the light that it emits.

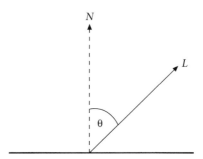

Figure 6.4
Lambert's law: the reflected intensity is proportional to cos θ, L is direction to the light source, N is the surface normal

Computing local diffuse reflection

Figure 6.4 shows the normal (N) to a surface at a point, and the direction vector to the light source from that point (L). Lambert's law states that the light intensity reflected at a point is proportional to the cosine of the angle between these two vectors: N and L. Since light is scattered equally in all directions for this perfectly diffuse model, the position of the observer does not have to be taken into account.

If we normalize N to be n, and L to be l, then Lambert's law states that:

$$I_r \propto n \cdot l \qquad \text{(EQ 6.16)}$$

However, the actual amount of light reflected depends precisely on the material surface properties – in particular, how much of the incident light is absorbed by the material. Moreover, the material will absorb light differentially in each wavelength. As we have seen, the *coefficient of diffuse reflection* specifies, for each wavelength, the proportion of incident light energy that is reflected back into the environment.

Now taking into account the coefficient of diffuse reflection, (EQ 6.16) becomes:

$$I_r = k_d I_i (n \cdot l) \qquad \text{(EQ 6.17)}$$

where I_i is the normalized intensity of the light energy due to the ray emitted from the light source.

(EQ 6.17) is quite straightforward. This model says that the intensity of light energy reflected from a surface at a point is determined by three factors:

- the normalized intensity of the light incident on the surface due to a ray from a point light source (I_i);

- the light reflected due to the operation of Lambert's Law – that is, depending on the angle of incidence (θ) of the ray with the surface;

- the proportion of light reflected rather than absorbed by the material from which the surface is fabricated (k_d).

One other component is usually added into the usual model. This is called *ambient light*, a constant intensity illumination throughout the scene (independent of the specific light source). If I_a is the total amount of ambient light then

$$k_a I_a \qquad \text{(EQ 6.18)}$$

is the amount of ambient light reflected for a particular surface where k_a is the *coefficient of ambient reflection* for that surface.

Since local models do not take into account the propagation of light between surfaces, this ambient term is introduced as a kind of global approximation to all of the interreflected light in the environment apart from that directly caused by the emitters.

Now putting (EQ 6.16), (EQ 6.17), and (EQ 6.18) together, we obtain the local model for a perfectly diffuse reflector with a single point light source:

$$I_r = k_a I_a + k_d I_i (n \cdot l) \qquad \text{(EQ 6.19)}$$

It must be remembered that this is evaluated three times, for the red, green, and blue primaries. Hence (EQ 6.19) is evaluated as:

$$
\begin{aligned}
I_{r,red} &= k_{a,red} I_{a,red} &+ k_{d,red} I_{i,red}(n \cdot l) \\
I_{r,green} &= k_{a,green} I_{a,green} &+ k_{d,green} I_{i,green}(n \cdot l) \\
I_{r,blue} &= k_{a,blue} I_{a,blue} &+ k_{d,blue} I_{i,blue}(n \cdot l)
\end{aligned}
\qquad \text{(EQ 6.20)}
$$

The coefficients k and the ambient and incident lighting intensities are chosen by the designer of the scene, and the computed reflectance intensities are then used to directly set the RGB color on the display.

We emphasize that in physical terms this model is wrong, as should be clear from the previous chapters. Nevertheless, it produces sufficiently acceptable results that a multi-billion-dollar industry is based on it, and specific hardware is produced that supports it.

Should there be multiple point light sources (say M such sources) then (EQ 6.19) becomes:

$$I_r = k_a I_a + k_d \sum_{j=1}^{M} I_{i,j}(n \cdot l_j) \qquad \text{(EQ 6.21)}$$

where $I_{i,j}$ is the intensity of the jth light source and l_j is the normalized direction vector to the jth source.

On a practical note, beware that the computation in (EQ 6.21) can lead to a light intensity that is outside the range [0, 1] for any particular color, so that color clipping is required, as discussed earlier (see "Color gamuts and undisplayable colors" on page 113). Note also that $n \cdot l < 0$ indicates a light source that is behind the surface, so that $n \cdot l$ can always be truncated at zero.

6.4   A simple model for local specular reflection

Here we consider only opaque surfaces, and defer consideration of transparent surfaces to a later section. In the case of specular reflection, the reflected ray

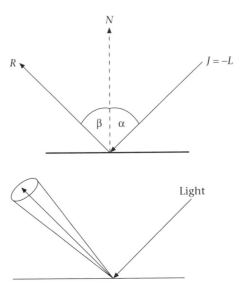

Figure 6.5
Perfect specular reflection.
J is the incident ray and
R is the reflected ray.
We must have $\alpha = \beta$

Figure 6.6
Glossy reflection

for an incident ray of light is such that the angle of incidence is equal to the angle of reflection.

In Figure 6.5, J is the incident ray, and R is the reflected ray. For perfect specular reflection we must have that the angle of incidence (α) is equal to the angle of reflection (β), and that the reflected ray, the incident ray, and the normal to the surface are all on the same plane. Hence only an observer positioned along the vector R will see the reflection of this particular incident ray. Bui-Tong, Phong (1975) introduced an approximating model based on this, known as the Phong Lighting Model. This introduces a type of reflection which is not ideally specular, but called glossy. The reflected light is a beam which can spread out from its origin, depending on a shininess parameter that we shall see below. The effect is illustrated in Figure 6.6.

In Figure 6.7 L and E are vectors which are the directions from the point on the surface to the light source and to the viewpoint respectively. H is the vector that bisects L and E. Then if k_s is the *coefficient of specular reflection* for the surface, and h is the normalization of H, the specular component of the illumination is given by:

$$I_i \cdot k_s \cdot (h \cdot n)^m \qquad \text{(EQ 6.22)}$$

where m, the *shininess*, is a positive number. Note that:

$$h = \frac{e+l}{|e+l|} \qquad \text{(EQ 6.23)}$$

where e, l are E and L normalized.

The idea of (EQ 6.22) is that when the angle of incidence is the same as the angle of reflection then H and N will coincide so that $h \cdot n = 1$, the maximum possible value. The value m is a constant, decided empirically, controlling the

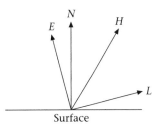

Figure 6.7
Specular reflection
(Phong model)

Surface

L is direction to the light. *E* is direction to the viewpoint. *H* bisects *E* and *L*

degree of "shininess." Large values of *m* will produce a greater degree of highlighting since small changes in the angle between *H* and *N* will cause large changes in the value of (EQ 6.22).

Real surfaces are both diffusely and specularly reflecting. Hence (EQ 6.19) and (EQ 6.22) are put together to produce one overall equation, for each RGB primary, shown in (EQ 6.24).

$$I_r = k_a I_a + k_d I_i (n \cdot l) + I_i \cdot k_s \cdot (h \cdot n)^m \qquad \text{(EQ 6.24)}$$

Where there are multiple sources, the diffuse and specular components are summed as before:

$$I_r = k_a I_a + \sum_{j=1}^{M} I_{i,j} (k_d (n \cdot l_j) + k_s (h_j \cdot n)^m) \qquad \text{(EQ 6.25)}$$

The equation may be further adjusted by taking into account the inverse square law for attenuation of radiant power with distance – the radiant power is inversely proportional to the square of the distance from the light source ((EQ 3.11) on page 79). Although the quantities used in (EQ 6.24) are nothing much to do with physical measures of light, such attentuation is nevertheless sometimes employed. Empirically, it is found that using this law exactly in the model given by (EQ 6.25) does not produce good effects. Instead, each contribution in the summation is divided by the distance plus a constant which may be varied empirically until acceptable results are achieved.

In practice, equation (EQ 6.25) is not used on a pixel-by-pixel basis, but instead an interpolation scheme is used, combining the computation of the color of a pixel with depth calculations for hidden surface removal. This is the topic of Chapter 13.

(EQ 6.25) is a simple empirical model that gives results that have been considered to be an acceptable trade-off between computational expense and realism. Once again we emphasize that this is not meant to be a true physical model.

6.5 Rendering the local illumination model with ray casting

Let's try to connect this local lighting model back to the radiance equation, and see what sort of approximation is being made. In the previous chapter, the

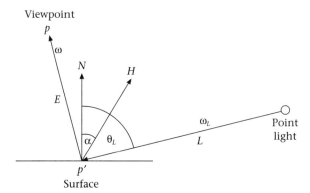

Figure 6.8
Local lighting model

approximation was very simple – make all objects emitters, and make all BRDFs zero. Here we can be a bit more sophisticated. First, note that we have introduced a new type of object into the scene – point light sources. In this model these are the only light emitters, and no substantial object itself emits light, only reflects it. So in this case $L_e(p, \omega) = 0$ for all points p on surfaces and in all directions. In this case the radiance equation becomes:

$$L(p, \omega) = \int_\Omega f(p, \omega_i, \omega)L(p, \omega_i)\cos\theta_i d\omega_i \qquad \text{(EQ 6.26)}$$

For simplicity of notation we will assume that there is only one point-light source. Consider the situation shown in Figure 6.8. The viewpoint is at p, and the direction from a particular scene pixel through the viewpoint is ω. We require $L(p, \omega)$. Now p is in free-space, it is not a point on a surface, and we know that radiance does not change along the ray. Therefore we can trace the ray backwards, until it strikes a first surface (if any) at point p'. Then we know that:

$$L(p, \omega) = L(p', \omega) \qquad \text{(EQ 6.27)}$$

We know from (EQ 6.26) that $L(p', \omega)$ may be found by integrating over the illumination hemisphere at p'. But there is only one direction in which this integral will be non-zero: in the direction (ω_L) from the point light source. (No other direction can contribute, because there is only local illumination from point light sources to surfaces, and no inter-object reflection.) Moreover, along this direction $L(p', \omega_L) = L_i$, i.e., a constant equal to the incident radiance emitted from the source.

Now putting this together, we must have:

$$\begin{aligned} L(p, \omega) &= L(p', \omega) \\ &= f(p', \omega_L, \omega)L_i\cos\theta_L \end{aligned} \qquad \text{(EQ 6.28)}$$

With this result, what must the BRDF be? A solution is to write, for any point p' on a surface:

$$f(p', \omega_i, \omega) = \delta(\omega_L - \omega_i)\left(k_d + k_s \cdot \frac{(\cos\alpha)^m}{\cos\theta_L}\right) \qquad \text{(EQ 6.29)}$$

Here it is α that depends on ω, the direction to the viewpoint (in fact a primary ray). The division by $\cos\theta_L$ is to remove the dilation due to diffuse reflection in this term, which only deals with the specular component. Using this then in (EQ 6.26), we get:

$$L(p, \omega) = L(p', \omega)$$
$$= L_i(k_d(n \cdot l) + k_s \cdot (h \cdot n)^m) \qquad \text{(EQ 6.30)}$$

So we take a couple of liberties here: normalize to "intensity" as before, and add in the "ambient lighting" for luck, and we get back to (EQ 6.24)!

In practical terms, what does this mean? It is actually provides a description of the next phase of the algorithm that was introduced in the previous chapter. There we saw that the rendering of the spheres resulted in flat disks, since each sphere was preassigned a color. Now we can be more sophisticated. As before, we trace primary rays backwards from the viewpoint into the scene until we hit an object (if any), essentially implementing (EQ 6.27). If the ray does not intersect any object, then we set it to some pre-specified background color such as (0, 0, 0) (black). Otherwise we have point p', we know the position and intensity of the point light, and we can therefore carry out the computation (EQ 6.24) for each of the red, green, and blue intensities, and then set this color on the appropriate display pixel.

There is one very important aspect of this algorithm that must be considered. It could be the case that the point p' on the surface of the intersected object *might not be visible* to the point light. This can occur for two reasons: there may be a self-shadow, or another object is causing the shadow. How can it be discovered whether this is the case or not? The answer is simple – trace a ray from p' in the direction of the light (i.e., in direction –L in Figure 6.8). If this ray intersects another object (or the same object) along the ray segment between p' and the point light, then p' is in *shadow*, and only the ambient term is non-zero.

Of course, if there is more than one point light, then (EQ 6.25) is used instead, and there is no real change in method. The calculations are repeated for each source, the results summed and the ambient lighting effect is added.

Figure 6.9 (color plate) shows a result of rendering the sphere world with diffuse reflection only. The objects now have depth, and no longer look like disks. However, they all look as if they have been made of a chalky substance. Figure 6.10 (color plate) shows the same scene rendered using the Phong model for specular reflection. Now the spheres look as if they could be billiard balls, or are made of plastic. It is certainly an improvement over the flat shading of the previous chapter, but still does not take any global, object-to-object inter-reflection into account. We move on to this in the next section.

6.6 Introduction to recursive ray tracing

Ray tracing embodies a more realistic model of how light passes through an environment where all the surfaces are ideal specular reflectors, but where the light emitters are point (or directional) sources. The method was originally

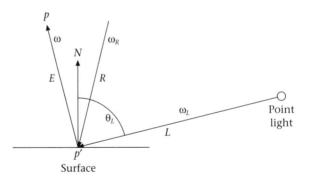

Figure 6.11
Contribution of a ray from
the reflected direction

introduced into computer graphics by Turner Whitted (1980). It takes into account the fact that an incident ray on a surface may, as well as directly illuminating that point on that surface, generate two further rays – a reflected and a transmitted (or refracted) ray, and that these will contribute to the illumination of other surfaces. In turn, reflections from other surfaces may illuminate this surface. In this sense it is a global rather than local illumination model: the illumination at a particular point is not now dependent solely on the interaction between point emitters and the surface, but every surface can have an effect on every other surface, taking into account occlusions. There is an enormous literature on ray tracing, and an excellent starting point is the book edited by Glassner (1989).

The fundamental principle then is that when a light ray strikes an object of course it may be further reflected and, if the object is transparent, transmitted through the object. These reflected and transmitted rays may strike further objects, and spawn yet more reflected and transmitted rays. For the moment we consider only *opaque* surfaces, since this suffices to introduce the main principles. Consider Figure 6.11, which shows the contributions to the ray labeled E in direction ω at point p as before. This could be thought of as a primary ray, with p as the viewpoint, though this interpretation is no longer necessary, as will be seen.

We require $L(p, \omega)$, and of course it is still the case that $L(p, \omega) = L(p', \omega)$. However, now there are two potential contributions to the light along ray direction ω: the point light source in direction ω_L, and also there could have been a ray from another object in exactly the direction ω_R to be reflected along the direction ω of interest. Hence $L(p', \omega)$ depends on the local point light as previously, but also it depends on $L(p', \omega_R)$. Hence the integral in (EQ 6.26) should only be non-zero at two values of ω_i: at $\omega_i = \omega_L$ when it should deliver the local lighting model, and at $\omega_i = \omega_R$ when it should deliver the light (if any) carried by the ray R. We write the BRDF therefore as a sum of two components:

$$f(p', \omega_i, \omega) = \delta((\omega_L - \omega_i) \cdot Local) + \delta(\omega_R - \omega_i) \cdot \frac{k_s}{\cos\theta_R}$$

$$= \delta(\omega_L - \omega_i)\left(k_d + k_s \cdot \frac{(\cos\alpha)^m}{\cos\theta_L}\right) + \delta(\omega_R - \omega_i) \cdot \frac{k_s}{\cos\theta_R}$$

(EQ 6.31)

The first term is just the contribution of the local lighting model. The second term allows the light on the incoming ray to be reflected in proportion only to the coefficient of specular reflection for this surface.

Now, carrying out the integral we obtain:

$$L(p, \omega) = L(p', \omega)$$
$$= L_i(k_d(n \cdot l) + k_s \cdot (h \cdot n)^m) + k_s L(p', \omega_R) \qquad \text{(EQ 6.32)}$$

Once again of course the first term is simply the local model, and the second term in the summation is the influence of the incoming ray R. This now gives us a recursive radiance equation, where $L(p', \omega)$ depends on $L(p', \omega_R)$. How can the latter term be evaluated? Well, by repeating the same computation. We trace *backwards* along R in direction $-\omega_R$ to find the first surface that this intersects, at say p'', and then evaluate $L(p'', \omega_R)$. Each time the form of the equation is the same. This seems still to have a problem, since it leads to a potentially infinite regress. However, the recursion does have a base case. It is possible that the backwardly traced ray does not intersect any object, in which case the result is a preassigned color (say black) or else the contribution is so small it is not worth including – in both cases the recursion stops.

Putting this together we arrive at a simple recursive ray tracing algorithm for opaque specularly reflecting objects. (Once again we use some "hey presto" magic here – normalize to intensities and introduce the ambient term.)

Algorithm 6.1 Recursive ray tracing for opaque materials

```
Color RayTrace(Point3D p, Vector3D direction, int depth)
/*ray tracing for a single light source and opaque materials*/
{
   Point3D pd;
   Vector3D R;
   bool intersection;
   Color ILocal;

   if(depth > MAX) return BLACK;

   /*intersect the ray from p in the given direction and return the
   nearest point pd along the ray. intersection is true if there is
   an intersection*/
   intersect(p,direction,&pd,&intersection);

   if(!intersection) return BACKGROUND_COLOR;

   /*there was an intersection, now compute the local color at pd -
   recall that this must be computed for each of R, G and B*/

   ILocal = kₐIₐ + Iₚ·v·(k_d(n·l) + k_s·(h·n)ᵐ);

      /*where v = 1 if pd is visible to the light, else 0*/

   /*continue recursion - compute reflection direction R - note that
   this is -R in Figure 96*/
   return ILocal + ks*Ray Trace(pd,R, depth+1);
}
```

Now this function must be called for every primary ray, that is, each ray from the COP through the center of a scene pixel. The return value is a color (an RGB value) and then this is used to set the corresponding screen pixel exactly as in the previous chapter. Note that the direction of flow here is opposite to the direction of light flow – as in the last chapter, it is going from the camera position out into the scene. Hence the direction of reflection R in the algorithm is the opposite to the direction of flow along R in Figure 6.11. Of course there is also a lot unsaid in the algorithm – we must know not simply the point of intersection with a ray but also sufficient information about the object so as to determine its normal at the point of intersection (in the case of spheres this is simple), and also its material properties (the k coefficients). Hence in practice the "intersect" function would return a pointer to the object that was intersected rather than just the point of intersection. Finally, of course, we are dealing with RGB intensities throughout, so the local color computation and the tolerance test (to see if the resulting color is so small that it is not worth continuing the recursion) must be carried out for each of R, G, and B.

Now we have assumed that the objects involved in the scene are always opaque. Clearly we could introduce another term in the equation allowing any light that comes through the object, if it is transparent, also to contribute. There is no point in writing down the radiance equation for this case (it is left as an exercise for the reader) since it adds nothing new to understanding the nature of the approximation being used. However, in the next section we revisit ray tracing in more detail, covering this and some other issues. Meanwhile Figure 6.12 (color plate) shows an example of this technique being used for the sphere scene.

6.7   Recursive ray tracing including transparent objects

We have seen how ray tracing traces rays backwards from the center of projection into the scene, and how this follows naturally from the unwinding of the recursive radiance equation. A special advantage of this is that it guarantees that we only trace rays which ultimately reach the viewpoint. The color at a particular pixel corresponding to a point on a surface that is visible to the viewer is therefore determined by the summation of all the effects of all rays ultimately spawned from the first generation, or *primary*, rays from the viewpoint through the pixel.

In Figure 6.13 we trace a ray from the viewpoint through a particular pixel, which strikes object A. From object A we trace two rays from the intersection point to the light sources (such rays are usually called *shadow feelers*). Note that shadow-feeler s_1 hits object C on route to light L1. Therefore, with respect to L1, this point on object A is in shadow. However, it is illuminated by L2. From object A, two further rays are spawned, a reflected ray (r_1) and a transmitted ray (t_1), since this surface is transparent. Consider r_1; this hits object B, from which further shadow feelers, and reflected and transmitted rays are spawned.

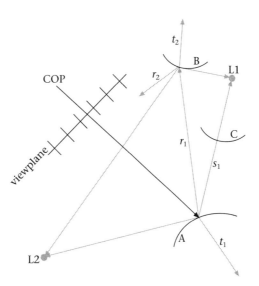

Figure 6.13
Ray tracing

This process continues until a ray goes out of the environment (hits nothing – for example t_2), or until further contributions do not add "significantly" to the ultimate color. At each successive stage, only a fraction of the received light is delivered onward with the spawned ray, hence ultimately, rays will be generated which for practical purposes make no contribution to the final color of the pixel. This ray tracing process lends itself to a simple recursive formulation as shown in Algorithm 6.2.

Algorithm 6.2 Recursive ray tracing for opaque and transparent surfaces

```
Color RayTrace(Point3D p, Vector3D direction, int depth)
{
   Point3D pd;
   Boolean intersection;

   if(depth > MAX) return BLACK /*(0,0,0)*/;
   else {
     /*intersect the ray from orgin in given direction
     with the scene to find the closest point of intersection
     pd. intersection = true if there is such an intersection
     */
     intersect(p,direction,&pd,&intersection);

     if(!intersection)return BACKGROUND_COLOUR;
     else {/*l*vi = 1 if pd is visible to the ith light, else 0*/
```

$$Ilocal = I = k_a I_a + \sum_i I_{pi} \cdot v_i \left((n \cdot l_i) k_d + (h_i \cdot n)^m k_s \right)$$

```
       R = reflection direction;
       Ir = RayTrace(pd,R,depth+1);
```

```
                    T = transmission direction;
                    It = RayTrace(pd,T,depth+1);

                    return (Ilocal + kr*Ir + kt*It )
                }
            }
        }
```

The recursion proceeds to a pre-set depth (*MAX*). The ray is fired into the environment and its intersection with all candidate objects computed. Amongst the set, where there is an intersection the intersection point which corresponds to the shortest path of the ray is computed (this is *pd*). In this case the boolean variable *intersection* is true, otherwise it is false. If the ray hits nothing, then it is assigned the background color – this means it has gone out of the environment.

The *Ilocal* term is based on the shadow feelers, so that the summation is over all shadow feelers which reach a light source without intersecting an opaque object. k_r and k_t are the coefficients of reflection in the reflection and transmission directions, respectively. We would normally have $k_r = k_t = k_s$.

This "local" model of light includes an ambient term, which stands for another kind of global illumination that is not taken care of at all in ray tracing – the global effects of diffuse reflection. In the next section we consider how to compute the new directions, *R* for the reflected and *T* for the transmitted rays.

Some details of the ray tracing algorithm

The direction of reflection (*R*)

In Figure 6.5 we show the incident ray (*J*) and the reflected ray *R*. *N* is the surface normal at the point of interest. There are two laws which allow the computation of *R* (assuming that all vectors are normalized):

• *R* is on the same plane as *J* and *N*, so that $R = aJ + bN$ for some constants *a* and *b*.

• The angles α and β are equal.

Since cosα = cosβ, we have

$$-J \cdot N = N \cdot R = N \cdot (aJ + bN) = a(N \cdot J) + b, \text{ since } N \cdot N = 1$$

Set $a = 1$, so that $b = -2(N \cdot J)$. Finally,

$$R = J - 2(N \cdot J)N \tag{EQ 6.33}$$

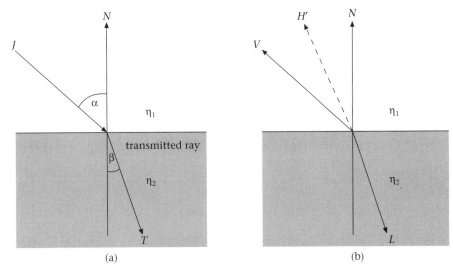

Figure 6.14
Direct specular transmission. (a) J is the incident ray and T is the transmitted ray (b) V is the direction to the eye. L is the direction to the light source

Perfect specular transmission

Figure 6.14(a) shows what happens when a ray passes from one medium to another. The path of the ray is bent according to the density of the medium, and as given by Snell's Law (Feynman *et al.*, 1977, pp. 26–3 to 26–4):

$$\frac{\sin\alpha}{\sin\beta} = \frac{\eta_2}{\eta_1} = \eta_{21} \qquad \text{(EQ 6.34)}$$

where η_2, η_1 are the indices of refraction of the two mediums.

The transmitted ray T will be on the same plane as J and N, so that $T = aJ + bN$.

Using these two laws it is possible to show (Glassner, 1989, p. 140):

$$T = \eta_{12}J + N(\eta_{12} \cdot \cos\alpha - \sqrt{1 + \eta_{12}^2 \cdot (\cos^2\alpha - 1)}) \qquad \text{(EQ 6.35)}$$

Now it may be the case that the value under the square root sign is negative. In this case there is so-called *total internal reflection* – which occurs when the ray passes from a dense to a relatively less dense medium, and the angle of incidence is greater than about 40 degrees. In this case the ray is only reflected. (This effect occurs, for example, under water in a swimming pool; at a certain angle the swimmer will see the bottom of the pool reflected when looking up at the surface.)

Direct specular transmission

In the *Ilocal* term of the ray tracing program, the $(h_i \cdot n)^m k_s$ represents the specular reflection component. However, this assumes that the light source is in front of the object. Another possibility is that the object is transparent and the light is behind it.

In this case the vector H' is computed, using Snell's Law as:

$$H' = \frac{V - \frac{\eta_2}{\eta_1}L}{\frac{\eta_2}{\eta_1} - 1} \qquad \text{(EQ 6.36)}$$

H' is then normalized as usual, and $k_t \cdot (h' \cdot n)^m$ is used in place of the specular reflection term. Here k_t is the coefficient of specular transmission. This is shown in Figure 6.14(b).

Intersection calculations

More than 90% of the computation in simple ray tracing consists of intersection calculations (Whitted, 1980). In the previous chapter we considered intersection with a sphere. In Chapter 8 we will find the intersection with planar polygons (see "Intersecting polygons by rays" on page 165).

Much of the research into ray tracing has centered on the problem of reducing the impact of the intersection calculations, by reducing either the cost of each ray or the total number of rays, or both. This is considered in detail in Chapter 16. However, one obvious method is to bound each object by the smallest sphere containing the entire object. If the ray intersects the sphere then it is worth testing the ray against the actual object, otherwise if the ray is outside of the sphere then it cannot possibly intersect the object. This is an example of a *bounding volume* method.

6.9   Illumination in OpenGL

OpenGL provides a straightforward representation of the illumination model described above. It supports the specification of ambient, diffuse, and specular material properties, and also a number of light sources. In this section we consider some examples of material specification and also of point-light sources. In OpenGL the system is put into a "state" whereby the current material properties are given, and it stays in this state until they are changed. In constructing a data structure for materials, the strategy could be adopted of providing a "material" for every facet of an object, for example polygons making up a more complex object. However, although simple, this has very great implications for efficiency, since a change in material properties on a polygon-by-polygon basis slows down OpenGL rendering enormously. Rather, here we adopt the strategy of changing materials on an object basis, but nevertheless allowing an individual polygon to override the object material setting. If an object does not select a material, then a default may be used.

We first construct a `Material` data structure, and then show how this may be used in OpenGL.

```
#define NOMATERIAL ((Material *)0)
typedef enum{
   FlatShading, SmoothShading
} ShadingModel;

typedef enum{
   Opaque, Transparent
} Opacity;

typedef struct{
   GLenum model;            /*GL_FLAT or GL_SMOOTH*/
   GLfloat ambient[4];      /*rgb alpha*/
   GLfloat diffuse[4];      /*rgb alpha*/
   GLfloat specular[4];     /*rgb alpha*/
   GLfloat shininess[1];    /*shininess for specular*/
   Opacity opacity;         /*transparent means glEnable(GL_BLEND)*/
} Material, *MaterialPtr;
```

The `Material` struct represents each component of the model discussed above, with the ambient, diffuse, and specular coefficients. The "shininess" is the m of (EQ 6.23) (it is represented as an array with one element for convenience in comparison with the OpenGL specification). This representation also allows for transparency, and two different types of model, smooth and flat shading. We will not be considering these in this chapter. In OpenGL pixels are actually RGBA values where the "A" stands for "alpha." This is explained where it is needed in Chapter 23 (see "Image-based rendering" on page 508).

```
void setDefaultMaterial(void)
/*sets a material for use when both object and face have NULL
materials*/
{

   GLfloat ambient[]  = {0.2,0.2,0.2,1.0};
   GLfloat diffuse[]  = {1.0,0.0,0.0,1.0};
   GLfloat specular[] = {1.0,1.0,1.0,1.0};
   GLfloat shininess[] = {20.0};

   glMaterialfv(GL_FRONT,GL_AMBIENT,ambient);
   glMaterialfv(GL_FRONT,GL_DIFFUSE,diffuse);
   glMaterialfv(GL_FRONT,GL_SPECULAR,specular);
   glMaterialfv(GL_FRONT,GL_SHININESS,shininess);
   glShadeModel(GL_FLAT);
}
```

In `setDefaultMaterial` we use the OpenGL `glMaterial` function to set the various coefficients of reflection. Note as usual that the "f" represents floating point and the "v" vector representation, so that, e.g., the ambient reflection coefficient is being set in a vector of four floating point values `GLMaterialfv`. The first three of these are the red, green, and blue components, and the last is called the "alpha" component, which may be used for transparency (see Section 23.4).

```
void setMaterial(Material *material)
/*sets the current material in OpenGL*/
{
  glMaterialfv(GL_FRONT,GL_AMBIENT,material->ambient);
  glMaterialfv(GL_FRONT,GL_DIFFUSE,material->diffuse);
  glMaterialfv(GL_FRONT,GL_SPECULAR,material->specular);
  glMaterialfv(GL_FRONT,GL_SHININESS,material->shininess);
  glShadeModel(material->model);
  if(material->opacity==Transparent) glEnable(GL_BLEND);
  else glDisable(GL_BLEND);
}
```

In `setMaterial` OpenGL is put into a state given by the supplied Material argument.

```
static void initialize(void)
{

  GLfloat light_ambient[] = {0.2,0.2,0.2,1.0};
  GLfloat light_diffuse[] = {1.0,1.0,1.0,1.0};
  GLfloat light_specular[] = {1.0,1.0,1.0,1.0};

  GLfloat light_position[] = {0.5,1.0,1.0,0.0};

  /*GL_FLAT or GL_SMOOTH*/
  glShadeModel (GL_SMOOTH);

  /*set the background (clear) Color to white*/
  glClearColor(1.0,1.0,1.0,0.0);

  /*enable normalization*/
  glEnable(GL_NORMALIZE);
  glEnable(GL_DEPTH_TEST);

  /*set the depth buffer for clearing*/
  glClearDepth(1.0);

  /*enable lighting*/
  glEnable(GL_LIGHTING);
  glEnable(GL_LIGHT0);
  glLightfv(GL_LIGHT0,GL_AMBIENT,light_ambient);
  glLightfv(GL_LIGHT0,GL_DIFFUSE,light_diffuse);
  glLightfv(GL_LIGHT0,GL_SPECULAR,light_specular);
  glLightfv(GL_LIGHT0,GL_POSITION,light_position);

  /*set up camera and scene here...*/
}
```

The function `initialize` is an example of a fragment of code to initialize various aspects of an OpenGL session, including the lighting. The ambient, diffuse, and specular components of the light (I_a, I_{pd}, I_{ps}) are defined (note that OpenGL supports the specular and diffuse components being different) and then set using `glLightfv`, which can also be used to set the position. Notice that the lighting must be enabled (`glEnable`). We defer discussion of different types of shading model (smooth or flat) until later.

6.10

Illumination in VRML97

The surface material model in VRML97 uses parameters that map almost directly onto those of OpenGL. The surface material properties are described with a `Material` node, which itself is a field in an `Appearance` node. The appearance node controls the overall look of a geometric object by specifying material, texture, and texture transformation attributes. (See "Texturing" on page 275. See "VRML97 Examples" on page 293 for a description of texture mapping in VRML.) The six fields of a Material node are `diffuseColor`, `specularColor`, `emissiveColor`, `ambientIntensity`, `shininess`, and `transparency`. The first three are specified as RGB triples, the others as single floating point values between 0 and 1.

The two basic components are `diffuseColor` and `specularColor` which perform as expected. Note that there is no "ambientColor" field but instead there is an `amibentIntensity` field which is a single floating point value which specifies what proportion of the total ambient light in the scene this material will reflect. This ambient color can be determined as `ambientIntensity * diffuseColor`. The `shininess` field acts as it does in OpenGL, that is as m of (EQ 6.22), though in VRML it is specified in the range 0 to 1 rather than the range 0 to 128. There is only a single `transparency` value that applies to all color components. Finally the `emissiveColor` field can be used to specify a color for the surface that is independent of the lighting in the world. This is useful for radiosity-type applications where a global lighting solution is pre-computed and "written" onto the geometry (see Chapter 15 for a description of the radiosity process).

Three of the fields in a material node have a non-zero default value. For `diffuseColor` there is a default color of (0.8 0.8 0.8), for `ambientIntensity` (0.2) and for `shininess` (0.2).

In the example in Figure 6.15(a) we specify three spheres. The first is a dull green color. The second is a shiny blue sphere. The third is a transparent, self-illuminating red sphere (see Figure 6.15(b), color plate).

We also specify a single `DirectionalLight` node in the example in Figure 6.15 in order to demonstrate the effects of local shading. Other lights available to the scene modeler are `PointLight` and `SpotLight`. See "Lights" on page 530 for an overview of lighting in VRML. If there are no lights specified in the VRML file then it is usual for the VRML browser to create a "headlight,"

```
#VRML V2.0 utf8                                     shininess 0.6
Group {                                           }
 children [                                       }
   DirectionalLight {                             geometry Sphere {
   color 1 1 1                                      radius 1
 }                                                }
                                                }
# Dull green sphere                            ]
 Shape {                                      ]
  appearance Appearance {
   material Material {                  # Transparent red sphere
    ambientIntensity 0.1                 Transform {
    diffuseColor 0.1 0.7 0.2              translation -3 0 0
    shininess 0.0                          children [
   }                                       Shape {
  }                                         appearance Appearance {
  geometry Sphere {                          material Material {
   radius 1                                   diffuseColor 0.0 0.0 0.0
  }                                           emissiveColor 0.7 0.2 0.1
 }                                            transparency 0.5
                                             }
# Shiny blue sphere                         }
 Transform {                                geometry Sphere {
  translation 3 0 0                          radius 1
  children [                                }
    Shape {                                }
     appearance Appearance {             ]
      material Material {               }
       ambientIntensity 0.3           ]
       diffuseColor 0.2 0.1 0.7      }
       specularColor 0.7 0.8 0.6
```

Figure 6.15(a)
VRML97 materials example

that is, a directional light that is attached to the viewpoint that always points along the line of sight.

6.11   Summary

This chapter has introduced the fundamental ideas and expressions for illumination computations in computer graphics. The ideas of perfectly diffuse and specularly reflecting surfaces were covered, and the illumination equations for point light sources derived. One global method of illumination was discussed, that of ray tracing, which provides a straightforward way of modeling specular–specular interreflections. We saw how both the local lighting models and the ray tracing method provide a particular type of solution of the radiance equation. Later chapters will deal with global illumination, and methods for rapid computation in greater depth. We concluded with a discussion of how the shading model may be accessed in OpenGL and in VRML. Our discussion has so far been in the context of an extremely simple camera viewing model, presented in the last chapter. We now begin to extend this in the next chapter.

7 Generalizing the camera

7.1 Introduction

7.2 Mapping from WC to the UVN viewing coordinate system

7.3 Using a general camera in ray tracing

7.4 VRML97 examples

7.5 Summary

7.1 Introduction

In the previous two chapters we used a very simple and restricted viewing model: the direction of view was along the negative Z axis, the COP was fixed somewhere along the positive Z axis, and the camera was always vertically aligned with the positive Y axis. Generally, we require the ability to view a scene from any position, with the camera in any orientation. We show how to do this now.

The scene in 3D World Coordinates is typically described in a right-handed coordinate system as has been discussed earlier. The simple abstract camera described earlier assumes the camera to be oriented along the Z axis of the scene, which is a very restrictive assumption. Here we introduce a set of parameters allowing an arbitrary orientation of the camera. The strategy will then be to apply transformations to this camera, and correspondingly to the scene to get the situation back to the simplicity of that shown in Figure 5.8, for example, and illustrated again in Figure 7.1.

In order to construct such a general camera, we define a new coordinate system in which the camera plays the central role. This is called the *Viewing Coordinate system*, or Viewing Coordinates (VC), also called sometimes *Eye Coordinates* in this book. It is a view-centered coordinate system, rather than WC where the origin is at any arbitrary position in space. For the purposes of

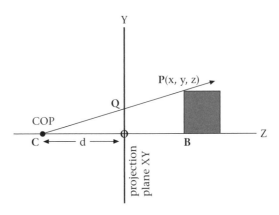

Figure 7.1
The simple camera model

exposition here, the viewing coordinate system is left-handed. (It is trivial to change from a right-handed to a left-handed system.)

There are a number of parameters defining the viewing coordinate system. These are:

The View Reference Point (VRP). This is a point in WC which specifies the origin of the new Viewing Coordinate system. Intuitively, it may be thought of as the point of interest in the scene, or alternatively as a point with respect to which the 'camera' (i.e., the view plane and the center of projection) is to be defined.

The View Plane Normal (VPN). This is a vector in WC whose direction specifies the positive Z axis of the viewing coordinate system. This axis is therefore obtained as the line through the VRP parallel to the VPN. Intuitively, it may be thought of as the direction in which the abstract camera is pointing. The Z axis is called the N axis of the new system. The view plane will be normal to this vector.

The View Up Vector (VUV). This is a vector in WC whose direction is used to define the positive Y axis of the new coordinate system. The Y axis is formed by projecting the VUV onto a plane which is perpendicular to the VPN and which passes through the VRP. This projection is the Y axis of the new system. The Y axis is also referred to as the V axis.

Finally, the X axis of the new system is constructed so as to make a left-handed system given the Y and Z axes (or a right-handed system if preferred). The X axis is often referred to as the U axis.

The names of the three principal axes of the viewing coordinate system give rise to the alternative name – UVN system. These ideas are illustrated in Figure 7.2. It should be clear that the new viewing space is a translation and rotation of the original world space – these two spaces have the same metric. The scene is described with respect to two different frames of reference: the measurements in the scene do not change, only the coordinates in terms of which the scene is described.

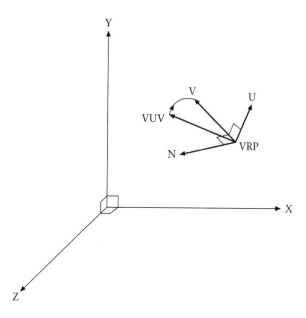

Figure 7.2
UVN coordinates

Mapping from WC to the UVN viewing coordinate system

This section derives a transformation matrix which maps WC space into the viewing coordinate system. Let n be a unit vector (relative to the origin of WC) in the direction of the VPN. Hence,

$$n = \frac{VPN}{|VPN|}$$

(EQ 7.1)

Let u be a unit vector in the direction of the required U axis of the new system. Hence, in order to form a left-handed VC system,

$$u = \frac{n \times VUV}{|n \times VUV|}$$

(EQ 7.2)

where $\times$ represents vector cross product. Finally, to obtain the unit vector v in the direction of the V axis,

$$v = u \times n$$

(EQ 7.3)

Now let M be the required 4×4 matrix that maps WC space into VC space. M can be partitioned into a 3×3 purely rotational part, R, and a translation vector t, as follows:

$$M = \begin{bmatrix} R & 0 \\ t & 1 \end{bmatrix}$$

(EQ 7.4)

The vectors u, v, n derived in (EQ 7.2) to (EQ 7.4) must rotate under transformation matrix R into the unit principal vectors i, j, k of VC space, where $i = (1, 0, 0)$, $j = (0, 1, 0)$, and $k = (0, 0, 1)$. Hence,

$$uR = i = (1, 0, 0)$$
$$vR = j = (0, 1, 0) \qquad \text{(EQ 7.5)}$$
$$nR = k = (0, 0, 1)$$

which becomes,

$$\begin{bmatrix} u \\ v \\ n \end{bmatrix} R = I \qquad \text{(EQ 7.6)}$$

where I is the 3×3 identity matrix. Since u, v, and n are orthonormal vectors (that is, they each have norm 1, but have dot product 0 with each other):

$$R = (u^T, v^T, n^T)$$
$$= \begin{bmatrix} u_1 & v_1 & n_1 \\ u_2 & v_2 & n_2 \\ u_3 & v_3 & n_3 \end{bmatrix} \qquad \text{(EQ 7.7)}$$

To obtain the translation vector t, note that the VRP must be transformed into the origin of the VC system. Let VRP be represented by q in

$$(q, 1)M = (0, 0, 0, 1) \qquad \text{(EQ 7.8)}$$

Therefore, from (EQ 7.4)

$$qR + t = 0 \qquad \text{(EQ 7.9)}$$

so that

$$t = -qR$$
$$= -\left(\sum_{i=1}^{3} q_i u_i, \sum_{i=1}^{3} q_i v_i, \sum_{i=1}^{3} q_i n_i \right) \qquad \text{(EQ 7.10)}$$

Putting all this together, results in the matrix for transforming from WC to VC:

$$M = \begin{bmatrix} u_1 & v_1 & n_1 & 0 \\ u_2 & v_2 & n_2 & 0 \\ u_3 & v_3 & n_3 & 0 \\ -\sum q_i u_i & -\sum q_i v_i & -\sum q_i n_i & 1 \end{bmatrix} \qquad \text{(EQ 7.11)}$$

Now it will also be useful to find the inverse matrix of M, a matrix that will transform from viewing coordinates back to world coordinates. This is easy to find. In (EQ 7.4) we know that R is an orthogonal matrix, i.e., its inverse is the same as its transpose. Also we can rewrite (EQ 7.11) more succinctly as:

$$M = \begin{bmatrix} R & 0 \\ -qR & 1 \end{bmatrix} \qquad \text{(EQ 7.12)}$$

From this it is easy to see that:

$$M^{-1} = \begin{bmatrix} R^T & 0 \\ q & 1 \end{bmatrix} \qquad \text{(EQ 7.13)}$$

This can be verified by multiplying the two matrices together to get the identity: $M \cdot M^{-1} = I$ as required.

7.3 Using a general camera in ray tracing

Now the matrix M defined in (EQ 7.12) will map any WC point $p = (x, y, z)$ into the same point (its actual position does not change!), but redescribed in the UVN viewing coordinate frame. Specifically, $(p, 1)M = (r, 1)$ where r is the point as expressed in VC.

The Center of Projection (COP) is expressed in the VC system. Similarly, the view plane, and therefore the center of each scene pixel, is described relative to the VC system. So one way to proceed in the implementation of an arbitrary camera is to first transform all scene (WC) objects so that they are re-expressed in VC and then do the ray tracing exactly as in Chapter 6.

With a scene made up wholly of spheres, this is an inexpensive operation. Recall that the transformation from WC to VC does not involve any change in scale, it is only a change in orientation and a translation. So the radii of the spheres cannot be affected, only the centers. Therefore, apply M to the center of each sphere, and then do exactly the same ray tracing as before. This is a very easy and elegant solution to the problem of rendering a scene from an arbitrary camera.

There is another way to proceed. As noted, the COP and the position of each scene pixel are points in VC. So, using the inverse transformation matrix, as defined in (EQ 7.13), applied to each ray, will give exactly the same effect. So in this situation, the objects are not transformed, but each ray is transformed from VC to WC.

Which method will be most efficient? Ray tracing is a slow business, so this is an important question. There are likely to be orders of magnitude more rays than objects. Even a very complex scene might have, say, 500,000 objects (an unlikely candidate for ray tracing in any case!). But if the display resolution (i.e., the number of scene pixels) is 1,000 by 1,000, then this is already 1,000,000 primary rays, let alone all the secondary rays that will be spawned as a result of the reflection and transmission. It is clear that a transformation of the objects into VC once, and then the ray tracing carried out in VC space, is the more efficient approach.

7.4　VRML97 examples

The properties of a camera to view a VRML scene are specified with a Viewpoint node. This contains a translation and orientation and a field of view. The size of the view plane window is either configured in the HTML if the VRML is viewed with a plug-in on a web page, or is configured by the VRML browser itself otherwise. The aspect ratio is automatically set so that the view does not appear to be stretched.

```
Viewpoint {
    eventIn  SFBool  set_bind
    exposedField SFFloat  fieldOfView  0.785398  #(0,Π)
    exposedField SFBool  jump  TRUE
    exposedField SFRotation orientation  0 0 1 0  #[-1, 1],(-∞,∞)
    exposedField SFVec3f position  0 0 10  #(-∞,∞)
    field SFString  description  ""
    eventOut  SFTime  bindTime
    eventOut  SFBool  isBound
}
```

Standard camera parameters can be inferred as follows. The translation and orientation fields specified are concatenated with the current transformation inherited from the Viewpoint position in the scene graph. The VRP is thus the local origin of this combined transformation, VUV is +Y and VPN is –Z. Note that the default camera is at position 0 0 10 and the orientation is 0 0 1 0 which is a null rotation. Thus the VPN is (0 0 –1) in world coordinates and the VUV is (0 1 0).

The description field defines a name for the camera. This name will usually be placed in a viewpoint list so that the user can jump to this viewpoint by selecting the viewpoint name.

The bindTime, isBound, jump, and set_bind fields allow switching between multiple viewpoints around the scene. Discussion of how this can be scripted is beyond the scope of this book, but refer to "VRML as interactive experience" on page 535 for a general introduction to scripting within VRML.

7.5　Summary

In this chapter we have considered one issue: how to specify a camera with arbitrary position and orientation. We defined the viewing coordinate system as a coordinate frame relative to the camera. This was based on three parameters: the origin of the new coordinate frame (VRP), the direction of view (VPN), and the specification of what is to be "vertical" in the image (VUV). These three parameters allowed the construction of a matrix that redescribes points in WC in terms of the VC frame. Ray tracing is then carried out in this new coordinate system, after all objects have been transformed into that system.

This makes our ray tracing system far more powerful than described earlier. However, we are still restricted to relatively simple scenes, and to spheres as the primary object.

We showed how to specify a view with VRML, but we defer continuing with the illustrations using OpenGL until we have developed some more understanding of the viewing process in a later chapter.

In the next chapter we will expand the range of primitives to include polygons and polyhedra, and show how to compose a scene made of composite objects.

8 Constructing a scene

8.1 Introduction

In this chapter we consider the fundamental subject of the representation of the geometry of 3D virtual environments. The real world is geometrically very complex – just look around wherever you are now and consider how a geometric description of that real environment might be achieved. Inevitably, in order to capture the geometry of an environment there must be a process of abstracting away from all the complexity and detail that there is in the real world, and an attempt to represent objects and the relationships between them using a succinct set of simplifying assumptions and mathematical constructs. The assumption that we make in this chapter, an assumption which is at the core of computer graphics, is that the geometry of the world may be adequately represented by using planar polygons. There are several forms of representation used in computer graphics, including curved surfaces, and fractal representations for the representation of such natural objects as rocks or mountain ranges, but polygons are the standard currency for representation in computer graphics practice. For example, most graphical hardware accelerators can cope only with polygons.

In this context it is important to remember a fundamental distinction between representation and rendering. The first is concerned wholly with the means for *describing* an object or scene independently of any particular rendering of that scene. A representation of a scene is usually externally achieved by means of a file containing geometric (and other) data, and internally, during a program execution, in the form of a data structure resident in memory. The second, rendering, is concerned with the problem of displaying the scene given a view (a camera oriented in a particular direction). In the final instance, whatever the form of representation, it is usually the case that this representation is mapped into a polygonal one for the purposes of rendering (for the reason already mentioned, that most graphics hardware deals only with polygons). So, for example, even though a scene may be described as a set of curved surfaces, when the scene is rendered, these surfaces are typically approximated by a large number of small polygons. In this chapter we are concerned only with the issue of representation, and not at all with rendering.

In the next sections we consider the following issues: first, all polygons that we consider are planar – their vertices all lie on the same plane. Knowing the equation of this plane is crucial for many operations in visibility determination, and illumination, and we will review the mathematics of this. Next we introduce the notion of polyhedra, a particular type of connected arrangement of polygons that may be used to represent objects. We consider a simple and more advanced data structure for the representation of polyhedra. Given that we can describe a single object, we consider a scene – a collection of objects, organized hierarchically. This requires an understanding of transformations applied to objects, and we introduce the necessary mathematics. Finally, we consider some examples of real systems for describing scenes, in particular the virtual reality modeling language VRML.

8.2   Polygons and planes

The plane equation

A *polygon* is defined by a sequence of points or *vertices*:

$$[p_0, p_1, \ldots, \ldots p_{n-1}], \; p_n \equiv p_0 \qquad \text{(EQ 8.1)}$$

with $p_i = (x_i, y_i, z_i)$. Each p_{i-1} to p_i, $i = 1, \ldots, n$ is an *edge*.

It is assumed that the points are *co-planar*, that is, they all lie on the same plane. Any three distinct points always lie on the same plane. However, a fourth point may not lie on the same plane as that defined by the first three. Therefore, requiring all points of a polygon to lie on the same plane is a very strong restriction. This is why in practice, in computer graphics there is a preference for three-sided polygons (i.e., triangles) because obviously triangle vertices are co-planar. A *convex polygon* is the simplest type of polygon with more than three sides that preserves a certain similarity to triangles: every

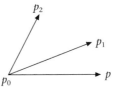

Figure 8.1
Three points defining
a plane

internal angle is less than 180 degrees. A triangle is obviously also a convex polygon. In computer graphics there is also a strong preference for convex polygons, since it is very easy to break a convex polygon up into a set of triangles. In computer graphics polygons are often called *faces* – that is, we think of a complex object being broken up into lots of "facets" which are small planar polygons. In this chapter we shall use the terms "polygon" and "face" interchangeably.

The equation of a plane is

$$ax + by + cz = d \qquad\qquad\qquad (EQ\ 8.2)$$

where x, y, and z are coordinates and the coefficients a, b, c, and d are known. Any point (x, y, z) on the plane must satisfy the equation, and any point that satisfies the equation is on the plane. We will now derive the meaning of the coefficients in the context of finding the plane equation from any three distinct points.

Suppose the plane is the surface on which this text is represented. Consider three points on this plane, p_0, p_1, p_2 as shown in Figure 8.1, and any other point $p = (x, y, z)$ on the plane. This point p can be thought of as a free variable.

The cross product $(p_1 - p_0) \times (p_2 - p_0)$ defines a vector (n) that points out perpendicular to the plane, pointing towards the reader. Such a vector is called a *normal vector* to the plane. Clearly, there are two normal vectors to a plane pointing in opposite directions. Now consider the vector $p - p_0$. Since this vector is orthogonal to the vector n, it must be the case that the inner product $n \cdot (p - p_0) = 0$.

Since p is any arbitrary point on the plane, this gives us the plane equation of the polygon as:

$$[(p_1 - p_0) \times (p_2 - p_0)] \cdot (p - p_0) = 0$$

or $\qquad\qquad\qquad\qquad\qquad\qquad\qquad\qquad (EQ\ 8.3)$

$$n \cdot p = n \cdot p_0$$

The general form of the plane equation is (EQ 8.2). If we write $n = (n_1, n_2, n_3)$, then it is clear that $a = n_1$, $b = n_2$, $c = n_3$, which shows that the normal vector is (a, b, c).

Also,

$$d = n \cdot p_0 = n_1 \cdot x_0 + n_2 \cdot y_0 + n_3 \cdot z_0 \qquad\qquad (EQ\ 8.4)$$

Notice that the particular labeling of the points is important. If we use (EQ 8.3) but swap the *spatial positions* of the points p_1 and p_2, then of course the final equation will still be the plane equation, but the normal will point in the opposite direction, that is, away from the reader. This is very important – since a plane obviously has two sides, and no side is mathematically preferred in any way. However, when we are using planar polygons to represent surfaces of objects, we need to know which side of the polygon (or plane) is the "front" side of the surface, and which is the "back." (EQ 8.3) gives us a criterion for determining the "front" faces of polygons: List the vertices of a polygon in *counterclockwise order* when looking at them from the *front* side. Then when any three successive vertices are chosen and used in formula (EQ 8.3) the normal will be front facing.

One very useful fact about the equation of a plane is that it allows us to determine the relationship of any other point in space to the plane. From equation (EQ 8.2) let's write:

$$l(x, y, z) = ax + by + cz - d \qquad \text{(EQ 8.5)}$$

Then clearly the plane equation can also be written as $l(x, y, z) = 0$. Now a plane divides all of 3D space into three disjoint regions: the so-called *half-space* consisting of all points on one side of the plane, all the points on the plane, and all the points on the other side of the plane (for this to make sense you have to remember that a plane is infinite!).

The half-space that contains the normal vector (a, b, c) is called the *positive half-space*, and the other half-space is called the *negative half-space*. The reason for this is that the positive half-space consists of all points such that $l(x, y, z) > 0$, and the negative half space all points with $l(x, y, z) < 0$.

Now suppose that (X, Y, Z) is any point. Then the following is true:

if $l(X, Y, Z) > 0$ then (X, Y, Z) is in the positive half-space (that is, it is on the same side of the plane as that in which the normal vector (a, b, c) points),

if $l(X, Y, Z) < 0$ then (X, Y, Z) is in the negative half-space, and obviously,

if $l(X, Y, Z) = 0$ then (X, Y, Z) is on the plane itself.

Recalling that we organize computation of the plane equation so that (a, b, c) points to the "front" side of the plane, these facts give us a way of determining whether any particular point is in "front" of or "behind" the plane. This is very useful for hidden-surface elimination.

Intersecting polygons by rays

As is obvious from the previous chapters, it is essential to be able to find the intersection (if any) between a ray (in other words, a line) and a polygon. There are two steps in this process, the first of which is very easy, and the second a bit more complex. The first is to find the intersection between the ray and the plane in which the polygon is embedded. There is only one situation in which no intersection results from that, which is when the ray is parallel to the plane.

Suppose the plane equation is that in (EQ 8.2), and that the ray origin is $q_0 = (u_0, v_0, w_0)$, and direction vector $dq = (du, dv, dw)$. Then the parametric equation of the ray is:

$$q(t) = q_0 + t \cdot dq$$
$$t \geq 0$$

(EQ 8.6)

Where the plane and polygon meet therefore:

$$a(u_0 + tdu) + b(v_0 + tdv) + c(w_0 + tdw) = d$$

(EQ 8.7)

Now rearrange and solve for t:

$$t = \frac{d - au_0 - bv_0 - cw_0}{adu + bdv + cdw}$$

(EQ 8.8)

The denominator will be zero when the ray is parallel to the plane, in which case no intersection exists. Otherwise, by substituting t into (EQ 8.6), we obtain the point $p = (x, y, z)$ where the ray hits the plane of the polygon. (We return to the issue of intersections between lines and planes in Chapter 10 in a very different context.)

Now assuming that we have the point p, although it is obviously on the plane of the polygon, it may or may not be inside the polygon itself. So now we have a 3D point and a polygon in 3D space, and we have to determine whether the point is inside the polygon. In general this is not an easy problem to solve in 3D. Instead we change the problem to a much easier 2D one, by projecting the vertices of the polygon and the point p onto one of the principal planes (XY, XZ, or YZ). The projected point will have the same relationship (inside or outside) to the projected polygon as the original point did to the original polygon.

To which of the three principal planes should the polygon be projected? One extreme situation to avoid is where we choose a plane which turns out to be orthogonal to the plane of the polygon, for in this case the projection would degenerate into a line. A good solution is to choose the principal plane which is somehow "most parallel" to the plane of the polygon. More formally, the angle between the normal to the plane of the polygon and the normal to the chosen principal plane should be minimized. The angle can be minimized by maximizing the dot product of the normals (assuming that they are normalized). Table 8.1 shows these dot products for the principal planes, which are c, b, and a for XY, XZ, and YZ respectively. Hence choose the principal plane corresponding to the maximum absolute value of the coefficient in the plane equation for the polygon. The projection itself is trivial: if XY is chosen then drop the z-coordinates for the polygon vertices and p, if XZ is chosen drop the y-coordinates, and if YZ is chosen drop the x-coordinates. In other words, we carry out the projection to 2D by dropping the coordinate x if $|a|$ is the maximum, drop y if $|b|$ is the maximum, and drop z if $|c|$ is the maximum.

Let's suppose without loss of generality that the principal plane chosen is the XY plane, and that the projected points are $p_i' = (x_i, y_i)$. We might end up

Table 8.1 Normals for principal planes and dot product with $n = (a, b, c)$

Principal plane	Plane equation	Normal n_{PP}	$n_{PP} \cdot n$
XY	$z = 0$	$(0, 0, 1)$	c
XZ	$y = 0$	$(0, 1, 0)$	b
YZ	$x = 0$	$(1, 0, 0)$	a

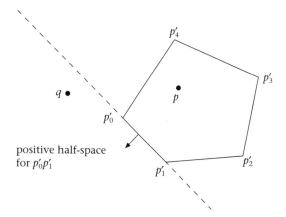

Figure 8.2
Is a point inside a polygon?

with a situation depicted as in Figure 8.2. In general it is a non-trivial problem to determine if a point is inside a polygon, even in 2D, if the polygon is allowed to be any shape at all. We discuss this in more detail in Chapter 12. Here we will assume that the polygon is convex.

We assume that the polygon vertices are organized in a counterclockwise order as in Figure 8.2. Suppose $p'_i = (x_i, y_i)$, then it is not difficult to show that the equations of the lines forming the polygon edges are:

$$e_i(x, y) = (x - x_i)dy_i - (y - y_i)dx_i = 0$$
$$dx_i = x_{i+1} - x_i$$
$$dy_i = y_{i+1} - y_i$$

(EQ 8.9)

Consider edge $e_0(x, y)$ for the moment. This is the dashed line shown in Figure 8.2. The positive half-space for this line, that is, all points on the same side as the normal to the line, are those (x, y) points such that $e_0(x, y) > 0$. The same is true for each of the line-equations corresponding to the edges of the polygon (provided that the counterclockwise ordering is valid, and the polygon is convex). Now consider a point such as q which is outside of the polygon. There will be some values of $e_i(q)$ which are positive (for edges 0 and 4) and the other values will be negative. However, for any point inside the polygon, all such values will be negative (a point inside the polygon will be in the negative half-space of every edge – or perhaps actually on one of the edges).

So an algorithm to determine whether a point is inside the polygon may be constructed from the following rule: if $e_i(p) \leq 0$ for each edge $i = 0, 1, \ldots, n-1$, then the point is inside the polygon, otherwise it is outside.

Having pursued this aside about intersecting polygons with rays, we return to the main issue of this chapter, which is representing 3D scenes by polygons.

8.3 Polyhedra

Objects in a 3D scene are usually represented by a large collection of polygons. Typically each polygon belongs to a larger structure, a *polyhedron*, where the polygons are connected edge to edge. A simple polyhedron has the following properties:

- Each edge connects exactly two vertices, and is the boundary between exactly two faces.
- Each vertex is a meeting point for at least three edges.
- No two faces intersect, except along their common edge.

The numbers of edges (E), faces (F), and vertices (V) in the polyhedron always satisfies Euler's rule (provided that the polygon has no holes):

$$V - E + F = 2 \qquad\qquad \text{(EQ 8.10)}$$

We do not consider here more complex structures, such as polyhedra with holes. Also, if we trace a closed path around the faces that meet at a vertex, that path should be unbroken, and not intersect the vertex itself. This rules out, for example, two cones joined together at their apex – such a structure is not a polyhedron following this definition. For an extensive mathematical treatment of polyhedra, see Coxeter (1973).

A polyhedron is an example of a *boundary representation* of objects, that is, where the object is represented by geometrical information about faces forming its boundary. There are other forms of representation, such as oc-trees, Binary Space Partition Trees, Constructive Solid Geometry, and these will be considered later.

The Vertex–Face data structure for polyhedra

The simplest data structure for representing a polyhedron would be as a collection of separate polygons. This is not very efficient in terms of space, nor useful in terms of modeling. For example, it is clear that each vertex would be stored at least three times, and each edge twice. The following is an example of what can be called the *Vertex–Face data structure*.

The wedge-shaped polyhedron in Figure 8.3 has 6 vertices, 9 edges, and 5 faces ($V - E + F = 2$). Label the faces as:

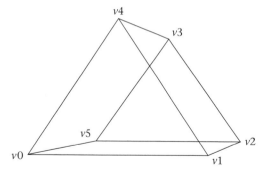

Figure 8.3
Example of a polyhedron

$$v_0 v_1 v_4 = F_0$$
$$v_5 v_3 v_2 = F_1$$
$$v_1 v_2 v_3 v_4 = F_2$$
$$v_0 v_4 v_3 v_5 = F_3$$
$$v_0 v_5 v_2 v_1 = F_4$$

The data structure involves two sequences, one an array of all vertices in the object, and the other a list of all faces, as shown in the table below:

Vertices	Faces
v_0	0, 1, 4
v_1	5, 3, 2
v_2	1, 2, 3, 4
v_3	0, 4, 3, 5
v_4	0, 5, 2, 1
v_5	

An implementation of this data structure is straightforward. The vertices can be represented as a dynamically allocated array of 3D points. A face would then be, for example, a linked list of integers, where each integer referred to a point in the vertex array. Suppose, for example, that the ith element of the vertex array is denoted $v[i]$, then the first face in the example above consists of the vertices $v[0]$, $v[1]$, $v[4]$. It is important to remember that the order in which the vertices for a face are listed is crucial, for it would signify the "front" side of that face. The vertices must be presented in such a way that when "looking" at the face from the required front side, the vertices are in counterclockwise order. This is because the function that computes the plane equation, and therefore the front-facing normal for the face, will assume that the vertices are in this order. (Alternatively, information must be stored with the face in order to indicate whether the front-facing order is clockwise or counterclockwise).

Finally, the data structure may be completed by storing the faces in a list, or an array – depending on the requirements of the application. As will be seen in the next section, the face data structure will contain not only the associated list of vertices, but also other information such as its plane equation, and information used to determine its material properties (and hence ultimately its color).

The Winged Edge data structure

The Vertex–Face data structure is very simple, but it is also very limiting. It can be made richer by having an Edge list, so that each edge points back to two entries in the vertex list, and then the faces are made from indices into the edge list. It can be made even more complex, with each vertex maintaining pointers to the edges and faces in which it participates, and edges maintaining pointers to the faces, and so on. It can be made more and more complicated, in an *ad hoc* way.

Why is this important? The reason is that this data structure may be queried in unexpected ways in some future use, and it is best to construct a rich data structure at the outset, rather than make *ad hoc* changes to it later.

The *Winged Edge data structure* defined by Baumgart (1975) is a complete data structure for polyhedra, which has stood the test of time, and is often employed. It attempts to provide a data structure which is rich enough to support reasonable queries which might be made of it, such as:

- for any face, find all of the edges, traversed in (counter)clockwise order;
- for any face, traverse all of the vertices;
- for any vertex, find all of the faces that meet at that vertex;
- for any vertex, find the edges that meet at that vertex;
- for any edge, find its two vertices;
- for any edge, find its two faces;
- for any edge, find the next edge on a face in a certain order (clockwise or counterclockwise).

Figure 8.4 shows the essential idea of the Winged Edge structure. For any edge there will always be an arrangement as shown (given the definition of a polyhedron). This is represented by a set of interrelated data structures.

The overall polyhedron is represented by a so-called *Body*. The Body contains rings (that is, doubly linked lists) called *Vertex*, *Edge*, and *Face*, and other information giving its geometrical relationship to other Bodies. Each node in the vertex ring consists of a 3D point, links to the next and previous vertices, and a link to the Edge ring. The Vertex ring holds the geometry of the object. The Edge ring holds the topology – it has links to the next and previous edges, but also the so-called "wings" as in the diagram, and also to its neighboring vertices and faces. The Face ring contains links to next and previous faces, and also to the Edge ring.

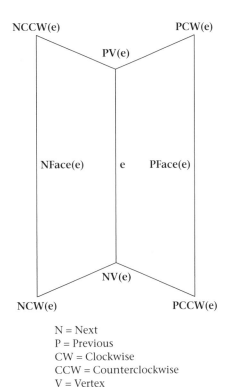

N = Next
P = Previous
CW = Clockwise
CCW = Counterclockwise
V = Vertex
e is a particular edge

Figure 8.4
The Winged Edge
data structure

The data structure is illustrated in C (see Appendix 8.1, "C specification of the Winged Edge data structure" on page 184). The main data structure is given, and then some example functions. The Edge data structure is the central one – it provides all the connectivity between edges and vertices. The vertex data structure provides the geometry.

The designer of an object has to build all of the primary links, such as the vertex, face, and edge rings, but does not have to work out the wings (`nextCWEdge`, `prevCWEdge`, `nextCCWEdge`, `prevCCWEdge`). These are constructed automatically by use of the `MakeWing` procedure shown in the appendix. For any pair of edges, it finds all of the winged connections between them.

Constructing the Winged Edge data structure from scratch is quite a difficult and time-consuming procedure. In practice, the data structure would be constructed from an initial Vertex–Face representation. Chan and Tan (1988) show how to convert data in the Vertex–Face form to the Winged Edge form – though actually the process is simpler than the method they describe.

We consider Figure 8.5 as an example where v_3 is behind the plane of the page. This has the following Vertex–Face data structure:

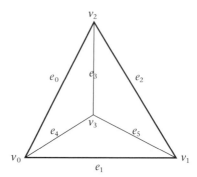

Figure 8.5
A tetrahedron

Vertices	Faces
v_0	F0 = 0, 3, 1
v_1	F1 = 0, 2, 3
v_2	F2 = 3, 2, 1
v_3	F3 = 0, 1, 2

Now to build the Winged Edge data structure, we need to identify each of the edges, and for each edge determine the previous vertex, next vertex, previous face, next face. For the two vertices that form an edge, which is labeled "previous" and which "next" is completely arbitrary, except that once this choice is made, the faces which are called "previous" or "next" for this edge are determined. Once these basic links are made, the MakeWing algorithm is used for each pair of edges that share a vertex, and hence the wings are formed.

In order to form the edges we need only traverse each face, recalling that the vertices in the face are stored in counterclockwise order. We choose to label the first vertex we encounter for an edge the "previous" and the subsequent one the "next." In the example, the first edge we encounter, belonging to face F0, is formed from vertices v_0 and v_3. (In the diagram, this edge is labeled e_4.) For this edge, v_0 is the "previous vertex" and v_3 is the "next" vertex, according to our choice. In this case, by construction the current face we are traversing (F0) must be the "previous face" for this edge, because the "previous face" is such that we move from previous to next vertex in a counterclockwise order.

Later, while traversing face F1, we will again meet this edge, only now in the order v_3 to v_0. However, this is still the same edge, and it would not be placed into the edge ring twice. The crucial new information, though, is that F1 must be the "next face" for this edge, and therefore this field can be added to this edge.

Traversing all edges of all faces in this way, we can build all the required initial links, and then use MakeWing to complete the structure. (This isn't as trivial as it seems; great care must be taken in constructing the basic elements.)

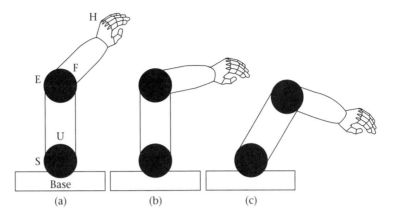

Figure 8.6
A simple robot arm in three orientations

8.4 The scene hierarchy

Basic concepts

Objects are specified by a data structure giving their geometry (vertices), topology (relationships between the edges and faces), and material properties. Objects can be manipulated in various ways – in particular, translated to another position, rotated about an axis, scaled, and various combinations of these operations. Such transformations can be accomplished by the use of the matrix transformations discussed in Chapter 2 (see "Standard transformations" on page 64). Matrix transformations are applied only to the vertices of objects; of course, the topology remains invariant.

However, objects do not stand in an isolated relationship to one another, but frequently are interdependent – a transformation applied to one object or part of an object often has ramifications for others. In this section we show how to build a data structure to represent these ideas, and where the notion of interdependent transformation is built in.

The concepts are best illustrated with respect to an example. Consider Figure 8.6, which shows a simple (2D) robot arm. The arm is composed of a number of elements: a base, shoulder joint (S), upper arm (U), elbow joint (E), forearm (F), and hand (H). The degrees of freedom are such that the robot arm as a whole can be moved, or the arm can be rotated on its base, or the forearm can be rotated on its elbow. The figure shows three situations. In (b) the forearm has been rotated compared to (a). In (c) the arm has been rotated on the base compared to (b).

The robot arm can be represented by a simple hierarchical model, shown in Figure 8.7. The hierarchy indicates the relationships between the parts, where the meaning of the arrows might be described as "contains" or "includes." Note that this is an asymmetrical relationship. When the base is moved or

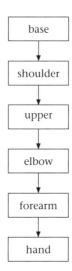

Figure 8.7
Hierarchical design for
a robot arm

rotated, each object (here only one) that is on it is similarly moved or rotated, and each object on that object is itself similarly transformed, and so on throughout the hierarchy. However, if the "shoulder" joint on the base is rotated, the base itself is not affected, but all of the descendants in the hierarchy of the shoulder joint itself are affected. Here the overall model of the arm is a hierarchical data structure reflecting the construction of the arm itself.

The data structure that models the arm should be distinguished from the images of the arm reflecting various instantiations of this underlying data structure. In graphical modeling, there is a clear and important separation between modeling and rendering. Modeling involves building the data structure representing the overall object. Rendering involves traversing that data structure and rendering each of its components.

The structure is usually more complex than a simple linear one. Suppose that there are two such robot arms, but now each is connected to the sides of a trunk, and the trunk itself is part of an overall robot, with head, trunk, arms, legs, and so on. The hierarchical model for this is shown in Figure 8.8. Note that in this case, the data structure is a tree, but in general it might be any acyclic graph.

If the robot were being built in reality, then each component would be manufactured separately, and then finally all would be assembled together to form the robot. In graphical modeling a similar method is employed. Each component is designed separately, usually in a coordinate space appropriate for its design. For example, in the (simple) case of the robot arm, the joints (elbow, shoulder) are circles, and might initially each be described in a coordinate space which is a unit square with center at the origin. Similarly, the designer of the hand might prefer to work in a unit square coordinate space (with origin at the lower left corner).

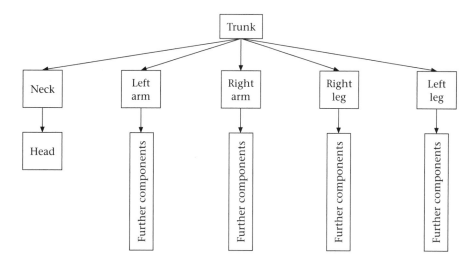

Figure 8.8
Hierarchical model for
a robot

The coordinate system in which a component is designed is usually called *Local Coordinates* (LC), and sometimes *Master Coordinates*, *Modeling Coordinates*, or *Object Coordinates*. Note that the LC systems for each individual component are independent of each other – each object is designed in its own space. Assembly is achieved by producing instances of these "master objects." This involves applying appropriate matrix transformations to locate objects in the required relationships to one another.

Specifically, each node in the graph represents an object. At each node there is a corresponding transformation matrix, which specifies how the object at that node is related to its parent node. For example, in the case of Figure 8.7, wherever and in whatever orientation the base might be, the relationship between the base and the shoulder joint (S) can be described by a transformation matrix (relative to the coordinate system in which the base is described). Similarly, the relationship of the upper arm (U) to S can also be described by a transformation matrix. Hence the relationships between the objects in the hierarchy can always be described by such matrices. It follows that the relationship between the object at any node, and an ancestor which is, say, two levels higher, can also be described by a single transformation matrix, which is formed by the multiplication of the matrices on the path connecting the nodes.

Simulation of the arm moving and generally going about its work is achieved by changing the appropriate transformation matrices at the various levels. For example, to simulate the movement of the arm as a whole, change the transformation matrix associated with the base. To simulate the rotation of the forearm, change only the transformation matrix associated with the forearm (or with the elbow). An instance of the model is therefore obtained as a particular set of such transformation matrices.

Figure 8.9
Hierarchy of
transformations

$b.B$
$s.SB$
$u.USB$
$e.EUSB$
$f.FEUSB$
$h.HFEUSB$

When the model is rendered, the entire structure is traversed starting at the root of the hierarchy. The matrix associated with the root can be thought of as transforming the root object into WC. This transformation is carried out and the root object rendered. Each child of the root is then transformed by its corresponding matrix. This transforms these objects into the *local coordinate system* of the root. These transformed objects are then again transformed by the matrix associated with the root (to get them into WC). Each can then be rendered. The same process now continues throughout the hierarchy, where at each node, the matrices on the path up to the root are multiplied together to form the appropriate transformation to WC.

Suppose that the matrices associated with the base, shoulder joint, upper arm, elbow joint, forearm, and hand are respectively B, S, U, E, F, and H. Suppose that b is a point on the base (described in the local coordinate system of the base). Then $b.B$ is in WC. Suppose, similarly, that s, u, e, f, and h are similarly points in the respective local coordinate systems of the shoulder joint, etc. Then Figure 8.9 shows the points in WC.

So note, for example, that a change in the matrix F will only affect the rendering of the forearm and hand. A change in B will affect the whole arm, whereas a change in H will only affect the hand. Although this example is in terms of a simple linear hierarchy, the same would apply to a general acyclic graph.

It is clear from the above discussion that modeling is a stage prior to rendering. Objects are first modeled in their own local coordinate systems (LC). The modeling transformations then produce WC points at the time when the hierarchy is traversed, which then feed into the rendering system.

Matrices associated with objects

Now consider the following table showing various matrices associated with each component object.

Object	Local transformation matrix (LTM)	Current transformation matrix (CTM)	Global transformation matrix (GTM)
Base	B	B	I
Shoulder joint	S	SB	B
Upper arm	U	USB	SB
Elbow joint	E	$EUSB$	USB
Forearm	F	$FEUSB$	$EUSB$
Hand	H	$HFEUSB$	$FEUSB$

The Current Transformation Matrix (CTM) converts a point from LC to WC. It is formed by multiplying the LTMs back through to the root. The Global Transformation Matrix (GTM) is essentially a convenience for computing the CTM. At any node the GTM is equal to the CTM of its parent. Hence we have the relationship:

$$CTM = LTM \times GTM \qquad\qquad\text{(EQ 8.11)}$$

It is important to realize that the notion of WC becomes *relative* from this point of view. WC corresponds at any moment to whatever is the root of the hierarchy to be rendered. Of course, this might be a subtree of a larger tree. For example, imagine a room containing various pieces of furniture and a picture on the wall (of a room containing furniture and a picture on the wall . . .). The room as a whole might be at the root of the hierarchy to be rendered, and so is in a sense "World Coordinates." However, if the subtree corresponding to the picture on the wall is rendered, then this now corresponds to WC. On the other hand, if the room is in a house, and the whole house is rendered, then the house supplies the WC frame, and so on.

Data structures

The basic descriptions of objects are typically collections of polygons, for example as in the Winged Edge data structure. We will call these basic descriptions *structures*. For example, a particular structure might be the Local Coordinate description of a desk. This structure can be used ("*instanced*") by one or many objects in the hierarchy. It is ultimately the coordinates of the vertices of the polygons in these structures that are multiplied by the transformation matrices. The data structure for the object hierarchy might then be as follows:

```
struct Object   {
  WingedEdge structure; /*representation of LC polys*/
  Matrix   CTM, LTM, GTM;
  int   noOfChildren;
  Object   child[]; /*array of children*/
}
```

Then in order to traverse any particular subtree of the hierarchy applying a function `f()` to each node:

```
traverseObject(Object object, Function f) {
    f(object);
    if(object.noOfChildren > 0){
      for(i=0; i< object.noOfChildren;++i){
        traverseObject(object.child[i],f);
      }
    }
  }
}
```

In particular, f() might involve multiplying the vertices of the polygons in the structure by the CTM, hence transforming to WC, and then rendering in the normal way.

The following two functions set the correct matrix connections between the objects.

```
setGlobalMatrixOfObject(Object object, Matrix m) {
  object.GTM = m;
  /* The "*" represents matrix multiplication*/
  object.CTM = object.LTM*object.GTM;
  if(object.noOfChildren > 0) {
    for(i=0; i< object.noOfChildren;++i){
      setGlobalMatrixOfObject(object.child[i], object.CTM);
    }
  }
}

setLocalMatrixOfObject(Object object, Matrix m) {
  object.LTM = m;
  object.CTM = object.LTM*object.GTM;
  if(object.noOfChildren > 0){
    for(i=0; i< object.noOfChildren;++i){
      setGlobalMatrixOfObject(object.child[i], object.CTM);
    }
  }
}
```

In order to describe a scene using an object hierarchy

(1) Model the relationships between the objects in the scene hierarchically – that is, establish the links.

(2) Design each structure, that is, measure the objects in a suitable coordinate system for each object.

(3) Establish the geometrical relationships between each child and its parent in terms of the LTM, which transforms the child coordinates into the coordinate system of the parent.

(4) Call the function setLTM() in order to set the LTM for each object.

8.5   Using OpenGL

OpenGL is a *rendering* system; it has no specific data structures for representing polyhedra. It does provide support for constructing a hierarchical object model, but has no particular policy on how this should be done. Rather OpenGL provides the capability for rendering graphical primitives (polygons), and applying matrix transformations to their vertices before rendering. We will see how this works in some detail in the next chapter, i.e., having constructed an object hierarchy how OpenGL may be used to render this efficiently.

In the example here we show how the *modelview matrix stack* in OpenGL can be directly used to create an object hierarchy. The way that this is done here is far from the ideal, but understanding this example will help in understanding the workings of the modelview matrix stack.

The objective of the code is to create a series of cubes stacked one on top of the other, each one scaled down by a factor of two with respect to the one that it "rests" upon. There is one instance of a cube created, and even that is created by six copies of instances of a single face, each one rotated and translated to the appropriate position.

In the function `cubebase` a single square is created with opposite corners (−0.5, −0.5, 0.0) to (0.5, 0.5, 0.0). This is the base of the cube to be created.

In `cube` this single side is invoked six times, each under a new matrix transformation. The first call in that function (`glMatrixMode`) sets the modelview matrix stack as the one to be manipulated in subsequent calls. The next function (`glPushMatrix`) pushes a copy of the current modelview matrix onto the stack. This is to isolate the succeeding modeling transformations from the viewing transformation (to be considered in the next chapter). There are then successful calls to the transformation functions (`glTranslate` and `glRotate`). The first (the "d" – double version is used throughout) constructs a translation matrix, and pre-multiplies the current modelview matrix by this. For example, if C is the current modelview matrix, and T is the translation matrix, then after the call to translate the new modelview matrix is TC.

`glRotate(a,x,y,z)` constructs a rotation matrix, which is an anti-clockwise rotation of a degrees about the vector from the origin to (x,y,z). Suppose this is matrix R, then the new modelview matrix is RC. Hence the sequence of calls:

```
glTranslated(a,b,c);/*matrix T*/
glRotated(theta,x,y,z); /*matrix R*/
```

causes the new modelview matrix to be RTC. (Note that the matrices impact the transformation in the reverse order in which they were specified.)

The `cube` function therefore constructs all six sides of the cube by making use of the original base.

Now the procedure `stack` specifies a cube, and then recursively calls itself n times, where in each subsequent call it embeds a new cube, translated on top of its predecessor and scaled by 0.5 in each dimension. By the end of this a stack of cubes has been defined.

It is worth emphasizing again that this is not an elegant or even efficient way in which to construct an object hierarchy. This method is too *ad hoc*, too basic, relying directly and only on the OpenGL matrix facilities. A more appropriate approach would be to build the object hierarchy data structures as discussed earlier in this chapter, and then use the OpenGL facilities to render this hierarchy. This is discussed in the next chapter.

```
static void cubebase(void)
/*specifies a side of a cube*/
{
  glBegin(GL_POLYGON);
    glVertex3d(-0.5,-0.5,0.0);
    glVertex3d(-0.5,0.5,0.0);
    glVertex3d(0.5,0.5,0.0);
    glVertex3d(0.5,-0.5,0.0);
  glEnd();
}

static void cube(void)
/*uses cube side to construct a cube, making use of the modelview
matrix*/
{
  /*make sure we're dealing with modelview matrix*/
  glMatrixMode(GL_MODELVIEW);

  /*pushes and duplicates current matrix*/
  glPushMatrix();

  /*construct the base*/
  cubebase();

  glPushMatrix();
  /*construct side on +x axis*/
  glTranslated(0.5,0.0,0.5);
  glRotated(90.0,0.0,1.0,0.0);
  cubebase();

  glPopMatrix();

  /*construct side on -x axis*/
  glPushMatrix();
  glTranslated(-0.5,0.0,0.5);
  glRotated(-90.0,0.0,1.0,0.0);
  cubebase();
  glPopMatrix();

  /*construct side on +y axis*/
  glPushMatrix();
  glTranslated(0.0,0.5,0.5);
  glRotated(-90.0,1.0,0.0,0.0);
  cubebase();
  glPopMatrix();

  /*construct side on -y axis*/
  glPushMatrix();
  glTranslated(0.0,-0.5,0.5);
  glRotated(90.0,1.0,0.0,0.0);
  cubebase();
  glPopMatrix();

  /*construct top*/
  glPushMatrix();
```

```
    glTranslated(0.0,0.0,1.0);
    glRotated(180.0,1.0,0.0,0.0);
    cubebase();
    glPopMatrix();

    glPopMatrix();

}

static void stack(int n)
/*creates a smaller cube on top of larger one*/
{

    cube();
    if(n==0)return;

    glPushMatrix();
    glTranslated(0.0,0.0,1.0);
    glScaled(0.5,0.5,0.5);
    stack(n-1);
    glPopMatrix();
}
```

8.6 Using VRML97

VRML97 supports the definition of polyhedra in a very similar manner to
that described above. Although a few basic primitives are supported directly
(see "Shapes and geometry" on page 528), most geometry is defined using an
IndexedFaceSet node, which follows a Vertex–Face data structure. The following example defines a prism and a cube (we are ignoring the built-in Box
node for the moment), demonstrates how an object hierarchy is built, and also
introduces the VRML instancing methodology.

A VRML scene graph is a hierarchical set of nodes. The semantics of the
scene graph are more than just a transformation hierarchy, but we can consider
a Group node to be an identity matrix pushed on the stack, so it forms a logical
partition of these nodes from others in the scene graph.

Visible objects in the scene are defined by Shape nodes. A Shape node has
two fields, *appearance* and *geometry*. Each of these fields are themselves nodes.
The first is an Appearance node (see "Illumination in VRML97" on page 153
for description of appearances) and the second is one of the geometry nodes
and in our case this is IndexedFaceSet.

In the example in Figure 8.10 the first object defined is a cube. The statment
DEF my_box labels this part of the scene graph for later instancing (see below).
The IndexedFaceSet for the cube consists of the specification of the vertices
in the coord field (itself a Coordinate node), and a list of indices into the
vertices in the coordIndex field. Each face is a list of vertices terminated by –1.
By default the faces should be defined in counterclockwise order.

```
#VRML V2.0 utf8
Group {
 children [
  Shape {# The first box
   appearance Appearance {
    material Material {# A green material
     diffuseColor 0.1 0.7 0.2
    } }
   # Define the geometry for a box
    geometry DEF my_box IndexedFaceSet {
     coord Coordinate {
      point [-1 0 -1,1 0 -1,-1 0 1,1 0 1,
             -1 2 -1,1 2 -1, -1 2 1, 1 2 1]
     }
     coordIndex  [0,1,3,2,-1,1,5,7,3,-1,
                  2,3,7,6,-1,0,2,6,4,-1,
                  0,4,5,1,-1,4,6,7,5,-1]
  } }
#Position the first prism on the first box
 Transform {
  translation -0.5 2 0
   children [
    Shape {#The first prism
     appearance Appearance {
#A reddish material
      material Material {
       diffuseColor 0.5 0.2 0.2
      } }
#Define the geometry for a prism
    geometry DEF my_prism IndexedFaceSet {
     coord Coordinate {
      point [-0.5 0 0.5, 0.5 0 0.5, 0.5 0 -0.5,
             0 1 -0.5, 0 1 0.5,-0.5 0 -0.5]
     }
     coordIndex  [0,1,4,-1,5,3,2,-1,
                  1,2,3,4,-1,0,5,2,1,-1,
                  3,5,0,4,-1]
    }
   }
  ]
 }
```

```
#Position the second box on the first box
 Transform {
  translation 0.5 2 -0.5
  scale 0.25 0.25 0.25
  children [
   Shape {# The second box
    appearance Appearance {
     material Material {# A blue material
      diffuseColor 0.3 0.4 0.8
    }
   }
#"Instance" the box geometry
   geometry USE my_box
  }

#Position the second prism on the second box
 Transform {
  translation 0 2 0
  rotation 0 1 0 0.7853
   children [
   Shape {# The second prism
    appearance Appearance {
     material Material {
      diffuseColor 0.7 0.7 0.7
     }
    }
#"Instance" the prism geometry
    geometry USE my_prism
   }
  ]
 }
]
}
]
}
```

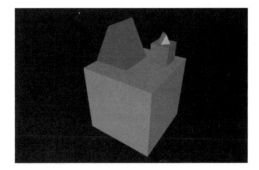

Figure 8.10
VRML97 example scene

The second visible object, a prism, is to be placed on top of the box, so we wrap this in a `Transform` node. A Transform allows a translation, rotation, and scale to be applied to objects lower in the scene graph. Again we have an `IndexedFaceSet` node, and this time we label it `my_prism` with the `DEF` keyword.

The third visible object is a another cube. This is at the same level of the hierarchy as the prism, that is, it is not a sub-object of the prism, but of the first cube. We scale the box this time by 0.25 in each direction and translate to one corner of the top of the first cube. Because we have already defined some geometry for a cube, we can just instance it by writing `USE my_box`. In VRML an instance is a reference to another piece of the scene graph and is not a complete copy of it. This mechanism can thus both reduce the memory costs of storing a scene graph and boost performance since the geometry that is shared can be optimized and reused multiple times by the rendering system (see "Groups, transformations, and scene graphs" on page 528 for further discussion of `DEF` and `USE`).

The fourth visible object is a second prism. This is a sub-object of the second cube and is placed on top and rotated $\pi/4$ radians. Note two things about its transformation. Because it is a sub-object of the second cube it is one quarter the size of the first prism, because the current transformation matrix still reflects the previous scale. Note also that this does not mean that the translation we need to make to stand the second prism on the second cube has changed from that required to stand the first prism on the first cube, since translation is performed relative to the current local coordinate system. In the local coordinate system, the second cube is still 2 units high, so we must move the second prism two units up.

8.7 Summary

In this chapter we have considered polygons in some detail, and considered the problem of object and scene creation. This involved data structures for the representation of polyhedra, and a hierarchical data structure for representing complex objects composed of multiple polyhedra. Indeed the scene as a whole may be thought of as such a complex "object," or the root of the entire object hierarchy. We saw that the creation of a hierarchy not only involves the creation of "links" representing parent–child relationships, but also transformation matrices in order to shift objects to the coordinate system of their parent. We defined the "local transformation matrix," and the "current transformation matrix," which transforms an object's vertices into the coordinate system of the object at the root of the hierarchy ("world coordinates"). Finally, we have glimpsed how widely used systems, such as OpenGL and VRML, may be used to create such hierarchies.

An important point about this chapter is the idea of thinking about the specification of scenes independently of how they are viewed: viewing and modeling are independent (in spite of the "modelview" matrix of OpenGL!). We create a scene, and then we may select arbitrary views of that scene. This is the subject of the next chapter.

Appendix 8.1   C specification of the Winged Edge data structure

```
/*winged edge data structure for representing polyhedra*/

#define NOWINGEDEDGE ((WingedEdge *)0)
#define NOVERTEXELEMENT ((VertexElement*)0)
#define NOEDGEELEMENT ((EdgeElement *)0)
#define NOFACEELEMENT ((FaceElement *)0)

typedef struct _vertexElement{
  Point3D *p;
  struct _vertexElement *nextVertexElement, *prevVertexElement;
  struct _edgeElement *edgeElement;
} VertexElement, *VertexElementPtr;

typedef struct _faceElement{
  Face *face;
  struct _faceElement *nextFaceElement, *prevFaceElement;
  struct _edgeElement *edgeElement;
} FaceElement, *FaceElementPtr;

typedef struct _edgeElement {
  struct _edgeElement *nextEdgeElement, *prevEdgeElement;
  VertexElement *nextVertexElement, *prevVertexElement;
  FaceElement *nextFaceElement, *prevFaceElement;
  struct _edgeElement *nextCWEdgeElement, *prevCWEdgeElement,
                      *nextCCWEdgeElement, *prevCCWEdgeElement;
} EdgeElement, *EdgeElementPtr;

typedef struct{
  VertexElementPtr vertexElement;
  FaceElementPtr faceElement;
  EdgeElementPtr edgeElement;
} WingedEdge, *WingedEdgePtr;

static void makeWings(EdgeElement *e1, EdgeElement *e2)
/*given two edges, this function finds all the wings*/
{
  VertexElement *e1pv, *e1nv, *e2pv, *e2nv;
  FaceElement *e1pf, *e1nf, *e2pf, *e2nf;

  if(e1==NOEDGEELEMENT || e2==NOEDGEELEMENT) return;

  e1pv = e1->prevVertexElement;
  e1nv = e1->nextVertexElement;
  e2pv = e2->prevVertexElement;
  e2nv = e2->nextVertexElement;
```

```
e1pf = e1->prevFaceElement;
e1nf = e1->nextFaceElement;
e2pf = e2->prevFaceElement;
e2nf = e2->nextFaceElement;

if((e1pv==e2pv) && (e1pf==e2nf) ) {
   e1->prevCWEdgeElement = e2;
   e2->nextCCWEdgeElement = e1;
   return;
}

if((e1pv==e2pv) && (e1nf == e2pf)  ) {
e1->nextCCWEdgeElement = e2;
   e2->prevCWEdgeElement = e1;
   return;
}

if((e1pv==e2nv) && (e1pf == e2pf)  ) {
   e1->prevCWEdgeElement = e2;
   e2->prevCCWEdgeElement = e1;
   return;
}

if((e1pv==e2nv) && (e1nf == e2nf)  ) {
   e1->nextCCWEdgeElement = e2;
   e2->nextCWEdgeElement = e1;
   return;
}

if((e1nv==e2pv) && (e1pf == e2pf)  ) {
   e1->prevCCWEdgeElement = e2;
   e2->prevCWEdgeElement = e1;
   return;
}

if((e1nv==e2pv) && (e1nf == e2nf)  ) {
   e1->nextCWEdgeElement = e2;
   e2->nextCCWEdgeElement = e1;
   return;
}

if((e1nv==e2nv) && (e1pf == e2nf)  ) {
   e1->prevCCWEdgeElement = e2;
   e2->nextCWEdgeElement = e1;
   return;
}

if((e1nv==e2nv) && (e1nf == e2pf)  ) {
   e1->nextCWEdgeElement = e2;
   e2->prevCCWEdgeElement = e1;
   return;
}
}
```

```
static short commonVertex(EdgeElement *e1, EdgeElement *e2)
/*returns 1 if edges share a vertex*/
{
   return(e1->prevVertexElement==e2->prevVertexElement) ||
         (e1->prevVertexElement==e2->nextVertexElement) ||
         (e1->nextVertexElement==e2->prevVertexElement) ||
         (e1->nextVertexElement==e2->nextVertexElement);
}

static void makeAllWings(EdgeElement *edgeElement)
{
   EdgeElement *e1, *e2;

   e1 = edgeElement;
   do{
     e2 = e1->nextEdgeElement;
     do{
       if(commonVertex(e1,e2)) {
         makeWings(e1,e2);
       }
       e2 = e2->nextEdgeElement;
     } while(e2 != edgeElement);
     e1 = e1->nextEdgeElement;
   } while(e1 != edgeElement);
}

EdgeElement *ccwEdgeAfterEdge(EdgeElement *edgeEl, FaceElement
*faceEl)
/*returns the next CCW edge belonging to the given face after this
edge*/
{
   if(edgeEl->prevFaceElement == faceEl) return(edgeEl-
   >prevCCWEdgeElement);
   else
   if(edgeEl->nextFaceElement == faceEl) return(edgeEl-
   >nextCCWEdgeElement);
}

EdgeElement *cwEdgeAfterEdge(EdgeElement *edgeEl, FaceElement
*faceEl)
/*returns the next CW edge belonging to the given face after this
edge*/
{
   if(edgeEl->prevFaceElement == faceEl) return(edgeEl-
   >prevCWEdgeElement);
   else
   if(edgeEl->nextFaceElement == faceEl) return(edgeEl-
   >nextCWEdgeElement);
}
```

```
EdgeElement *ccwEdgeAfterVertex(VertexElement *vel, FaceElement
*faceEl)
/*returns the next CCW edge belonging to the given face after this
vertex*/
{
  EdgeElement *edge;

  /*get the edge for the vertex*/
  edge = vel->edgeElement;
  /*this will always be such that vel is the nextV for this edge*/

  if(faceEl == edge->nextFaceElement) return edge;
  else
  if(faceEl == edge->prevFaceElement) return edge-
  >prevCCWEdgeElement;
  else
  return edge->nextCWEdgeElement;
}

EdgeElement *cwEdgeAfterVertex(VertexElement *vel, FaceElement
*faceEl)
/*returns the next CW edge belonging to the given face after this
vertex*/
{
  EdgeElement *edge;

  /*get the edge for the vertex*/
  edge = vel->edgeElement;
  /*this will always be such that vel is the nextV for this edge*/

  if(faceEl == edge->nextFaceElement) return edge->nextCWEdgeElement;
  else
  if(faceEl == edge->prevFaceElement) return edge;
  else
  return edge->prevCCWEdgeElement;
}

VertexElement *ccwVertexAfterVertex(VertexElement *vel, FaceElement
*faceEl)
/*returns the next CCW vertex belonging to the given face after this
vertex*/
{
  EdgeElement *edge;
  VertexElement *v;

  /*get the next CCW edge*/
  edge = ccwEdgeAfterVertex(vel,faceEl);

  if((v=edge->prevVertexElement)==vel) return edge-
  >nextVertexElement;
  else return v;
}
```

```
VertexElement *cwVertexAfterVertex(VertexElement *vel, FaceElement
*faceEl)
/*returns the next CW vertex belonging to the given face after this
vertex*/
{
  EdgeElement *edge;
  VertexElement *v;

  /*get the next CCW edge*/
  edge = cwEdgeAfterVertex(vel,faceEl);

  if((v=edge->prevVertexElement)==vel) return edge-
  >nextVertexElement;
  else return v;
}

void applyCCWEdgesOfFace(FaceElement *faceEl, void (*f)(EdgeElement
*edge))
/*runs through all edges of face in CCW order, applying function f*/
{
  EdgeElement *e0,*edgeEl;

  /*get any edge of this face*/
  e0 = edgeEl = faceEl->edgeElement;

  do{
    (*f)(edgeEl);
    edgeEl = ccwEdgeAfterEdge(edgeEl,faceEl);
  } while(edgeEl != e0);
}
```

9 Projection: completing the camera model

9.1 Introduction

In Chapter 7 we showed how to construct a camera that looked on the scene from an arbitrary viewpoint and in arbitrary orientation. We then went on to show how to extend the scene beyond spheres, to include polyhedra, which are the basic building blocks for scene description. Given the discussion of ray tracing polygons in Chapter 8 (see "Intersecting polygons by rays" on page 165) we have now given the tools for the definition and rendering of quite sophisticated scenes using ray tracing. There is a problem, however. The more rich and interesting these scenes are, the longer it will take to render them: from minutes to days.

In this chapter we are going to start the process of moving away from the type of illumination realism offered by ray tracing and towards a real-time solution.

What is it about ray tracing that takes a long time? As we noted earlier, it is the huge number of intersection calculations. Each ray must (in principle) be intersected with each object in order to find the closest intersection, if any. This can be substantially reduced, as we shall see in Chapter 16. But even if it is reduced, there is still an enormous number of rays, bearing in mind the reflected and transmitted rays in addition to the primary rays from the COP through the pixels.

The first thing we can do then is to drop the requirement for reflections and transmissions. In other words, we will only compute the illumination that occurs directly as a result of the light on the objects, and not interreflections between objects. This reduces realism substantially.

We are still left with primary rays. Primary rays still have to be compared with objects in the scene in order to find the closest intersection. So this is nevertheless very slow, without any hope of achieving real-time performance. For example, each time that the camera moves, the entire set of primary rays have to be fired again, and each time an object moves, at least a subset of the primary rays have to be reconsidered.

So the second way to speed things up is to drop the whole idea of firing rays from the eye into the scene.

Instead, we can do something that is much faster. Let's return to the idea that each polygon has a preordained color (i.e., forget the lighting computations). If you ray cast such a polygon onto the view plane, the result will be a polygon on the view plane. This polygon would be identical to one produced by tracing a ray through each polygon vertex and the COP, and finding its intersection on the view plane. The projected vertices on the view plane then form a polygon on the view plane (recall the discussion of affine transformations: see "Flatness-preserving transformations" on page 59). The polygon on the view plane is then shaded with the preordained color of the polygon. The change in speed is enormous. Instead of ray casting through each pixel, and looking for rays that happen to hit the polygon, we have found just a few ray–view plane intersections – one for each vertex, which, by construction, we know for sure hit the polygon.

Restricting ourselves to scenes described wholly with polygons our new method will be as follows (Figure 9.1):

(1) Project polygons onto the view plane. For any polygon, find all the intersections on the view plane of the rays through the COP and the polygon vertices. This defines a 2D polygon on the view plane. Transform the projected (2D) vertices into display coordinates, and draw the polygon with the required shading in 2D.

(2) Repeat this for each polygon.

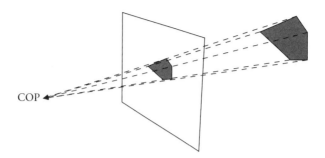

Figure 9.1
Project a polygon onto
the view plane and render

Instead of tracing millions of rays, we are finding (for a complex scene) perhaps several tens of thousands of ray–view plane intersections. Moreover, there is no "tracing" involved – each ray is, of course, guaranteed to lie on an object (since each ray is through the defining vertices of the objects).

Of course, in arriving at this method we have introduced several additional problems:

- Ray tracing implicitly solved the "visibility" problem for us. Now in the new approach we just have a set of polygons. How is the visibility relationship between them to be resolved? This is a major issue.

- Ray tracing was used in conjunction with a lighting model. Now we seem to be rendering 2D polygons. How can the lighting effect be reintroduced?

- Given a polygon in 2D, how do we efficiently determine the set of pixels that comprise it? In other words, how do we render a 2D polygon?

- Ray tracing implicitly solved the "view volume visibility" problem: no rays outside of the view volume would ever be generated. Now this is not the case with the new method. Polygons outside of the view volume have to be ignored, and those partially inside the view volume have to be trimmed to just those parts which are inside the view volume. This is the process known as "clipping."

We seem to have taken a major step forward and several steps back. It is the purpose of the next few chapters to show how each of these issues can be resolved, enabling an efficient "rendering pipeline" to be implemented.

In this chapter we concentrate on the process of projection of polygons onto the view plane. After that, we consider the various issues raised above in subsequent chapters.

9.2 Full camera specification

Before going any further, we have to complete the description of all the parameters that go into specifying a virtual camera. So far we have seen the VRP, VPN, VUV, and COP. In addition, there is the view plane window. Some more are needed.

There is sometimes confusion about the role of the "eye" in a camera model such as the one we are describing – for example, the COP is sometimes said to be an "eye." However, in reality we use our eyes to position and orient a real camera in a real scene, to capture an image. We use our eyes to look at the image on the photograph afterwards. In the case of this abstract camera, we write a program which has *functions to position and orient a view plane and a center of projection* in relation to the abstract scene. Recall that the scene only "exists" as a database of objects, as described in Chapter 8. Once this scene has been projected to the view plane and rendered on the display we use our real eyes to look. Here we mention the functions that are required in order to specify a camera. Having determined the viewing coordinate system, using the VRP, VPN, and VUV, these remaining parameters can be specified, and *all remaining parameters are in VC*:

View plane distance. The view plane is a plane orthogonal to the VPN, onto which the scene is projected. The view plane distance is the distance of the view plane, along the VPN, measured from the VRP (i.e., from the origin of the viewing coordinate system, along that system's N axis).

Type of projection. The two major types of projection are *perspective* and *parallel*. In the case of perspective projection, rays from every point of the scene converge to a specific point – the center of projection (COP). The intersection of these rays with the view plane forms the projection. The COP is *specified as an offset from the VRP* (that is, as a point in the viewing coordinate system). A parallel projection is constructed by parallel rays from the points in the scene, again whose intersection with the view plane forms the projection. The direction of these parallel rays is known as the direction of projection (DOP). An orthographic parallel projection has direction of projection $(0, 0, -1)$, that is, the rays are parallel to the N axis. Conceptually, the parallel case can be thought of as the perspective case where the COP is at "minus infinity."

In the case of perspective projection, parallel lines in the scene that are not parallel to the view plane will converge to a *vanishing point* in the projection image. Lines that are parallel to a principal axis converge to a *principal vanishing point*. There are at most three principal vanishing points in a projection. The number of principal vanishing points is equal to the number of principal axes which the view plane intersects. People therefore sometimes distinguish these different "classes" of perspective projection, as 1-point, 2-point and 3-point perspective, which characterise the particular class. An *isometric* projection is one where the view plane has equal angles with the principal axes.

Amongst parallel projections, orthographic projections, as we have seen, are where the direction of projection is normal to the view plane. This is not the case with an *oblique* parallel projection. Carlbom and Paciorek (1978) give a full survey of types of projection.

View plane window. This is a window on the view plane – specified as a rectangle with sides parallel to the U and V axes. In the case of perspective projection, rays from the COP through the four corners of this window determine the view volume as a (possibly irregular) doubly infinite pyramid. The view volume is analogous to a cone of vision; it includes only what can be seen from this particular view in the scene. A similar construction holds for the parallel projection case (further exposition will only consider the perspective case). Clearly, the view volume acts as a 3D clipping region.

Front and back clipping planes. The construction so far does not actually exclude objects in the scene which are behind the COP. In addition, the observer may wish to exclude parts of the scene which are "too close" or "too far away" from the COP. The latter might be excluded for rendering efficiency (don't attempt to render objects that are so far away they cannot contribute to the image). The former need to be excluded to avoid objects behind the COP, and also to avoid numerical instability. This can be accomplished by specifying front and back clipping planes. These are planes which are parallel to the view plane, and placed at specified distances from the VRP.

The ideas of this section are illustrated in Figure 9.2.

In order to represent these ideas in a programming language, we assume a data structure called a `Camera`, which would be represented as a structure containing instances of the various parameter settings.

```
typedef struct{
  /*camera parameters and implementation information*/
  /*...*/
} Camera;

Camera *newCamera(void);
/*creates a new camera for a perspective view*/

void setVRP(Camera *camera, double x, double y, double z);
/*sets the View Reference Point*/

void setVPN(Camera *camera, double x, double y, double z);
/*sets the View Plane Normal*/

void setVUV(Camera *camera, double x, double y, double z);
/*sets the View Up Vector*/

void setCOP(Camera *camera, double x, double y, double z);
/*sets the Centre of Projection*/

void setVPWindow(Camera *camera, double xmin, double xmax, double
ymin, double ymax);
/*sets the View Plane Window*/

void setVPDistance(Camera *camera, double vpd);
/*sets the View Plane Distance*/
```

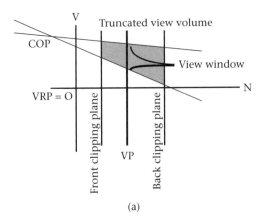

(a)

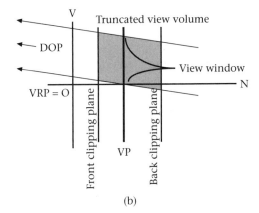

Figure 9.2
(a) Perspective projection and
(b) parallel projection

(b)

```
void setClipPlanes(Camera *camera, double front, double back);
/*sets the front and back clipping planes*/

void clickView(Camera *camera);
/*does the transformation to viewing coordinates: using VRP, VPN, VUV.
Transforms to a RHS looking down negative z-axis*/
```

9.3   Projection

Projection is the process of representing a 3D scene on a 2D plane. Human beings have represented the world in 2D since prehistoric times; everyone knows about cave paintings. However, on this immense historical scale, it is only comparatively recently that we have understood the principles behind correct 2D representations of 3D scenes. This was discovered in the Renaissance period.

The problem is: given a 3D object, how can it be represented on a 2D plane? The answer arrived at by artists and mathematicians is in the notion of a *projection*. A projection is a way of associating each point in 3D space with a unique point in the 2D space in which the representation is to appear. Note that this is always a one-to-many mapping, that is, one point in the 2D space will typically represent an infinite number of possible points in the 3D space.

There are two fundamentally different ways of doing a projection, as discussed above. The first is *parallel* and the second *perspective*. Within these there are many subtypes.

Parallel projection

Consider parallel projection first and the following example. (You should do the following yourself to help understand it.)

The following sequence of points defines a simple pyramid shape in 3D. We will give the coordinates for each side or face of the pyramid:

Base: $(-1, -1, 0)$, $(1, -1, 0)$, $(1, 1, 0)$, $(-1, 1, 0)$
side 1: $(-1, -1, 0)$, $(1, -1, 0)$, $(0, 0, 2)$
side 2: $(1, -1, 0)$, $(1, 1, 0)$, $(0, 0, 2)$
side 3: $(1, 1, 0)$, $(-1, 1, 0)$, $(0, 0, 2)$
side 4: $(-1, -1, 0)$, $(-1, 1, 0)$, $(0, 0, 2)$

Carry out the following steps:

(1) Sketch this pyramid using a 3D coordinate system. (Draw and label the axes with appropriate values, then insert the edges of the pyramid's sides. Note that this coordinate system as shown, including your drawing, will itself be a projection! Until books can be given as holograms or in Virtual Reality, there is no alternative to this.)

(2) Now draw this pyramid again on a 2D (x, y) coordinate system; just ignore the z-coordinate of every point.

(3) What do you see? If you have done this correctly, you will see a square, with the diagonal lines from corner to corner drawn. To what does this correspond? It is as if you are looking at the pyramid from the top down, and the projection plane is parallel to the base of the pyramid.

(4) Now repeat the exercise, but this time, ignore the y-coordinate. What do you see? Give a geometrical interpretation to the kind of view which you have obtained in this case.

The kind of projection which you have been using is an *orthographic parallel projection*. In such a projection the direction of view is always parallel to one of the principal axes, the projection plane is at right angles to the direction of view, and the viewpoint is from infinitely far away.

These kinds of projections give "unrealistic" views, in the sense that they don't agree with everyday observation. We know that if we look down a very long road, far away from our viewpoint the edges of the road will converge to

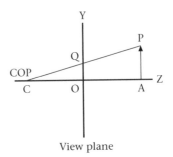

Figure 9.3
Perspective projection

View plane

a point ("at infinity"). A parallel projection does not result in this – in a parallel projection, parallel lines in the scene remain parallel in the projected image. (Of course the road really *does* have the same width throughout, so in this sense the parallel projection preserves an aspect of reality – which is why it is rather more important in, say, engineering drafting than it is in the kind of computer graphics interested in producing realistic images).

Perspective projection

In order to get the projection to look right we need perspective projection. This works rather more like natural vision. Simple perspective projection is illustrated in Figure 9.3. Here the view plane is the XY plane (the X axis may be thought of as pointing out of the page to form a left-handed system). The X, Y, and Z axes may be thought of as the UVN system as in Chapter 7.

The center of projection (COP) is distance d = OC behind the view plane and on the Z axis. The point P(x, y, z), in 3D, will be projected to the point Q on the XY plane. The triangles COQ and CAP are similar. Therefore,

$$\frac{OQ}{OC} = \frac{AP}{AC}$$ (EQ 9.1)

Translating this into coordinates, if Q is the point (x', y', z'):

$$x' = \frac{xd}{d+z}$$ (EQ 9.2)

$$y' = \frac{yd}{d+z}$$

Now given the parameters defining a particular camera (VRP, VPN, and VUV), the matrix M defined in (EQ 7.11) on page 158 may be constructed. Any polygon in WC can be redescribed in viewing coordinates, that is, the coordinate frame corresponding to Figure 9.3, using M. Then (EQ 9.2) can be used to project the polygon onto the view plane. Finally, the method described in Chapter 5 (see "Forming the displayed image" on page 126) can be used to map the polygon vertices into display space.

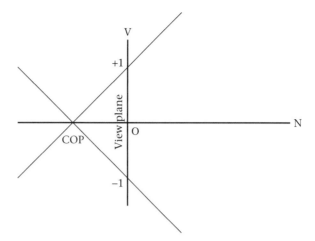

Figure 9.4
Canonical frame for
perspective projection

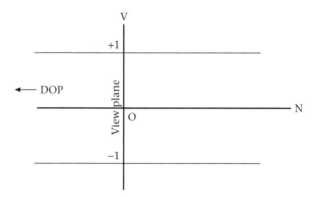

Figure 9.5
Canonical frame for
parallel projection

Canonical frames

The *canonical frames* are the fundamental arrangements that capture the essence of perspective and parallel projections. The canonical perspective frame is shown in Figure 9.4. The COP is at point $(0, 0, -1)$, the view plane is coincident with the U–V plane, and the view plane window is bounded by -1 to $+1$ for both U and V. Hence the view volume is a regular pyramid with apex at the COP (theoretically extending to infinity in both directions).

In the case of parallel projection, shown in Figure 9.5, the canonical frame forms an orthographic parallel projection, with the direction of projection $(0, 0, -1)$, and the same view-plane window as for the perspective case. The view volume in the parallel case is an infinite parallelepiped, formed by the planes $U = \pm 1$ and $V = \pm 1$.

Let $p = (x, y, z)$ be a point in VC, and let p' be the equivalent projected point on the viewplane. In the case of orthographic parallel projection, clearly

$$p' = (x, y, 0) \tag{EQ 9.3}$$

From Figure 9.4, the similar triangles argument results in the perspective projection as:

$$p' = \left(\frac{x}{z+1}, \frac{y}{z+1}, 0 \right) \tag{EQ 9.4}$$

Transforming to the canonical perspective frame

Perspective projection in the general case is tackled by first constructing a matrix to transform to the canonical perspective frame, and then a further matrix to transform this into the canonical parallel frame. This last space is, in this context, called *Projection Space* and is useful for a variety of reasons in the rendering pipeline.

First consider transforming the space illustrated in Figure 9.6 into the canonical space shown in Figure 9.4. Let the COP be point (c_x, c_y, c_z). Let d be the VP distance, and (U_1, U_2, V_1, V_2) the VP window. There are a number of steps involved in constructing matrix P, which transforms the general VC system into the canonical coordinate system.

(1) Translate the VP so that it is coincident with the U–V plane. This requires application of the matrix:

$$\begin{bmatrix} 1 & 0 & 0 & 0 \\ 0 & 1 & 0 & 0 \\ 0 & 0 & 1 & 0 \\ 0 & 0 & -d & 1 \end{bmatrix} \tag{EQ 9.5}$$

where d is the viewplane distance.

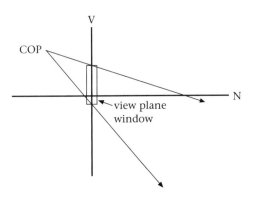

Figure 9.6
The COP in the viewing coordinate frame

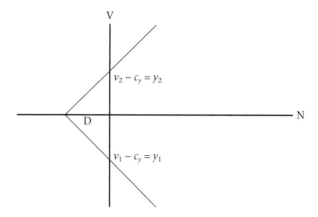

Figure 9.7
Towards the canonical frame

(2) Now translate the COP from its new position so that it lies on the N axis. Hence the required matrix is

$$\begin{bmatrix} 1 & 0 & 0 & 0 \\ 0 & 1 & 0 & 0 \\ 0 & 0 & 1 & 0 \\ -c_x & -c_y & 0 & 1 \end{bmatrix}$$

(EQ 9.6)

This results in the situation shown in Figure 9.7.
Note that (with $i = 1, 2$):

$$D = d - c_z$$
$$x_i = U_i - c_x$$
$$y_i = V_i - c_y$$

(EQ 9.7)

(3) Change the view volume into a regular pyramid, i.e. the clipping planes will be $x = \pm(z + D)$ and $y = \pm(z + D)$. It is easy to show that this can be achieved with the following matrix (see Appendix 9.1 on page 224):

$$\begin{bmatrix} \dfrac{2D}{dx} & 0 & 0 & 0 \\ 0 & \dfrac{2D}{dy} & 0 & 0 \\ -\dfrac{px}{dx} & -\dfrac{py}{dy} & 1 & 0 \\ -\left(\dfrac{px}{dx}D\right) & -\left(\dfrac{py}{dy}D\right) & 0 & 1 \end{bmatrix}$$

(EQ 9.8)

where

$$dx = x_2 - x_1$$
$$dy = y_2 - y_1$$
$$px = x_2 + x_1$$
$$py = y_2 + y_1$$

(EQ 9.9)

(4) Scale by $(1/D)$ for X, Y, and Z with the matrix

$$\begin{bmatrix} \frac{1}{D} & 0 & 0 & 0 \\ 0 & \frac{1}{D} & 0 & 0 \\ 0 & 0 & \frac{1}{D} & 0 \\ 0 & 0 & 0 & 1 \end{bmatrix}$$

(EQ 9.10)

Now multiply matrices (EQ 9.5), (EQ 9.6), (EQ 9.8), and (EQ 9.10) to arrive at the final matrix:

$$Q = \begin{bmatrix} \frac{2}{dx} & 0 & 0 & 0 \\ 0 & \frac{2}{dy} & 0 & 0 \\ -\left(\frac{px}{dx}\right)\left(\frac{1}{D}\right) & -\left(\frac{py}{dy}\right)\left(\frac{1}{D}\right) & \frac{1}{D} & 0 \\ -c_x\left(\frac{2}{dx}\right)+\left(\frac{1}{D}\right)\left(\frac{px}{dx}\right)c_z & -c_y\left(\frac{2}{dy}\right)+\left(\frac{1}{D}\right)\left(\frac{py}{dy}\right)c_z & -\left(\frac{d}{D}\right) & 1 \end{bmatrix}$$

(EQ 9.11)

The matrix in (EQ 9.11) will transform the general VC (Figure 9.6) to the canonical system illustrated in Figure 9.4.

Canonical projection space

The final step in the transformation part of the 3D viewing pipeline is to transform into the canonical projection space shown in Figure 9.5. This can be seen to be achieved by the following matrix:

$$P = \begin{bmatrix} 1 & 0 & 0 & 0 \\ 0 & 1 & 0 & 0 \\ 0 & 0 & 1 & 1 \\ 0 & 0 & 0 & 1 \end{bmatrix}$$

(EQ 9.12)

The space obtained after transforming by this matrix is the *projection space* (PS).

Now given any homogeneous point in canonical VC, $(x, y, z, 1)$, the equivalent point in PS is $(x, y, z, z + 1)$ (after multiplying by P). Hence the equivalent Euclidian 3D point, obtained by dividing the X, Y, and Z components by the W component, is:

$$\left(\frac{x}{z+1}, \frac{y}{z+1}, \frac{z}{z+1}\right)$$

Since this is a point relative to PS, the projection of this point to the X–Y plane is clearly obtained simply by ignoring the Z component, obtaining:

$$\left(\frac{x}{z+1}, \frac{y}{z+1}\right)$$

Comparing with (EQ 9.4) this is the required perspective projection of the original point (x, y, z).

This final transformation to PS therefore implicitly performs the perspective projection. Its fundamental importance is that it simplifies the problem of visibility computations (hidden surface removal) to be discussed in Chapter 13.

Incorporating the front and back clipping planes

In the derivation of the final matrix, no account has been taken of the front and back clipping planes. What has happened to these? How can these be incorporated, so that in the final Projection Space, the front clipping plane is at 0, and the back clipping plane is at 1?

The solution is as follows: suppose that *before* the application of (EQ 9.12), the front and back clipping planes have become *Dmin* and *Dmax*. Then consider the transformation:

$$z' = \left(\frac{Dmax+1}{Dmax-Dmin}\right)\left(\frac{z-Dmin}{z+1}\right)$$

$$y' = \frac{y}{z+1} \tag{EQ 9.13}$$

$$x' = \frac{x}{z+1}$$

This accomplishes the perspective transformation. Moreover, when $z = Dmin$, $z' = 0$, and when $z = Dmax$, $z' = 1$. In matrix terms this can be written as:

$$\begin{bmatrix} 1 & 0 & 0 & 0 \\ 0 & 1 & 0 & 0 \\ 0 & 0 & \dfrac{Dmax+1}{Dmax-Dmin} & 1 \\ 0 & 0 & -\dfrac{Dmin\cdot(DMax+1)}{Dmax-Dmin} & 1 \end{bmatrix} \tag{EQ 9.14}$$

Now use this matrix in place of (EQ 9.12) and the final space will have the required front and back clipping planes at 0 and 1.

Transforming the plane distances

Recall that the COP is (c_x, c_y, c_z). Let d be the view plane distance, and *dmin* and *dmax* be the front and back clipping plane distances respectively. Matrix

Q in (EQ 9.11) transforms the VC space into the *canonical* viewing space shown in Figure 9.4.

Examine what happens to the VPD, d, under these transformations. In order to transform the VPD (which is only a distance) by the matrices, we need to represent it as a point. We can represent the VPD as any point of the form (__, __, d, 1) where we use the "__" to indicate a "don't care" value, since the only thing important about the VPD is its z distance from the origin. Now applying the matrix in (EQ 9.5) results in the point (__, __, 0, 1). Matrices (EQ 9.6), (EQ 9.8), and (EQ 9.10) have no further effect on the z-coordinate, so that in the canonical VCS, the VPD has become 0, which is the required result.

Now we need to use the same technique to see what happens to the FCP and BCP under these transformations. The FCP may be represented as (__, __, $dmin$, 1). Using (EQ 9.5) results in (__, __, $dmin - d$, 1); matrices (EQ 9.6) and (EQ 9.8) have no effect on the z-coordinate, and (EQ 9.10) scales by D. Hence in canonical VCS the front and back clipping planes have been transformed to:

$$Dmin = \frac{dmin - d}{D}$$

$$Dmax = \frac{dmax - d}{D}$$

(EQ 9.15)

where $D = d - c_z$ from (EQ 9.7).

9.4   A composite matrix

Now when we begin with a WC point, it must be transformed into the canonical VC, first by transforming it to the VC, and then on to the canonical VC. In order to accomplish this, first multiply by the matrix M and then by Q. So given a WC point $p = (x, y, z)$, the resulting point in canonical VC is $(x, y, z, 1)MQ$. Now rather than compute the two matrix multiplications, we give the combined matrix that is the product of M and Q. Let's call this T, then $T = MQ$, and can be shown to be as follows:

$$T =
\begin{bmatrix}
\dfrac{2u_1 D - n_1 px}{Ddx} & \dfrac{2v_1 D - n_1 py}{Ddy} & \dfrac{n_1}{D} & 0 \\[2ex]
\dfrac{2u_2 D - n_2 px}{Ddx} & \dfrac{2v_2 D - n_2 py}{Ddy} & \dfrac{n_2}{D} & 0 \\[2ex]
\dfrac{2u_3 D - n_3 px}{Ddx} & \dfrac{2v_3 D - n_3 py}{Ddy} & \dfrac{n_3}{D} & 0 \\[2ex]
-\left(\dfrac{2(qu)D - (qn)(px) + 2c_x D - (px)c_z}{Ddx}\right) & -\left(\dfrac{2(qv)D - (qn)(py) + 2c_y D - (py)c_z}{Ddy}\right) & -\left(\dfrac{qn + d}{D}\right) & 1
\end{bmatrix}$$

(EQ 9.16)

where the following were defined earlier:

U_1, U_2, V_1, V_2 give the VP window, and

$$x_i = U_i - c_x \ (i = 1, 2)$$
$$y_i = V_i - c_y \ (i = 1, 2)$$
$$dx = x_2 - x_1 = U_2 - U_1$$
$$dy = y_2 - y_1 = V_2 - V_1 \qquad \text{(EQ 9.17)}$$
$$px = x_1 + x_2 = U_1 + U_2 - 2c_x$$
$$py = y_1 + y_2 = V_1 + V_2 - 2c_y$$

(q_1, q_2, q_3) is the VRP and

$$qu = \sum_{i=1}^{3} q_i u_i$$

$$qv = \sum_{i=1}^{3} q_i v_i \qquad \text{(EQ 9.18)}$$

$$qn = \sum_{i=1}^{3} q_i n_i$$

the inner products of the VRP with the u, v and n vectors defined by equations (EQ 7.1), (EQ 7.2), and (EQ 7.3).

So, the final result is, given a WC point (x, y, z), that the equivalent point in the canonical VC is $(x, y, z, 1)T$, where T is given in (EQ 9.16).

9.5 Computing the view matrix T

When implementing the result of the previous sections in C, it is best to treat the camera as an abstract data type (or class). The `Camera` should contain all of the information necessary to define the matrix T, as follows:

```
/*we distinguish between points and vectors for semantic reasons*/

typedef double Matrix[4][4];

typedef struct{
   double x,y,z;
} Vector;

typedef struct{
   double x,y,z;
} Point3D;
```

```
/*we assume a number of functions:*/

double normVector3D(Vector3D *v);
/*returns the norm of the Vector3D *v*/

double dotProductVector3D(Vector3D *v1, Vector3D *v2);
/*returns the dot project (*v1).(*v2)*/

void crossProductVector3D(Vector3D *v1, Vector3D *v2, Vector3D *vout);
/*returns the cross project (*v1)*(*v2) and puts the result in vout*/

void differencePoint3D(Point3D *p1, Point3D *p2, Vector3D *vdiff);
/*returns the vector that is the difference of two points p1-p2*/

void normalizeVector3D(Vector3D *v, Vector3D *vout);
/*normalizes *v to have length 1, with result returned in vout*/

void transformPoint3D(Point3D *p, Matrix m);
/*does the matrix multiplication (p->x,p->y,p->z,1)*m
to return a new point in p*/

typedef struct{
  /*public:*/
  DRAWABLE drawable;          /*a drawing surface e.g. an X Window*/
  Point3D vrp;                /*view reference point*/
  Vector3D vpn;               /*view plane normal*/
  Vector3D vuv;               /*view up vector*/
  Point3D cop;                /*centre of projection*/
  double vpd,fcp,bcp;         /*view plane distance*/
                              /*front and back clipping planes*/
  double u1,u2,v1,v2;         /*view plane window*/
  int width, height;          /*of drawable*/

  /*private:*/
  double aX,bX,aY,bY;         /*converts from 2D window -> display*/
  Point3D wc_cop;             /*COP expressed in WC*/
  double Dmin,Dmax,dr;
  Matrix T;
} Camera;
```

Now let's look at the implementation of a few of the functions:

```
void setVRP(Camera *camera, double x, double y, double z)
/*sets the View Reference Point*/
{
  camera->vrp.x = x;
  camera->vrp.y = y;
  camera->vrp.z = z;
}

void setVPN(Camera *camera, double x, double y, double z)
/*sets the View Plane Normal*/
```

```
{
   camera->vpn.x = x;
   camera->vpn.y = y;
   camera->vpn.z = z;
}

void setVPWindow(Camera *camera, double xmin, double xmax, double
ymin, double ymax)
/*sets the View Plane Window*/
{
   camera->U1 = xmin;
   camera->U2 = xmax;
   camera->V1 = ymin;
   camera->V2 = ymax;
}
```

and similarly for the other functions, where each parameter set by the application would have a corresponding function that simply stores the appropriate values in the data structure. These functions should also, of course, do error checking, for example, checking that the VPN vector does not form a 0 or 180 degree angle with the VUV.

Now we need another function that computes the matrix *T* given the information stored in the structure. In terms of the model, we can say that such a function fixes the camera parameters to be those specified so far. It is equivalent to "clicking" the camera with these fixed parameters. The implementation of this function is now given in full.

```
void click(Camera *camera)
/*computes viewing matrix based on existing parameter settings*/
{
   Vector3D u,v,n,vout;
   double px,py,dx,dy,qu,qv,qn,D,Ddx,Ddy;
   int i;
   double U[3],V[3],N[3],c[3],cx,cy,cz;

/*(a) create the M matrix*/
   /*(EQ 212) to (EQ 214)*/
   /*normalize VPN and put into n*/
   normalizeVector3D(&camera->vpn,&n);

   /* vout = n x VUV */
   crossProductVector3D(&n,&camera->vuv,&vout);
   /*computes u = (n x VUV)/|n x VUV| */
   normalizeVector3D(&vout,&u);
   /*computes v = u x n */
   crossProductVector3D(&u,&n,&v);

   /*for last row of M matrix (have to cast point to vector)*/
   /*(EQ 221), (EQ 222) and (EQ 9.18)*/
   qu = dotProductVector3D((Vector3D *)&camera->vrp,&u);
   qv = dotProductVector3D((Vector3D *)&camera->vrp,&v);
   qn = dotProductVector3D((Vector3D *)&camera->vrp,&n);
```

```
/*(b) compute the T matrix*/
  /*(EQ 9.16)*/
  dx = camera->U2 - camera->U1;
  dy = camera->V2 - camera->V1;
  px = camera->U1 + camera->U2 - 2.0*camera->cop.x;
  py = camera->V1 + camera->V2 - 2.0*camera->cop.y;

  /*(EQ 9.15)*/
  D = camera->vpd - camera->cop.z;
  camera->Dmin = (camera->fcp - camera->vpd)/D;
  camera->Dmax = (camera->bcp - camera->vpd)/D;
  Ddx = D*dx;
  Ddy = D*dy;

  /*need for transformation to Projection Space. See "Incorporating
  the Front and Back Clipping Planes" on page 000.*/
  camera->dr = (camera->Dmax + 1.0)/(camera->Dmax - camera->Dmin);

  /*now we have all the ingredients for computing T:)*/
  /*first do the first three rows and columns*/
  /*convert u,v,n to arrays -- for convenience*/
  U[0] = u.x; U[1] = u.y; U[2] = u.z;
  V[0] = v.x; V[1] = v.y; V[2] = v.z;
  N[0] = n.x; N[1] = n.y; N[2] = n.z;

  for(i = 0; i<3; ++i){
     camera->T[i][0] = (2*U[i]*D - N[i]*px)/Ddx;
     camera->T[i][1] = (2*V[i]*D - N[i]*py)/Ddy;
     camera->T[i][2] = N[i]/D;
     camera->T[i][3] = 0.0;
  }

  /*now do the last row*/
  camera->T[3][0] =
    -(2*qu*D-qn*px+2*camera->cop.x*D-px*camera->cop.z)/Ddx;
  camera->T[3][1] =
    -(2*qv*D-qn*py+2*camera->cop.y*D-py*camera->cop.z)/Ddy;
  camera->T[3][2] = -(qn + camera->vpd)/D;
  camera->T[3][3] = 1.0;

/*(c) compute the WC cop*/
  /*compute the COP expressed in WC = cop*R'+vrp,
    where R = rotation part of M
    R' is the transpose of R, ie, has rows: [u1,u2,u3]
    [v1,v2,v3][n1,n2,n3]
  */
  for(i=0;i<3;++i)  c[i] = camera->cop.x*U[i]+camera->
  cop.y*V[i]+camera->cop.z*N[i];
  camera->wc_cop.x = c[0] + camera->vrp.x;
  camera->wc_cop.y = c[1] + camera->vrp.y;
  camera->wc_cop.z = c[2] + camera->vrp.z;

/*(d) do the 2D window->display transformation*/
  /*set up the 2D window->display transformation*/
```

```
/*now the view plane window will have been transformed to
-1 <= x <= +1, -1 <= y <= +1 */

camera->bX = (double)camera->width/2.0;
camera->aX = camera->bX;

camera->bY = (double)camera->height/2.0;
camera->aY = camera->bY;

/*adjust y to turn the y axis right way up*/
camera->aY = camera->height - 1 - camera->aY;
camera->bY = -camera->bY;
}
```

This function `click` computes everything needed to transform from WC to Projection Space, including the final perspective projection, in other words the information to render a WC polygon. The function falls into four major parts:

Create the *M* matrix. This uses the VRP, VPN, and VUV to compute the *M* matrix using (EQ 7.1) to (EQ 7.11).

Compute the *T* matrix. This computes the overall *T* matrix given in (EQ 9.16).

Compute the WC COP. The COP is specified in VC. However, one of the operations that we require later is to be able to determine whether the COP is on the "front" or "back" side of the plane corresponding to any polygon (Chapter 8). This is used for back-face elimination – for any properly defined polyhedron (satisfying Euler's equation, and organized so that polygons have their vertices specified in anti-clockwise order with respect to their "front"), a polygon that faces away from the COP cannot be visible to the COP, since it will be obscured by at least one other face of the polyhedron. Suppose the plane equation is:

$$l(x, y, z) = ax + by + cz - d = 0 \qquad \text{(EQ 9.19)}$$

then if (X, Y, Z) is any point $l(X, Y, Z) > 0$ if (X, Y, Z) is in the "positive half-space" of the plane, that is, if (X, Y, Z) is on the "front" side of the plane. Therefore, to determine if the COP is on the front side, we need to substitute the COP into (EQ 9.19).

However, the COP is expressed in VC rather than WC, whereas (EQ 9.19) requires a WC point (since the plane equation is expressed in WC). We therefore have to transform from VC to WC. This turns out to be very easy. We know that matrix *M* transforms from WC to VC. Therefore the inverse of *M* is needed.

Now, from (EQ 7.4) and (EQ 7.10) we have:

$$M = \begin{bmatrix} R & 0 \\ -qR & 1 \end{bmatrix} \qquad \text{(EQ 9.20)}$$

where q is the VRP.

Also, we know by construction that R is an orthogonal rotation matrix (that is, its inverse is equal to its transpose R^T). It is therefore easy to see that the inverse of M is given by:

$$M^{-1} = \begin{bmatrix} R^T & 0 \\ q & 1 \end{bmatrix}$$

(EQ 9.21)

The position of the COP expressed in WC is therefore:

$$(cop, 1)M^{-1} = cop \cdot R^T + vrp$$

(EQ 9.22)

Geometrically, if we treat the COP as a vector in VC, then the R^T matrix converts it to the equivalent vector in WC. Translate this by the VRP to obtain the required WC expression.

The 2D window to display transformation.   This makes use of the material in Chapter 5 (see "Forming the displayed image" on page 126). After applying the projection transformation, the view plane window will have become $-1 \le x \le 1$, and $-1 \le y \le 1$. After clipping (next chapter) all points will be within the bounds of this window. We assume that the display area is of size (in pixels) $width \times height$. Using the earlier result we express the relationship between a display (viewport) point (x', y') and a window point (x, y) as follows:

$$x' = Vxmin + \left(\frac{dVx}{dWx}\right)(x - Wxmin)$$

$$y' = Vymin + \left(\frac{dVy}{dWy}\right)(y - Wymin)$$

(EQ 9.23)

In this case we have $Wxmin = -1.0$, $Wxmax = 1.0$, $dWx = 2.0$ and similarly for y. Moreover, $dVx = width$ and $dWx = height$, reducing to the equations:

$$x' = \left(\frac{width}{2}\right)(x + 1)$$

$$y' = \left(\frac{height}{2}\right)(y + 1)$$

(EQ 9.24)

and x' and y' should be rounded to integers.

Finally, many display systems have the Y axis with increasing y from top to bottom, so that $y = 0$ is at the top of the display. We *may* therefore need to reverse the direction of y by subtracting it from the maximum pixel value ($height - 1$).

9.6   Putting it all together

In practice, we have a polygon in WC, such as $p_i = (x_i, y_i, z_i)(i = 0, \ldots, n - 1)$, $p_n \equiv p_0$. We have to transform the polygon to canonical VC, then clip it and then transform the result to canonical Projection Space (PS) (i.e., the box-shaped space).

In order to do this last step, take each point and use the matrix `view->T` to transform it to the canonical VC. (In practice, we would use a copy of the point, rather than overwrite the values stored in the scene data structure.)

If we apply this to each point in the polygon, its vertices will be expressed in canonical VC. We can then clip it against the clipping planes:

$$X = \pm(Z + 1) \text{ and } Y = \pm(Z + 1), Z = Dmin \text{ and } Z = Dmax$$

The clipping process results in a new polygon, (or maybe none at all), given by canonical VC vertices $q_0, q_1, \ldots, q_{m-1}$. Now each of these must be transformed to canonical PS, using the result above (see "Transforming to the canonical perspective frame" on page 198). For example, the point q would be transformed to the point, say, r in PS as follows:

```
zplus1 = q.z + 1.0;
r.x = q.x/zplus1 ;
r.y = q.y/zplus1 ;
r.z = view->DR*((q.z - view->Dmin)/zplus1);
```

The final point `r = (r.x, r.y, r.z)` is in PS, so that the projected point is (r.x, r.y). This becomes `(round(aX + bX*r.x), round(aY + bY*r.y))` in display coordinates, using (EQ 9.23). The corresponding z depth of the point is r.z. We make use of the z depth in solving the hidden surface problem.

9.7 Combining view implementation with the scene graph

In practice, the scene is stored as an object hierarchy, where each object is represented in its own local coordinate system. Recall from Chapter 8 that a CTM (current transformation matrix) is associated with each object in the hierarchy, and the role of this matrix is to transform from local to global (i.e., world coordinates). Rather than, first, transforming the vertices of an object by multiplying through by its CTM, and then again traversing the same object's vertices to multiply by T, it is more efficient to combine, on an object-by-object basis, the CTM and T together. This is illustrated by the following function, which displays an object node with respect to a camera.

```
void displayObject(Camera *camera, GObject *object)
/*This displays all the faces associated with the object of the  camera*/
{
   FaceArray *farray;
   register int i;
   Matrix T,M;
   Point3D p;

   farray = object->farray;
```

```
/*update the camera transformation matrix by the CTM of this object*/
copyMatrix(camera->T,T);
multiplyMatrix(object->CTM,camera->T,M);
copyMatrix(M,camera->T);

/*transform the wc_cop into the local coord system -
  for back face elimination*/
p = camera->wc_cop;
transformPoint3D(&camera->wc_cop,object->invCTM);

for(i=object->startFace; i < object->startFace+object->numFaces; ++i)
  displayFace(camera,atFaceArray(farray,i));

/*restore camera transformation matrix*/
copyMatrix(T,camera->T);

/*restore wc_cop*/
camera->wc_cop = p;
}
```

This function carries out the following operations:

(1) Save the current camera transformation matrix (camera->T) into a local matrix T.

(2) Overwrite camera->T with the product of the object's CTM and camera->T, to form a new overall matrix that transforms from local to canonical viewing coordinates.

(3) Transform the WC representation of the COP into the local coordinate space of the object (by multiplying by the inverse CTM matrix – this is for the purposes of back-face elimination).

(4) Render the faces of the object as usual. Now that this object has been rendered, restore the previous state of the camera and the COP.

9.8 Viewing in OpenGL

In Chapter 8 (see "Using OpenGL" on page 178) we discussed OpenGL's minimalist approach of providing fundamental structures and operations rather than enforcing any particular policy. (This is of course within the scope set by basic assumptions such as that the scene is ultimately to be displayed as polygons.) In the context of viewing, OpenGL follows the same idea: it provides a matrix (stack), the modelview matrix for transforming from local object coordinates to (what we have called) viewing coordinates (eye coordinates), and also a projection matrix. In Chapter 8 we considered the "model" part of the modelview matrix; here we consider the "view" part, and also the projection matrix.

First, we consider how we would use the OpenGL facilities to implement the camera model discussed earlier in this chapter. First consider computation of the matrix to transform to the VC system. This is shown in clickView_GL.

```
typedef struct{
  Matrix m;
} RotationMatrix;

void clickView_GL(Camera_GL *camera)
/*does the transformation to viewing coordinates: using VRP, VPN, VUV.
Transforms to a RHS looking down negative z-axis*/
{
  Vector3D u,v,n,vout;
  GLfloat m[16];
  RotationMatrix r;

  /*normalize VPN and put into n*/
  normalizeVector3D(&camera->vpn,&n);

  /* vout = VUV x n */
  crossProductVector3D(&n,&camera->vuv,&vout);
  normaliseVector3D(&vout,&u);  /*computes u = (VUV x n)/|VUV x n| */
  crossProductVector3D(&u,&n,&v);  /*computes v = n x u */


  /*construct the viewing matrix, and also store it*/

  r.m[0][0]=m[0]=u.x; r.m[0][1]=m[1]=v.x; r.m[0][2]=-(m[2]=(-n.x));
  m[3]  = 0.0;
  r.m[1][0]=m[4]=u.y; r.m[1][1]=m[5]=v.y; r.m[1][2]=-(m[6]=(-n.y));
  m[7]  = 0.0;
  r.m[2][0]=m[8]=u.z; r.m[2][1]=m[9]=v.z; r.m[2][2]=-(m[10]=(-n.z));
  m[11]  = 0.0;
  m[12]  = 0.0;  m[13]  = 0.0;  m[14]  = 0.0;  m[15]  = 1.0;


  camera->R = r;

  /*the OpenGL calls*/
  glMatrixMode(GL_MODELVIEW);
  glLoadIdentity();
  glLoadMatrixd(m);
  glTranslated((GLdouble)(-camera->vrp.x),
    (GLdouble)(-camera->vrp.y),
    (GLdouble)(-camera->vrp.z));
}
```

The first part of the procedure is the same as before, compute the n, u, and v vectors. These are used to construct the M matrix. Two representations are stored, one internally in the RotationMatrix, and the other only for use with OpenGL (m). It is important to note that OpenGL assumes a right-handed coordinate system throughout, so that the negative is required in the third column of the m matrix.

It is also important to note that OpenGL actually defines points as column vectors, and that matrices therefore pre-multiply the points (in this book we are using the complementary convention). Therefore in OpenGL the transposes of the matrices in this book should be used. However, note that a matrix given as a single-dimension array of 16 doubles, m, is represented in OpenGL as:

$$\begin{bmatrix} m[0] & m[4] & m[8] & m[12] \\ m[1] & m[5] & m[9] & m[13] \\ m[2] & m[6] & m[10] & m[14] \\ m[3] & m[7] & m[11] & m[15] \end{bmatrix}$$

(EQ 9.25)

Having constructed the M matrix, glMatrixMode (GL_MODELVIEW) sets the current matrix stack to be the modelview stack, which is initialized with the identity matrix. Then glLoadMatrix(m) multiplies the current modelview matrix by m, and since the current matrix was the identity, this achieves the required result – almost – in fact it achieves matrix (EQ 7.7). However, note that we need to take account of the VRP (EQ 7.10). The glTranslated call multiplies the current modelview by the corresponding translation matrix, achieving matrix (EQ 7.11) as required.

Next we have to construct the equivalent of the matrix Q (EQ 9.11) – the projection matrix. OpenGL specifies a function:

```
glFrustum(GLdouble left, GLdouble right,
          GLdouble bottom, GLdouble top,
          GLdouble near, GLdouble far)
```

which determines a projection matrix for the view plane window (left, bottom, –near) and (right, top, –near) on the near clipping plane. These corners are mapped to the bottom left and top right corners of the viewing window. The center of projection is assumed to be at (0, 0, 0). Note that this assumes the "scene" to be on the negative Z axis (in fact it is exactly the same as using a left-handed system for viewing, except that the Z axis has a negative label!).

Now in our model, we have the view plane window located on the view plane (which is at distance camera->vpd) rather than on the front clipping plane. Also, the COP need not be at the origin but at some arbitrary point (cx, cy, cz). Therefore in order to use this OpenGL function we must find the projection of the view plane window onto the front clipping plane, and also adjust for the COP not being at the origin.

Figure 9.8 shows how the appropriate VP window on the front clipping plane can be computed. Consider a VP window coordinate y on the VP, which is at distance d from the origin. We wish to find the equivalent coordinate (y') on the front clipping plane (FCP) which is at distance f from the origin. By similar triangles,

$$\frac{y}{d} = \frac{y'}{f} \text{ and hence}$$

(EQ 9.26)

$$y' = \left(\frac{f}{d}\right)y$$

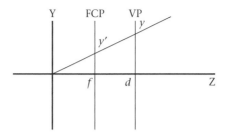

Figure 9.8
Computing the VPW on
the front clipping plane

This is all put together in the `clickProject_GL` function. Notice how the current matrix (stack) is set to the projection matrix, and then set to the identity, since the matrix determined by `glFrustum` will multiply the current matrix.

```
void clickProject_GL(Camera_GL *camera)
/*sets up the projection transformation*/
{
   GLdouble fcp,bcp,a,cx,cy,cz,umin,umax,vmin,vmax;

   /*compute the VPW given the COP at the origin, and assume that
   the VPW has been specified on the VPD*/
   cx = camera->cop.x; cy = camera->cop.y; cz = camera->cop.z;
   fcp = (camera->fcp - cz);
   bcp = (camera->bcp - cz);
   a = fcp/(camera->vpd - cz);
   umin = a*(camera->U1 - cx);
   umax = a*(camera->U2 - cx);
   vmin = a*(camera->V1 - cy);
   vmax = a*(camera->V2 - cy);

   glMatrixMode (GL_PROJECTION);         /*  prepare for and then  */
   glLoadIdentity ();                    /*  define the projection */
   glFrustum(umin,umax,vmin,vmax,fcp,bcp);
   glTranslated(-cx,-cy,cz);
}
```

Having constructed these matrices, the next issue is how to use them for rendering. We consider two issues, first the rendering of a single face, and next displaying an object in an object hierarchy, where the object is represented in local coordinates.

```
void displayFace_GL(Face *face)
/*This displays the (convex) polygon associated with the face*/
{
   int n,i;
   VertexArray *va;
   Index *index;
   Point3D p;
   PlaneEq plane;
```

```
    /*determine material properties according to rules above*/
    determineMaterial(face);

    /*get the vertex array and index to first point*/
    va = vertexArrayOfFace(face);
    index = face->first;

    glBegin(GL_POLYGON);
        plane = *planeEqOfFace(face);
        glNormal3d(plane.a,plane.b,plane.c);

        n = numVerticesInFace(face);
        for(i=0; i<n; ++i){
            p = *atVertexArray(va,valueAtIndex(index));
            glVertex3d(p.x,p.y,p.z);
            index = nextIndex(index);
        }
    glEnd();
}
```

Displaying a face is straightforward. The coordinates of the face are extracted from the Face data structure, and called within a `glBegin(GL_POLYGON)`, `glEnd()` block. Note that for illumination considerations the normal appropriate to the face must be set, and the material properties determined. This was discussed in Chapter 6.

```
void displayObject_GL(GObject *object)
/*This displays all the faces associated with the object*/
{
    FaceArray *farray;
    int i;
    Material *material;
    short disable;

    /*do nothing if this object has no geometry*/
    if(!HASGeometry(object)) return;

    /*determine the material*/
    if(material=object->material) {
        glMaterialfv(GL_FRONT,GL_AMBIENT,material->ambient);
        glMaterialfv(GL_FRONT,GL_DIFFUSE,material->diffuse);
        glMaterialfv(GL_FRONT,GL_SPECULAR,material->specular);
        glMaterialfv(GL_FRONT,GL_SHININESS,material->shininess);
        glShadeModel(material->model);
        disable=0;
        if(material->opacity==Transparant) {
            glEnable(GL_BLEND);
            disable=1;
        }
    }
    else setDefaultMaterial();
```

```
    /*get the object's face array*/
    farray = object->farray;

    /*make sure we're dealing with modelview matrix*/
    glMatrixMode(GL_MODELVIEW);

    /*pushes and duplicates current matrix*/
    glPushMatrix();

    /*multiply CurrentMatrix*CTM*/
    glMultMatrixd((GLdouble *)object->CTM); /*works because of double
    transpose*/

    for(i=object->startFace; i < object->startFace+object->numFaces; ++i){
        displayFace_GL(atFaceArray(farray,i));
    }

    /*restore camera transformation matrix*/
    glPopMatrix();

    if(disable) glDisable(GL_BLEND);
}
```

Displaying an object is also straightforward (ignore the part concerned with materials). First, in an object hierarchy it is not mandatory for each node to actually store geometry (it may just be a placeholder for a transformation) – in which case there is nothing to do. Next, after making sure that the modelview matrix is current, we push and duplicate the current modelview matrix to the top of the modelview stack (for later reinstatement), since each object has its own current transformation matrix. Next we multiply the current modelview matrix by the CTM of this object and this product becomes the new modelview matrix. The current modelview matrix should just be the one corresponding to the current camera settings. Then each face is displayed (remember that each face's coordinates are local). Finally the original modelview matrix is restored.

Suppose M is the current camera matrix for transforming from WC to VC. Suppose C is the CTM of this object. Then,

(1) M becomes the top of the stack, and the current modelview matrix is also M.

(2) The current modelview matrix becomes CM.

(3) The faces are rendered.

(4) The current modelview matrix becomes M.

```
void displayObjectTree_GL(GObject *object)
/*displays the entire subtree starting with object as root*/
{
    int i;

    /*do nothing if nothing there*/
    if(object == (GObject *)0) return;
```

```
        displayObject_GL(object);

        /*display the children*/
        if(object->n > 0){
           for(i=0; i<object->n; ++i) displayObjectTree_GL(*(object->child+i));
        }
}
```

Rendering an entire subtree of the hierarchy is simple, with a recursive function displayObjectTree. If the object is null, do nothing, otherwise render the object, and then recursively display all of its children, if any.

Finally, we consider the viewing model provided by the GLU utility library. This does provide "policy" – two functions for specifying the transformation to VC and the Projection matrix.

```
gluLookAt(GLdouble eyex, GLdouble eyey, GLdouble eyez,
          GLdouble centerx, GLdouble centery, GLdouble centerz,
          GLdouble upx, GLdouble upy, GLdouble upz)
```

The point e = (eyex, eyey, eyez) may be thought of as a WC point specifying the COP. The point c = (centerx, centery, centerz) may be thought of as the interpretation of the VRP corresponding to a point of interest in the scene. Hence the VPN is $n = c - e$. The vector u = (upx, upy, upz) is the view up vector.

This generates a matrix that maps n to the negative Z axis (recall the RHS assumed by OpenGL), e to the origin, and c to the center of the display viewport.

In order to determine the projection matrix, the gluPerspective function may be used:

```
gluPerspective(GLdouble fovy, GLdouble aspect, GLdouble znear,
GLdouble zfar)
```

This determines the angle of the field of view in the y direction (fovy in degrees), the aspect ratio of width to height of the VP window located on the front clipping plane znear. The back clipping plane is at zfar.

In Appendix 9.2 we continue the "stack of boxes" example of Chapter 8. We use the GLUT utilities library for making the OpenGL windows and specifying callbacks. Starting from main we initialize GLUT, set the window size, set the display mode (more of which in a later chapter), create and map a window. The callback functions specified determine what will occur:

- whenever the display needs to be refreshed (glutDisplayFunc)
- whenever the window is reshaped (glutReshapeFunc)
- whenever nothing else is happening (glutIdleFunc).

In initialize the only part to observe at the moment is the use of gluLookAt to determine the view.

In the callback function `reshape` the `gluPerspective` is called, because the window aspect ratio may have changed as a result of the window reshape event.

Whenever nothing else is happening, the callback function `rotate` is executed, which applies a rotation matrix, thus spinning the object displayed.

The `display` callback displays the stack of cubes, and swaps the rendering buffer in order to ensure flicker-free animation. The remainder of the program was discussed in Chapter 8.

9.9 Creating 3D stereo views

Setting up a stereo view

In Chapter 1 (see "Seeing in 3D" on page 36) we introduced the notion of stereo views of a 3D scene, by constructing separate left- and right-eye images, and allowing the visual mind to fuse these into one overall 3D image in stereo. We noted that there are many other depth cues in an image than stereo, such as linear perspective, texture gradients, and so on, but that stereo may be particularly important for near-field objects. In this section we consider how we can use the apparatus of our camera model to create 3D stereo views very simply.

Figure 9.9 shows a schematic view of a left and right eye, and an image plane on which points in the scene are to be projected. The IPD is the *inter-pupilary distance*, that is, between the two eyes. Point p_1 is on the near side of the image plane, and projects to points R_1 for the right eye, and L_1 for the left eye. Similarly p_2 is on the far side of the image plane, and projects to R_2 and L_2 respectively. The projected image points of a single scene point are called *homologous*. For example, R_1 and L_1 are homologous. Generally when $R - L > 0$ this is called *positive horizontal parallax* (as in the case of p_2) and $R - L < 0$ is *negative horizontal parallax*. Corresponding terms can similarly be defined for *vertical parallax*. When the left- and right-eye images fuse, p_1 and p_2 will be seen as virtual points in 3D space, the first in front of the stereo view plane (negative horizontal parallax) and the second behind the stereo window (positive horizontal parallax). All points on the image plane are invariant under this projection, i.e., the image plane maps to itself.

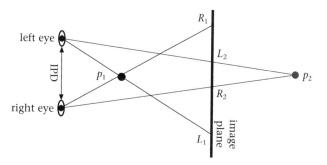

Figure 9.9
Horizontal parallax for stereo pairs

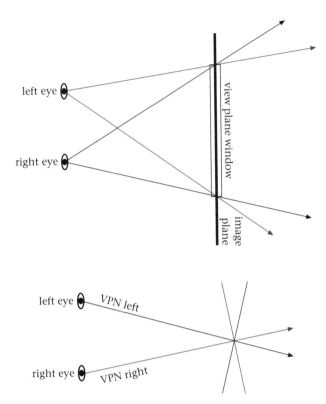

Figure 9.10
Stereo overlap

Figure 9.11
Forming stereo
images by rotation

Figure 9.10 illustrates the idea of *stereo overlap*. Although there are two separate images, one for each eye, they use the same overall viewing setup – they operate with the same image plane, the same view plane normal, view up vector, and view plane window. Only the centers of projection are different. Now since each eye uses the same view plane window, there will be an overlap in their respective view volumes. The situation shown here is 100 percent stereo overlap, since each view has exactly the same view plane window. It is possible to have a separate view plane window, one for each eye, such that there is a common overlap region between the two windows and hence the projections. The percentage of such overlap determines how much of the final overall view is in stereo, and also the size of the (non-stereo) peripheral image. Wide IPD separation and smaller overlap will influence the depth in the virtual image, but may lead to greater difficulty or discomfort in fusing the two images.

The idea that only the centers of projection are different in the left- and right-eye views may be surprising. Figure 9.11 shows an alternative method for producing stereo pairs. Here the left- and right-eye positions may be thought of as the view reference points, with the corresponding COPs as (0, 0, 0). Now each would have its own view plane normal, and view plane (the view up vector must be the same for each). So they may be considered as rotations of

Table 9.1 Viewing parameters for Figure 9.12

Parameter	Value
VRP	(5, 5, 100)
VPN	(0, 0, −1)
VUV	(0, 1, 0)
COP	(0, 0, 0)
VPWindow	−10 to 10 for X and Y
VPDistance	80

one another. However, it is not difficult to show (Hodges and McAllister, 1993) that this kind of setup produces a non-flat virtual image plane, and that there is also resulting vertical parallax. The first produces distortions, and both cause discomfort in maintaining a fused image.

A comprehensive discussion of the computation of stereo views can be found in Hodges and McAllister (1993). In particular they list a number of factors that should be taken into account in the ideal construction of stereo views, some of which are:

- Aim for congruence between left and right images. This means that the two images should be the same except for the horizontal parallax. In particular, the color and brightness should be the same for homologous points in the two images.

- Vertical parallax should be zero, in order to avoid discomfort in fusing the images.

- A good compromise between depth and comfort is to place the view plane so that approximately half of the parallax values are positive and half negative. However, in general, the greater the distance of the observer from the display, the greater the parallax that can be tolerated.

Stereo views with the camera model

Figure 9.12 (color plate) shows a view of a pyramid looking from the top. A description of the pyramid and the basic viewing setup are shown in Figure 9.13. Note that the VRP is 100 units away from the XY axis, which forms the base of the pyramid. The viewing parameters for the mono view of Figure 9.12 are shown in Table 9.1.

Now we will create three stereo views of this scene, the first with the view plane behind the pyramid, the second with the view plane cutting the pyramid halfway up its length, and the third with the view plane in front of the pyramid. In each case we will use an inter-pupilary distance of 3, by setting the COP to (0, 0, −1.5) for the left-eye view and to (0, 0, 1.5) for the right-eye view.

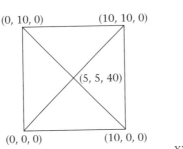
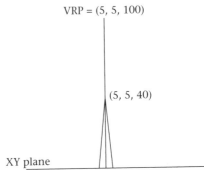

Figure 9.13
Viewing setup for the pyramid

Figure 9.14 (color plate) shows the view plane behind the pyramid. If the two images are fused then the pyramid should be seen as coming out of the page. Try to see the texture of the page itself; this will help to locate the page relative to the virtual pyramid. Note that this corresponds to negative horizontal parallax.

Figure 9.15 (color plate) shows the image with everything unchanged except that the view plane is now at a distance of 80. Hence it intersects the pyramid halfway up its length from base to apex. Note how now the virtual pyramid starts from behind the page and then comes out of the page. This corresponds to a use of both negative and horizontal parallax for this object.

Finally Figure 9.16 (color plate) shows the image with the view plane now at 60, so that it just touches the apex of the pyramid, so that for all other points it is in front of the pyramid. Notice how now the virtual pyramid appears to be behind the paper. This corresponds to positive parallax.

Perhaps the most interesting aspect of this set of figures is how remarkably different the mono image of Figure 9.12 is from all the others, and how much additional information is conveyed by the stereo depth cue in this case. The mono-view figure just looks like a 2D pattern of triangles arranged in a square; there is no hint that it could be the description of a 3D object, or at least the viewer has to use imagination to interpret this as a 3D object. The depth of the stereo views literally stands out for the other figures.

The code that was used for this example is shown below.

```
static Camera_GL *TheCamera;

static Point3D Pyramid[] = {{0.0,0.0,0.0},{10.0,0.0,0.0},
                            {10.0,10.0,0.0},{0.0,10.0,0.0},
                            {5.0,5.0,40.0}};

/*read in command line argument*/
int Eye;          /*- for L, + for R*/
float VPDistance; /*view plane distance*/

/*preset half inter-pupilary distance*/
#define HIPD  1.5
```

```c
static void displayPyramid(void)
{
  /*base*/
  glBegin(GL_POLYGON);
    glColor3f(0.0,0.0,0.0);
    glVertex3f(Pyramid[0].x,Pyramid[0].y,Pyramid[0].z);
    glVertex3f(Pyramid[3].x,Pyramid[3].y,Pyramid[3].z);
    glVertex3f(Pyramid[2].x,Pyramid[2].y,Pyramid[2].z);
    glVertex3f(Pyramid[1].x,Pyramid[1].y,Pyramid[1].z);
  glEnd();

  /*front*/
  glBegin(GL_POLYGON);
    glColor3f(1.0,0.0,0.0);
    glVertex3f(Pyramid[0].x,Pyramid[0].y,Pyramid[0].z);
    glVertex3f(Pyramid[1].x,Pyramid[1].y,Pyramid[1].z);
    glVertex3f(Pyramid[4].x,Pyramid[4].y,Pyramid[4].z);
  glEnd();

  /*right*/
  glBegin(GL_POLYGON);
    glColor3f(0.0,1.0,0.0);
    glVertex3f(Pyramid[1].x,Pyramid[1].y,Pyramid[1].z);
    glVertex3f(Pyramid[2].x,Pyramid[2].y,Pyramid[2].z);
    glVertex3f(Pyramid[4].x,Pyramid[4].y,Pyramid[4].z);
  glEnd();

  /*back*/
  glBegin(GL_POLYGON);
    glColor3f(0.0,0.0,1.0);
    glVertex3f(Pyramid[4].x,Pyramid[4].y,Pyramid[4].z);
    glVertex3f(Pyramid[2].x,Pyramid[2].y,Pyramid[2].z);
    glVertex3f(Pyramid[3].x,Pyramid[3].y,Pyramid[3].z);
  glEnd();

  /*left*/
  glBegin(GL_POLYGON);
    glColor3f(1.0,1.0,0.0);
    glVertex3f(Pyramid[0].x,Pyramid[0].y,Pyramid[0].z);
    glVertex3f(Pyramid[4].x,Pyramid[4].y,Pyramid[4].z);
    glVertex3f(Pyramid[3].x,Pyramid[3].y,Pyramid[3].z);
  glEnd();
}

static void display ()
{
  glClear(GL_COLOR_BUFFER_BIT|GL_DEPTH_BUFFER_BIT);
  displayPyramid();
  glFlush();
}

static void reshape(int width, int height)
{
```

```
    setCOP_GL(TheCamera,(float)(HIPD*Eye),0.0,0.0);
    setVPDistance_GL(TheCamera,VPDistance);
    setClipPlanes_GL(TheCamera,0.1,200.0);
    setVPWindow_GL(TheCamera,-10.0,10.0,-10.0,10.0);

    clickProject_GL(TheCamera);
    glViewport (0, 0, width, height); /*define the viewport*/
}

static void initialize(void)
{

    /*GL_FLAT or GL_SMOOTH*/
    glShadeModel(GL_FLAT);

    /*set the background (clear) Color to white*/
    glClearColor(1.0,1.0,1.0,0.0);

    glEnable(GL_DEPTH_TEST);

    /*set the depth buffer for clearing*/
    glClearDepth(1.0);

    /*initialize the camera*/
    TheCamera = newCamera_GL();
    setVRP_GL(TheCamera,5.0,5.0,100.0);
    setVPN_GL(TheCamera,0.0,0.0,-1.0);
    setVUV_GL(TheCamera,0.0,1.0,0.0);

    clickView_GL(TheCamera);
}

int main(int argc, char** argv)
{
    int window;

    glutInit(&argc,argv);

    if(argc != 3){
        printf("stereo eye(-1 or 1) vpdistance\n");
        exit(0);
    }

    Eye = atoi(argv[1]);
    VPDistance = (float)atof(argv[2]);

    /*record the window height*/
    Height = 200;

    glutInitWindowSize(Height,Height);

    glutInitDisplayMode(GLUT_RGBA|GLUT_DEPTH);
```

```
if(Eye < 0)   window = glutCreateWindow("Left");
else
if(Eye == 0)  window = glutCreateWindow("Mono");
else          window = glutCreateWindow("Right");

glutSetWindow(window);

initialize();

/*register callbacks*/
glutDisplayFunc(display); /*display function*/
glutReshapeFunc(reshape);

glutMainLoop();
}
```

The function `displayPyramid` simply takes the coordinates out of the array `Pyramid` and forms polygons in the appropriate (counterclockwise) order. The function `display` clears the color buffer and depth buffer, and then renders the pyramid, flushing the output buffer. The function `reshape` sets the projection matrix. Note that it sets the COP (which might be for a left or right eye) and the view plane distance, and view plane window. The COP and view plane distance values are determined from the command line argument in `main()`. Notice that the `clickProject` function is called to set the projection matrix as discussed in the previous section. The `initialize` function sets the shading type to be flat (there are no lights in this example, so that each polygon has a preassigned color). It clears the background color to white (and whenever the color buffer bit is reset, as in `display`, this is the color that will be set throughout the frame-buffer). It enables z depth testing (Chapter 13), and sets the maximum z value to 1.0 (which is what the z buffer will be set to when the depth buffer bit is cleared as in `display`). It then creates a new camera object and sets the VRP, VPN, and VUV. It sets the M matrix as described in the previous section.

Now we are taking the opportunity here to show how to embed such a program within the GLUT system. GLUT is a utility program (GL utility) which enables programmers to quickly create interactive programs using OpenGL (remember that OpenGL is only a renderer – and does not deal with the setting up of display windows or interaction). GLUT will not be described in this book, except for its use in examples. The code in `main` should be self-explanatory. GLUT uses a callback system, so that it enters a main loop, and whenever certain specific events occur it calls the relevant function. In this example, whenever it needs to redisplay the frame buffer it will call the function `display`, and whenever the window in which the frame buffer is rendered is changed (e.g., made visible or uncovered or stretched) it will call `reshape`.

The reader is encouraged to try out this program, and change the parameters in order to examine the effects on the stereo views.

Now in the context of a virtual reality system, the situation is more complex. For a head-mounted display, the stereo system must not only take into account the geometric viewing system, but also the optics and distortions introduced by the lenses. This is discussed in detail in Robinett and Rolland (1992) and also considered in Chapter 20. For a CAVE there are several projections, one for each wall, and again the viewing system must take this into account, and especially consider what happens when the images join together at the corners. A full discussion of this can be found in Cruz-Neira *et al.* (1993).

(9.10)   Summary

This chapter has examined the process of transforming a WC point into a projection space, suitable for carrying out the perspective projection, and further computations such as clipping. From the parameters describing a view, view reference point, view plane normal, view up vector, a matrix (M) is constructed which performs a transformation to a viewing coordinate system. Further parameters of the view, the center of projection, the view plane distance, and view plane window, are used to construct a matrix (Q) which transforms the VC into a canonical viewing coordinate system. Finally, a matrix P is used to transform to projection space. Hence the matrix MQP transforms a WC point into the PS. In the next chapter we discuss a further critical aspect of this process, the process of clipping to the view volume.

We considered the implementation of viewing using the facilities of OpenGL. First we looked at the basic facilities (the modelview and projection matrix stacks), and then how to specify a view using the GLU utility library.

Finally we saw how stereo views can be created very simply given the apparatus of the viewing model, and provided an example program for further exploration of this topic.

Appendix 9.1   Derivation of matrix in (EQ 9.8)

The matrix in equation (EQ 9.8) transforms the planes of Figure 9.7 into the simpler form $y = \pm(z + D)$ and $x = \pm(z + D)$. This transformation must be affine, since the planarity is preserved in the transformation. The original planes in Figure 9.7 have equation $Dy = y_i(z + D)$ and $Dx = x_i(x + D)$, $(i = 1, 2)$. Each point on the plane $Dy = y_2(z + D)$ must be transformed into a point on the plane $y = z + D$, and the same must be true for each of the remaining three planes. Moreover, under this transformation the distance D is preserved, and some specific results we know are that $(\_\_, 0, -D) \rightarrow (\_\_, 0, -D)$, and $(\_\_, y_2, 0) \rightarrow (\_\_, D, 0)$ and $(\_\_, y_1, 0) \rightarrow (\_\_, -D, 0)$, where $\_\_$ represents any value. A similar result holds for x. It is clear that z must be unaffected by the transformation, and also that x and y can be treated separately. Hence, supposing (y, z) becomes mapped into (y', z'), this must be of the form:

$$y' = Ay + Bz + C$$
$$z' = z$$

(EQ 9.27)

where the constants *A*, *B*, and *C* can be determined by substituting in the three specific results above and solving the resulting equations. In fact then:

$$A = \frac{2D}{dy}$$

$$B = -\frac{py}{dy}$$

(EQ 9.28)

$$C = -D\left(\frac{py}{dy}\right)$$

resulting in the matrix in (EQ 9.8).

Appendix 9.2   OpenGL rendering of an object hierarchy

This appendix shows an example of using OpenGL to render a simple object hierarchy. In practice it wouldn't be done this way – there would be an object hierarchy data structure, which would then be rendered using OpenGL. This code illustrates some simple ideas about how OpenGL may be used to render the hierarchy.

```
#include <GL/glut.h>
#include <stdio.h>

/*This next is referred to in several places, and because of the callback
interface, cannot be passed as a parameter, hence, global*/

static void cubebase(void)
/*specifies a side of a cube*/
{
    glBegin(GL_POLYGON);
        glVertex3d(-0.5,-0.5,0.0);
        glVertex3d(-0.5,0.5,0.0);
        glVertex3d(0.5,0.5,0.0);
        glVertex3d(0.5,-0.5,0.0);
    glEnd();
}

static void cube(void)
/*uses cube side to construct a cube, making use of the modelview
matrix*/
{
    /*make sure we're dealing with modelview matrix*/
    glMatrixMode(GL_MODELVIEW);

    /*pushes and duplicates current matrix*/
    glPushMatrix();

    /*construct the base*/
    cubebase();
```

```
    glPushMatrix();
    /*construct side on +x axis*/
    glTranslated(0.5,0.0,0.5);
    glRotated(90.0,0.0,1.0,0.0);
    cubebase();

    glPopMatrix();

    /*construct side on -x axis*/
    glPushMatrix();
    glTranslated(-0.5,0.0,0.5);
    glRotated(-90.0,0.0,1.0,0.0);
    cubebase();
    glPopMatrix();

    /*construct side on +y axis*/
    glPushMatrix();
    glTranslated(0.0,0.5,0.5);
    glRotated(-90.0,1.0,0.0,0.0);
    cubebase();
    glPopMatrix();

    /*construct side on -y axis*/
    glPushMatrix();
    glTranslated(0.0,-0.5,0.5);
    glRotated(90.0,1.0,0.0,0.0);
    cubebase();
    glPopMatrix();

    /*construct top*/
    glPushMatrix();
    glTranslated(0.0,0.0,1.0);
    glRotated(180.0,1.0,0.0,0.0);
    cubebase();
    glPopMatrix();

    glPopMatrix();

}

static void stack(int n)
/*creates a smaller cube on top of larger one*/
{

    cube();
    if(n==0)return;

    glPushMatrix();
    glTranslated(0.0,0.0,1.0);
    glScaled(0.5,0.5,0.5);
    stack(n-1);
    glPopMatrix();
}
```

```
static void display()
{
   glClear(GL_COLOR_BUFFER_BIT | GL_DEPTH_BUFFER_BIT);

   stack(6);
   glutSwapBuffers();

}

static void rotate(void)
/*rotates around z-axis*/
{
   static GLdouble a = 0.0;

   /*make sure we're dealing with modelview matrix*/
   glMatrixMode(GL_MODELVIEW);
   glPushMatrix();
   glRotated(a,0.0,0.0,1.0);
   cube();
   display();
   glPopMatrix();
   a += 5.0;
}

static void reshape(GLsizei width, GLsizei height)
{
   /*define the viewport - width and height of display window*/
   glViewport (0, 0, width, height);

   glMatrixMode(GL_PROJECTION);
   glLoadIdentity();
   /*define view frustrum*/
   gluPerspective(50.0,(GLdouble)width/(GLdouble)height,0.01,10.0);
   /*35deg field of view vertically, with aspect ratio, and
   front and back clipping planes of -1.0 and 10.0*/
}

static void initialize(void)
{
   /*material properties*/
   GLfloat mat_diffuse[] = {1.0,1.0,0.0,0.0};

   /*lighting*/
   GLfloat light_diffuse[] = {1.0,1.0,1.0,1.0};

   /*light position*/
   GLfloat position[] = {1.0,1.0,1.0,1.0};

   /*flat shading*/
   glShadeModel (GL_FLAT);

   /*create normals which are normalized automatically*/
   glEnable(GL_NORMALIZE);
   glEnable(GL_AUTO_NORMAL);
```

```
    /*set the background (clear) Color to white*/
    glClearColor(1.0,1.0,1.0,0.0);

    /*enable lighting*/
    glEnable(GL_LIGHTING);
    glEnable(GL_LIGHT0);

    /*for 2D the modelview matrix is the identity*/
    glMatrixMode(GL_MODELVIEW);
    glLoadIdentity();

    gluLookAt(3.0,3.0,4.0,/*eye*/
              0.0,0.0,0.0,/*looking here*/
              0.0, 0.0, 1.0);/*up vector*/

    /*set the light position in eye (viewing) coordinates*/
    glLightfv(GL_LIGHT0,GL_POSITION,position);
    /*actually this is direction, since by default an infinite
    light source is assumed*/

    /*set the material*/
    glMaterialfv(GL_FRONT,GL_DIFFUSE,mat_diffuse);

    glLightfv(GL_LIGHT0,GL_DIFFUSE,light_diffuse);

    /*enable the depth buffer*/
    glEnable(GL_DEPTH_TEST);

    /*set the depth buffer for clearing*/
    glClearDepth(1.0);

}

int main(int argc, char** argv)
{
    int window;

    glutInit(&argc,argv);

    glutInitWindowSize(500,500);
    glutInitDisplayMode(GLUT_RGBA|GLUT_DOUBLE|GLUT_DEPTH);

    window = glutCreateWindow("House");
    glutSetWindow(window);

    initialize();

    /*register callbacks*/
    glutDisplayFunc(display); /*display function*/
    glutReshapeFunc(reshape);
    glutIdleFunc(rotate);

    glutMainLoop();
}
```

10 Clipping polygons

10.1 Introduction

In the previous chapter we considered the sequence of transformations that take a point described in coordinates with respect to an object's local coordinate system, through to the projection onto a display. The projection was mediated through a very general virtual camera. A crucial aspect of that viewing pipeline not covered was *clipping*. In ray tracing this is not an issue, since no primary ray can be outside of view volume, that region bounded by four planes through the edges of the view plane window, and the front and back clipping plane. However, in the new approach, where we are projecting polygons onto the view plane, we must explicitly clip them so that only objects and parts of objects that are within the view volume are considered. In this chapter we consider only the clipping of polygons.

Recall that a polygon is a sequence of points $[p_0, p_1, \ldots, \ldots p_{n-1}]$, $p_n \equiv p_0$ connected by straight-line segments, with a closing line from p_{n-1} to p_0. The p_i are called the *vertices* of the polygon, and the connecting straight line segments the *edges*. All polygons are considered as planar (all vertices lie on the same plane). A polygon is called *simple* if no edges intersect one another – except where adjacent edges intersect at their common vertex. A polygon is called *convex* if each of its interior angles, i.e., angles between adjacent edges facing the inside of the polygon, are less than 180 degrees. We consider simple polygons in this chapter.

To maintain consistency of primitive type, the clipping of a polygon should result in a polygon (or nothing if the polygon is entirely outside of the clipping region). If, after clipping, the original polygon is reduced to a sequence of partially unconnected lines, then algorithms designed for rendering a polygon on the display would not longer work. Hence on clipping, some of the original polygon edges are replaced by boundaries of the clip region.

We first consider the clipping of polygons in 2D and then extend to 3D, in the context of the spaces described in the previous chapter.

10.2

The Sutherland–Hodgman algorithm (2D)

This section considers the clipping of polygons to a rectangular window in 2D. The general problem in 2D is to clip one polygon (the candidate) to another polygon (the clipping region). Both polygons, of course, are on the same plane. The edges of the clipping region are called *boundaries*.

The end result is a new polygon (which may be "null") consisting of the intersection of the candidate and the clipping region. Each edge of this new polygon is a fragment or entire edge of one of the candidate or clipping region edges. Here we only consider axis aligned rectangles as clipping regions, although the algorithms we discuss are trivially generalizable to more complex regions.

The procedure for polygon clipping invented by Sutherland and Hodgman (1974) is to clip the polygon against a boundary of the clip region, say the top boundary. The resulting polygon is then clipped against a second boundary, say the right boundary. The result is clipped against the bottom and finally against the left boundary. The method is illustrated in Figure 10.1.

Clipping the polygon against a clip boundary is straightforward. The procedure is to iterate through each of the polygon edges, constructing a new sequence of vertices – representing the polygon after clipping against that boundary. Let this new sequence of vertices (P) be initialized to the empty sequence. Then, for each edge, represented here by p_0 to p_1, there are four possible cases to consider:

(1) The line p_0 to p_1 is entering into the clip region (i.e., p_0 is outside the relevant clip boundary, and p_1 is inside). In this case, let p be the intersection of the line p_0 to p_1 with the clip boundary, and concatenate p and then p_1 to the end of P.

(2) The line is leaving the clip region (i.e., p_0 is inside and p_1 is outside). Again, let p be the intersection with the clip boundary, and concatenate p to the end of P.

(3) The line is entirely outside of the clip region – do nothing.

(4) The line is entirely on the visible side of the clip boundary – in which case concatenate p_1 to the end of P.

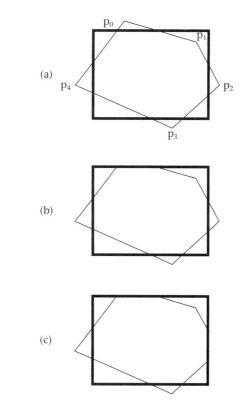

(a)

p_0

p_1

p_4

p_2

p_3

(b)

(c)

Figure 10.1
Clipping a polygon (a):
(b) against top,
(c) against right

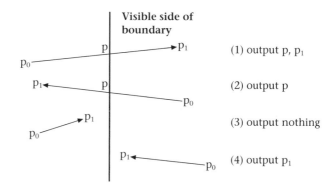

Visible side of boundary

p p_1 (1) output p, p_1

p_0

p_1 p (2) output p

p_0

p_1 (3) output nothing

p_0

p_1 (4) output p_1

p_0

Figure 10.2
Clipping a polygon
against a boundary

Steps 1 to 4 are illustrated in Figure 10.2. After carrying out these steps for each edge in turn of the polygon, the sequence P will contain the vertices of the polygon as clipped by the relevant boundary. The tests involved in (1) to (4) can be carried out very simply. Suppose the boundary being considered is the "left" one, with equation $x = xmin$. Then for the polygon edge $p_0(x_0, y_0)$ to $p_1(x_1, y_1)$:

$$x_0 < xmin \text{ and } x_1 > xmin \rightarrow (1)$$
$$x_0 > xmin \text{ and } x_1 < xmin \rightarrow (2)$$
$$x_0 < xmin \text{ and } x_1 < xmin \rightarrow (3)$$
$$x_0 > xmin \text{ and } x_1 > xmin \rightarrow (4)$$

(EQ 10.1)

10.3 Clipping polygons – the Weiler–Atherton algorithm

Consider polygon B in Figure 10.3. An application of the SH algorithm would result in the clipped polygon with vertices i, b, l, 4, 5, k, b, j, 9, 0 – there would be a single output polygon, with "degenerate" edges, that is, some edges of the output polygon would coincide. Note that this is still a valid polygon, according to our original definition – it is a sequence of vertices, which is closed. Also, such a polygon can be processed correctly by a polygon rendering procedure. However, there are examples where the degenerate edges could be a problem. For example, clipping is required for some hidden surface and shadow detection algorithms, where the output in the case of polygon B should ideally be two distinct polygons.

Weiler and Atherton (1977) produced an algorithm that would allow the clipping of any simple polygon to any other polygon forming the clip region. The algorithm is discussed here, though, in the context of a rectangular clipping region. It is based on the idea that there are no edge segments in the output polygon which were not already in the input polygon or the boundaries of the clip region. Moreover, any portion of a clip region boundary that is

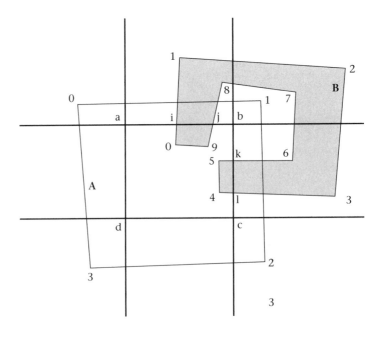

Figure 10.3
Clipping of polygon B
to polygon A

inside the polygon partitions the polygon into an inside and an outside region. These portions of clip region boundaries always start and end at intersection points of the polygon with the clip region boundaries.

We assume that the polygon and clip region are traversed in a consistent order – for example, clockwise. The first step is to compute all of the intersections of polygon edges with clip region boundaries. In polygon B this results in the set {i, j, k, l}. Each of these intersection vertices may be classified as points where the polygon enters the clip region (E) or leaves the region (L). So the classification in the example is L: {i, k} and E: {j, l}.

We require a data structure which represents the original polygon vertices and also the clip region vertices. This data structure should consist of two sequences, but such that the last point in the sequence points back to the first point – representing the clockwise ordering of the two sets of vertices. Finally, the intersection vertices must be referenced from the two sequences, so that at an intersection vertex a traversal from the polygon vertex list to the clip vertex list can be made (and vice versa). So there are two complete contours that can be traced, around the polygon (and intersection) vertices and around the clip region (and intersection) vertices. An example is shown in Figure 10.4.

Now we start from the set E, and choose one of the points, for example j. Since at j the polygon path is entering inside the clip region, we follow the polygon path until the next intersection is met. This results in the sequence 9, 0, i. The next vertex i is an L, so we follow the clip path, which would take us back to j. This completes the output of this polygon. Now we go back to the set E and choose another vertex. In this case there is only one left, which is l. This results in the sequence 4, 5, k. The last is a leaving vertex, so we follow the clip path which takes us back to k. So this completes the second polygon. Now the set E is empty so we are finished.

Figure 10.4
Data structure for insertion of the intersection vertices: the bold path follows the clip region vertices. The other path follows the polygon vertices. The E intersection points are in shaded circles and the L intersection points in the unshaded circles

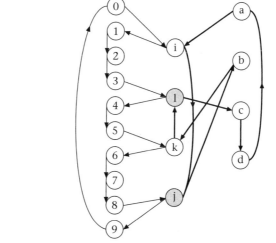

To summarize:

- Form the circular linked lists for the polygon and the clip region vertices.
- Find all of the intersections of edges with boundaries, inserting the intersection vertices into the lists, so that it is possible to traverse from one list to the other at an intersection vertex.
- Partition the set of intersection vertices into the set E containing those vertices where the polygon is entering into the clip region from outside, and L containing those where the polygon is leaving the clip region.

```
while (E is not empty){
  select and remove v from E;
  start a new empty polygon P;
  initialize w = v;
  do{
    w = nextPolygonVertex(w); append(P,w);
    while(w ≠ intersection vertex){
      w = nextPolygonVertex(w);
      append(P,w);
    };

    w = nextClipVertex(w); append(P,w);
    while(w ≠ intersection vertex){
      w = nextClipVertex(w);
      append(P,w);
    };
  } while(w ≠ v);
}
```

Notice that this algorithm relies on functions `nextPolygonVertex` and `nextClipvertex` which return the next vertex in the polygon or clip vertex list, respectively. The algorithm will output one polygon for each of the vertices in E.

Weiler (1980) produced an improved version of this algorithm, which relied on a data structure with greater complexity than the one above. Notice that the major difficulty in the algorithm is computing the intersection values and storing them correctly in the linked lists describing the vertices. It is possible to show that this can be done efficiently using a plane sweep algorithm (Preparata and Shamos, 1985).

10.4 Clipping polygons in 3D

The Sutherland–Hodgman algorithm is almost trivially generalizable to 3D. Before doing so, however, we must first identify exactly the 3D clipping boundary. In the canonical viewing space, the view volume is a regular pyramid, truncated by the front and back clipping planes. In projection space the view volume is a cuboid. First we consider clipping to the view volume in projection

Table 10.1 Clipping planes and intersections for projection space. Consider the line segment: (x_0, y_0, z_0) to (x_1, y_1, z_1)

Name of plane	Plane equation in projection space	t-values for intersection
Left	$x = -1$	$-\left(\dfrac{1 + x_0}{dx}\right)$
Right	$x = 1$	$\dfrac{1 - x_0}{dx}$
Bottom	$y = -1$	$-\left(\dfrac{1 + y_0}{dy}\right)$
Top	$y = 1$	$\dfrac{1 - y_0}{dy}$
Front	$z = 0$	$-\dfrac{z_0}{dz}$
Back	$z = 1$	$\dfrac{1 - z_0}{dz}$

space. Next we highlight the problems of this, and consider clipping in the canonical viewing space. Finally, we consider the advantages of clipping in the homogeneous coordinate space that is defined by the application of the matrix in (EQ 9.16) followed by P as defined in (EQ 9.14).

Generally, clipping algorithms for 3D have the same structure as those for 2D. The detailed changes are:

- the clipping boundaries are planes, and there are six of them;

- the intersection calculations between line segments or edges and these planes are obviously different.

Clipping in projection space

The view volume in projection space is defined by:

$$-1 \le x \le 1$$
$$-1 \le y \le 1 \quad\quad\quad\quad \text{(EQ 10.2)}$$
$$0 \le z \le 1$$

Hence the six clipping planes and associated intersection t-values for a parametrically defined line are shown in Table 10.1.

The Sutherland–Hodgman polygon clipping algorithm relies on clipping the entire polygon against each boundary and then passing the resulting polygon (if any) to the next boundary. This requires two operations:

(1) determining the relationship between a polygon edge and the boundary (Figure 10.2):

- p_0 inside and p_1 inside
- p_0 inside and p_1 outside
- p_0 outside and p_1 inside
- p_0 outside and p_1 outside

(2) finding the intersections between a polygon edge and the boundary.

Considering the $x = 1$ (right) clipping plane, the four conditions of 1 would be:

- $x_0 \leq 1$ and $x_1 \leq 1$
- $x_0 \leq 1$ and $x_1 > 1$
- $x_0 > 1$ and $x_1 \leq 1$
- $x_0 > 1$ and $x_1 > 1$

The conditions for the other planes are similar. The SH algorithm can now be structured identically to the 2D version with the changes in detail described above.

Clipping in canonical viewing space

There are circumstances where clipping in PS can lead to incorrect results. Figure 10.5 shows a situation where there is a line segment p_1 to p_2 with p_1 behind and p_2 in front of the COP. The projection of this line to the view plane actually generates two infinite lines, as shown in the figure. Consider the projection of p_1 – this projects through the COP onto the view plane at q_1. The fact that it is behind the COP makes no difference to the projection (by

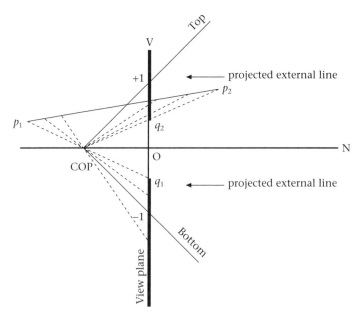

Figure 10.5
Clipping the line p_1 to p_2
in canonical viewing space

definition, the projection of a point on the view plane is the intersection between the ray starting at this point through the COP and the view plane). The projection exists provided that the point is not on the plane that is parallel to the view plane and which passes through the COP. Now if we choose another point close to p_1 but still on the line segment, this projects to another point on the view plane. If we continue in this manner, we generate a line (the lower one shown on the view plane) that is infinitely long. Similarly, if we start with a projection from p_2 through the COP, this intersects the view plane at q_2 and then choosing other points near to p_2 generates a second infinite line (the upper one shown on the view plane in the figure). Hence the correct projection of a single line segment is a so-called "external line."

This situation can lead to a serious error, since typically the two line segment end-points, p_1 and p_2, would be projected, and the line segment q_1 to q_2 would be formed on the view plane. Yet the line segment joining q_1 to q_2 is exactly the *complement* of the correct line, which, in the example, should be from "minus infinity" to q_1 and from q_2 to "infinity." This seems strange but it is mathematically correct. In real vision it doesn't happen, of course, because the part of the scene behind our eyes is "clipped" by our heads. Similarly, if we impose a front clipping plane that is in front of the COP, all parts of the scene behind the COP will be removed, and this situation cannot arise.

Now recall that transforming to projection space is equivalent to carrying out the projection (for example, once in PS we are in a viewing situation that is equivalent to orthographic parallel projection – so that the perspective projection must have already been carried out). Therefore, transforming to PS and then clipping will lead to the incorrect results whenever there are parts of the scene behind the COP. In other words, whenever the COP is inside the scene that is being viewed, it is incorrect to first project and then clip. Interactive walkthrough applications involve the COP moving anywhere in the scene, so clearly for this class of application, clipping in PS is wrong.

This is not a problem, however. It is just as easy to perform clipping in the canonical viewing space, defined by the inequalities:

$$-(z + 1) \leq x \leq z + 1$$
$$-(z + 1) \leq y \leq z + 1 \hspace{3cm} \text{(EQ 10.3)}$$
$$Dmin \leq z \leq Dmax$$

Once again clipping to this space is straightforward and requires trivial changes to the SH algorithm. The changed details are the tests for visibility of a point with respect to a boundary, and the intersection tests. The various plane equations and the intersection t-values are shown in Table 10.2.

For example, consider one of the clipping planes: $y = z + 1$. Now substitute the parametric equation of the line, to find where it meets this plane in terms of the parameter t:

$$y(t) = z(t) + 1$$
$$y_0 + tdy = z_0 + tdz + 1 \hspace{3cm} \text{(EQ 10.4)}$$

Table 10.2 Clipping planes and intersections for canonical viewing space
Consider the line segment: (x_0, y_0, z_0) to (x_1, y_1, z_1)

Name of plane	Plane equation in projection space	t-values for intersection
Left	$x = -(z + 1)$	$-\left(\dfrac{z_0 + x_0 + 1}{dx + dz}\right)$
Right	$x = z + 1$	$\left(\dfrac{z_0 - x_0 + 1}{dx - dz}\right)$
Bottom	$y = -(z + 1)$	$-\left(\dfrac{z_0 + y_0 + 1}{dy + dz}\right)$
Top	$y = z + 1$	$\left(\dfrac{z_0 - y_0 + 1}{dy - dz}\right)$
Front	$z = Dmin$	$\dfrac{Dmin - z_0}{dz}$
Back	$z = Dmax$	$\dfrac{Dmax - z_0}{dz}$

and solve for t to give:

$$t(dy - dz) = z_0 - y_0 + 1$$
$$\therefore t = \frac{z_0 - y_0 + 1}{dy - dz} \qquad \text{(EQ 10.5)}$$

This can be substituted into the parametric line equation, to find the intersection point.

Clipping in homogeneous space

A WC point is represented as a 4D homogeneous point and then multiplied by the matrix T (EQ 9.16) to transform it to canonical viewing space. Now suppose that instead of clipping there, we continue and use the projection matrix (EQ 9.14). This transforms points into the general homogeneous form (x, y, z, w) where the equivalent 3D point in PS is (X, Y, Z) with:

$$X = \frac{x}{w}, \; Y = \frac{y}{w}, \; Z = \frac{z}{w}, \; w \neq 0 \qquad \text{(EQ 10.6)}$$

This division by w in fact projects points in 4-space onto the hyperplane $w = 1$, as illustrated in Figure 10.6, where a line is projected to the hyperplane $w = 1$. Figure 10.7 shows that if one of the end-points of the line has negative w, then the line projects to an external line segment – i.e., it "wraps round" to infinity. Note that points on the $w = 0$ plane are projected to infinity (they have no projection on $w = 1$).

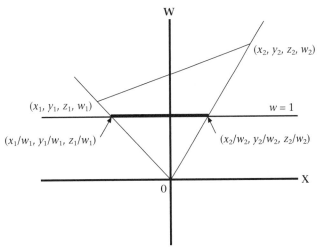

Figure 10.6
The transformation from homogeneous coordinates to 3D coordinates: an internal line segment

The line (x_1, y_1, z_1, w_1) to (x_2, y_2, z_2, w_2) is mapped

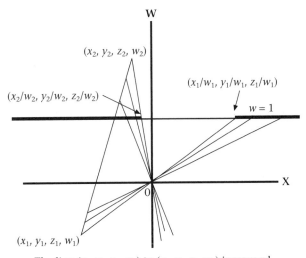

Figure 10.7
The transformation from homogeneous coordinates to 3D coordinates: an external line segment

The line (x_1, y_1, z_1, w_1) to (x_2, y_2, z_2, w_2) is mapped

Now an interesting thing occurs when the projection matrix P

$$P = \begin{bmatrix} 1 & 0 & 0 & 0 \\ 0 & 1 & 0 & 0 \\ 0 & 0 & 1 & 1 \\ 0 & 0 & 0 & 1 \end{bmatrix}$$ (EQ 10.7)

is applied to the canonical viewing space. This is shown in Figure 10.8. The COP at $(0, 0, -1, 1)$ is transformed to the $w = 0$ plane. Therefore lines in view

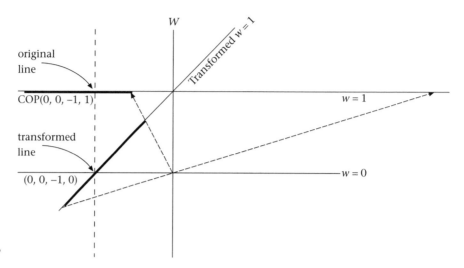

Figure 10.8
Transformation of the COP

space which have one point behind the COP will generate external line segments on projection. Blinn and Newell (1978) show that this problem can be overcome by the clipping process, but where, and crucially, the clipping is performed *before* the transformation from homogeneous space to 3D PS space (i.e., before the division by w). Hence, instead of first transforming to PS space, and then clipping, first clip and then divide by w. This is the same issue dealt with above, but considered in a different space. The clipping can therefore be done in 4D space, rather than in canonical viewing space.

The clipping in 4D space is performed similarly to clipping in canonical 3D viewing space. However, the clipping boundaries are expressed differently. For example, the 3D PS boundaries are of the form:

$$-1 \le \frac{x}{w} \le 1 \qquad\qquad \text{(EQ 10.8)}$$

which is the same as

$$-w \le x \le w(w > 0) \text{ or}$$
$$w \le x \le -w(w < 0) \qquad\qquad \text{(EQ 10.9)}$$

illustrated in Figure 10.9. Clipping to these boundaries is performed as easily as in all the other spaces. However, considering the problem in homogeneous coordinates clearly brings out the fact that external line segments can occur, and it easily allows them to be generated (if this is required by the application). Hence, clipping at this level can incorporate the possibility of a front clipping plane being behind the COP (though the physical interpretation of this is far from clear).

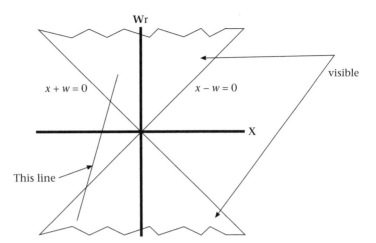

Figure 10.9
The clipping region
in 4D space

The clipping region is therefore specified by the following inequalities:

$$-w \leq x \leq w (w > 0) \text{ and } w \leq x \leq -w, (w < 0)$$
$$-w \leq y \leq w (w > 0) \text{ and } w \leq y \leq -w, (w < 0) \qquad \text{(EQ 10.10)}$$
$$0 \leq z \leq w (w > 0) \text{ and } w \leq z \leq 0, (w < 0)$$

Finding the intersections is straightforward: consider the plane $x = w$ (i.e., $w - x = 0$) and the line in homogeneous coordinates

$$p(t) = (x_1, y_1, z_1, w_1) + t(dx, dy, dz, dw) \qquad \text{(EQ 10.11)}$$

Then the intersection occurs when:

$$(w_1 + tdw) - (x_1 + tdx) = 0$$
$$\therefore t = \frac{x_1 - w_1}{dw - dx} \qquad \text{(EQ 10.12)}$$

The intersection point is therefore obtained by substituting this value for t into the equation for the line. The remaining intersections are computed accordingly. The construction of the equivalents of Tables 10.1 and 10.2 is left as an exercise for the reader.

In Figure 10.7 a line segment is shown which straddles the $w = 0$ plane. Such a line segment on clipping should generate two output segments. This can be achieved as follows:

- If the line has both end-points with $w > 0$, then clip the line as usual.
- If the line segment has both end-points with $w < 0$, then mirror the line about the $w = 0$ plane and clip as usual.
- If the line segment has one end-point with $w > 0$ and the other with $w < 0$ then first clip the line to the positive (in w) part of the clip region, then mirror the line about the $w = 0$ plane and repeat.

If this procedure is followed, then two output segments will be correctly generated in the required case. Further details can be found in Blinn, *op. cit.*, where an example is presented of clipping a parametric curve when the situations described naturally occur.

When the clipping region includes a front and a back clipping plane it is possible to avoid two clips (for $w > 0$ and $w < 0$) in the case of clipping lines and polygons, where the front clipping plane is in front of the COP. In terms of z the clipping region is $0 \leq z \leq w$. Hence, if clipping to $z \geq 0$ and $z \leq w$ is performed first, then the clipped points must have $w \geq 0$. Hence, for example, when using the Sutherland–Hodgman algorithm:

- clip to $z = 0$
- clip to $z = w$
- clip to the remaining planes in any order.

10.5 Summary

This chapter has completed the viewing pipeline, by showing how the process of clipping is combined with the transformations associated with the implementation of a camera with arbitrary position and orientation. We have only dealt with quite limited aspects of the clipping problem: in 2D to rectangular windows, and in 3D to the pyramid-shaped view volume bounded by the six clipping planes. Moreover, we have only dealt with clipping polygons. We will take up the issue of clipping lines when this topic is needed in Chapter 17.

To return to the overall rendering pipeline, we now have the capability to render hierarchical scenes constructed ultimately from polygons, and from any camera setup. This process is much faster than our original starting point in ray tracing, since we are projecting polygons onto the view plane instead of carrying out millions of ray–polygon intersection tests. Of course, we have lost the inter-object reflections that ray tracing easily deals with. The realism we can sacrifice on the altar of speed. However, we cannot sacrifice something else that ray tracing handles with ease – visibility. If we simply run through the scene graph rendering each polygon as we encounter it, the result will be hopelessly wrong. We have to take into account visibility relationships as "seen" through the current camera setup. It would be ideal to have a way of sorting our polygons so that they are rendered in the correct order with respect to visibility – those "further away" would be rendered before those that are nearer, with the nearer ones overwriting the further ones. This can be very elegantly achieved with a special data structure called a "Binary Space Partition Tree" – the subject of the next chapter. We shall also see that this data structure allows us to reintroduce shadows – something else that was lost with the move away from ray tracing.

Visibility determination

11.1   Introduction

In previous chapters we have studied how to create a scene, and view that scene through a virtual camera. This was achieved by projecting each polygon of the scene onto a 2D image plane. In this chapter we introduce the problem of computing visibility. This falls into two parts, one of which we have already considered. Only objects that are in the view volume should be visible – we saw how to use clipping to achieve this in the previous chapter. However, a much more significant, and difficult, problem is to take account of inter-object visibility. From any viewpoint, some objects obscure others, and as you move your head different parts of objects are obscured, and come into view. Hence it is in general incorrect simply to project each polygon in the scene database in the order given by the scene database. This does not take visibility into account, and will produce an incomprehensible rendering of the scene. The problem of determining the part of each object visible in each region of the image is called the *visible surface determination* problem. A classic reference for this is Sutherland *et al.* (1974).

There are many methods for performing this inter-object visibility; they can be broadly classified into three groups. *Object precision* methods compare objects with each other to decide exactly which part of each one is visible in the image. One of the first examples of this class was presented by Weiler and Atherton (1977). They used a general clipping method to partition polygons which were further away from the viewpoint using the boundaries of those closer, discarding the regions where they overlapped. Object precision algorithms can be thought of as a continuous solution (to the extent that machine precision allows) but often suffer from scalability problems as the size of the environment grows and can be difficult to implement robustly. *Image precision* algorithms on the other hand operate at the discrete representation of the image. The overall idea is to produce a solution at the resolution of the required image by determining the visible object at each pixel of the image. Ray casting is one example of this class. Another example is the z-buffer which we will see in Chapter 13. These methods tend to be much simpler to implement and more robust, thus are very popular. Finally, the third class, which is the one we will consider in this chapter, is the hybrid methods which combine object and image precision operations.

In particular, we will look at the so-called *list priority* algorithms. The idea behind these is the following: We try to determine an order of all polygons such that for any pair of polygons P and Q, P will be before Q in the ordering if Q might hide part of P. Then we render the polygons in the order given so that those polygons that obscure others will be rendered after them, thus covering over those parts that are obscured. A not quite accurate, but nevertheless helpful way to think about this is that "further" polygons are rendered before "nearer" polygons, with respect to the viewpoint. This overwriting is called the *Painters' Algorithm*, being similar to how a painter paints first the background followed by the objects in the foreground. Algorithmically the hardest part here is ordering the polygons correctly.

In this chapter we will first consider the issue of visibility for one closed polyhedron, and introduce the notion of "back-face elimination." Next we will consider some List Priority algorithms. The Depth-Sort algorithm first projects all polygons into projection space, and then achieves an order in this space. Note that this is a view-dependent solution, since the ordering is carried out after projection, hence with each change of view it must be executed again from the start. Finally we consider more view-independent solutions, the object-based partitioning tree and the "Binary Space Partition" (BSP) trees. These build data structures in world space, from which it is very easy to construct an ordering for a given viewpoint. We then show how objects can be dynamically changed while maintaining a correct BSP tree.

11.2 Back-face elimination

Back-face elimination can be used where the scene is described as a data structure representing a set of planar polygons, so that all objects are closed polyhedra. Each facet of a polyhedron will face either toward or away from the camera. Those facing away from the camera can be eliminated from all further computation. It is easy to compute whether a face is pointing away from the camera, for this can be determined from the plane equation of the polygon.

Assuming a right-handed WC system, choose three successive vertices of the polygon, where these are anticlockwise observing from the outside (i.e., from in front) of the polygon. Then, the plane equation can be computed as $l(x, y, z) = ax + by + cz - d = 0$, as discussed in Chapter 8 (see "Polygons and Planes" on page 163).

The front-facing normal vector for this polygon is (a, b, c) which will point to the desired "outside" (front) of the polygon. If this vector points away from the camera then the polygon is back-facing and may be eliminated.

Suppose COP $= (c_x, c_y, c_z)$ is the COP *represented in WC* then

$l(c_x, c_y, c_z) > 0$ if (c_x, c_y, c_z) is in front of the plane of the polygon, < 0 if behind, and $= 0$ if on.

Alternatively, suppose that the polygon has been transformed to projection space. Then if the z component of the normal (*computed in PS*) is positive, this normal must face away from the viewer (remember that the COP is at $(0, 0, -\infty)$ in this space). However, this approach requires computation of the plane equation in PS. This can be carried out directly, using three successive points of the transformed polygon, or computed from the original WC plane equation as follows:

The WC plane equation can be represented as:

$$p \cdot l = 0 \qquad\qquad (EQ\ 11.1)$$

where $p = (x, y, z, 1)$ is any point on the plane, and $l = \begin{bmatrix} a \\ b \\ c \\ -d \end{bmatrix}$.

Suppose S is a matrix which transforms each point on the plane. Hence, for any point p, let

$$q = pS \qquad\qquad (EQ\ 11.2)$$

be the transformed point.

Post-multiplying throughout by S^{-1} results in:

$$qS^{-1} = p \qquad\qquad (EQ\ 11.3)$$

Post-multiply throughout by l and use (EQ 11.1) to give:

$$qS^{-1} \cdot l = p \cdot l = 0 \qquad\qquad (EQ\ 11.4)$$

Finally, write $m = S^{-1} \cdot l$ to give

$$q \cdot m = 0 \qquad\qquad (EQ\ 11.5)$$

The meaning of this derivation is that if l represents the plane equation in some space, and then the objects in that space are transformed by a matrix S, m represents the transformed plane equation.

It is interesting to note that for a single convex object, back-face elimination is enough to solve the visibility problem. By definition a convex object is one

Figure 11.1
For a closed convex object, any order of the polygons is valid provided that back-face elimination is used

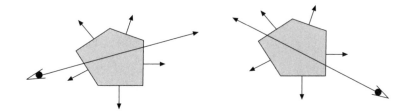

where any given ray will intersect it at most at two points (there is only one point of intersection when the ray is tangent to an object edge or face). It is easy to prove that of the two points, the closest one will always be front facing while the other will be back facing, and hence the polygons can be tested and rendered if not back facing, in any order (Figure 11.1).

11.3 List priority algorithms

As already mentioned, the overall idea in a list priority algorithm is to sort the polygons "far-to-near" with respect to the COP and use the Painters' Algorithm for the rendering.

Let's have a closer look at what we mean by this ordering. Given n polygons in the environment we want an ordering $\{P_1 \ldots P_n\}$ such that any polygon P_i does not obscure any of the polygons $\{P_{i+1} \ldots P_n\}$. Intuitively we can think of it as polygon P_i being further away from the COP than $\{P_{i+1} \ldots P_n\}$ and thus can be rendered before them. Although we'll see soon that the distance criterion is not enough.

Ordering in projection space

The simplest implementation of this idea is the *z-sort*. Once the polygons have been transformed to projection space, find the distance of the mid-point of each polygon to the COP (this is the z-coordinate of the mid-point) and then do a 1D sort based on these distances. This low-dimensional sorting works very fast but it's not always correct. Similar ideas were very often used in games before the wide availability of the z-buffer and were responsible for the unpredictable appearance or disappearance of objects for small steps of the viewpoint. To understand why this happens, we can look at the example of Figure 11.2. As the COP moves from COP1 to COP2 we go from $d_Q < d_P$ to $d_Q > d_P$, so at some point Q will start being rendered before P and Q disappear from view.

We can make our criteria stricter to avoid such errors. For a pair of polygons P, Q, instead of making our decision on the distance of the two mid-points we can check whether their Z-extents overlap. If $Z_{maxQ} < Z_{minP}$ or $Z_{maxP} < Z_{minQ}$ then one is clearly in front of the other. But if that is not the case, it might be that

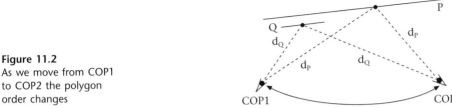

Figure 11.2
As we move from COP1 to COP2 the polygon order changes

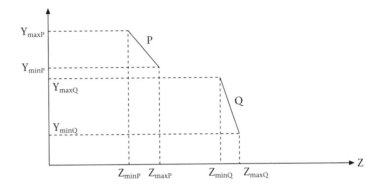

Figure 11.3
The extents of P, Q have no Z or Y overlap

the two polygons do not project on the same region of the image, in which case the ordering between them can be arbitrary. An easy way to test if they don't project on the same region is to compare the extents of the polygons along the X axis and the Y axis (Figure 11.3).

Depth-sort

The *depth-sort* algorithm (Newell, Newell and Sancha, 1972) uses the above ideas to order the polygons. The approach is interesting for historical reasons, and the ideas are important even if the algorithm would not be used in practice today. Given two polygons P and Q, P can be rendered before Q if any one of the following tests succeeds. The tests are applied in the order given.

(1) The Z-extent of Q is wholly in front of that of P.

(2) The Y-extent of Q does not overlap the Y-extent of P.

(3) The X-extent of Q does not overlap the X-extent of P.

(4) All points on P lie on the opposite side of the plane of Q than the viewpoint.

(5) All points on Q lie on the same side of the plane of P as the viewpoint.

(6) The projections of P and Q on the XY plane do not overlap.

The algorithm is as follows:

- Sort all polygons in order of their maximum Z value, and let P be the last polygon in this list.
- Let Qset be the set of polygons which have Z-extent overlapping that of P. If Qset is empty then render polygon P, otherwise:
- For each Q in Qset, apply the tests (2) to (6) above until one succeeds or they all fail. If each succeeds then render P.
- For any Q that fails all tests, swap its place with P (i.e., it takes the role formerly occupied by P), mark Q as having been moved, and apply the tests again in this new situation.
- If a situation arises where an attempt is made to swap a Q which has already been marked as having been moved once, then the planes of P and Q intersect. In this case polygon Q can be split into two by the plane of polygon P, and the two new polygons which formerly made up Q are inserted into the list.

Once a polygon has been rendered in this way, remove it from the list, and continue processing from the back of the list. When all polygons have been processed, the scene will be rendered with hidden surfaces removed.

Ordering of polygons in object space

Now we look at methods of ordering the polygons while in world coordinates but first let's look at a more precise definition of the visibility relation between two polygons. We will say that a polygon P_1 can obstruct P_2 from a given COP position C if and only if there exists a ray that starts from C and intersects both P_1 and P_2, with $t_1 < t_2$, as in Figure 11.4. If no such ray can be found then the two polygons can be rendered in any order.

Now think of two objects O_1 and O_2 and a plane H_1 that separates them, as shown in Figure 11.5. If the COP is on the positive side of H_1 then it is easy to show that there can exist no ray starting from the COP and intersecting O_2 before O_1; such a ray would intersect H_1 twice. Therefore we can safely render object O_2 before O_1. A similar argument can be made also when the COP is in the negative side of H_1.

This idea, due to Schumacker *et al.* (1969), can be extended to the case where we have more than two objects in our scene, as in Figure 11.6. Testing the COP against H_1 will decide the order of the two groups that it separates,

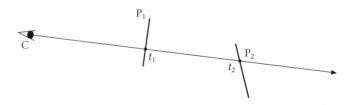

Figure 11.4
Polygon P_1 obstructs polygon P_2

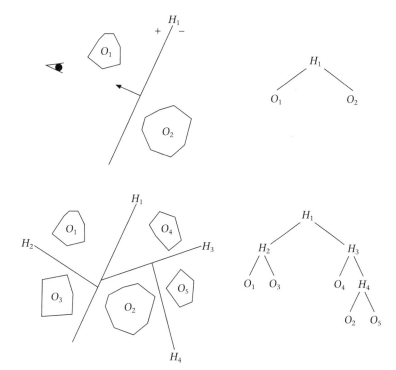

Figure 11.5
Deciding the order between objects using separating planes

Figure 11.6
A set of objects and the corresponding tree

but how do we decide the order within the two groups? We can keep placing more and more separating planes until we have only individual objects in each of the set of regions being defined. This partition can be represented as a tree structure with the internal nodes holding the separating planes and the leaves storing the objects. The tree is built once at a pre-processing stage. The order can then be decided by testing the COP against the plane at each level and displaying the far side first and then the near side.

In the original implementation polygons were manually arranged into clusters, corresponding to what we called objects here, and these were kept at the leaves. For the polygons in each of these clusters an invariant ordering was found in advance. For convex or fairly simple objects such order can be found if we take in account back-face elimination, as we discussed earlier.

One of the difficult aspects of building such a tree lies in finding suitable separating planes. In fact it is easy to come up with situations where it is impossible to find any, requiring the splitting of the objects into separate pieces. Again this was done manually in the original implementation.

Algorithms such as the above were predominantly what were used in flight simulations and other similar systems in the 1980s, before fast hardware z-buffers were widely available. However, they are still quite relevant today, if not for visible surface determination then for higher-level operations such as collision detection (Chapter 20) and visibility culling (Chapter 23).

Binary space partition trees

The binary space partitioning algorithm was introduced several years later by Fuchs *et al.* (Fuchs *et al.*, 1980; Fuchs *et al.*, 1983) as a simple and automatic extension of Schumacker's partitioning tree. It resolves each of the problems of inseparable objects and intra-object ordering present in the earlier work.

The BSP tree method relies on the fact that polygons can be defined to have a "front" and a "back" (see "Polygons and planes" on page 163). To recall, if the plane equation of a polygon is $l(x, y, z) = 0$, where $l(x, y, z) = ax + by + cz - d$, then the front-facing normal is (a, b, c). For any point (X, Y, Z), if $l(X, Y, Z) > 0$ then the point is in "front" of (or "outside") the plane, if $l(X, Y, Z) < 0$ then the point is "behind" (or "inside") the plane, and *on* the plane when $l(X, Y, Z) = 0$.

The BSP tree algorithm for visible surface determination has two parts: first the tree is built from the set of scene polygons, and then given a viewpoint it is traversed to get the required back-to-front order.

Constructing a BSP tree

A BSP tree represents a recursive subdivision of space. In general a plane is chosen by some means, and all polygons in the scene are classified as being in front of the plane, behind, or on it. Those on the plane are kept together with that plane. The space in front of the plane, with its corresponding polygons, is recursively subdivided in the same manner, and similarly for those in the back space. The planes chosen in which to subdivide the various spaces are called *partitioning planes*. Typically, especially for the visibility application considered in this chapter, the partitioning planes are chosen as planes that embed polygons in the scene. From this discussion, a data structure for a BSP tree can be represented as follows:

```
typedef struct _bspTree{
  FaceList *face; /*list of faces belonging to this node*/
  PlaneEq plane; /*partitioning plane*/
  struct _bspTree *front; /*front node*/
  struct _bspTree *back; /*back node*/
} BSPTree;
```

Given a scene defined by a set of polygons, one is chosen to define the root. All other polygons are partitioned into three sets – a front (or outside) set and a back (or inside) set, according to whether the polygon is behind or in front of the root, and a set consisting of those on the same plane as the root. Polygons which have some vertices behind and some in front of the root are split into two by the plane of the root. The tree construction algorithm proceeds recursively on the front and back sets, until the entire polygon set has been exhausted. This procedure is carried out in object space. A pseudocode implementation is shown in Program 11.1.

Program 11.1 Making a BSP tree

```
BSPTree *makeTree(face_list)
{
  if Empty(face_list) return EMPTY_TREE;
  else{
    root = select(face_list);
    on_list = NULL;
    back_list = NULL;
    front_list = NULL;

    for(each face in face_list){
      c = splitFace(root,face,front,back);
      switch(c) {
        case ON :appendList(on_list,face);
              break;

        case IN_FRONT :appendList(front_list,face);
              break;

        case AT_BACK :appendList(back_list,face);
              break;

        case SPLIT :appendList(front_list,front);
                 appendList(back_list,back);
              break;
      }
    }
    return Combine_tree(makeTree(front_list),
            on_list,makeTree(back_list) );
  }
}
```

The `Combine_tree` function simply constructs the tree which has the first parameter as its front node, the middle parameter is the list of polygons in the root, and the third parameter is the back node.

Thibault and Naylor (1987) showed that a BSP tree can also be constructed incrementally. A polygon supplies the plane for the root, and then successive polygons are filtered down the tree. For a given polygon, if it lies wholly in front or behind the root then it is added (recursively) to the appropriate child of the root, otherwise it is split by the plane of the root and each fragment is added recursively to the corresponding child. Clearly, polygons on the same plane of the root are added to the root node.

The main computational effort in constructing BSP trees is the testing and possibly splitting of a polygon against a plane. The algorithm for accomplishing this involves stepping through the vertices of the target polygon, $p_0, p_1, \ldots, p_{n-1}$, and computing $l(p_i)$ for each. When there is a change in sign of l, this signifies that the polygon crosses the plane. If $l(p_i) = 0$ (all i) then the polygon is embedded in the plane. This is shown in Program 11.2.

Program 11.2 Classification of a polygon by a plane

```
/*evaluate plane equation at point p=(x,y,z)*/
float l(p, (a,b,c,d)) = return a*p.x + b*p.y + c*p.z - d;


void splitFace([p0 ,p1 ,...pn-1 ], (a,b,c,d), front, back, on)
/*splits the face by the plane equation*/
{
  front = back = on = NULL;

  /*find a first vertex of face that is not on the plane*/
  j = -1;
  for(i=0;i<n;++i){
    L0 = l(pi );
    if(L0 ≠ 0.0) {j = i; break;}
  }
  if(j == -1) {/*face on the plane*/
    on = face;
    return;
  }

  /*if reached here then the face isn't on the plane*/
  if(L0 > 0) {/*front side of plane*/
    addVertex(front,pj );
    currentFace = front; otherFace = back;
  }
  else{/*back side of plane*/
    addVertex(back,pj );
    currentFace = back; otherFace = front;
  }

  /*assume that vertices are stored cyclically, ie, pn+k == pk*/
  for(i=j+1; i < n+j; ++i){
    L1 = l(pi );
    if (sign(L0 ) == sign(L1 )) addVertex(currentFace,pi );
    else{/*change of sign*/
      p = intersection(pi-1 ,pi ,plane);
      addVertex(currentFace,p);
      addVertex(otherFace,p); addVertex(otherFace,pi );
      swap(currentFace,otherFace);
    }
    L0 = L1 ;
  }
  if(L1 >0) {
    front = currentFace;
    back = otherFace;
  }
  else {
    front = otherFace;
    back = currentFace;
  }
}
```

Rendering a scene represented as a BSP tree

To render the polygons in the tree from any camera position the tree is traversed in a special in-order manner. This is based on Schumacker's central idea that objects on the same side of a plane as the viewpoint cannot be obscured by objects on the far side. In particular, for any plane represented at a tree node, the subtree on the far side of that node with respect to the COP should be rendered first, then the polygons at the node, and finally the subtree in the near side of the node. This leads to an elegant and simple algorithm for tree traversal with linear complexity on the number of tree nodes.

The COP (in WC) is classified by the plane of the root polygon. If it is in front of the root, then the traversal algorithm is first applied recursively to the back set of the root, followed by displaying the root polygon, followed by applying the traversal algorithm to the front set. If it is behind the root then the traversal is applied to the front set, then the root is displayed, and then traversal applied to the back set. Note that the display function is responsible for clipping, projection, and rendering. This is shown in Program 11.3. Gordon and Chen (1991) have shown that, for high depth complexity scenes, a significant improvement in rendering speed can be attained when the tree is traversed in front-to-back order in conjunction with a dynamic data structure for scanline polygon filling.

Program 11.3 Traversing a BSP tree to produce a back-to-front list with respect to the COP

```
void TraverseTree(tree,COP) {
  if(EMPTY(tree)) return;
  else{
    if(COP in front of rootPolygonOf(tree)){
      TraverseTree(BackDescendent(tree));
      Display(rootPolygonOf(tree));
      TraverseTree(FrontDescendent(tree));
    }
    else{
      TraverseTree(FrontDescendent(tree));
      Display(rootPolygonOf(tree));
      TraverseTree(BackDescendent(tree));
    }
  }
}
```

The BSP tree implementation by Fuchs et al. (1983) showed that a near real-time frame rate could be achieved for their models with this method without extraordinary special graphics hardware, although the computation time for the tree itself could be significant. BSP trees are therefore particularly suited for applications where the scene itself is static, but where the camera frequently moves. This is the case, for example, in architectural walkthroughs where the camera moves through a set of buildings (an early example being Brooks, 1986) and other similar applications.

Constructing a better tree

In this chapter we concentrate on using BSP trees for solving the visibility ordering problem but in fact BSP trees are a useful tool that can help to solve many other problems – collision detection, view volume culling, visibility culling, and so on (Naylor, 1993). Building a tree that performs well for all operations is a very difficult task since they might have different requirements. There are two attributes of the tree that need to be adjusted, size and shape, and they tend to have different importance depending on the application.

As shown in Paterson and Yao (1989) and Paterson and Yao (1990), for a set of n initial polygons the upper bound for space and time complexity for building a BSP tree is $O(n^2)$, although the expected case is closer to $O(nlog\ n)$. There can be great variation depending on the partitioning polygon selected as the root at each iteration.

One method that is often used for controlling the size and shape of a tree is to select a few candidate polygons (maybe 5 or 10) at each iteration and find the best of these to use as the root (Fuchs *et al.*, 1983). The evaluation of each one is done by comparing it against the rest of the polygons in the subspace and computing the weighted sum of two quantities, size (number of resulting splits) and distribution (difference in the number of polygons in each of the resulting subsets).

The weights used depend on the application. For visible surface determination every node of the tree is visited at each frame, and there is no searching involved. Therefore the balance of the tree is irrelevant. The number of nodes and polygons is important. There is a problem if too many polygons are split, for then the polygon database can increase dramatically in size with a corresponding slowdown in the rendering process. On the other hand, for ray tracing applications or algorithms involving classifications, balance is more important than size. Also, balanced trees are generally faster to build (if the number of splits created is not overwhelming) even if this doesn't reflect the run-time performance.

Another idea was first mentioned in Slater (1992a). Here the polygons are presented to the tree construction procedure in an approximate "periphery" to "center" order – that is, those polygons at the periphery of the scene are used as roots for those nearer the center. This is suitable for scenes that describe interiors of buildings – so that the larger, peripheral polygons, for example, representing walls, are unlikely to split polygons belonging to more centrally located objects, such as furniture within the room.

A different measurement of "goodness," based on expected cost of various operations given by probability models, is presented by Naylor (1993). In simple terms, the idea is to keep the larger cells (with a great probability of being visited) on shorter paths and the smaller ones on longer paths. In a sense this is a sequence of approximations similar to bounding volumes.

When using BSP trees for visible surface determination, a dot product operation needs to performed with the viewpoint and each partitioning plane of the tree. This could potentially be a costly operation. In recent years a number of variations on the BSP tree theme have been proposed which aim at minimizing this cost (Chen and Wang, 1996; James and Day, 1998; Sadagic and Slater, 2000). In these methods there is always a sacrifice to be made for the added speed. This is usually in terms of memory and in the functionality of the resulting tree (none of these can be used for merging trees together, for example).

Using BSP trees in dynamic scenes

The BSP tree representation is certainly useful for applications where the scene remains geometrically unchanged, and the application's main concern is navigating through the scene, since a change of camera position only requires traversing the tree in a different order. When the geometry of the scene changes, the original BSP tree is no longer a valid representation since some of the planes defining the partitioning nodes might have changed. Nevertheless, algorithms can be constructed which "repair" the damage to the tree as a result of geometric transformations or deletions of objects.

In the object-based partitioning tree of Schumacker, where the internal nodes are defined by separating planes rather than polygon planes, the objects can move freely without causing any problems, as long as they do not cross any of the separating planes. A similar idea was later suggested by Torres (1990). In this algorithm the individual objects at the leaves are also represented by a BSP tree constructed by considering the polygons of the object alone. As an object moves, its tree remains valid – if it does not intersect a separating plane – and can be just translated.

Fuchs *et al.* (1983) suggested that if we know the dynamic objects and their path in advance then it is possible to allow for them. A tree can be constructed such that the movement region is enclosed within a tree cell. Then the objects can move in that region independently with regard to the rest of the tree.

A different method that again involves knowing the objects that will be moving in advance but not their path was used by Naylor (1990). This is probably the most elegant method for dynamic changes; however, it makes use of tree merging (Thibault and Naylor, 1987) which is beyond the scope of this book. In brief, first the static objects are built into one tree, and for each dynamic object we also build its individual tree separately. At the beginning of each frame we can put all the trees together by merging them, which gives us the complete scene tree. By using some tree duplication the individual trees are available for subsequent frames. Naylor described an application of this where a tool was interactively added or subtracted from a work piece.

A method that requires no prior knowledge of the moving objects and is very simple to implement, if not as efficient as Naylor's method, was suggested by Chrysanthou and Slater (1992). In the rest of this section we will look at this in more detail.

In virtual environments most often a very small part of the scene changes, for example the user walks to an object and picks it up while the rest of the scene remains unchanged. In such cases we can make use of this simple method. Whenever an object is transformed, whether it be by translation, rotation, scaling, or even deformation, this can be reflected on the tree by first deleting the polygons of the object, next applying the transformation to the object's geometry (vertices of the polygons), and then adding these transformed object polygons back into the tree. Using the incremental approach to building BSP trees, it is easy to see how the polygons can be added back; they can be filtered down the tree as usual. The main problem in this algorithm is how to remove the polygons.

Deleting a polygon from the tree seems a difficult operation, since the plane defined by the polygon might have been used to form a node which further splits a subspace. In this case deleting the polygon and its node would split the tree into two separate pieces. However, a more careful analysis reveals four cases – the polygon to be deleted might be:

(1) On a leaf node: in this case deletion of the polygon is easy. This deletion is valid because the plane defined by this polygon was used to split an "empty" subspace.

(2) On a node with other faces (i.e., on the same plane): in this case the polygon can be deleted from this node, since the plane is still defined by the other polygons on that node. However, if the first two polygons on this node face in opposite directions, and we are deleting the first one, then the front and back subtrees of the node must be swapped, in order to maintain the correct front and back ordering of the tree.

(3) A node with exactly one non-empty child: in this case, the plane was used to split the subspace into an empty region and a non-empty region. So if this node is removed, it can be replaced by the node representing the non-empty region. In other words, the child of the deleted node directly becomes the child of the parent of this node.

(4) A node with two non-empty children: this is the most difficult case. The polygon was used to split the subspace into two non-empty regions. So if the polygon is removed we would be left with two unconnected subtrees. These can be rebuilt into a single BSP tree again, by filtering the polygons of the smaller subtree down the largest tree, using the incremental BSP tree-building algorithm discussed earlier. This method is also used by Torres, when a separating plane cannot be found between objects.

These four cases can be illustrated using the scene in Figure 11.7 and corresponding tree in Figure 11.8. Case 1 would be used in the case of deleting polygons 4 or 7. Case 2 would be used in the case of polygons 3 or 6. Note that if 3 is deleted, then the two subtrees must be swapped. Case 3 would be used in the case of polygons 1 or 5. Case 4 would be used when 2 is deleted, in which case the resulting tree is shown in Figure 11.7.

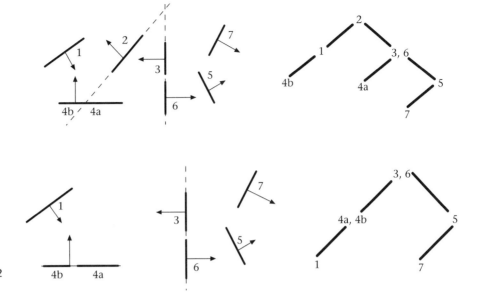

Figure 11.7
A 2D representation of
a set of polygons and
their BSP tree

Figure 11.8
The tree after polygon 2
is deleted

The algorithm runs in two stages. For each polygon in the moving object, the node in the tree is marked as being "deleted," in the case where it is the only polygon at that node. This can be done either by searching for the polygons, or better by following location pointers that each polygon stores when inserted into the tree. In the case where there is more than one polygon at the node (Case 2) the polygon is removed immediately rather than marking the node, and if it was the first polygon and the second polygon faces in the opposite direction, then the front and back subtrees at that node are swapped.

After all the relevant nodes have been marked, a recursive function (*Restore*) is called that goes through each node once and removes the marked ones. The *Restore* function is described in Program 11.4(a). In brief, at each iteration the root is checked and if it is not marked the function proceeds to the left and right subtrees. If the root is marked and it has only one non-empty subtree, the algorithm will process the subtree and then return it. If both subtrees are non-empty then it will find the largest of the two, restore it and return the tree generated by inserting the polygons of the smaller tree into it (*FilterIntoTree*).

Program 11.4(a) Restoring the BSP tree to take account of deleted polygons

```
BSPTree Restore(tree)
{
    if(Empty(tree)) return NULL;
    if(tree.root is not marked as "deleted") {
        tree.front = Restore(tree.front);
        tree.back = Restore(tree.back);
```

```
      return(tree);
  }
  else{
    if(any child of the tree is empty) return(Restore(other child
    of tree))
    else
    return( FilterIntoTree(polygons of smaller sub-tree,
    Restore(largest subtree) ) );
  }
}
```

One of the factors that make this algorithm practical is that when a target object is being transformed, for example in an interactive application, the `Restore` function is only relevant for the very first transformation. The reason for this is that after the object polygons have been deleted from the tree, when they are transformed and then reinserted, they will end up in one of three places: at the leaf nodes of the tree; at a node shared with other polygons on the same plane; at a node near the leaf nodes of the tree, that is on subtrees consisting wholly of polygons belonging to the target object. In each case only the simpler deletion cases would need to be used in subsequent transformations of this object in this particular interactive sequence.

Second, a consequence of the algorithm is that objects whose polygons are near the leaf nodes of the BSP tree can be deleted in essentially constant time. Therefore objects which are likely to be transformed often, for example a 3D cursor object in an interactive application, or smaller objects in the interior of a room in an application involving, say, room layout, should be placed into the tree last of all.

Third, in the `Restore` function the way it is presented in Program 4(a), in the case where the node to be deleted has two children, the smaller subtree is filtered into the larger, no matter what the sizes of the two trees. This could be an expensive operation, and could be wasteful, since the polygons in the unified subtree might anyway have only a short lifetime. An alternative strategy is to adopt some criterion which determines when the filtering operation should be carried out, or when the nodes are just left marked as "deleted" but not actually deleted from the tree. The criterion adopted is to do the filtering only when the smaller subtree is less than some maximum size. In this case, the `Restore` function should be altered so that the second "if" statement reads as in Program 11.4(b).

Program 11.4(b)   A modified clause of Algorithm 1(a)

```
if(ree.root is not marked as "deleted" || the smaller subtree is
too large){
  tree.front = Restore(tree.front);
  tree.back = Restore(tree.back);
  return(tree);
}
else{/*as before*/
}
```

It should be noted that in a scene there might just be a very small proportion of polygons which result in most of the splitting in the creation of the tree. It is precisely these polygons which will, of course, have large subtrees. Therefore the operation of leaving polygons marked as "deleted" in the tree will not occur very often, and therefore will not unduly increase the size of the tree. Also, if these "deleted" polygons are left in the tree, further transformations of other objects may diminish the size of the subtrees of the "deleted" polygons, and so they would anyway eventually be deleted.

11.5 Summary

In this chapter we have introduced list priority algorithms which order polygons in terms of visibility with respect to the COP. In terms of the "big picture," having lost the visibility "credentials" that come with ray tracing, this is our first attempt to "put back" visibility into the new system that we are constructing. In fact, now we almost have a complete system again: we can describe scenes in terms of a hierarchy of graphical objects with polygons as the base primitive, we can render the scene from any viewpoint, and in correct visibility order. But there are still problems.

First, note that the BSP tree approach to visibility, although elegant and fast, is very memory intensive. The size of the data structure could increase quadratically with the number of polygons if care is not taken during construction, and therefore would be difficult for scenes with many hundreds of thousands of polygons. A more telling problem, though, is the splitting process involved in the construction of BSP trees: smaller and smaller polygon fragments would be produced, leading to the potential for greater and greater inaccuracy. The second problem is that we have yet to reintroduce illumination into the picture. How are the displayed polygons to be shaded? Where does the lighting computation of Chapter 6 come into the picture? Third, the BSP tree method, of course, ends up requiring the rendering of 2D polygons on the view plane. How are 2D polygons rendered? All of these problems – an incremental algorithm without an ever-increasing memory requirement, reintroduction of shading, and the rendering of polygons – all have one solution; in fact the solution is, surprisingly, very much tied up with the rendering of 2D polygons.

In the next chapter we will introduce a 2D polygon rendering algorithm. We will then show, in the following chapter, how this can be used in another method for solving the visibility problem, called the z-buffer. We will then use the same ideas to show how shading can be very cheaply factored into the rendering process.

12 Rendering polygons

12.1   Introduction

The BSP tree approach is an example of a *priority list* algorithm. It pre-computes a data structure which, when traversed according to a particular camera setup, will produce an ordering of the scene polygons. The computation of the data structure is (theoretically) with the scene expressed in world coordinates, i.e., independent of any particular camera. It is a view-independent method. For correct visual effect it can rely on the overpainting properties of raster displays – rendering the polygons in a back-to-front order will produce a correct visualization of the final scene with respect to visibility.

As we have seen, after projection, polygons may be considered as 2D objects on the projection XY plane. The priority list algorithms pre-sort the polygons such that the correct depth-ordering is maintained. Therefore the z-depths associated with the polygons are no longer relevant at all, provided that we render them in a correct order. Hence, the back-to-front ordering produced by the BSP algorithm simply requires the rendering of a sequence of 2D polygons.

This begs the question – how are 2D polygons efficiently rendered? This question is answered in this chapter. We will see in the next chapter that the resulting algorithm has some surprising extensions – it can be used to provide an entirely different solution to the visibility problem, and can also be used to enhance shading. At the moment though, we concentrate on the 2D polygon rendering algorithm as an end in itself.

12.2 Polygon rasterization

Inside a polygon

Back-face elimination is typically an important first step in the rendering pipeline. The rasterization of polygons, that is, finding the "best" set of pixels to represent a polygon, is (almost) the last step. We use the notation for a planar polygon as discussed in Chapter 8 (see "Polygons and planes" on page 163). We assume that the vertices have already been converted to pixel positions – i.e., are expressed in an integer coordinate space.

Recall that a polygon is *simple* if no edges intersect (except, by definition, at vertices). A polygon is *convex* if it is simple and every interior angle $\Delta p_{i-1} p_i p_{i+1} < \pi$. Otherwise we call a polygon *arbitrary* or *complex*. (A simple polygon is an example of a so-called *Jordan curve*, that is, any curve which is topologically equivalent to a circle).

In order to fill a polygon, that is, find and shade all the pixels on its boundary and interior, there must be some explicit definition of what is "inside" or "outside" the polygon. If the polygon is not complex, then everyone can agree about what is inside (although in different circumstances the edges themselves might be taken as inside or outside). If the polygon is complex, then there is no "true" answer about what is inside or outside, only rules that give results which may or may not be satisfactory for a particular application.

Two common rules are the following:

Odd–even rule. For any point draw a horizontal line to infinity. Count the number of intersections which this line makes with polygon edges. If the number of intersections is odd then the point is inside.

If the line touches a vertex, then the line might be perturbed so that this no longer happens, otherwise the rule does not work. Alternatively, count maximal or minimal vertices as 0, and all other vertices as 1. Points on edges or vertices (which are obviously on edges) receive the same classification as edges themselves.

Non-zero winding number rule. This assumes that the edges are traversed in a consistent order such as clockwise or anticlockwise. Figure 12.1 shows a

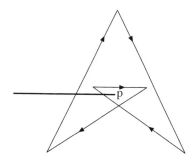

Figure 12.1
Non-zero winding
number rule

Figure 12.2
Scan-line coherence. The *x*-intersection values for one scan-line can be computed from the previous scan-line

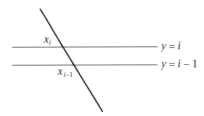

clockwise example. From any point draw a horizontal line to infinity as before. Count the number of up-directed edges, *u*, and the number of down-directed edges, *d*, which cross the line. If $u - d = 0$ then the point is outside, otherwise it is inside. (This has the physical meaning of counting the number of times the polygon wraps around the point of interest.)

Exploiting coherence

Obviously filling a polygon requires identifying all pixels inside the polygon, and setting them to the required colors. This could be done crudely – by directly carrying out an inside test for each pixel. This would be grossly inefficient as a sequential algorithm, but it is not inappropriate for parallel machines. This approach ignores *pixel coherence* – i.e., if one pixel is inside/outside then the same is likely to be true of its neighbors.

A better approach would be to identify the upper and lower vertices of the polygon, with y-coordinates `ymin` and `ymax` respectively, and then for each scan-line between `ymin` and `ymax` compute its intersections with the edges of the polygon, and then fill these horizontal spans with the appropriate colors. This will work, but is still inefficient; it ignores *scan-line coherence* – the x-intersection points for any given scan-line are simply related to the intersection values for the scan-lines above and below it. An efficient algorithm would make use of this information, which is shown in Figure 12.2.

Consider here the intersection of two successive scan-lines with an edge which has equation $y = a + bx$, where *b* is the slope of the line (*dy/dx*). It is assumed that $b \neq 0$.

$$i = a + bx_i$$
$$i - 1 = a + bx_{i-1}$$
(EQ 12.1)

Hence,

$$x_i = x_{i-1} + \frac{1}{b}$$
(EQ 12.2)

Edge tables

The following algorithm makes use of scan-line coherence, and is based on the approach of Appel (1968), Bouknight and Kelley (1970) and Watkins (1970).

Consider an edge $(x1, y1)$ to $(x2, y2)$ with the labels chosen so that the y-value of the first point is always less than that of the second $(y1 < y2)$. *Horizontal edges are ignored throughout.* This edge is represented by a structure:

```
struct Edge {int y2; float x1; float Dx;}
with Dx = dx/dy
where dx = x2-x1, dy = y2-y1.
```

All edges are bucket sorted according to their smaller y-values $(y1)$. This sorted sequence is called the edge table (ET). The ET therefore contains all the edges in the original polygon, but now ordered according to the height at which they start (i.e., the lower y-value). Therefore, associated with every bucket in ET there will be a set of edges which have their lower y-value equal to the bucket index.

More specifically, represent ET as an array with bounds 0 to the maximum possible scan-line on the display (YMAX). Each array entry is a sequence of triples representing the edges, using the edge structure. In order to make the edge table,

```
Initialize ET[i] = Ø (the empty sequence), for i = 0 to YMAX;
```

For each edge $(x1, y1)$ to $(x2, y2)$ ensure that $y2 > y1$ (which may involve swapping values, and ignoring horizontal edges):

```
append(ET[y1],{y2,x1,Dx})
```

which puts the new triple at the end of this list (or alternatively it could be put at the head, or even insert sorted with respect to *x*1 into the list). Also during construction of the ET, keep track of the maximum and minimum y-vertices (ymin and ymax).

Next, process the ET as follows, constructing a new object AET (active edge table) which is of type "sequence of Edges" (i.e., the same type as any particular ET[i]).

```
processET(void)
{
  AET = Ø;                    /*initialise to the empty sequence*/
  for(i = ymin; i <= ymax){   /*for each scan-line*/
                              /*delete from AET entries with y==i,*/
                              /*and compute x1 += Dx for remainder*/
    update(AET,i);
    append(AET,ET[i]);        /*join ET[i] to the AET*/
    sort(AET);                /*sort the entries by x1*/
    JoinLines(AET,i);         /*join horizontal lines between*/
                              /*pairs of x1, at height i*/

  }
}
```

The active edge table is the sequence of edges that intersect the current scan-line sorted according to increasing x1 value (the intersections between the polygon edges and the scan-line). Initially it is empty – any scan-line below the lowest vertex (at y = ymin) of the polygon obviously intersects none of its edges. The `update` function deletes any entries in the AET which have their y-coordinate equal to the current scan-line at height `i` (since these edges have now been completely processed and are below the current scan-line). For the edges that are not deleted, it increments their $x1$-coordinate by `Dx`, implementing the scan-line coherence idea shown in Figure 12.2. These $x1$-coordinates are the x-coordinates of the intersections of the active edges with the current scan-line. The `append` function appends to the AET those edges which start at height `i`. The `sort` function now sorts the edges in the AET according to their $x1$-values. The reason for this is that the next function, `JoinLines`, must join horizontal spans determined by pairs of $x1$ values. This relies on the odd–even inside test to assure correctness. (It is assumed that update has no effect when the AET is empty.)

Figure 12.3 shows an example polygon to illustrate these ideas. The polygon has edges a, b, c, and d as shown in Table 12.1

The edge table for this figure is shown in Table 12.2 and the AET in Table 12.3.

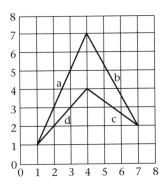

Figure 12.3
An example polygon

Table 12.1 The edges of the polygon in Figure 12.3

Edge label	Coordinates	$y1$	Structure
a	(1, 1) to (4, 7)	1	(7, 1, 3/6)
b	(7, 2) to (4, 7)	2	(7, 7, –3/5)
c	(7, 2) to (4, 4)	2	(4, 7, –3/2)
d	(1, 1) to (4, 4)	1	(4, 1, 3/3)

Table 12.2 The edge table for Figure 12.3

$y1$	Sequence of edges
1	(7, 1, 3/6), (4, 1, 3/3)
2	(7, 7, –3/5), (4, 7, –3/2)

Table 12.3 The active edge table for Figure 12.3

Scan-line i	Active edge table	Spans at height i
0	empty sequence	
1	(7, 1, 0.5), (4, 1, 1)	1 to 1
2	(7, 1.5, 0.5), (4, 2, 1), (7, 7, –0.6), (4, 7, –1.5)	1.5 to 2, 7 to 7
3	(7, 2.0, 0.5), (4, 3, 1), (4, 5.5, –1.5), (7, 6.4, –0.6)	2.0 to 3, 5.5 to 6.4
4	(7, 2.5, 0.5), (7, 5.8, –0.6)	2.5 to 5.8
5	(7, 3.0, 0.5), (7, 5.2, –0.6)	3.0 to 5.2
6	(7, 3.5, 0.5), (7, 4.6, –0.6)	3.5 to 4.6
7	empty	
8		

Figure 12.4
A 3D object is composed of contiguous polygons

Note how the $x1$ values and consequently the horizontal spans are floating point numbers, ideally representing the exact intersections. However, the spans must correspond to exact pixel locations, and hence the fractional values are another illustration of how aliasing can occur – this time along the edges of the displayed polygon.

It is easy to show (indeed is shown in the example) that this algorithm does not display maximal vertices, nor maximal horizontal edges. This is easy to fix, in a variety of ways – for example, rendering such missing elements directly, or in the case of a maximal vertex or horizontal edge, do the increment $x1 += Dx$ and draw the span, before deleting the entry. From another point of view, however, this deficiency may be desirable.

In 3D applications it is most often the case that a large number of polygons are rendered, where these polygons join together edge on edge, as shown in Figure 12.4. For rendering, these 3D polygons are converted (through a process of projection) into 2D polygons on the display, as we have seen. Clearly some edges are in common between adjoining polygons. In such cases we may adopt a rule such that where an edge is in common with a neighboring polygon, it should only be processed once. A rule often adopted is that right- and upper-most pixels of scan-lines are not rendered where it is known that the current polygon is joined to the right or top by another. In this way these edges will not be rendered twice.

12.3 Summary

The central feature of this chapter was the 2D polygon fill algorithm. The polygon fill can clearly be implemented in very efficient manner – especially if the original polygons are further decimated into triangles. There is then no need even to keep an edge table (since there are only two intersections per scan-line per polygon, and no local minima or maxima) but scan-line coherence is obviously maintained. For an interesting alternative approach to rendering polygons, based on the exploitation of parallel hardware, see Pineda (1988).

In the next chapter we show how to adapt the 2D polygon algorithm to solve the problem of depth computation and smooth shading. This will complete our pass through the complete 3D graphics pipeline.

13 Image space rendering and texturing

13.1 Introduction

In this chapter we turn to *image space* algorithms. Here the visibility computation is made "in the last instance" – at the pixel level. In the case of ray tracing we trace a ray through a pixel, and search among all objects to find the nearest one that it intersects (if any). As we have seen, this is a slow process. Here we discuss algorithms that do the opposite: project each polygon onto the view plane (in any order). Set the color of each pixel according to which polygon "seen" through this pixel had the smallest depth (z) value so far. At the end of projecting all scene polygons, the pixels will only show the colors of the polygon that could be seen through that pixel (or else a background color). This has the same effect as ray casting, but is orders of magnitude faster. With ray casting, for each ray we search all objects for the nearest intersection. With this type of image space approach we project each polygon, and for each pixel that it covers, we only set the color of that pixel according to the polygon if this polygon is "closer" (smaller z-depth) than any other polygon that covered this pixel so far. Hence with the image space approach, the total rendering time is proportional to the number of polygons in the scene.

This image space approach begs some questions:

- How do we efficiently determine the set of pixels covered by a polygon?
- How do we maintain the required depth information with each pixel?
- How do we determine the color to which the pixel should be set?

These three questions, surprisingly enough, have one unified answer – the algorithm for the rendering of 2D polygons introduced in Chapter 12. That algorithm might be called the "central algorithm of the 3D graphics pipeline" – but it is actually inherently an algorithm that operates essentially in 2D space.

In this chapter we will describe three image space visibility algorithms. After that, we will show how the same 2D polygon rendering algorithm also can be used for shading. *It is assumed throughout that clipping has been carried out and that the scene has been transformed into projection space*, which considerably simplifies the computation. Finally, we discuss in detail one of the most import- ant aspects of rendering, a method that greatly adds to the realistic appearance of the final image at relatively cheap computational cost: the idea of texture mapping.

13.2 The z-buffer visibility algorithm

Basic idea

The 2D polygon rendering algorithm is used for an efficient implementation of the most famous of image space visibility algorithms, the *z-buffer algorithm* (due to Catmull, 1974). This is based on the idea of an array associated with the frame buffer (i.e., a one-to-one pixel to array element association) which at any moment during the execution of the algorithm holds the "depths" corres- ponding to the pixels which have so far had their colors set. Suppose the display resolution is $M \times N$. Let z be an array of this dimension, with each element initially set to be 1.0 (the maximum z-value in PS). The algorithm proceeds as follows for each object in the scene:

(1) Each point (x, y, z) on the surface of the object corresponds to a pixel (x_s, y_s) on the display (with a translation and scaling to get from PS to display coordinates). Let $I(x, y, z)$ be the color intensity for this point, within the appropriate shading model for the scene.

(2) If $z < Z[x_s, y_s]$ then set the intensity of pixel (x_s, y_s) to be $I(x, y, z)$ and get $Z[x_s, y_s]$ to be z; otherwise do nothing.

Hence for the pixel currently being processed the pixel color is only overwrit- ten by the new one if this new color represents a point in the scene which is closer to the COP than the distance represented by the current color. The role of the z-buffer is to record the distances which correspond to the color intens- ities currently set in the frame buffer.

Use of the polygon scan-line renderer

If, as is often the case, the scene is represented as polyhedra, then each polygon can be processed on a scan-line basis using the algorithm in Chapter 12. The obvious modification to the algorithm is that each individual pixel must be checked and the z-buffer updated, rather than simply drawing the current span with a horizontal line in the `JoinLines` procedure.

We consider three approaches here to computing the z value for each pixel, from least to most efficient.

Method 1: directly from the plane equation. The plane equation is $ax + by + cz + d = 0$. Hence, given (x, y) we can find z as:

$$z = \frac{d - ax - by}{c} \qquad\qquad \text{(EQ 13.1)}$$

This is an expensive calculation to have to make for each pixel. Alternatively:

Method 2: incremental calculation.   Consider two successive pixel positions on scan-line y, (x, y, z_x), $(x + 1, y, z_{x+1})$. Then substituting these into the plane equation and subtracting, we obtain:

$$z_{x+1} = z_x - \frac{a}{c} \qquad\qquad \text{(EQ 13.2)}$$

A similar argument holds for vertical traversal of pixels.

Method 3: interpolation.   Recall that in the filling algorithm, each edge of the polygon (x_1, y_1) to (x_2, y_2) with $y_2 > y_1$ is represented by a data structure:

```
{int y2,  float x1,  float Dx;}
where  Dx  =  dx/dy;
```

Extend this data structure to include z,

```
{int y2,  float x1,  float Dx,  float z1,  float Dz;}
where  Dz  =  dz/dy;
```

This now represents an edge (x_1, y_1, z_1) to (x_2, y_2, z_2) with $y_2 > y_1$. In the update stage of the fill algorithm z is treated exactly the same as x, i.e., z_1 is replaced by $z_1 + D_z$ where $D_z = dz/dy$. This provides for interpolation of z-values from one scan-line to the next, up a polygon edge.

In addition, interpolation horizontally across a polygon span is required. This is carried out in the stage of the polygon fill algorithm that renders the horizontal spans. Suppose that two successive entries in the active edge table at scan-line height y are $(y_{a2}, x_{a1}, D_{ax}, D_{az})$ and $(y_{b2}, x_{b1}, D_{bx}, D_{bz})$. Then interpolate from z_{a1} to z_{a2} by adding

$$D_{zx} = \frac{z_{b1} - z_{a1}}{x_{b1} - x_{a1}} = -\frac{a}{c} \qquad\qquad \text{(EQ 13.3)}$$

to the z-value each time, starting from z_{a1}. It should be clear that the first pixel has z-value z_{a1}, and the last pixel has z-value

$$z_{a1} + (x_{b1} - x_{a1}) \times D_{zx} = z_{b1}$$

as required.

This process is called *bi-linear interpolation*. We will return to this when considering shading below ("Smooth shading" on page 273).

z-buffer polygon fill example

Consider the polygon shown in Figure 13.1 and the corresponding edge table. This polygon exists in projection space, and the z-values are given. (Such z-values are normally between 0 and 1, but here for illustrative purposes we use z-values outside that range). We show how to compute the z-values incrementally, as part of the scan-line algorithm for polygon filling.

The ET entries are of the general form: $\left(y2, x1, \dfrac{dx}{dy}, z1, \dfrac{dz}{dy} \right)$, with

$$ET[4] = \left[cb \rightarrow \left(7, 7, -1, 2, \frac{2}{3} \right) \right]$$

$$ET[1] = \left[ac \rightarrow \left(7, 3, \frac{1}{6}, 1, \frac{3}{6} \right), ab \rightarrow \left(4, 3, \frac{4}{3}, 1, \frac{1}{3} \right) \right]$$

and all other $ET[i] = \varnothing$.

Scan-line y = 1.

$$AET = \left[ac \rightarrow \left(7, 3, \frac{1}{6}, 1, \frac{3}{6} \right), ab \rightarrow \left(4, 3, \frac{4}{3}, 1, \frac{1}{3} \right) \right]$$

This corresponds to a single pixel (3, 1) where the z-depth is 1.

Scan-line y = 2.

$$AET = \left[ac \rightarrow \left(7, 3.1667, \frac{1}{6}, 1.5, \frac{3}{6} \right), ab \rightarrow \left(4, 4.3333, \frac{4}{3}, 1.3333, \frac{1}{3} \right) \right]$$

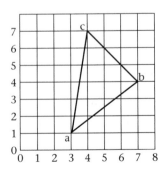

Figure 13.1
Example polygon.
a = (3, 1, 1)
b = (7, 4, 2)
c = (4, 7, 4)

This represents a span at height y = 2, from x = 3.16667 to x = 4.3333, that is, pixels (3, 2) and (4, 2). The corresponding z-depths are 1.5 and 1.3333.

Scan-line y = 3.

$$AET = \left[ac \rightarrow \left(7, 3.3333, \frac{1}{6}, 2.0, \frac{3}{6} \right), ab \rightarrow \left(4, 5.6667, \frac{4}{3}, 1.6667, \frac{1}{3} \right) \right]$$

This represents a span at height y = 3, from x = 3.3333 to x = 5.6667, that is, pixels (3, 3), (4, 3), (5, 3), and (6, 3). As x ranges from 3 to 6, z ranges from 2.0 to 1.6667. Therefore, a unit increase in x results in a change of dz/dx = −0.1111. Hence each new z value can be computed by adding dz/dx to each old one. For example:

- when x = 3, z = 2.0
- when x = 4, z = 2.0 − 0.1111 = 1.8889
- when x = 5, z = 1.8889 − 0.1111 = 1.7778
- when x = 6, z = 1.7778 − 0.1111 = 1.6667.

The scan-line visibility algorithm

This is a more sophisticated modification of the standard 2D polygon fill scan-line algorithm referred to above, since it processes *all polygon edges* in the scene in one pass, rather than a single polygon at a time as with the z-buffer. (This approach has a long history: Wylie *et al.*, 1967; Bouknight, 1970; Bouknight and Kelley, 1970; Watkins, 1970). The following discussion assumes that polygons do not intersect one another (except at common edges). To render a solid shaded polygon there are two main stages: first, the construction of a data structure (the edge table, ET) which provides an alternative representation of the polygon edges, and second, the processing of this edge table (i.e., the construction of the dynamic active edge table, AET). In the first step each edge of the polygon is traversed, and a corresponding record $\left(y_2, x_1, \frac{dx}{dy} \right)$ appended into an edge table at element y_1 (for edge (x_1, y_1) to (x_2, y_2) with $y_2 > y_1$). This 3D version of this algorithm is similar, except that in construction of the ET, ignoring the z-coordinates, the edges of *all polygons in the scene* are represented in the ET. Each edge is represented by a record containing four elements $\left(y_2, x_1, \frac{dx}{dy}, pt \right)$, where *pt* is a "polygon pointer." The *pt* entry is a pointer to information about the polygon of which the edge is a member. In particular, (*a*, *b*, *c*, *d*), the coefficients of its plane equation would normally be stored, together with any further information needed for shading (such as the color coefficients).

Processing of the AET is similar to the 2D case, up to the interpretation of the `JoinLines` procedure, responsible for joining together successive horizontal line segments on a scan-line. What happens in this case is discussed with

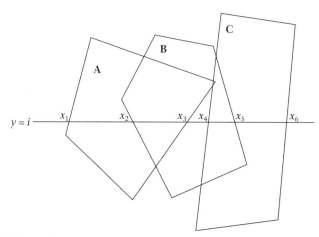

Figure 13.2
Polygon scan-line
algorithm

Polygons A, B, C are such that A is in front of B which is in front of C

reference to Figure 13.2. Consider the situation at scan-line $y = i$. Here the AET would consist of six entries corresponding to $x_1, x_2, \ldots, x_6$. From the polygon pointer corresponding to x_1, the scan-line from x_1 to x_2 is processed as belonging to polygon A. However, at point x_2, there are two polygons to be considered, A and B. Hence the plane equation coefficients in the respective polygon pointers for x_1 and x_2 are used to resolve the issue as to which polygon is closer (by computing the z-depth at point (x_2, i) for each polgyon). In this case, polygon A would be found to be the closest, and therefore the line from x_2 to x_3 is rendered as belonging to polygon A. From x_3 to x_4 there is only one candidate polygon, which is B. However, at x_4 polygon C must also be considered, and a similar resolution of the distance as between B and C at (x_4, i) is required. Continuing in this way, each segment of the scan-line can be processed, until, after x_6, there are no further polygons to be considered.

Although this algorithm might be considered in some sense more elegant than the z-buffer approach, it is generally slower for a large number of polygons (over about 500 100-pixel sized polygons). However, for a small number of polygons it can be much faster than the z-buffer. The factors which slow it down are that:

- even for convex polygons sorting is required when appending entries into the AET (since all edges are processed rather than a single polygon at a time);
- if the number of polygons is large, the computation involved in determining the polygon with the minimum z-value among the set of overlapping polygons can be considerable.

The algorithm exploits the idea of scan-line coherence, which, as the name implies, means horizontal coherence across scan-lines. However, coherence can also be added across sets of scan-lines. Given the ordered set of visible polygons for scan-line y, the ordered set of visible polygons for scan-line $y + 1$ is likely to be the same. This observation can be exploited in more or less complex ways. One cheap (but not so efficient) method is to cache the ordering of polygons for a scan-line, and provided nothing changes when the active edge list is processed for the next scan-line, this immediately ensures which polygon segments are visible across the scan-line, thus removing the need for depth calculations. In practice, this approach is of limited use but Crocker (1984) describes a more complex algorithm to exploit this vertical or invisibility coherence.

A recursive subdivision visibility algorithm

This is a divide and conquer algorithm due to Warnock (1969). This kind of approach is one often used in computer graphics (and other areas of computer science). The clipping rectangle on the XY plane represents the view plane window of the camera model (as transformed into PS). If this rectangular window contains a scene in which the hidden surface problem is easily solved, then solve it and render the scene; otherwise split the rectangle into four quadrants, and recursively apply the same principle to each.

The scene is considered easy to render according to whether it fits one of four cases:

(1) The window is covered by a polygon, and there are no other polygons in the scene closer to the XY plane than this. Then render the window according to the shading required by this polygon.

(2) There are no polygons intersecting the window – then take no further action with respect to this window.

(3) A single polygon intersects the window, in which case render the polygon (using the window as a clipping region).

(4) The window contains a single polygon, in which case render the polygon.

Hence the algorithm involves initially coloring the entire scene with the shade of the required background color, and then applying the four tests to the current window. If all tests fail, then split the window into four, and apply the procedure recursively to each of the four in turn.

13.3 Smooth shading

Gouraud shading

Earlier (EQ 6.1) we introduced shading based on Lambert's Law ("Diffuse reflection and Lambert's law" on page 135):

$$I = k_a I_a + k_d \sum_{i=1}^{N} I_{pi} \cdot (n \cdot l_i)$$

(EQ 13.4)

for multiple light sources. Computing this expression at each pixel is expensive, and best avoided. Alternatively, a bi-linear interpolation scheme is used, based on computing of the color values using the (EQ 13.4) vertices of polygons only. Then exactly as with the z-value interpolation, the basic data structure is extended:

`(y2, x1, Dx, z1, Dz, r1, Dr, g1, Dg, b1, Db),` where

$$Dr = \frac{r2 - r1}{y2 - y1}$$

$$Dg = \frac{g2 - g1}{y2 - y1} \qquad\qquad\text{(EQ 13.5)}$$

$$Db = \frac{b2 - b1}{y2 - y1}$$

to represent an edge from (x1, y1, z1, r1, g1, b1) to (x2, y2, z2, r2, g2, b2). The changes to the `update` and `JoinLines` functions are on the same lines as the z-buffer algorithm.

This method, called *Gouraud shading* after Gouraud (1971), is used for "smooth shading." Suppose that a surface is represented by a set of polygons. Then it may be possible (when there is an analytic specification of the surface) to compute the true surface normals at the polygon vertices. Hence the colors at the vertices are computed using these true normals, and then interpolated. So although polygons are being rendered, the interpolation of the colors gives the effect of a smooth shaded surface.

If the normals to the underlying surface cannot easily be computed, then an alternative method is to approximate the normal at each vertex by taking the average of the normals for each of the faces to which the vertex belongs.

Since abutting polygons belonging to a larger polyhedral object have shared vertices, as the color is interpolated across the polygons, the interpolation smooths the color changes across multiple polygons. This has the impact of making the polygon edges almost imperceptible, and it looks as though the polyhedron is a smoothly varying surface. This is shown in Figure 13.3 (color plate. Note that Gouraud shading will not produce acceptable results if a light source is close to the center of a large polygon. What should happen in such circumstances is that the center of the polygon should be brightest, with the polygon becoming darker towards its edges. This will not happen because the color in the center would have been interpolated from the colors at the vertices. Polygons must be sufficiently small with respect to their distance from the light sources for Gouraud shading to be effective. Of course, the same remarks would apply to any such interpolation scheme.

Phong shading

This includes specular reflection in the interpolation scheme, instead of only diffuse reflection as with Gouraud shading. The equation:

$$I = k_a I_a + \sum_{i=1}^{N} I_{pi} \cdot ((n \cdot l_i) k_d + (h_i \cdot n)^m k_s) \qquad \text{(EQ 13.6)}$$

originally introduced as (EQ 6.25) is used. Instead of a bi-linear interpolation of colors, this method uses interpolation of *normals*. The "true" normals at the vertices are interpolated, and then at each pixel equation (EQ 13.6) is used to determine the color. This method is due to Bui-Tong, Phong (1975). See Figure 13.4 (color plate).

It is important to note that with each interpolation the normals have to be re-normalized (since given two unit normals their interpolation will not in general be a unit normal). The calculation is expensive, involving a square root. There are methods to speed up Phong shading, for example as in Bishop and Weimer (1986) and Claussen (1989). Bishop and Weimer exploit a Taylor expansion of the Phong expression, to provide a useful simplified approximation. Claussen notes that good results can be obtained by expressing the normals in spherical coordinates form, so that angles can be interpolated avoiding the normalization.

13.4 Texturing

Introduction

Figure 1.11 (color plate) shows a scene inside a room with a number of virtual characters sitting around a table. How would such a scene be created and rendered? The scene would be created as a hierarchical scene graph, as discussed in Chapter 8. There are, however, significant items in the scene that would be very hard to model geometrically – in particular the faces, hair, and clothes of the characters, and also the patterns that can be seen on the chairs and table. If you examine the window you may see that there is also an outside scene. Would this also have to be modeled in detail, so that behind the part of the scene corresponding to the room there is in fact another complex model – with all the cost of rendering this too? How is such fine detail managed in computer graphics?

Of course, the faces, hair, and clothes *can* be modeled geometrically, but this would add an enormous number of polygons to the scene graph, and thus slow the rendering considerably. In some applications (particularly those where hair and clothes might be significant aspects of the application) this may be worth the effort. But suppose, as in this case, that the purpose is only to give a good impression of these aspects of the scene, and that it is known for sure that no participant in such a virtual environment is going to have the chance to closely inspect this fine detail?

The answer to these questions is to employ a rendering method known as *texture mapping* (Catmull, 1974; Blinn and Newell, 1976). A texture map is just a rule that assigns a color to a pixel – independently of any lighting model. For example, suppose that during the scan-line rasterization of a polygon, blocks of successive n pixels were set to red, and the next block set to white, and so on throughout the rendering of the polygon. Then the polygon would be red-and-white striped, although the stripes would always be in the same orientation independently of the polygon. Somehow the stripes would have to be attached to the polygon in its object coordinate representation, and then the striping effect taken through the rendering pipeline – so that the stripes would always be correctly oriented with the polygon. If the polygon were clipped during the pipeline, then somehow the stripes would have to be clipped too. Finally, the stripe colors may be combined with colors computed from a lighting model – it is not a question of either texture or lighting, both may be used simultaneously. This simple example has introduced many of the ideas and problems of texture mapping which we now consider in more detail.

The above example was a very simple *procedural texture*, i.e., the color is determined by a formula (Blinn, 1978). In the vast majority of applications of texture mapping a "texture" is a two-dimensional image, an array of color values as would be used to set pixels, stored in computer memory. The idea of texture mapping is to somehow "paint" this texture onto a graphical object so that it appears to be stuck on the polygon at the time of rendering. In other words, instead of determining the color of each pixel in the object solely according to a lighting model, as discussed in the previous section, the color of each pixel may also or be solely determined by a color in the texture. There is therefore some rule which associates each pixel in the rendered object to a color value from the texture. How can this be done?

Texels

The individual elements within the two-dimensional texture array are called *texels*. So a texel has a color, and a position in the array. The texture is parameterized with coordinates (s, t), where $0 \leq s, t \leq 1$, with s and t refering to the horizontal and vertical axes respectively. Suppose, for example, that the texture consists of an $M \times N$ image, then the st coordinate system is superimposed upon this, and there would be a correspondence between the integer texel coordinates and the st coordinates. Figure 13.6 shows a situation where the image is not square. Given any s and t we can identify the corresponding texel by:

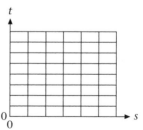

Figure 13.6
Texel coordinate system

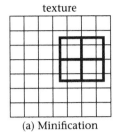
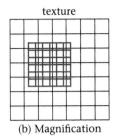

texture   texture

Figure 13.7
The relationship between
pixels and texels

(a) Minification   (b) Magnification

$$i = \text{round}(s \times N)$$
$$j = \text{round}(t \times M)$$

(EQ 13.7)

where (i, j) picks out the texel which is i along the columns and j going up the rows.

Mapping

Let's take the simplest case of a square polygon and a square texture map. Two examples are shown in Figure 13.7. In each case the polygon vertices are mapped into st space. Then each pixel of the polygon is associated with the corresponding texel that it covers, and rendered with this color.

However, Figure 13.7 shows that the situation is more complex than this – there will very rarely be an exact match between the pixel and texel resolution. Each pixel may overlap several texels, as is the case in Figure 13.7(a), or each pixel may be a fragment of a texel as in Figure 13.7(b) (or both). So there is no simple rule to assign the colors of the pixels from the colors of the texels.

In Figure 13.7(a) each pixel covers several texels. This is called *minification*. The question arises as to the color to which the pixel should be set. One rule is to choose the center of the texel that is nearest the center of the pixel, and set the pixel color to be the color of that texel. The advantage of this is that it is fast. The disadvantage is that it can lead to very severe aliasing in the final rendered image. Another method is to set the pixel color to be a weighted average of the (say) four texels closest to it, but weighting by the proportions of area covered. This would be slower, but would result in significantly improved images. *Magnification* occurs when each texel covers several pixels. Here the simplest strategy is to choose the pixel color closest to the center of the texel to which the pixel belongs. Again there will be circumstances where the pixel may overlap more than one texel, so a weighted average approach would be useful in reducing aliasing.

Recall that the texture is applied to the graphical object expressed in its original object coordinates. Now the object is passed through the rendering pipeline and eventually (if not entirely clipped) is mapped to a set of display pixels. Suppose that the object is far away from the center of projection. Then it will occupy few pixels, and therefore each pixel will occupy a relatively large proportion of the area of the object. Hence each pixel will likewise be large compared to the texels, and overlap several texels. This is how minification can arise. Magnification is the converse of this, where the object is close to the COP, and hence each pixel occupies a very small fraction of the area of the object, therefore being sub-texel size.

Note that implicit in the above is a two-stage mapping. The object coordinates are mapped to pixels as usual. Also, the object coordinates are mapped into the st texture space. The st texture space coordinates are further mapped into the texels, and it is these that determine the color. This requires that there is some representation of the object such that the mapping to st can be computed. First we show that such a mapping is possible in the case of a triangle. Suppose the triangle has three non-colinear vertices p_0, p_1 and p_2. We can construct a barycentric combination of the vertices to represent the triangle as shown in "Barycentric combinations: flatness" on page 59). As α_0 and α_1 sweep over their permitted range, so the point p sweeps out the complete triangle:

$$p = \alpha_0 p_0 + \alpha_1 p_1 + (1 - \alpha_0 - \alpha_1) p_2$$

where

$$0 \le \alpha_0, \alpha_1 \le 1$$

$$0 \le \alpha_0 + \alpha_1 \le 1$$

(EQ 13.8)

If we identify α_0 as s, and α_1 as t, then each point p of the triangle corresponds to a position in the texture map. This is illustrated in Figure 13.8. The texture space point $s = 0$, $t = 0$ corresponds to the object space point p_2, $s = 1$, $t = 0$ corresponds to p_0, and so on. Each point belonging to the triangle (including of course its edges) corresponds to a unique point in texture space. Moreover, given any point in the triangle, it is easy to compute s and t, and therefore implement this mapping. In practice, this approach requires that as the triangle is rasterized to pixels, each pixel coordinate must be transformed back into object space, then the corresponding texture coordinate computed, and finally

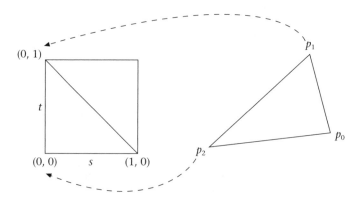

Figure 13.8
Example mapping from a triangle to texture space

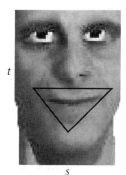

t

s

Figure 13.9
A triangle in texture space

that is used to enter into the image and compute the color based on the set of texels overlapped. However, each pixel is itself a finite size, of rectangular shape. Ideally therefore, the corners of the pixel are transformed back to object space, forming a quadrilateral in object space, and therefore a quadrilateral in texture space, overlapping a set of texels. Then an integration of color over the set of texels must be formed in order to determine the color for the pixel.

This relatively simple example has been used to illustrate the process of texturing a simple object such as a triangle. This particular example is quite restrictive, however, because it sets the portion of the texture image to be mapped to the object space triangle as precisely that bounded by the triangle in *st* space (0, 0), (1, 0), and (0, 1).

Figure 13.9 shows an example where this would not be appropriate. In this case we wish to map just the region of the mouth to a specific triangle in object space. In general the specific regions of the texture image are required to be mapped onto particular objects, and such regions can in general be of arbitrary shape. In practice, the texture coordinates corresponding to each vertex of the object space polygon would be specified, and therefore only the region bounded by those texture coordinates would be mapped to the polygon.

In this common case the user is required to assign texture coordinates to the vertices in texture space that form the boundary of that part of the image to be mapped to an object. It is simplest to stay with an example of a triangle with object space 3D vertices p_0, p_1 and p_2. Suppose that texture coordinates (s_0, t_0), (s_1, t_1) and (s_2, t_2) correspond to the vertices. Then we require a map such that:

$$p_i \rightarrow (s_i, t_i), i = 0, 1, 2 \tag{EQ 13.9}$$

and a method for finding the *st* coordinates corresponding to any point in the triangle. In general,

$$p = f(s, t), 0 \leq s, t \leq 1$$
$$p_i = f(s_i, t_i) \tag{EQ 13.10}$$

provides a parametric form for the graphical object. We will explore this type of relationship in substantial detail when we consider representations for curves and surfaces in Chapter 19. For texture mapping we also need the inverse relationship:

$$s = s(x, y, z) = s(p)$$
$$t = t(x, y, z) = t(p) \quad \text{(EQ 13.11)}$$
$$(s_i, t_i) = (s(p_i), t(p_i))$$

where $p = (x, y, z)$ ranges across the object surface (in object space). In general these functions will not be known. However, making the simplifying assumption that (s, t) varies *affinely* with p locally, then we can construct such a mapping. For example, suppose that the object surface is represented by a patchwork of triangles, then we can find a mapping for each triangle. In this case Heckbert (1986) suggests

$$x_i = A_x + B_x s_i + C_x t_i, \ i = 0, 1, 2 \quad \text{(EQ 13.12)}$$

giving a system of three equations in three unknowns which can be solved for the unknown constants. A similar computation can be carried out for y_i and z_i, leading to a map of the form:

$$(x, y, z) = (s, t, 1) \begin{bmatrix} B_x & B_y & B_z \\ C_x & C_y & C_z \\ A_x & A_y & A_z \end{bmatrix} \quad \text{(EQ 13.13)}$$

This can be re-expressed in the form (EQ 13.11) by inverting the matrix.

Watt and Watt (1992) discuss another approach to this (essentially the same but expressed by a geometric argument). Consider only the s parameter (the same argument will hold for t) and suppose that the relationship is of the affine form:

$$s_i = s_0 + (p_i - p_0) \cdot v$$
$$i = 1, 2 \quad \text{(EQ 13.14)}$$

where v is a vector that lies in the same plane as the triangle, and such that the direction along v corresponds to the greatest rate of change in parameter s. Rewrite (EQ 13.14) as:

$$s_i - s_0 = (p_i - p_0) \cdot v \quad \text{(EQ 13.15)}$$

Hence $s_i - s_0$ is proportional to the cosine of the angle between the two vectors $(p_i - p_0)$ and v.

Some examples are shown in Figure 13.10. In Figure 13.10(a) all the variation in s is along s_0 to s_1, and hence the gradient vector for s corresponds exactly to $p_i - p_0$ (the cosine between this vector and v is maximized, and hence the angle between them must be 0). In Figure 13.10(b) the distance from s_0 to s_1 is the same as that between s_0 and s_2, so v must bisect the angle at p_0. A similar explanation can be given for Figure 13.10(c) where the distance from

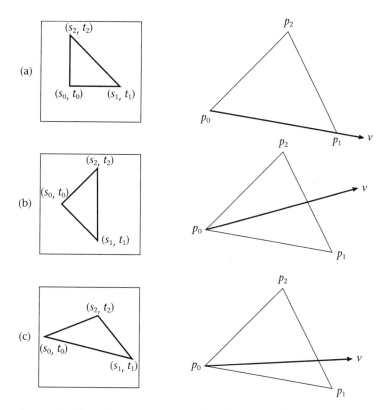

Figure 13.10
Gradiant of *s* for different
configurations of the
texture triangle

s_0 to s_1 is greater than from s_0 to s_2, and so the angle between v and $p_1 - p_0$ is smaller than between v and $p_2 - p_0$. Now suppose $v = (a_s, b_s, c_s)$ and the normal to the polygon is $n = (n_x, n_y, n_z)$. Then since $v \cdot n = 0$, we have with (EQ 13.14) three equations in the three unknowns a_s, b_s, and c_s. Putting this together with a similar result for t, we would have:

$$(s, t) = (s_0, t_0) + (p - p_0) \begin{bmatrix} a_s & a_t \\ b_s & b_t \\ c_s & c_t \end{bmatrix} \qquad \text{(EQ 13.16)}$$

which is of the same general form as (EQ 13.13).

Now to summarize the texture mapping process as we have described so far, a large surface is tesselated into a number of triangles in object space. Each triangle has associated texture coordinates and a map from object space to texture space. The triangle is passed through the rendering pipeline. The corners of each pixel are mapped back to object space, and the mapping to texture coordinates determines a quadrilateral in texture space. An appropriate weighted average of the overlapped texels is computed, and used to set the color of the pixel.

There is still the problem of clipping. Suppose that a triangle is clipped by the view volume and split along two of its edges. The result will be a quadrilateral,

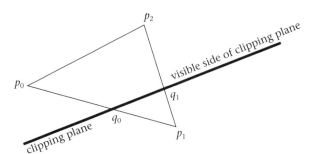

Figure 13.11
Texture coordinates
for clipped triangle

and if triangles are the only primitives available, this can easily be split into two triangles. A more difficult problem is to clip the texture coordinates. Of course the texture coordinates belonging to the vertex that was clipped can no longer be used. This is shown in Figure 13.11 where vertex p_1 is outside the visible region. There are two possible solutions for this.

Each new intersection point (here q_0 and q_1) can be mapped back to object space, and then the mapping (EQ 13.11) (for example, as given by (EQ 13.16)) used to find the new texture coordinates. An alternative method uses inter-polation. Clipping takes place before the perspective projection, and therefore clipping the actual texture coordinates will not result in texture distortions (see the next section). Now suppose that the edge p_0 to p_1 has parametric equation $p(h) = (1 - h)p_0 + hp_1$, and $p(h_0) = q_0$. Then the texture coordinates can be interpolated in the same ratio along the edge:

$$s_0' = (1 - h_0)s_0 + h_0 s_1$$
$$t_0' = (1 - h_0)t_0 + h_0 t_1$$

(EQ 13.17)

where (s_0', t_0') are the interpolated texture coordinates for q_0.

Incremental texture mapping

It is costly to have to do an inverse transformation from pixel coordinates to object coordinates for each pixel. Instead we examine the possibility of exploiting the same kind of method as is used for z-buffering and interpolated smooth shading, which is to update the texture coordinates incrementally as part of the process of polygon rasterization. In this approach each object space polygon vertex p_i has its associated texture coordinates (s_i, t_i) and these are carried through the rendering pipeline and interpolated in the same manner as colors for Gouraud shading. However, in general, as it stands this produces incorrect results. In order to see this, we concentrate for the moment on the simplified case of a line segment in object coordinates, with an associated one-dimensional texture. It may be helpful to think of this line segment as the edge of a polygon.

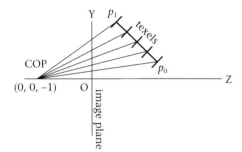

Figure 13.12
Projection of a textured
edge onto the image
plane

Suppose the line segment is from p_0 to p_1, parameterized as:

$$p(s) = p_0 + s(p_1 - p_0), \ 0 \le s \le 1 \tag{EQ 13.18}$$

Then s is the texture coordinate, and without loss of generality we assume that the texture coordinates at the vertices are $s = 0$ and $s = 1$.

Also without loss of generality, we assume the simple perspective viewing model of Figure 9.3 on page 196. The center of projection is at $(0, 0, -1)$. The line segment is textured, with equally spaced texels along the segment, as shown in Figure 13.12. In general for this viewing model, if (x, y, z) is a point in object space, then the corresponding point in projection space is shown in (EQ 13.19).

$$X = \frac{x}{z+1}$$

$$Y = \frac{y}{z+1} \tag{EQ 13.19}$$

$$Z = \frac{z}{z+1}$$

The equivalent point on the screen is then of course (X, Y). Hence the projected line segment has its Y range from Y_0 to Y_1. Now it should be clear from the figure that equally spaced intervals in s on the original object space line do not map to equally spaced intervals on the projected line on the image plane. Hence simply choosing the texture coordinates for each pixel corresponding to the line by interpolating between texture coordinates 0 and 1 will not produce the correct mapping. The effect of the projection is not taken into account in this procedure.

We examine this now in more detail. If this were an edge of a polygon, then it would be represented by a tuple:

$$\left(Y_1, \ X_0, \ \frac{dX}{dY}, \ Z_0, \ \frac{dZ}{dY}, \ \dots, \ s_0, \ \frac{ds}{dY} \right) \tag{EQ 13.20}$$

("Method 3: interpolation" on page 269). Hence the screen coordinate corresponding to the ith scan-line up from Y_0 is:

$$\left(X_0 + i \cdot \frac{dX}{dY}, \ Y_0 + i, \ Z_0 + i \cdot \frac{dZ}{dY} \right) \tag{EQ 13.21}$$

Now from (EQ 13.19) the inverse map from screen coordinates to object co-ordinates is:

$$x = \frac{X}{1-Z}$$

$$y = \frac{Y}{1-Z} \qquad \text{(EQ 13.22)}$$

$$z = \frac{Z}{1-Z}$$

Applying this to (EQ 13.21), the object space point corresponding to the inter-polated screen space point is:

$$\left(\frac{X_0 + i \cdot \frac{dX}{dY}}{1 - \left(Z_0 + i \cdot \frac{dZ}{dY}\right)}, \frac{Y_0 + i}{1 - \left(Z_0 + i \cdot \frac{dZ}{dY}\right)}, \frac{Z_0 + i \cdot \frac{dZ}{dY}}{1 - \left(Z_0 + i \cdot \frac{dZ}{dY}\right)} \right) \qquad \text{(EQ 13.23)}$$

We again make use of (EQ 13.19) to re-express the x-coordinate in terms of the original object space coordinates:

$$x' = \frac{(y_1 z_0 - y_0 z_1 + dy)x_0 + i(z_0 + 1)(x_1 z_0 - x_0 z_1 + dx)}{(y_1 z_0 - y_0 z_1 + dy) - i(z_0 + 1)dz} \qquad \text{(EQ 13.24)}$$

Similar expressions can be found for y- and z-coordinates. Since the projection of the line segment is a line segment, and the projection is invertible, x' must be an x-coordinate on the object space line segment. Hence using (EQ 13.18), we can find the corresponding parameter value as:

$$s = \frac{x' - x_0}{dx} \qquad \text{(EQ 13.25)}$$

Using (EQ 13.24) and simplifying we obtain:

$$s = \frac{i(z_0 + 1)^2}{y_1(z_0 + 1) - y_0(z_1 + 1) - idz(z_0 + 1)} \qquad \text{(EQ 13.26)}$$

This value is the *true texture coordinate* corresponding to the projected point on the line segment which is i scan lines above Y_0, the projection of y_0.

Now suppose that the texture coordinate is itself interpolated as part of the rendering of this line segment. Then, at the ith scan line for this edge, the interpolated texture coordinate would be:

$$s' = \frac{i}{dY}$$

$$= \frac{i}{\dfrac{y_1}{z_1 + 1} - \dfrac{y_0}{z_0 + 1}} \qquad \text{(EQ 13.27)}$$

$$= \frac{i(z_0 + 1)(z_1 + 1)}{y_1(z_0 + 1) - y_0(z_1 + 1)}$$

Comparing (EQ 13.27) with (EQ 13.26) we see that interpolating the texture coordinates directly does not produce the correct result. The relationship between s', the interpolated coordinate, and s, the true coordinate, can be seen from the following:

$$\frac{1}{s'} = \frac{1}{i}\left(\frac{y_1}{z_1+1} - \frac{y_0}{z_0+1}\right) \tag{EQ 13.28}$$

Also:

$$\frac{1}{s} = \frac{1}{i}\left(\frac{y_1}{z_0+1} - \frac{y_0(z_1+1)}{(z_0+1)^2}\right) - \frac{dz}{z_0+1} \tag{EQ 13.29}$$

Hence:

$$\begin{aligned}\left(\frac{z_0+1}{z_1+1}\right)\frac{1}{s} &= \frac{1}{i}\left(\frac{y_1}{z_1+1} - \frac{y_0}{z_0+1}\right) - \frac{dz}{z_1+1} \\ &= \frac{1}{s'} - \frac{dz}{z_1+1}\end{aligned} \tag{EQ 13.30}$$

Finally:

$$\frac{z_0+1}{s} = \frac{z_1+1}{s'} - dz \tag{EQ 13.31}$$

From (EQ 13.31) we can see that $s' \rightarrow s$ as $dz \rightarrow 0$. The flatter the line segment is, in other words, the closer it is to being parallel to the image plane, the closer the interpolated texture coordinate will be to the true one. Although we have derived this result for a single line, clearly this situation is reproduced for each scan-line belonging to a polygon. The result therefore generalizes to polygons. Interpolating the texture values will produce reasonable results for small polygons where the depth hardly varies over the polygon. Alternatively, the texture values can be interpolated, and then a correction formula such as (EQ 13.31) used in order to obtain the true texture coordinates.

A way to carry out an interpolation scheme that leads to correct results on each interpolation is to use homogeneous coordinates. Staying with the example of the line segment, we represent the texture coordinate in homogeneous form (sw, w). In other words, to recover the texture coordinate, divide the first element by the second, in the usual interpretation of homogeneous coordinates. Express (EQ 13.26) in this form:

$$(sw, w) = (i(z_0+1)^2, \; y_1(z_0+1) - y_0(z_1+1) - idz(z_0+1)) \tag{EQ 13.32}$$

Re-express this in screen coordinates:

$$(sw, w) = \left(\frac{i}{(1-Z_0)^2}, \; \frac{dY}{(1-Z_0)(1-Z_1)} - i\left(\frac{dZ}{(1-Z_0)^2(1-Z_1)}\right)\right) \tag{EQ 13.33}$$

Now we can multiply throughout by $(1 - Z_0)$ since this does not change the value of the homogeneous expression to achieve:

$$(sw, w) = \left(\frac{i}{1-Z_0}, \frac{dY}{1-Z_1} - i\left(\frac{dZ}{(1-Z_0)(1-Z_1)}\right)\right)$$

(EQ 13.34)

Hence, the iteration scheme is as follows:

```
Initialize: sw = 0;  w = dY/(1 - Z₁)
       for i = 0 . . . dY:
         sw = sw + 1/(1 - Z₀);
         w = w - (dZ/((1 - Z₀)(1 - Z₁)));
         s = sw/w;
```

It is left to the reader to check that at the start of the iteration s is 0, and by the end of the iteration s is 1, as required.

Filtering and mipmapping

We have mentioned the problems of minification and magnification – generally the problem of filtering over the texels in order to produce a reasonable color value for a corresponding pixel. This is essential in order to avoid severe aliasing. Such aliasing may be acceptable for a single image, but would be completely unacceptable for animation – as objects or the viewpoint moved around, the textures would shimmer and distort, rather than seem to be invariant on the surfaces of objects.

There are several methods of filtering, discussed in some detail by Heckbert (1986). In OpenGL the simplest method is to choose the texel which has coordinates nearest to the center of the pixel being rendered. This is the computationally cheapest method, but also the one prone to result in severest aliasing. An alternative is to find the four nearest texels (a 2 × 2 array) to the center of the pixel, and linearly interpolate the colors of these.

OpenGL also provides a method known as *mipmapping* (Blinn and Newell, 1976) which is an efficient way to try to overcome the problems caused by minification and magnification. The idea is to store several versions of a texture map, each of a different resolution. Suppose that the highest resolution texture map (level 0) has dimension $2^m \times 2^n$. By averaging each block of 2 × 2 texels, a (level 1) texture can be defined which has resolution $2^{m-1} \times 2^{n-1}$. This same averaging process is repeated until finally there is a 1 × 1 texture map. If $m > n$ this will be the level m texture. Now based on the screen size of the object the appropriate resolution texture can be dynamically selected during the rendering process.

Filtering and mipmapping can be used together. In the case of magnification, where the pixel sizes are fractions of the texel sizes, it only makes sense to use the highest resolution (level 0) texture. In the case of minification the interpolation can be across the mipmaps as well as within each mipmap, in order to avoid sudden changes as the texture resolution changes across mipmaps. OpenGL provides for the following possibilities (Neider *et al.*, 1993, p. 266):

- Within any mipmap, the nearest texel is chosen, or else a linear interpolation of the nearest 2×2 block, as before.
- In each of the two "nearest" mipmaps, the centers of the closest texels are chosen, and these are linearly interpolated.
- In each of the two "nearest" mipmaps, the 2×2 nearest blocks are interpolated, and the two resulting values are then interpolated across the mipmaps.

The above assumes that there is essentially a linear map from the discrete set of mipmap images available to the continuous range of sizes (i.e., the degree of minification) of the objects. Hence the word "nearest" is used in the context of that mapping.

Methods for choosing texture coordinates

In all of the above discussion we have worked with a single object – in fact a polygon, or more specifically a triangle. Assigning texture coordinates to a single polygon is relatively straightforward, as we have seen. However, this isn't too useful. It would be fine for the table top shown in Figure 13.5, but not for the faces. Each face is a polygon mesh and one texture needs to be applied across the whole mesh. The texture coordinates must be chosen in a way that results in a consistent overall application of the texture across the whole mesh.

There is no "correct" answer to this problem. Some types of surfaces have a natural parameterization (for example, the Bézier and B-Spline surfaces to be discussed in Chapter 19). But polygon meshes do not have such a natural parameterization, but a map from vertices to texture coordinates has to be chosen somehow. A good review of methods that have been used is provided by Watt and Watt (1992). The fundamental idea is to choose a surface which does have a natural parameterization, and which is computationally efficient and easy to use. This surface is then wrapped around the polygon mesh, and a projection method used from the mesh vertices onto the surrounding surface. The texture coordinates of the surrounding surface are then used as the texture coordinates for the vertices.

We illustrate this with a common technique, based on cylinders. Without loss of generality, assume that a cylinder of radius r, with center at the origin, and height h is to be used as the surrounding surface. The equation of such a cylinder is:

Figure 13.13
Map from mesh vertices
to cylindrical texture
coordinates

$$x(\theta) = r\cos\theta$$
$$y(\theta) = r\sin\theta$$
$$0 \le \theta \le 2\pi$$
$$0 \le z \le h$$

(EQ 13.35)

The cylinder can be flattened into a rectangle of width $2\pi r$ and height h. Hence a natural parameterization is:

$$s = \frac{\theta}{2\pi}$$
$$t = \frac{z}{h}$$

(EQ 13.36)

with $0 \le s, t \le 1$. Now, given a convex polygon mesh, a map can be defined between its vertices and the surrounding cylinder. This is illustrated with a 2D analogy in Figure 13.13. Here the vertices are projected to the cylinder such that the ray from vertex is normal to the cylinder. The intersection point can be used to compute (s, t) texture coordinates.

Representation of a polyhedral mesh by a cylinder is simple though problematic for polygons at the "top" and "bottom" extremes of the mesh – where no part of the cylinder matches. An alternative is to use a bounding sphere. Again simple representation can be constructed from (EQ 2.20) on page 56. A radial projection can be used, such that the vertices are projected to the sphere using the center of the sphere as the center of projection. Here the problem is that this mapping does not produce a uniform parameterization around the sphere, so that the texture will be "squashed" at its poles.

It is something of an art to produce a mapping from polygon mesh vertices to texture coordinates – often this is tried interactively with substantial trial and error.

An OpenGL example

In this section we consider a simple OpenGL program, which adds texture to the example from Chapter 8 of constructing a stack of cubes, one on top of the other ("Using OpenGL" on page 178). A simple texture is added to the cubes. The comments in the program are self-explanatory.

```
#include <GL/glut.h>
/*
   An example of using OpenGL to render a simple object with
   a texture. The texture is saved in a ppm format file.
   You can also use the program dmconvert to tell you more about
   the image file.
*/

#include <stdio.h>
#include <stdlib.h>
#include <string.h>

/*This next is referred to in several places, and because of the callback
interface, cannot be passed as a parameter, hence, global*/

/*WARNING - using the PPM file format, you must delete the first few
lines of text, starting only from the image size data*/
typedef GLubyte Pixel[3]; /*represents red green blue*/

int Width, Height; /*of image*/

/*array of pixels*/
Pixel *Image;

/*name of image file*/
/*char Filename[30];*/
char *Filename = "../filename.ppm";

int allowedSize(int x)
/*returns max power of 2 <= x*/
{
   int r;

   r = 1;
   while(r < x) r=(r<<1);

   if(r==x) return r;
   else return r>>1;
}

void readImage(void)
/*reads the image file assumes ppm format*/
{
   int w,h,max;
   int i,j;
   unsigned int r,g,b;
   int k;

   FILE *fp;

   fp = fopen(Filename,"r");

   /*read the width*/
   fscanf(fp,"%d",&w);
```

```
   /*read the height*/
   fscanf(fp,"%d",&h);

   /*I think that this is max intensity - not used here*/
   fscanf(fp,"%d",&max);

   /*width and height must be powers of 2 - taking the simple option
   here of finding the max power of 2 <= w and h*/

   Width = allowedSize(w);
   Height = allowedSize(h);

   printf("filename = %s\n",Filename);
   printf("Width = %d, Height = %d\n",Width,Height);

   Image = (Pixel *)malloc(Width*Height*sizeof(Pixel));

   for(i=0;i<Height;++i){
      for(j=0;j<Width;++j) {
         fscanf(fp,"%d %d %d",&r,&g,&b);
         k = i*Width+j; /*ok, can be more efficient here!*/
         (*(Image+k))[0] = (GLubyte)r;
         (*(Image+k))[1] = (GLubyte)g;
         (*(Image+k))[2] = (GLubyte)b;
      }
      /*better scan to the end of the row*/
      for(j=Width; j<w; ++j) fscanf(fp,"%c %c %c",&r,&g,&b);
   }
   fclose(fp);
}
```

The function readImage reads the image from a file referenced by Filename. The image is assumed stored in the PPM (portable pixmap format), which is simply the width, the height, the maximum intensity, followed by each pixel color represented by a triple of RGB values, in this case stored as bytes. Note that a PPM file has some additional information at the top – but this has been deleted for the purposes of the example. The image is stored in the Pixel array Image.

```
void initializeTextures(void)
{
   GLint level = 0;    /*only one level - no level of detail*/
   GLint components = 3; /*3 means R, G, and B components only*/
   GLint border = 0;    /*no border around the image*/

   /*read the image file*/
   readImage();

   /*each pixelrow on a byte alignment boundary*/

   glPixelStorei(GL_UNPACK_ALIGNMENT,1);
```

```
    /*define information about the image*/
    glTexImage2D(GL_TEXTURE_2D,level,components,
      (GLsizei)Width, (GLsizei)Height,
      border, GL_RGB, GL_UNSIGNED_BYTE,Image);

    /*ensures that image is not wrapped*/
    glTexParameterf(GL_TEXTURE_2D,GL_TEXTURE_WRAP_S,GL_CLAMP);
    glTexParameterf(GL_TEXTURE_2D,GL_TEXTURE_WRAP_T,GL_CLAMP);

    /*chooses mapping type from texels to pixels*/
    glTexParameterf(GL_TEXTURE_2D,GL_TEXTURE_MIN_FILTER,GL_LINEAR);
    glTexParameterf(GL_TEXTURE_2D,GL_TEXTURE_MAG_FILTER,GL_LINEAR);
    /*this chooses the texel for minification and magnification
    GL_NEAREST chooses the texel nearest the center of the pixel.
    GL_LINEAR performs a linear interpolation on the 4 surrounding
    texels*/

    /*GL_DECAL - this says overwrite pixel with texture color*/
    glTexEnvf(GL_TEXTURE_ENV,GL_TEXTURE_ENV_MODE,GL_DECAL);
    /*an alternative is GL_MODULATE which modulates the lighting
    by the texel value by multiplication*/

    /*this enables texturing*/
    glEnable(GL_TEXTURE_2D);
}
```

The function initializeTextures actually reads in the image, and declares information about it using glTexImage2D. There is no use of mipmaps in this example, so that only one level (0) is defined. There is no assumed border to the image, and the pixels are interpreted as RGB unsigned byte values. When a texture coordinate goes outside the range [0, 1] one possibility is to "wrap around," so that the texture is tiled over the object. In this case we ensure that there is no wrap-around; the image is clamped to the object. We show the choices for dealing with filtering. The program uses linear interpolation between the block of four nearest neighbour texels for the center of the pixel. An alternative (GL_NEAREST) would just choose the nearest texel.

A texture color may be combined with a pixel in various ways. It can completely determine the pixel color, which is achieved using the GL_DECAL parameter. An alternative is to let the texture modulate the lighting calculation value by multiplication. Finally texture mapping is set into force with glEnable(GL_TEXTURE_2D).

```
static void cubebase(void)
/*specifies a side of a cube*/
{
  glBegin(GL_POLYGON);
    glTexCoord2f(0.0,0.0);
    glVertex3d(-0.5,-0.5,0.0);

    glTexCoord2f(0.0,1.0);
    glVertex3d(-0.5,0.5,0.0);
```

```
        glTexCoord2f(1.0,1.0);
        glVertex3d(0.5,0.5,0.0);

        glTexCoord2f(1.0,0.0);
        glVertex3d(0.5,-0.5,0.0);
    glEnd();
}
```

The function cubebase defines the object space cube base. Note, however, that texture coordinates are now given along with each vertex. The entire texture space is mapped to the base.

```
static void cube(void)
/*uses cube side to construct a cube, making use of the modelview matrix*/
{
  /*make sure we're dealing with modelview matrix*/
  glMatrixMode(GL_MODELVIEW);

  /*pushes and duplicates current matrix*/
  glPushMatrix();

  /*construct the base*/
  cubebase();

  glPushMatrix();
  /*construct side on +x axis*/
  glTranslated(0.5,0.0,0.5);
  glRotated(90.0,0.0,1.0,0.0);
  cubebase();

  glPopMatrix();

  /*construct side on -x axis*/
  glPushMatrix();
  glTranslated(-0.5,0.0,0.5);
  glRotated(-90.0,0.0,1.0,0.0);
  cubebase();
  glPopMatrix();

  /*construct side on +y axis*/
  glPushMatrix();
  glTranslated(0.0,0.5,0.5);
  glRotated(-90.0,1.0,0.0,0.0);
  cubebase();
  glPopMatrix();

  /*construct side on -y axis*/
  glPushMatrix();
  glTranslated(0.0,-0.5,0.5);
  glRotated(90.0,1.0,0.0,0.0);
  cubebase();
  glPopMatrix();
```

```
        /*construct top*/

    glBegin(GL_POLYGON);
       glTexCoord2f(0.0,0.0);
       glVertex3d(-0.5,-0.5,1.0);

       glTexCoord2f(1.0,0.0);
       glVertex3d(0.5,-0.5,1.0);

       glTexCoord2f(1.0,1.0);
       glVertex3d(0.5,0.5,1.0);

       glTexCoord2f(0.0,1.0);
       glVertex3d(-0.5,0.5,1.0);
    glEnd();

    glPopMatrix();

    glFlush();
}

static void stack(int n)
/*creates a smaller cube on top of larger one*/
{

    cube();
    if(n==0)return;

    glPushMatrix();
    glTranslated(0.0,0.0,1.0);
    glScaled(0.5,0.5,0.5);
    stack(n-1);
    glPopMatrix();
}
```

The function cube is the same as that originally defined – making a cube out of rotating copies of the master base. The function stack recursively creates the hierarchy, as before. An example of the output of the program is shown in Figure 13.14 (color plate).

13.5 VRML97 examples

As noted in this chapter, the main difficulty for the modeler is in choosing the texture coordinates for the vertices of geometry. For each of the basic primitives (see "Shapes and geometry" on page 528 for their definitions), there is a pre-defined set of texture coordinates that map a texture on to each side. For the IndexedFaceSet geometry node (see "Using VRML97" on page 181), the texture coordinates for each vertex must be defined.

The full range of texture mapping options is beyond the scope of this brief introduction. The actual images used for texture maps can be specified as one,

```
#VRML V2.0 utf8
Transform {
 translation 0 0 0
 children [
   Shape {
   appearance Appearance {
     texture DEF my_tex ImageTexture {
      url ["default.jpg"]
     }
    }
   }
    geometry DEF my_box Box {
     size 2 2 2
    }
   }
  ]
 }
}
Transform {
 translation 3 0 0
   children [
    Shape {
     appearance Appearance {
      texture USE my_tex
      textureTransform TextureTransform {
       scale 3.0 3.0
      }
     }
     geometry USE my_box
    }
   ]
  }
 }
```

```
Transform {
 translation -3 0 0
  children [
   Shape {
    appearance Appearance {
     texture USE my_tex
     textureTransform TextureTransform {
      translation 0.5 0.5
     }
    }
    geometry USE my_box
   }
  ]
 }

Transform {
 translation 0 3 0
  children [
   Shape {
    appearance Appearance {
     texture USE my_tex
     textureTransform TextureTransform {
      rotation 0.785
     }
    }
    geometry USE my_box
   }
  ]
 }
```

Figure 13.15(a) Texture mapped primitives example

three or four channel images. If a one component (gray-scale image) is used, then this is used to modulate the base color of the polygon. If a three- or four-component image is used, then the texture color replaces the base color of the polygon. The fourth component, if it exists, is treated as the transparency, or alpha, channel. The image source is specified by one of three texture nodes. It can be an external image file (ImageTexture), an external movie (MovieTexture), or an image specified directly within the VRML file (PixelTexture). For the ImageTexture nodes, the PNG and JPEG file formats are preferred.

VRML97 has a facility for applying a 2D transformation to the texture coordinates of an object using a TextureTransformation node. Both the texture and texture transformation nodes are fields within the appearance node.

Figure 13.15(a) shows some simple examples of texture transformation in action. With a texture transformation the texture can be stretched, rotated or displaced on the surfaces of the box. (See Figure 13.15(b), color plate.)

The application of texture coordinates to an IndexedFaceSet can be done in one of two principal ways. Each vertex can have the same texture coordinate in each face that is coincident at that point, or the vertex can have a different texture coordinate for each face that is coincident. Typically when wrapping a texture around an object, a vertex will have the same coordinate in each face. In both situations the texCoord field of the IndexedFaceSet is required. If the vertex has the same texture coordinate for each face, then texture coordinates

```
#VRML V2.0 utf8                              Transform {
                                               translation 1.5 0 0
Transform {                                    children [
 translation -1.5 0 0                           Shape {
 children [                                       appearance USE my_app
  Shape {                                         geometry IndexedFaceSet {
   appearance DEF my_app Appearance {              coord USE my_coord
    texture ImageTexture {                         texCoord TextureCoordinate {
     url ["default.jpg"]                            point [0 0, 0.333 0, 0.666 0, 1 0,
    }                                                      0 1, 0.333 1, 0.666 1, 1 1]
   }                                              }
   geometry IndexedFaceSet {                      coordIndex [1 5 6 2 -1, 3 2 6 7 -1,
    coord DEF my_coord Coordinate {                 0 4 5 1]
     point [-1 0 -1, 1 0 -1, 1 0 1, -1 0 1,      }
            -1 2 -1, 1 2 -1, 1 2 1, -1 2 1]     }
    }                                           Shape {
    texCoord TextureCoordinate {                 appearance USE my_app
     point [0 0, 0.333 0, 0.666 0, 1 0,          geometry IndexedFaceSet {
            0 1, 0.333 1, 0.666 1, 1 1]           coord USE my_coord
    }                                             texCoord TextureCoordinate {
    coordIndex [0 1 2 3 -1, 1 5 6 2 -1,           point [0.666 1, 1 1, 1 0, 0.666 0,
     3 2 6 7 -1, 0 3 7 4 -1,                             0.333 1, 0 1, 0 0, 0.333 0 ]
     0 4 5 1 -1, 4 7 6 5]                        }
    texCoordIndex [6 7 3 2 -1, 1 5 6 2 -1,        coordIndex [0 1 2 3 -1, 0 3 7 4 -1,
     3 2 6 7 -1, 6 2 1 5 -1,                       4 7 6 5]
     0 4 5 1 -1, 5 1 0 4]                       }
   }                                            }
  }                                            ]
 ]                                            }
}
```

Figure 13.16(a) Texture mapped IndexedFaceSet example

can be indexed using the same indices from the array in the coordIndex field. Thus the number of texture coordinates in the texCoord field must be the same as the number of coordinates in the coord field.

If the vertex has a different texture coordinate in each face, then the array in the texCoordIndex field will have to be set. The length of this array will be the same length as the array in the coordIndex field.

Figure 13.16(a) shows examples of both of these texture application methods. Two cubes have been built manually from arrays of points. For the first cube, the texture mapping is specified with texture coordinate per vertex per face. For the second cube each vertex has a unique texture coordinate. For the second cube we have had to break the shape into two smaller shapes in order to get a sensible texture mapping. (See Figure 13.16(b), color plate.)

13.6 Summary

The fundamental objective of the chapter was a completion of the rendering pipeline – to include image space visibility, local illumination with smooth shading, and texturing. We saw how the polygon fill algorithm could be used to deal with all of these in a very efficient manner. We can now also see that the rendering pipeline consists of two fundamental stages: a geometry pipeline and a rendering process. The first takes a scene graph where object geometry is represented in local coordinates. Relationships between objects are expressed through the structure of the graph (topologically) and the local transformation matrices (geometrically). The polygons are transformed into projection space, taking into account the modeling and viewing transforms, and then the clipping and projection. The rendering process takes the individual polygons pushed out of the geometry pipeline and renders them with the polygon fill algorithm, taking into account the z-buffer, shading and texturing information. The polygon fill can clearly be implemented in very efficient manner – especially if the original polygons are further decimated into triangles. There is then no need even to keep an edge table (since there are only two intersections per scan-line per polygon, and no local minima or maxima) but scan-line coherence is obviously maintained.

We have thus completed the first stage of the journey of "realism" to "real-time." We started out with ray tracing in the early chapters, embodying an element of realism, abandoned those elements that made ray tracing impossible to achieve in real-time, and now have ended at a potentially real-time solution, but which in itself produces images that are based only on local illumination. In the next chapter we show how to add shadows into the scene. In the subsequent chapter we complete the circle: we introduce a new method, radiosity, which does offer (a different kind of) realism in the way that it treats global illumination, and where static scenes can be rendered in a real-time walkthrough.

Figure 1.3
A person inside a virtual
kitchen, displayed in a
Trimension ReaCTor, a
system similar to a CAVE

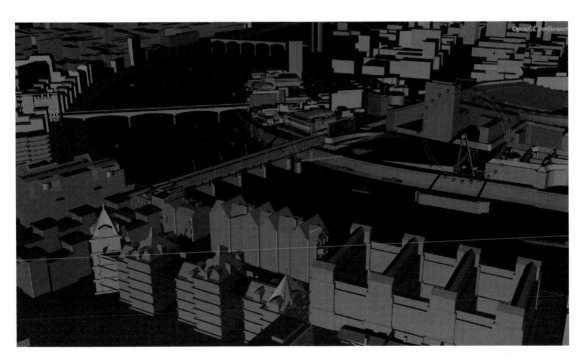

Figure 1.7
Virtual Millennium Eye
Courtesy of Rick Mather Architects

Figure 1.8
The Maitreya Project
© Maitreya Project
International Ltd.
http://www.maitreyaproject.org

(a)

(b)

Figure 1.9
Outlet valves
© Real-Time Visualisation.
Produced using form Z
RenderZone and the
integrated Light Works
renderer. These fire pump
outlet valves were part
of an animated presentation
produced by Real-Time
Visualisation for an operator's
training guide

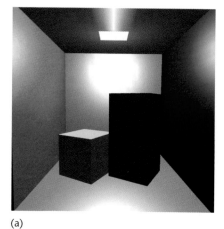 

(a)   (b)

Figure 1.10
The Cornell Box,
a scene rendered
with (a) local and
(b) global illumination
Courtesy of Jesper Mortensen,
Department of Computer
Science, UCL

Figure 1.11
Fear of public speaking – an
example of texture mapping
Courtesy of David-Paul Pertaub,
Department of Computer Science,
UCL

Figure 1.13
The Starry Night, 1888
by Vincent Van Gogh
Lauros-Giraudon/Bridgeman
Art Library

Figure 1.16
A virtual model of UCL

Figure 1.17
Object placement
© ACM 1999 used with
permission

Figure 1.18
Simulating the behavior of cloth
Courtesy of Bernhard Spanland and Tzvetomir Vassilev,
Department of Computer Science, UCL

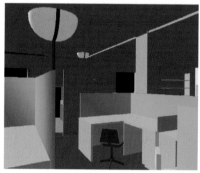
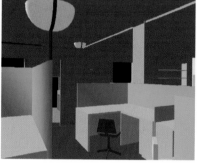

(a) Virtual laboratory

Figure 1.21
Virtual and real
views of a
laboratory

(b) Same view of the real laboratory

Figure 1.33
Stereo pairs
Runner courtesy of
Computoons; Shop scene
courtesy of O.W. Holmes
Stereoscopic Research Library
http://www.stereoview.org

Figure 4.3
Visible spectrum

400 nm

700 nm

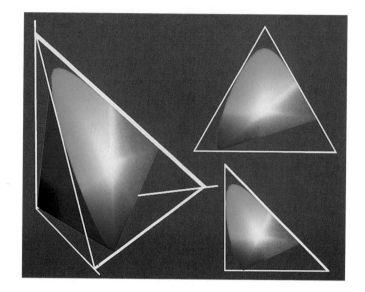

Figure 4.9
CIE-XYZ chromaticity
diagram
Image provided courtesy
of Barbara Meier

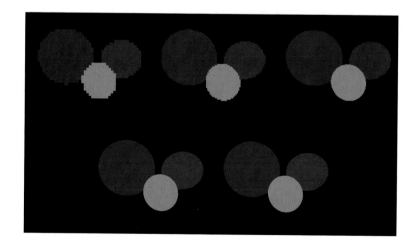

Figure 5.6
A sequence of images with
increasing resolution

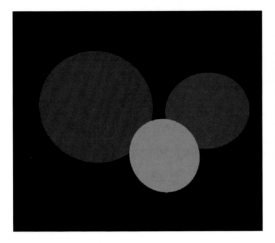

Figure 6.9
Ray casting using diffuse reflection

Figure 6.10
Ray casting using specular reflection

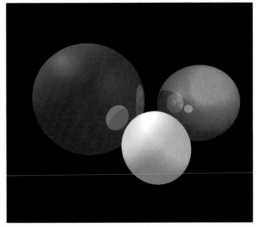

Figure 6.12
Ray tracing example – opaque surfaces

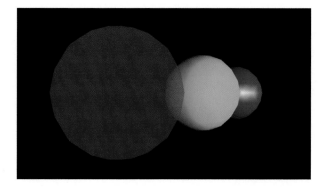

Figure 6.15(b)
VRML97 materials example

Figure 9.12
Looking at a pyramid from the top

Figure 9.14
Stereo view with VPDistance at 100
(VP behind the pyramid)

Figure 9.15
Stereo view with VPDistance at 80
(VP intersects the pyramid)

Figure 9.16
Stereo view with VPDistance at 60
(VP intersects the pyramid)

Figure 13.3
Illustrating Gouraud shading
Courtesy of Jesper Mortensen
and Alican Met, Department
of Computer Science, UCL

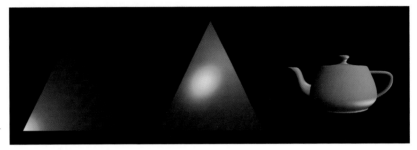

Figure 13.4
An illustration of Phong shading
Courtesy of Jesper Mortensen and
Alican Met, Department of Computer
Science, UCL

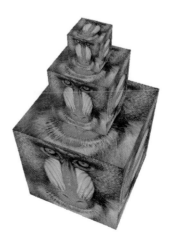

Figure 13.14
The textured stacked cube example

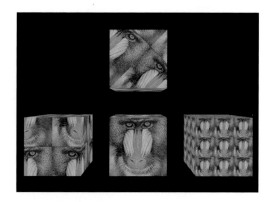

Figure 13.15(b)
Texture mapped primitives example

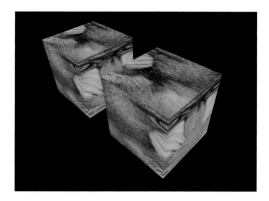

Figure 13.16(b)
Texture mapped IndexedFaceSet Example

Figure 14.19
Left: A 1000 input polygon scene. Direct illmination only, which took 29.3 CPU minutes
(on an SCI Indigo 2 R4000) for discontinuity meshing, back projection and lighting
calculations. Computed using the Drettakis–Fiume algorithm
Right: The same scene with the discontinuity mesh superimposed
Courtesy of George Drettakis, iMAGIS-GRAVIR, France

Figure 20.2
The VR-CUBE at Center
for Parallel Computers
(PDC), Royal Institute
of Technology (KTH),
Stockholm, Sweden

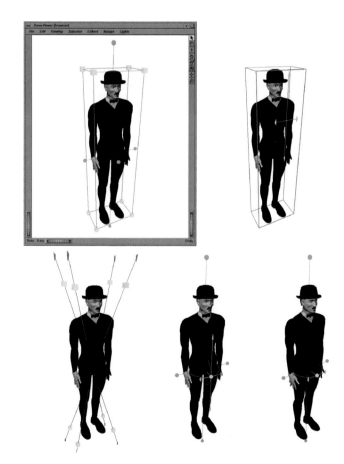

Figure 21.6
A transform manipulator
in SceneViewer
Body model courtesy of
Computer Graphics
Laboratory (LIG) Swiss Federal
Institute of Technology (EPFL).
Directed by Professor Daniel
Thalmann, Lausanne,
Switzerland. H-Anim prod:
Christian Babski. Body design:
Mireille Clavien

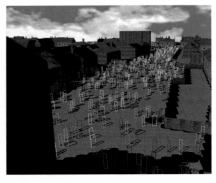

Figure 23.16
An example of image-based rendering for large environments
Courtesy of Franco Tecchia, Deparment of Computer Science, UCL

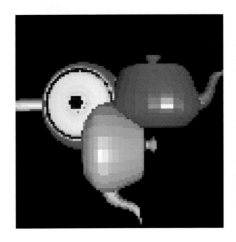
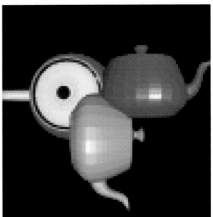

Figure 23.25
Full screen anti-aliasing

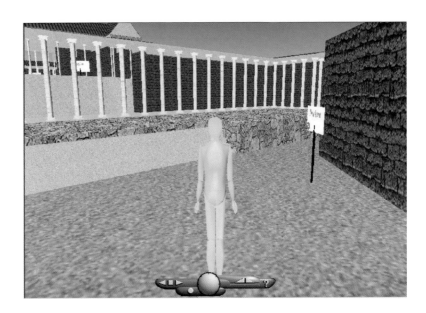

Figure A.1
Example VRML world

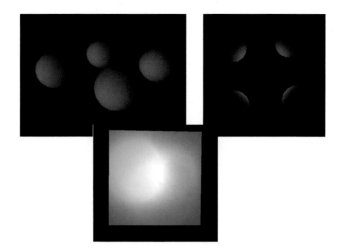

Figure A.4
DirectionalLight, PointLight,
and SpotLight examples

Figure P.1
Light shelf office: furnished
interior view
Copyright © 1997 by
Greg Ward

Figure P.2
Using LightWorks radiosity, architectural designers can simulate daylight flooding through a window. In addition, the system simulates lighting effects for complex geometry, such as curved surfaces, and variation in lighting levels in a scene
© LightWork Design Limited

Figure P.3
A light field of Michaelangelo's statue of *Night*
Courtesy of Professor Marc Levoy, Digital Michaelangelo Project, Stanford University
http://graphics.stanford.edu/ projects/mich/lightfield-of-night/lightfield-of-night.html

14 Shadows: toward real-time realism

14.1 Introduction

14.2 Shadow umbras

14.3 Shadow penumbras

14.4 Summary

14.1 Introduction

Ray casting discussed in Chapter 5 and ray tracing in Chapter 6 naturally incorporate the rendering of shadows. You may recall that "shadow feelers" are traced from any point of intersection of a ray with an object to the set of (point) light sources in the scene. Those rays that reached light sources without obstruction by another object contributed a local illumination term. Those rays towards a light source that were obstructed by another object contributed nothing to the illumination. Clearly shadows are automatically produced by this process.

As we relaxed the requirements for global illumination, and moved from ray tracing to the rendering pipeline, we lost shadows. Yet shadows add a great degree of realism to a scene. This chapter considers whether shadows can be added back into the rendering of a scene, while still maintaining the possibility of real-time rendering.

It is interesting to note that the problem of visibility is closely related to shadows. The simplest meaning to attribute to the idea of a "shadow" is that it is a part of the scene that is not visible to a light. If we consider the light to be a single point (or direction), this idea of shadows is true, hence whenever studying visibility with respect to a viewer, we are also considering at least part of the problem of shadows – visibility with respect to a light source instead of with respect to a viewer. Realistic sources, however, are not simply points, but have a certain extent. Although computation of shadows can still be considered

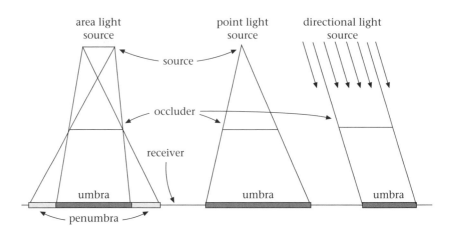

Figure 14.1
Soft and sharp shadows

as a visibility problem in this case, it is a much harder problem to solve. In this case we are considering what is visible from any point within an area or volume.

In the real world, light sources emit light through a surface which has non-zero area (*area light sources*). The intensity of shadows created by such sources varies gradually as it goes from completely lit to fully in shadow. They can be divided into two regions. The innermost one which receives no light is called the *umbra* while the outer region is called the *penumbra*. Finding the exact boundaries of the umbra and penumbra as well as the intensity at each point in the penumbra (as we will see later the intensity in the penumbra does not vary continuously) is a very difficult and computationally-intensive problem.

In computer graphics we usually tend to simplify the shadow determination problem. If we aim to have a real-time system we cannot afford the cost of area light sources. In practice, we usually assume that the light source is defined either as a mathematical point (*point light source*) or as if it is placed at infinity (*directional light source*). The shadows created by such sources have no penumbra. In this case the shadow has only one well-defined boundary, an umbra, which can be assumed to be the same intensity all over since it is all fully hidden from the source. Such shadows look very hard (*sharp shadows*), even artificial; however, they are still useful for providing spatial cues and making the images a bit more realistic (see Figure 14.1).

One very important attribute of shadows is that they are view independent. Shadows depend only on the geometry and relative positions of the objects and the light source in the scene and they do not change as we change the viewing parameters. This can be exploited to pre-compute some or all of the shadow information in the cases where the scene is static.

In the rest of this chapter we will use the term *occluder* to refer to the polygon causing the shadow and the term *receiver* to refer to the polygon on which the shadow is cast.

We will start by looking at algorithms for sharp shadow generation (shadow umbras), including a partial solution often used used in practice (fake shadows). Then we will go on to touch on the subject of soft shadow generation. The aim is to look at some representative algorithms to demonstrate some of the ideas in shadow generation. For a more comprehensive survey the reader is encouraged to read Woo *et al.* (1990).

14.2 Shadow umbras

General approaches

Computing shadows from point light sources, even though not very realistic, is often the best we can do. Since these methods are so similar to the Visible Surface Determination (VSD) methods (Chapter 11 and Chapter 13), we will follow a similar classification. We will classify the different methods – and there are a large number of them – into *image precision*, *object precision*, and *hybrid*.

Image precision methods compute the shadow information at the pixel level. We have already seen one such method, ray tracing. In this chapter we will look at another method from this class, the shadow buffer. In this category we can possibly also include the scan-line methods, where shadow edges are projected onto the polygon being displayed, and during the scan-line process such shadow edges mark a transition into or out of shadow (Appel, 1968; Bouknight and Kelley, 1970). Even though the calculation is not strictly per pixel it is still at image precision.

Object precision methods compute shadow information independently of the viewpoint, often storing it along with the geometric database. Since shadow information is the same from whatever viewing position, it does not need to be recalculated as long as the geometry remains static. Atherton *et al.* (1978) described one of the first such methods. It is a two-pass hidden surface algorithm: In the first pass the light source position is used as viewpoint, distinguishing fragments of polygons which are visible to the light source, and those which are hidden, and therefore in shadow. The shadow polygons are added to the original scene, and in the second pass the scene is traversed from the camera viewpoint and hidden surface elimination and rendering are performed. For both passes they used a VSD algorithm based on general polygon clipping. Slater (1992a) presented a method which uses regular subdivision of space, in the form of a tiled cube, to find the shadow relations between the polygons and then used the shadow volume on these to find the exact shadow. This resembles the Light Buffer of Haines and Greenberg (1986), which was used in the context of ray tracing. Another algorithm of this class based on binary space partitioning, the Shadow Volume BSP (SVBSP) trees, was presented by Chin and Feiner (1989). We will study this in more detail later in this chapter. Even though shadows are computed in a pre-processing phase, it doesn't mean that shadows in these methods come with no cost to the frame rate, since we can get an increase in the complexity of the scene.

Hybrid methods do part in the complexity of object precision and part in image precision. The example that we will see here, Shadow Volumes (Crow, 1977; Bergeron, 1986), is one of the oldest and still very popular methods. In this, the volume of space covered in shadow (shadow volumes) is computed in object space and remains valid while the scene is static, but the final shadow determination on the surface is derived from that on each pixel-by-pixel basis for each given viewpoint.

And finally we will look at "fake shadows" (Blinn, 1988). This method is only capable of computing a subset of the shadows – those lying on a planar surface – but it is also the easiest to implement and less restrictive in terms of dynamic objects since it is fully recomputed at each frame.

Shadow z-buffer

This method was first described by Williams (1978). It is a two-step method. For the first step we use the light as the viewpoint and render the scene into the z-buffer. Note that we are not interested in the contents of the color buffer in this step, just the depth information for each pixel from the light source. We can turn off illumination and texturing to speed things up. We only keep the z-buffer which we call the *shadow depth buffer* or *shadow map*. This shadow map can be used repeatedly as long as we don't change the scene geometry or move the light source. We will call the coordinate system defined by the light the *light space*.

For the second pass we render the objects as usual from the viewpoint with the only difference that as we scan-convert them, before writing each visible pixel we test it for shadows. To do this we transform the pixel's (x_v, y_v, z_v) coordinates from viewing space to (x_s, y_s, z_s) in light space (Figure 14.2) and compare the z_s value against the depth stored at the (x_s, y_s) position of the shadow depth buffer. If the pixel has a greater depth than that stored it means that from the light point of view there is something closer that occludes it and

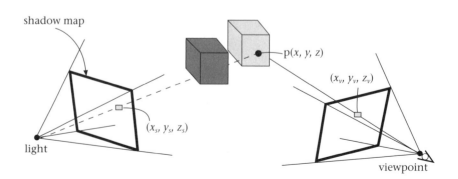

Figure 14.2
A point is transformed from view space to light space to test if it is visible to the source (z-comparison)

hence it is in shadow. If the z_s value is the same as that in the shadow buffer, that indicates that it is the same point that is visible from the light at that point.

One of the benefits of this method is that it is not limited to polygonal models. Any surface that can be scan-converted into a z-buffer can be used for shadows. On the other hand, because of its image precision nature, it is prone to aliasing and quantization errors. One source of error is the transformation of the points from viewpoint space to light space for the depth comparison. Due to the limited precision the z-comparison might result in "greater-than" in cases where it should be "equal," creating what is known as "shadow ackne," where a lit surface has random lit points on it. This effect can be minimized with the inclusion of a tolerance in the comparison. Filtering and dithering can be used for minimizing other aliasing problems (Williams, 1978; Reeves *et al.*, 1987).

The method as described above can be quite expensive to execute since it has to do a shadow comparison for every pixel written into the color buffer. A lot of this time is wasted since we are testing many pixels which will in any case be overwritten during the visibility z-buffer process, and will not appear in the final image. One acceleration we can do is defer the shadow testing unil after we finish the rendering of the image. In this case the second step of the shadow computation is independent of the scene complexity. However, we lose on image quality. That's because we have already performed the illumination for the image pixels and all we can do is just reduce the value of each one by a constant amount, so we might end up having highlights in shadow regions.

If we take the latter approach mentioned above, although the per frame shadow computation is independent of the scene complexity we still need to perform a large number of individual pixel comparisons which can be quite expensive. A variation of this method which uses texture mapping hardware to do the comparisons was described by Segal *et al.* (1992). The hardware transformations allow for very fast run-time; however, this requires special texturing hardware which is not always available.

Multiple light sources can be simulated by using a separate shadow buffer for each source. If we are taking the post-processing approach, then the same buffer can be used for all sources by doing the shadowing of each source sequentially; however, the shadow maps will have to be recomputed for every frame.

Shadow volumes

There are several algorithms that make use of the idea of shadow volumes. In this section we will study a hybrid method presented by Crow (1977) and in the next we will see an object precision method, the SVBSP tree.

The *shadow volume* (SV) of a polygon, with respect to a point light source, is the volume of space hidden from the view of the light behind the polygon. It is a semi-infinite pyramid defined by the *shadow planes* (SPs) and bounded on top by the polygon itself. Given a light source L and a polygon P defined by the vertices $[v_1, v_2, \ldots, v_n]$ arranged as in Figure 14.3(a), a *shadow plane* is

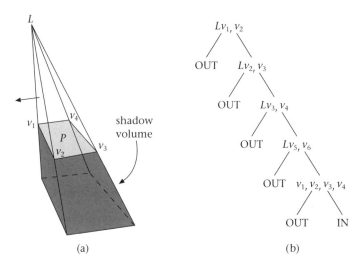

Figure 14.3
A shadow volume
(a) and a BSP
representation of it (b)

the plane defined by a triple (L, v_i, v_{i+1}) where $i = 1, \ldots, n, n + 1(v_{n+1} \equiv v_1)$. The shadow volume of P is then defined as the frustum enclosed by the shadow planes of (P, L) and bounded on top by P.

When a plane belonging to the shadow volume is computed it is vital that the correct "back" and "front" sides are represented by the polygon plane equation. Adopting the convention that the vertices are described in counter-clockwise order when viewed from the front side, in Figure 14.3 the correct order for the vertices for computing the shadow plane equation is, in the situation shown, v_2Lv_1. In this case the polygon is described by vertices v_1, v_2, v_3, v_4 in the appropriate anticlockwise order so that it is facing towards the light source. The convention has been adopted that the "back" side of the shadow plane is on the shadow side.

The shadow volumes method, first described in Crow (1977) and later revis-ited by Bergeron (1986), is still one of the most popular methods for shadow computation. It is based on the following idea, shown in Figure 14.4. Given a viewpoint that is not in shadow itself, then if we draw a vector v from the eye to a point p in the scene we can decide whether the point is in shadow by counting the number of front-facing and back-facing shadow planes that v intersects before it reaches p. If the difference between the number of front-facing and back-facing shadow planes is zero then the point is lit (p_2 in Figure 14.4) otherwise it is in shadow (p_1 in Figure 14.4). Note that the difference might be greater than one since some regions might be in the shadow volume of more than one polygon (p_3 in Figure 14.4). There is a special case when the eye is in shadow. Here we need to modify the counting to take that into account.

The algorithm proceeds in two steps:

(1) creation of the shadow volumes in object space;

(2) shadow determination per pixel by shadow plane count.

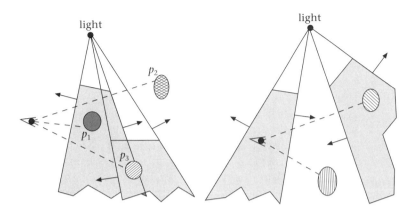

Figure 14.4
A point *p* is in shadow if *v* intersects more front-facing shadow planes than back-facing

The generation of the shadow planes can be thought of as pre-processing since it is only performed once independently of the viewpoint and then can be used repeatedly as long as the objects do not change. The shadow planes are included in the scene database and taken through the graphics pipeline. Since a polygon representation of these planes is necessary, they are bounded by clipping against the field of view or the sphere of influence of the light.

For the second step, in Bergeron (1986) the rendering is done using a scan-line algorithm similar to that presented in Chapter 13. The shadow planes are processed in the same way as the scene polygons except that they are invisible. When they are encountered on a scan-line they are not used for setting the pixel color but instead for incrementing/decrementing the pixel's shadow-plane counter. We start with the counter being equal to 0 or to the number of shadow volumes that contain the viewpoint, if that is in shadow, and during the rendering we add one every time we cross a front-facing SP and subtract one when we cross a back-facing SP.

If we are using OpenGL then the second step can be done in hardware using the z-buffer and the stencil buffer (Heidmann, 1991). (A *stencil buffer* is a bitmap – although it can be deeper on some hardware – such that the corresponding pixel to any bit in the bitmap can be changed only if a test on the bit succeeds. In this case when z-test succeeds the corresponding bit in the stencil buffer is modified.) This is done in three steps. First the scene is rendered with the lighting turned on, without taking into account the shadows. Then the shadow planes are rendered. In this step we allow comparison with the z-buffer but whenever that comparison succeeds, instead of modifying the color buffer we increment/decrement the value at the corresponding position in the stencil buffer. At the end of this rendering the stencil buffer will contain the difference of front-facing minus back-facing shadow planes for each pixel. In the third step we render the scene with the lighting turned off and we use the stencil buffer to restrict the rendering only in the areas where we had more front-facing SPs.

If our scene is made of closed polyhedra then creating the SPs for each polygon separately is very wasteful since at every non-silhouette edge we will have two SPs, one front facing and one back facing which will cancel each other out. It is much more efficient if we first compute the silhouette of the objects as seen from the light source and use the edges of that instead. In any case the generation of the shadow planes can be a time-consuming process when the scene is of some complexity. An interesting alternative method for computing shadow planes was suggested by McCool (2000). The scene is drawn first from the light position and the z-buffer read. The shadow volumes are then reconstructed based on the edges of the discretized shadow map. The discretization can introduce artifacts, though.

One of the drawbacks of the shadow volume method is that the shadow planes tend to be very large (in fact they are semi-infinite) and they have a detrimental effect on the rendering time. In practice, we can limit this effect by using the method not for a complete solution but rather for shadows only from the "important" objects. We do that by creating and adding only their shadow volumes to the scene for shadow computation. Like the shadow z-buffer we can use this method to cast shadows onto any object that can be scan-converted. But unlike the shadow z-buffer, the objects causing the shadows need to be polygonal. Multiple light sources can be handled by creating separate shadow volumes and keeping a separate counter for each source.

Shadow volume BSP trees

Given a shadow volume for each polygon in the scene, we can compute the shadows directly in object space and store them in the database rather than storing the shadow planes as above. The shadow between two polygons, an occluder (*O*) and a receiver (*R*), can be found by clipping *R* against the shadow volume of *O*. Any part of *R* falling within the volume is in shadow. This shadow can be represented either as a detail polygon on top of *R* or by splitting *R* using the shadow edges, into lit and shadowed pieces.

The brute force method for performing the calculations in object space would be to compare each of, say, the *n* polygons facing the light against the shadow volume of each other such polygon. This, however, is wasteful. An improvement to this n^2 algorithm can be achieved by observing that only a polygon closer to the light source can cast a shadow on one further away. The polygons can be sorted by building a scene BSP tree and traversing it in a *front-to-back* manner from the light position. The polygons can then be processed in this order and each one only needs to be compared against the SV of those before it. This method can reduce the number of comparisons involved, if the number of splits produced by the BSP tree is not too large, but much better performance can be achieved by using space subdivision, as we will see soon.

In Chapter 11 we saw the BSP tree as a data structure for ordering polygons. However, a much more useful interpretation of the BSP tree is as a hierarchical decomposition of space into subspaces or regions. The plane of each node does

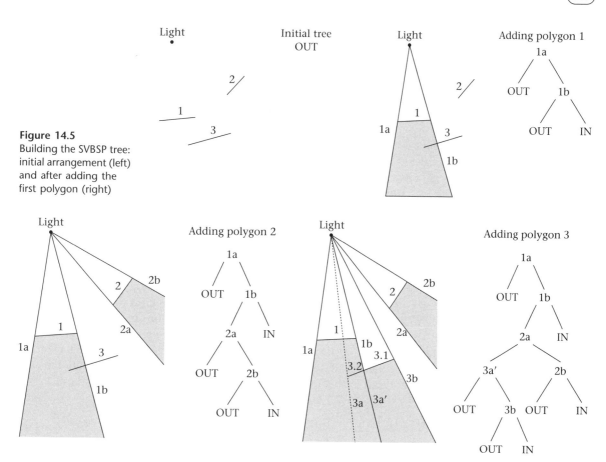

Figure 14.5
Building the SVBSP tree: initial arrangement (left) and after adding the first polygon (right)

Figure 14.6
Building the SVBSP tree: polygon 2 reaches an *OUT* cell and augments the tree (left). Polygon 3 is split, with 3.2 reaching an *IN* region

not just split polygons into two subsets, *front* and *back* (and possibly *on*), but also at the same time it splits space into two subspaces, *positive* and *negative*. Each child then recursively splits the corresponding subspace further (Thibault and Naylor, 1987). At the root of the tree we have the whole of R^3 (or R^2 or indeed any space in which our scene is defined, since BSP trees work the same way in any dimension), while at the leaves are the individual convex regions. In the case of the shadow volume we can label these regions as IN or OUT depending on whether they correspond to a lit or shadowed volume of space. See the example in Figure 14.3(b).

Chin and Feiner (1989) extended this idea to build a unified shadow volume of all the polygons which face the light source, the Shadow Volume BSP tree. We will explain the method by using the example in Figures 14.5 and 14.6.

Given a set of polygons *S* and a light source *L* we proceed as follows. First we build a BSP tree and traverse it from the point of view of the light source to get a front-to-back ordering of the polygons. Then we take each one of these polygons in order and add them to the SVBSP tree. The polygon insertion is done using a similar proceedure to that used for the incremental building of the BSP tree in Chapter 11. The polygon is compared against the plane at the root of each subtree to decide whether to insert it at the front or the back or split it and send each piece to the corresponding subtree. The difference here is when a leaf node is reached.

If the leaf node is marked as *OUT* then the tree is not enlarged by adding the polygon's plane but it is enlarged with the shadow planes defined by the edges of that fragment. The polygon itself is classified as "lit." We can see this in Figure 14.5. Initially the SVBSP tree is just an *OUT* node (left). Polygon 1 is inserted in the OUT node and hence its shadow volume is used to replace that node. The same happens for polygon 2 in Figure 14.6 (left). As we insert it from the top of the tree it is behind SP 1a, thus sent down the back subtree; there it is found to be in front of SP 1b and ends up at the OUT node which it replaces with its shadow volume.

Any fragment reaching an *IN* node is classified as shadowed but does not change the tree. Polygon 3 in Figure 14.6 (right) is split as it inserted into the tree and one of the fragments (3.2) ends up at an *IN* node.

The polygons themselves do not need to be included into the tree since the order of processing ensures that they will always be behind those already in the tree. An alternative way is to process the scene polygons in any order. This has the benefit of not requiring a BSP tree for the ordering and thus avoiding the increase in the number of scene polygons. In such a case the polygons have to be included in the SVBSP tree along with each shadow volume. If a z-buffer is used for rendering then this method often works much faster (Chrysanthou, 1996).

Program 14.1 Building a SVBSP tree

```
buildSVBSP(Tree bsp, Light light)
{
  /* the svbsp tree is initially set to null */
  svbsp = OUT;

  /* the BSP gives the back-to-front order */
  order[] = traverseBSP(bsp, light);

  /* each polygon is inserted in order */
  for(i = 0; i<=n;++i){
    svbsp = insert(svbsp, order[i], light);
  }

  /* tree is not needed any more, discard */
  free(svbsp);
}

SVBSP insert(SVBSP svbsp, Poly poly, Light L)
{
  if (leaf(svbsp)){ /* svbsp is a cell */
    if (svbsp == IN) {
        /* polygon in IN leaf, in shadow */
      add poly as a shadow polygon;
```

```
      } else
          /* polygon in OUT leaf, lit. expand tree*/
        return constructSV(poly, L);
      }
  } else
      /* find which side of the root is polygon */
      classifyPolygon(svbsp.rootplane, poly, pf, pb);
    if (notNull(pf)) {
      svbsp.front = insert(svbsp.front, pf, L);
    }
    if (notNull(pb)) {
      svbsp.back = insert(svbsp.back, pb, L);
    }
  }

  return svbsp;
}
```

The pseudocode for this process is shown in Program 14.1. In function `buildSVBSP` the SVBSP is first initialized to a single *OUT* node, then the polygons are ordered using the scene BSP tree and they are inserted into the SVBSP in that order. A polygon is inserted using the recursive function *insert*. At each call of *insert*, if the tree is a leaf, then if it has an *IN* value the polygon is marked as shadowed, if it has an OUT value the leaf is replaced by the shadow volume of the polygon. If the tree is an internal node the polygon is classified against the plane at the root of the tree and sent to the appropriate subtree. At the end of the proceedure the tree is deleted.

It is important to realize that the computations involved in this are the same needed for the construction of the original BSP tree. This too, of course, requires the splitting of polygons by planes. It follows that the shadow-generating algorithm can easily be constructed given the software tools required for the BSP tree.

There remains the question of representing the shadows in the data structure. This can be done in two ways. The first is to allow the scene polygons to be split as they are inserted into the SVBSP tree, into lit and shadowed fragments. This seems the obvious thing to do although it will result in a large increase in the number of polygons since each original scene polygon will be split into several lit pieces for each shadow that falls on it. An alternative is to keep the original polygons intact and store the shadows as detail polygons associated with each original one. In this case the scene polygons can be rendered with full lighting and the shadow polygons will cover the appropriate regions. The shadow polygons can be rendered either as opaque with only ambient illumination or as transparent gray. Here the increase in the number of rendered polygons is much smaller but they cover a larger area since effectively regions in shadow are rendered twice.

Multiple light sources can be incorporated into this algorithm straightforwardly. There is one pass for each light source. The first light source is treated as above. After this has been processed, the position of the second light source is used to traverse the original BSP tree, to obtain the list of polygons in back-to-front order from the point of view of this light source. These polygons are treated exactly as in the case of the first light source. The only additional requirement now is that when each target polygon is encountered, the shadows inscribed on it (i.e., the list of detail shadow polygons) must also be considered as targets. Since these are ordinary polygons, these too will have a list of shadows inscribed on them as computed during this process. Care must be taken to ensure that a shadow polygon is treated as a target only when it was produced by a different light source than the one currently being processed. Hence each polygon also stores the set of lights which have been "removed" from contributing to its color if the first method of shading is used. In the case of the original scene polygons, these sets will be empty. If the second method is used, then each polygon stores the set of lights which do contribute to it.

What is required is that during the rendering process, shadow polygons associated with a scene polygon are displayed in the order necessary to achieve the correct shadow effect. First, the original scene polygon must be displayed. Next, all of the first-level shadow polygons must be displayed. First-level shadow polygons are those produced directly from intersecting the scene polygon with the shadow volumes from the different light sources. Next, all of the second-level shadow polygons must be displayed. These are those generated by intersecting the shadow volumes with the first-level polygons – and so on.

The process is illustrated in Figure 14.7. This shows three light sources throwing shadows onto a polygon labeled 0. The shadows are labeled 1, 2, and 3 in an obvious way. It is assumed that the lights are processed in order 1, 2, and 3. First, light source L1 is processed, producing shadow 1. Next, L2 is processed, producing shadow 2 and 1∩2. Finally, L3 is processed, producing shadows 3, 1∩3, 2∩3, and 1∩2∩3. When polygon 0 is displayed, it is displayed in the order of levels shown in Figure 14.7, i.e., 0, 1, 2, 3, 1∩2, 1∩3, 2∩3, 1∩2∩3.

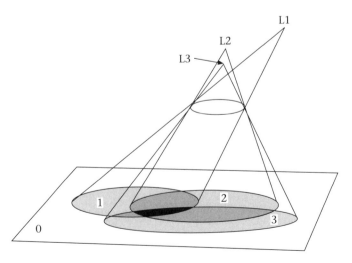

Figure 14.7
Shadows for multiple light sources

A detailed analysis of the SVBSP tree and a comparison with other methods is given in (Slater, 1992a).

The tree is only used for creating the shadows and then it can be discarded. As long as the scene remains static the shadows can be used from frame to frame without any recomputation. Chrysanthou and Slater (1995) retained the tree and showed how it can be efficiently updated in cases where small changes in the scene occur.

Fake shadows

This is probably the easiest and fastest way of creating the impression of shadows in the scene, though it is not complete or always accurate. This method was first described by Blinn (1988). The shadows are just the projections of the original polygons onto the ground plane. Here for ground we will assume the plane $z = 0$ but it can be generalized to work for any plane. The attraction of this method is that it can be done using the same graphics pipeline that we normally use for rendering. After displaying the scene without shadows, we just apply an additional transformation matrix which causes the environment to "flatten" down to the ground and re-render everyting, letting the z-buffer deal with the composition of the final image.

Given a directional light source which emits light parallel to a direction L (x_l, y_l, z_l) and a point p (x_p, y_p, z_p) in the scene then we can find g, the shadow of p on the ground, by projecting it along the direction of light. The projection will be of the form $(x_g, y_g, 0)$. We need to define a matrix S such that $p \cdot S = g$.

g lies on the equation defined by point p and the light direction:

$$g = p + t \cdot L$$

But we know that $z_g = 0$ so we can find t:

$$0 = z_p + t \cdot z_l$$
$$t = -z_p/z_l$$

And so find

$$x_g = x_p - (z_p/z_l)x_l$$
$$x_g = y_p - (z_p/z_l)y_l$$

which can be done using the following transformation matrix:

$$\begin{bmatrix} 1 & 0 & 0 & 0 \\ 0 & 1 & 0 & 0 \\ -x_l/z_l & -y_l/z_l & 0 & 0 \\ 0 & 0 & 0 & 1 \end{bmatrix}$$

Along the same lines we can also compute a matrix for projecting shadows for a point light source, rather than a directional one (Figure 14.8).

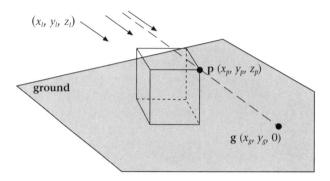

Figure 14.8
Projecting the vertices
onto the ground plane

There are no inter-object shadows in this method and extra clipping against the edge of the ground plane will need to be done if we want to avoid shadow polygons running over the edge. In a case where we have geometry below the ground plane, a naive implementation will also cast shadows from these upwards.

We need to render the whole model for each surface onto which we want to have shadows. If that is only one ground plane then it can be fairly fast but if we want something more complex then it becomes impractical. Of course, if we know which objects in our model will be visually important then we might decide just to project those for shadow creation, hence accelerating this method considerably.

14.3   Shadow penumbras

Shadows from point sources provide a lot of information about the spatial relations of the objects in the scene. In the real world most of the light sources have a non-zero area.

To add to the realism of the images the effect of such sources should be modeled. Shadows due to area sources have soft edges, they are no longer defined by a singular sharp boundary (umbra), but also have partially lit areas (penumbra). A more precise definition of umbra and penumbra is given later in this section.

The algorithms for finding shadows from area light sources can be classified into two broad categories:

Analytical determination: methods in this category analytically compute the boundaries of the shadows and other discontinuities within the penumbra. Some also compute the visible part of the source before performing the illumination. With the exception of Amanatides (1984), who computes shadows from circular or spherical sources, the other methods in this category are restricted to models made entirely of planar polygons, including the source. The calculations are done in object space.

Sampling: these are approximate solutions. Often the source is treated as a collection of point sources whose contribution is combined. The visible part of the source can then be taken as a proportion of point sources visible from the given position. Point sampling techniques can be computationally expensive, especially if an accurate solution is required, but they tend be more general than the analytical determination. It is possible to implement sampling techniques using modern graphics hardware, thus making them more practical. We will also include in this category convolution methods since although they do not exactly point sample the source, they still offer an approximate solution. These tend to be more accurate and faster than the point sampling methods.

We will start by looking at the analytical methods. We will go through the principles and describe in some detail methods such as discontinuity meshing. Finally we will briefly look at some of the sampling methods.

Analytical determination

In these methods the shadows and other discontinuities of the illumination function on the scene surfaces are computed by forming the "shadow planes" explicitly and tracing them into the scene. We will see a more appropriate name than "shadow planes" soon. We will see later that if we want to compute the complete solution accurately, the contribution of successive occluders should be combined and then some of these "planes" are actually quadratic surfaces, but let us start from the simpler cases. We will start from the umbra and penumbra boundaries caused by a single occluder.

Extremal shadow boundaries

Shadows from area light sources consist of a totally blocked area, the umbra, and a partially blocked area, the penumbra. The boundaries between lit and penumbra and between penumbra and umbra areas are called the extremal boundaries of the shadow.

The first to compute the exact extremal boundaries were Nishita and Naka-mae (1983). They described how to build the penumbra and umbra volumes formed by the *extremal planes* (Figure 14.9). Assuming that all shadow planes face outwards, away from the shadow volume, then these extremal planes are:

For penumbra: planes defined by a pair of (source vertex, occluder edge) or (source edge, occluder vertex) which have the source totally in the front half-space and the occluder on the back half-space (Figure 14.9).

For umbra: planes defined by a vertex of the source and an edge of the occluder which have both the source and the occluder in their back half-space (Figure 14.9).

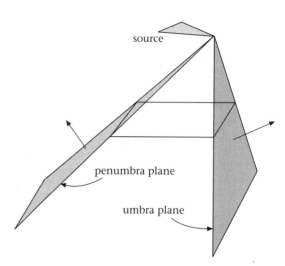

source

penumbra plane

umbra plane

Figure 14.9
Extremal shadow planes

The umbra shadow volume, then, is the intersection of the back (negative) half-spaces of the umbra planes and the back half-space of the polygon. Similarly, the penumbra shadow volume is the intersection of the back half-spaces of the penumbra planes and the back half-space of the polygon.

In their method, the shadow boundaries, umbra and penumbra, on the scene polygons are computed in object space. This is done by comparing each receiver polygon against the penumbra shadow volume of every other polygon; if there is an intersection then the receiver is also compared against the umbra volume of that polygon. It should be clear that where we say "every other polygon" we only refer to the polygons that face, at least partly, the light source and which lie, at least partly, in front of it (we will call these *light-facing* polygons). Any polygon that is behind or has the source behind it is irrelevant to any shadow algorithm.

Once the boundaries are found they are transformed to image space where they are used in the illumination of the polygons during rendering. While the image is scan-converted to the screen the intensity is calculated whenever a shadow boundary is met and at regular intervals along the rest of the scan-line. The intensity of the unoccluded points is computed using (EQ 14.1) on the next page. For points in the umbra this value is zero and only an ambient intensity is used. For points in the penumbra (EQ 14.1) is used on the visible parts of the source, from the point.

To find the visible parts of a source from a penumbra point p, first the set of occluders (O) of that point are found. Then for each polygon in O a pyramid using the polygon edges and with apex at p is constructed. This is very similar to the point shadow volume described earlier in this chapter, but with p as source. The source is compared against this pyramid and only the parts of it falling outside are visible. These visible parts are then compared against the pyramids of the rest of the polygons in O.

The shadow boundaries and illumination intensities are not explicitly stored in object space so whenever the viewpoint changes the whole process has to be repeated. Also, the shadow boundary determination is an $O(n^2)$ process, where n is the number of light-facing scene polygons.

Campbell and Fussell (1991) presented a more efficient algorithm that performs all the calculations in object space. The penumbra and umbra shadow volumes of all light-facing polygons are built as BSP trees and then put together to form two SVBSP trees, one for the penumbra and one for the umbra. The SVBSP trees are constructed by the shadow volumes using the BSP tree merging algorithm described in Naylor *et al.* (1990). Then each of the light-facing polygons is inserted into the penumbra tree to determine the shadow boundaries. If it is found to lie even partly in an *IN* cell of the penumbra SVBSP then it is also tested against the umbra tree. In the point source SVBSP method (Chin and Feiner, 1989), the classification of the polygons can be done while inserting the polygons at the construction of the tree. Here the algorithm uses the two-pass process, first constructing the SVBSPs and then inserting the polygons in them. This was necessary because, unlike the point source case, it is not so easy to find an ordering of the polygons with respect to the light source.

Chin and Feiner (1992) dealt with the problem of ordering from an area by splitting the source whenever it is found to straddle the plane of a scene polygon. The scene BSP tree can then be unambiguously traversed from each resulting source fragment to give the front-to-back ordering. Two SVBSP trees are constructed for each source fragment and the shadows are calculated during the construction in a manner similar to the point SVBSP tree.

These two methods don't have an easy way of knowing exactly which polygons are blocking the source at the penumbra vertices, which is needed for computing the illumination. Campbell and Fussell build the convex hull for each receiver and the source and clip all the scene polygons against it. The penumbra vertices on the receiver need only to test the source against the remaining polygons. Chin and Feiner use the BSP tree to find the set of polygons (O) that lie between the source and a receiver. For each penumbra vertex v_i on this receiver a point SVBSP tree is built using the polygons in O and v_i as the apex. Then the source is inserted into this tree and the visible parts are those reaching the *OUT* cells.

The visible parts of the light source as seen from a penumbra vertex are calculated as convex polygons which can be used as separate sources with their sum giving the total illumination at that vertex.

The illumination I_p from a convex polygonal source with n vertices at point p is approximated by the following equation, as described in Nishita and Nakamae (1983):

$$I_p = \frac{I_s}{2} \sum_{v=1}^{n} \theta_v \cos(\phi_v)$$ (EQ 14.1)

where

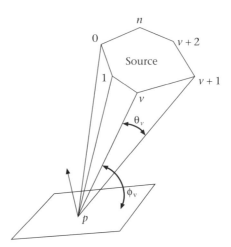

Figure 14.10
Illumination calculation
from an area light source

I_s = intensity of the light source

θ_v = the angle formed by source vertex v, p, and source vertex $v + 1$, Figure 14.10

ϕ_v = the angle between the plane on which p lies and the triangle v, p, $v + 1$, Figure 14.10

In all methods mentioned above, only the umbra and penumbra boundaries are determined explicitly, but in fact the illumination function has local maxima, minima, and discontinuities within the penumbra regions (Heckbert, 1991; Campbell and Fussell, 1991).

Aspect graphs

More insight into the problem of the variation within the penumbra can be gained through the aspect graph approach used for object recognition in computer vision. In this approach the 3D objects in the scene are represented by a set of 2D views and the viewpoint space is partitioned into regions such that in each region the qualitative structure of the line drawing does not change. The qualitative measure of the structure of each image is called the *aspect* (Gigus *et al.*, 1991). By considering only views from the light source, that is, finding the regions of space in which the visible part of the source is qualitatively constant, this becomes the same as the problem we are trying to solve.

In the aspect graph theory, the surfaces that bound these homogeneous regions are called *critical surfaces*, which when crossed produce *visual events*. The critical surfaces are defined by the interaction of edges and vertices in the scene and, as described by Gigus in Gigus and Malik (1990) and Gigus *et al.* (1991), they can be grouped into two classes:

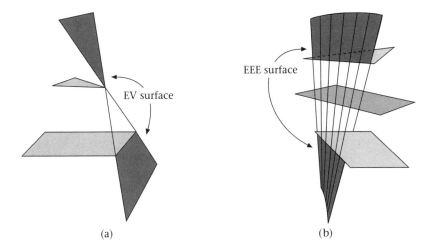

Figure 14.11
(a) An EV surface defined by an edge and a vertex, (b) an EEE surface defined by three non-adjacent edges

(a)   (b)

- *EV surfaces*: the planes defined by an edge and a vertex, Figure 14.11(a).
- *EEE surfaces*: the quadratic surfaces defined by three non-adjacent edges, Figure 14.11(b).

For the shadow computation problem most of these surfaces are irrelevant. We are only interested in EV and EEE surfaces that contain a source feature (edge or vertex) and in EV and EEE surfaces that cut the source polygon (Drettakis, 1994). The intersection of these surfaces with the scene polygons generates critical curves which correspond to discontinuities in the illumination function. These critical curves are also called discontinuity curves (or edges for the EV events).

The penumbra volumes, as defined earlier, are made entirely of EV surfaces involving a feature of the source while the umbra volumes might consist of EV and EEE surfaces. All the discontinuities are enclosed by the penumbra.

Discontinuity meshing

A function f is said to be continuous (C^0) over an interval (t_1, t_2) if and only if

$$\forall a \in (t_1, t_2), \lim_{x \to a-\varepsilon} f(x) = \lim_{x \to a+\varepsilon} f(x) = f(a), \text{ as } \varepsilon \to 0 \qquad \text{(EQ 14.2)}$$

A function that fails this criterion is said to have a zero degree (D^0) discontinuity. A function whose k^{th} derivative satisfies (EQ 14.2) is said to be C^k continuous. A function that is C^{k-1} but not C^k is D^k.

Discontinuities in the illumination function of a polygon are caused at its intersection with the critical surfaces. As said before, the only relevant critical events are those caused by EV or EEE surfaces involving a source edge or vertex, which are called *emitter events*, and those caused by EV or EEE surfaces not involving a source feature but intersecting the source with their surface, which are called *non-emitter events*.

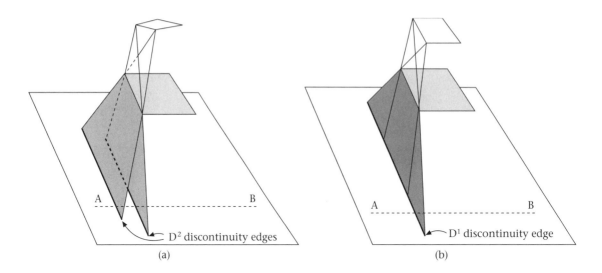

(a) (b)

Figure 14.12
(a) Discontinuities of the second degree (D^2) and (b) D^1 discontinuity

As described by Heckbert (1991), critical surfaces due to point, linear, area light sources cause in general D^0, D^1, D^2, respectively but when two discontinuities coincide the degree of discontinuity can decrease.

As we are dealing with area sources, discontinuities from both EV and EEE surfaces will in general be of the second degree. For example, in Figure 14.12(a) as we move along line AB on the polygon, the illumination function has D^2 discontinuities at the points where it crosses the marked edges.

In cases where an edge of the source and an edge of the occluder are parallel then two EV surfaces have a combined effect and produce D^1 edges. In Figure 14.12(b) as we move along line AB on the polygon, the illumination function has a D^1 discontinuity at the point where it crosses the marked edge.

D^0 edges can also be generated. These occur along touching surfaces and they can cause some of the most severe artifacts if they are not represented explicitly. They are usually found by using a separate pass through the database before doing any further subdivision (Baum *et al.*, 1991) (see Figure 14.13).

Higher-order discontinuities can be generated when the radiance of the source is non-uniform. This can be the case with secondary sources in radiosity (see the next chapter). In general a D^k on the source can cause D^{k+1} and D^{k+2} on the receiver (Heckbert, 1991). Higher-order discontinuities are less noticeable and anything above D^2 is not usually considered.

The first study on discontinuity meshing was presented by Heckbert (1992a) for a 2D domain. A complete mesh was constructed by considering every possible interaction between the edges and vertices in the scene, an operation with N^3 cost for N vertices. He later extended his work to a 3D environment (Heckbert, 1992b) by using a similar algorithm which traces every EV surface; EEE surfaces were ignored. At the same time a different 3D algorithm was proposed by Lishinski *et al.* (1992). They also considered only the EV discontinuities but used a more "progressive" approach for locating them. A separate computation

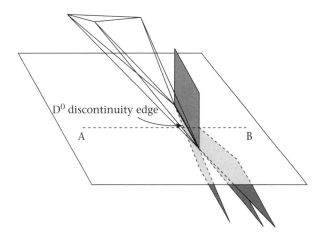

Figure 14.13
A D^0 discontinuity

is made for each emitting polygon. The highest-energy polygon is selected to be the source at each pass, the discontinuities on the other polygons caused from this are found and the intensities are calculated. At the end, the resulting meshes are merged in order to produce the final subdivision. This approach was adopted in later DM research.

EEE surfaces were partly treated by Teller (1992), in a related computation where the visible region of a source through a sequence of portals is calculated. This method finds what would be the extremal umbra boundary in our problem, but the algorithm is based on a 5D Plucker coordinate representation that does not generalize so easily to a complete DM solution, and is computationally expensive.

Algorithms that include all EV and EEE events, even non-emitter ones, were later presented by Drettakis and Fiume (1994) and Stewart and Ghali (1994). Most often EEE and non-emitter EV surfaces are ignored since the error produced by their exclusion is small compared to their cost.

Following Lishinski's progressive algorithm, discontinuity meshing can be broken down into four main operations:

(1) The discontinuity curves are found by tracing the critical surfaces of the emitter through the environment.

(2) These curves are used to construct the mesh, on each of the scene polygons/patches, due to the particular emitter.

(3) The illumination intensities at the vertices of the mesh and other selected points are calculated. Calculating the intensities requires the determination of the visible part of the source from each point.

These three steps are repeated for each of the major emitters and then finally:

(4) The meshes created on each surface are merged together to form the final subdivisions.

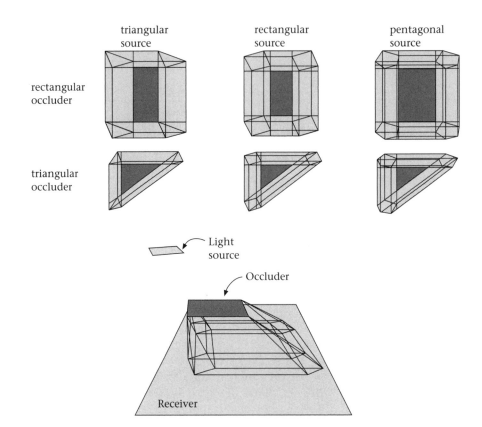

triangular source   rectangular source   pentagonal source

rectangular occluder

triangular occluder

Light source

Occluder

Receiver

Figure 14.14
Shadows and discontinuities for pairs of different geometry

Figure 14.15
The arrangement of source/receiver for the previous image

This last step is important only for multiple light sources (such as for a radiosity solution) so it will not be described here. In most algorithms, the tasks of locating the discontinuities and constructing the mesh are interleaved but we will discuss them separately here.

In Figure 14.14 we see example shadows and discontinuities cast onto a receiver from pairs of different source/receiver geometries. For the rectangular-source/rectangular-occluder case we can see the arrangement in Figure 14.15. In Figure 14.14, the black region is the umbra while the gray is the penumbra. All the edges are D^2 discontinuities, which follows from our discussion above since the occluder does not touch the receiver to create D^0 and none of source edges are parallel to the occluder edges to create D^1.

Locating the discontinuities

Most DM algorithms locate the D^0 edges and the D^1 and D^2 edges using separate methods. The D^0, which lie at the contact between surfaces, are computed first by considering only object proximity. This involves visiting each object and comparing it against the adjacent ones. The efficiency of this operation

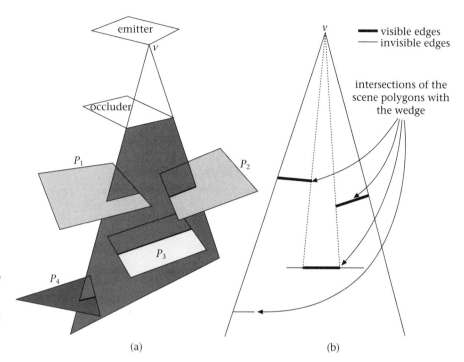

Figure 14.16
(a) Intersecting the wedge with the scene polygons, and (b) intersections are transformed to the wedge space to determine visibility

depends on the efficiency of the method used for determining proximity. Tampieri (1993) uses a hierarchy of bounding volumes while Drettakis and Fiume (1994) use a voxel-based subdivision structure.

To find the rest of the discontinuities, which are EV emitter edges if we ignore EEE or non-emitter EV, the most common method is to form the semi-infinite *wedges* using a vertex of the source and an edge of an occluder or an edge of the source and a vertex of an occluder and find their intersection with the scene polygons. For the rest of this discussion we will differentiate between the wedges caused by a source vertex and those formed by a source edge by calling the former VE and the latter EV wedges. A VE wedge with its intersections in the environment can be seen in Figure 14.16(a).

These algorithms process each EV wedge separately to find its intersections with the environment, but differ mainly by whether they sort the scene polygons and compare it against them in that order or not. In the latter group we have Heckbert and Drettakis. Heckbert compares each scene polygon against each wedge, requiring excessive computations. Drettakis greatly reduces the number of comparisons by using a voxel-based subdivision which limits the candidate polygons to only those sharing voxels with a wedge.

One problem with processing the polygons in an unsorted manner is that it is not possible to tell immediately if the intersection of a polygon with a wedge is a discontinuity (critical edge). Only the intersection edges that are visible from the apex of the wedge form discontinuity edges and should be added to the mesh. For example, the intersection of polygon P_4 in Figure 14.16(a)

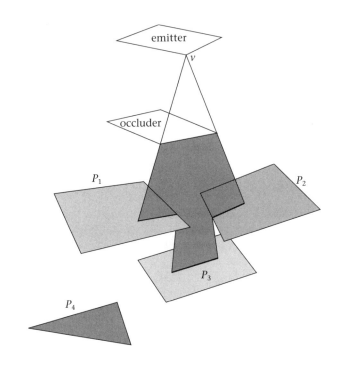

Figure 14.17
Clipping the wedge
when compared against
ordered polygons

cannot be seen by v, because it is blocked by polygons closer to v, and hence should not be added to the mesh.

To find the critical edges from each wedge all the intersections are transformed into the wedge plane and put into a sorted list. A 2D visibility test, a variant of the Weiler–Atherton visible surface algorithm (Atherton *et al.*, 1978; Weiler and Atherton, 1977) is performed from the point of view of the wedge apex and the critical edges are found. In Figure 14.16(b) only the thick edges correspond to discontinuities.

Alternatively, the scene polygons can be built into a BSP tree which will provide the order from the apex of each wedge, eliminating the need for the 2D visibility test (Lischinski *et al.*, 1992). As the polygons are compared against the wedge in front-to-back order, the intersections are found and at the same time the wedge is clipped against the intersected polygons so that only the unobstructed parts of it are traced further. The tracing can stop as soon as the wedge is completely clipped, avoiding unnecessary polygon/wedge comparisons. This can be seen in Figure 14.17: intersections that do not form discontinuity edges are not found and the tracing of the wedge stops at polygon P_3.

In Chrysanthou (1996) an alternative approach is given. The set of EV wedges corresponding to one occluder are treated as one entity (a shadow volume) and they are traced together in the scene. The shadow volume is compared against a candidate list of receiver polygons which is found using a tiling cube based method. The D^0 are found in the same pass.

Constructing the mesh on the faces

Once the discontinuity edges on each polygon are found they are combined to form the mesh on the polygons. A common data structure is used for representing the mesh, which is the *discontinuity meshing tree* (DM-tree). One such tree is used per scene polygon.

The DM-tree consists of two parts: a 2D BSP tree and a Winged Edge data structure (WEDS) (Baumgart, 1974, 1975). The WEDS is an edge-based structure suitable for maintaining the consistency and accelerating access to the adjacency information, as we saw earlier (see "The Winged Edge data structure" on page 170). It has three basic elements: a vertex, an edge, and a face structure. Most of the topological information is held on the edge structure. This has pointers to the two faces lying on either side, to the two vertices on its endpoints, and to four other edges sharing these vertices. Each vertex structure holds a 3D point as well as a reference to an edge of which it is an end-point and each face structure holds a pointer to one of the edges that define its boundary.

The WEDS is central to the DM-tree because it allows for the intensity of each vertex to be calculated only once and shared between the incident faces. Also, it ensures that no T-vertices are introduced as the faces are split.

The 2D BSP tree is an augmented version of the structure described in Chapter 11. As before, each internal node holds a sub-hyperplane (edge) and it is defined by its hyperplane (line). Each node corresponds to a region of space which is partitioned by the node hyperplane with the leaf nodes corresponding to unpartitioned regions (cells or mesh faces). At the leaf nodes, however, in this case we store an explicit representation of the region of 2D space that corresponds to the leaf by keeping a pointer to the mesh face.

Initially the DM-tree is a single leaf node holding one face (the whole polygon), as in Figure 14.18(a). When a discontinuity edge is added, splitting the polygon, the tree is updated to store the edge at the root and the two new faces at its leaves. If the edge does not span the face completely then it is augmented by adding another segment, called a *construction* edge, to keep the subdivision convex (Figure 14.18(b)). As more discontinuity edges are added they are filtered down the DM-tree, possibly being subdivided on the way, until they reach the leaves where they subdivide the faces held there.

One of the potential problems of this method for building the mesh is that it relies on machine precision to connect the discontinuity edges at the right point. Take, for example, edges e_1 and e_2 in Figure 14.18. These two edges were caused by wedges formed by consecutive edges of the occluder (or consecutive vertices) and that is why they share a common end-point (v). As each wedge is traced independently and the discontinuities are inserted into the structure one by one, they will only correctly connect at v if no precision errors occur in the calculations. This is a common problem, occuring in many applications, and it is usually tackled by using a tolerance value that gives thickness to the lines. Of course, this creates other problems if we have very small or closely placed edges.

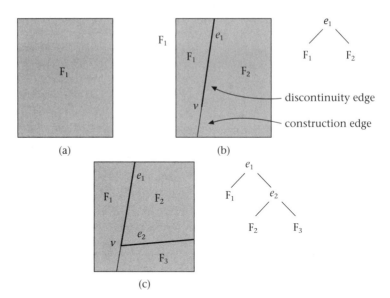

Figure 14.18
Building the DM-tree

The work of Drettakis (1994) goes some way towards limiting this problem. The EV wedges are created and traced in the order of the occluder's edges and each new discontinuity edge on the same receiver is connected to the end of the previous one. This is made possible because of the use of an extended WEDS to accommodate temporarily dangling edges without the use a 2D BSP. Yet this can only correctly connect half the edges, and the *ve* events still rely on machine precision. The algorithm presented in Chrysanthou (1996) connects all EV discontinuities cast from an individual occluder onto the the plane of the receiver and forms a *single* DM-tree. This tree is then merged into the *total* DM-tree of the receiver; in this way such errors are minimized further.

Using a BSP tree for storing the discontinuities (the DM-tree) is not without its problems. It can generate mesh elements with bas aspect ratios and also the discontinuities inserted earlier in the tree can have undue influence on the rest of the mesh. Heckbert (1992b) used constrained Delauney triangulation while Drettakis (1994) suggests the use of a regular grid as the underlying mesh onto which the discontinuities are to be inserted.

Illuminating the mesh vertices

Each vertex in the mesh created above (as well as any generated by further mesh refinement, like triangulation) must be illuminated. The illumination calculation of the mesh is usually the most costly part of DM. This is because for each vertex the visible parts of the source must be found before applying (EQ 14.1) on them. The usual method for finding the visible parts of a source

(S) as seen from a vertex (v) is to project the occluders of v onto the source plane and then use them to clip away any hidden parts of the source. Of course, only vertices in penumbra need to do this source/occluder comparison but most of the DM-methods do not provide immediate information on which vertices are in the penumbra or which polygons are causing the penumbra if the vertex is found to be in one.

Using every polygon in the scene as a potential occluder would be extremely inefficient. Lischinski *et al.* (1992) limit the number of potential occluders by using a shaft culling technique (Haines and Wallace, 1991). For each vertex v in the mesh a pyramid is constructed using v as apex and the source as its base. The scene polygons are compared against this and only those that intersect the pyramid's interior are projected onto the source plane for clipping the source.

Gatenby (1995) uses spatial coherence to provide a much smaller set of potential occluders for each vertex. It relies on the fact that if an occluder O does not obstruct any part of a given receiver R from the source then no vertex on R can be in the penumbra of O and hence O is excluded from the potential occluder set of the vertex. Before illuminating the vertices in the mesh of a receiver polygon R, a two-step "pre-processing" is performed involving the whole of R, to find only the polygons that affect at least a part of it. First the BSP tree is traversed, front-to-back, from each of the source vertices until R is found. The sets of polygons encountered by the traversals are put together to form one set L_0'. The receiver is then compared against the penumbra shadow volume of each polygon in L_0'. When R is found to intersect the penumbra of a polygon in L_0', this polygon is added to another list L_0. The potential occluders of vertices in the mesh of R is the set L_0. Those receivers totally in umbra or unoccluded are therefore treated particularly fast.

In the algorithm described by Chrysanthou (1996) the IDs of the occluders for each region are inserted into the mesh elements during the construction of the mesh so no searching is required at illumination time. This is possible because the discontinuities from each occluder are merged all together with the tree of the receiver, thus allowing the classification of the different regions from the start.

An altogether different way of calculating the visible parts of the light source, based on the aspect graphs, was suggested by Drettakis and Fiume (1994) and Stewart and Ghali (1994). They use a data structure called the *backprojection* which stores the exact structure of the visible part of the source. This is computed once for each point on a surface and then it can be updated incrementally each time a discontinuity edge is crossed to get to a neighboring cell. It is fast compared to the alternatives but it has the disadvantage of requiring a full mesh to be constructed, one that includes non-emitter EV and EEE edges.

In Figure 14.19 (color plate) we can see on the left an example image generated with Drettakis' backprojection method and the underlying discontinuities on the right.

Figure 14.20
Complexity of discontinuity meshing. On the left the input scene of 5,742 polygons, on the right a close-up of the floor underneath one of the tables showing some of the 500,000 discontinuity lines
Courtesy of David Hedley, PhD thesis, *Discontinuity Meshing for Complex Environments*, Department of Computer Science, University of Bristol, 1998

Discontinuity meshing in practice

Discontinuity meshing methods can produce highly accurate solutions. However, they generally suffer from scalability and robustness problems. This is mainly due to the excessive number of edges in the resulting discontinuity meshes on the surfaces. In complex scenes a large number of discontinuities contribute little to the final image. This is especially true when the scene is lit by more than one light source since illumination of one source might wash out discontinuities from another. This can be nicely demonstrated in Figure 14.20. The input scene consists of 5742 polygons but there are almost 500,000 discontinuity lines generated with over 4 million triangular elements in the mesh. Admittedly this is an extreme example because the illumination comes from 24 strip-lights on the ceiling and because of the arrangement of the geometry. However, it clearly shows that we need to be selective.

There have been a number of suggestions in the literature on how to cull discontinuities with little visual effect. Tampieri (1993) takes some samples on each edge and if its strength, in terms of a radiometric measure, is below a threshold then it is not included. Hardt and Teller (1996) also use a radiometric measure. Hedley (1998) on the other hand suggests methods based on a visual perception measure which seem to be more successful than the others.

Computing a DM solution can be quite time consuming: it can take minutes, even hours. It can be done as a pre-processing task and then used in a walk-through application. However, for dynamic environments where a small part of the geometry changes, when interacting with a small object for example, it will be wasteful to recompute the solution anew.

Some of the methods mentioned in the previous sections have been extended to allow for dynamic modifications. Worrall and colleagues (Worrall, *et al.*, 1995; Worrall, *et al.*, 1998) build a triangulated discontinuity meshing and then *relocate* the discontinuity edges from one surface to another when the casting object moves. They suggest a number of techniques for reducing the polygons considered during the process. They use ray casting on the new mesh vertices for computing the illumination, which might be expensive. Chrysanthou and Slater (1997) take advantage of a modified hemicube to quickly identify the relevant objects that might be affected in an animation (see Chapter 15). They also use the BSP tree merging to find exactly what the occluders are for each new mesh vertex. Although the method seems promising, it was only tested on scenes of less than 200 polygons and thus it is difficult to assess. Finally, Loscos and Drettakis (1997) extended Drettakis' (1994) method. They use space coherency to localize changes in events when an object moves. A motion volume is used to select voxels of a 3D grid in which information had been pre-stored. The update algorithm uses an extension of Worral to find visibility modification and update the intersections between discontinuity surfaces and objects. An analysis of intersections between EV discontinuity meshes was used to detect when EEE surfaces should be created, maintained and destroyed. However, they still have the full mesh as a requirement for computing the illumination through backprojection.

Sampling

The methods that we will see in this section might not provide accuracy to the level that we have seen above, but they are much simpler and easier to implement. Many of them make use of the specialized graphics hardware and as the latter becomes faster and more common we expect to see these methods becoming more popular as well.

Most of the point source shadow methods can be extended to simulate soft shadows by applying them repeatedly on a cluster of point sources that approximate the area source. For example, the ray tracing method can be extended naturally to do this by casting several sample shadow rays towards the light source instead of one. In distributed ray tracing these points are jittered to minimize aliasing (Cook *et al.*, 1984). The hemicube or similar methods used in radiosity could also be mentioned here but we will study those in more detail in the next chapter.

The shadow buffer method that we saw at the begining of this chapter can be extended to soft shadows using hardware-supported depth buffers (Haeberli and Akeley, 1990). The scene is rendered multiple times, using a different point on the area source, and the result is averaged using the hardware accumulation buffer. (See Section 23.6 for a description of the accumulation buffer and another application of it). This method requires many sample lights for good shadow quality but that can be accelerated by computing only a few samples and applying view interpolation to generate the in-between ones (Chen and Williams, 1993). Herf and Heckbert (1996) also use the accumulation buffer. A number of shadow images are created, one for each sample point on the source. These are then registered and averaged on the receiver and combined using the accumulation buffer. The result is then stored as a texture to be applied on the receiver.

Brotman and Badler (1984) used shadow volumes from several sample points on an area light source and then used an extended z-buffer algorithm with linked lists at each pixel to store the information needed for the multiple shadow volumes. Heidmann (1991) also used shadow volumes but with a hardware implementation. In his method the scene is rendered through the stencil buffer created from each light source.

Finally, soft shadows have also been computed using convolution on blocker images (Soler and Sillion, 1998), when smoothing or anti-aliasing the shadows from point sources (Reeves *et al.*, 1987), and through image-based techniques (Keating and Max, 1999).

(14.4) Summary

In this chapter we looked at the shadow determination problem in some detail. Throughout we have stayed within the "real-time" paradigm. Although shadow umbras and penumbras are treated in detail, there is still no inter-object reflection, and hence no global illumination. Shadows with penumbras look more "real" than shadow umbras, but they are still not realistic. In the next chapter we switch back to a global illumination solution. Just as ray tracing naturally computes shadow umbras, but cannot easily handle penumbras, so almost the opposite is true for radiosity – it naturally computes shadow penumbras, but there are difficulties in distinguishing the sharp edges of umbras. Nevertheless, many of the techniques discussed in the current chapter have a direct application to the radiosity computation, as well as wider issues in computer graphics rendering.

15 An introduction to radiosity

15.1 Introduction

In ray tracing (Chapter 6) we considered an illumination model and algorithm which adequately deals with light which is specularly reflected and transmitted throughout the scene. It is a global illumination model. For specularly transmitted light it deals with the interactions between the light sources and the objects, and between the objects themselves. It does not correctly take into account the global aspects of diffuse light transport, and uses the constant "ambient light" term instead. For many realistic scenes (for example, look around you right now) most of the light energy in the scene is from diffusely reflecting surfaces, whereas only a small proportion of the scene might have specular highlights, reflections, and refraction (transmission). This is possibly the reason why many ray traced images, although often spectacular, do not usually show everyday scenes but various objects (in particular spheres) multiply reflected on each other.

The radiosity illumination model takes account of the global aspects of diffuse reflection but does not model specular reflection. It is based on methods employed by thermal engineers to compute the exchange of radiant energy between surfaces in closed environments. The method was first introduced into computer graphics by Goral *et al.* (1984).

In this chapter we give a basic introduction to radiosity. This will also be an "integrative" chapter, for it will pull together both of the themes of this book: the real-time aspect (radiosity requires *Gouraud shading* for fast walkthrough of globally illuminated scenes), it is a global illumination method, and it can also make use of ray casting (Chapter 5) for a crucial aspect of its computation.

15.2   Form-factors: energy between two patches

The radiosity paradigm provides a global illumination model which takes into account interreflections of light in a closed diffuse environment, that is, where all light energy in the environment is accounted for by sources within the environment itself, and no light escapes from the environment. We suppose that the scene is described as a number of surfaces (for example, polygons), and that these surfaces are further subdivided into small differential areas, referred to as *patches*.

Recall (Chapter 3) that light energy may measured as "radiant power" or "flux" – which is the energy flow per unit time (measured in watts) over a real or imaginary surface. *Radiosity* is the radiant power leaving the surface per unit area (watts per unit area (w/m^2)). *Irradiance* is a similar measure, but the flux per unit area incident on a surface. Radiosity and irradiance are wavelength dependent – their values should be computed at all wavelengths, although we will advance this discussion without explicitly referring to wavelength in the remainder of this chapter.

We first consider the energy relationship between two patches, a source patch S and a receiver patch R, and for convenience reproduce a relabeled Figure 3.2 as Figure 15.1. We suppose that the radiance from source to receiver is L, and therefore from (EQ 3.10):

$$d\Phi = L \cdot dS \cdot \cos\theta_S \cdot d\omega_R \tag{EQ 15.1}$$

where Φ is the flux transmitted from S to R. Expanding out the differential solid angle, using (EQ 2.28) on page 59:

$$d\Phi = \frac{L \cdot dS \cdot \cos\theta_S \cdot dR \cdot \cos\theta_R}{r^2} \tag{EQ 15.2}$$

We now consider the total flux (Φ) from S across all directions. Using (EQ 15.2):

$$\Phi = \int_{\Omega} L(p, \omega)dS\cos\theta_S d\omega \tag{EQ 15.3}$$

where Ω is the set of all directions corresponding to the illumination hemisphere over S, with centre p. Now we assume that the environment consists

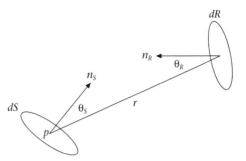

Figure 15.1
Radiant power between
two patches

only of diffusely reflecting surfaces. In this case $L(p, \omega) = L$ since radiance is the same for all directions, and we drop p for succinctness. We also make use of (EQ 2.26) on page 58, to give:

$$\Phi = LdS \int_0^{2\pi} \int_0^{\pi/2} \cos\theta \sin\theta \, d\theta \, d\phi \qquad \text{(EQ 15.4)}$$

$$= LdS\pi$$

From (EQ 15.2) and (EQ 15.4) the *proportion of flux* that leaves S which reaches R *per unit area* of R is therefore:

$$F_{dS,dR} = \frac{d\Phi}{\Phi} = \frac{\cos\theta_S \cdot \cos\theta_R}{\pi r^2} \qquad \text{(EQ 15.5)}$$

This quantity is known as the *differential form-factor* from S to R. It is the proportion of energy (measured radiant power or flux) from a source differential patch which arrives at a receiver differential patch, per unit area of receiver.

If we repeat the same argument, but this time consider the proportion of energy from the differential area dS to the patch R, we obtain:

$$F_{dS,R} = \int_R \frac{\cos\theta_S \cdot \cos\theta_R}{\pi r^2} \, dR \qquad \text{(EQ 15.6)}$$

Finally, if we now integrate over the whole of the source patch, then the proportion of energy per unit area of source that reaches the receiving patch is:

$$F_{S,R} = \frac{1}{A_S} \int_S \int_R \frac{\cos\theta_S \cdot \cos\theta_R}{\pi r^2} \, dR dS \qquad \text{(EQ 15.7)}$$

This is the *form-factor* from source patch S to receiver patch R.

In general we refer to patches i and j, with areas A_i and A_j, and corresponding angles θ_i and θ_j. Then the form-factor from i to j, the proportion of energy that leaves i and reaches j, per unit area of source and receiver is:

$$F_{ij} = \frac{1}{A_i} \cdot \int_{A_i} \int_{A_j} \frac{\cos\theta_i \cos\theta_j}{\pi r^2} \, dA_j dA_i \qquad \text{(EQ 15.8)}$$

Note that there is a symmetry relationship that follows from this:

$$A_i F_{ij} = A_j F_{ji} \qquad \text{(EQ 15.9)}$$

The form-factor plays a crucial role in the radiosity algorithm to be described below.

15.3 The radiosity equations

Since we are assuming a closed environment, the radiant power that leaves a patch must be equal to any power that is directly emitted from the patch (if it is itself a light source) plus the total reflected from the patch. This is the same argument that led to the radiance equation (EQ 3.23), except now in a specific context of an environment consisting of a number of diffusely reflecting patches ($i = 1, 2, \ldots, n$). If we denote the flux leaving the ith patch as Φ_i, then:

$$\Phi_i = \Phi_{ei} + \rho_i \sum_j \Phi_j F_{ji} \qquad \text{(EQ 15.10)}$$

where Φ_{ei} is the emitted flux from patch i, and ρ_i is the reflectivity of i (the proportion of flux received by i that is reflected). The summation accounts for all of the flux from all other patches j times the appropriate form-factors – so that only the total that actually reaches i from j is counted.

This equation is expressed in terms of flux. In order to convert this into radiosity, we recall that radiosity is flux per unit area. Hence if B_i is the radiosity for patch i, and A_i the area, then $\Phi_i = B_i A_i$, and therefore:

$$B_i A_i = E_i A_i + \rho_i \sum_j B_j A_j F_{ji} \qquad \text{(EQ 15.11)}$$

where E_i is the emitted radiosity from i.

Using (EQ 15.9) we obtain:

$$B_i A_i = E_i A_i + \rho_i \sum_j B_j A_i F_{ij} \qquad \text{(EQ 15.12)}$$

or

$$B_i = E_i + \rho_i \sum_j B_j F_{ij} \qquad \text{(EQ 15.13)}$$

The meaning of this equation (of course there is one copy of this equation for each wavelength considered) is quite straightforward. It shows that the radiosity from patch i is equal to the radiosity directly emitted from i, plus the proportion of incoming irradiance that it reflects out again. The incoming energy is the sum of the irradiance received from each other patch (j) but modified by the proportion of energy from such a patch that arrives at i (determined by the form factor).

Assuming that all terms other than the radiosities are known, we have a system of n linear equations in n unknowns, which can be expressed in matrix form as:

$$FB = E \qquad\qquad\qquad\qquad\qquad\qquad \text{(EQ 15.14)}$$

where:

$$F = \begin{bmatrix} 1 - \rho_1 F_{11} & -\rho_1 F_{12} & \cdots & -\rho_1 F_{1n} \\ -\rho_2 F_{21} & 1 - \rho_2 F_{22} & \cdots & -\rho_2 F_{2n} \\ \cdots & \cdots & \cdots & \cdots \\ -\rho_n F_{n1} & -\rho_n F_{n2} & \cdots & 1 - \rho_n F_{nn} \end{bmatrix} \qquad \text{(EQ 15.15)}$$

$$B = \begin{bmatrix} B_1 \\ B_2 \\ \cdots \\ B_n \end{bmatrix} \text{ and } E = \begin{bmatrix} E_1 \\ E_2 \\ \cdots \\ E_n \end{bmatrix} \qquad\qquad \text{(EQ 15.16)}$$

Solving this set of equations for B gives the required radiosity solution. It would be convenient if this were all there was to it, but unfortunately this isn't the whole story.

The method requires that the E and ρ terms be known. These are determined by the properties of the materials the surfaces represent, and are chosen by the scene designer (Note again that these are wavelength-dependent quantities). Much more problematic is the computation of the form-factors.

Computing the form-factors

The major component of the method requires that the form-factors F_{ij} be computed. The form-factor is a purely geometric quantity, independent of the actual illumination conditions in the scene. If an object is obscured or partially obscured by another, then a proportion of light energy that would otherwise have reached it will not do so, and this is not taken into account in (EQ 15.5) to (EQ 15.8).

In practice, the form-factors cannot be evaluated analytically, and in any case must take into account the visibility relationships between objects. In the original radiosity paper (Goral *et al.*, 1984), the integral expression (EQ 15.8) was converted into a complex contour integral using Stoke's Theorem, and then a numerical method used to integrate along the contour. This is impractical for all but the simplest scenes.

The Nusselt Analog and hemicube approximation

A later paper (Cohen and Greenberg, 1985) used a result called the *Nusselt Analog*. This shows that the form-factors can be computed by putting a hemisphere over one patch, projecting another patch onto this hemisphere, and then projecting vertically down to the circle at the base of the hemisphere. It turns out that the fraction of the circle taken up by the projection is equal to the differential area to finite area form-factor F_{dA_i, A_j}. This is illustrated in Figure 15.2.

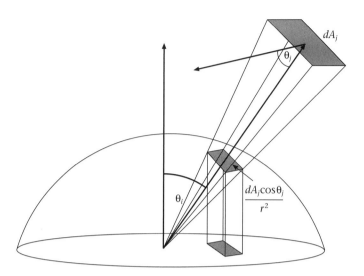

Figure 15.2
The Nusselt Analog

This result can be shown straightforwardly. Suppose the total area of the patch A_j is partitioned into many differential areas dA_j as before. Then the projection of the differential area onto the hemisphere is the solid angle subtended by dA_j:

$$\frac{dA_j \cos\theta_j}{r^2} \qquad\qquad\qquad \text{(EQ 15.17)}$$

where r is the distance to dA_j. Therefore the projection of this onto the circle occupies the projected area:

$$\left(\frac{dA_j \cos\theta_j}{r^2}\right)\cos\theta_i \qquad\qquad\qquad \text{(EQ 15.18)}$$

The proportion of the area of the circle occupied by this project is then:

$$\left(\frac{dA_j \cos\theta_j}{\pi r^2}\right)\cos\theta_i \qquad\qquad\qquad \text{(EQ 15.19)}$$

Now integrate this over the area of the patch, and the result for $F_{dA_i A_j}$ is obtained, equivalent to (EQ 15.6).

Figure 15.2 also illustrates another important point, that all patches which have the same projection onto the hemisphere have the same form-factor with respect to the differential area dA_i. On this basis a practical method for computation of form-factors was devised by Cohen and Greenberg (1985). It is assumed that patches are small enough so that the form-factors $F_{A_i A_j}$ can be approximated by $F_{dA_i A_j}$.

Figure 15.3 shows patch i with a hemicube erected above its center, and polygon j which is projected onto the hemicube of patch i, in order to determine the form-factor from j to the "differential area" i. Each polygon in the

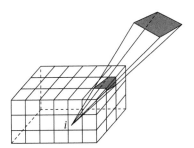

Figure 15.3
Computing form-factors
with a hemicube

environment is projected onto i in this way, and a hidden surface algorithm used to determine which polygons can be seen from i. The surface of the hemicube is tiled, and the identifiers of polygons which project onto the surface are stored in the tiles. A lookup table can be constructed which gives the result of the contributions of the surface tiles to the center of the patch. For example, it is easy to show that a patch on the top surface of the hemicube contributes:

$$\frac{1}{\pi(x^2 + y^2 + 1)^2}$$

(EQ 15.20)

These are called "delta form-factors." The final form-factor is the sum of the delta form-factors for a particular patch and hence computed as a summation of such terms as (EQ 15.20) across the set of tiles covered.

The z-buffer is suggested as a means for hidden surface elimination on the faces of the hemicube where one "pixel" corresponds to a tile on the cube. Hence each face is tiled, and the identifier of a patch is written to a tile only when the corresponding entry in an associated z-buffer will permit. Using this method all patches must be projected, and then the tiles have to be traversed to count the contributions of the delta form-factors for the various patches.

An alternative is to use BSP trees. This would work as follows:

- Form a BSP tree of the original polygons (not the patches on the polygons).
- Let the center of the hemicube base be the COP and traverse the tree from this position, but forming a list of the polygons in front-to-back order.
- For the ith polygon in this list, project each of its patches one by one onto the hemicube. Each tile need only be a Boolean value, containing *true* when this tile has been reached by any patch, but initialized to *false*. Once *true* it can never be used by any other patch.

In this method, all delta form-factors for the patch are found at the time of projection (rather than projecting all patches and then determining the form-factors as with the z-buffer).

Computing form-factors with ray casting

Now we turn full circle and apply some of the ideas of Chapter 5 to the computation of form-factors. Wallace *et al.* (1989) introduced a method for computing form-factors based on ray casting. Unlike the hemicube approach, which computes radiosity for a small surface patch, and then averages these for vertices in order to do smooth shading, the ray casting method directly computes the radiosities at the vertices. Recall that the form-factor relating a differential area to a surface patch was given in (EQ 15.6).

This could be solved by summation (numerical integration) over small delta areas of A_j. This is numerically unstable where A_j is large compared to r, the distance between the patches. Instead the new method relies on an approximation based on a known analytic solution. A form-factor from a differential area dA_i to an orthogonally opposite receiving disk of radius a is given by

$$F_{dA_iA_j} = \frac{a^2}{r^2 + a^2} \tag{EQ 15.21}$$

The reciprocity principle for form-factors gives:

$$dA_i F_{dA_iA_j} = A_j F_{A_jdA_i} \tag{EQ 15.22}$$

so that the form-factor from a disk as source to differential area as receiver is given by:

$$F_{A_jdA_i} = \frac{dA_j}{\pi r^2 + A_j} \tag{EQ 15.23}$$

This follows because $A_j = \pi a^2$, the area of the disk.

This relationship is for an orthogonally opposing disk. To generalize it, include the cosines of the angles between the normal at each surface, and the direction between the source and the receiver.

$$F_{A_jdA_i} = \frac{\cos\theta_i \cos\theta_j dA_j}{\pi r^2 + A_j} \tag{EQ 15.24}$$

The additional approximation is to assume that the area is disk shaped!

Now the evaluation of the form-factors in this representation is achieved by ray casting. The *source patch* (A_j) is divided into differential areas, and the receiver (dA_i) is a particular *vertex*. Hidden surface occlusion is achieved by tracing a ray from the vertex into the scene toward the particular delta area, and stopping if the ray intersects anything before reaching the center of the source.

The final form-factor for this vertex is the sum of the form-factors for the delta areas which are visible from the vertex. This is shown in (EQ 15.25).

$$F_{A_jdA_i} = \sum_{k=1}^{n} d_i \cdot \frac{\cos(\theta_{ik})\cos(\theta_j)dA_{ik}}{\pi r^2 + A_j} \tag{EQ 15.25}$$

Here n is the number of sample points on the source, and $d_i = 0$ or 1 depending on whether the sample point on the source is visible to the vertex.

This method of computing form-factors is, as would be expected, more accurate the closer the shape of the source regions is to disks. For example, squares give quite good results but oblongs do not. Generally, quite a small number of samples are needed to give good effects, compared to the size of the grid that would be required in the hemicube method.

Finally, since radiosities are now computed directly at the vertices, the interpolation stage during rendering does not require a shift from the centers of the patches to the vertices (see "Rendering", Section 15.7). This is another advantage for this method.

15.5 The progressive refinement method

Algorithm

This method of computing radiosities is due to Cohen *et al.* (1988). In (EQ 15.12) a single term in the summation determines the contribution to the radiosity of patch *i* from patch *j*.

$$B_i \text{ due to } B_j = \rho_i B_j F_{ij} \qquad \text{(EQ 15.26)}$$

Since $F_{ij}A_i = F_{ji}A_j$ we have (swapping *i* and *j*):

$$B_j \text{ due to } B_i = \rho_j B_i F_{ji} = \rho_j B_i F_{ij}\frac{A_i}{A_j} \qquad \text{(EQ 15.27)}$$

Hence for all patches *j*: B_j due to $B_i = \rho_j B_i F_{ij}\dfrac{A_i}{A_j}$

We "shoot" light out from patch *i*, allowing it to make a contribution to all other patches *j* in the environment, adjusting the radiosities of each of these other patches. The important point here is that in this formulation the form-factors needed (F_{ij}) are still those based on the hemicube at patch *i*. At each iteration there will be an improvement to the estimate of B_i, which will already include the previous estimate of B_i. Hence only the change in B_i needs to be considered; this is called the *unshot radiosity* ΔB_i.

Initially set B_i and ΔB_i to zero for all non-light sources, and to E_i for the remainder. Then an iterative process starts by finding the brightest patch and using it to shoot out energy. This is repeated at each step, with the brightest patch being the one with the greatest unshot energy. It terminates when the total unshot energy is below a threshold or when the result is deemed satisfactory.

```
while not converged {
    Find patch i with the greatest A_iΔB_i;
    compute the form factors F_ij using a hemi-cube at i;
    for each patch j {
        ΔRad = ρ_jΔB_iF_ij(A_i/A_j);
        ΔB_j = ΔB_j + ΔRad;
        B_j = B_j + ΔRad;
    }
    ΔB_i = 0;
    /*render scene here if desired*/
}
```

This method benefits from the observation that the global illumination in a scene is mostly determined by a small number of elements (the primary sources and a few secondary ones). Therefore by processing them in order of importance it quickly converges close to the full solution. It also avoids the quadratic storage requirement of the complete form-factor matrix since only the form-factors relating to the current patch are computed at each iteration and then discarded.

Including an ambient term

Using the progressive refinement method allows for rendering of the scene after each iteration. Since the patches are sorted in descending order of radiosity, the light sources will be treated first, and thus some light will be added to the environment after the first iteration. However, in practice, it can be seen that these initial scenes will be dark. So a heuristic correction for this, purely for display purposes, is to add a constant ambient term to the illumination, where this term gets progressively smaller for each iteration.

The argument for this provided in Cohen *et al.* (1998) is that an initial form-factor from i to j can be approximated by a ratio of areas:

$$F_{\square j} = \frac{A_j}{\sum\limits_{i=1}^{n} A_i} \qquad \text{(EQ 15.28)}$$

The average reflectivity of the environment can be computed as:

$$\rho_{ave} = \frac{\sum\limits_{i=1}^{n} \rho_i A_i}{\sum\limits_{i=1}^{n} A_i} \qquad \text{(EQ 15.29)}$$

A fraction ρ_{ave} of energy sent into the environment will be reflected, and part of that will be reflected, and so on, leading to overall average interreflection R:

$$R = 1 + \rho_{ave} + \rho_{ave}^2 + \rho_{ave}^3 + \ldots = \frac{1}{1 - \rho_{ave}} \qquad \text{(EQ 15.30)}$$

The overall ambient radiosity is equal to the area average of the radiosity which has not yet been "shot" via the form-factor, times the reflection factor R:

$$Ambient = R \sum\limits_{j=1}^{n} \Delta B_j F_{\square j} \qquad \text{(EQ 15.31)}$$

Hence for display purposes only, use the radiosity

$$B_i' = B_i + \rho_i Ambient \qquad \text{(EQ 15.32)}$$

Meshing

In practice, in the radiosity method we attempt to capture the variations of the illumination across the scene surfaces by discretizing each one into a mesh of pieces small enough that they can be assumed to have constant radiance distribution over their whole area. This can be achieved in a number of ways discussed below.

Uniform meshing

The first radiosity methods were based on uniform meshing. This is the easiest to implement. Here each surface is partitioned into a regular grid of rectangular patches and the radiosity is computed at the center of each one of them. The resolution of the grid controls the accuracy and the speed of the solution.

Achieving an appropriate resolution for each surface is not an easy task and it is usually left to the user. This method, however, has several problems, for example:

- missing shadows and/or blocky shadows due to undersampling;
- shadow leaks and light leaks – this is more apparent where there is a large gradient in the illumination (such as a D^0 discontinuity, see below) which does not coincide with boundary of a patch.

Adaptive subdivision

A substructuring method was presented by Cohen *et al.* (1986) for use with the full matrix radiosity solution. However, it can also be used with progressive refinement.

We require the mesh to be fine enough to capture all the illumination variations on the surfaces (shadows, highlights, etc.) but we also want to minimize the processing cost which is quadratic on the number of patches. One observation which can help us here is that although we need the small patches for receiving the illumination to capture the detail, we can get away with using larger patches to emit the radiosity.

Substructuring is based on this idea. The environment is partitioned initially into a coarse set of *patches*. These will act as the emitters throughout the solution process. We will partition these patches further into *elements* as needed.

In the full matrix solution substructuring is used as follows. We first obtain a full solution based on the patches. Then we go through the mesh and refine the solution by subdividing the patches. We compare the radiosities of neighboring patches and where we find that they differ by more than a predefined threshold we assume that there is an important gradient in the radiosity and we subdivide these patches further into elements.

The radiosity on the new elements is computed by gathering radiosity from the other patches in the environment (rather than from the elements).

$$B_{i_e} = E_{i_e} + \rho_{i_e} \sum_j B_j \cdot F_{i_e j}$$

(EQ 15.33)

Here, B_{i_e}, E_{i_e}, and ρ_{i_e} are the radiosity, emmitance, and reflectivity of an element e on a patch i, B_j is the radiosity of patch j, and $F_{i_e j}$ is the form-factor from element i_e to patch j.

The B_j are already known and the $F_{i_e j}$ could be computed by using the hemicube on the element, for example. Once the radiosities on the new elements have been computed, the radiosities on the patches can be updated with a more accurate estimate to be used for any further iterations:

$$B_i = \frac{1}{A_i} \sum_e B_{i_e} \cdot A_{i_e}$$

(EQ 15.34)

where B_i and A_i are the radiosity and area of the patch and B_{i_e} and A_{i_e} are the radiosity and area of element e on patch i.

Then we can continue with more iterations to split the elements where needed and refine the mesh further. If we assume that the patches are rectangular then usually the subdivision can be stored using a quad-tree data structure on each patch (see "Non-uniform space subdivision" on page 348).

If we have an initial number of patches N and a final number of elements M then in this solution we compute $N \times M$ form-factors which is significantly smaller than $M \times M$ since $M > N$ by far.

For progressive refinement we use a similar idea. We use the patches to emit the radiosity. At each progressive refinement iteration we choose the patch with the greatest unshot energy and shoot that out to the elements in the environment. When there is a large difference in the radiosity received from this step among the elements, they are subdivided and a new shot is performed from the current emitting patch.

Hierarchical radiosity

Hierarchical radiosity (HR) (Hanrahan et al., 1991) takes the ideas above one step further. While, in substructuring, the exchange of energy goes from patches to elements regardless of the importance of the individual interaction, HR creates a hierarchy of subpatches on each patch and connects individually each one with each of the others at the right level of subdivision where the energy is to be exchanged.

We start with a very coarse set of initial patches. We take each pair and try to "link" them for energy exchange. The main idea is that if the form-factor (FF) between the two is large then there is potential for a large error in the exchange. In such a case we subdivide them and check the FFs of each pair of subpatches. If they are below the threshold we link the pair, if not we subdivide further, until either the FF is low enough or the area of the subpatch is too small. In the process a hierarchy is built on each patch, for example a quad-tree, although it could be another type of hierarchy. Then we go through this process again, trying to pair up with other patches. In this linking, parts of the hierarchies will already exist, so all we need to add are the links at the right nodes and refine where necessary. The exchange of energy happens only along the links.

In HR, for a pair of patches *i, j* which are close by, leaves at the bottom of the hierarchy will be linked with lots of fine exchanges happening, while if *j* is far away there might be one collective exchange from the root of the hierarchies. And of course there are intermediate cases.

The algorithm runs in two stages. First the hierarchy is built on each initial patch and all the links are established. Then through an iterative process the radiosity is distributed along the links.

To build the hierarchy and form the links we call the `refine` procedure between each pair of initial patches.

```
void refine (p, q, F_eps, A_eps) {
   estimate F_pq and F_qp;
   if (F_pq < F_eps and F_qp < F_eps)
      link (p, q);
   else {
      if (F_pq > F_qp and A_p > A_eps)
         for each child c of p
            refine(p_c, q, F_eps, A_eps);
      else if (A_q > A_eps)
         for each child c of q
            refine(p, q_c, F_eps, A_eps);
      else
         link(p, q)
   }
}
```

Here, F_{eps} and A_{eps} give bounds on the maximum form-factor between the two patches and the minimum area of subdivision. We can see an example of the hierarchies built on two perpendicular polygons in Figure 15.4.

The most expensive part of the linking process is the computation of the form-factors. This will happen so often that it is not practical to do it accurately. Instead an estimation is used. For example, one could use the following:

$$F_{ij} = \frac{\cos\theta_i \cos\theta_j A_j}{\pi r^2 + A_j}.$$

What we said above doesn't take account of visibility between patches. This is essential for any realistic environment. Since we are considering links between pairs of patches rather than between a patch and the rest of the environment, a hemicube approach would be wasteful. Ray casting is more appropriate here. A number of rays can be sent between the pair to find an estimate of the visibility. This computation can be done either after we have

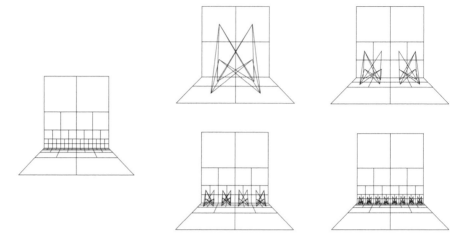

Figure 15.4
Hierarchical subdivision on two perpendicular polygons. Line segments indicate linked pairs at different levels in the hierarchies
Courtesy of Pat Hanrahan, Computer Science and Electrical Engineering Department, Stanford University, USA

subdivided based purely on the FFs, in which case we use the visibility to adjust the FFs of the links downward. Or it can be done during the `refine` procedure, while building the hierarchy. In the latter case partial visibility can be used to encourage further subdivision for better capturing of the shadow boundaries.

Once the links have been established we proceed to propagate the radiosities using an iterative process. At each step we first gather radiosity on the patches through their links. The contribution of a link of patch i to some other patch j can be computed as: $B_i \mathrel{+}= \rho_i F_{ij} B_j$. In the pseudocode below we use `Bg` to denote the radiosity gathered by the patch at this iteration.

```
void gather (patch p) {
   Bg_p = 0;
   for each link of p connecting to patch j
      Bg_p += r_p F_pj B_j;
   for each child c of p
      gather (p_c)
}
```

Each subpatch, however, is only linked directly to a subset of the scene. To have a representation of the *total* energy arriving at the region we need to take into account what has been gathered by the links higher and lower in the hierarchy. After the gathering, a depth-first traversal from the top of the tree is used to update the energies for the next iteration. The gathered energy is *pushed* down to the leaf nodes, adding to each internal patch on the way. Then it is *pulled* upwards again to the root using an area weighted average to complete the update.

Hanrahan argued that the complexity of this method can be as low as $O(M)$, where M is the number of final elements in the scene. To this we need to add the $O(N^2)$ cost of the initial pairing of the patches. The initial patches are much larger and thus fewer than for the adaptive subdivision method.

Discontinuity meshing

Although adaptive or hierarchical techniques reduce the error in the resulting solutions by providing more elements in regions of greater illumination variations, they just minimize rather than fully treat the problems we mentioned in the uniform meshing section above. To eliminate artefacts such as light/shadow leaks etc. we need to construct our mesh so that it includes the illumination discontinuities caused by the visual events. In Chapter 14 we described how to compute these and add them to a mesh; however, we concentrate on illumination from a single light source. For discontinuity meshing radiosity we need to compute the discontinuities from multiple sources and add them together (Lischinski *et al.*, 1992; Drettakis and Fiume, 1994). The results are highly accurate but the method can be quite costly, difficult to implement robustly and often excessive. A better solution should select only a subset of these discontinuities and ignore those with little contribution (Gibson and Hubbold, 1997).

15.7 Rendering

Suppose one of the methods above is used and the radiosities have been computed for all the patches in the scene. How is the scene rendered? Let's ignore the very serious complication as to how the radiosity values are transformed to appropriate RGB values for display – this was considered with respect to radiance in Chapter 4. Suppose now that this has been accomplished by some method. The radiosities belong to the centers of the patches. If we naively rendered each patch with a uniform color according to the radiosity associated with that patch, of course we would obtain a faceted image – the edges between adjoining patches would be clearly noticeable. We have met this problem before. It would be as if we are treating the radiosities as the "preordained" colors associated with the polygons. In Chapter 13 we overcame this problem with interpolated smooth shading (see "Smooth shading" on page 273). In particular, Gouraud shading was used for diffuse reflection.

Now the radiosity method only simulates diffuse reflection. So Gouraud shading could be used. The only problem is that for Gouraud shading the radiosity values must be associated with the vertices rather than with the centers of the patches. The way to overcome this should be familiar – produce radiosities at each vertex as the average radiosities of the surrounding patches. This is the same as computing approximated normals. It is also a very good reason for using a Winged Edge data structure (Chapter 8, see "The Winged Edge data structure" on page 170).

15.8 Summary

This chapter has provided a brief introduction to a method for global illumination in scenes consisting of diffusely reflecting surfaces. The major computational expense of the method is the computation of the form-factors – just as the intersection calculations were the major effort in ray tracing. However, here there is a difference. The radiosity solution can be carried out "off line" – it is not part of the rendering process itself. Once the radiosity solution has been obtained, a real-time walkthrough of the scene is possible, since only Gouraud shading and a z-buffer – i.e., standard graphics hardware – is required for rendering. This emphasizes the point that since radiosity simulates diffuse reflection, and since diffuse reflection is view-independent, the radiosity computation can be carried out independently of the view. Ray tracing, however, is very much view dependent – the entire rendering process starts from the center of projection.

Very realistic images can be generated with radiosity (see, for example, color plate P.2). However, the radiosity solution is only valid for the given scene geometry and lighting. If the lighting is changed, then at least the form-factors do not have to be recomputed, but progressive refinement would still be needed to shoot light out into the scene. On the other hand, if the geometry of any object in the scene is changed, for example by translation, then the computations have to be done again. Chen (1990) has shown how to compute the changes incrementally given changes in scene geometry.

Radiosity and ray tracing are complementary, and need integration. There has been some work towards achieving this, although the algorithms are very costly. Two examples are Wallace *et al.* (1989) and Chen *et al.* (1991).

16 Faster ray tracing

16.1 Introduction

In the previous chapter we saw how to render a globally illuminated scene, provided that all the surfaces are diffuse reflectors. To some extent this meets the goal of real-time global illumination – since we are at least able to walk through such a scene in real-time. However, there is clearly a large pre-processing step to compute the radiosity solution, and in general it is not possible to compute changes to the scene in real-time.

In this chapter we return to ray tracing. Up to now we have used a "brute force" approach to ray tracing, where each ray is intersected with each object in the scene. In this chapter we will discuss some ideas that increase the speed of ray tracing by orders of magnitude. Unfortunately, this is still nowhere near real-time, but minutes rather than hours, or hours rather than days, depending on the complexity of the scene.

We start with the problem of intersection calculations, and then introduce a number of data structures that allow culling of large collections of rays that would otherwise be traversed, with no ultimate impact on the final image. Many of these data structures have uses that go beyond ray tracing, and are therefore worth studying for their own sake.

16.2 Intersection calculations

Most of the work in ray tracing consists in intersection calculations. The most common primitive used is a polygon. We considered the intersection of a ray with a polygon in Chapter 8 (see "Intersecting polygons by rays" on page 165). In Chapter 5 we saw how to intersect a ray with a sphere, and in Chapter 18 we will examine the intersection with a more general class of objects of which a sphere and a plane are instances, called a quadric surface.

Most of the research into ray tracing has centered on the problem of reducing the impact of the intersection calculations, either by reducing the cost of each ray, or reducing the total number of rays, or both.

Existing algorithms for speeding up the visibility computation for a ray are based on the use of *space coherence*. Only those objects passing through the regions lying on a ray's path need to be considered in the visibility calculation; other objects will not intersect the ray and therefore can be simply ignored. The key issue with these algorithms is to partition world space properly so as to minimize the number of objects to be tested, and reduce the overhead for traversing the space in order to find the candidate objects. These algorithms fall into the following categories:

- hierarchical bounding volumes: these bounding volumes are determined by the position and extent of the objects;

- uniform space subdivision: a fixed uniform partition of the space is constructed that is independent of the distribution of objects;

- adaptive space subdivision: an adaptive subdivision scheme is used that is based on the distribution of objects;

- ray direction techniques: coherence among rays induces a classification in object space, such that bunches of similar rays can be treated together.

We consider these in turn.

16.3 Bounding volumes and hierarchies

Bounding volumes

An obvious way to reduce the cost of intersection is to fit a bounding volume, such as a sphere or a box, around each primitive object. There is a trade-off here between the tightness of fit and the simplicity of computing the ray-bounding volume intersection. If the ray does not intersect the bounding volume then no further action is necessary. However, if the ray does intersect it, a further test is required to see if the ray actually intersects the enclosed object. If the bounding volume is not a tight fit to the objects, there will be a high proportion of instances where the ray intersects the bounding volume but does not intersect the object it encloses. Here more work than would

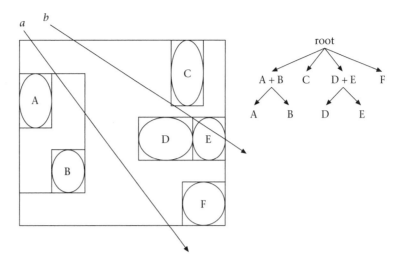

Figure 16.1
Hierarchical bounding volumes

originally have been necessary may sometimes be carried out. Bounding volumes are rarely used by themselves in ray tracing, but rather are used to form hierarchies.

Hierarchical bounding volumes

In this method bounding volumes are fitted to primitives. Then higher-level bounding volumes are fitted to groups of first-level volumes and so on (Goldsmith and Salmon, 1987; Kay and Kajiya, 1986). This is illustrated in Figure 16.1. In this case there are a number of objects, labeled A to F. Each has a bounding volume placed around it, and clusters of bounding volumes are formed to create a hierarchy of bounding volumes. The root volume bounds the entire scene. Each ray is successively intersected with the bounding volume, and if the ray does intersect the bounding volume it is traversed down the tree until it meets (or not) an actual object. Two rays, *a* and *b*, are shown. Ray *a* intersects the root bounding volume. It is then tested against A + B, and the result is a "hit" (it does intersect this volume). It is then tested against A and B and misses both. It intersects no other bounding volume at that level of the tree and hence the ray is rejected. Note that although the ray is intersected with a number of bounding volumes, there is still a great potential saving compared to intersecting it with all objects in the scene. Of course, one bounding volume that the ray misses may contain thousands of objects – and the ray is not intersected against those. Ray *b* misses A + B but intersects C. It does not intersect the primitive inside C. It does intersect D + E and finally the primitive inside E.

Care must be taken to ensure that the nearest intersection (if any) is returned. This could be achieved by pre-sorting the bounding volumes, so that the ray is processed along its length from origin to termination (inside the scene bounding volume). This could be achieved by using a BSP data structure, where the faces of the bounding volumes are used for the priority list, or else another similar data structure that takes advantage of the fact that the faces of the bounding volumes are axis aligned – such as a KD-tree (see, for example, Samet, 1990).

The selection of bounding volumes

The cost of the traversal algorithm depends on two factors. The first is the cost of testing the intersection between a ray and a bounding volume. Testing against an object's bounding volume should ideally be very much cheaper than testing against the object itself, otherwise the advantage of bounding volumes can be lost. The second is the total number of intersection calculations carried out against bounding volumes, which depends on how tightly a bounding volume fits with a surface and how the bounding volume hierarchy is built. Usually, a more expensive ray-bounding volume intersection is required for a tighter fit, which is a trade-off situation.

Some simple geometry types have been used for bounding volume, including spheres, boxes, ellipses, cylinders, and cones. In (Kay and Kajiya, 1986) a *bounding slab* method was suggested. In this approach, a slab is defined by two parallel infinite planes. To define a completely closed bounding volume, at least three bounding slabs are required. The *t*-values for the intersections between a ray and a slab are given as:

$$\frac{d_i - (n \cdot p_0)}{n \cdot v}, \ i = 1, 2 \qquad \text{(EQ 16.1)}$$

where n is the plane normal of the slab; d_1 and d_2 are the distances between the planes of the slab and the coordinate origin; p_0 is the ray origin; and v is the ray direction (see (EQ 8.8)). Since the normals for the slabs will be known and fixed, $n \cdot p_0$ and $n \cdot v$ need only be computed once. Therefore, the intersection is reduced to one subtraction and one division.

The hierarchical bounding volume method can result in a large reduction in the number of intersection calculations, but still every object (even if only its bounding volume) may be considered by a ray during a computation. A better approach would be one where only objects obviously along the path of the ray are tested, and all others are ignored. We can achieve this with space subdivision methods.

16.4 Uniform space subdivision

The idea of uniform space subdivision is to bound the scene with an axis aligned box, and divide the space up into a uniform partition, where each small cuboid

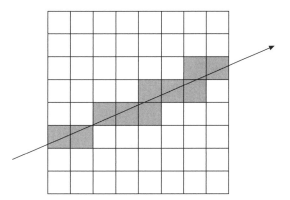

Figure 16.2
Tracing a ray through
a space subdivision
(2D example)

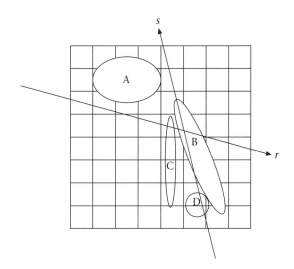

Figure 16.3
Only intersections in
the current cell can
terminate the ray

cell (sometimes called a "voxel") stores the identifiers of the objects which intersect it. This idea, due to Fujimoto *et al.* (1986), Amanatides (1987) and Cleary and Wyvill (1988), dramatically reduces the number of ray–object intersections, since the path of a ray through the cells may be enumerated, and only those objects encountered along this path need be considered for intersections. As soon as the first valid intersection with an object is found, the ray path may be terminated.

The algorithm requires enumeration of the cells encountered by the ray. This is achieved by an adaptation of a 3DDA (digital differential analyzer) algorithm, which will be discussed in the next chapter. Such an algorithm (see Figure 16.2) shows how the ray must be traced, in a 2D example, where all cells encountered by the ray must be considered.

Figure 16.3 illustrates a number of pitfalls which must be avoided. First, notice that the ray *r* will pass through two cells, both of which contain object

A. Obviously, it is pointless to test A twice. Hence each ray is given a unique identifier, and each object keeps a list of ray identifiers corresponding to rays that have already been tested against it (and the associated intersections, if any). Second, B and C are encountered in the same cell. It might just happen that B is tested before C, and the intersection found. In this case C would be missed, unless the rule were adopted that the ray intersections terminate only on intersection points which are inside the current cell, and are sorted among all objects with intersections on that ray within the current cell. Ray *s* shows that D and B will be encountered in the same cell. However, the intersection with B does not occur inside that cell, and hence would not be included when consideration is given to the intersections within that cell.

Uniform subdivision schemes have the useful property that it is very cheap to compute the path of a ray through the space subdivision, as we shall see in the next chapter. However, a major disadvantage is that the subdivision does not take into account the distribution of the objects. If most of the objects were bunched together in one corner of the space, then the subdivision would not be efficient, since the cells in that densely populated area would each contain a large number of objects. Hence the saving in ray–object intersection calculations would be substantially reduced.

16.5 Non-uniform space subdivision

Octrees

The uniform subdivision approach can achieve a very significant speed-up over the brute force approach for scenes containing objects that are uniformly distributed throughout the enclosing box. However, if objects are concentrated within small regions of the scene, a large number of empty cells may need to be traversed before the first non-empty cell is encountered. This may not always be a serious problem though, since 3DDA allows very fast traversal of cells. The major problem is that since objects are concentrated in a relatively small number of cells, these cells are mostly likely to contain a large number of objects. Therefore, rays which encounter these cells will require a large number of intersection calculations. A better approach is to use an adaptive hierarchical subdivision so that the space is subdivided according to the distribution of objects in a region. In the hierarchical subdivision, a cell is further subdivided if it contains more than a pre-set number of objects. This allows empty regions to be quickly skipped while also minimizing the number of intersection calculations. In addition, a maximum level of subdivision is also maintained so that a cell will not be subdivided too deeply.

The data structure typically used for this is an *octree*. The use of octrees for ray tracing was first proposed by Glassner (1995). An octree is a hierarchical subdivision scheme that allows the space to be subdivided adaptively according to the distribution of objects in space. In the octree approach, a cell is divided

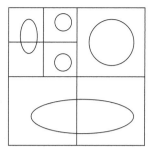

Figure 16.4
A quadtree – no cell is allowed to intersect more than one object in this example

along the middle of each axis into $2 \times 2 \times 2$ equal octants. A 2D analogue of an octree called a *quadtree* is shown in Figure 16.4. Compared to the uniform space subdivision scheme, the octree is more expensive to traverse. To traverse children of an interior cell, the incremental algorithm for the uniform subdivision method can be used. However, the incremental approach is more effective when a large number of incremental steps is required. This is unfortunately not the case with the octree. Alternatively, the following algorithm that recursively subdivides a ray's path into intervals can be used.

In order to construct the octree the world is enclosed in an axis aligned box. If there are fewer than a maximum number of elements intersecting the box, then stop this process of space subdivision. Alternatively, divide each of the axes into two, thus forming eight equal partitions, and recursively apply the same principle to each.

The advantage of this method is clear – the subdivision adapts to the distribution of the objects in the scene. The disadvantage compared to uniform subdivision is the increased cost of passing the ray through the partition. A straightforward method of doing this is as follows:

- Intersect the ray with the box, and move it slightly inside.
- Traverse the octree to see which node it is in.
- Intersect with the faces of the cube represented by that node, to find out which one it exits the corresponding cell from in order to find the next cell.

BSP trees

Another non-uniform space subdivision scheme uses BSP trees. In an axis aligned BSP tree, a cell is divided into two children using an axis aligned plane. Each of the three principal axes is selected in turn as the depth of the subdivision increases. (Such a tree is a 3-dimensional example of a *KD-tree*, which we will meet again in Chapter 22). The position of the partitioning plane can be selected in several ways. For example, we can always subdivide a cell at its center. This yields a binary tree representation of the octree data structure. The disadvantage is that it can result in redundant subdivisions in which a cell is subdivided into two cells; one contains no objects and the other contains the original set of objects. A better approach may be to divide the objects into two equal sets. Hence the bounding space is partitioned into a BSP tree where the nodes are axis aligned planes. This method was considered by Kaplan (1985) and Jansen (1986), and has the following characteristics:

- If the dividing planes are at the mid-points of the principal axes then the same subdivision as an octree is achieved.

- An adaptive subdivision can be achieved by choosing planes so that, for example, the number of objects are always divided into two equal sets.

When BSP trees are used, there is an efficient recursive algorithm for ray traversal:

```
procedure BSPIntersect(ray,node) {
  if(ray interval empty or node == nil)   return;

  if(node is leaf then intersect ray with each associated object)
  else{
    near = ray clipped to near side of node plane;
    BSPIntersect(near, node->near);
    if(no intersection) {
      far = ray clipped to far side of node plane;
      BSPIntersect(far,node->far)
    }
  }
}
```

16.6   Ray coherence methods

Partitioning the space either into non-overlapping cells or into a bounding volume hierarchy requires us to traverse the resulting data structure in order to find the path of the ray. Although this can give a very significant speed-up, it includes an overhead due to traversal which should be minimized. One possible approach to reduce the overhead is to take ray coherence into consideration (Arvo and Kirk, 1987; Ohta and Maekawa, 1987). By ray coherence we mean that the set of objects that a given ray is likely to intersect is likely to be very similar to the set of objects that its neighbors will intersect. In this situation, we can cache objects tested by a ray and use them for nearby rays. This is a useful approach for testing shadows. Alternatively, we can bound a set of rays in a volume in rayspace and enumerate the candidate objects for the volume together with these objects being tested against the rays in the rayspace. Arvo and Kirk (1987) proposed a ray classification scheme to take such ray coherence into account. They perform subdivision in the space of rays rather than the space of objects.

We consider the ray coherence idea in relation to shadow feeler testing, and then the Arvo and Kirk method.

The Light Buffer – efficient shadow testing

The Light Buffer, due to Haines and Greenberg (1986), is a method for reducing the amount of work when firing the shadow-feeler rays. The approach can be summarized as follows:

- Construct a virtual box around each light source position.
- Consider a particular box – project the environment onto the faces of the box, using a rectangular subdivision on each face of the box.
- When the shadow feeler hits a box face, examine the corresponding tile. The set of objects in this tile are those that potentially cast shadows on the object from which the ray was fired. Keep this set in depth-sorted order.

Ray classification

Ray classification is quite a different approach to space subdivision, since it is the space of rays which is subdivided rather than the space of objects (Arvo and Kirk, 1987). Note that a ray can be represented as a point in 5D space: (x, y, z) is the origin and (u, v) is the direction. In outline the method makes use of this by finding the candidate set likely to be intersected by a set of 'similar' rays – rays within some relatively small hypercube of 5D space.

The algorithm employs five steps:

(1) *Find the a subset E of R^5 containing the 5D point which is the equivalent of every possible ray in the scene. E must be a bounded set.* A ray can be represented as a 5D point – the direction is determined by choosing an axis aligned cube around the scene. Each face +X, –X, +Y, –Y, +Z, –Z is represented by a coordinate system, UV, where each is in the range –1 to +1. Hence where in terms of UV the ray hits the face gives the additional 2 degrees of freedom. Hence a ray is represented by (x, u, z, U, V) and the 'dominant axis' (that is, which face the (U, V) point refers to). The set of all such points (x, u, z, U, V) gives the bounded subset E.

(2) *Let $E_1, E_2, \ldots, E_n$ be a partition of E (i.e., each pair is disjoint and their union is equal to E).* The partition of E is in the 5D equivalent of an octree. That is, a hypercube in 5D can be divided in two along each of its axes, to form 32 partitions. Each such partition can be similarly divided according to some criterion. There will be such a 32-tree for each of the six dominant axes.

(3) *For each E_i there is a C_i which represents the complete set of objects intersected by at least one of the rays of E_i.* A hypercube in 5D corresponds to a beam in 3D. The set of objects which this beam intersects is the candidate set for this hypercube. Note that as we progress down the 32-tree, a smaller and smaller number of objects will be intersected, and associated with each node.

(4) *For any ray, find the particular E_i which contains it. (From (2) there will be only one).* Since a ray is equivalent to a 5D point, finding the node of the 32-tree which contains it is a simple tree traversal algorithm.

(5) Given the ray and a set C of objects, find the intersections.

The overall algorithm can be outlined as follows:

(1) Initialization

```
Create the roots of the six 32-trees for each of the axes;
each 32-tree root, corresponding to the 5D hypercube, inherits
the entire set of objects.
```

(2) Ray classification

```
p = 5-tuple for the ray;
axis = dominant axis;
H = leaf hypercube of the 32-tree containing p;
```

(3) Candidate list creation

```
if C(H) is "inherited" then C(H) = C(H) ^ Beam(H);
while (C(H) > max_H and size(H) > min_H) {
   split H along 5 axes creating 32 children;
   let all new children "inherit" C(H);
   H = child which contains p;
   C(H) = C(H) ^ Beam(H);
};
```

(4) Candidate processing

```
for each candidate in C(H) (considered in ascending order of
minimum extent) {
   check ray with bounding volume;
   if(intersects bounding volume) {
     intersect ray with object;
     if(intersects object){
       return this intersection;
     }
   }
}
```

Initially the six 32-trees are set up, representing the entire 5D bounding volume of rayspace. Each of the trees is associated with the entire set of objects. Then, for any ray, find its dominant axis, and the cell (H) in the 32-tree which contains it. If the set of objects associated with H is "inherited" then actually compute the intersection of the 3D beam with this set of objects, in order to narrow down the set. This method of only computing the sets when required is termed "lazy evaluation" of the sets by Arvo and Kirk. Now keep splitting and creating child nodes until either a node is created which is too small, or the corresponding number of objects associated with the node is small enough. Let the node which now contains p again be H, and find the set of objects to be associated with H by intersecting its corresponding beam with the objects in the set.

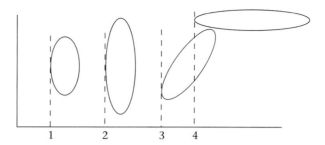

Figure 16.5
No objects with minimum extent on the dominant axis which is further from an intersection point need to be considered

The candidate processing makes use of the fact that we know the dominant axis for this ray. Hence the objects are kept sorted according to their minimum extent on this dominant axis. Once an intersection point has been found, no objects that have their minimum extents beyond this point on the dominant axis need to be considered. This is shown in Figure 16.5.

16.7 Summary

This chapter has briefly considered some methods for reducing the number of ray–object intersections. These methods make ray tracing a practical proposition on standard PCs or workstations. More recent developments, showing that real-time ray tracing on PCs may not be too far off, can be found in Wald, Slusalleck and Benthin (2001).

There are important details not considered in this chapter, which are also of importance more widely in computer graphics. The first is how to efficiently intersect a ray with a bounding box, and the second is how to trace a ray through a regular space subdivision. These are taken up in the next chapter.

17 Clipping and rendering lines

17.1   Introduction

In the last chapter we used various techniques to speed up ray tracing. Fundamentally the methods involved tracing rays through various subdivision spaces, whether uniformly subdivided or adaptively subdivided. There are two problems here: the first is to determine efficiently how a ray intersects with another object – in particular, a cell of a subdivision space or a bounding volume. In 3D such a volume is a cuboid, in 2D it is a rectangle. In this chapter we will focus on the determination of the intersection between a ray and a rectangle, the extension to higher dimensional spaces being straightforward. This is called "line clipping." In Chapter 10 we considered the clipping of polygons.

The second problem is to compute efficiently the path of a ray through a subdivision space. In particular, given a uniform subdivision, the problem is to determine the sequence of cells that the ray intersects. Now this could be solved by repeated use of line clipping: clip the ray by a bounding box around the whole scene, and determine a starting cell containing the first end-point of the ray. Then test each neighboring cell for intersection with the ray, and continue with this process until the other end-point of the clipped ray is reached. However, this is very inefficient – in particular, it does not take into account coherence – making use of the solution for one cell to find efficiently which neighboring cell the ray enters.

Although we have motivated this discussion from the point of view of the requirements of fast ray tracing, another very strong motivation is at the 2D level of computer graphics. In Chapter 5 (see "Forming the displayed image" on page 126) we saw that objects are mapped to a display window from a higher-level (world space) representation. This process of mapping does not, of course, ensure that objects are truncated or clipped – to avoid displaying parts of the object that are outside of the display window. We saw this with polygons in Chapter 5, but we have to find efficient algorithms for clipping lines to the display window as well.

Finally, we saw in Chapter 12 how to render polygons into the display. We have yet to see how to rasterize lines. If a line is vertical, horizontal, or has a slope of ±1, then the problem is easy to solve. But in general it is not easy. Finding a set of pixels that correspond as closely as possible to a given line segment is a fundamental problem at the 2D level in computer graphics. The generalization of the solution to higher-dimensional spaces also gives us a way to trace a ray through a uniformly subdivided 3D space for the purposes of fast ray tracing.

In this chapter we first consider a number of algorithms for clipping lines. Then we consider the problem of rendering lines – finding the "closest" set of pixels for a given line segment.

17.2 Clipping line segments

Line equations and intersections

In this section we consider the mathematical representation of a line, and of a line segment. There are three types of equation that can be used to represent a straight line:

Implicit equation of a line (I). This is in the form:

$$Ax + By = C \qquad \text{(EQ 17.1)}$$

for constants A, B, and C.

One very good use of the implicit form is that it helps us to determine the relationship between any point $p = (x, y)$ and the line. We say that the line partitions space into three exclusive sets. Let us write $L(x, y) = Ax + By - C$. Then the three sets are:

- the set of all points *on the line*, i.e., where $L(x, y) = 0$;

- the set of all points on one side of the line, called the *positive half-space*, where $L(x, y) > 0$;

- the set of all points on the other side of the line, called the *negative half-space*, where $L(x, y) < 0$.

(See also page 165.)

For example, suppose we have two points (x_1, y_1) and (x_2, y_2) and we wish to check whether the line segment joining these two points crosses the line defined by $Ax + By = C$. Then, if $L(x_1, y_1)$ and $L(x_2, y_2)$ have *opposite* signs, the line segment must cross the line. We made use of this approach in Chapter 8 (see "Intersecting polygons by rays" on page 165).

Explicit equation of a line (E).　This is in the familiar form:

$$y = a + bx \qquad\qquad\qquad (EQ\ 17.2)$$

Here b is the "slope" of the line, that is, the change in y for a unit change in x. The value a is the intercept on the Y axis where $x = 0$. It is very easy to re-express form I in terms of E and vice versa. In other words, find the formula for a, b in terms of A, B, and C, and also for A, B, and C in terms of a and b.

The line that passes through two points (2P).　Suppose that (x_1, y_1) and (x_2, y_2) are distinct points, then the equation of the line that passes through these points is:

$$\frac{y - y_1}{y_2 - y_1} = \frac{x - x_1}{x_2 - x_1} \qquad\qquad\qquad (EQ\ 17.3)$$

provided that the line is not exactly horizontal or vertical.

This can be formulated as an either implicit or explicit equation (hence, find A, B, and C, and also a and b in terms of x_1, y_1, x_2, and y_2).

The parametric equation of a line (P).　Consider the point described by

$$p(t) = (\alpha_1 + t\beta_1, \alpha_2 + t\beta_2) \qquad\qquad\qquad (EQ\ 17.4)$$

If we think of t as a parameter, then for any value of t we have a particular point $p(t)$. For example, suppose $p(t) = (1 + 2t, 3 + 4t)$ then $p(1) = (3, 7)$, $p(2) = (5, 11)$, $p(3) = (7, 15)$.

It is easy to show that the locus of the point $p(t)$ as t varies continuously is a straight line. In fact you should show that the formula for $p(t)$ satisfies (EQ 17.1) and (EQ 17.2).

A line segment (LS).　The line equations above describe lines that are infinite. In computer graphics we are concerned with finite *line segments*, that is, continuous subsets of lines between two points $p_1 = (x_1, y_1)$ and $p_2 = (x_2, y_2)$. Using the parametric form it is very easy to specify exactly the set of points on a line segment. Consider:

$$p(t) = (x_1 + t(x_2 - x_1), y_1 + t(y_2 - y_1)) \text{ for } t \in [0, 1] \qquad (EQ\ 17.5)$$

In other words, we consider $p(t)$ defined as before but this time we *restrict* t to be within the range 0 to 1 (inclusive).

Clearly, $p(0) = (x_1, y_1)$ and $p(1) = (x_2, y_2)$. For any t between 0 and 1 the point $p(t)$ is on the line segment between these two points. For example, $p(0.5)$ is halfway between p_1 and p_2.

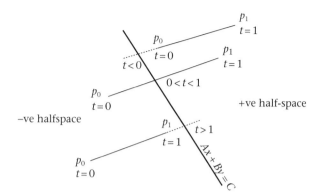

Figure 17.1
Parametric and
implicit line equations
and intersections

Intersections of lines. The different forms for the representations of lines and line segments allow a straightforward solution to the problem of finding the point of intersection between two lines. Suppose we have a line represented implicitly by

$$L(x, y) = Ax + By - C = 0 \qquad\qquad \text{(EQ 17.6)}$$

and a line segment as in (EQ 17.5).

We wish to find the point of intersection (if any) between these two. We can check if the line segment crosses the line by using the argument of (I) above. So suppose we know that it does cross the line, at what point does this happen?

At the point where the two lines meet, both of (EQ 17.5) and (EQ 17.6) must be satisfied. In other words, the point $p(t)$ must be on the line $L(x, y) = 0$, which implies that there is a $t \in [0, 1]$ with $L(x(t), y(t)) = 0$. Unscrambling this:

$$A(x_1 + t\,dx) + B(y_1 + t\,dy) = C$$
$$\text{where } dx = x_2 - x_1 \text{ and } dy = y_2 - y_1 \qquad\qquad \text{(EQ 17.7)}$$

If we solve this equation for t, we get:

$$t = \frac{C - Ax_1 - By_1}{A\,dx + B\,dy} \qquad\qquad \text{(EQ 17.8)}$$

If we substitute this result for t back into $p(t)$, we get the required point of intersection. Some of these ideas are illustrated in Figure 17.1.

The 2D clipping region

In this section we treat the clipping of line segments to a 2D rectangular region, called the "window" or "clipping region." This clipping region is defined by the following:

$$Xmin \leq x \leq Xmax$$
$$Ymin \leq y \leq Ymax$$

(EQ 17.9)

In particular, there are four boundary lines:

$$x = Xmin$$
$$y = Ymin$$
$$x = Xmax$$
$$y = Ymax$$

(EQ 17.10)

The *visible* side of each boundary is determined by the corresponding half-spaces:

(1) $x \geq Xmin$ is the visible side of the boundary $x = Xmin$ (this is the *positive half-space* of the line $x = Xmin$).

(2) $x \leq Xmax$ is the visible side of the boundary $x = Xmax$ (this is the *negative half-space* of the line $x = Xmax$).

(3) $y \geq Ymin$ is the visible side of the boundary $y = Ymin$ (this is the *positive half-space* of the line $y = Ymin$).

(4) $y \leq Ymax$ is the visible side of the boundary $y = Ymax$ (this is the *negative half-space* of the line $y = Ymax$).

The intersection of the visible half-spaces determines the clipping region. Note that the boundaries themselves are inside the clipping region.

The Cohen–Sutherland algorithm

The Cohen–Sutherland line clipping algorithm (Newman and Sproull, 1979) is based on the ideas illustrated in Figure 17.2. In (a) the line is completely inside the clip region, so that the clipped line is the same as the original. In (b) the line is clearly outside of the clipping region, since both end-points are to the left of the left boundary. In (c) the line is partly inside the clipping region, and the resulting clipped line is shown in (d).

The major work involved in any clipping algorithm is computing intersections between the object to be clipped and the clip region. These intersection calculations are straightforward if the clipping region is rectangular, since it involves computing the intersection of arbitrary lines with the horizontal and vertical boundaries forming the region.

Suppose the line segment to be clipped is from (x_1, y_1) to (x_2, y_2). Then the equation of the line is:

$$\frac{y - y_1}{dy} = \frac{x - x_1}{dx}$$

(EQ 17.11)

where $dx = x_2 - x_1$ and $dy = y_2 - y_1$

The intersections of this line with a horizontal boundary $y = Y$ and with a vertical boundary $x = X$ are at the points:

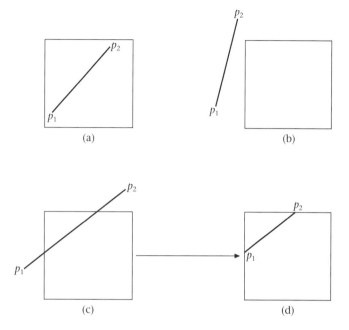

Figure 17.2
Clipping lines

$$\left(x_1 + \left(\frac{dx}{dy}\right)(Y - y_1),\ Y \right)$$

$$\left(X,\ y_1 + \left(\frac{dy}{dx}\right)(X - x_1) \right)$$

(EQ 17.12)

However, it would clearly be inefficient to compute the intersection of the line with all four boundaries of the clip region using (EQ 17.12) – since it is known that the line intersects at most two of these boundaries in the visible part of the clip region. Cohen and Sutherland introduced an algorithm that attempts to reduce the number of intersection computations that need to be performed, by carrying out a simple test to eliminate certain cases – such as when the line is clearly outside or inside of the clipping region.

Consider Figure 17.3, which shows a clipping classification table. The bounded cell in the center of the figure represents the clipping region, and those surrounding it represent quadrants of space outside of the clipping region. Now the two end-points of the line, p_1 and p_2, can be classified with respect to this table. Let *Outside* be a function that returns the classification for a given point. For example, for the line shown in Figure 17.2(b), with p_1 as the lower point:

$$Outside(p_1) = \{Left\}$$
$$Outside(p_2) = \{Left,\ Top\}$$

(EQ 17.13)

A way of thinking about this *Outside* function is that it returns the set of boundaries which the point is outside. Hence, if the intersection of two such

Top left	Top	Top right
Left	**Clip**	Right
Bottom left	Bottom	Bottom right

Figure 17.3
Clipping classification table

sets is not empty, then the line must be completely outside of the clip region – because both of its end-points are to the left, or right, or below or above the clip region. In the case of the line in Figure 17.2(b),

$$Outside(p_1) \cap Outside(p_2) \neq \varnothing \qquad \text{(EQ 17.14)}$$

meaning that the line is completely outside of the clipping region. Similarly, consider the line in Figure 17.2(a). This is completely inside the clipping region, so that the set of boundaries that its two end-points are outside should be the empty set. In this example,

$$Outside(p_1) \cup Outside(p_2) = \varnothing \qquad \text{(EQ 17.15)}$$

since both end-points are inside the region.

Finally, consider the line in Figure 17.2(c).

$$\begin{aligned} Outside(p_1) &= \{Left\} \\ Outside(p_2) &= \{Top\} \end{aligned} \qquad \text{(EQ 17.16)}$$

This satisfies neither (EQ 17.14) nor (EQ 17.15), so that it cannot be trivially rejected as being outside nor accepted as being inside of the clip region. In such a case the union of the two *Outside* sets contains the set of boundaries which the end-points of the line is outside. Choose any one of these boundaries, and intersect the line against this boundary, discarding the portion of the line projecting outside of this boundary. Now re-apply the procedure to the remaining line segment.

The entire clipping process therefore relies on two functions – to find the intersection of lines with horizontal or vertical boundaries, and to find the set of boundaries a point is outside. The intersection function can be constructed from (EQ 17.12). The *Outside* function is very simple, for it only involves the comparison of the coordinate of the point with the boundaries. For example, suppose that the coordinate is (x, y) and the equations of the boundaries are as in (EQ 17.12).

Figure 17.4
Four-bit encoding
for line segment
classification

1001	1000	1010
0001	0000	0010
0101	0100	0110

Then the *Outside* function would deliver a value outside constructed as follows:

```
outside = Ø;
if x < Xmin then outside = outside ∪ {Left}
else
if x > Xmax then outside = outside ∪ {Right};

if y < Ymin then outside = outside ∪ {Bottom}
else
if y > Ymax then outside = outside ∪ {Top};
```

Notice that this implies that the clip region boundaries are themselves inside the clip region.

Implementation of Cohen–Sutherland line segment clipping

To clip the line joining p_1 to p_2:

- Let $o_1 = Outside(p_1)$ and $o_2 = Outside(p_2)$.
- If $o_1 \cap o_2 \neq \varnothing$ then reject the line as being completely outside the clip region.
- If $o_1 \cup o_2 = \varnothing$ then accept the line as being completely inside the clip region.
- If $o_1 \cup o_2 \neq \varnothing$ then choose one of the boundaries in either o_1 or o_2 and find the intersection of the line with this boundary. Call the intersection point p_i.
- If the boundary chosen was from o_1 then clip the line p_i to p_2 else clip the line p_1 to p_i.

For implementation the regions in Figure 17.3 are usually represented by a four-bit encoding (Figure 17.4).

Now intersection and union can be represented by bit-ORing and -ANDing. (Dorr, 1990) provided a useful summary of the algorithm:

```
c0 = region_code(p0);
c1 = region_code(p1);
while (c0 OR c1 ≠ 0) {
   if(c0 AND c1 ≠ 0) then reject line_segment;
   i = if c0 ≠ 0 then 0 else 1;
   j = position of most significant bit in ci ;
   pi = intersection point of line p0 p1 with boundary j;
   ci = region_code(pi)
}
```

Parametric line clipping

The algorithm above for line clipping is the most popular in the sense of the most widely known and used. This does not mean to say that it is the only one. This section discusses the Liang–Barsky line clipping algorithm as an alternative (Liang and Barsky, 1984).

This is a so-called *parametric* line clipping algorithm, since it is based on the parametric form of the equation for the line segment from (x_1, y_1) to (x_2, y_2). As discussed above:

$$x(t) = x_1 + tdx$$
$$y(t) = y_1 + tdy \qquad \text{(EQ 17.17)}$$
$$0 \le t \le 1$$

Suppose that the clipping region is defined as in (EQ 17.1). Using (EQ 17.17) these inequalities can be rewritten as:

$$-tdx \le x_1 - Xmin$$
$$tdx \le Xmax - x_1$$
$$-tdy \le y_1 - Ymin \qquad \text{(EQ 17.18)}$$
$$tdy \le Ymax - y_1$$

Write these four inequalities as:

$$tp_i \le q_i$$
$$i = 1, 2, 3, 4 \qquad \text{(EQ 17.19)}$$

where, for example, $p_1 = -dx$, $q_1 = x_1 - Xmin$, and i is an index to the four boundaries, left, right, bottom, top. For any particular i, the ratio

$$r_i = \frac{q_i}{p_i} \qquad \text{(EQ 17.20)}$$

is the value of t for the intersection between the line and the corresponding clipping boundary.

The relationship between the line and a clipping boundary can be classified as "entering" or "leaving." Consider the situation when $p_i < 0$. Then, from (EQ 17.19)

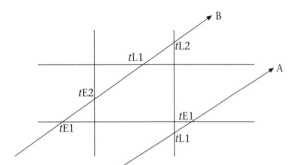

Figure 17.5
Parametric line
clipping: *t*E2 replaces
*t*E1; *t*L1 replaces *t*L2

$$t \geq \frac{q_i}{p_i}$$

(EQ 17.21)

This set of values for t represents the portion of the line which is inside the boundary. Since q_i/p_i is the t value at the intersection, and the intersection has the minimum t value for those values of t on the inside of the boundary, this must be an "entering" line.

Similarly, when $p_i > 0$, this will be a "leaving" line, i.e., the line is crossing from the visible to the invisible side of boundary i.

When $p_i = 0$, the inequality (EQ 17.19) reduces to $q_i \geq 0$, so that the line can be rejected if $q_i < 0$.

The idea behind the algorithm is shown in Figure 17.5. Any (non-vertical/horizontal) line will intersect all four boundaries, with a corresponding t value for each boundary. Each t value can be classified as an "entering" (tE) or "leaving" (tL) value. If ever tE > tL then the line must be outside the clipping region, as in line A. Otherwise, the required line is represented by the largest tE (≥ 0) and the smallest tL (≤ 1) such that tE $\leq$ tL.

The algorithm can therefore be stated as follows:

Parametric line clipping algorithm.   Initialize tE = 0 and tL = 1

```
for each boundary (i = 1,2,3,4)
   if pi < 0 then
      if qi < pi then reject the line, since this is an E line yet
      ri > 1
      if qi ≥ 0 then do nothing, since ri would be negative, which
      cannot change tE
      if qi < 0 then if ri > tL then reject the line else tE =
      max(ri,tE)

   if pi > 0 then
      if qi < 0 then reject the line, since this is line is L, yet
      ri < 0
      if qi ≥ pi then do nothing, since ri ≥ 1, which cannot change tL
      if qi > 0 then if ri < tE then reject the line else tL =
      min(ri,tL).
```

```
if pi = 0 then
    if qi < 0 then reject the line, since this contradicts the
    inequalities(EQ 17.18)

if the iteration has survived this far without a rejection of the
    line then the clipped line is given by the two parameter values
    tE and tL substituted into (EQ 17.17).
```

Note that if a trivial reject test (as in the Cohen–Sutherland algorithm) is carried out before entering this main loop, then cases such as $p_i < 0$, $q_i < p_i$ and $p_i > 0$, $q_i < 0$ cannot occur. Similarly, the "do nothing" cases cannot occur if a trivial accept test is performed first.

Nicholl–Lee–Nicholl line clipping

The Cohen–Sutherland (CS) algorithm relies on a coding scheme of the line end-points in order to quickly reject lines with end-points outside a particular clipping boundary, and quickly accept lines totally inside the clipping region. In other cases the line segment is intersected with one of the boundaries it is known to cross, and the procedure repeated with the truncated line. Cyrus and Beck (1978) and, as we have seen, Liang and Barsky (1984) introduced an alternative approach where the line is represented in parametric form. In the case of LB, the values of the parameter t corresponding to the points where the extended line segment intersects the clipping boundaries are used to find the clipped line. Initially these values are 0 and 1, corresponding to the line end-points, but are successively "squeezed down" by intersecting with the boundary lines. It has been argued by Liang and Barsky, based on empirical evidence that this parametric approach is faster than CS, for the case of a large number of "random" lines distributed over the display space, and various sizes of clipping region. However, this claim is doubtful (see Slater and Barsky, 1994).

Each of CS and LB necessitate computing intersection points that might not form one of the end-points of the clipped line. Nicholl, Lee, and Nicholl (1987) (NLN) introduced a new approach which computed intersection points of the line with the clip boundaries only when the new point is definitely one of the end-points of the clipped line. They use the space subdivision of Figure 17.3, but superimpose on it a further subdivision based on the location of the "first" end-point of the line. A particular case is shown in Figure 17.6, where the first end-point (p_1) is in cell {Left,Top}. The second end-point might be in any of the other regions, and the bold labels in the regions indicate that the Left, Top, or Bottom boundaries would be intersected by the line segment (the empty regions are trivial reject cases). A similar analysis holds for the other possibilities.

NLN show that their algorithm has the smallest number of arithmetic operations compared to many of the other known line-clipping algorithms. On the

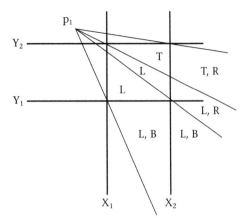

Figure 17.6
The NLN clipping algorithm. The bold labels indicate the boundaries which the line intersects, depending on the position of the second end-point

other hand, although the algorithm is quite simple to follow, its implementation is rather lengthy because of the large number of cases that need to be considered.

These three algorithms, CS, LB, and NLN, are well-known algorithms for line clipping in computer graphics. There are, however, lesser known variants of these, in addition to other algorithms. Improvements to the CS algorithm have been developed in Andreev (1989), Duvanenko *et al.* (1990), Shi *et al.* (1990) and Blinn (1991), who have concentrated on speeding up the algorithm by minimizing the work involved in recomputing line segment end-point encodings. In Liang and Barsky (1990) the original LB algorithm is improved by reducing the number of divisions in favor of more comparisons. Dorr (1990) provides a further improvement by showing that the LB algorithm can be performed entirely in integer arithmetic. Sobkow *et al.* (1987) developed an algorithm which is similar to NLN in substance (if not in form) in the sense that they enumerate all possible relationships between a line and the clipping region, and only compute intersection points where these are required as part of the output.

Another approach by Slater and Barsky (1994) traces the line segment through the subdivided space shown in Figure 17.3, much in the sense that Bresenham's algorithm (see later in this chapter) traces a line segment through the grid of pixels. The advantage of this algorithm is that it is "adaptive" in the sense that the boundaries are dealt with in the order in which they occur along the line segment, rather than in fixed order, as is the case with each of the other algorithms.

The complexity of the general clipping problem, of line segments against polygons, has been given attention in the computational geometry literature (where it is known as the Line-Polygon Classification problem, LPC), and is discussed, for example, in Tilove (1981), Skala (1989) and Rappaport (1991a).

17.3 Rasterization of line segments

A line segment has been clipped, is visible, and is now ready for display. In this section we consider how to do this. Given a frame-buffer and a function for setting individual pixels, we need to compute the pixel locations corresponding to the line segment.

We immediately encounter a fundamental problem of computer graphics – *sampling* and *aliasing*. A line is a continuous, infinitesimally thin entity, yet we are only able to sample it at the discrete locations available in the raster grid. Pixels are not infinitesimally small, but have a finite area, the area over which the light energy emitted from the pixel is distributed. Hence a line rendered on a raster display is a rather lumpy, discontinuous, jagged object – not at all a straight line! – as shown, for example, in Figure 17.7, depicting at large scale the set of pixels that might be chosen to represent a line fragment.

Generally, a displayed line has artifacts called *aliases* – aspects that do not exist in the ideal specification, but which emerge through the process of sampling a continuous entity on a discrete grid. Yet, given large enough display and colour resolutions, it is possible to fool the human perceptual system into seeing a straight line. In this section, we focus on computing the "best" pixel locations corresponding to a line.

A simple method

We assume the line to be (x_1, y_1) to (x_2, y_2) with slope dy/dx making use of (EQ 17.11). We further assume that the slope of the line is greater than 0 and less than 1. From (EQ 17.2) and (EQ 17.3) we can see that a possible algorithm for computing the pixels corresponding to a line segment would be as follows:

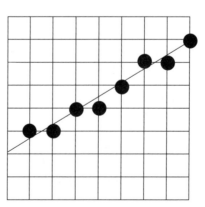

Figure 17.7
Ideal rasterization of
a line segment

```
void line0(int x1, int y1, int x2, int y2, Color color)
{
    float y;
    int x;
    for{x = x1; x <= x2; ++x){
        y = (dy/dx)*(x-x1) + y1;
        setPixel(x,round(y),color);
    }
}
```

This approach is naive. It ignores a characteristic property of the linear rela-tionship between x and y, that is, for each unit increment in x, y increments by a constant amount given by the slope dy/dx. Hence a better algorithm would be:

```
float line1(int x1, int y1, int x2, int y2, Color color)
{
    float y = y1 , m = dy/dx;
    setPixel(x1,y1,color);
    for(x=x1+1; x<=x2; ++x){
        y = y + m;
        setPixel(x,round(y),color);
    }
}
```

There are many ways in which line1 is preferable to line0, but even line1 involves floating point arithmetic, including a division, and rounding. In fact it is possible to construct a line drawing algorithm using only integer arith-metic, with additions, and multiplications by 2. This algorithm is due to Bresenham (1965). See also Foley *et al.* (1990).

Bresenham's line drawing algorithm

In this section, we assume that $x_1 = y_1 = 0$, and $dx > 0$, $dy > 0$, and that the slope is less than 1 ($0 < dy < dx$). These restrictions are useful only for developing the concepts of the algorithm, and can easily be overcome in implementation.

The task is to find the pixels which are, in some sense, "close" to the line. In Figure 17.8, the pixel positions are at the intersections of the vertical and horizontal lines, and suppose that the line is in the region shown. Now we adopt the criterion that at each successive x value, we will choose the pixel that has the minimum vertical distance from the line. Then at pixel $x = i$, pixel (i, y_i) was chosen, and the problem is to choose between $U(i + 1, y_i + 1)$ and $L(i + 1, y_i)$ for the next pixel along the line.

The line intersects $x = i + 1$ at the point $\left(i+1, \left(\dfrac{dy}{dx}\right)(i+1)\right)$. Call this point I (for intersection). According to our criteria, if the distance from U to I is less than that from I to L then we should choose U, otherwise choose L. (If the distances are equal, choose either.) Hence,

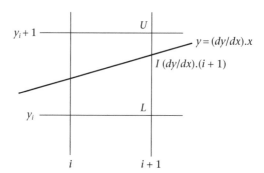

Figure 17.8
Choosing between
pixels U and L

if $U - I < I - L$ choose U else choose L (EQ 17.22)

This is equivalent to:

if $y_i + 1 - \dfrac{dy}{dx}(i + 1) < \dfrac{dy}{dx}(i + 1) - y_i$ choose U else choose L (EQ 17.23)

Since $dx > 0$ by our assumption, we can multiply throughout by dx, without changing the sense of the inequality:

if $dx(y_i + 1) - dy(i + 1) < dy(i + 1) - y_i dx$ choose U else choose L (EQ 17.24)

Now rearrange terms to bring everything to the left-hand side, to get:

if $dx(2y_i + 1) - 2dy(i + 1) < 0$ choose U else choose L (EQ 17.25)

Let

$e_i = dx(2y_i + 1) - 2dy(i + 1)$ (EQ 17.26)

then our condition becomes:

if $e_i < 0$ choose U else choose L (EQ 17.27)

Replacing i throughout by $i + 1$, in (EQ 17.26):

$e_{i+1} = dx(2y_{i+1} + 1) - 2dy(i + 2)$ (EQ 17.28)

Subtract (EQ 17.26) from (EQ 17.28) to see that:

$e_{i+1} = e_i + 2dx(y_{i+1} - y_i) - 2dy$ (EQ 17.29)

Now consider the meaning of "choose U" and "choose L." "Choose U" means that $y_{i+1} = y_i + 1$, and "choose L" means that $y_{i+1} = y_i$. We can therefore rewrite (EQ 17.27) as:

if $(e_i < 0)$ $\{y_{i+1} = y_i + 1\}$ else $\{y_{i+1} = y_i\}$ (EQ 17.30)

Now, using (EQ 17.29):

$$\text{if } (e_i < 0)\{y_{i+1} = y_i + 1; \; e_{i+1} = e_i + 2(dx - dy)\}$$
$$\text{else } \{y_{i+1} = y_i; \; e_{i+1} = e_i - 2dy\} \tag{EQ 17.31}$$

What this says is that at each successive x-coordinate, we can examine the sign of the variable e. If it is negative, then we choose the upper y-coordinate, and increment e by $2(dx - dy)$, otherwise we choose the lower y-coordinate and decrement e by $2dy$.

The variable e is an error term; it is the difference between the upper y-value at the pixel and the intersection of the line segment with the vertical line at the x-value, multiplied through by dx, to turn it into an integer value.

In order to construct a complete algorithm, we need to find a suitable starting value for e, that is, e_0. Substitute $i = 0$ in equation (EQ 17.26), to give

$$e_0 = dx - 2dy \tag{EQ 17.32}$$

since $y_0 = 0$ by our earlier assumption.

Now putting everything together we construct the following program:

Bresenham's algorithm. The line starts at $(0, 0)$ and ends at (dx, dy) with $dx > 0$, $dy > 0$ and $dy/dx < 1$

```
void bresenhamLine(int x1, int y1, int x2, int y2, Color color)
{
    int dx = x2-x1, dy = y2-y1;

    int e = dx - 2*dy;
    int y = 0;
    setPixel(0,0,color);
    for(int x=1; x<= dx; ++x) {
        if(e < 0){
            y = y + 1;
            e = e + 2*(dx - dy);
        }
        else{
            e = e - 2*dy;
        }
        setPixel(x,y,color);
    }
}
```

In practice, of course, we would not use multiplication to compute the multiplication by 2, but bit shifts, for example in C, $2*y$ may be computed by `y<<1`.

The algorithm has been developed for a special case – it assumes that the line starts at the origin and that x is the dominant axis ($0 < dy < dx$). If the line does not start at the origin, then the algorithm may be changed trivially by setting the starting value of y at y_1 and the starting value of x at x_1. If x is not the dominant axis, then swap the roles of x and y in the algorithm. If $dx < 0$ then decrement rather than increment, and the cases of lines that are exactly horizontal or vertical can be dealt with specially. A paper by Nicholl and Nicholl

(1990) shows how to construct program transformations corresponding to geometric transformations, and deals with the various cases of Bresenham's algorithm as an example.

We have presented the core of the algorithm for the rasterization of line segments. For the time being, we are not taking into account the complicating factor of aliasing, nor many improvements that can be made to this core. However, it is important to note that there has been research aimed at improving the performance of Bresenham's algorithm. The basic idea is that instead of looking at the possibilities of which pixel can be set just one step ahead (either U or L), consider the possible patterns several (say, four) steps ahead. In this way it is possible to quickly identify which pixels should be set between each successive four pixels, without doing any arithmetical computations. This and similar work is described in Rokne and Wyvill (1990), Rokne and Rao (1992) and Fung et al. (1992). Also, similar techniques to Bresenham's line drawing algorithm have been applied to other primitives such as circles and ellipses (see Pitteway, 1967; Bresenham, 1977).

17.4 Tracing a ray through a uniformly subdivided space

Bresenham's algorithm is fundamental for 2D graphics, but we motivated it by a problem in ray tracing: to efficiently trace a ray through a uniformly subdivided space, for reasons discussed in "Uniform space subdivision" on page 346). Although the problem of finding the best set of pixels corresponding to a line is similar to the problem of finding the set of cells that a ray traverses in a uniformly subdivided space, there are some crucial differences that do not admit a simple adaptation of a 3D version of Bresenham's algorithm to solve the ray traversal problem. More important is the way of thinking introduced by Bresenham's algorithm that we can apply in this slightly different context.

Figure 17.7 illustrated the problem of finding pixels corresponding to a line. Compare this with Figure 17.9. In the ray tracing case (in 3D of course) we need to enumerate the cells through which the ray passes. In our 2D example, for ray A the traversal algorithm should report: (0, 2), (1, 2), (1, 3), (2, 3), (3, 3), (3, 4), (4, 4), (5, 4), (5, 5), (6, 5). For ray B it should report: (1, 0), (2, 0), (2, 1), (3, 1), (4, 1), (5, 2), (6, 2).

Note that something happened in ray B which did not happen in ray A. There was a cell transition in the case of B when each cell coordinate increased by 1 (from (4, 1) to (5, 2)). This relates to the *connectedness* allowed by the traversal algorithm. Consider the 3D case, with the cell coordinates denoted as (u_1, u_2, u_3). Now when the ray moves into the next cell, each coordinate may either stay the same, increment by 1, or decrease by 1. For example, the next cell's coordinates might be $(u_1 + \Delta u_1, u_2 + \Delta u_2, u_3 + \Delta u_3)$ with each $\Delta u_i = 0$ or ± 1. There are 27 such possible transitions. Take away the null transition which has each $\Delta u_i = 0$, and we arrive at 26 possible transitions from one cell to the next. This is called a *26-connected path*. Another way to think about this is that the

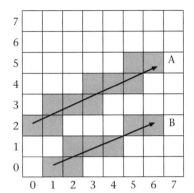

Figure 17.9
Rays traversing the cells in a uniformly subdivided space

next transition may involve the ray going through one of the *faces* of the cuboid cell (6 possibilities, where only one of the u_i changes) or exactly through one of the *edges* (12 possibilities, where exactly two of the u_i change) or exactly through one of the *vertices* (8 possibilities, where all three of the u_i change). Hence there are 26 possible transitions altogether. A traversal algorithm that supports all 26 possible transitions is a 26-connected algorithm. Of course, there is also the possibility of an *18-connected* algorithm (the algorithm only reports one or two coordinate changes per cell transition) or a *6-connected* algorithm, where at each transition only one u_i is allowed to change. In the context of ray tracing it is important to try to minimize the set of cells reported by a traversal, since for each enumerated cell we must intersect the ray with the set of object identifiers stored at that cell, which is a costly operation. Hence the 26-connected path should be reported. On the other hand, we are typically working in floating point arithmetic, a level of imprecision where it would be unlikely for a ray to pass exactly through a vertex of a cell. In the remainder of this section we will develop a 6-connected algorithm only. (A full derivation of a 26-connected algorithm can be found in Slater, 1992b.)

Suppose that the width (X axis), depth (Y axis) and height (Z axis) of each cell is s_1, s_2 and s_3 respectively. Let the ray be $p = (p_1, p_2, p_3)$ to $q = (q_1, q_2, q_3)$, with $du_j = q_j - p_j$, and $du = (du_1, du_2, du_3)$. We assume without loss of generality that $du_j > 0$ and $p_j > 0$. The equation of the ray is therefore:

$$p(t) = p + t\,du$$
$$t \in [0, 1]$$

(EQ 17.33)

As t varies from 0 to 1 the ray will intersect cells with successive integer coordinates $c(0), c(1), \ldots, c(m)$, where:

$$c(i) = (c_1(i), c_2(i), c_3(i)) \quad i = 0, \ldots, m$$

with

$$c(0) = (p_1/s_1, p_2/s_2, p_3/s_3)$$
$$c(m) = (q_1/s_1, q_2/s_2, q_3/s_3)$$

(EQ 17.34)

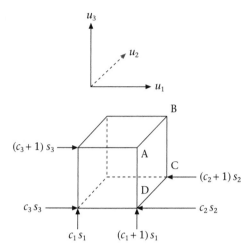

Figure 17.10
The cell with coordinates
(c_1, c_2, c_3)

and where the divisions are truncated to their integer part only. (For example, in this notation we would have 21/5 = 4).

Figure 17.10 shows a particular cell with cell coordinates (c_1, c_2, c_3). Notice how the actual 3D coordinates are obtained by multiplying by the width, depth, and height respectively.

Suppose the ray has entered cell $c(i)$, and consider the circumstances when $c_1(i + 1) = c_1(i) + 1$, so that the transition occurs along the x direction. This can only happen when the intersection between the ray and the cell faces is such that face ABCD is intersected. Suppose the intersection point is (v_1, v_2, v_3), then this implies that:

$$v_2 < (c_2 + 1)s_2$$
$$v_3 < (c_3 + 1)s_3$$

or

$$v_k < (c_k + 1)s_k \text{ for } k \neq 1$$

(EQ 17.35)

(We sometimes drop the "i" argument to the c values for notational convenience.) The intersection between the ray and the cell face with equation $u_1 = (c_1 + 1)s_1$ occurs when

$$(c_1 + 1)s_1 = p_1 + tdu_1$$

(EQ 17.36)

and therefore:

$$v_k = p_k + ((c_1 + 1)s_1 - p_1)\frac{du_k}{du_1}$$
$$k = 1, 2, 3$$

(EQ 17.37)

Using (EQ 17.37) and (EQ 17.35),

$$c_1(i+1) = c_1(i) + 1 \text{ when}$$

$$p_k + ((c_1+1)s_1 - p_1)\frac{du_k}{du_1} < (c_k+1)s_k \text{ for } k \neq 1 \qquad \text{(EQ 17.38)}$$

There is nothing special in this derivation about c_1, and the same argument can be followed through for any c_j. We arrive at:

$$c_j(i+1) = c_j(i) + 1 \text{ when}$$

$$p_k + ((c_j+1)s_j - p_j)\frac{du_k}{du_j} < (c_k+1)s_k \text{ for } k \neq j \qquad \text{(EQ 17.39)}$$

Recall that we are deriving a 6-connected algorithm, so that at each iteration one and only one of the c_j will be incremented.

Rearrange (EQ 17.39) to obtain:

$$\frac{(c_j+1)s_j - p_j}{du_j} < \frac{(c_k+1)s_k - p_k}{du_k} \qquad \text{(EQ 17.40)}$$

Write:

$$e_j(i) = \frac{(c_j+1)s_j - p_j}{du_j} \qquad \text{(EQ 17.41)}$$

Now the algorithm can be stated as:

$$c_j(i+1) = c_j(i) + 1 \text{ when}$$
$$e_j(i) < e_k(i) \text{ for } k \neq j \qquad \text{(EQ 17.42)}$$

Suppose it is the case that $c_j(i + 1) = c_j(i) + 1$, then from (EQ 17.41),

$$e_j(i+1) = e_j(i) + \frac{s_j}{du_j} \qquad \text{(EQ 17.43)}$$

Take the case $i = 0$ in (EQ 17.41), and use (EQ 17.34)

$$e_j(0) = \frac{((p_j/s_j)+1)s_j - p_j}{du_j}$$
$$= \frac{s_j - (p_j \% s_j)}{du_j} \qquad \text{(EQ 17.44)}$$

where "%" is the "mod" or remainder operator. This gives us the initialization for the "error" term which plays exactly the same role as the "e" in Bresenham's algorithm. From all these elements we can put together the following algorithm:

```
void UniformRay(p, q, s₁, s₂, s₃)
{
    /*initialization*/
    for(j=1,2,3){
        du_j = q_j - p_j;
        c_j = p_j/s_j;
        c_qj = q_j/s_j;
```

$$e_j = \frac{s_j - (p_j \% s_j)}{du_j} \, ;$$

$$r_j = \frac{s_j}{du_j} \, ;$$

```
  }
  Report(c);

  /*main loop*/
  while(c ≠ c_q){
    for(j=1,2,3){
      if(for each k ≠ j e_j < e_k){
        c_j = c_j + 1;
        e_j = e_j + r_j;
        break; /*out of for loop*/
      }
    }/*end for*/
    Report(c);
  }/*end while*/
}
```

Report means that the corresponding cell coordinates are returned to the calling program (the ray tracing program) and processed. This algorithm is similar to the one presented by Cleary and Wyvill (1988) for the case with all of the s_j equal.

Algorithms for reporting all cells traversed by a ray in a uniformly subdivided space have a long history, and, as can be seen, employ similar reasoning to Bresenham's algorithm in their derivation. Such algorithms are discussed by Dippe and Swensen (1984), Glassner (1984), Kaplan (1985), Fujimoto *et al.* (1986), Kaplan (1987), Amanatides (1987) and Cleary and Wyvill (1988). For a more recent discussion of the issues involved in tracing a ray through a non-uniformly subdivided space, see Havran and Bittner (2000).

17.5 Summary

In this chapter we have considered the basic geometric primitive: a straight line. Earlier in the chapter we were concerned with the problem of efficiently clipping a line to a rectangular boundary. The motivation was for intersecting rays by bounding volumes or cells in ray tracing. We have shown a solution for 2D, which is important in its own right. The extension to 3D is trivial, and the ideas presented in Chapter 10 on polygon clipping may be referred to help with this. The Cohen–Sutherland and Liang–Barsky algorithms extend easily to 3D, but the NLN algorithm does not extend to 3D.

In the second part of this chapter we considered the problem of efficiently rendering a line into a 2D grid (a pixelized display space) and derived Bresenham's algorithm. The original motivation for this was tracing the path of a ray in a 3D space subdivision. We returned to the issue of tracing a ray through a uniformly subdivided space, and showed how such an algorithm can be derived by an argument similar to Bresenham's.

18 Constructive solid geometry

18.1   Introduction

We started with ray casting and ray tracing spheres, and then moved exclusively to polygons. This chapter and the next one introduce additional primitives – in this chapter quadric surfaces, essentially a general class of object in which spheres are a special case, involving the representation and combination of solids that are based on implicit quadric equations. In the next chapter we consider another form, boundary representations that make use of higher-order parametric representations – the B-Spline curves and surfaces.

This chapter also introduces constructive solid geometry (CSG) which provides a representation for and a means of constructing solid objects. The idea is to represent primitive objects as point sets in 3D space, and then form more complex objects from unions, intersections, and differences of these primitives. These primitives can be as simple as half-spaces, that is, all points on one side of a plane. In this chapter we use quadric surfaces as the basic primitives, and a half-space is a special (degenerate) case of a quadric surface.

Rendering of CSG objects is, in this chapter, by means of ray casting, introduced in Chapter 5. As the reader will recall, this is "backwards ray tracing" to a first level, where light rays are traced from the center of projection through each pixel on the display, and the intersection with the nearest surface computed. Further reflected and refracted rays are not followed in this method.

Set operations are fundamental to CSG. However, when the point sets represent solids, non-solid results can be obtained by naively applying the

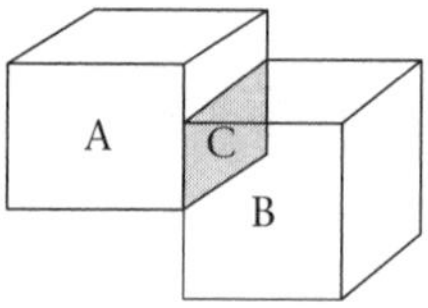

Figure 18.1
A∩B = C

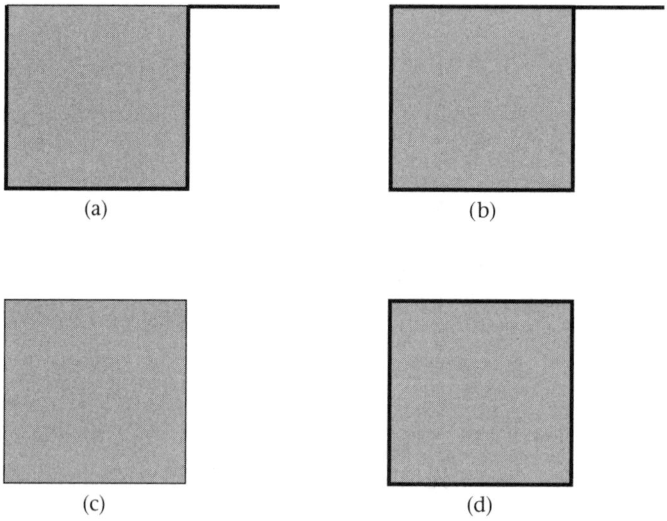

(a)   (b)

Figure 18.2
Regularized set operations:
the set (a) is closed in
(b), its interior is (c) and
the closure of its interior
(regularization) is (d)

(c)   (d)

intersection (∩), union (∪), and difference (−) operators to such solids. This is illustrated in Figure 18.1 where the intersection of the cuboids A and B results in an object C which has only one dimension.

In order to overcome this problem, the idea of *regularized set expressions* is used. In order to explain this, some straightforward ideas from topology are introduced. Given the space R^3 and a point $p \in R^3$ and $\varepsilon > 0$, define

$$B(p, \varepsilon) = \{q \in R^3 \mid \|q - p\| < \varepsilon\} \qquad \text{(EQ 18.1)}$$

where $\|q - p\|$ is the distance from q to p. $B(p, \varepsilon)$ represents an open ball of points with p at the center.

A *boundary point* of S is any point p such that $B(p, \varepsilon)$ contains points in S and also points in ~S (the complement of S) for any ε. The *boundary* of S is the set of all its boundary points. The boundary of S may or may not be a subset of S. S is an *open set* if it does not contain its boundary. S is a *closed set* if it does contain its boundary. The closure of S is defined by:

$$closure(S) = S \cup boundary(S) \qquad \text{(EQ 18.2)}$$

The *interior* of S is S minus all of its boundary points.

The *regularization* of S is the closure of *interior(S)*. This is illustrated in Figure 18.2.

Figure 18.3
An example of CSG:
the composite object
is constructed by
subtracting the cylinder
from the block

Block (B)   Cylinder (C)   Composite Object
                                                              (B – C)

Given any Boolean set operation, it is the regularization of the result which is required. Hence if *op* is one of intersection (∩), union (∪), or difference (–), then the regularized Boolean set operator is defined by:

A op* B = closure(interior(A op B))   (EQ 18.3)

18.2   Quadric surfaces

This section reviews the ideas of CSG and the use of ray casting in this context. The standard reference is Roth (1982), who shows how basic primitives such as a block, cylinder, sphere, cone, and torus can be combined to produce more complex shapes. The combination is achieved by set operators, union, difference, and intersection. An example is shown in Figure 18.3 where, for the sake of illustration, a block has a hole cut through it by a cylinder, making use of the subtraction operator. This shows just a single-level operation. Of course, expressions can be arbitrarily complex, with the CSG formula therefore forming a binary tree. At the leaves of the tree are the basic primitives, with interior nodes representing sub-components of the whole object, which is represented by the root.

First consider the intersection calculations. The parametric equation of a ray through two points was given in the previous chapter. In the present context, one of the points is the COP and the other represents the pixel through which the ray passes. Intersection of the ray with a block is essentially the same calculation as that of clipping to a 3D box discussed in the previous chapter. The other case to be considered here is that of quadric surfaces (which can represent, for example, cylinders, cones, and spheres). (See, for example, Heckbert, 1984.) A quadric surface is represented by the second-degree equation:

$$s(x, y, z) = pQ\,p^T = 0 \qquad\qquad (EQ\ 18.4)$$

where p is the row vector $(x, y, z, 1)$, and Q a symmetric 4×4 matrix of constants.

The quadric solid is expressed by the inequality:

$$s(x, y, z) = pQ\,p^T \le 0 \qquad\qquad (EQ\ 18.5)$$

Hence a quadric partitions space into three regions: points on the surface of the quadric, points inside the quadric, and points outside the quadric.

It is easy to ray cast quadric surfaces. Clearly a sphere is a special case, and this was considered in detail in Chapter 5. It is easy to generalize to any quadric as follows. The ray equation can be represented by:

$$p(t) = c + td \tag{EQ 18.6}$$

where c is the origin of the ray, and d the direction vector.

Substitution of (EQ 18.6) into (EQ 18.4) results in a quadratic equation in t. Depending on whether the ray intersects the quadric, the roots will be either both real or both imaginary (assuming Q non-singular). In other words, the ray intersects a non-degenerate quadric in two places or not at all.

Quadrics can be used to represent a number of useful solids by appropriate choice of the constants a to j in the expression for Q, where in its general form:

$$Q = \begin{bmatrix} a & b & c & d \\ b & e & f & g \\ c & f & h & i \\ d & g & i & j \end{bmatrix} \tag{EQ 18.7}$$

If we multiply out (EQ 18.4), we obtain:

$$s(x, y, z) = ax^2 + ey^2 + hz^2 + 2bxy + 2cxz + 2fyz + 2dx + 2gy + 2iz + j = 0 \tag{EQ 18.8}$$

Now we can obtain each of the following primitives, by appropriate choices for the constants in Q.

Plane

$$Ax + By + Cz - D = 0$$
$$a = e = h = b = c = f = 0 \tag{EQ 18.9}$$
$$2d = A,\ 2g = B,\ 2i = C,\ j = -D$$

Sphere

$$x^2 + y^2 + z^2 = r^2$$
$$a = e = h = 1$$
$$b = c = f = d = g = i = 0 \tag{EQ 18.10}$$
$$j = -r^2$$

Cylinder

$$x^2 + y^2 - 1 = 0$$
$$a = e = 1$$
$$h = b = c = f = d = g = i = 0 \tag{EQ 18.11}$$
$$j = -1$$

Cone

$$x^2 + y^2 - z^2 = 0$$
$$a = e = 1$$
$$h = -1$$
all other coefficients 0

(EQ 18.12)

Paraboloid

$$x^2 + y^2 + z = 0$$
$$a = e = 1$$
$$2i = 1$$
all other coefficients 0

(EQ 18.13)

Hyperboloid (of two sheets)

$$x^2 + y^2 - z^2 + 1 = 0$$
$$a = e = 1$$
$$h = -1$$
$$j = 1$$
all other coefficients 0

(EQ 18.14)

Hyperboloid (of one sheet)

$$x^2 + y^2 - z^2 - 1 = 0$$
$$a = e = 1$$
$$h = -1$$
$$j = -1$$
all other coefficients 0

(EQ 18.15)

In addition a *torus*, although not a quadric surface, can also be used relatively easily in ray casting, since the intersection equation is 4th degree and an analytic solution is available:

Torus

$$(x^2 + y^2 + z^2 - (a^2 + b^2))^2 = 4a^2(b^2 - z^2)$$

(EQ 18.16)

This represents a torus where a cross section would show two circles with distance between centers as $2a$ and radii b.

Roth also used a *unit cube* as a fundamental primitive.

In the case of quadrics, the normal at a point $p = (x, y, z)$ on the surface is particularly easy to find. This normal is the vector:

$$2pQ$$

(EQ 18.17)

Finally, it is easy to show that if all the points p belonging to a quadric are transformed by a transformation matrix M, then the resulting surface is also a quadric.

Let $q = pM$ be the point on the transformed surface corresponding to p on the surface of the quadric. Then assuming M to be non-singular:

$$qM^{-1} = p \qquad \text{(EQ 18.18)}$$

Using (EQ 18.5):

$$qM^{-1}Q(qM^{-1})^T = 0 \qquad \text{(EQ 18.19)}$$

If we write $R = M^{-1}Q(M^{-1})^T$ then it is clear that each transformed point q also belongs to a quadric surface.

18.3 Ray classification and combination

The CSG tree is a binary tree, where each interior node contains a left tree, a right tree, and a combination operator such as union, intersection, or difference. Hence we might represent this as the structure:

```
typedef struct _csgtree{
    Operator op; //defines the combination operator at this node - 0
    for a primitive
    Quadric primitive; //the primitive if this is a leaf node - 0 for
    an interior node
    struct_csgtree *left;
    struct_csgtree *right;
} CSGTree;
```

Each leaf node represents a primitive, typically a quadric solid. For any given ray, the result of its intersection computations against the objects in the CSG tree will be an ordered sequence of parametric t-values $t_1, t_2, \ldots, t_n$, where n is the number of intersections. However, in order to take account of the combination primitives in the CSG tree, the tree is traversed according to the following recursive algorithm, and then the t-values combined as described below.

```
Classification RayCast(Ray ray, CSGTRee *solid)
{
    if(solid->op){
        left = RayCast(ray,solid->left);
        right = RayCast(ray,solid->right);
        Combine(solid->op,left,right);
    }
    else{
        //transform ray to local primitive coordinates
        switch(solid->primitive){
            CASE cube:.........................
            CASE sphere:{intersection
            CASE cone:calculations}
            CASE cylinder:........................
            //etc......................
        }
    }
}
```

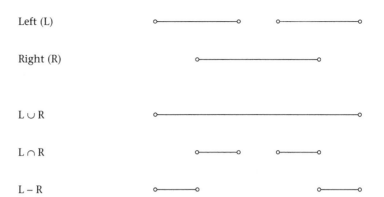

Figure 18.4
The CSG combination
function

The `RayCast` function takes as arguments the ray and a pointer to the CSG tree representing the solid, and returns a sequence of t-values representing the intersections. (Together with each t-value will typically be a pointer to a record giving the properties of the surface to which the t-value corresponds). If the pointer points to an interior node or the root, then the function is called recursively for the left and right branches of the tree at this node. Then the results of these recursive calls are combined to produce the overall sequence of values for the tree. If the pointer is to a primitive then the intersection calculations for the primitive are performed.

Roth's paper describes a unifying method for representation of the primitive solids, which aids in the computation of the intersection calculations. Each primitive is represented in a local coordinate system, for example a unit cube for the block, and unit sphere centered at the origin in the case of the sphere. Now when a user of the system inserts a primitive into WC space, this is stored internally by the system as a 4×4 transformation matrix from the local coordinate system to the WC space (the inverse of this matrix is also stored). When a ray is to be intersected with a primitive, only the ray needs to be transformed to the local coordinate space for the primitive (by using the inverse matrix), so that all intersection calculations can take place in the local space. This also avoids the computation involved in applying the matrix to the description of the primitives in order to transform them into WC. Hence the system stores the current translation, rotation, and scaling of all primitives entirely by storing the matrix and its inverse.

The `Combine` function produces a classification of the t-values according to the set operator to be used. This is illustrated in Figure 18.4.

Given the two sets of t-values, they are combined according to the operator as shown, with an obvious interpretation for each of the three operators.

Ray casting is clearly computationally very expensive. Roth estimates that more than 50% of the processing time is spent in intersection calculations. For full ray tracing this is more like 90%. In order to reduce the computational overhead Roth suggested the use of bounding boxes for each primitive, in order to construct a 'trivial' acceptance/rejection test, as we discussed in Chapter 16. The various methods discussed in that chapter can also be applied.

18.4 Summary

This chapter essentially extended Chapter 5 by showing how spheres are a special case of a more general primitive, a quadric. There is an elegant way to represent all quadrics, and we examined a class of primitives, including planes, that fall into this category. Second, we have introduced a new way of constructing objects from set-theoretic combinations of such primitives. We also saw how to ray cast such CSG objects. Also in this chapter we have considered objects as solids, rather than only the representation of boundaries. Note that a CSG scene can be rendered (with ray casting) without the use of polygons at all. For an alternative method see Salesin and Stofi (1990).

In the next chapter we return to a boundary form of representation, and a parametric rather than the implicit equation approach of quadrics. We will introduce the important topic of B-Spline curves and surfaces, and show how these may be rendered with line segments (for curves) and polygons (for surfaces).

19 Introduction to computer aided geometric design

19.1 Introduction

Computer aided geometric design (CAGD) is concerned with the specification, properties, and rendering of curves and surfaces that are to be used in the computer design of some artefact. The field has its origins in the car and shipbuilding industries – two of the most notable researchers in the field carried out their pioneer work while working for Renault and Citroen in France.

A brief history of geometric modeling is given by Mortenson (1985, pp. 5–7), and the introductory comments of Forrest in Bartels *et al.* (1987) and Bézier in Farin (1996) provide further information. (See also the tutorial by Farin, 1992.) They trace the origins of CAGD from problems in numerically controlled (NC) machinery in manufacturing, especially in the shipbuilding, aircraft, and automobile industries. Limitations in NC specifications, and also problems in curve and surface fitting in statistics, stimulated research into curves, sculptured surfaces, and solids, leading to mathematical descriptions of lofting, Coons patches, and the work of Bézier and de Casteljau with parametrically defined triangular and rectilinear surface patches.

In this chapter we introduce the fundamental ideas of CAGD using a mathematical approach based on *polar forms* (or *blossoms*). The curves and surfaces used in CAGD are represented as piecewise polynomials with continuity constraints imposed on the "joins" where two polynomial curves or surfaces meet. Polar forms were first used by de Casteljau (1986), and later by Ramshaw (Ramshaw, 1987a, 1987b, and see also Lee, 1989) as a way of representing polynomials, elegantly demonstrating their intrinsic connection with Bézier curves. Ramshaw used the term "blossom" for polar forms, and we will use this terminology interchangeably with "polar form." We introduce polynomials and blossoms in the next section. Then we use blossoms to define Bézier curves, in order to specify a single polynomial curve segment. Realistic designs require many curve segments to be joined together end-to-end to construct a curve more complex in shape than can be realized by any one curve corresponding to a polynomial of relatively low degree (usually no more than 3). Yet when curves join together continuity constraints must be satisfied at the joins. Continuity is discussed and then exploited in the construction of B-Spline curves. These ideas are shown to extend easily to surfaces.

19.2   Polynomials and blossoms

Polynomials

In this section we consider the following ideas – functions (or maps), affine interpolation, polynomials and their blossoms. Polynomials are fundamental to CAGD; although polynomials are expressions involving only additions and multiplications, they may be used to represent a large variety of curve and surface shapes, as we shall see.

A polynomial is an expression of the form:

$$a_0 + a_1 t + a_2 t^2 + \ldots + a_n t^n \qquad \text{(EQ 19.1)}$$

This is called an nth degree polynomial, since the highest power of t is n. For example: $1 + 2t + 3t^2$ is a second degree polynomial, and $4 + 5t + 6t^2 + 9t^3$ is a third degree polynomial.

It should be noted that a polynomial of any degree can also be considered as a "degenerate" polynomial of higher degree. For example, although $1 + 2t + 3t^2$ is a second degree polynomial, we might under certain circumstances agree to call it a degenerate third degree polynomial: $1 + 2t + 3t^2 + 0t^3$.

We shall also see that a polynomial is a special case of a richer entity known as a *blossom*. It is this connection between polynomials and blossoms that allows a full expression of CAGD theory and methods in a relatively simple and elegant manner.

Revision of functions and affine maps

A function is a rule that associates each member of a given set, the *domain*, with a unique member of a set, the *image* or *co-domain*. (The domain and image may be the same set in some cases.) For example, consider the function, x, that given any number, t, produces the square of that number t^2. Then

$$x(t) = t^2 \qquad \text{(EQ 19.2)}$$

Suppose y is another function that adds 1 to any number, then

$$y(t) = 1 + t \qquad \text{(EQ 19.3)}$$

and finally, consider

$$\begin{aligned} p(t) &= (x(t), y(t)) \\ &= (t^2, t) \end{aligned} \qquad \text{(EQ 19.4)}$$

then p is a function that maps any number t into a point in 2-dimensional space.

A function such as p in (EQ 19.4) is an example of a parametric equation. Imagine that $p(t)$ specifies the position of a point at time t, then as t varies over some range, the point will move in 2-dimensional space on a path given by the rule specified by (EQ 19.4). It would be useful if the reader would sketch the path of p for t in the range 0 to 1.

We introduced the idea of an affine map in Chapter 2 (see "Affine transformations" on page 62). Consider the following affine function:

$$f(t) = a + bt \qquad \text{(EQ 19.5)}$$

For example, $f(t)$ might represent the distance of an object from a given point, while travelling at constant velocity b, and initial distance a. Now suppose that the distance is known at two particular times t_1 and t_2 – in other words, $f(t_1)$ and $f(t_2)$ are known values. We require the distance at some other time t, where t is, for example, in the interval t_1 to t_2 (inclusive) (i.e., the interval $[t_1, t_2]$).

Of course, we could find $f(t)$ by using (EQ 19.5), but let us consider another route instead.

The following identity is easy to show:

$$t = \left(\frac{t_2 - t}{t_2 - t_1}\right)t_1 + \left(\frac{t - t_1}{t_2 - t_1}\right)t_2 \qquad \text{(EQ 19.6)}$$

This expresses t as a weighted average (in fact a barycentric combination) of t_1 and t_2.

f in (EQ 19.5) is an affine function that maps the real line R to itself, and we know from Chapter 8 that affine functions preserve barycentric combinations. It follows that:

$$f(t) = \left(\frac{t_2 - t}{t_2 - t_1}\right)f(t_1) + \left(\frac{t - t_1}{t_2 - t_1}\right)f(t_2) \qquad \text{(EQ 19.7)}$$

Equations (EQ 19.6) and (EQ 19.7) give us a fundamental result that will be used throughout this chapter.

Multi-affine maps

Examine the following function:

$$f(t_1, t_2) = 1 + 2t_1 + 3t_2 + 7t_1t_2 \qquad \text{(EQ 19.8)}$$

For example, $f(4, 5) = 1 + 2 \times 4 + 3 \times 5 + 7 \times 4 \times 5 = 164$. Suppose that t_1 is considered as a fixed number, for example $t_1 = 1$. Then: $f(1, t_2) = 1 + 2 + 3t_2 + 7t_2 = 3 + 10t_2$ which is obviously of the same form as (EQ 19.5). Similarly, for any fixed value of t_2, (EQ 19.8) becomes an affine function of t_1. An equation such as (EQ 19.9) is called a multi-affine function of t_1 and t_2, since it is affine in each of the variables considered separately.

Here are some more examples:

$$f(t_1, t_2) = 4 + 5t_1 + 4t_2 - t_1t_2$$
$$f(t_1, t_2, t_3) = 1 + 3t_1 - 2t_2 + 6t_3 + t_1t_2 - t_1t_3 + 10t_2t_3 - 24t_1t_2t_3$$

the second case being a multi-affine function of three arguments.

In general, a multi-affine function of n arguments, $t_1, t_2, \ldots, t_n$, is a sum consisting of

- a constant (independent of t);
- the sum of constants times each of the arguments separately (e.g., $3t_1 - 2t_2 + 6t_3$);
- the sum of constants times each of the arguments taken two at a time (e.g., $t_1t_2 - t_1t_3 + 10t_2t_3$);
- the sum of constants times each of the arguments taken three at a time, . . . ;
- a constant times the product of each of the arguments (e.g., $-24t_1t_2t_3$).

Properties of multi-affine maps

Affineness. A multi-affine map is affine separately in each of its arguments.

Symmetry. A multi-affine map is *symmetric* when any permutation of the arguments results in the function having the same value.

Consider a general 3-argument multi-affine map:

$$f(t_1, t_2, t_3) = c_0 + c_1 t_1 + c_2 t_2 + c_3 t_3 + c_4 t_1 t_2 + c_5 t_1 t_3 + c_6 t_2 t_3 + c_7 t_1 t_2 t_3 \quad \text{(EQ 19.9)}$$

For this to be symmetric we must have $c_1 = c_2 = c_3$ and $c_4 = c_5 = c_6$.

This is a consequence of the requirement that $f(t_1, t_2, t_3) = f(t_i, t_j, t_k)$ where (i, j, k) is, in turn, each of the six permutations $(1, 2, 3)$, $(1, 3, 2)$, $(3, 1, 2)$, $(3, 2, 1)$, $(2, 3, 1)$, $(2, 1, 3)$.

Diagonal. The diagonal of a multi-affine map is obtained by setting all arguments to be the same value, say t. The diagonal of an n-argument multi-affine map is a polynomial of degree n.

For example, consider the 4-argument multi-affine map:

$$f(t_1, t_2, t_3, t_4) = 1 + t_1 + t_1 t_2 + 5 t_2 t_3 t_4 - 11 t_1 t_2 t_3 t_4 \quad \text{(EQ 19.10)}$$

Then the diagonal is a 4th degree polynomial:

$$f(t, t, t, t) = 1 + t + t^2 + 5t^3 - 11t^4 \quad \text{(EQ 19.11)}$$

Blossoming theorem

There is a strong connection between multi-affine maps and polynomials that is at the heart of CAGD:

- Every n-argument multi-affine map has a unique nth degree polynomial as its diagonal.

- Every nth degree polynomial corresponds to a unique symmetric n-argument multi-affine map that has that polynomial as its diagonal.

The first part of the theorem is obvious; the second part is less obvious but easy to prove. We shall look at an example. Consider the polynomial:

$$F(t) = 1 + 3t + 9t^2 + 5t^3 \quad \text{(EQ 19.12)}$$

Now the diagonal of any 3-argument multi-affine map is a third degree polynomial. Hence the multi-affine map for which (EQ 19.12) is the diagonal must be of the general form given in (EQ 19.9).

There are eight unknowns, c_0 to c_7, in this expression. For symmetry we know that $c_1 = c_2 = c_3 = A$ (say), and $c_4 = c_5 = c_6 = B$ (say), so that (EQ 19.9) becomes:

$$f(t_1, t_2, t_3) = c_0 + A(t_1 + t_2 + t_3) + B(t_1 t_2 + t_2 t_3 + t_1 t_3) + c_7 t_1 t_2 t_3 \quad \text{(EQ 19.13)}$$

Now setting $t_1 = t_2 = t_3$,

$$f(t, t, t) = c_0 + 3At + 3Bt^2 + c_7 t^3 \quad \text{(EQ 19.14)}$$

Equating the coefficients in (EQ 19.12) and (EQ 19.14) we get:

$$c_0 = 1$$
$$3A = 3, \text{ and so } A = 1$$
$$3B = 9 \text{ and so } B = 3 \qquad \text{(EQ 19.15)}$$
$$c_7 = 5$$

There is no other symmetric 3-argument multi-affine map that corresponds to (EQ 19.12). In the general case of an nth degree polynomial, we can follow a similar argument, and find that the number of unknowns (c_i) exactly matches the number of linear equations in those unknowns, to arrive at the unique symmetric multi-affine map of n arguments.

This multi-affine map is called the *blossom* (or *polar form*) of the polynomial. Ramshaw pointed out that, in a sense, the blossom and the polynomial represent the same underlying abstract entity; however, the blossom is a richer representation.

In order to find the blossom of any polynomial we can use the following rules:

For an nth degree polynomial, the kth power, t^k is represented by the average of products of all selections of k terms from the n arguments $t_1, t_2, \ldots, t_n$. For example, in the case where $n = 3$ and $k = 2$:

$$\frac{t_1 t_2 + t_1 t_3 + t_2 t_3}{3} \qquad \text{(EQ 19.16)}$$

Two further examples:

$$F(t) = 1 + t + t^2$$
$$f(t_1, t_2) = 1 + \frac{t_1 + t_2}{2} + t_1 t_2 \qquad \text{(EQ 19.17)}$$

$$F(t) = a + bt + ct^2 + dt^3$$
$$f(t_1, t_2, t_3) = a + b\left(\frac{t_1 + t_2 + t_3}{3}\right) + c\left(\frac{t_1 t_2 + t_1 t_3 + t_2 t_3}{3}\right) + dt_1 t_2 t_3 \qquad \text{(EQ 19.18)}$$

19.3   Blossoms and Bézier curves

de Casteljau triangles

Suppose $f(t_1, t_2)$ is a multi-affine symmetric function, and r, s are numbers with $r < s$. Constants x_0, x_1, x_2 are given, such that

$$x_0 = f(r, r)$$
$$x_1 = f(r, s) \qquad \text{(EQ 19.19)}$$
$$x_2 = f(s, s)$$

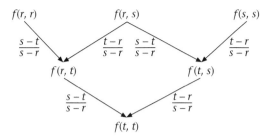

Figure 19.1
Computing the diagonal

The problem is to find $f(t, t)$ for any $r \leq t \leq s$.

Note first of all that in finding $f(t, t)$, the diagonal, we are evaluating the second degree polynomial $F(t) = f(t, t)$ (recall the diagonal property of a multi-affine function). Now since $f(t_1, t_2)$ is multi-affine, it is affine in t_1 and t_2 separately. Therefore, we can use the result (EQ 19.7), to find that

$$f(r, t) = \left(\frac{s-t}{s-r}\right) f(r, r) + \left(\frac{t-r}{s-r}\right) f(r, s)$$

$$f(t, s) = \left(\frac{s-t}{s-r}\right) f(r, s) + \left(\frac{t-r}{s-r}\right) f(s, s)$$

(EQ 19.20)

Since f is supposed to be symmetric, we know that $f(t, s) = f(s, t)$ and therefore we can again interpolate between r and s to get:

$$f(t, t) = \left(\frac{s-t}{s-r}\right) f(r, t) + \left(\frac{t-r}{s-r}\right) f(s, t)$$

(EQ 19.21)

to get the required value. We can represent this calculation in graphical form as a tree structure as shown in Figure 19.1. The first row represents the original given values. The second row and the edges leading to that row represent the equations (EQ 19.20). The final row and edges leading to it represent (EQ 19.21). The labels on the edges are the interpolation coefficients in those equations. The notation expresses the general equivalence shown in Figure 19.2. This type of representation is called a *de Casteljau triangle*.

Exactly the same technique can be used to solve the equivalent 3-parameter problem: $f(t_1, t_2, t_3)$ is a symmetric multi-affine function, $r < s$, and the following values are known:

$$x_0 = f(r, r, r)$$
$$x_1 = f(r, r, s)$$
$$x_2 = f(r, s, s)$$
$$x_3 = f(s, s, s)$$

(EQ 19.22)

Figure 19.2
Graphical notation for interpolation: $C = xA + yB$, for $x + y = 1$

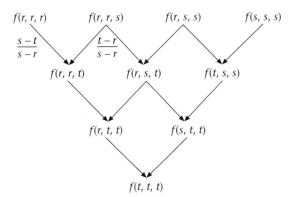

Figure 19.3
Evaluating the diagonal
$F(t) = f(t, t, t)$

The problem is to find $F(t) = f(t, t, t)$ where t is some number between r and s. The calculation can be set out as shown in Figure 19.3. This uses the same convention as before, and the labeling of the edges is the same.

The reader should write down the equivalent 4-parameter case and obtain the solution $F(t) = f(t, t, t, t)$.

Bézier curves

In this section we introduce a fundamental form for CAGD – Bézier curves. Suppose we are given three *points* p_0, p_1, p_2, and the equations:

$$p_0 = f(r, r)$$
$$p_1 = f(r, s) \tag{EQ 19.23}$$
$$p_2 = f(s, s)$$

Now $f(t_1, t_2)$ consists of *two* functions – one for the x component and one for the y component:

$$f(t_1, t_2) = (x(t_1, t_2), y(t_1, t_2))$$
$$F(t) = (X(t), Y(t)) \tag{EQ 19.24}$$

In other words, $F(t)$ is a vector-valued polynomial, consisting in this case of two polynomials $X(t)$ and $Y(t)$, each of which is a polynomial, and each of which has its corresponding polar form. In this example, both polynomials are quadratics.

Now carry out the same interpolation algorithm as above, in order to compute, for any t in the range r to s (inclusive), the *point* associated with $f(t, t)$. The geometry of this process is shown in Figure 19.4.

Each edge of this graph is interpolated with the same ratio, $(s - t):(t - r)$, as in (EQ 19.20) and (EQ 19.21).

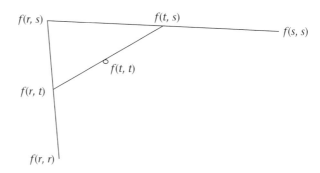

Figure 19.4
Geometric interpretation
of a de Casteljau triangle
(degree 2)

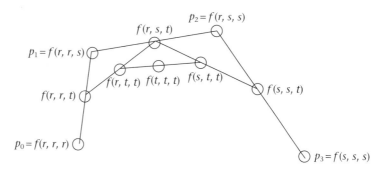

Figure 19.5
Evaluating a point on
a cubic Bézier curve

Notice that these interpolations are carried out for a particular value of
t. If we repeated the calculation for each value of t between r and s, then
all such points $f(t, t)$ would lie on a curve – which is called a *second degree
Bezier curve*. The original points p_0, p_1, p_2 are called the *control points* of the
curve.

Exactly the same process can be carried out with the three argument case,
as shown in Figure 19.5.

Here we start with four control points:

$$p_0 = f(r, r, r)$$
$$p_1 = f(r, r, s)$$
$$p_2 = f(r, s, s)$$
$$p_3 = f(s, s, s)$$

(EQ 19.25)

We use the algorithm shown in Figure 19.3 to evaluate $f(t, t, t)$ for any t in the
range r to s. Any particular t (e.g., $t = 0.5$ as in the diagram) would give us one
point on the curve. If we repeated the process for all t, we would obtain the
Bézier curve of degree 3, for $t \in [r, s]$. A Bézier curve of any degree can be
defined in a similar way.

Properties of the Bézier curve

We can derive the following properties based on the way that the curves are constructed. Let us consider cubic Bézier curves (degree 3) and call the point on the curve at value t, $f(t, t, t) = F(t)$. Then (show these results for yourself):

(1) End-point interpolation: $F(r) = p_0$ and $F(s) = p_3$.

(2) Invariance under change of parametric interval: if we transform the interval $[r, s]$ into the interval $[a + br, a + bs]$ (i.e., an affine map of the interval) then the shape of the curve is unaltered.

(3) Convex hull property: any point on the curve must be within the convex hull defined by the control points.

(4) Affine invariance: if we take an affine transformation of the control points p_i ($i = 0, 1, 2, 3$) and draw the curve based on these transformed points, then this will be the same curve as we would get by applying this transformation to each point on the original curve.

(5) If the control points p_i are on a straight line, then the Bézier curve is a straight line.

(6) The tangent vectors to the curve at the end-points are
$$F'(r) = 3(p_1 - p_0) \qquad F'(s) = 3(p_3 - p_2)$$

The de Casteljau algorithm

In Figure 19.5 let us relabel as follows:

$$q_0 = f(r, r, r) \qquad q_1 = f(r, r, t) \qquad q_2 = f(r, t, t)$$
$$r_0 = q_3 = f(t, t, t)$$
$$r_1 = f(t, t, s) \qquad r_1 = f(t, s, s) \qquad r_2 = f(s, s, s)$$

(EQ 19.26)

as shown in Figure 19.6.

Examine the pattern for the q points – this gives us the control points for a Bézier curve in the range r to t, say Q. Similarly, the r points gives us a Bézier curve in the range t to s, say R. These two curves end-to-end give us the original Bézier curve, based on the p points, P. Hence we have the basis of a simple recursive divide-and-conquer algorithm for generating the curve P:

> If the points p_i are in a straight line, draw the line (property 5), otherwise split into the two sets of points Q and R, and apply the same principle recursively to each set of points. Of course, it is unlikely that the points will lie exactly on a straight line, but we can adopt a tolerance level, and so draw a line when the points are within some tolerance of a straight line.

This algorithm can be written as:

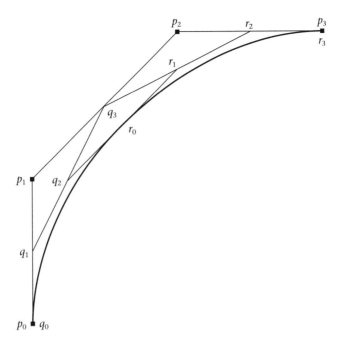

Figure 19.6
Cubic de Casteljau

```
void bezier(Point p[]){
   Point q[], r[];
   if(colinear(p)) Line(p0 ,p3 );
   else{
      /*split p into q and r*/
      split(p,q,r);
      bezier(q);
      bezier(r);
   }
}
```

The Boolean function `colinear` returns as "true" when the 4 points are approximately on a straight line, and `split` computes the points at some convenient value such as $t = 0.5$, using the algorithm above.

In order to test whether the four points are approximately on a straight line, find the equation of the line joining p_0 to p_3 in the form $ax + by + c = 0$. Then the distance $D(X, Y)$ of any point (X, Y) from this line is given by:

$$D^2(X, Y) = \frac{(aX + bY + c)^2}{a^2 + b^2}$$
(EQ 19.27)

Therefore if $D(p_1)$ and $D(p_2)$ are each less than some predefined tolerance, the four points can be said to be approximately colinear. The inequality $D^2(X, Y) < T$, for some tolerance T, can be organized in such a way that there are no divisions involved in its evaluation (by multiplying throughout by the denominator, which is always positive).

19.4 **Bézier curves and the Bernstein basis**

Polynomial form of the Bézier curve

Consider the second degree Bézier as defined in (EQ 19.23) and (EQ 19.24). Without loss of generality (given property 2) we restrict the parametric range to [0, 1], i.e., $r = 0$ and $s = 1$. Then from (EQ 19.20):

$$f(0, t) = (1 - t)f(0, 0) + tf(0, 1) = (1 - t)p_0 + tp_1$$
$$f(t, 1) = (1 - t)f(0, 1) + tf(1, 1) = (1 - t)p_1 + tp_2$$
(EQ 19.28)

and therefore using (EQ 19.21):

$$F(t) = f(t, t) = (1 - t)^2 f(0, t) + tf(t, 1)$$
$$= (1 - t)^2 p_0 + 2t(1 - t)p_1 + t^2 p_2$$
(EQ 19.29)

We could construct a similar argument for the cubic case, starting from (EQ 19.25). In this case:

$$F(t) = f(t, t, t)$$
$$= (1 - t)^3 p_0 + 3(1 - t)^2 t p_1 + 3(1 - t)t^2 p_2 + t^3 p_3$$
(EQ 19.30)

In (EQ 19.35) the coefficients of the points are successive terms in the binomial expansion of $((1 - t) + t)^2$, and in (EQ 19.36) of $((1 - t) + t)^3$. In general, if we carried out a similar derivation for any degree n, we would find the same result. (This can be proven, for example, by induction.)

Therefore a way to define a point on a general (nth degree) Bézier curve is to start with the $n + 1$ control points, identified with multi-affine functions:

$$p_0 = f(0, 0, \ldots, 0)$$
$$p_1 = f(0, 0, \ldots, 1)$$
$$\ldots$$
$$p_n = f(1, 1, \ldots, 1)$$
(EQ 19.31)

where in the blossom for p_i there are i 1s and $(n - i)$ 0s.

Now if we apply the rules for finding the diagonal $F(t) = f(t, t, \ldots, t)$ for any $t \in [0, 1]$, then we would obtain:

$$F(t) = \sum_{i=0}^{n} B_{n,i}(t)p_i, \quad t \in [0, 1]$$
(EQ 19.32)

where

$$B_{n,i}(t) = \binom{n}{i} t^i (1 - t)^{n-1}$$

and
(EQ 19.33)

$$\binom{n}{i} = \frac{n!}{i!(n - i)!}$$

Bernstein basis

The functions $B_{n,i}(t)$ are known as *Bernstein basis* functions. A *basis* has the property that any polynomial at all can be expressed uniquely as a linear combination of basis functions. For example, suppose we were to restrict our attention to polynomials of maximum degree 3, then any such polynomial has the form:

$$a_0 + a_1t + a_2t^2 + a_3t^3 \qquad \text{(EQ 19.34)}$$

Now the *monomial* (or *power*) basis consists of the polynomials $1, t, t^2, t^3$. It is obvious that any polynomial of the form (EQ 19.34) can be written as an affine combination of these basic polynomials. It is also true that any such polynomial can be written in the form:

$$\alpha_0 B_{3,0}(t) + \alpha_1 B_{3,1}(t) + \alpha_2 B_{3,2}(t) + \alpha_3 B_{3,3}(t) \qquad \text{(EQ 19.35)}$$

In this sense these functions $B_{3,i}(t)$ are a basis for all third degree polynomials. In general the Bernstein polynomials of degree n are a basis for all nth degree (or lower) polynomials.

The properties of these basis functions are:

$$B_{n,i}(t) \geq 0, \text{ all } t \in [0, 1]$$

$$\sum_{i=0}^{n} B_{n,i}(t) = 1 \qquad \text{(EQ 19.36)}$$

The first should be clear from the definition, and the second follows since these functions are the successive terms in the expansion of $((1 - t) + t)^n = 1$. From these properties and (EQ 19.33) we can deduce:

- any point on the Bézier curve is a barycentric combination of the control points;
- in fact a convex combination since the coefficients sum to 1; and hence
- any point on the curve must lie inside the convex hull of the control points.

Tangent vectors

Given a parametric equation defining a curve, e.g.

$$F(t) = (X(t), Y(t)) = (1 + 3t^2 - t^3, 1 + 3t - t^3), \qquad \text{(EQ 19.37)}$$

we will need to investigate certain properties of the curve using the traditional tools of analysis (e.g., gradient of the curve). We define the tangent vector

$$F'(t) = (X'(t), Y'(t)) \qquad \text{(EQ 19.38)}$$

where the dash denotes differentiation with respect to the parameter. This tangent vector is a vector that indicates the direction of the curve at the point on the curve associated with t, and the magnitude of the tangent vector says something about the "flatness" of the curve at that point. Hence for the curve above,

$$F'(t) = (6t - 3t^2, 3 - 3t^2) \tag{EQ 19.39}$$

Of particular interest are the tangent vectors at the beginning and end of the curve. Suppose that this curve was defined over the range $t \in [0, 1]$, then at the start of the curve $F'(0) = (0, 3)$ and at the end $F'(1) = (3, 0)$. The length and direction of these tangent vectors give an indication of the shape of the curve at the start and end.

Let's find the Bézier control points for the curve defined by (EQ 19.37). The polar form is, using (EQ 19.18):

$$f(t_1, t_2, t_3) = (x(t_1, t_2, t_3), y(t_1, t_2, t_3))$$
$$x(t_1, t_2, t_3) = 1 + (t_1 t_2 + t_2 t_3 + t_1 t_3) - t_1 t_2 t_3$$
$$y(t_1, t_2, t_3) = 1 + (t_1 + t_2 + t_3) - t_1 t_2 t_3$$

Substituting (t_1, t_2, t_3) by $(0, 0, 0)$, $(0, 0, 1)$, $(0, 1, 1)$, and $(1, 1, 1)$ respectively, we get:

$$p_0 = (1, 1)$$
$$p_1 = (1, 2)$$
$$p_2 = (2, 3)$$
$$p_3 = (3, 3)$$

Using the properties of the Bézier curve, together with the tangent vectors, the shape of the curve (shown in Figure 19.7) can be intuitively ascertained.

Consider the cubic curve defined by (EQ 19.30). If we differentiate the expression with respect to t, and find the result for $t = 0$ and $t = 1$, we obtain:

$$F'(0) = 3(p_1 - p_0)$$
$$F'(1) = 3(p_3 - p_2) \tag{EQ 19.40}$$

In other words, at the beginning and end of the curve, the tangent vector has the same direction as the beginning and end of the edges of the polygonal *control graph* defined by the control points p_0 to p_3.

This is a general result: it is quite straightforward to show that in the case of the nth degree Bézier curve (EQ 19.32):

$$F'(0) = n(p_1 - p_0)$$
$$F'(1) = n(p_3 - p_2) \tag{EQ 19.41}$$

This further property is very important in aiding a designer to quickly learn the relationship between control points and the final shape of the curve.

$$F'(t) = \frac{n!}{(n-r)!} \sum_{i=0}^{n-r} \Delta^r p_i B_{n-r,i}(t) \tag{EQ 19.42}$$

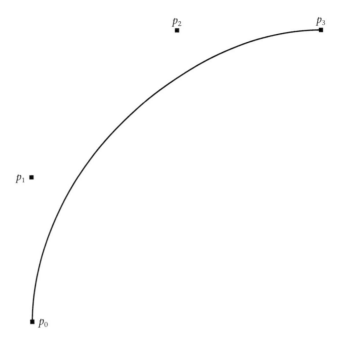

Figure 19.7
Bézier curve for
(EQ 19.37)

where Δ is the forward difference operator:

$$\Delta^0 p_i \equiv p_i$$
$$\Delta p_i = p_{i+1} - p_i$$
$$\Delta^r p_i = \Delta^{r-1} p_{i+1} - \Delta^{r-1} p_i, \; r = 1, 2, 3, \ldots$$

(EQ 19.43)

Hence the derivatives of Bézier curves are Bézier curves formed from forward differences of the original points (note that the control points are vectors in this case).

19.5 Degree-raising Bézier curves

Making use of degenerate polynomials

A Bézier curve of degree n can have a maximum of $n - 1$ "turning points" – for example, maxima and minima. One way to get greater flexibility in curve design is to join a sequence of relatively low-degree curves together end-to-end, in such a way that there is continuity at the joins. Another way is to start with a curve of lower degree, and find a new set of control points that describes the same curve, but of higher degree. This is only another way of expressing the fact that any given polynomial can be thought of as a "degenerate" polynomial of higher degree: degenerate in the sense that coefficients of the higher powers are zero. For example, the polynomial $1 + 2t + 3t^2$ may be thought of as a cubic polynomial except that the coefficient of t^3 happens to be zero. It may be thought of as any degree polynomial of three or higher, except that the relevant coefficients are zero.

Blossoms and degenerate polynomials

Consider the polynomial

$$F(t) = a_0 + a_1 t + a_2 t^2 \qquad \text{(EQ 19.44)}$$

Its blossom is

$$f(t_1, t_2) = a_0 + a_1\left(\frac{t_1 + t_2}{2}\right) + a_2 t_1 t_2 \qquad \text{(EQ 19.45)}$$

Now consider (EQ 19.44) as a "degenerate" cubic. Then the blossom in this case is:

$$g(t_1, t_2, t_3) = a_0 + a_1\left(\frac{t_1 + t_2 + t_3}{3}\right) + a_2\left(\frac{t_1 t_2 + t_1 t_3 + t_2 t_3}{3}\right) \qquad \text{(EQ 19.46)}$$

It is left as an exercise and it is easy to show that there is a relationship between (EQ 19.45) and (EQ 19.46), in fact:

$$g(t_1, t_2, t_3) = \frac{f(t_1, t_2) + f(t_1, t_3) + f(t_2, t_3)}{3} \qquad \text{(EQ 19.47)}$$

From first principles, we know that f is the blossom of F, so that f is symmetric and multi-affine, and its diagonal is F. Hence g must also be symmetric and multi-affine, and its diagonal is also clearly F. Hence g must be the unique polar form of F when F is considered as a cubic polynomial.

Application to Bézier curves

Suppose we are given a quadratic Bézier curve based on control points p_0, p_1, and p_2. Then we know that if we take the parameter range as $t \in [0, 1]$,

$$\begin{aligned}
p_0 &= f(0, 0) \\
p_1 &= f(0, 1) \\
p_2 &= f(1, 1)
\end{aligned} \qquad \text{(EQ 19.48)}$$

where f is the blossom of the curve. Now we wish to express the same curve as a cubic Bézier curve. What are the corresponding control points? Suppose these are

$$q_0,\ q_1,\ q_2,\ q_3. \qquad \text{(EQ 19.49)}$$

We know from the end-condition property of Bézier curves that $q_0 = p_0$ and $q_3 = p_2$. How about the other points?

Suppose the blossom of the corresponding cubic is $g(t_1, t_2, t_3)$. Then

$$
\begin{aligned}
q_0 &= g(0, 0, 0) \\
q_1 &= g(0, 0, 1) \\
q_2 &= g(0, 1, 1) \\
q_3 &= g(1, 1, 1)
\end{aligned}
\qquad \text{(EQ 19.50)}
$$

From (EQ 19.47):

$$
\begin{aligned}
q_0 &= g(0, 0, 0) = f(0, 0) = p_0 \\
q_1 &= g(0, 0, 1) = \frac{1}{3}f(0, 0) + \frac{2}{3}f(0, 1) = \frac{1}{3}p_0 + \frac{2}{3}p_1 \\
q_2 &= g(0, 1, 1) = \frac{2}{3}f(0, 1) + \frac{1}{3}f(1, 1) = \frac{2}{3}p_1 + \frac{1}{3}p_2 \\
q_3 &= g(1, 1, 1) = f(1, 1) = p_2
\end{aligned}
\qquad \text{(EQ 19.51)}
$$

The new points can therefore be computed from the old.

General result

Suppose we have a Bézier curve from $n + 1$ control points, and we require the same Bézier curve from $n + 2$ control points. Suppose the polar form for the $n + 1$ case is $f(t_1, t_2, \ldots, t)$, and for the $n + 2$ case $g(t_1, t_2, \ldots, t_{n+1})$. Then:

$$
\begin{aligned}
&g(t_1, t_2, \ldots, t_{n+1}) = \\
&\frac{f(t_1, t_2, \ldots, t_n) + f(t_1, t_2, \ldots, t_{n-1}, t_{n+1}) + \ldots + f(t_2, t_3, \ldots, t_{n+1})}{n + 1}
\end{aligned}
\qquad \text{(EQ 19.52)}
$$

where each term in the sum omits one of the t_i parameters. This result is seen to be correct since the expression on the right is symmetric, multi-affine, $g(t, t, \ldots, t) = f(t, t, \ldots, t)$, and polar forms are unique.

Suppose the original control points are p_i, and the new q_i. Then,

$$
q_i = g(\underbrace{0, 0, \ldots, 0}_{n - i + 1}, 1, 1, \ldots, 1)
\qquad \text{(EQ 19.53)}
$$

where there are $n + 1 - i$ zero terms and i ones. Substituting this into the expression for g gives:

$$
q_i = \frac{(n - i + 1)p_{i-1} + ip_i}{n + 1} = \left(1 - \frac{i}{n+1}\right)p_{i-1} + \left(\frac{i}{n+1}\right)p_i
\qquad \text{(EQ 19.54)}
$$

19.6 Rational Bézier curves

Introduction

Bézier curves provide a flexible method for curve design; however, some important curves that are very useful in CAGD cannot be represented exactly by any
degree Bézier curve no matter how high the degree. This is the case with the
conic sections, for example a circle. Bézier curves are invariant under affine
transformations (that is, the same curve is obtained whether the control points
are transformed and then the curve rendered from these transformed control
points, or the original curve itself is transformed), but they are not invariant
under projective transformations – that is, the transformation used when projecting onto a view plane.

For example, given the control points (x_i, y_i, z_i) $i = 0, \ldots n$ for a Bézier curve,
and with the view-plane as the XY plane, and center of projection at $(0, 0, -1)$,
with direction of view along the Z axis, then the projections of these points
are at

$$\left(\frac{x_i}{z_i + 1}, \frac{y_i}{z_i + 1}, 0 \right)$$ (EQ 19.55)

Now if a Bézier curve is constructed from these points, it is clearly not the same
curve as would be obtained by projecting points $(x(t), y(t), z(t))$, $t \in [0, 1]$ on
the original curve. It might help the reader to show that this is the case.

In general a *rational polynomial* is a ratio of two polynomials. For example:

$$\frac{a_0 + a_1 t + a_2 t^2 + \ldots + a_n t^n}{b_0 + b_1 t + b_2 t^2 + \ldots + b_n t^n}$$ (EQ 19.56)

A rational parametric curve is one where the expressions for $x(t)$, $y(t)$ (and $z(t)$
if a space curve) are rational polynomials.

For example, consider:

$$x(t) = \frac{1 - t^2}{1 + t^2}$$

$$y(t) = \frac{2t}{1 + t^2}$$ (EQ 19.57)

$$t \in [0, 1]$$

It is easy to verify that $x(t)^2 + y(t)^2 = 1$, showing that this parametric curve
represents a quadrant of a circle. Thus a second degree rational parametric
curve can exactly represent a circle, but no finite degree non-rational curve can
exactly represent a circle.

Rational Bézier curves

In order to define a rational Bézier curve, we attach a number $w_i > 0$ as a *weight*
at each point. Given the control points (x_i, y_i) we represent these in homogen-

eous form as $(w_i x_i, w_i y_i, w_i)$ (if 3D curves then $(x_i, y_i, z_i) \equiv (w_i x_i, w_i y_i, w_i z_i, w_i)$). Recall that the homogeneous point $(w_i x_i, w_i y_i, w_i)$ in general is equivalent to the 2D point (x_i, y_i), and this is always obtained by dividing by the last element (the weight).

Now we construct the Bézier curve as usual, in homogeneous space as $(x(t), y(t), w(t))$ based on control points $(w_i x_i, w_i y_i, w_i)$, and the actual points on the curve in 2D space are obtained by dividing by the last element. Hence:

$$X(t) = \frac{x(t)}{w(t)} = \frac{\sum\limits_{i=0}^{n} B_{n,i}(t) w_i x_i}{\sum\limits_{i=0}^{n} B_{n,i}(t) w_i}$$

$$\text{(EQ 19.58)}$$

$$Y(t) = \frac{y(t)}{w(t)} = \frac{\sum\limits_{i=0}^{n} B_{n,i}(t) w_i y_i}{\sum\limits_{i=0}^{n} B_{n,i}(t) w_i}$$

Note that when all the w_i are equal, (EQ 19.58) reduces to a non-rational Bézier curve, since the w_i cancel and the denominator is equal to one for all t.

Evaluating a rational curve

A rational Bézier curve may be evaluated by any method we know for ordinary Bézier curves, except that at the last stage, the x- and y-coordinates are each divided by the w-coordinate. For example, consider the quadtratic rational curve with control points (0, 0), (1, 1), and (2, 0), and corresponding weights 1, 2, and 3. Then we construct the homogeneous control points (0, 0, 1), (2, 2, 2), and (6, 0, 3). Now let's evaluate the curve at t-value 0.5 using subdivision (de Casteljau's algorithm) (Table 19.1).

The final point is (2.5, 1, 2) in homogeneous space, which is (2.5/2, 1/2, 1) $\equiv$ (1.25, 0.5).

Table 19.1 Evaluating a rational Bézier curve

CPs	mid-points	mid-point
(0, 0, 1)		
	(1, 1, 1.5)	
(2, 2, 2)		(2.5, 1, 2)
	(4, 1, 2.5)	
(6, 0, 3)		

Similarly, the forward difference method (see later) may be used to evaluate points on $(x(t), y(t))$ and $w(t)$, and then the ratios are computed at the last step.

Converting from general to Bézier form

Consider (EQ 19.57) representing a quadrant of a circle on the parametric interval [0, 1]. Suppose that we wish to find the control points and weights for this when expressed in Bézier form. The homogenous representation is $(x(t), y(t), w(t)) = (1 - t^2, 2t, 1 + t^2) = F(t)$, say. Then find the blossoms for each of the quadratics, so that the equivalent blossom functions are:

$$f(t_1, t_2) = (1 - t_1 t_2, t_1 + t_2, 1 + t_1 t_2) \tag{EQ 19.59}$$

The control points are $f(0, 0)$, $f(0, 1)$ and $f(1, 1)$ with

$$\begin{aligned}
f(0, 0) &= (1, 0, 1) \\
f(0, 1) &= (1, 1, 1) \\
f(1, 1) &= (0, 2, 2)
\end{aligned} \tag{EQ 19.60}$$

Now convert these to 2D space, obtaining the control points $(1, 0)$, $(1, 1)$, and $(0, 1)$ with weights 1, 1, and 2. The reader should write a program to generate a complete circle using these ideas.

Properties

In general, the greater the weight attached to a control point, in relation to the other weights, the greater the influence of that control point. Hence the weights may be used to adjust the shape of the curve interactively (for example, by providing a slider attached to each control point, so allowing adjustment of the weight).

Rational Bézier curves share the affine transformational invariance of non-rational curves, but they are also invariant under projective transformations.

19.7   Joining curves together: continuity

Piecewise polynomial curve segments

In order to design complex shapes (e.g., Figure 19.8), we must either use polynomials of very high dimensions, or else join separate curve segments together. Degree raising in order to increase complexity is finally self-defeating, for it is typically impractical and not useful to use curves of high degree:

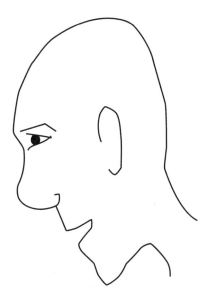

Figure 19.8
A complex shape:
constructed by
smoothly joining curves

- The polynomials become numerically unstable.
- The computational overhead increases greatly compared to lower degree curves.
- The overall shape does not have the property of local control – that is, it is impossible to change one part of the curve without the whole curve changing.

The alternative is to join a number of lower degree curves together, and in such a way that certain continuity requirements are met at the joins. We introduce the idea of parametric continuity where two curves join together.

Parametric continuity

Suppose that $F(t)$, $t \in [t_0, t_1]$ and $G(t)$, $t \in [t_1, t_2]$ are two kth degree polynomials. Then $F(t)$ and $G(t)$ join with C^0 *continuity* at t_1 if $F(t_1) = G(t_1)$, that is, they simply join together at the parametric value $t = t_1$. C^1 continuity requires that they have the same first derivative at $t = t_1$, that is $F'(t_1) = G'(t_1)$. In general C^r continuity requires that all derivatives up to and including the rth match at $t = t_1 : F'(t_1) = G'(t_1)$. The parametric values where the curves join together are generally called *knots*.

In the context of CAGD we are interested in continuity for parametrically defined curves of the form $F(t) = (X_F(t), Y_F(t))$ and $G(t) = (X_G(t), Y_G(t))$ at the knot $t = t_1$. The result is the same except that now we give the interpretation that $F^r(t) = (X_F^r(t), Y_F^r(t))$.

Hence when $r = 1$, $F'(t)$ is the tangent vector, representing the rate of change of the point $(X_F(t), Y_F(t))$ along the curve at t, which would be interpreted as velocity if t were time. Similarly, $r = 2$ is equivalent to acceleration in this case.

Note that given two polynomials it is a relatively simple, but tedious matter to ensure that they join together with a required continuity. The problem always becomes one of solving a set of linear equations. For example:

$$F(t) = a_0 + a_1 t + a_2 t^2 + a_3 t^3$$
$$G(t) = b_0 + b_1 t + b_2 t^2 + b_3 t^3$$

(EQ 19.61)

Suppose that the polynomial F (i.e., the coefficients a_i) are known, and we require G to join to F at $t = 1$ with C^2 continuity. Then, we require:

$$F(1) = G(1) \Rightarrow a_0 + a_1 + a_2 + a_3 = b_0 + b_1 + b_2 + b_3$$
$$F'(1) = G'(1) \Rightarrow a_1 + 2a_2 + 3a_3 = b_1 + 2b_2 + 3b_3$$
$$F^2(1) = G^2(1) = 2a_2 + 6a_3 = 2b_2 + 6b_3$$

(EQ 19.62)

There are four unknowns $b_0, \ldots, b_3$ and three equations, so that the requirement imposes constraints with one degree of freedom on the coefficients b_i.

Notice that with degree 3 polynomials, C^3 continuity would require that G and F were exactly the same polynomial (since equating the third derivatives gives $a_3 = b_3$, and then substituting this back into the second degree requirement results in $b_2 = a_2$, and so on, so that $b_i = a_i$, all i). In general, for kth degree polynomials it is only interesting to require up to C^{k-1} continuity.

Geometric continuity

In this section we show that parametric continuity is a very strict requirement. Suppose $P(t)$ and $Q(t)$ are two kth degree Bézier curves, defined over the range [0, 1] and [1, 2] respectively. We require C^1 continuity at $t = 1$. Then we know the tangent vectors at the ends and beginnings of the curves:

$$P'(1) = k(p_k - p_{k-1}) = Q'(1) = k(q_k - q_{k-1})$$

(EQ 19.63)

Also we require:

$$P(1) = p_k = Q(1) = q_0$$

(EQ 19.64)

From this we deduce that for C^1 continuity:

$$q_0 = p_k$$
$$q_1 = 2p_k - p_{k-1}$$

(EQ 19.65)

Therefore, parametric continuity requires that q_1 must be located at a precise distance along the ray defined by the control points p_{k-1} and p_k. Yet we know that there would be a first order visual continuity between the two curves provided that q_1 was *any* distance along this ray. Parametric continuity is seen to be a very specific and strict requirement. G^1 (*geometric*) *continuity* would be satisfied provided that q_1 was along the appropriate ray; the actual distance would not be of concern from the point of view of continuity, though it would affect the shape of the overall curve.

It turns out that even though parametric continuity is a requirement that is stricter than we usually need to satisfy our intuitive understanding of "continuity," it is mathematically easier to treat than geometric continuity. Here we concentrate exclusively on parametric continuity.

Derivatives from blossoms

Suppose that $F(t)$ is a kth degree polynomial, and $f(t_1, \ldots, t_k)$ is its polar form. Then we can express the rth derivative of F as:

$$F^r(t) = \frac{k!}{(k-r)!} \cdot \sum_{i=0}^{r} \binom{r}{i}(-1)^{r-i}f(t^{[k-i]}, (t+1)^{[i]}) \tag{EQ 19.66}$$

where we use the notation $t^{[k-i]}, (t+1)^{[i]}$ to mean a sequence $t, t, \ldots, t, (t+1)$, $\ldots, (t+1)$ with $k-i$ occurences of t and i occurrences of $(t+1)$.

This formula looks complex, but a simple example illustrates it:

Suppose $F(t) = t^3$. Then the polar form is $f(t_1, t_2, t_3) = t_1 t_2 t_3$. Now use the formula to find $F'(t)$. Here $k = 3$, $r = 1$. Then:

$$\begin{aligned} F'(t) &= \frac{3!}{2!} \cdot (-f(t, t, t) + f(t, t, t+1)) \\ &= 3(-t^3 + t^2(t+1)) \\ &= 3t^2 \end{aligned} \tag{EQ 19.67}$$

Of course, in a case like this it is easy to work out the derivative directly, but later we will see applications where this result is very useful. An outline of the proof follows:

Proof. Consider for some a and t' the expression

$$F(t + a(t' - t)) = f(t + a(t' - t), t + a(t' - t), \ldots, t + a(t' - t)) \tag{EQ 19.68}$$

Now

$$t + a(t' - t) = (1 - a)t + at' \tag{EQ 19.69}$$

Therefore, using the multi-affine property:

$$\begin{aligned} f((t + a(t' - t)), \ldots, t + a(t' - t)) &= (1-a)f(t, t + a(t' - t), \ldots, \\ t + a(t' - t)) + af(t', t + a(t' - t), \ldots, t + a(t' - t)) \end{aligned} \tag{EQ 19.70}$$

Continue to use the multi-affine property to expand out the terms, eventually yielding (by induction):

$$F(t + a(t' - t)) = \sum_{i=0}^{k} \binom{k}{i} a^i (1-a)^{k-i} f(t^{[k-i]}, t'^{[i]}) \tag{EQ 19.71}$$

By Taylor's expansion:

$$F(t + a(t' - t)) = \sum_{i=0}^{k} \frac{a^i (t' - t)^i}{i!} F^{(i)}(t) \tag{EQ 19.72}$$

(since all after the kth derivative are zero). The result follows by expanding $(1 - a)^{k-i}$ in powers of a in (EQ 19.71), rearranging the indices of the summation, and then equating coefficients of powers of a. In particular, choose $t' = 1 + t$.

Continuity condition

Suppose we have two k degree polynomials, $F(t)$, $t \in [a, s]$ and $G(t)$, $t \in [s, b]$. Then at the parametric value s, these join with C^r continuity if and only if

$$f(u_1, u_2, \ldots, u_r, s^{[k-r]}) = g(u_1, u_2, \ldots, u_r, s^{[k-r]}) \tag{EQ 19.73}$$

for any sequence $u_1, u_2, \ldots, u_r$. The proof can be found in (Seidel, 1989). Note that implicit in this is that C^r continuity implies continuity of all lower degrees, since the u sequence can of course include instances of s.

Suppose, for example,

$$\begin{aligned} F(t) &= t^2 \\ G(t) &= a_0 + 2a_1 t + a_2 t^2 \end{aligned} \tag{EQ 19.74}$$

with domains $[0, 1]$ and $[1, 2]$ respectively. We shall determine the conditions for C^1 continuity at the knot $t = 1$.

$$\begin{aligned} f(t_1, t_2) &= t_1 t_2 \\ g(t_1, t_2) &= a_0 + a_1(t_1 + t_2) + a_2 t_1 t_2 \end{aligned} \tag{EQ 19.75}$$

In this example, we have $k = 2$, $s = 1$.

Consider first C^0 continuity. According to the requirement we must have:

$$f(1, 1) = g(1, 1) \text{ and therefore } a_0 + 2a_1 + a_2 = 1 \tag{EQ 19.76}$$

Now consider C^1 continuity. This requires:

$$f(u_1, 1) = g(u_1, 1) \text{ for any } u_1 \tag{EQ 19.77}$$

Hence:

$$u_1 = a_0 + a_1(u_1 + 1) + a_2 u_1 \tag{EQ 19.78}$$

From (EQ 19.76) substitute $a_0 = 1 - 2a_1 - a_2$ into (EQ 19.78) and rearrange to get:

$$a_1(u_1 - 1) + a_2(u_1 - 1) = u_1 - 1 \tag{EQ 19.79}$$

From (EQ 19.79) we obtain the requirement that $a_1 + a_2 = 1$. (Note – we can divide by $u_1 - 1$, safely assuming that $u_1 \neq 1$ since if $u_1 = 1$ we would be back to equation (EQ 19.78)).

B-spline curves

Piecewise polynomial curves

In this section we show how to construct piecewise continuous polynomial curve segments of degree k that join with C^{k-1} continuity. These are the so-called B-spline curves. We specialize for the case $k = 3$, cubic B-splines, but the results generalize to any degree. A single curve segment is examined first, showing some fundamental results, and then it is shown that several such curve segments can be joined together with the required parametric continuity.

A single polynomial segment

Suppose we have a sequence of scalar values t_1, t_2, ..., t_{2k}. These are called *knots*. We require the values to be non-decreasing:

$$t_i \le t_j \text{ for } i < j$$
$$t_i < t_{i+k}, \text{ always}$$

(EQ 19.80)

These knot values are chosen by the curve designer. Often they are at equally spaced intervals, such as 1, 2, 3, ..., called a *uniform knot sequence*. Suppose v_0, v_1, ..., v_k is a sequence of arbitrary points in space. Then it can be shown (Ramshaw, 1989) that there is a unique k degree polynomial $F(t)$ with blossom f, such that

$$v_i = f(t_{i+1}, t_{i+2}, \ldots, t_{i+k})$$
$$i = 0, 1, \ldots, k$$

(EQ 19.81)

This is not difficult to prove. (EQ 19.81) actually gives us $k + 1$ linear equations in $k + 1$ unknowns, if we take the general form of the blossom. The unknowns are the coefficients a_i. The matrix representing the linear equations is of full rank, and therefore invertible. This is particularly straightforward to show in the specific cases $k = 2, 3$.

Take the case $k = 2$, so that we have knots t_1, t_2, t_3, t_4 and control points v_0, v_1, v_2. Then the theorem asserts that there exists a unique polynomial with blossom f such that:

$$v_0 = f(t_1, t_2) = a_0 + a_1\left(\frac{t_1 + t_2}{2}\right) + a_2 t_1 t_2$$

$$v_1 = f(t_2, t_3) = a_0 + a_1\left(\frac{t_2 + t_3}{2}\right) + a_2 t_2 t_3$$

(EQ 19.82)

$$v_2 = f(t_3, t_4) = a_0 + a_1\left(\frac{t_3 + t_4}{2}\right) + a_2 t_3 t_4$$

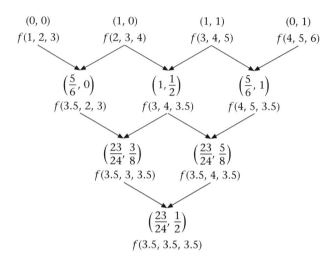

Figure 19.9
de Casteljau triangle for
f(3.5, 3.5, 3.5) for
(EQ 19.83)

The a_i are unknown, but all the other values are known. This gives us three equations in three unknowns. (In fact, since we are dealing with points, there will be two sets of such equations in 2D and three sets in 3D.)

In general, in order to evaluate a point on the curve, we can use the multi-affine property of the polar form, and "blossom out" the values by repeated interpolation. By doing this it will be seen that there are enough knots defined to find, by interpolation, any value between t_k and t_{k+1}. Hence for any t in this range we need to find $f(t, t, \ldots, t)$.

For example, suppose we have the knots 1, 2, 3, 4, 5, 6 and the control points v_i: (0, 0), (1, 0), (1, 1), and (0, 1). We want to find the point on the curve for $t = 3.5$. Then, by (EQ 19.81), we must have:

$$(0, 0) = f(1, 2, 3)$$
$$(1, 0) = f(2, 3, 4)$$
$$(1, 1) = f(3, 4, 5)$$
$$(0, 1) = f(4, 5, 6)$$

(EQ 19.83)

We can therefore construct a de Casteljau triangle to perform the evaluation, as shown in Figure 19.9.

The reader will find it useful to sketch a graph showing the interpolations on the control points. This exercise should be repeated for several values of t between 3 and 4, thus identifying several points on the cubic curve.

Two-polynomial curve segments

Continuing the case of the single curve segment, suppose we add one further point v_{k+1} and a further knot, t_{2k+1}, and now consider the sequence $t_2, t_3, \ldots, t_{2k+1}$. This, by the result of the previous section, corresponds to control points $v_1, \ldots, v_{k+1}$, with the polynomial curve G and polar form g defined over the

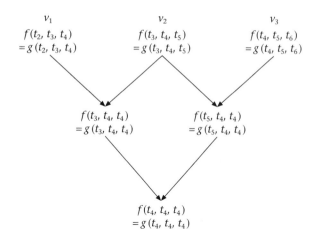

Figure 19.10
Evaluating f and g at the knot t_4

range $[t_{k+1}, t_{k+2}]$. For example, $v_{k+1} = g(t_{k+2}, \ldots, t_{2k+1})$. Now suppose we wish to evaluate a point on this curve, $g(t, t, \ldots, t) = G(t)$, $t \in [t_{k+1}, t_{k+2}]$. Of course, we would proceed in the usual way, finding the interpolated values.

Take the particular case $t = t_{k+1}$. This is at the end of the first curve segment and the beginning of the next. If we evaluated $f(t_{k+1}, t_{k+1}, \ldots, t_{k+1})$ and $g(t_{k+1}, t_{k+1}, \ldots, t_{k+1})$, the f and g blossom values must, by construction, be equal wherever they coincide in the respective de Casteljau triangles. They must be equal because they are interpolated from the common set of control points $v_1, \ldots, v_k$. A check on the various equalities that arise shows that the relations between the f and g blossoms exactly satisfy the requirements of the equations for C^{k-1} continuity, given in (EQ 19.73).

Consider the case $k = 3$, and the two triangles, for f and g, then evaluating at t_4 gives the triangle shown in Figure 19.10. The top row gives the condition for C^2 continuity at t_4. The second row gives the condition for C^1 continuity, and the bottom row, the condition for C^0 continuity.

The conclusion is that constructing polynomial curve segments in this way gives us exactly what is meant by the B-spline curves. In fact we can take this as a definition.

Definition of B-spline curves. We are given a sequence of knot values satisfying (EQ 19.80). On each interval $[t_i, t_{i+1}]$ there is a kth degree parametric curve $F(t)$ defined with corresponding B-spline control points $v_{i-k}, v_{i-k+1}, \ldots, v_i$ (for example, $k = 3$ for cubic B-splines). The following may be taken as a constructive definition of the B-spline:

Suppose that $f()$ is the k-parameter polar form associated with the curve segment on $[t_i, t_{i+1}]$. Then,

(1) The control points are defined by $v_j = f(t_{j+1}, \ldots, t_{j+k})$, $j = i - k, i - k + 1, \ldots, i$.

(2) The k-degree Bézier curve corresponding to this curve segment has control points:

$$p_j = f(\underbrace{t_i, t_i, \ldots, t_i}, t_{i+1}, t_{i+1}, \ldots, t_{i+1})$$

$$= f(t_i^{[k-j]}, t_{i+1}^{[j]}) \qquad \text{(EQ 19.84)}$$

$$j = 0, 1, \ldots, k$$

(3) Evaluation of the point on the curve at $t \in [t_i, t_{i+1}]$ is given by $F(t) = f(t, t, \ldots, t)$.

Examples and relations to Bézier points

Consider now the case of quadratic B-splines ($k = 2$), and limit attention to the ith interval $t \in [t_i, t_{i+1}]$. Then the quadratic Bézier curve corresponding to this curve segment has control points:

$$p_0 = f(t_i, t_i)$$
$$p_1 = f(t_i, t_{i+1}) \qquad \text{(EQ 19.85)}$$
$$p_2 = f(t_{i+1}, t_{i+1})$$

The B-spline control points are

$$v_{i-2} = f(t_{i-1}, t_i)$$
$$v_{i-1} = f(t_i, t_{i+1}) \qquad \text{(EQ 19.86)}$$
$$v_i = f(t_{i+1}, t_{i+2})$$

We have the interpolation:

$$f(t_i, t_i) = \left(\frac{t_{i+1} - t_i}{t_{i+1} - t_{i-1}} \right) v_{i-2} + \left(\frac{t_i - t_{i-1}}{t_{i+1} - t_{i-1}} \right) v_{i-1}$$

$$\text{(EQ 19.87)}$$

$$f(t_{i+1}, t_{i+1}) = \left(\frac{t_{i+2} - t_{i+1}}{t_{i+2} - t_i} \right) v_{i-1} + \left(\frac{t_{i+1} - t_i}{t_{i+2} - t_i} \right) v_i$$

From this we can see that (Figure 19.11):

- p_0 is an interpolation between v_{i-2} and v_{i-1};
- $p_1 = v_{i-1}$;
- p_2 is an interpolation between v_{i-1} and v_i.

A similar construction can be made for the cubic case, $k = 3$. Again consider the jth knot interval $[t_j, t_{j+1}]$ and associated B-spline control points $v_{j-3}, v_{j-2}, v_{j-1}, v_j$. The required Bézier points are:

$$f(t_j, t_j, t_j), f(t_j, t_j, t_{j+1}), f(t_j, t_{j+1}, t_{j+1}), \text{ and } f(t_{j+1}, t_{j+1}, t_{j+1})$$

with construction as shown in Figure 19.12.

This figure shows two triangles involved in the computation of the Bézier points. Note that all four Bézier points are contained in this table. p_1 and p_2 are linear interpolations of the same two B-spline control points (but in different ratios), whereas p_0 and p_3 are quadratic interpolations in their parameter values

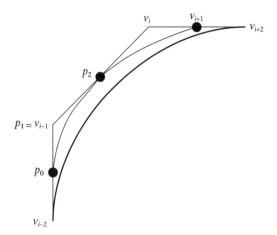

Figure 19.11
B-spline points and
Bézier points for the
quadratic case

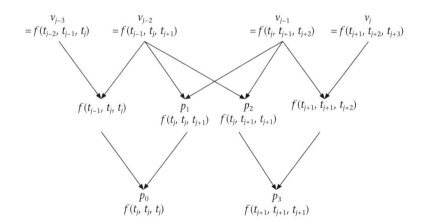

Figure 19.12
Constructing Bézier points
from B-spline points

based on the B-spline control points. Also, p_0 and p_3 correspond to the join in successive curves, with the p_0 of the next curve equal to the p_3 of the previous curve. It should be clear from the table that the joins are C^2 continuous. The cubic B-spline curve shown in Figure 19.13 was rendered by converting the B-spline control points in the figure to the Bézier control points. Note how the curve is within the convex hull of each successive sequence of four B-spline control points.

Computation (de Boor algorithm)

Consider now the problem of computing the point on the B-spline corresponding to parameter value $t \in [t_i, t_{i+1}]$. We know that this can be computed by $f(t, t, \ldots, t)$.

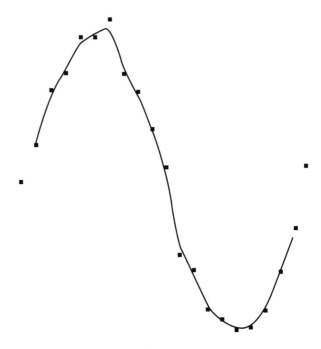

Figure 19.13
B-spline curve rendered
from Béziers

From Figure 19.14 we can establish the following recursion formula, called de Boor's algorithm, for computing the B-spline curve of kth degree:

$$P_j^0(t) = v_j, j = i - k, i - k + 1, \ldots, i$$

$$P_j^r(t) = \left(\frac{t_{k+1+j} - t}{t_{k+1+j} - t_{r+j}}\right)P_j^{r-1}(t) + \left(\frac{t - t_{r+j}}{t_{k+1+j} - t_{r+j}}\right)P_{j+1}^{r-1}(t)$$ (EQ 19.88)

for $r = 1, 2, \ldots, k$ and $j = i - k, i - k + 1, \ldots, i - r$

Then the required point on the curve is $P_{i-k}^k(t)$.

Remarks about knot sequences and control points

Suppose we have the cubic B-spline control points $v_0, v_1, \ldots, v_n$. What corresponding knot vector must exist for this sequence? Let the knots be denoted by $t_1, t_2, \ldots$.

Suppose f is the polar form, so we know that in the cubic case $v_0 = f(t_1, t_2, t_3)$ and $v_n = f(t_{n+1}, t_{n+2}, t_{n+3})$. At the start of the curve, the knots $t_1, \ldots, t_6$ allow evaluation of the curve in the parameter range $[t_3, t_4]$ and make use of the control points $v_0, \ldots, v_4$. Similarly, at the end of the curve, the final parameter range is $[t_n, t_{n+1}]$.

Therefore, the following conclusions can be reached in the cubic case:

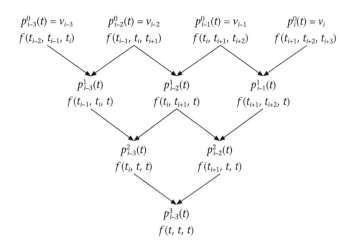

Figure 19.14
de Boor algorithm for
evaluating B-splines

- For control points $v_0, v_1, \ldots, v_n$ the required knot sequence is $t_1, t_2, \ldots, t_{n+3}$.
- The curve is defined over the range $t \in [t_3, t_{n+1}]$.
- There will be $n-2$ curve segments altogether, since each interval $[t_i, t_{i+1}]$, $i = 3, 4, \ldots, n$ defines a curve segment.

Construct the triangular array corresponding to an evaluation of the curve in the first interval $[t_3, t_4]$. Now suppose that the first three knots are equal, that is, $t_1 = t_2 = t_3 = t_0$. It is then easy to see that evaluation of the curve at $t = t_0$ results in v_0. A similar conclusion can be drawn about what happens if the last three knot values are equal:

> If the first three knot values are equal, then the B-spline curve will start at the first control point. Similarly, it will end at the last control point if the last three knots are equal.

This is a special case of a more general result:

> Each time a knot value is repeated, one degree of continuity is lost at the junction point corresponding to that knot value. In general, if the B-spline is based on k degree polynomials, and a particular knot value has multiplicity m, then at that junction point, the degree of continuity is $k - m$.

Knot insertion

Inserting new knots into the sequence while maintaining the same B-spline curve is a fundamental operation. Two applications are:

- rendering;
- adding greater flexibility to the curve shape.

There are many algorithms for this (Goldman, 1990), we will consider only Boehm's knot insertion algorithm in this section, and for the cubic case. The idea is that in an interval $[t_i, t_{i+1}]$, a new knot $\hat{t}$ is inserted. Hence in this local region the knot sequence will be:

$$t_{i-2}, t_{i-1}, t_i, \hat{t}, t_{i+1}, t_{i+2}, t_{i+3} \tag{EQ 19.89}$$

with corresponding control points:

$$
\begin{aligned}
f(t_{i-2}, t_{i-1}, t_i) &= v_{i-3} \\
f(t_{i-1}, t_i, \hat{t}) &= w_1 \\
f(t_i, \hat{t}, t_{i+1}) &= w_2 \\
f(\hat{t}, t_{i+1}, t_{i+2}) &= w_3 \\
f(t_{i+1}, t_{i+2}, t_{i+3}) &= v_i
\end{aligned}
\tag{EQ 19.90}
$$

Let the old control points be $v_0, v_1, \ldots, v_n$, and insert a knot in the interval $[t_i, t_{i+1}]$ and let the complete new set of control points be $w_0, w_1, \ldots, w_n, w_{n+1}$.

Then the following relationships can be seen to hold:

$$
\begin{aligned}
w_j &= v_j, \, j = 0, 1, \ldots, i-3 \\
w_j &= f(t_{j+1}, t_{j+2}, \hat{t}), \, j = i-2, i-1, i \\
w_j &= v_{j-3}, \, j = i+1, i+2, \ldots, n+1
\end{aligned}
\tag{EQ 19.91}
$$

It remains to find an explicit formula for the $f(t_{j+1}, t_{j+2}, \hat{t})$, $j = i-2, i-1, i$. This is easily done using the multi-affine property of polar forms. The control point represented by $f(t_{j+1}, t_{j+2}, \hat{t})$ falls between $f(t_j, t_{j+1}, t_{j+2})$ and $f(t_{j+1}, t_{j+2}, t_{j+3})$. We can therefore use the usual interpolation result, interpolating on $\hat{t} \in [t_j, t_{j+3}]$ to give:

$$f(t_{j+1}, t_{j+2}, \hat{t}) = \left(\frac{t_{j+3} - \hat{t}}{t_{j+3} - t_j}\right) f(t_j, t_{j+1}, t_{j+2}) + \left(\frac{\hat{t} - t_j}{t_{j+3} - t_j}\right) f(t_{j+1}, t_{j+2}, t_{j+3}) \tag{EQ 19.92}$$

and so

$$w_j = \left(\frac{t_{j+3} - \hat{t}}{t_{j+3} - t_j}\right) v_{j-1} + \left(\frac{\hat{t} - t_j}{t_{j+3} - t_j}\right) v_j \tag{EQ 19.93}$$
$$j = i-2, i-1, i$$

This is called *Boehm's knot insertion formula*. In order to insert many knots, this process is repeated for each one.

Knot insertion is useful for rendering, since it can be shown that when more and more knots are inserted into the knot sequence, in between the two endpoints, the sequence of control vertices more and more closely approximates the B-spline curve.

Multiple knot insertion – Oslo algorithm

In Boehm's knot insertion algorithm we insert one new knot in an interval at a time, and get k new control points (where k is the degree of the parametric polynomials), although only one additional control point compared with the

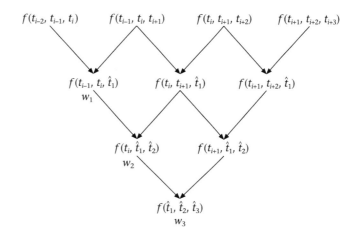

Figure 19.15
Insert knots in increasing order

previous situation. The Oslo algorithm inserts many knots in an interval simultaneously. We present a simple version of the Oslo algorithm, due to Goldman (1990), based on blossoming.

Continue with the case $k = 3$, and consider inserting three knots in the interval $[t_i, t_{i+1}]$. Then the new knot sequence near this interval is:

$$t_{i-2}, t_{i-1}, t_i, \hat{t}_1, \hat{t}_2, \hat{t}_3, t_{i+1}, t_{i+2}, t_{i+3} \tag{EQ 19.94}$$

Therefore the control points are:

$$v_{i-1} = f(t_{i-2}, t_{i-1}, t_i) \text{ (original control point)}$$
$$\text{(new control points):}$$
$$w_1 = f(t_{i-1}, t_i, \hat{t}_1)$$
$$w_2 = f(t_i, \hat{t}_1, \hat{t}_2)$$
$$w_3 = f(\hat{t}_1, \hat{t}_2, \hat{t}_3) \tag{EQ 19.95}$$
$$w_4 = f(\hat{t}_2, \hat{t}_3, t_{i+1})$$
$$w_5 = f(\hat{t}_3, t_{i+1}, t_{i+2})$$
$$v_i = f(t_{i+1}, t_{i+2}, t_{i+3}) \text{ (original control point)}$$

The question then becomes how to arrange a suitable computation to obtain these new control points. This can be done by constructing two de Casteljau triangles. The first inserts the knots, row by row in the order $\hat{t}_1, \hat{t}_2, \hat{t}_3$ (Figure 19.15) and the second in the reverse order (Figure 19.16).

19.9　B-spline basis functions

Earlier we saw how the Bézier curves can be represented using the Bernstein basis (see "Bézier curves and the Bernstein basis" on page 394). The familiar approach to B-splines is to represent kth degree B-spline curves as a similar weighted sum of B-spline basis functions:

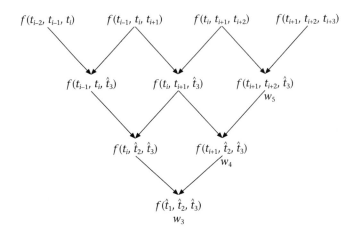

Figure 19.16
Insert knots in decreasing order

$$F(t) = \sum_{i=0}^{n} N_{k,i}(t) v_i \qquad \text{(EQ 19.96)}$$

where the basis functions are defined by the recursive formula:

$$N_{0,i}(t) = \begin{cases} 1 \text{ if } t \in [t_i, t_{i+1}] \\ 0 \text{ otherwise} \end{cases} \qquad \text{(EQ 19.97)}$$

$$N_{r,i}(t) = \left(\frac{t - t_i}{t_{i+r} - t_i} \right) N_{r-1,i}(t) + \left(\frac{t_{i+r+1} - t}{t_{i+r+1} - t_{i+1}} \right) N_{r-1,i+1}(t), \; t \in [t_i, t_{i+r+1}]$$

$N_{r,i}(t)$ is a polynomial of degree r, with local support on $[t_i, t_{i+r+1}]$, i.e., it is non-zero only over this range. It consists of $r + 1$ polynomial curve segments of degree r, joined with C^{r-1} continuity. Seidel (1989) shows how the blossoming approach can be derived from this B-spline representation. Here we illustrate how, starting from the blossoming representation, we end up with the basis functions (EQ 19.97) given the requirement to express the B-spline curve in form (EQ 19.96).

First consider the case $k = 1$, and the segments including the point v_i. Let the blossom be f throughout. The first of these is the segment $t \in [t_i, t_{i+1}]$, with $v_{i-1} = f(t_i)$ and $v_i = f(t_{i+1})$ (these being the one-parameter polar forms for degree 1 polynomials). Then,

$$F(t) = \left(\frac{t_{i+1} - t}{t_{i+1} - t_i} \right) v_{i-1} + \left(\frac{t - t_i}{t_{i+1} - t_i} \right) v_i, \quad t \in [t_i, t_{i+1}] \qquad \text{(EQ 19.98)}$$

However, v_i also contributes to the next segment, $t \in [t_{i+1}, t_{i+2}]$, with $v_i = f(t_{i+1})$ and $v_{i+1} = f(t_{i+1})$. Hence,

$$F(t) = \left(\frac{t_{i+2} - t}{t_{i+2} - t_{i+1}} \right) v_i + \left(\frac{t - t_{i+1}}{t_{i+2} - t_{i+1}} \right) v_{i+1}, \quad t \in [t_{i+1}, t_{i+2}] \qquad \text{(EQ 19.99)}$$

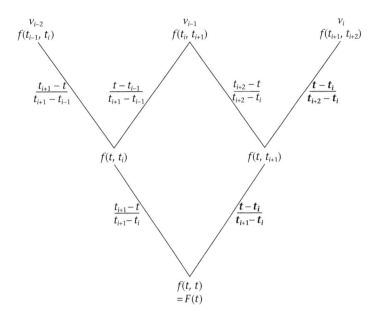

Figure 19.17
The coefficient of v_i is obtained along the bold path

In order to write $F(t)$ in form (EQ 19.96) each v_i must be associated with a single coefficient $N_{1,i}(t)$. Equating coefficients of v_i in (EQ 19.98) and (EQ 19.99) with (EQ 19.96), we have:

$$N_{1,i}(t) = \left(\frac{t - t_i}{t_{i+1} - t_i}\right)N_{0,i}(t) + \left(\frac{t_{i+2} - t}{t_{i+2} - t_{i+1}}\right)N_{0,i+1}(t), \quad t \in [t_i, t_{i+2}] \qquad \text{(EQ 19.100)}$$

which is a special case of (EQ 19.97) with $r = 1$.

Let's go one step further and consider the case $r = 2$. Again consider the three segments to which v_i makes a contribution:

(1) The segment $t \in [t_i, t_{i+1}]$, including $v_{i-2} = f(t_{i-1}, t_i)$, $v_{i-1} = f(t_i, t_{i+1})$, and $v_i = f(t_{i+1}, t_{i+2})$. By using the de Casteljau triangle (Figure 19.17) it is easy to see that the coefficient of v_i in $F(t)$ is:

$$\left(\frac{t - t_i}{t_{i+2} - t_i}\right)\left(\frac{t - t_i}{t_{i+1} - t_i}\right) \qquad \text{(EQ 19.101)}$$

(2) The segment $t \in [t_{i+1}, t_{i+2}]$, including $v_{i-1} = f(t_i, t_{i+1})$, $v_i = f(t_{i+1}, t_{i+2})$ and $v_{i+1} = f(t_{i+2}, t_{i+3})$. Here the coefficient of v_i is (Figure 19.18):

$$\left(\frac{t - t_i}{t_{i+2} - t_i}\right)\left(\frac{t_{i+2} - t}{t_{i+2} - t_{i+1}}\right) + \left(\frac{t_{i+3} - t}{t_{i+3} - t_{i+1}}\right)\left(\frac{t - t_{i+1}}{t_{i+2} - t_{i+1}}\right) \qquad \text{(EQ 19.102)}$$

(3) The segment $t \in [t_{i+2}, t_{i+3}]$, including $v_i = f(t_{i+1}, t_{i+2})$, $v_{i+1} = f(t_{i+2}, t_{i+3})$ and $v_{i+2} = f(t_{i+3}, t_{i+4})$. The coefficient of v_i is:

$$\left(\frac{t_{i+3} - t}{t_{i+3} - t_{i+1}}\right)\left(\frac{t_{i+3} - t}{t_{i+3} - t_{i+2}}\right) \qquad \text{(EQ 19.103)}$$

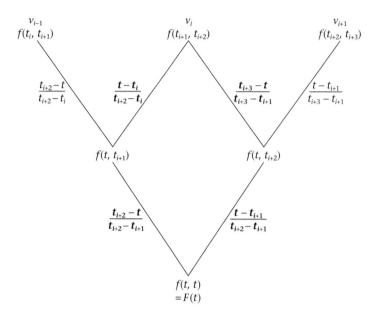

Figure 19.18
The coefficient of v_i is obtained along the bold paths

Now, using 1, 2, and 3 the coefficient of v_i in (EQ 19.96) for $r = 2$ must be:

$$N_{2,i}(t) = \left(\frac{t - t_i}{t_{i+2} - t_i}\right)N_{1,i}(t) + \left(\frac{t_{i+3} - t}{t_{i+3} - t_{i+1}}\right)N_{1,i+1}(t), \quad t \in [t_i, t_{i+3}] \qquad \text{(EQ 19.104)}$$

This is the special case of (EQ 19.97) with $r = 2$. The general result can be shown by induction on r.

19.10   Introduction to surfaces

In the next few sections we show how the theory for curves can easily be applied to form a certain class of surface, known as *tensor product surfaces*, *rectilinear surfaces*, or *rectangular patches* (these terms are interchangeable). The theory for curves applies very straightforwardly to such surfaces, and no fundamentally new ideas need to be introduced. Whereas a curve is specified by a sequence of control points and a sequence of knots (or parametric intervals), so in 3D there is a rectangular array of control points, and two knot sequences specifying the parametric intervals.

A surface is specified parametrically by a function of the form

$$F(t, u) = (X(t, u), Y(t, u), Z(t, u)), \quad t, u \in [0, 1] \qquad \text{(EQ 19.105)}$$

(The parametric ranges are arbitrary, and [0, 1] is chosen for convenience.)

It is easy to see why this specifies a surface. For any fixed t, as u varies between 0 and 1, a curve will be mapped out by the path of $(X(t, u), Y(t, u), Z(t, u))$. Take any point on that curve, and now allow t to vary, and it is clear that the point will again travel on some curve. In this way it can be seen that we have a curve of curves, so defining a surface.

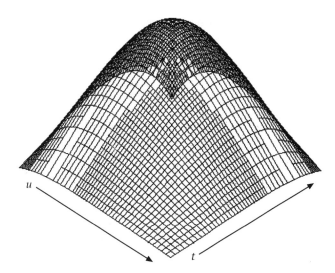

Figure 19.19
A parametric surface: this is a Bézier surface with control points on a Gaussian

This is shown in Figure 19.19, where the u and t direction on the surface are illustrated. Consider curve A which occurs at a fixed value of u and the range of values of t. Then take any point on that curve, and allow u to vary; this maps out, for example, curve B. The entire surface is defined in this way.

In computer-aided geometric design the form of $(X(t, u), Y(t, u), Z(t, u))$ is, as for curves, polynomial expressions in t and u. The exact form of the representation determines the type of surface – we concentrate on the Bézier and B-spline form, as with curves.

19.11 Parametric surfaces

The Bernstein basis representation

Suppose we have an $(m + 1) \times (n + 1)$ array of Bézier control points as follows:

$$\begin{bmatrix} p_{00} & p_{01} & \cdots & p_{0n} \\ p_{10} & p_{11} & \cdots & p_{1n} \\ \multicolumn{4}{c}{\cdots\cdots\cdots\cdots} \\ p_{m0} & p_{m1} & \cdots & p_{mn} \end{bmatrix} \qquad \text{(EQ 19.106)}$$

Each row or column defines a Bézier curve. We can form a surface, as curves of curves, by the so-called *tensor product* of the Bézier curves:

$$F(t, u) = \sum_{i=0}^{m} \sum_{j=0}^{n} B_{m,i}(t) p_{ij} B_{n,j}(u) \qquad \text{(EQ 19.107)}$$
$$t, u \in [0, 1]$$

where the basis functions are the same as in (EQ 19.33).

We can rearrange (EQ 19.107) as:

$$F(t, u) = \sum_{i=0}^{m} B_{m,i}(t) \left(\sum_{j=0}^{n} p_{ij} B_{n,j}(u) \right) \qquad \text{(EQ 19.108)}$$

For fixed t and i, the term in brackets is a Bézier curve for the ith row of the control points. For any fixed u, the expression in brackets evaluates to a point on that curve. Across each value of i, therefore, another Bézier curve is generated. Hence the Bézier surface may be thought of as a Bézier curve of Bézier curves.

To render the Bézier curve we may apply the de Casteljau algorithm to split each row, and then each resulting column. Hence the original array of $m \times n$ control points becomes four sets of such arrays. Continue splitting in this way until the array approximates a co-planar set of control points that can be approximated by a four-sided polygon. Therefore, the Bézier patch is approximated by a set of four-sided planar polygons.

```
typedef struct{
   float x,y,z;
}Point3D;

typedef Point3D ControlPointArray[4][4];

void Bezier3D(ControlPointArray p){
   ControlPointArray q,r,s,t;
   if(Coplanar(p)) RenderPolygon(p[0][0],p[3][0],p[3][3],p[0][3]);
   else{
      /*split p into q,r,s,t*/
      Split3D(p,q,r,s,t);
      Bezier3D(q);
      Bezier3D(r);
      Bezier3D(s);
      Bezier3D(t);
   }
}
```

In order to implement `Split3D`, the de Casteljau algorithm may be used for each row, and then for each resulting column, with the split at parametric value 1/2 each time. In order to test for co-planarity, it is possible to use the result that the perpendicular distance (D) of the point (X, Y, Z) from the plane with equation $ax + by + cz - d = 0$ is given by:

$$D^2 = \frac{(ax + by + cz - d)^2}{a^2 + b^2 + c^2} \qquad \text{(EQ 19.109)}$$

This is a costly calculation, since in the case of a bi-cubic Bézier surface, it must be performed for each of 13 points of the 16, except for the 3 used to compute the plane equation. There are some approximate methods that have been proposed which are far less costly (Rappaport, 1991b).

Blossoms for rectangular Bézier patches

The idea of polar forms for Bézier surfaces follows directly from Bézier curves, though the notation is inevitably more messy. As an example, consider a bi-quadratic Bézier surface as follows:

$$
\begin{aligned}
F(t, u) &= \sum_{i=0}^{2} B_{2,i}(t) \left(\sum_{j=0}^{2} p_{ij} B_{2,j}(u) \right) \\
&= \sum_{i=0}^{2} B_{2,i}(t)(p_{i0}(1-u)^2 + 2p_{i1}(1-u)u + p_{i2}u^2) \\
&= (1-t^2)(p_{00}(1-u)^2 + 2p_{01}(1-u)u + p_{02}u^2) \\
&\quad + 2(1-t)t(p_{10}(1-u)^2 + 2p_{11}(1-u)u + p_{12}u^2) \\
&\quad + t^2(p_{20}(1-u)^2 + 2p_{21}(1-u)u + p_{22}u^2)
\end{aligned}
$$

(EQ 19.110)

Such an expression is clearly a bi-quadratic function in terms of t and u, and is of the general form:

$$
\begin{aligned}
F(t, u) &= a_0(b_0 + b_1 u + b_2 u^2) + a_1 t(c_0 + c_1 u + c_2 u^2) \\
&\quad + a_2 t^2(d_0 + d_1 u + d_2 u^2)
\end{aligned}
$$

(EQ 19.111)

Suppose we blossom this expression first on t, treating the u as constants, we get:

$$
a_0(b_0 + b_1 u + b_2 u^2) + a_1 \left(\frac{t_1 + t_2}{2} \right)(c_0 + c_1 u + c_2 u^2) + a_2 t_1 t_2(d_0 + d_1 u + d_2 u^2)
$$

(EQ 19.112)

Now take this expression and blossom on the u, to get:

$$
\begin{aligned}
&a_0 \left(b_0 + b_1 \left(\frac{u_1 + u_2}{2} \right) + b_2 u_1 u_2 \right) \\
&+ a_1 \left(\frac{t_1 + t_2}{2} \right) \left(c_0 + c_1 \left(\frac{u_1 + u_2}{2} \right) + c_2 u_1 u_2 \right) \\
&+ a_2 t_1 t_2 \left(d_0 + d_1 \left(\frac{u_1 + u_2}{2} \right) + d_2 u_1 u_2 \right)
\end{aligned}
$$

(EQ 19.113)

Obviously, this is not a very elegant expression, although easily derived. The point is that it shows that the blossom can be formed, and may be written in the form $f(t, t_2; u_1, u_2)$, the semi-colon indicating that the polynomial is first blossomed with respect to one parameter, and then the result with respect to the other.

Now, the relationship between the Bézier control points and blossoms follows directly from the curve case. In general, for an $m \times n$ Bézier surface with parameter values $t \in [a, b]$ and $u \in [c, d]$:

$$p_{ij} = f(a, a, \ldots, a, b, b, \ldots, b; c, c, \ldots, c, d, d \ldots d)$$
$$= f(a^{[m-i]}b^{[i]}; c^{[n-j]}d^{[j]})$$

(EQ 19.114)

(recall that $b^{[i]}$ means $b, b, \ldots, b$ – i.e., a sequence of b values of length i).

B-spline surfaces

The theory again follows directly from curves. Consider the case of bi-cubic surfaces. We have an array of $m \times n$ B-spline control points v_{ij}. We have two knot sequences, one for the rows, and the other for the columns:

- $t_1, t_2, \ldots, t_{m+3}$ for each column, and
- $u_1, u_2, \ldots, u_{n+3}$ for each row.

Now all the theorems from curves apply directly. For example:

(1) The connection between control points and blossoms for any row or column is as before. Hence, using the notation of the previous section:

$$v_{ij} = f(t_{i+1}, t_{i+2}, t_{i+3}; u_{j+1}, u_{j+2}, u_{j+3})$$
$$i = 0, 1, 2, \ldots, m$$
$$j = 0, 1, 2, \ldots, n$$

(EQ 19.115)

(2) From (EQ 19.115) we can separately use interpolation on the rows and columns in order to derive the Bézier control points for any individual patch. For example, from (EQ 19.114) we know that the control points for the patch defined by the range $[t_i, t_{i+1}]$ and $[u_j, u_{j+1}]$ will have Bézier control points of the form:

$$p_{ab} = f(t_i^{[3-a]}t_{i+1}^{[a]}; u_j^{[b]}u_{j+1}^{[3-b]})$$
$$a, b = 0, 1, 2, 3$$

(EQ 19.116)

(3) Knot insertion, probably the easiest way to render the surface, can be performed by inserting knots for each row, and again for each column, following the scheme presented earlier (see "Knot insertion" on page 413).

19.12 Triangular Bézier patches

The previous sections have considered rectangular patches, that is, where the parameter domain is over some interval $[a, b] \times [c, d]$. Moreover, the degree of the polynomial that generates the surface is of the form $m \times n$, where the first parameter is of degree m, and the second independently of degree n. Here we consider an alternative form, in many ways simpler, where the parametric domain is a triangle, and the *total* degree of the corresponding polynomial is of degree n. These are called triangular patches.

Figure 19.20
Triangular parametric
domain: any parameter
value **u** can be expressed
in barycentric coordinates
(α, β, γ)

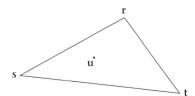

Figure 19.20 shows a triangular parametric region defined by vertices **r**, **s**, and **t** in R^2. Any parameter value $\mathbf{u} \in R^2$ can be expressed as a barycentric combination of the vertices:

$$\mathbf{u} = \alpha\mathbf{r} + \beta\mathbf{s} + \gamma\mathbf{t}$$
$$\alpha + \beta + \gamma = 1 \tag{EQ 19.117}$$
$$\alpha, \beta, \gamma \geq 0$$

Let $F(\mathbf{u})$ be an nth degree polynomial expression from $R^2 \to R^3$ expressed in these Barycentric coordinates and with total degree n. Then:

$$F(\mathbf{u}) = \sum_{i+j+k=n} a_{ijk}\alpha^i\beta^j\gamma^k \tag{EQ 19.118}$$

where the $a_{ijk} \in R^3$. (Recall that (α, β, γ) is a Barycentric coordinate for $\mathbf{u}$.)

Now a blossom can be constructed for such polynomials in much the same way as for polynomials with parametric domain in R. For example, suppose $n = 3$, with

$$F(\mathbf{u}) = \alpha^3 + 6\alpha^2\beta + \beta\gamma^2 + \alpha\beta\gamma \tag{EQ 19.119}$$

Then

$$f(\mathbf{u}_1, \mathbf{u}_2, \mathbf{u}_3) = \alpha_1\alpha_2\alpha_3 + 6\left(\frac{\alpha_1\alpha_2 + \alpha_1\alpha_3 + \alpha_2\alpha_3}{3}\right)\left(\frac{\beta_1 + \beta_2 + \beta_3}{3}\right)$$
$$+ \left(\frac{\beta_1 + \beta_2 + \beta_3}{3}\right)\left(\frac{\gamma_1\gamma_2 + \gamma_1\gamma_3 + \gamma_2\gamma_3}{3}\right) \tag{EQ 19.120}$$
$$+ \left(\frac{\alpha_1 + \alpha_2 + \alpha_3}{3}\right)\left(\frac{\beta_1 + \beta_2 + \beta_3}{3}\right)\left(\frac{\gamma_1 + \gamma_2 + \gamma_3}{3}\right)$$

Clearly (EQ 19.120) has all the properties required of the blossom – it is multi-affine, symmetric, and its diagonal is equal to the corresponding polynomial (EQ 19.119).

Generally, corresponding to any polynomial function $F(\mathbf{u})$ of total degree n, there is a unique corresponding blossom $f(\mathbf{u}_1, \mathbf{u}_2, \ldots, \mathbf{u}_n)$ which is multi-affine, symmetric, and has diagonal $f(\mathbf{u}, \mathbf{u}, \ldots, \mathbf{u}) = F(\mathbf{u})$.

This can be exploited to construct Bézier triangular patches. Consider:

$$F(\mathbf{u}) = f(\mathbf{u}, \mathbf{u}, \ldots, \mathbf{u}) \tag{EQ 19.121}$$

From (EQ 19.117) we can use the multi-affine property to write:

$$F(\mathbf{u}) = \alpha f(\mathbf{r}, \mathbf{u}, \ldots, \mathbf{u}) + \beta f(\mathbf{s}, \mathbf{u}, \ldots, \mathbf{u}) + \gamma f(\mathbf{t}, \mathbf{u}, \ldots, \mathbf{u}) \tag{EQ 19.122}$$

Continuing to expand out the blossoms in this way, we arrive at:

$$F(\mathbf{u}) = \sum_{i+j+k=n} \left(\frac{n!}{i!j!k!} \right) \alpha^i \beta^j \gamma^k f(\mathbf{r}^{[i]}, \mathbf{s}^{[j]}, \mathbf{t}^{[k]}) \qquad \text{(EQ 19.123)}$$

If we identify the blossom values with points in 3D space:

$$p_{ijk} = f(\mathbf{r}^{[i]}, \mathbf{s}^{[j]}, \mathbf{t}^{[k]}) \qquad \text{(EQ 19.124)}$$

we obtain the Bézier triangular patch of degree n.

Consider the case $n = 2$, then the triangular arrangement:

$$
\begin{array}{ccc}
p_{200} & & \\
p_{110} & p_{101} & \\
p_{020} & p_{011} & p_{002}
\end{array}
\qquad \text{(EQ 19.125)}
$$

corresponds to the arrangement of blossoms:

$$
\begin{array}{ccc}
f(\mathbf{r}, \mathbf{r}) & & \\
f(\mathbf{r}, \mathbf{s}) & f(\mathbf{r}, \mathbf{t}) & \\
f(\mathbf{s}, \mathbf{s}) & f(\mathbf{s}, \mathbf{t}) & f(\mathbf{t}, \mathbf{t})
\end{array}
\qquad \text{(EQ 19.126)}
$$

Similarly for the case $n = 3$:

$$
\begin{array}{cccc}
p_{300} & & & \\
p_{210} & p_{201} & & \\
p_{120} & p_{111} & p_{102} & \\
p_{030} & p_{021} & p_{012} & p_{003}
\end{array}
\qquad \text{(EQ 19.127)}
$$

corresponding to:

$$
\begin{array}{cccc}
f(\mathbf{r}, \mathbf{r}, \mathbf{r}) & & & \\
f(\mathbf{r}, \mathbf{r}, \mathbf{s}) & f(\mathbf{r}, \mathbf{r}, \mathbf{t}) & & \\
f(\mathbf{r}, \mathbf{s}, \mathbf{s}) & f(\mathbf{r}, \mathbf{s}, \mathbf{t}) & f(\mathbf{r}, \mathbf{t}, \mathbf{t}) & \\
f(\mathbf{s}, \mathbf{s}, \mathbf{s}) & f(\mathbf{s}, \mathbf{s}, \mathbf{t}) & f(\mathbf{s}, \mathbf{t}, \mathbf{t}) & f(\mathbf{t}, \mathbf{t}, \mathbf{t})
\end{array}
\qquad \text{(EQ 19.128)}
$$

Using the multi-affine property we can immediately use this arrangement to evaluate any point $f(\mathbf{u}, \mathbf{u}, \mathbf{u})$ on the surface. This is shown in Figure 19.21, where we interpolate on each of the inner triangles to obtain new triangles, and repeat this until $f(\mathbf{u}, \mathbf{u}, \mathbf{u})$ is obtained. Each interpolation is of the form given in (EQ 19.122). First the original control points are interpolated to produce the inner points labeled 1. Then these are interpolated to produce the points labeled 2. Finally the required point is shown labeled 3.

Notice that the interpolation in Figure 19.21 gives rise to three triangles each of the same form as (EQ 19.128). (Consider the triangle of four rows whose apex is $f(\mathbf{u}, \mathbf{u}, \mathbf{u})$, and whose last row is the last row of the original triangle.) This shows that the triangular patch can be decomposed as a de Casteljau subdivision, and hence a simple recursive rendering scheme can be applied as above (see "The Bernstein basis representation" on page 419).

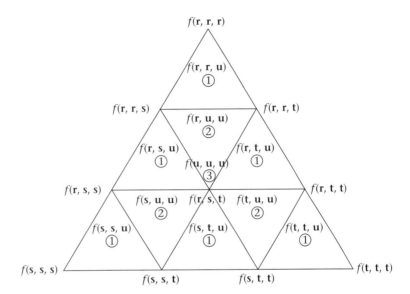

Figure 19.21
Interpolation scheme
for triangular patches

(19.13) ## Cubic B-spline interpolation

The curve interpolation problem

Throughout this chapter we have concentrated on the problem of curve and surface design based on the relationship between a set of control points and a curve or surface. In this section we consider the converse problem: we are given some points on a curve, and we require the control points that could have given rise to this curve. In particular, we are given a sequence of n distinct *data points* $p_1, p_2, \ldots, p_n$ such that for some cubic B-spline curve F,

$$F(t_i) = p_i$$
$$i = 1, 2, \ldots, n$$

(EQ 19.129)

where the t_i consist of a given sequence of knot values, in increasing order. We are required to find the control points v_j that construct such a B-spline curve. We suppose that the blossom corresponding to F is the three-parameter polar form $f(u_1, u_2, u_3)$.

A solution for cubic B-spline curves

In order to solve this problem we first look at the knot sequence that is required. Since we know that the curve must start at p_1, the first three knot values should be t_1, thus giving

$$p_1 = f(t_1, t_1, t_1) \tag{EQ 19.130}$$

Similarly, at the other end of the curve:

$$p_n = f(t_n, t_n, t_n) \tag{EQ 19.131}$$

Hence the knot sequence must be of the form:

$$t_1, t_1, t_1, t_2, t_3, t_4, \ldots, t_{n-4}, t_{n-3}, t_{n-2}, t_{n-1}, t_n, t_n, t_n \tag{EQ 19.132}$$

By definition of a B-spline curve, over the usual knot sequence

$$t_1, t_2, t_3, t_4, \ldots, t_{n-4}, t_{n-3}, t_{n-2}, t_{n-1}, t_n \tag{EQ 19.133}$$

we have:

$$\begin{aligned} v_i &= f(t_{i+1}, t_{i+2}, t_{i+3}) \\ i &= 0, 1, 2, \ldots, n-3 \end{aligned} \tag{EQ 19.134}$$

The de Casteljau triangle for this range of knot values, leading to the evaluation of p_i, is shown in Figure 19.22.

From this we can derive the set of equations:

$$\begin{aligned} p_i &= a_{i-3}v_{i-3} + b_{i-2}v_{i-2} + c_{i-1}v_{i-1} \\ i &= 3, 4, \ldots, n-2 \end{aligned} \tag{EQ 19.135}$$

where the coefficients a_{i-3}, b_{i-2}, and c_{i-1} are functions of the knot values, and which can be easily evaluated over the triangle in the usual way. The unknowns in these equations are, of course, the control points v_j. So far we have $n - 4$ equations and $n - 2$ unknowns.

Now consider the start of the knot sequence and the evaluation of p_2, as shown in Figure 19.23.

It follows that:

$$p_2 = a_{-1}v_{-1} + b_0v_0 + c_1v_1 \tag{EQ 19.136}$$

The other end of the knot sequence is shown in Figure 19.24. From this it follows that:

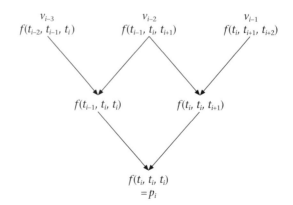

Figure 19.22
Evaluation of data point
for knots in (EQ 19.133)

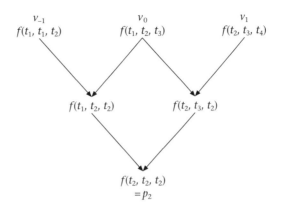

Figure 19.23
Evaluation of p_2

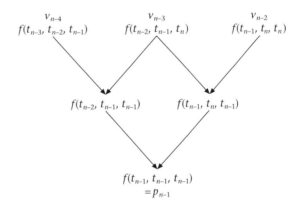

Figure 19.24
Evaluation of p_{n-1}

$$p_{n-1} = a_{n-4}v_{n-4} + b_{n-3}v_{n-3} + c_{n-2}v_{n-2} \qquad \text{(EQ 19.137)}$$

Putting (EQ 19.135), (EQ 19.136), and (EQ 19.137) together, we find:

$$p_i = a_{i-3}v_{i-3} + b_{i-2}v_{i-2} + c_{i-1}v_{i-1}$$
$$i = 2, 4, \ldots, n-1 \qquad \text{(EQ 19.138)}$$

Altogether now we have $n - 2$ equations in n unknowns $v_{-1}, v_0, \ldots, v_{n-2}$. This leaves us with two degrees of freedom – set

$$v_{-1} = q_1$$
$$v_{n-2} = q_n \qquad \text{(EQ 19.139)}$$

arbitrarily (these will affect the shape of the curve near the ends), thus giving the same number of equations as unknowns.

Matrix equation

The overall set of equations can now be written as:

$$v_{-1} = q_1 \text{ (chosen)}$$
$$a_{-1}v_{-1} + b_0 v_0 + c_1 v_1 = p_2$$
$$a_0 v_0 + b_1 v_1 + c_2 v_2 = p_3 \tag{EQ 19.140}$$
$$\ldots$$
$$a_{n-4}v_{n-4} + b_{n-3}v_{n-3} + c_{n-2}v_{n-2} = p_{n-1}$$
$$v_{n-2} = q_n \text{ (chosen)}$$

This can be written in matrix form (EQ 19.141), showing that this is a tri-diagonal matrix equation that is particularly straightforward to solve.

$$
\begin{bmatrix}
1 & 0 & 0 & 0 & 0 & \ldots & \ldots & \ldots & 0 \\
a_{-1} & b_0 & c_1 & 0 & 0 & \ldots & \ldots & \ldots & 0 \\
0 & a_0 & b_1 & c_2 & 0 & \ldots & \ldots & \ldots & 0 \\
\ldots & & & & & & & & \\
0 & \ldots & & & 0 & a_{n-4} & b_{n-3} & c_{n-2} & \\
0 & 0 & 0 & 0 & \ldots & 0 & 0 & 0 & 1
\end{bmatrix}
\begin{bmatrix}
v_{-1} \\
v_0 \\
v_1 \\
\ldots \\
v_{n-3} \\
v_{n-2}
\end{bmatrix}
=
\begin{bmatrix}
q_1 \\
p_2 \\
p_3 \\
\ldots \\
p_{n-1} \\
q_n
\end{bmatrix}
\tag{EQ 19.141}
$$

It is important to remember that of course the v_j and the p_i are points either in 2D or 3D. Hence there could be two or three such systems of linear equations to solve.

19.14   Evaluating polynomials

Forward differences

Finally for this chapter we consider a fundamental issue: the efficient evaluation of polynomials. This section first considers the problem of evaluating cubic polynomials, and then these results are applied to B-splines. Consider the polynomial:

$$g(t) = a_0 + a_1 t + a_2 t^2 + a_3 t^3 \tag{EQ 19.142}$$

Evaluation of this directly involves six multiplications and three additions. Horner's method rewrites the polynomial as:

$$g(t) = ((a_3 t + a_2)t + a_1)t + a_0 \tag{EQ 19.143}$$

This involves three multiplications and three additions – a significant saving, especially taking into account that the polynomial may have to be computed at many values of t. This result can trivially be generalized to an nth degree polynomial.

If the polynomial is to be evaluated at equally spaced intervals, $t = 0$, h, $2h$, ..., then an alternative method is available, which in its iterative loop requires only additions. This is called the *forward difference* method.

Assuming a constant increment (h) throughout, the first difference applied to $g(t)$ is defined as:

$$\Delta g(t) = g(t + h) - g(t) \tag{EQ 19.144}$$

Similarly, higher orders are defined by:

$$\Delta^0 g(t) = g(t)$$
$$\Delta^i g(t) = \Delta^{i-1} g(t+h) - \Delta^{i-1} g(t) \tag{EQ 19.145}$$
$$i = 1, 2, \ldots$$

In general, for an nth degree polynomial the first difference will be a polynomial of degree $n - 1$, the second difference of degree $n - 2$, and so on. Hence the nth difference will be a constant (degree 0). In the case of a cubic polynomial $\Delta^3 g(t)$ will be a constant – i.e., independent of t. It is these facts which allow a simple algorithm to be constructed.

Using (EQ 19.145) it is easy to show that the following results hold:

$$\Delta g(t) = (a_1 h + a_2 h^2 + a_3 h^3) + (2a_2 h + 3a_3 h^2)t + (3a_3 h)t$$
$$\Delta^2 g(t) = h^2(2a_2 + 6a_3 h) + (6a_3 h^2)t \tag{EQ 19.146}$$
$$\Delta^3 g(t) = 6a_3 h^3$$

Also from (EQ 19.145) it is easy to see that

$$g(t+h) = g(t) + \Delta g(t)$$
$$\Delta g(t+h) = \Delta g(t) + \Delta^2 g(t) \tag{EQ 19.147}$$
$$\Delta^2 g(t+h) = \Delta^2 g(t) + \Delta^3 g(t) = \Delta^2 g(t) + 6a_3 h^3$$

(EQ 19.146) and (EQ 19.147) together therefore imply the following: Suppose that the values of $g(t)$, $\Delta g(t)$, $\Delta^2 g(t)$ are known ($\Delta^3 g(t)$ is obviously always known since it is a constant). Then using (EQ 19.147) $g(t + h)$, $\Delta g(t + h)$, and $\Delta^2 g(t + h)$ can be found incrementally. Typically, in the application to curve rendering, the polynomial will be evaluated in the range 0 to 1, with h chosen according to the number of increments required. (EQ 19.142) and (EQ 19.146) can obviously be used to compute the starting values $g(0)$, $\Delta g(0)$, $\Delta^2 g(0)$. The remaining values are computed incrementally from (EQ 19.147). This calculation is set out in tabular form in Figure 19.25. The first row is pre-computed. For each subsequent row the values are computed by summing the terms immediately above and to the right, making use of (EQ 19.147), except for the last column which is constant. The required evaluations at equi-distant intervals of the parameter are given in the first column. Note that the entire calculation (apart from the first row) is based on additions only.

$g(0)$	$\Delta g(0)$	$\Delta^2 g(0)$	$\Delta^3 g(0) = 6a_3 h^3$
$g(h)$	$\Delta g(h)$	$\Delta^2 g(h)$	$\Delta^3 g(h) = 6a_3 h^3$
$g(2h)$	$\Delta g(2h)$	$\Delta^2 g(2h)$	$\Delta^3 g(2h) = 6a_3 h^3$
$g(3h)$	$\Delta g(3h)$	$\Delta^2 g(3h)$	$\Delta^3 g(3h) = 6a_3 h^3$
$\ldots$			

Figure 19.25
Forward difference
computation for third
degree polynomial

Adaptive forward differences

In the previous section we saw the idea of forward differences. Although fast, this method results in a traversal of the curve at equally spaced parameter values, which may not be suitable if there are sections of the curve which are essentially flat. Too much computation is being done in this case. On the other hand, recursive subdivision methods adaptively subdivide the curve and find the relatively flat segments, but this is at the cost of a recursive implementation. We would like a combination of these two approaches, which has the advantages of the simplicity of forward differencing, and of recursive subdivision, but without actually doing any recursion.

One potential solution to this problem was given by Shue-Ling Lien *et al.* (1987), called *Adaptive Forward Differences*. First, some background. Consider a cubic Bézier curve:

$$F(t) = (1 - t)^3 p_0 + 3(1 - t)^2 t p_1 + 3(1 - t)t^2 p_2 + t^3 p_3 \qquad \text{(EQ 19.148)}$$

This can be rewritten in matrix form:

$$F(t) = [t^3 \ t^2 \ t \ 1] \begin{bmatrix} 1 & 0 & 0 & 0 \\ -3 & 3 & 0 & 0 \\ 3 & -6 & 3 & 0 \\ -1 & 3 & -3 & 1 \end{bmatrix} \begin{bmatrix} p_0 \\ p_1 \\ p_2 \\ p_3 \end{bmatrix} \qquad \text{(EQ 19.149)}$$

$$= tBp$$

The fact that this is a Bézier curve is expressed by the B matrix. This is what defines it as a Bézier curve, for this matrix is the only component of the expression which depends on the Bézier formulation.

Now suppose we do some *transformation* on the parameter, for example replace t by $a + bt$ ($t \leftarrow a + bt$), then we can go through the process again of finding this new curve as a cubic polynomial, and again find a similar expression:

$$F(a + bt) = tCp \qquad \text{(EQ 19.150)}$$

for some matrix C. Since the Bernstein functions form a basis, we know that any polynomial can be re-expressed in the Bézier form, and again we can see this now. Suppose we can find a matrix A such that:

$$BA = C \qquad \text{(EQ 19.151)}$$

then substituting this into (EQ 19.150) gives

$$F(a + bt) = tB(Ap) \qquad \text{(EQ 19.152)}$$

So the points Ap are the Bézier points corresponding to the curve given by (EQ 19.150).

Consider in particular the parameter transformation given by:

$$L: t \leftarrow \frac{t}{2} \qquad \text{(EQ 19.153)}$$

This describes the portion of the curve over the parametric range $[0, \frac{1}{2}]$.

We already know how to construct the Bézier control points corresponding to this part of the curve by using the de Casteljau algorithm (see "The de Casteljau algorithm" on page 392). So the matrix A in this special case would be such that the set of points Ap are the Bézier points on the curve $[0, \frac{1}{2}]$. A similar argument holds for (R):

$$R\text{:}t \leftarrow \frac{t+1}{2} \qquad\qquad \text{(EQ 19.154)}$$

This represents the part of the curve over the parametric interval $[\frac{1}{2}, 1]$.

In general, for any curve, these two transformations, L and R, give the left and right curve segments corresponding to a de Casteljau subdivision at $t = \frac{1}{2}$. It was the insight of the authors Shue-Ling Lien *et al.* (1987) to realize that a further transformation:

$$E\text{:}t \leftarrow t + 1 \qquad\qquad \text{(EQ 19.155)}$$

is such that:

$$R = EL \qquad\qquad \text{(EQ 19.156)}$$

That is, first L is applied, and then E, and the result R is obtained.

The sets of points produced by the application of L and R correspond to the points which would be obtained in a de Casteljau recursive subdivision. However, using (EQ 19.156), it is possible to avoid the recursion. The Adaptive Forwards Difference algorithm is such that:

(1) Apply L sufficient times to get a small segment of the curve (e.g., so that the curve is within 1 pixel, or the control points are in approximately a straight line, or whatever criterion).

(2) Keep applying E to get the subsequent points on the curve, while the criterion holds true. (This is the forward differences part of the algorithm.) If the curve segment becomes too small, then apply L^{-1}. When the criterion ceases to be true, then apply L.

This method requires a concrete representation for the operations E and L. We know from above, that since they are parameter transformations we can find a matrix A which transforms the control points. In fact $A = B^{-1}C$. So the three operations in fact correspond to three (A) matrices which are used to transform the control points.

It is obviously possible to use this method directly on Bézier curves; however, the corresponding matrices for E, L, and L^{-1} are not particularly convenient for computation. Instead of the Bernstein basis functions (i.e., for Bézier curves), the authors Shue-Ling Lien *et al.* (1987) proposed the so-called *forward difference* basis, which results in matrices for efficient computation. This is defined as follows:

$$D_0(t) = 1$$
$$D_1(t) = t$$
$$D_2(t) = \frac{1}{2}t(t-1)$$

(EQ 19.157)

$$D_3(t) = \frac{1}{6}t(t-1)(t-2)$$

Since this is a basis, any polynomial function of degree at most 3 can be written in the form:

$$F(t) = p_0 + p_1 D_1(t) + p_2 D_2(t) + p_3 D_3(t)$$

(EQ 19.158)

Expand this out as a polynomial in the power basis:

$$F(t) = t^3\left(\frac{p_3}{6}\right) + t^2\left(\frac{p_2 - p_3}{2}\right) + t\left(\frac{p_3}{3} - \frac{p_2}{2} + p_1\right) + p_0$$

(EQ 19.159)

Now do the substitution $L : t \leftarrow \dfrac{t}{2}$ to obtain:

$$F(t) = \frac{t^3}{8}\left(\frac{p_3}{6}\right) + \frac{t^2}{4}\left(\frac{p_2 - p_3}{2}\right) + \frac{t}{2}\left(\frac{p_3}{3} - \frac{p_2}{2} + p_1\right) + p_0$$

(EQ 19.160)

We want to rewrite (EQ 19.160) in the form (EQ 19.159) in order to get back to the same basis, that is, to find the set of points q_0, q_1, q_2, q_3, so that

$$F(t) = t^3\left(\frac{q_3}{6}\right) + t^2\left(\frac{q_2 - q_3}{2}\right) + t\left(\frac{q_3}{3} - \frac{q_2}{2} + q_1\right) + q_0$$

(EQ 19.161)

is equal to (EQ 19.160). We can do this by equating the coefficients of powers of t, which gives us:

$$q_0 = p_0$$
$$q_1 = \frac{p_1}{2} - \frac{p_2}{8} + \frac{p_3}{16}$$
$$q_2 = \frac{p_2}{4} - \frac{p_3}{8}$$

(EQ 19.162)

$$q_3 = \frac{p_3}{8}$$

Finally, this can be written in matrix form:

$$L = \begin{bmatrix} 1 & 0 & 0 & 0 \\ 0 & \frac{1}{2} & -\frac{1}{8} & \frac{1}{16} \\ 0 & 0 & \frac{1}{4} & -\frac{1}{8} \\ 0 & 0 & 0 & \frac{1}{8} \end{bmatrix}$$

(EQ 19.163)

The following can be computed from this:

$$L^{-1} = \begin{bmatrix} 1 & 0 & 0 & 0 \\ 0 & 2 & 1 & 0 \\ 0 & 0 & 4 & 4 \\ 0 & 0 & 0 & 8 \end{bmatrix}$$

(EQ 19.164)

A similar analysis yields:

$$E = \begin{bmatrix} 1 & 1 & 0 & 0 \\ 0 & 1 & 1 & 0 \\ 0 & 0 & 1 & 1 \\ 0 & 0 & 0 & 1 \end{bmatrix}$$

(EQ 19.165)

Looking at the values in these matrices, their use involves only additions and multiplications by powers of 2. Hence they are very efficient for use in practice (and in hardware).

Therefore, to render any curve using adaptive forward differences, first it must be expressed in the forward difference basis, and then application of the E, L, and L^{-1} matrices can be used to generate points on the curve.

19.15   Summary

In this chapter we have presented some of the major results in computer aided geometric design. This has been introduced using the blossoming approach, from which we derived Bézier curves and considered the properties of these curves and the de Casteljau subdivision algorithm. This was generalized to B-spline curves, where a sequence of curve segments can be joined together end-to-end to form a more complex curve, and with continuity constraints at the joints. We showed how the blossoming approach can be used to derive the B-spline basis functions, the more usual approach to the definition of B-spline curves. Once the ideas for curves are understood, there is an easy transition to surfaces. We introduced Bézier and B-spline tensor product surfaces, and triangular Bézier patches. An application of the blossoming approach to B-splines was used to generate a particular result for curve interpolation: given a set of data points on a curve, find the control points that would generate such a curve. Finally, we introduced some fundamental ideas useful for rendering polynomial curves – forward differences and adaptive forward differences.

20 Human dynamics in a virtual world

20.1 Introduction

So far we have only considered the rendering of virtual environments. However, a major component of most real-time systems is interaction between people and the virtual environment. The term "users" is often employed to describe people interacting within a virtual environment. We find this term inappropriate in the context of an immersive virtual environment, because such people are part of, are participating in, the environment (often along with others). Hence we tend to employ the term "participant" rather than "user." The most basic interaction capability is the ability to move the virtual camera(s) through the virtual environment under the control of the participant. This capability is referred to as *exploratory navigation* or *locomotion*. Real-time systems that allow this locomotion capability are often called *walk-through* systems because the participant cannot touch objects or affect how the system evolves, but only observe it.

Systems that are more interactive might allow the participant to interact with individual objects to activate their built-in behavior or change their properties.

In this book we do not consider abstract user-interface devices such as 3D menus and widgets, but concentrate on how to touch, select, or manipulate objects.

How interaction is specified and activated by the participant is a complex process that depends greatly on the input and output devices involved. We start this discussion by introducing the *virtual reality model*, that is, the style of human–computer interface where the participant is *immersed* within the computer displays and *directly manipulates* the virtual world. These techniques are very demanding in terms of scene modeling, interaction, and behavior. In particular, we will focus on how the participant is represented within the virtual environment and the techniques for tracking and sensing the participant in order to animate this representation.

We will then discuss some of the limitations encountered with today's systems both in hardware and software and spend some time outlining the problem of *collision detection*. The following chapter will describe more general interaction techniques that are in common use today for *non-immersive* systems.

20.2   Virtual reality model

Virtual reality systems have a particular goal, that of convincing participants that they are actually located in the environment displayed to their sensory systems. This sense of "being there" in the environment has been called *presence* or *telepresence* (Held and Durlach, 1992; Draper *et al.*, 1998) as discussed in Chapter 1. A presence-generating environment is often equated with an environment that is *intuitive* to use and has a *natural* set of interaction metaphors. If the participant is present in an environment that is modeled in a realistic manner, then we can expect the participant's prior knowledge of the interactions expected in similar real situations to be employed. Conversely, situations where the participant's expectations of behavior or interaction are not fulfilled can lead to a break in presence. For example, it would be difficult to feel present in a simulation of a social gathering if you were not able to respond to a person putting out their hand by putting out your own in order to perform a handshake. Furthermore, the participant's response to their non-ability to fulfill the expected action can lead to trepidation or confusion in future encounters.

In the virtual reality model, the displays try to completely surround the participant with visual, audio, tactile, smell, and taste information. The unrealized ambition is to create Ivan Sutherland's *ultimate display* (Sutherland, 1965), or more popularly, *Star Trek*'s Holodeck, where simulations of reality are so authentic that physical harm might befall the participant.

We should point out that most virtual environment display systems concentrate on the visual system. Indeed, the existence of this book belies the authors' own biases and we do not consider audio outside the scope of this section. However, it is our experience that audio display is essential in some situations, and the existence of suitable background noise and contextual cues

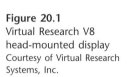

Figure 20.1
Virtual Research V8
head-mounted display
Courtesy of Virtual Research
Systems, Inc.

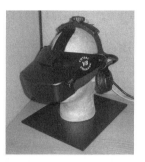

can heighten the sense of presence. Audition has some unique properties over vision, in that the audio cues can be located in any direction, and the auditory system has an ability to segregate and focus on one sound among several simultaneous streams (Wenzel, 1992).

Finally we note that very few systems employ any form of tactile, smell, or taste display. Research into such systems continues, but there are fundamental problems in display that pose major technological hurdles (e.g., the display being large areas of skin). We refer the interested reader to Kalawsky's review of the physiological requirements of such displays and some of the technologies currently employed (Kalawsky, 1993).

Immersion

In the virtual reality model, the first requirement is that the participant be *immersed* in the display system. We take immersion to be a combination of several display properties. Firstly, the displayed information *surrounds* the participant, for example the display covers as much of the visual field as possible and, when the participant turns around, they do not see darkness. The display is *extensive*, covering a range of sensory modalities. The display is *inclusive*, that is, distracting information (such as reality) is excluded. Finally, the display is *vivid*, that is, it has a high resolution, is rich in color, covers the full range of audition and so on, as described in Chapter 1.

Typical immersive systems include the head-mounted display (Melzer and Moffitt, 1996) and the Cave Automatic Virtual Environment (CAVE[1]) (Cruz-Neira *et al.*, 1992; Cruz-Neira *et al.*, 1993). In a head-mounted display there is usually a pair of displays, one for each eye, that are kept stationary relative to the participant's head. The rest of the visual field is then blanked out with some form of mask. Figure 20.1 shows a Virtual Research V8, a typical mid-range HMD in the year 2000. Each screen has 800×600 colour triads. The head will be tracked in order to dynamically adjust the properties of the virtual

---

1. CAVE is a trademark of the board of trustees of University of Illinois. The term is still commonly used as a generic name for such displays.

cameras which define the image in the left and right eyes. We introduced stereo rendering in "Creating 3D stereo views" on page 217. The reader is referred to McAllister (1993) and Melzer and Moffitt (1996) for details of head-mounted display design.

CAVE-like displays take the opposite extreme view of immersion: a series of large display surfaces surround the participant who is free to move about in that volume of space. Figure 20.2 (color plate) shows the VR-CUBE at Center for Parallel Computers (PDC), Royal Institute of Technology (KTH), Stockholm, Sweden. This was one of the first six-sided CAVE-like displays.

Although the aim of CAVE-like and HMD systems is to immerse the participant in visual information, they do actually have quite different properties. In the CAVE-like display participants can see their own body and objects can not appear to be in front of the body. For example, any attempt to track the hand and place a virtual object in the palm of the hand will fail because the hand will obscure the display screen. In a HMD the real body can not be seen and a virtual body is often created. This removes the problem of near-space objects being occluded because the whole display is computer generated. Note that we do not consider a whole class of system, often term *augmented reality systems*, where real and virtual imagery are mixed inside a HMD (Azuma, 1997).

In an immersive system, then, the display aims to provide as broad a range of input to the sensory system as possible. However, immersion only refers to display properties and not what is displayed. An immersive system, though, has the potential to display hyper-realistic or totally fantastic worlds. It is up to the designers and programmers (including the graphics programmers) to make the world appear to be consistent and believable.

Human–computer interface

Interaction between humans and the desktop computer involves the participants making actions with the mouse and keyboard that activate a variety of windows, icons, and menus. Such interfaces suffer from two problems: the difficulty of forming the appropriate actions to perform a task, *gulf of execution*, and then understanding and evaluating the response, *gulf of evaluation* (Hutchins *et al.*, 1986). That is, it is often difficult to find that some functionality is available to be used at the interface, and even when it has been activated, there may be no immediate feedback, or if there is it may not be readily comprehensible. To alleviate these problems, interface designers often use a *direct manipulation* paradigm in which a world model is built where objects can be directly moved, selected, or edited by the participant (Hutchins *et al.*, 1986). Examples include What You See is What You Get (WYSIWG)-style text editors and computer-aided design packages.

The direct manipulation style of interface pervades the virtual reality model. Indeed, at one level the participant's own body is the interface, since three-dimensional displays completely surround and include the participant and he or she is tracked. For example, when using a stereo head-mounted display-type unit, the displays are stationary relative to the participant's head. If the head is tracked (see "Tracking the participant" on page 440) the virtual cameras that generate the views can be moved in direct correspondence to the motions of the participant's head. This one-to-one mapping in both translation and rotation is a very intuitive mapping and although, in our experience, people who first put on a HMD might not realize it is head-tracked, once they do realize (or have been told to "look around"), they will not forget how to turn the view.

Compare this with the desktop case. Positioning a camera is a six degree of freedom task. In order to utilize the mouse and keyboard for this task, some mapping must be constructed that takes several separate control dimensions and combines them. Typical ways of doing this involve either mapping different devices to different dimensions (e.g., the mouse rotates the camera and arrow keys effect translation relative to the current camera rotation) or by making the interface *modal* (e.g., making mouse movements map onto translations in the XZ plane unless the left shift key is pressed, in which case mouse movements map onto translations in the XY plane). The next chapter will talk at length about some common interaction techniques and the issues in implementing them.

It should hopefully be apparent that the camera control task in the virtual reality model has a lower cognitive overhead than the techniques described above. It is also the case that we have both hands free to do other tasks, whereas with the desktop condition we were using one or both of the hands to use the keyboard and mouse. This is one of the powers of the virtual reality model; it maximizes the opportunities for input control by tracking the participant's body as closely as possible. We note that it is common in virtual reality systems for the participant's hands to be tracked in addition to the head, so picking and interaction tasks should be similarly easier.

Interaction within the virtual reality model

Once the participant is immersed and is accurately tracked it is assumed that input and output are registered. Registration implies that motions of the participant's limbs are accurately measured relative to one another. If this is done then participants can expect, for example, that if they place their real hand in front of their real face, a virtual hand or cursor will appear in view at the correct position.

Already we can see that some of the usability problems associated with desktop systems become non-issues. For example, it is possible to lose the mouse cursor among screen clutter when operating a windowing system, but it difficult to see how participants could lose their hand in a virtual reality system. This suggests that the gulf of execution should be lower for the virtual reality model. However, it is important to note that the gulf can still exist because of inconsistencies in how the virtual environment is modeled or how it reacts.

Is the gulf of evaluation narrowed in a virtual reality system? Consider the hand-waving example. If participants see a virtual hand waving, it is easy for them to evaluate what is happening and make the connection between effect and affect. However, if they see a cursor then perhaps they might be confused because they were expecting to see a real hand. Certainly there is evidence to show that not only a hand, but a complete virtual body is useful in a virtual reality system (Slater and Usoh, 1994; Mine *et al.*, 1997). The answer to our original question is thus unclear. In the general case, with the weird and wonderful types of environment that we can display in a virtual environment system, we can only hope that the fact that the displays are immersive gives the participant a good comprehension of 3D space. As virtual environment designers, we can use that third dimension to good effect when designing our virtual environments. To put it another way, it is as easy to make bad, hard to understand and difficult to operate virtual environments as it is to make bad desktop environments. Participants should be able to build a cognitive model of how the world operates and how they can interact with it. This does not necessarily mean the application need be realistically modeled, but this approach is commonly used since it is easy for naive participants to comprehend what they are experiencing.

20.3 Simulation of body

From the discussion of the previous section it should be obvious that a vital component of any virtual environment system is a model of the participant within that environment. In one sense the body model *is* the description of the interface to the virtual environment system – the eyes are the visual interface, the ears are the audio interface, and the hands are the effectors in the world. As we have seen, it also can be useful to have a geometric description of the body drawn from an egocentric point of view. This is not only for the purposes of showing participants their own body. The geometric description of the hand and fingers can be used as the basis of a realistic grasping simulation for picking up objects (Boulic *et al.*, 1996).

In describing the virtual reality model, we talked about participants being immersed and tracked so that movements of their body are mapped into consistent changes in the display. If we ignore, for the moment, some of the limitations of tracking systems such as limited range, the virtual reality model allows us to avoid "fantastic" interaction metaphors since participants are able to interact freely.

Building the body model

Extremely sophisticated tracking systems that track dozens of points do exist. For example, the Ascension MotionStar can track up to 90 points. Such systems

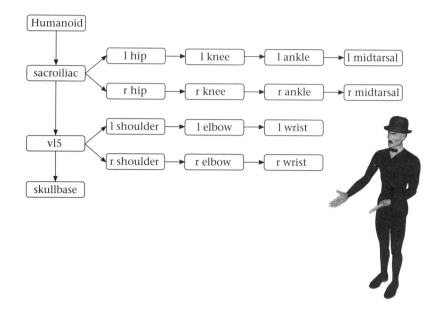

Figure 20.3
Excerpt from the
H-Anim body hierarchy
and an example avatar
driven by motion capture
data
Courtesy of Computer
Graphics Lab (LIG) directed by
Daniel Thalmann, Lausanne,
Switzerland. H-Anim prod.:
Christian Babski. Body design:
Mireille Clavien

are most commonly used for motion capture for off-line animation rather than immersive displays, but when used interactively potentially each joint in the humanoid model can be tracked separately. To complement tracking systems, some very complex skeleton hierarchies exist, and there is an emerging standard for the human skeleton, H-Anim (H-Anim, 1999), see Figure 20.3.

However, a much more typical human modeling situation is one where the head, torso, and both hands are tracked. We can create a very simple avatar model with disconnected components, but preferably we try to determine some of the articulation of the body from this limited sensor information.

Inferring multiple connected limb positions from limited tracker data is an example of an *inverse kinematics* problem. Because the skeleton has many degrees of freedom, there are multiple ways to configure it so that the tracked limbs are in their required position. For example, given the position of the shoulder and the hand, there are an infinite number of positions for the elbow. Finding a consistent constraint is a problem. Continuing the example, it might seem sensible just to make the elbow hang in the lowest position, but this would be visually incorrect for some motions such as moving the hand from the front of the face to behind the head. Badler *et al.* (1993) describe a solution for this problem for the four-tracker situation.

Tracking the participant

There are many different tracking technologies in use (Meyer *et al.*, 1992). The Polhemus Fastrak (Polhemus, HTTP) is a commonly used magnetic tracking device that consists of a base transmitter that generates a switching magnetic field. This field induces current in a receiver device from which the relative positions of the receiver and transmitter can be deduced. A common problem with magnetic trackers is that they suffer from interference with metal in the environment and other electronic systems.

Due in part to these problems of interference, tracking systems usually have a limited operating range. A top of the range commercial system such as the Ascension MotionStar can support tracking in a volume approximately 10 meters across (Ascension, HTTP), but more commonly used systems typically have a usable range of only a couple of meters.

Vision, ultrasonic, and inertial alternatives exist, but again these are less commonly used, being either technically less desirable or significantly more expensive. A promising area of research is in hybrid technologies such as trackers from Intersense that combine inertial and ultra-sonic tracking (Intersense, HTTP).

The choice between different tracking systems depends primarily on five factors: accuracy (both angular and positional), resolution, range, total system lag, and update rate. The implications of poor accuracy, resolution, and range should be fairly obvious. The implications of system lag and update rate are slightly more involved. Total system lag is the total time taken between the participant's making, say, a head motion, and the picture appearing on the screen. This lag is very important in immersive systems since it affects the reliability with which the participant can effect motor control. If, say, the virtual hand lags considerably behind the real hand motions, participants may find it hard to touch objects naturally since they fall into a pattern of waiting for the visual feedback to catch up with their actions before carrying on with another action. If the update rate is not very rapid then the scene can lose its sense of continuity for the participant. A typical figure suggested in the liter- ature is that the frame-rate, and thus the tracker update rate, should not fall below 15 Hz (Barfield and Hendrix, 1995).

20.4   Interacting with the virtual body

The limitations of tracking mean that we have to introduce interaction metaphors for object manipulation (grasping and moving) and locomotion (movement). There are other limitations that require us to employ metaphors. Limitations in haptic display, for instance, mean that the participant can not walk into objects in the virtual environments.

Interaction metaphors are quite perfidious since the participant must re-member how to activate the techniques enshrined in the metaphor. Even if we could make the display very highly immersive we still have distanced ourselves from the ideal of the ultimate display where virtual reality is indistinguishable from reality since these interaction metaphors rarely match appropriate real-world tasks.

Figure 20.4
Specifying object
manipulation in the
virtual reality model

grasping

releasing

We will discuss interaction metaphors in more depth in the next chapter when we relax the requirement to track the participant's body and instead rely on more abstract input devices.

Object manipulation

The first problem that is often experienced with object manipulation is that the hand might be tracked by a single point and, because hand posture is not tracked, the virtual hand has a static shape. This makes grasping gestures difficult to perform, and the usual interaction metaphor is to effect a grasp by touching the virtual object with the virtual hand and then pressing a button on a handheld device. The ease with which the grasp metaphor can be remembered by the participant will depend on the form of the button device. These vary from buttons on billiard balls (3BALL from Polhemus Inc.) to gloves such as the Pinch Glove (Fakespace, HTTP) that create button "clicks" when the participant touches thumb to finger.

An essential part of the grasp interaction metaphor is some facility to test intersection between the virtual hand and other virtual objects. Once an object to grasp has been identified we can attach it to the hand and thus it will move when the hand moves. We can implement this by removing the object from its position in the scene graph and replacing it as a child of the hand when the object is grasped. During the grasp, the object's position is affected by the global transformation of the hand and thus it moves with it. When the object is released it is removed from the hierarchy of the hand and replaced in its original position in the scene graph.

This process is illustrated in Figure 20.4. The first step involves calculating M_R, the relative transformation from the hand to the object. This is given by the equation

$$M_R = (M_B \cdot M_H)^{-1} \cdot M_O \cdot M_P \qquad \text{(EQ 20.1)}$$

where M_B is the transformation from body to world coordinates, M_H is the transformation from hand to body coordinates, M_O is the transformation from object O coordinates to world coordinates, and M_P is the transformation from object P to object O coordinates.

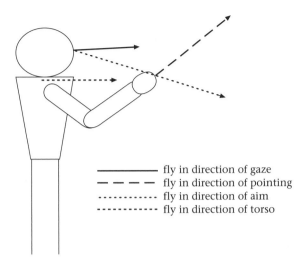

fly in direction of gaze
fly in direction of pointing
fly in direction of aim
fly in direction of torso

Figure 20.5
Specifying the direction
for locomotion

After the manipulation the new local transformation of the object $M_{P'}$ can be calculate thus:

$$M_{P'} = M_O^{-1} \cdot M_B \cdot M_H \cdot M_R \qquad \text{(EQ 20.2)}$$

Robinett and Holloway (1992) describe a second method for doing this style of manipulation that does not involve removing and replacing the object in the scene graph.

Locomotion

The limitations of tracker range mean that for distances greater than one or two meters participants must use an interaction metaphor to locomote. A common practice is to have a second button on the handheld device that can be used to start locomotion. The direction of locomotion can be taken from the direction they are looking, the direction their hand is pointing or the direction their torso is facing, see Figure 20.5, and the velocity might be fixed or might be participant-controlled. See Mine *et al.* (1997) for other examples for the immersive case.

It is also common to constrain participants to locomote in a horizontal plane so that their eye level remains constant. This becomes problematic when moving over uneven surfaces. We can not (yet) physically display ground surfaces at different heights, so obstacles either prevent movement, or the participant is raised or lowered onto the new surface based on some heuristic of allowable steps up and down. Again we need a form of collision detection here and again the model of the participant's body can be employed. For example, if the object hits the participant below the knee, then the participant is moved up so that his or her feet rest on the obstacle, but otherwise the participant is moved back so the body just touches the obstacle.

Interesting approaches to the locomotion problem have been developed. Both linear (Brooks, 1986) and omni-directional treadmills (Darken *et al.*, 1997) have been used as input devices. These address the problem of tracker range directly, but they have serious shortcomings that prevent their widespread use.

Body-centered navigation

Once the participant can locomote about the environment, an obvious question to ask is how their virtual body interacts with the environment. In addition to surface following mentioned in the previous section, it is usually desirable to stop the participant walking through or placing parts of their virtual body through walls in the environment because of the likely disorientation this might cause. This requires detection of collisions between the participant's virtual body and the virtual environment, so that locomotion in the virtual world can be halted when the body is touching an obstacle. However this rapidly becomes more complex; if a participant moves up to a wall and then stretches out an arm, we might have to move them away from the wall and so prevent the hand penetrating it. Many systems avoid this problem by making a large bounding object around the participant which prevents them getting within arms length of walls, but this has its own problems. Any of these techniques has the potential to confuse the participant because it is physically impossible to stop them making physical actions that might result in a collision response. The next section will outline some techniques that can be used for collision detection tests between the body and the scene.

20.5 Object pair collision detection

A vital component of the interaction of the virtual human with the virtual environment is a facility to test for collisions between pairs of objects. Essentially we tackle this problem by describing an exhaustive test for when two objects intersect, and then describing how in reality we avoid doing this test if at all possible.

Exhaustive test

We assume that all objects under consideration for collision testing can be considered as collections of triangles. Consider a pair of objects, one consisting of m triangles, the other consisting of n triangles. If we have a reliable triangle–triangle intersection test, we can test for intersection of the two objects by exhaustively testing all pairs of triangles. This requires $m.n$ triangle–triangle tests, and we will briefly list methods to reduce this after describing the triangle–triangle intersection test.

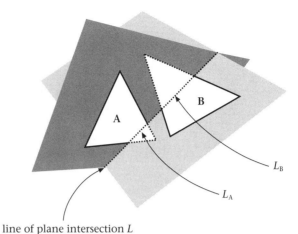

Figure 20.6
Example triangle–
triangle intersection
test

line of plane intersection L

The following method is due to Möller (1997). In the comparison of two triangles A and B:

(1) Reject triangles A and B (they do not intersect) if all the vertices in A lie completely on one side of the plane containing B and vice versa.

(2) Otherwise, the planes containing A and B must therefore intersect on a line L.

(3) Find the line segment intersection of L with A (L_A) and L with B (L_B).

(4) A and B intersect if and only if L_A and L_B overlap.

This process is illustrated in Figure 20.6.

This test is obviously expensive to perform for large objects and although there are methods to speed up this test, a lot of attention has been devoted to finding rapid rejection tests that can quickly determine if it is impossible for two objects to overlap.

Basic rejection tests

The simplest object rejection test is one based on distance. Each scene element is surrounded by a bounding sphere. Two objects cannot overlap if the distance between the two bounding sphere centers is greater than the sum of the radii of the bounding spheres.

This test is very simple to perform but is very conservative in use. A tighter test is the *separating plane* test. Two objects can not collide if any plane can be found where all the points of one objects lie on one side and all the points of the other on the reverse. The key to this test is finding a good separating plane.

See Figure 20.7 for some examples. Objects A and B do not overlap because there is an axis aligned plane that separates them. Objects B and C do not overlap because the plane formed by one of the edges of C separates them.

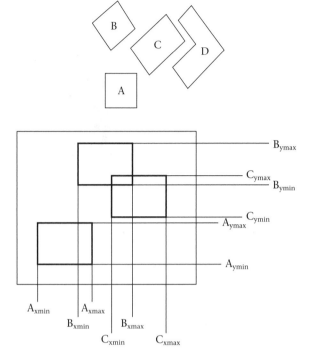

Figure 20.7
Simple tests for rejection of collision candidates

Figure 20.8
Performing collision detection using a series of 1D overlap tests

However, objects C and D do not overlap, but there is no separating plane. In this case we must revert to an exhaustive test.

Bounding box range tests

If axis aligned bounding boxes are created for the scene elements, then another simple rejection test becomes available. The bounding box is defined by three ranges in x, y, and z. The key insight is that two boxes can overlap in 3D if and only if both their x-ranges overlap and both their y-ranges overlap and both their z-ranges overlap. Conversely, two boxes do not overlap if any of the projections onto x, y, and z do not overlap. This is illustrated in Figure 20.8. We can see that the elements A and B overlap in the x-axis ($A_{xmax} > B_{xmin}$), but not in the y-axis ($A_{ymax} < B_{ymin}$). Elements A and C overlap in neither axis, so can be rejected by either the X or Y axis test. Elements B and C overlap in both axes and so are candidates for collision.

20.6 General collision detection

The problem of detecting collisions between a set of objects is more involved than the single pair case. With n objects there are order n^2 possible pairs of

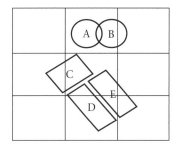

Figure 20.9
Finding likely collision pairs with a regular space subdivision

objects that would potentially need testing for overlap. In general, the strategy is to find a spatial partitioning that discards as many pairs as possible and for this we can use some of the techniques discussed in Chapter 16 in the context of speeding up ray-tracing. For all remaining pairs, we then use one of the techniques in the previous section to determine whether the pair is actually in collision.

In the section "Uniform space subdivision" on page 346 we introduced the concept of uniform space subdivision for acceleration of ray tracing. We can use a similar technique to accelerate collision detection.

An axis aligned box is placed around the scene and is uniformly subdivided along each axis. In each resulting cell, a list is kept of all scene elements that intersect this cell. This is usually done conservatively, say by using the bounding box of the scene element. Then for each cell whose element list contains more than one element, we must test all pairs of objects in that list for actual overlap. Obviously once a pair of objects has been tested once, there is no need to test them again, so a list of tests performed must be kept.

This process is illustrated in Figure 20.9. Elements A and B share a common cell, and the object pair do overlap. However, elements C, D, and E share a common cell, but none of the pairs CD, DE, EC overlap.

Obviously, choosing a denser spatial subdivision will increase the likelihood of discarding pairs that really do not overlap. The cost is, as always, increased memory usage and more expensive maintenance of the cell lists, especially if the objects are dynamic. It is of course possible to use similar methods with octree, BSP tree or hierarchical bounding box structures.

20.7 A note on VRML

The H-Anim standard for describing human models within VRML97 has been mentioned earlier in this chapter. Note that the use of H-Anim avatars is limited to the visual description of the participant, and the avatar can not be used in the general way as the basis for interaction that we have described in this chapter.

VRML97 does itself provide a facility to describe a very basic virtual body that can be used for collision detection when locomoting about the scene. We will discuss this is the following chapter.

20.8 Summary

We have introduced interaction by considering a virtual reality model of inter-action. If we model the participant and track their movements, then we can use techniques such as gestures and touch as input. Conversely, we can customize the rendering and other displays such that the participant is immersed and feels as if he or she is surrounded by the displays.

With current technology this approach is limited because of the form of the displays, the range or accuracy of tracking, latency in the display system, or limitation of the programming model.

We also provided an introduction to the problem of collision detection between objects. First we described a test for collision between two objects and then we discussed how to avoid testing all possible pairs of objects by looking at spatial subdivisions of space.

In the next chapter we will investigate the very different approach to interactions that are found in non-immersive systems.

21 Real-time interaction

21.1 Introduction

The techniques of interaction within the virtual reality model are at one end of a spectrum of possible interaction methods for real-time systems. In this chapter we take a different view that starts not from a model of the user, but from consideration of simple interaction tasks and how the user can perform these tasks using common interaction devices.

The model of real-time 3D interaction where the user sits at a monitor using a keyboard, mouse or other desk-bound interaction device has sometimes been called *desktop virtual reality*, *fish tank virtual reality*, or *non-immersive virtual environments*. These terms have been applied to a very broad range of systems and a plethora of different devices and displays.

In this chapter we will review some common interaction devices, and then illustrate how they can be used for the basic interaction tasks of selection, manipulation and locomotion.

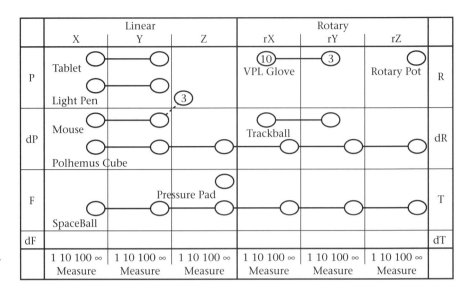

Figure 21.1
Some input devices plotted on the taxonomy of Mackinlay *et al.*

Desktop interaction devices

An interaction device recognizes some physical action of the user such as rotation of a dial, and reports that action at some granularity over a certain range. For example, a dial might report an integer value between 0 and 99 that corresponds to actual rotation values between 0 and 2π radians, that is, a over a full rotation. It is then up to the virtual environment software to map that value to, perhaps, the rotation of the camera about the Y axis of the local coordinate system. The design of interaction devices is vast and a comprehensive review is beyond the scope of this chapter. The reader is referred to reviews in Foley *et al.* (1984), Buxton (1986) and Mackinlay *et al.* (1990).

Using the taxonomy of Mackinlay *et al.* and examples from Buxton *et al.*, a few demonstrative devices are illustrated in Figure 21.1.

This taxonomy breaks devices down into individual components that they sense, classifies these components and then composes them back into complete description of the device. Each circle on the diagram represents a transducer of a physical property. The classification uses the categories of physical action mentioned below and for each action gives a rough idea of the granularity of response from binary through to continuous.

The classification is:

- Linear/Rotary
- Position, Rotation/Force, Torque (P,R/F,T)
- Relative/Absolute

- Direction
- Sensitivity (1 = discrete, 10 = small range, 100 = large range, ∞ = continuous range)

Thus a simple button is a sensor that can be classified as linear, position, absolute in the Z direction at a sensitivity of one, that is, it senses a discrete binary value.[1]

In actuality a single device might sense more than one value and such devices can be considered to be composed of simpler, one-dimensional sensors (Mackinlay *et al.*, 1990). For example, a mouse is composed of one linear, position, relative sensor that reports continuous values in the X direction, one linear, position, relative, sensor that reports continuous values in the Y direction, and usually two or three simple buttons as described above. Three types of composition are given.

The first type is *merge composition*. Merge composition of two devices creates a single device that generates output in the merged domain of both original devices simultaneously. The second type of composition is *layout composition*. Layout composition of several devices generates a single device that can sense the separate properties of each device independently. A button panel is so composed since each button is independently sensed and can be operated individually. The third type is *connection composition*. Good examples of these include *virtual devices* such as sliders within widgets, that map output of the mouse into the input for a secondary device which then outputs values in a different domain.

In Figure 21.1 merge composition is indicated by a solid line, and layout composition by a dotted line. A tablet or light pen is thus a merge of two absolute position-sensing devices, one in the X direction, one in the Y direction. The mouse is thus a merge compose of two position sensors and a layout compose with two to three buttons.

Several other popular devices are plotted in Figure 21.1, though there are several variations for most of the devices, particularly where there is a possibility of adding buttons.

The Polhemus Fastrak and Spaceball 2003 are radically different devices, though each senses the same number of degrees of freedom. The Polhemus Fastrak is a free-space magnetic tracking device that was introduced in the previous chapter. The Spaceball senses force and torque applied to a ball fixed to a stationary base. Even though both devices sense the same number of degrees of freedom, they are very different in use for similar tasks. An advantage of the Spaceball over the Polhemus Fastrak or any similar free-space tracking device is that it rests on the desk and doesn't need to be held in the air. However, with the Spaceball it is trickier to apply a torque to the ball without

---

1. For the purposes of this exposition, a body-centered axis system is used, X being to one's right, Y away, and Z up.

a resultant force, and vice versa. Thus it is common to have only one of rotation or translation enabled at any one time, at least for non-experts.

Also shown in the diagram is the VPL dataglove (Zimmerman *et al.*, 1987), which has been used in desktop systems though it is more usually associated with immersive systems. The dataglove senses the angle of bend for the two proximal joints of each digit, and has an option for sensing the abduction of the thumb and first and middle fingers. Overall this makes it a 13 degree of freedom sensing device.

21.3   Selection

Selection is simply the ability to be able to look at, point at, or touch an object to indicate that it is the focus of attention. We introduce it here, because in the virtual reality model it is not a separable component of object manipulation or locomotion. In fact, selection is a technique derived from desktop metaphors where objects can be selected by clicking once upon them, or lassoing them with a rubber-band type metaphor. In the virtual reality model where a realistic metaphor is being employed, indicating an object has no effect. However, in more fantastic environments objects might themselves react to such gestures. In the desktop model prior selection of objects is often useful since it allows more freedom in the design of interaction control.[2]

In the virtual reality model the definition of "point at" will depend on whether the posture of the user's hand is sensed. If no hand posture is available, a common approach is to test for the first object that intersects a ray centered on the user's hand and pointing in the direction of the hand.

Ray-based selection metaphors are applicable to any system where there is a 2D or 3D cursor under the control of the user. For example, in a 2D system with a mouse, we can select an object based on casting a ray from our virtual camera, through the pixel on the screen at the location of the cursor, in much the same way as we did when painting using ray casting. Note how this is different to selection in the virtual reality model. Selection in the virtual reality model does not require the user even to look at the target object since the ray originates at the hand, not the eye. See Figure 21.2 for a comparison.

The advantage of such ray-casting based approaches is that objects can be selected at a distance whereas in the virtual reality model, users must position themselves within reaching distance first. The disadvantage comes when we then try to manipulate objects that have been selected at such distances. First, errors in manipulation are scaled because of the distance to the object. Second, it is not possible to rotate the object in place about any axis except that of the ray itself.

---

2. For example, in the VRML browser examine mode, see "Vehicles" on page 462, selection is used to specify the object about which to circle, and subsequently the mouse motions move the viewpoint. Thus there are two separable states for the control method.

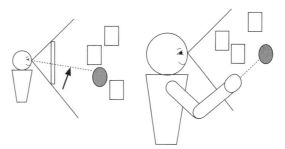

Figure 21.2
Comparing selection
in the desktop models
with selection in virtual
reality model

21.4 Manipulation

Computer users will be very familiar with the techniques of object manipulation on the standard 2D desktop. Object manipulation in 3D is considerably harder than 2D for several reasons. Not only are there simply more degrees of freedom to control (six rather than two or three) but common interaction devices can not control all those degrees of freedom at once. With two degree of freedom devices being so widespread, many approaches have used mice and joysticks to control objects either directly using mode switches to enable translations and rotations in different directions, or indirectly through the use of virtual devices.

Translation with a 2D device

There are many possibilities for control of objects using a 2D device. Given the relative positions of the input device, these can be simply mapped into translations in two out of three axes in some coordinate system. The problem is that there are several possible coordinate systems to choose from: world coordinates, the selected object's local coordinates, or potentially the coordinate system of any relevant parent object of the selected object (Figure 21.3). Given the multitude of possibilities it is usual to draw the coordinate axes on the screen, but even so control might be un-intuitive. To cope with covering only two dimensions an alternative mode should be provided either to toggle movement in the third dimension or to switch between different pairs of axes.

An alternative to object coordinate based manipulation is to map the movement of the 2D device into translation relative to the coordinate space of the camera. This is more intuitive since, for example, left–right movements of the device map onto left–right movements on the screen. If the 2D device controls an on-screen cursor, it is common to scale the translation based on depth into the screen, so that the apparent motion keeps the object fixed relative to the cursor.

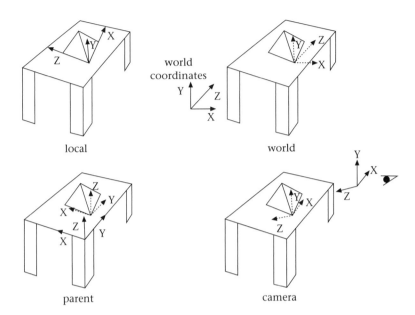

Figure 21.3
Controlling objects
in different coordinate
systems

Rotation with a 2D device

Again there are many possibilities for rotational control. Movement of the mouse can be mapped into rotation about any two axes, with the same broad selection of axes to choose from.

Viewpoint-centered control techniques are again useful. Chen *et al.* (1988) describe a virtual sphere technique, where the object is considered to be contained within a sphere. Two-dimensional device motion over the sphere rolls the sphere about the U and V axes of the camera, 2D device motion outside the sphere rotates about the N axis. A full sweep across the sphere rotates 180 degrees, while a full circle around the sphere rotates by 360 degrees about the N axis.

21.5 Locomotion

Controlling the viewpoint is also a difficult task with the same degrees of freedom as object manipulation. We discussed locomotion in the virtual reality model in "Body-centered navigation" on page 444. With the desktop model, locomotion control is very different since, as with object manipulation, we must map control from a 2D device to a 6D task.

Two basic approaches exist, moving the viewpoint through the workspace (what we have referred to as locomotion) or moving the workspace around the viewpoint. Essentially the difference is the choice of coordinate system in which to perform translations and rotations. Ware and Osborne (1990) give three navigation metaphors that illustrate the difference.

Scene in hand. The scene itself is slaved to the input device.

Eyeball in hand. The movements of the input device correspond directly to movements of the eye.

Flying vehicle control. The input device provides the controls for the vehicle such as velocity and rotation.

Operating the scene in hand metaphor is equivalent to an object manipulation metaphor. It is well suited for the viewing of small scenes where the eye orbits around a specified object. It is common to provide a zoom facility alongside the rotation functionality. A VRML browser's "examine mode" is a good example of such a metaphor (see "Vehicles" on page 462). When the scene becomes larger and the eye must traverse interior spaces, this metaphor becomes cumbersome.

The difference between eyeball in hand and flying vehicle control is one of whether the input device maps directly to position and rotation, or to velocity of the eyepoint. There is a spectrum of techniques possible, and we will discuss examples in the following section.

Specifying locomotion with a 2D device

For control of the viewpoint, viewpoint coordinate-centered techniques are obviously the most sensible approach. However, the modal separation of translation and rotation actions is more varied.

A common technique for free navigation is to have forward and backward motion of the 2D device effect viewpoint motion, along the positive and negative N axis of the viewpoint coordinate system, and to have left and right motions translate into rotation about the V axis.

For situations where most navigation is on a plane (e.g., a walkthrough simulation) two changes are often made. Firstly, rotation of the camera is about the world Y, not V. Note the difference between choosing world Y and V. One rotates the camera in the XZ plane of world coordinates, the other in the UN plane of the camera. Secondly, translation of the viewpoint would be by the projection of the VPN into the XZ plane of the world. The difference between the two techniques is illustrated in Figure 21.4.

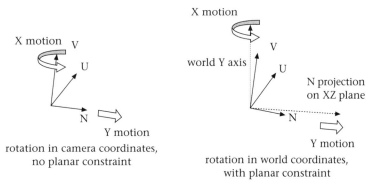

Figure 21.4
Effecting locomotion with a 2D device

rotation in camera coordinates, no planar constraint

rotation in world coordinates, with planar constraint

As with object manipulation metaphors, a series of modes is required to effect rotation and translation about the remaining axes if required. Another common technique involves the mouse normally controlling pitch and yaw (rotation about U and V) with a second mode for translation along U and N, and a third mode for rotation about N and translation along V.

Scale and accuracy

Positional control is accurate, but inefficient over long distance. Velocity control allows rapid movement over large distances (Ware and Slipp, 1991), but is inaccurate when approaching an object. Switching between the two control methods is possible, or the application might force the switch based on some knowledge about current working scale.

A more general solution is found in the application of a logarithmic approach technique (Mackinlay et al., 1990). In this technique the user specifies a point of interest by selecting an object. Once done, the user's viewpoint is smoothly animated along the path toward the point using a logarithmic approach. Distance away from the point of interest can be given by the following equation, where d is the original distance away, and k is a constant which can be used to control the rapidity of the approach.

$$f(t) = d - de^{-kt} \qquad \text{(EQ 21.1)}$$

This is often used in combination with the scene-in-hand metaphor where the selection point becomes the center of the rotation of the world (see the discussion of the examine mode in "Vehicles" on page 462).

A technique that is applicable in some situations where an object is the focus of attention is that of automatic camera control (Phillips et al., 1992). In this technique the camera automatically seeks a useful position from which to carry out the expected task. The main problem with automatic camera placement is choosing a view from which the focus object is not occluded. This can be computed using a hemicube approach (refer to "Computing the form-factors" on page 331). The scene is projected onto the hemicube surrounding the focus object. Uncovered areas on the hemicube are possibilities for the camera position. If the scene encloses the focus object then the projected depth of objects on the hemicube will have to be taken into account.

Use of a virtual body

Although we have seen that a virtual body is useful in the immersive case, it is not so obviously useful in the desktop case. Often the sole element of the virtual body is a 3D cursor in the world, and even that might be superfluous if the techniques are effected with a 2D locating device such as a mouse.

The use of an egocentric body is thus limited, but walkthrough systems, especially 3D games, often use an exocentric body, where the viewpoint is

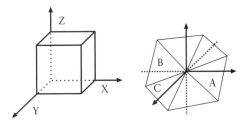

Figure 21.5
Mapping 2D motions into 3D based upon correlation with the projection of the object axes

placed behind and above a rendered avatar that represents and interacts with the environment as a sort of proxy. User control then is mapped onto translations and rotations of that avatar, and the viewpoint is slaved to remain fixed relative to that avatar. Unfortunately, this means that in enclosed environments the avatar might very easily become occluded from the camera, and thus some form of automatic camera control will have to employed to resolve a suitable position. Many times this can simply be done by moving the camera closer in, but often this will fail and the camera will need to be moved from its position behind the avatar. Figure A.1 (color plate) shows a VRML browser with an over-the-shoulder avatar view.

21.6 Avoiding modality in the interface

In the virtual reality model, we avoid modality because viewpoint control and object manipulation are performed by different devices (trackers) that can be manipulated simultaneously. Unfortunately, with most combinations of desktop devices there is no such luxury and some concessions need to be made.

With object manipulation there is little that can be done to reduce the complexity if the user does require fine control. One technique that can alleviate some of the burden is described by Nielsen and Olsen (1986). They take the 2D movements and map them onto motion along the virtual world coordinate axis that has the closest 2D projection to the direction of mouse movement. Thus the plane of motion of the 2D device is separated into six regions which map to motion in the positive and negative directions along the respective axes. This is illustrated in Figure 21.5. Thus if the local axes of the selected object project as shown on the left, mouse motion in sector A maps onto movement along the positive local X axis, motion in sector B maps onto negative local X axis, motion in sector C maps onto positive local Y axis, and so on.

Constraints

One method of reducing complexity of either object manipulation or viewpoint control is to reduce the number of degrees of freedom that can be controlled. For example, an object on a table might be constrained only to move in the plane of the table top and not vertically off the table (see "Virtual widgets" below for an example of a rotational constraint). When locomotion is controlled by a mouse, it is common not to provide a mechanism to roll the camera, or only to make this available in a special mode (e.g., pressing one of the Ctrl keys). This might be useful, and even desirable, for walkthrough systems but it is an impediment for general inspection of objects.

In 2D the use of imposed constraints such as grid-based or gravity snapping is quite common. Numerous analogous 3D techniques exist, for example see (Bier, 1990).

Virtual widgets

The use of virtual devices has been discussed before within the context of connection composition. We can take that further and describe virtual widgets that allow the user to control object manipulation by manipulating 3D objects that represent the operation to perform. Figure 21.6 (color plate) gives an example.

The Open Inventor manipulator illustrated in Figure 21.6 consists of a series of virtual widgets that allow the complete transformation for the object to be changed (Wernecke, 1994). Several modes exist, each enabled by selecting and grabbing one of three elements visible in the first figure: faces of the wire-frame cube, cubic handles of the wire-frame cube, and spherical handles on the axes centered on the object. The first effects translation in the plane defined by that face of the box (Figure 21.6, top right). The second effects scaling (lower left). The third effects rotation. Rotation occurs in two stages, firstly (lower middle) we see that a rotation control is created, but rotation is only allowed in one of the two indicated axes. Once we move the mouse a significant distance in one of the directions indicated, we are then constrained to rotate only in that direction (lower right). Many other examples of such controls can be found in the literature (e.g. Brookshire Conner *et al.*, 1992).

21.7   C examples

A common method of interacting with 3D games is to have rotation of the camera attached to the mouse, but locomotion attached to the cursor keys. The GLUT library has a series of helper functions that allow programmers to build simple interfaces very quickly (see "Setting up a stereo view" on page 217 for an introduction to the GLUT toolkit). In particular, it allows registration of callbacks for key press, key release, and mouse events, and it provides a very simple menuing system. The following code segment illustrates registration of interest in mouse move events, a simple menu system, and key press events:

```
glutIdleFunc(idle);
glutMouseFunc(mouseButton);
glutMotionFunc(mouseMotion);
glutKeyboardFunc(keyboard);
glutSpecialFunc(specialDown);
glutSpecialUpFunc(specialUp);
glutCreateMenu(menu);
glutAddMenuEntry("Toggle planar constraint", M_PLANAR);
glutAddMenuEntry("Move Faster", M_FASTER);
glutAddMenuEntry("Move Slower", M_SLOWER);
glutAddMenuEntry("Rotate Faster", M_RFASTER);
glutAddMenuEntry("Rotate Slower", M_RSLOWER);
glutAttachMenu(GLUT_RIGHT_BUTTON);
```

The role of `glutIdleFunc` is discussed below. Note there are two types of key press functions: `glutKeyboardFunc` is for keys that generate ASCII codes, and `glutSpecialFunc` is for other keys such as the cursor keys and functions keys. In GLUT3.7 additional functions `glutKeyboardUpFunc` and `glutSpecialUp-Func` were added to provide notification of key release events.

We create a simple menu system that allows the user to alter translational and rotational velocity and also toggle a planar constraint on and off. The following code segment shows how this is done:

```
enum {
  M_PLANAR,
  M_FASTER,
  M_SLOWER,
  M_RFASTER,
  M_RSLOWER
};

int usePlanarConstraint = 1;
double velocity = 0.05;
double angularVel = 0.005;

void menu(int item)
{
  switch (item) {

  case M_PLANAR:
    usePlanarConstraint = 1 - usePlanarConstraint;
    break;
  case M_FASTER:
    velocity*=1.5;
    break;
  case M_SLOWER:
    velocity*=0.5;
    break;
  case M_RFASTER:
    angularVel*=1.5;
    break;
  case M_RSLOWER:
```

```
      angularVel*=0.5;
      break;
   }
   glutPostRedisplay();
}
```

The actual translational movement is attached to the cursor keys:

```
static short Move = 0;
static void specialDown(int key, int x, int y)
{
   switch (key){
   case GLUT_KEY_UP:
     Move = 1;
     break;
   case GLUT_KEY_DOWN:
     Move = -1;
     break;

   }
}


static void specialUp(int key, int x, int y)
{
   switch (key) {
   case GLUT_KEY_UP:
     Move = 0;
     break;
   case GLUT_KEY_DOWN:
     Move = 0;
     break;

   }
}
```

Normally in a full screen game, movement of the mouse would be permanently attached to rotation of the camera. However, in this case, we are operating within a windowing environment, so we activate camera rotation on left mouse down:

```
static GLint XC, YC;/*current mouse position*/
short Rotate = 0;

static void mouseButton(int button, int state, int x, int y)
{
   if(button==GLUT_LEFT_BUTTON){
     XC = x;
     YC = Height - y;
     if(state==GLUT_DOWN) Rotate = 1;
     else Rotate = 0;
   }
}
```

If the mouse moves we then apply a rotation and possible translation to the camera:

```
static void mouseMotion(int x, int y)
{

  if(Rotate){/*for left button*/
    rotateVPN(x,y);
  }

  if(Move!=0){/*for right button*/
    moveVRP();
  }

  clickView_GL(TheCamera);

  /*force a call to display*/
  glutPostRedisplay();
}
```

We also apply the translation periodically using the idle function since we only get key press and release events and do not get events while the cursor key is held down:

```
static void idle(void)
/*if nothing else happening*/
{
  if(Move!=0) {
    moveVRP();
    clickView_GL(TheCamera);

    /*force a call to display*/
    glutPostRedisplay();
  }
}
```

Finally then, we provide the moveVRP (camera translation) and rotateVPN (camera rotation) functions:

```
static void moveVRP(void)
/*move the VRP along the VPN*/
{
  Vector3D n;
  Point3D vrp;

  vrp = TheCamera->vrp;

  /*normalize the vpn - pity this happens also in camera code*/
  normalizeVector3D(&TheCamera->vpn,&n);
```

```
    vrp.x += (velocity*n.x)*Move;
    vrp.y += (velocity*n.y)*Move;
    if (!usePlanarConstraint) {
      vrp.z += (velocity*n.z)*Move;
    }

    setVRP_GL(TheCamera,vrp.x,vrp.y,vrp.z);
}

static void rotateVPN(int x, int y)
{
    double dx, dy; /*change in mouse position*/
    double nx,ny,nz; /*new vpn*/
    RotationMatrix r;
    /*trial and error value affecting angular velocity*/

    /*difference between old and new coordinates*/
    dx = angularVel*(x - XC);
    dy = angularVel*((Height-y)- YC);

    XC = x;
    YC = Height-y;

    /*treat (dx,dy,1) as the new offset VPN, expressed in VC*/
    /*transform back to WC, using transpose of RotationMatrix*/
    r = TheCamera->R;
    nx = r.m[0][0]*dx + r.m[0][1]*dy + r.m[0][2];
    ny = r.m[1][0]*dx + r.m[1][1]*dy + r.m[1][2];
    nz = r.m[2][0]*dx + r.m[2][1]*dy + r.m[2][2];

    setVPN_GL(TheCamera,nx,ny,nz);
}
```

21.8 VRML examples

VRML not only describes animation and scripting but it allows a variety of interactive techniques. There are two basic categories of interaction: user control of the viewpoint in the scene, and interaction of the user with objects in the scene. These are described in very different ways. Viewpoint control is effected by the world author selecting one of a number of prescribed vehicles and only one vehicle is active at a time. In contrast, interaction with objects is effected by *Sensor* nodes in the scene graph that detect use interaction with geometry that is underneath that sensor in the scene graph.

Vehicles

VRML itself is not explicit about exactly how navigation about the world is to be effected. It does, however, describe two common interaction metaphors that a browser may supply. These are the walk and examine vehicles. The walk vehicle is analogous to a simple flying vehicle (see "Locomotion" on page 454). The user is assumed to be navigating about the virtual world mainly in a horizontal plane, and the mouse controls are mapped onto yaw and forward and backward motion. In the examine vehicle, navigation is effected around a focus point, with both mouse controls mapped to rotation about that focus. This is similar to the scene-in-hand metaphor (see "Locomotion" on page 454).

The vehicle also says some very basic things about the avatar representation of the user in the scene. This avatar is not rendered, but is used for collision detection between the user and the scene. Elements in the scene can be made solid so that the user cannot walk through them. Gravity can also be enabled, in the world so that the user follows and sticks to surfaces when he or she locomotes about the environment. The avatar is specified within the `NavigationInfo` node. This contains a field `avatarSize` of type `MFFloat` whose default value is [0.25, 1.6, 0.75]. The first two values give the radius and height of a simple cylindrical avatar. This cylinder is prevented from penetrating any solid objects. The third value specifies a step height. If the cylinder hits any scene geometry below this height from the bottom, it is moved up onto that geometry. This allows the avatar to follow surfaces over small steps.

Sensors

VRML allows objects to be programmed to respond to the user's pointing at, selecting, or manipulating part of the scene graph. This is done by attaching a *Sensor* node to a node in the scene graph. When a sensor is attached to a branch of the scene graph, it can receive certain input events from the user when the pointing device is interacting with any geometry under that branch. The actual details of how sensors are activated are dependent on the actual device used, but we describe how they are usually activated when a mouse is employed for interaction.

A `TouchSensor` responds to the user's placing the mouse cursor over the geometry. Once the mouse cursor is over the geometry, it can then generate a second response when the user clicks a mouse button. A `PlaneSensor` similarly responds to the user placing the mouse cursor over the geometry, but if the user presses and holds down the mouse button, his or her drag motions are mapped onto a plane, and the planar movement is available as a `SFVec3f` `eventOut` of the sensor. This vector can be used to drive a `Transform` node, and thus the geometry itself can be dragged around.

Other interaction sensors include: `SphereSensor`, `CylinderSensor`, `Anchor`, and `Collision`. `SphereSensor` and `CylinderSensor` are similar to `PlaneSensor`, but the mouse motion is mapped onto 2D and 1D rotation respectively. An `Anchor` node is the 3D equivalent of a HTML hyperlink; i.e., it can cause a new world or other type media file to be loaded in a frame of the browser. `Collision` can be used to detect when the user's avatar hits a piece of scene geometry.

The VRML specification is deliberately unclear about how sensors are activated since this depends on the input device, and it is up to the browser to provide some appropriate mechanism. The usual case on a 2D desktop will be that a sensor is enabled by the mouse cursor moving over the object and the user clicking an object, a form of ray-based selection. When VRML is employed in immersive systems this can be replaced by the metaphor of sensors activating when the user touches them (Stiles *et al.*, 1997). See "VRML as interactive experience" on page 535 for an example of a SphereSensor.

21.9 Summary

In this chapter we have reviewed interaction with desktop virtual reality systems. We have seen that a wide range of devices are used with these systems, and thus there is a very broad range of applicable interaction techniques. Indeed, unlike 2D interface systems, there is very little standardization and 3D applications differ, sometimes quite subtly, in their approach to interaction.

We looked at three basic tasks that one might undertake:

- selection – indicating one object on the screen as the focus for subsequent actions;
- manipulation – moving or otherwise altering an object;
- locomotion – moving a specific object, the camera viewpoint, through the environment.

Given that each of these tasks might involve up to six degrees of freedom, we also looked at a selection of techniques that can reduce or eliminate modality in the interface. In particular, we looked at widget interfaces.

22 Ray-based methods for global illumination

22.1   Introduction

This chapter briefly reviews a number of approaches to global illumination all with the common feature of being ray based. However, the techniques vary radically, with the most powerful employing stochastic (Monte Carlo) solutions to the radiance equation. Some of the techniques presented have been considered in earlier chapters, but are reviewed here in a more general context. The radiance equation of Chapter 3 is also reconsidered and expanded.

22.2   Ray tracing methods

Ray tracing

Ray tracing was introduced by Whitted (1980). Ray tracing requires a pin-hole camera model and point light sources, and a non-participating medium (in fact a vacuum representing an approximation to air). Its fundamental operation is to trace a ray with origin at the center of projection (COP) through a point on an image plane. The point is a pixel (or "subpixel" in the case when some anti-aliasing method is required) – the purpose being to find the "intensity" for the pixel, by tracing the ray back through the scene, bouncing from object to object, until it goes out of the scene or makes a negligible contribution to the intensity.

In order to achieve this the nearest object intersected by the ray is found (at point p). A bidirectional reflectance (BRDF) function, in the most general case, will determine the subsequent path of the ray. In fact ray tracing classically only follows three specific paths at each object intersection. The first is a "shadow feeler" ray – the rays from the object intersection point p to the set of point light sources are followed, and each such ray that does not intersect another (opaque) object before reaching the light source adds a local illumination contribution to the point. This intensity is computed as the sum of an "ambient" term, representing all background light in the scene, and terms for each light source based on Lambert's Law for ideal diffuse reflectors plus a highlighting term based on the Phong model. Notice that there is no global illumination for diffuse reflection, but only the local contribution of each light source to p (and therefore to the current pixel). If the object is an ideal specular reflector, then a new ray is computed in the direction of specular reflection, based on the law of angle of incidence equal to angle of reflection, and the reflected and incident rays being in the same plane. The ray tracing function is recursively invoked with this reflected ray, and the result added to the intensity at p. Similarly, if the object is transparent, then using Snell's Law new ray directions through the object and out again can be computed, and again, the ray tracing function recursively invoked to produce an intensity to be added to that for p. This ray tracing function is called for each primary ray with origin at the COP and through each relevant point (pixel or subpixel) on the image plane. The result is an image where specular reflection and transmission have been simulated.

Ray tracing was a major advance in the synthesis of photo-realistic images in computer graphics. It is very computationally intensive – most of the computational effort is involved in ray–object intersection calculations. A naive implementation would need to test each ray against each object, for example. Much of the (vast) research on ray tracing has concentrated on speeding up this process by substantially reducing the number of ray–object intersection tests. As we saw in Chapter 16, such methods have included bounding volumes and hierarchies (see also Clark, 1976; Rohlf and Helman, 1994) where rays are tested first against simpler objects that encapsulate the actual scene objects. Only if the test against the simple bounding object (an axis aligned box, or a sphere) succeeds is there any need to test the ray against the actual scene object. As we saw, such bounding volumes can be organized hierarchically, making use of spatial coherence of objects in the scene – so that groups of objects close together can be grouped into a bounding volume, and then groups of bounding volumes put together in a larger volume, and so on. The bounding volumes may be organized as a tree with its root enclosing the entire scene, and the objects at the leaves. The ray is filtered down the tree until either it intersects no bounding volume, or else finally intersects an object at the leaves.

Spatial partitioning methods exhaustively partition the space occupied by the scene into smaller regions each of which maintains a list of identifiers of objects that intersect it. Uniform partitioning (Fujimoto *et al.*, 1986; Cleary and Wyvill, 1988) divides the scene space into a regular three-dimensional grid of small cuboids or cells. The path of a ray through this space-subdivision can be quickly computed, and only objects in the cells along the ray path are candidates for intersection. Adaptive partitioning, such as octrees (Glassner, 1984), subdivide the space in a way that depends on the distribution of objects – so that more densely occupied regions are subdivided to a greater extent.

Notwithstanding the great deal of research, ray tracing remains a computationally expensive process. Clearly, with each change in viewpoint the entire ray-tracing algorithm must be carried out again. There have been some efforts to exploit coherence from image to image as the camera moves (for example Chapman *et al.*, 1991; Teller *et al.*, 1996), but these have not yet achieved results sufficient for real-time walkthrough.

Ray space methods for ray tracing

Ray classification schemes provide another type of approach to speeding up ray tracing. The primary space of interest in this case is the space of rays rather than the usual space of objects. The most notable and elegant example of this was introduced by Arvo and Kirk (1987), discussed in Chapter 16. A ray has an origin (x, y, z) and a direction given by angles (θ, ϕ) and hence may be considered as a point in 5D space. Arvo and Kirk in fact represented all possible rays in the scene as six sets of 5D points. An axis aligned bounding box is placed around the scene, and each face of the box has a 2D UV coordinate system. Hence a ray can be represented by its origin (x, y, z), the side of the bounding box that it intersects (Left, Right, Top, Bottom, Near, Far), and the UV coordinate of intersection. Hence all possible rays can be represented by the six sets of all points (x, y, z, U, V).

The algorithm exploits ray-coherence – that is, rays that are "close" to one another are likely to intersect similar sets of objects. In brief, as each ray is considered a 32-tree subdivision (a 5D version of an octree) is lazily formed for each of the six faces, where at any moment any leaf of the tree represents a bundle of (similar) rays and has a corresponding "candidate" set of objects – i.e., any object in the candidate set is likely to be intersected by at least one of the rays in the corresponding ray subset.

The important point to note is the idea that it is the space of "all possible rays" that is of primary importance rather than the space of objects. The algorithm forms a partition of ray space rather than of object space.

Muller and Winckler (1992) introduced another ray-space method – though for quite different reasons. "Breadth-first ray tracing" is designed not especially for speed, but to save on the substantial memory requirements that occur when there is a huge object database. The idea is that rays are kept in main memory and object information may be stored on disk. Each ray is stored as an origin, parameters representing the line equation of the ray, the current intersection point along the ray, and the object corresponding to that intersection point. In a naive implementation of this algorithm, each object is read from disk into memory and intersected against all primary rays. Using a kind of "z-buffer" all primary rays that intersect anything would point to the nearest object intersected, with, of course, the corresponding intersection point. A similar process is repeated for all "shadow feeler" rays. It is then continued for all reflected rays, then transmitted rays, and so on, to any required level of depth. The ray tracing is therefore breadth first – dealing with all rays in each iteration rather than recursively moving through object space. Nakamaru and Ohno (1997) improved this approach later by using uniform space subdivision for the rays. In fact this space subdivision was carried out in object space – which was partitioned into a regular grid of cuboid cells, and then each cell maintains a list of pointers to rays that pass through it. In this way, as objects are read from the database, only those rays that pass through the cells occupied by the object need be tested. Although the breadth-first ray tracing avoids recursion and therefore can deal with extremely large databases, it is generally slower than the normal depth-first ray tracing, and, of course, has all the usual properties of ray tracing – dealing only with specular reflection at the global level, and being viewpoint dependent.

Discrete ray tracing

Discrete ray tracing (DRT) belongs to the volume visualization approach to computer graphics (Kaufman, 1996). It is a quite different approach to ray tracing, introduced by Yagel *et al.* (1992). In conventional computer graphics the fundamental entity is the "pixel," representing a location on a display device, which may be independently set to a color intensity. In volume rendering the display space is three-dimensional, and the smallest corresponding entity is the *voxel*, which may contain both color information and information regarding the (solid) object of which it is a part. In practice, voxels are small, cuboid, non-overlapping regions, small enough so that at most one object can intersect a voxel.

In DRT objects are first "rendered" into the voxel space. Each intersected voxel records information regarding the exact normal to the original object, information about the material properties of the object, and also rays are traced, through the voxel space, to each of the light sources. For each light source the voxel records a two-bit code to indicate that it is visible, invisible, or visible through another translucent object.

Tracing rays through the voxel space involves finding the "best" set of voxels along the path of a ray, much like the Bresenham or DDA algorithms for finding the best line representations in 2D pixel space (see "Rasterization of line segments" on page 366).

The rendering phase begins the same way as in conventional ray tracing. A ray is traced through the 2D image plane with origin at the COP. The ray is followed along the voxel path, until it reaches a non-empty voxel. Of course the first one that it finds is the relevant intersection point. The "shadow feeler" rays are already known (they were pre-computed immediately following the object rendering phase). DRT then follows the standard recursive ray tracing method – of spawning reflected and transmitted rays.

The advantages of DRT over conventional ray tracing are:

- The intersection computations are no longer dominant – since rays are followed until they hit the first non-empty voxel. There is no searching for the nearest intersection point, but the time spent by rays traversing the voxel space is instead significant.

- The ray tracing time is essentially independent of the number of objects. As pointed out by the authors, the greater the number of objects in fact the less time spent ray tracing, since the rays will hit non-empty voxels sooner in more densely occupied regions of space. Of course, the ray tra- cing time does depend on the 3D resolution of the voxel space, since this determines the path-length for ray traversals.

- Many view-independent attributes are pre-computed – such as the shadow feelers, normals, and textures. Hence a change of view requires signific-antly less new computation compared to conventional ray tracing.

DRT is clearly a highly view-dependent approach – the majority of the computa-tion (the construction of the ray tracing tree for each image plane pixel) needs to be carried out for each change in view.

22.3 Distributed ray tracing

Monte Carlo methods

Monte Carlo is a general class of estimation method based on statistical samp-ling. The most famous example is the estimation of π. Inscribe a unit circle in a square of side length 2. Now randomly select a large number of random points in the square (for example, by throwing pins at the square!). The area of the square is 4, and the area of the circle is π. Hence the proportion of pins that land inside the circle will be an estimator for $\pi/4$. The statistical Law of Large Numbers guarantees that with probability one any error bound can be attained with a sufficiently large sample size. Now the same kind of technique can be employed in the solution of the radiance equation. Rather than firing a single ray through pixels, and reflecting a single ray from each surface in a geometrically computed direction (reflected or refracted), we send a number of rays in a random sampling scheme, and then combine the results of the rays

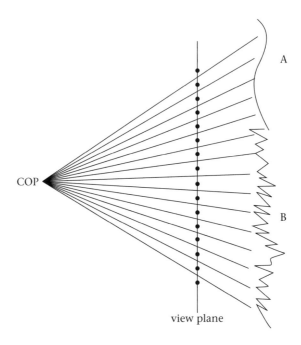

Figure 22.1
Aliasing caused by
pixel sampling

together. There are many different ways to do this. We consider distributed ray tracing first and path tracing next.

Distributed ray tracing (Cook *et al.*, 1984) significantly extends what can be achieved with classical ray tracing by tracing multiple primary rays through each pixel and multiple rays at each subsequent step. In particular, distributed ray tracing can model glossy rather than just specular reflection, translucence rather than only sharp transparency, shadow penumbras rather than just umbras, depth-of-field effects by tracing through a lens rather than only using a pin-hole camera, and motion blur by sampling rays through time. It also is a way of overcoming aliasing in ray traced images, not just by supersampling but by distributing rays over the pixel area in a specific type of random pattern. This reduces aliasing and replaces it by perceptually tolerable noise in the final image.

Aliasing

Figure 22.1 illustrates a set of primary rays from the COP through the pixels on a view plane. There are two components to the scene labeled A and B. The "signal" that comprises the scene is continuous. Clearly we are sampling the scene based on a discrete set of rays through the pixel locations. From the pixel samples it is easy to see that it is theoretically possible to exactly reproduce the scene component labeled as A. However, it is impossible to reproduce B. The difference is made clear by a comparison of the sampling rate compared to the frequencies of the two signals. With signal A the frequency in the signal (the number of changes within the bounds between two pixel locations in our 2D analogy) is less than one cycle. For signal B the number of cycles in the space between two successive pixel sample locations is two or more. The Nyquist limit allows a maximum of one cycle between two pixels in order for a signal to be reproducible, and if that limit is exceeded then the signal cannot be reconstructed from the sampling scheme. When an undersampled signal such as B is rendered, it will produce aliases, effects in the image reconstruction that are not in the original signal.

One way to reduce the impact of such aliasing is to increase the sampling rate. In a ray tracing context this is normally called *supersampling*. What this means is that each pixel is uniformly divided into subpixels, and normal ray tracing is carried out at this subpixel level. When results for all subpixels within a pixel are computed the results may be averaged over the pixel in order to produce the final pixel intensity. Such supersampling can reduce aliasing, but there will of course still be signals that break the sampling limit and cause aliasing.

In distributed ray tracing a stochastic sampling scheme is employed. One possibility is to distribute sample points uniformly randomly over the pixel area. However, a scheme that produces smaller variance in sample estimates is *stratified* sampling. Suppose, for example, that an estimate of the mean annual income over adults living in a certain city were required. Then one technique would be to obtain a list of all people living in the city (for example, such a list would be approximated by the electoral register) and then choose a random sample of *n* people from this list, and interview them to find out their annual income. However, suppose that certain features of the whole population were known in advance: such as the proportion of males to females, the age distribution, the distribution of people employed in different sectors of the economy, and so on. Now the closer that the random sample reflects these population characteristics, the lower the variance (i.e., the greater the chance for accuracy) of the sample estimator. A stratified sample is one that samples randomly within known strata, so that the proportions of the strata in the sample match the proportions in the population. In the simplest example, if it were decided to stratify only by gender, and the proportion of males in the population were 54%, then for a sample size of 1000, 540 would be randomly selected from the male population and 460 from the female population.

Now a random collection of points within a pixel location (imagine this as a square) does not imply that the points would be evenly spread out over the pixel. Randomness does not in any way imply an even spread (as anyone who plays a lottery knows). A random selection is just that – "random." In a lottery selection of 6 numbers from 1 through 40, the result 1, 2, 3, 4, 5 and 6 has exactly the same probability as any other selection. A stratified sampling scheme often used to sample pixels is called *jittered* sampling, and is illustrated in Figure 22.2. Here the pixel is divided (for example) into 16 subpixels. A

Figure 22.2
Jittered sampling over
a pixel

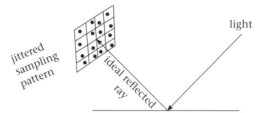

Figure 22.3
Jittered sampling pattern
for glossy reflection

random location is chosen within each subpixel. Hence we are guaranteed appropriate area coverage (this is the stratification) and within that we have randomness. Hence each pixel is sampled in this jittered way, and rays are fired through the selected locations within each subpixel. The final result for the pixel is then (in the simplest case) just the mean of the results for all the subpixels within the pixel.

Such a jittered sampling scheme can dramatically reduce the level of aliasing, since there is now some probability that any part of a cycle within a signal might be sampled with such a scheme.

The reflection and lighting model

When a ray strikes a surface in ray tracing two new rays may be spawned, one in the reflection direction and, if the surface is transparent, another in the refracted direction. Therefore, all reflections and transparencies are sharp. Distributed ray tracing allows for glossy rather than sharp reflections, and translucent rather than sharp transparency. Consider first the reflection. For an ideal specular surface there is one reflection direction (see "The direction of reflection (*R*)" on page 148). A glossy surface will reflect rays in a distribution around this perfectly specular ray (as shown in Figure 6.6 on page 140). In order to simulate this a jittered sampling pattern can be set up around the ideal specular reflection direction (Figure 22.3).

Now when a ray strikes a surface a sample of rays is generated over the jittered random sample directions rather than along the ideal specular path. The probabilities assigned to the different directions should be derived from the BRDF for the surface concerned. The final result at this intersection point may be taken as the average of the results of the individual rays.

Exactly the same procedure can be used for transparent surfaces. Many real surfaces are not purely transparent but the view seen through the surface is hazy rather than sharp. If just the computed ideal refracted ray is followed (see "Direct specular transmission" on page 149) then only sharp transparencies can be achieved. However, a jittered sampling pattern can be constructed around the ideal refraction direction in the same way as for the ideal specular direction in order to achieve a translucent effect.

Classical ray tracing uses point light sources. When a ray strikes a surface, one "shadow feeler" ray is traced to each light source point (or direction), and it is either blocked by another object (in shadow) or else not blocked (it is visible to the light source). Such a binary choice leads to the result that classical ray tracing can only simulate shadow umbras. However, real lights have areas, and as we have seen (Chapter 14), these cause shadow penumbras – where a point on the surface may be visible to part of the light. Distributed ray tracing accounts for this in much the same way as reflected and refracted rays. A jittered sampling scheme is established for the area light source. Hence a shadow feeler ray from each surface intersection is not sent along a predetermined path to a light source point, but rather the area light source is sampled such that the probability of any particular ray is based on the radiance distribution over the light source.

Depth of field

Computer graphics, including classical ray tracing, overwhelmingly employs the pin-hole camera model (Figure 5.4 on page 123). Distributed ray tracing can simulate views through a lens system, and therefore such effects as depth of field, normally seen on real film. For a pin-hole camera model the entire image is in focus. Where an image is formed through a lens system typically one part of the image will be in focus, and other parts not in focus. First we briefly discuss geometric optics for thin convex lenses (Jenkins and White, 1981), and then show how this can be used in the distributed ray tracing context.

Figure 22.4 shows a schematic of a thin convex lens. The *axis* of the lens is through its center, and orthogonal to the *plane* of the lens. For calculation purposes the lens may be identified with its plane. There are two significant points called the primary and secondary *focal points*, located equidistant from the center of the lens along its axis. (Which is primary and which is secondary depends on the direction from which light is thought to be coming – the primary focal point is on the same side of the lens as the scene, and the secondary on the other side of the lens where the image is formed). The primary focal point is such that all rays from this point to the lens are refracted in a direction parallel to the lens axis. All parallel rays perpendicular to the plane of the lens, parallel to the axis, are refracted through the secondary focal point. (To emphasize, there is complete symmetry here; the direction of light may be reversed and the same results hold – the primary becomes the secondary

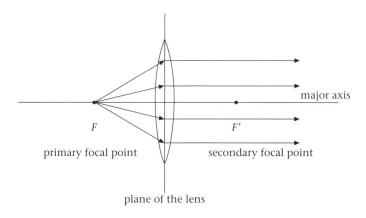

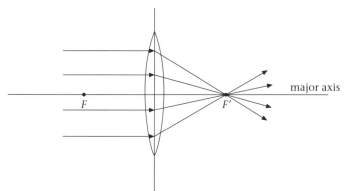

Figure 22.4
Thin convex lens

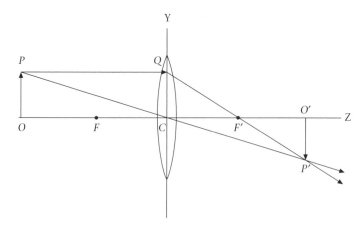

Figure 22.5
Computing an image
point

and vice versa). The *focal planes* are parallel to the plane of the lens containing the focal points.

Figure 22.5 shows how an image point is formed from an object point (in the scene). Note that any ray through the center of the lens (*C*) is not bent but passes through C in a straight line. So given an object point P in the scene, we can form a ray parallel to the axis, and this will be refracted through the secondary focal point. Also we can form a ray from P through the center C. The image point is where these two rays intersect. If an image plane (parallel to the plane of the lens) is located at that distance, then the point P has its image in focus on the image plane (at P'). Every ray from P through the lens will intersect with P', in other words the lens focuses P at P'. (Strictly speaking, this is only for rays that are almost parallel to the main axis – *paraxial* rays.)

Suppose that we are in viewing coordinates forming a left-hand coordinate system, and that C is at the origin of this system. Suppose P is at $(x, y, -a)$ $(a > 0)$, and the focal distance is f, hence the secondary focal point F' is at $(0, 0, f)$. The ray PQ will intersect the plane of the lens at $(x, y, 0)$. The ray QF' will have parametric equation

$$(x - tx,\ y - ty,\ tf) \qquad \text{(EQ 22.1)}$$

Suppose that there is an image plane at $z = d$, then the intersection of QF with this image plane is at

$$t = \frac{d}{f} \qquad \text{(EQ 22.2)}$$

i.e., at the point:

$$\left(x\left(1 - \frac{d}{f}\right),\ y\left(1 - \frac{d}{f}\right),\ d \right) \qquad \text{(EQ 22.3)}$$

Similarly, the ray PC will have equation

$$(x - tx,\ y - ty,\ -a + ta) \qquad \text{(EQ 22.4)}$$

and will intersect the image plane at:

$$\left(x\left(-\frac{d}{a}\right),\ y\left(-\frac{d}{a}\right),\ d \right) \qquad \text{(EQ 22.5)}$$

Now for the image point for P to be in focus, (EQ 22.3) and (EQ 22.4) must be the same point. Equating these, we must have:

$$1 - \frac{d}{f} = \left(-\frac{d}{a}\right)$$

$$d = \frac{fa}{a - f} \qquad \text{(EQ 22.6)}$$

$$a > f$$

Substituting this into (EQ 22.5) gives the image point.

Suppose that the position of the image plane does not satisfy (EQ 22.6), then each ray from P through the lens will be projected to a different point on the image plane. P will not be in focus; instead there will be a circular blurred representation of this point. In practice, P would be in focus for a narrow band of possible image planes close to the ideal distance d, or putting this another

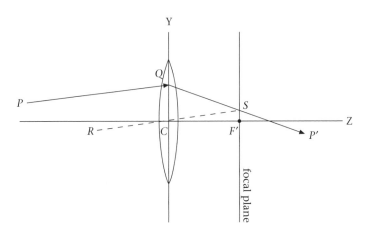

Figure 22.6
Refracting rays not
parallel to the lens axis

way, a small sphere of points around P will be almost in focus on an image plane at d. Depth of field effects occur precisely because the image plane focuses points only within a narrow band within the scene, and all other points become blurred.

Figure 22.6 shows how to refract a ray that is not parallel to the lens axis. Consider the ray PQ. RC is parallel to PQ but through the lens center. RC intersects the focal plane at S, and the refracted ray is then constructed as QS. Note that RC is not an actual ray, but just a geometric construction to show how the actual rays (shown in solid with arrows) are formed. Given any image plane at $z = d$, it is easy to compute the intersection point of such a ray with the image plane. It is easy to show in this way that all rays from P through the lens will converge at exactly the same image point.

In distributed ray tracing we have a jittered sampling scheme per pixel over the image plane. We also introduce a tessellation of the lens to produce a jittered sampling scheme over the lens. Now given a selected sample point on the image plane within a pixel, and a sample point on the lens, we need to determine the primary ray that goes out into the scene. In Figure 22.7, suppose that the sampled ray from image plane to lens is $P'Q$. Find the intersection point S with the focal plane. Find the ray SR from S through the center of the lens. This gives us the direction of the required primary ray, so that the primary ray is the ray starting at Q parallel to SR. Again, this is easy to find from the parametric ray equations as shown above. Notice that in the figure we have reversed the directions of the arrows. Now the rays are pointing in the opposite direction to the light paths, since these are rays that are being traced out into the scene. So for each jittered sample point (e.g., P') a jittered sample point on the lens is found (e.g., Q), and the primary ray QP constructed as above. These primary rays are traced as normal for distributed ray tracing, as described above. The final pixel value is taken as usual as the average from all the jittered sample points within the pixel.

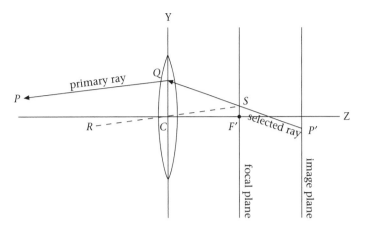

Figure 22.7
Determining a primary
ray from a selected ray

6	10	9	13
16	1	8	12
3	5	7	2
14	11	15	4

Figure 22.8
Sampling through time

Motion blur

So far we have shown how distributed ray tracing can be used to construct an image at a snapshot in time. It is a solution of the radiance equation (for primary rays through a lens system) allowing for depth of field, glossy and translucent surfaces, and tackling the problem of aliasing, but for a scene which is frozen in time. It is also possible, however, to extend the solution through time, so that if the camera or objects are moving then a motion blur effect will also be rendered. This can be extremely useful, for example, in situations where the ray tracing is used to produce a sequence of successive images in an animation sequence.

Without loss of generality let's assume that the time interval is [0, 1] and any moment in time is represented by $t \in [0, 1]$. Now we will associate each ray through the jittered sampling scheme with an instant of time. In Figure 22.8 an example is shown where the pixel is subdivided into 16 subpixels. The time interval is likewise divided into 16 intervals, labeled 1 through 16, and these are randomly assigned over the subpixels. Now suppose t_{ij} is the time period for the subpixel in the ith row and jth column. Then the time instant for that subpixel is:

$$T = \frac{t_{ij} - 0.5}{16}$$

(EQ 22.7)

For example, $t_{12} = 10$, so $T = 19/32$. Now a random jitter is added to this (of $\pm(1/32)$, so that T becomes a randomly selected instant of time in the range $(18/32) \leq T < 20/32$. Once this T value is known, the objects and camera are moved to their correct positions for this time period, and then the appropriate primary ray traced out into the scene, as described above.

Summary of distributed ray tracing

We have spent some time on the distributed ray tracing approach, since it was an important breakthrough in realistic image synthesis after ray tracing itself. It also allowed us to discuss some important additional issues, such as aliasing and lens effects. The overall algorithm can be summarized as follows (see also Glassner, 1989, Chapter 5):

```
for each pixel {
   for each jittered sample point within each pixel {
      find the corresponding jittered time instant
      Move the objects and camera to their position at this time
      interval
      select the jittered sample point on the lens and find the
      primary ray
      trace the primary ray into the scene to intersect the first
      surface in the scene
      determine the reflection ray direction and a jittered sample ray
      around this, according to the BRDF of the surface
      determine the transmitted ray direction and a jittered sample
      ray around this, according to the BRDF of the surface
      determine a jittered ray direction for each light source
         and trace the shadow feeler rays
      call the ray tracing algorithm recursively
         from the reflected and transmitted directions
   }
   average the returned radiance values for each subpixel to determine
   the colour for the pixel
}
```

Distributed ray tracing, as we have seen, greatly improves the ray tracing solution. However, it is still not in itself a full solution for the radiance equation; for example, it does not properly deal with diffuse reflection. In the next section we will examine another Monte Carlo solution, path tracing, which does provide a solution for the set of primary ray directions by sending multiple rays through the center of each pixel but where each ray's reflected and transmitted descendents follow random paths based on the BRDFs of the intersected surfaces. (Of course, distributed ray tracing and path tracing could be combined by adopting a path tracing solution at each subpixel.)

Path tracing

Kajiya (1986) unified a number of computer graphics lighting models into one overall model based on a *rendering equation* for the intensity of light $I(x, y)$ passing from point y to x, where y and x are constrained to be on surfaces in the scene (or, x may be on the view plane, receiving light from surfaces in the scene). The resulting integral equation is shown in (EQ 22.8) where the integral is taken over the union of all points on surfaces S, where S includes one bounding surface that encapsulates the whole scene (for example, a surrounding sphere):

$$I(x, y) = g(x, y)\left[\varepsilon(x, y) + \int_S \rho(x, y, z)I(y, z)dz\right] \qquad \text{(EQ 22.8)}$$

$g(x, y)$ is a geometry term which is either 0 if x and y are not visible to one another and $1/r^2$ otherwise, where r is the distance between them. $\varepsilon(x, y)$ is the intensity of emitted light from y to x, and $\rho(x, y, z)$ is a dimensionless quantity representing the unoccluded reflectance from z to x via y. Hence the equation states that if x is visible to y, then the intensity of light energy from y to x is given as that directly emitted from y to x (if y is a light emitter) plus the integral, over all surfaces, of light that arrives at y from any other point z that ultimately reaches x. In other words, $I(x, y)$ consists of the light emitted from y to x plus the total light reflected from y to x.

If x is considered as a point on the surface of the view plane, and y considered as the point of intersection with a surface visible from the COP on a line of sight through y, then a solution to (EQ 22.8) for each such x would provide an image accounting for all the relevant interreflection of light through the environment.

The radiance equation of Chapter 3 can be derived from (EQ 22.8) and we will use the radiance equation, reproduced for convenience in (EQ 22.9) for our subsequent discussion.

$$L(p, \omega) = L_e(p, \omega) + \int_\Omega f(p, \omega_i, \omega)L(p, \omega_i)\cos\theta_i d\omega_i \qquad \text{(EQ 22.9)}$$

The radiance equation (EQ 22.9) may be viewed as a decomposition of the radiance in a certain direction at a certain position into the emitted portion and the reflected portion. We can consider this more formally by using the idea of an "integral operator." An integral operator applied to a function results in a new function, with properties that are determined by the form of the operator. In this case the function will be $L(p, \omega)$, and the integral operator, denoted by R, will return the component of L due to reflection only (i.e., excluding emission). Obviously, R can be defined as:

$$RL(p, \omega) = \int_\Omega f(p, \omega_i, \omega) L(p, \omega_i)\cos\theta_i d\omega_i \qquad \text{(EQ 22.10)}$$

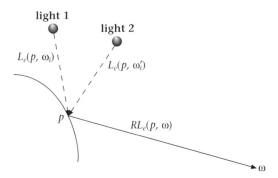

Figure 22.9
Illustrating RL_e

Note that the result of applying R to L results in another function over the same domain, which we will denote as $L^1(p, \omega)$.

Using this notation, we can rewrite (EQ 22.9) entirely in operator form:

$$L = L_e + RL \qquad (EQ\ 22.11)$$

where it is understood that the domain is given by the parameters (p, ω). Operator theory allows us to rewrite (EQ 22.11), treating R in much the same way as if it were an algebraic term:

$$L - RL = L_e$$
$$\therefore (1 - R)L = L_e \qquad (EQ\ 22.12)$$

Here "1" is the identity operator, which when applied to L results in L itself. We can further rearrange (EQ 22.12) as:

$$L = (1 - R)^{-1}L_e \qquad (EQ\ 22.13)$$

Finally the operator expression can be expanded out in a power series:

$$L = (1 + R + R^2 + R^3 + \ldots)L_e \qquad (EQ\ 22.14)$$
$$\therefore L = L_e + RL_e + R^2L_e + R^3L_e + \ldots$$

Of course, R^iL_e means that R is applied to L_e resulting in function L_e^1, and then R is applied again to this resulting in L_e^2, and so on for a total of i applications.

Now let's consider the meaning of the successive terms. Consider first:

$$RL_e = \int_\Omega f(p, \omega_i, \omega)L_e(p, \omega_i)\cos\theta_i d\omega_i \qquad (EQ\ 22.15)$$

$L_e(p, \omega_i)$ is the radiance corresponding to direct lighting (from light sources) in direction ω_i at point p. Therefore RL_e is the total radiance reflected, from point p in direction ω, that is due only to radiance that had its origin in the light sources. This is illustrated in Figure 22.9 which shows the contribution of two light sources, and how their effect only is combined to produce RL_e.

Let's write $RL_e = L_e^1$. Then

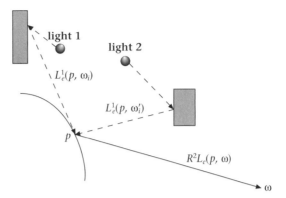

Figure 22.10
Illustrating $R^2 L_e$

$$R^2 L_e = R L_e^1 = \int_{\Omega} f(p, \omega_i, \omega) L_e^1(p, \omega_i) \cos\theta_i d\omega_i \qquad \text{(EQ 22.16)}$$

Now L_e^1 is reflected light that is just one step removed (reflected once) from the original light sources. Hence $R^2 L_e = L_e^2$ is the radiance corresponding to light that is "twice removed" from the original light sources – i.e., it has gone through two reflections. This is illustrated in Figure 22.10 which shows light reflected from two different objects, which had its origin directly from the light sources themselves.

In general, $R^i L_e(p, \omega)$ is the contribution to radiance from point p in direction ω from all light paths of length $i + 1$ back to the original light sources. In particular, $R^0 L_e(p, \omega) = L_e(p, \omega)$ is non-zero only in the case where the surface is itself a light emitter (since it represents a 1 path route back to a light source).

After all this, we have reached the mathematical formulation for a rather obvious result. The radiance $L(p, \omega)$ may be decomposed into that due to the emissive properties of the object itself, plus that reflected once removed from light sources, plus that twice removed, and so on to infinity.

Now consider successive approximations to the radiance equation by truncating the series at successive terms. If we adopted as our solution just the first term, then we would only be rendering objects that directly emitted light. In fact the "flat shading" method introduced Chapter 5 is somewhat like this – every object is considered as a light source, and every object has zero reflectance. Now the approximation that truncates the series after the second term is like the standard graphics pipeline: only direct reflection caused by the light sources themselves is taken into account, and there is no inter-object reflection. In fact the standard pipeline is generally simpler than this – since the light sources are only points, and there are typically no shadows. Moreover, the point lights themselves are typically not rendered, only their effect on other objects. Similarly ray tracing is another special case. By considering the situation where all surfaces are perfectly diffuse reflectors, Kajiya also reduces the radiance equation to the radiosity equation introduced by Goral *et al.* (1984).

Kajiya showed how to solve the equation by (Markov Chain) Monte Carlo integration, calling the method "path tracing" since it involves following the path of a photon on a random walk from surface to surface – as in ray tracing, a "backward" path from the viewpoint into the scene. Consider a ray starting at the viewpoint and through a point (p) on the view plane, intersecting the first visible surface at point q. Compute random rays to each of the light sources (the distributions determined by the radiant properties of the sources), and note that the sources need not be points. For each such visible ray compute the local contribution of intensity at point q, and add this to the intensity for p. Depending on the material properties of the surface (in terms of the coefficients of diffuse and specular reflection, and the degree of transparency of the object) choose another ray at random, determine its intersection with the environment (w), and repeat the process, each time adding to the intensity of the pixel. Surfaces may have both diffuse and specular material properties – these determine the distribution of random rays to be fired at each surface intersection. Hence at each ray intersection, rays are always fired to the light sources (to get the local contribution), and then one further ray is fired with probability distribution determined by the material properties of the surface. Unlike standard ray tracing, where at each intersection point all rays (specularly reflecting and transmitting) are followed, here only one such ray is followed. For each pixel (or subpixel) a number (N) of such paths are followed, and the final intensity is the average of all of these. Kajiya used N = 40 for all examples. If any particular path is of length $n + 1$ then this is like truncating the series expansion after term n.

The advantages of such Monte Carlo path tracing are clear: all types of surface can be considered, and greater weight is attached to the most important rays (the primary rays, rays to the light sources) without following paths that contribute little to the final intensities. In standard ray tracing, the trees may recurse to enormous depth, but with little contribution of the rays at and near the leaves of the tree.

Much of the research following from this approach has been on variance reduction techniques. Each pixel intensity is provided by an estimator based on the ray path samples. *Importance sampling* is a powerful variance reduction technique. This is where visibility and the material properties of the surface are taken into account in path generation. There have been considerable advances in this approach (for example, Arvo and Kirk, 1990).

Very efficient methods of handling diffuse reflection have been introduced into path tracing by keeping an illumination cache over diffusely reflecting surfaces. Specular interreflections account for most of the high frequency component of the radiance equation and are directly sampled during the path tracing. Diffuse reflection accounts for the slower-changing, but absolutely fundamental component for the realism of the solution. However, it is prohibitively computationally expensive to sample the large number of rays over the illumination hemisphere at a surface point in order to adequately represent diffuse interreflection (and of course each of those rays needs to be followed from its intersection point, and so on). Instead, since the diffuse component varies relatively slowly over a surface, the illumination hemisphere is adaptively sampled at a few points, the results cached (for example, in an octree) and then used for interpolation. This scheme was introduced in Warnock (1969) and Ward and Heckbert (1992) and is embodied in the Radiance software (Ward-Larson and Shakespeare, 1997). An example Radiance image is shown in Plate P.1.

22.5   Integrating radiosity and ray tracing

Ray tracing, as we have seen, is ideally adapted for the simulation of specular surfaces, and radiosity only for diffuse. Real scenes integrate light between each of these types of reflecting surfaces, and so realistic solutions must simulate this. Specular effects may be added in to radiosity in a post-process (Immel *et al.*, 1986) but of course, as pointed out by Jensen and Christensen (1995), and by Arvo and Kirk (1990), this cannot be used to properly model diffuse–specular interreflections, since each of these phases is carried out independently.

Heckbert (1990) introduced a notation for a photon path that helps explain this. Let L represent a light and E the eye. So photons that enter the eye start from L and finish at E. An encounter with a specular surface generates an S and with a diffuse surface a D. Then a regular expression of the form $L(S|D)^*E$ represents all possible eye-visible paths, where | stands for "or" and * is a multiple instance operator. For example $LS \ldots SE = LS^*E$. Ray tracing can simulate paths of the form: LDS^*E or LS^*E (see Figure 6.1). In ray tracing we start "backward" from the eye, tracing the ray from specular to specular surface. However, the algorithm cannot proceed after a diffuse surface has been encountered because of the sheer computational complexity involved in tracing rays from such a surface. Radiosity can simulate paths of the form: LD^*E. Now if we add a ray tracing pass to a radiosity algorithm, we can achieve paths of the form: LD^*S^*E.

Heckbert showed how to achieve a full solution for $L(S|D)^*E$ paths using a two-pass *bidirectional ray tracing* method. The first pass is *light tracing*. Photons are distributed from the light sources (in other words, rays through the light sources are distributed into the environment) and followed with their energy adjusted as in ray tracing. Photons encountering specular surfaces are reflected (or transmitted) in the usual way. When a diffuse surface is encountered the photon energy is stored in a texture map called an *adaptive radiosity texture* (or *rex*) associated with the surface. In fact it is not simply light sources that form the origins of these photon paths, but all diffusely (or partially diffusely) reflecting surfaces are used, exactly as in the manner of progressive refinement radiosity, in descending order of brightness (Chapter 15, see "The Progressive refinement method" on page 335). At the end of this phase the rex's will store a radiosity solution. The second pass is "eye tracing" – which is a conventional path tracing from the eye to form an image. However, instead of the lights only serving to illuminate the specular surfaces, the rex's associated with all surfaces that have had a diffuse reflection solution computed are used – in other words, there are "shadow feelers" to the surfaces that have been lit in the light trace phase. The light tracing pass simulates paths of the form: $L(S^*D)^*$, since many specular surfaces may be followed before a diffuse surface, and there may be many such sequences from the light. The eye path can produce sequences of the form DS^*E, since ray or path tracing is used and terminated by using lighting from the rex's in the diffusely reflecting surfaces instead of the lights. Hence putting these together we have paths of the form $L(S^*D)^*S^*E = L(S|D)^*E$.

Bidirectional ray tracing, where rays are distributed through the light sources as well as traced from the eye, is a general technique with many different instances. In the next section we discuss what is probably today's most popular general global illumination, photon mapping.

22.6 Photon tracing

Density estimation

In the bidirectional ray tracing method by Heckbert discussed above, a kind of density estimation of the radiance was stored in the textures. An explicit and full density estimation technique was proposed by Shirley et al. (1995) and extended by Walter et al. (1997). This is a multi-stage method which has the advantage of producing a globally illuminated scene for real-time walkthrough, which makes use of statistical density estimation techniques.

The method involves producing a fine triangulation of all (polygonal) objects in the scene. Photons are traced from light sources, with energy determined by the energy distribution of the emitters. Intersections with objects are followed by further Monte Carlo based tracing, until the particles are finally absorbed. When there is a hit on an object surface, the information is stored in the corresponding triangle. Each triangle potentially has an associated distribution of particle hits, which is then used to estimate the radiance density function. Finally adjacent triangles which are similar enough according to some tolerance criterion are merged together (this last step only to reduce the total number of triangles in the interest of rendering speed). The scene can then be rendered in real-time using Gouraud shading.

The method results in very impressive photo-realistic images – though with a number of drawbacks. Specular reflecting and transmitting surfaces are used correctly in the particle tracing phase, but due to the final Gouraud shading, they are not displayed as such. The method relies on all primitives in the scene being represented as polygons. Darker regions may not receive enough particle hits to illuminate them at all, with brighter regions taking up all the storage space since there is a non-uniform distribution of the emitted light across the scene.

KD-trees

In the illumination cache mentioned earlier, an octree was used as a spatial data structure in order to store the cached irradiance values across diffusely reflecting surfaces. Generally, however, global illumination techniques typically involve a finite element approach, where surfaces are tesselated into a mesh, and illumination information stored within the mesh elements. As we have seen, this is the case for radiosity solutions, where an extensive discontinuity meshing must be used for the most accurate shadow computations, and it was also used in the bidirectional ray tracing approach discussed above. Jensen (1996) introduced a full global illumination solution that stores typically hundreds of thousands of photons distributed on surfaces in the scene, but he had the goal to store these in a data structure independent of the surface geometry. There are two advantages to this: first, the solution does not depend on the vagaries of the resolution used for meshing, and the difficulty of finding an appropriate mesh is anyway avoided. Second, the meshing approach is really only suitable for surfaces that have a parametric representation; it is not suitable, for example, for fractals, a case where it would be impossible to provide a surface mesh (because there is no continuous surface). Jensen used KD-trees for this purpose (Bentley, 1975; Samet, 1990; see also de Berg *et al.*, 1997, pp. 97–103). We briefly describe these in this section, and then show how they are used in Jensen's *photon map* approach.

Given a large number of points $p_1, p_2, \ldots, p_n$ in a d-dimensional space, the problem is to classify them, and make queries of the form: find all the points within a specific axis aligned parallelepiped (or cuboid in 3D space), or find all the points in a neighborhood of a point. In the context of photon mapping these points will actually represent photons striking surfaces. A KD-tree is actually just an axis aligned BSP tree. Each node of the tree stores a separating plane, defined by the median value along one of the coordinates. The leaves of the tree contain the original data points.

Suppose $p_i = (x_{1i}, x_{2i}, \ldots, x_{di})$. The root of the tree will be the separating hyperplane $x = x_1$, where x_j represents the median of the values of jth coordinate. This will partition the original set into two equal subsets (by convention, if a value is exactly on the separating hyperplane it should be added to the left set). Now the same procedure is applied recursively to each of the left and right subsets, except that each of these sets is split along the x_2 coordinate. In general, the coordinate $x_{k \bmod d}$ is used at the kth invocation. This process continues until each leaf of the tree contains a data point. An outline is given below:

```
KDTree makeKDTree(int n, point_kd p[], int depth)
/*returns a kd-tree for the n k-dimensional points in p - assume all
indices start from 1*/
{
   if n==1 return a leaf containing p[1]; /*base case*/

   x = median of values of (depth mod d) coordinate in the points;
```

```
        pLeft is the set of points to the left of x and pRight is the
        set to the right;

        leftNode = makeKDTree(n/2,pLeft,depth+1);
        rightNode = makeKDTree(n/2,pRight,depth+1);
        /*assumes that the median splits the points exactly in two*/

        /*compose a new node and return*/
        return compose(leftNode,x,rightNode);
}
```

It can be shown that a KD-tree requires storage $O(n)$, and the construction time is $O(n\log n)$. A query with an axis aligned parallelepiped can be made in $O(n^{1-\frac{1}{d}} + k)$ time where k is the number of points in the output.

Photon maps

A photon is a packet of flux energy, containing also the position where it strikes a surface, and its incoming direction. A photon map is a spatial data structure, in particular a KD-tree representing a large number of photons. In the method described by Jensen (1996) (see also Jensen and Christensen, 1995) two such photon maps are created, the first very high density one is called the *caustics photon map*, and the second the *global photon map*.

A caustic can be represented as a path of the form: *LS*D*; ultimately a sharp beam strikes a diffuse surface. A good example is shown in Figure 1.13 (color plate). If we imagine that from a certain distance a lake is a diffuse surface (we are too far away to see the individual ripples and waves) then a beam of light striking the surface will form a pattern on the surface. Such caustics are notoriously difficult to model, certainly from any standard ray tracing scheme, since the last type of surface before entry to the eye is a diffuse reflector. Caustics are highly complex types of reflection in a scene, and therefore a lot of resource must be devoted to adequately capturing them. Hence Jensen's approach devotes one type of photon map specifically to sample these. Photons are distributed from the light sources only toward specularly reflecting surfaces. When a photon strikes a surface it is reflected according to the surface's BRDF, and on to the next specular surface, until the process stops at a diffuse surface. Hence only such *LS*D* paths are followed for the caustics photon map. The photons are stored in the KD-tree as they encounter the surfaces.

In Jensen and Christensen (1995) a light buffer was used on the light sources, in order to demarcate specular and diffuse surfaces (see "The Light Buffer – efficient shadow testing" on page 351). Photons would be sent only to specular surfaces from the light sources.

The global photon map is created by distributing photons to all objects from the light sources, following any type of path. It is created with a much lower density than the caustics photon map, since the latter will be visualized directly in the rendering process, whereas the global map is only used for indirect reflections (that is, reflections that do not immediately end up in the eye). The global photon map can be thought of as a rough global solution to the radiance equation. Information about where shadows might be is also stored, since when a ray carrying a photon strikes a surface it is continued on beyond the surface and thence marked as a shadow photon. This information can be used later in the rendering phase to reduce the need for shadow feeler rays, at least in the case of indirect illumination.

A variant of path tracing is used for the rendering phase. This is of course an attempt to provide a specific solution to the radiance equation for the set of directions relevant for the view. Consider the integral on the right-hand side of (EQ 22.9), and rewrite as:

$$\int_{\Omega} f(p, \omega_i, \omega) \, L(p, \omega_i) \cos\theta_i d\omega_i \tag{EQ 22.17}$$

Decompose the incoming radiance as follows:

$$L(p, \omega_i) = L_l(p, \omega_i) + L_c(p, \omega_i) + L_d(p, \omega_i) \tag{EQ 22.18}$$

where L_l is the direct contribution from the light source, L_c from a specularly reflecting surface (representing the caustics component), and L_d is the contribution from photons that have been diffusely reflected at least once.

Similarly, decompose the BRDF as:

$$f(p, \omega_i, \omega) = f_s(p, \omega_i, \omega) + f_d(p, \omega_i, \omega) \tag{EQ 22.19}$$

where f_s is the specular part, and f_d is the diffuse part.

Then substituting (EQ 22.18) and (EQ 22.19) into (EQ 22.17) (dropping the function arguments for notational convenience):

$$\int (fL) = \int (fL_l) + \int (f_s(L_c + L_d)) + \int (f_d L_c) + \int (f_d L_d) \tag{EQ 22.20}$$

This equation is used during the rendering phase. It may be solved accurately (if the direction is into the eye) or approximately (if this is an indirect ray). We consider each term successively:

Direct $\int(fL_l)$. This is the radiance direct from light sources. For the approximate solution a radiance as estimated from the global photon map is used. For the accurate solution, shadow feeler rays are only used if the information in the global photon map is ambiguous about whether this point is in shadow or not. If it is surrounded by shadow photons then it is in shadow. Otherwise, if it is an area with a mixture of shadow and non-shadow photons, or of course all non-shadow photons, then shadow feeler rays must be used.

Specular $\int(f_s(L_c + L_d))$. This is radiance from specular surfaces, and the solution is obtained via path tracing.

Caustics $\int(f_d L_c)$. This is radiance from caustics on diffuse surfaces. This is taken directly from the caustics photon map.

Diffuse $\int(f_d L_d)$. For the approximate solution the information in the global photon map can be used. For the accurate solution the BRDF is used to determine a set of directions for path tracing, those likely to make the greatest contribution to the solution, and these are followed as in path tracing.

The solution to the radiance equation is then the sum of the emitted light from the surface point through the ray toward the eye (the L_e term in (EQ 22.9)) plus the sum of the four effects: direct, specular, caustics, and diffuse, described above.

Clearly the method requires the ability to extract radiance in a given direction from a surface point from the photon maps. An estimator used by Jensen is the following:

$$L(p, \omega) \approx \sum_{i=1}^{N} f(p, \omega_i, \omega) \frac{\Delta\Phi(p, \omega_i)}{\pi r^2} \qquad \text{(EQ 22.21)}$$

where p is the surface point and the N nearest photons are found closest to p, with incoming directions ω_i and flux $\Delta\Phi(p, \omega_i)$. This forms a disk of radius r with πr^2 as its projected area on the surface. Since radiance is the BRDF times the irradiance, the sum of all such products gives the desired estimate.

Jensen described some typical execution properties of the system, on a number of scenes of up to about 5000 polygons. The largest photon map used contained about 390,000 photons for the caustic map, and 166,000 photons for the global map. On today's computers these kinds of scenes can be rendered in minutes. We have outlined the photon map method due to its importance in today's repertoire of rendering techniques. There is a lot more that could be written about it than has been described here. A recent application and extension has been to relax the usual assumption of light traversing only in a vacuum, to light in participating media (Jensen and Christensen, 1998).

22.7 Summary

This chapter has reviewed the major ray-based approaches for global illumination. We have shown how the radiance equation may be expanded, and how the problem of rendering may be considered as solutions to the equation, and how types of rendering are approximations to a series expansion of the integral radiance equation. We have reviewed stochastic (Monte Carlo) approaches – in particular, path tracing and photon tracing. The reader is referred to (Shirley, 2000) for further in-depth reading on these topics.

23 Advanced real-time rendering for virtual environments

23.1 Introduction

One of the main requirements for a believable experience in a VE is a high and constant frame rate. One might think that this will eventually be achieved through exploiting the faster and more powerful machines that are (always) coming onto the market. However, the size and complexity of the models as well as the expectations of the user tend to more than cancel out any benefits provided by hardware improvements. In spite of the exponential improvement in hardware performance, there remains a need for algorithms that can reduce the rendered geometry to a manageable size, without compromising the resulting image. There are in general three broad categories of algorithms often employed for this purpose: visibility culling, level-of-detail (LOD) representations, and image-based rendering (IBR). Basically the strategy is threefold:

Visibility culling. Don't send polygons through the rendering pipeline unless they have a high probability of being visible.

LOD. If objects are sent through the rendering pipeline, don't send them in any more complex form than is needed to represent them given their size in relation to the screen size and importance to the overall image.

IBR. If you can get away with repeatedly rendering an image (texture map) of an object instead of its geometry, then do so.

We will look briefly at each one of these methods. We will also see a control method that allows us to adjust the fidelity of the image (using more aggressive culling, lower LODs, etc.) in order to maintain the required frame rate.

23.2 Visibility processing

Let us start with visibility processing. Often as the models grow larger, only a subset of the scene is visible from any given viewpoint. There are three reasons why some part of the geometry (say a polygon) might not be visible. It might be outside the view frustum, facing away from the viewer, or be hidden from view behind other polygons closer to the eye. We have seen in previous chapters methods for dealing with each of these cases. In Chapter 10 we saw how to clip polygons and get rid of any part that falls outside the view volume. In Chapter 11 we saw how to determine if a polygon is front or back facing and also saw visible surface determination algorithms that can tell us exactly what is visible through each pixel (Chapter 13).

However, all the above methods share a common drawback. They have to visit and process each and every polygon in the scene at least once. As models grow larger and the numbers of polygons go into the millions these techniques on their own become impractical and wasteful. The techniques we will see in this section pre-process the geometry into data structures that can be queried in sub-linear time to quickly reject geometry that does not contribute to the final image.

These methods don't operate per polygon but rather on groups, for example on whole objects or collections of objects. Since a z-buffer or even a complete pipeline exists in hardware on most computers nowadays, the general idea of these methods is to find the relevant objects and leave the fine-grain visibility determination to the hardware.

Visibility algorithms can be described based on their output using the following classification (Cohen-Or *et al.*, 2000):

- *Exact visibility algorithms* output the set of all polygons which are at least partially visible, and only these polygons.

- *Approximate visibility algorithms* output a set that includes most of the visible polygons plus maybe some hidden ones.

- *Conservative visibility algorithms* output a set that includes at least all the visible polygons plus maybe some non-visible ones.

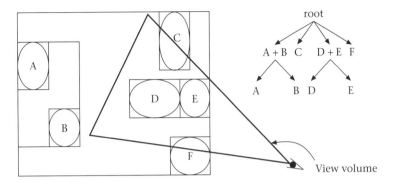

Figure 23.1
View volume culling against a hierarchy of bounding boxes

Obviously, if we have the exact set then the workload on the graphics hardware, for producing the correct image, will be minimized. However, exact culling methods are often very expensive and that is why the majority of visibility algorithms are designed to be conservative. They compute a *potentially visible set* (PVS) which, as we said, includes all the visible polygons plus some non-visible ones. This over-estimation might require slightly more processing but at least we are sure that it will produce the correct image. Nevertheless, some algorithms can allow for an approximate solutions (Slater and Chrysanthou, 1996; Zhang *et al.*, 1997) which can be useful when the load on the system is too high. They can trade accuracy in exchange for a faster run-time by allowing for objects to be skipped when they are potentially not contributing much to the final image.

View volume and backface culling

The first thing to do is to decide what parts of the scene are outside the view volume.

This is usually done hierarchically (Clark, 1976), depending on how the scene is stored. If it is in a hierarchy of bounding volumes, say for example bounding boxes (BBs), then we do the following. Start from the root of the hierarchy and test the BB there against the view volume. The result can be one of the following three:

- Completely outside, in which case all the objects enclosed are outside and thus they can all be ignored for this frame, node $A + B$ in Figure 23.1.

- Completely inside, in which case we don't need to test any other of the volumes below the node, for example $D + E$ in Figure 23.1. In fact we don't even need to do any clipping, we just render all the enclosed geometry with clipping off. This is normally faster, although not necessarily by much on some of today's hardware.

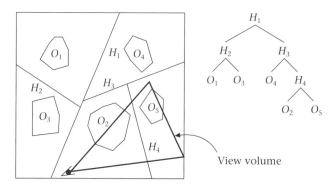

Figure 23.2
View volume culling
against a space
partitioning

- Or there is an intersection, in which case we test each child of the root separately, e.g., the *root* or nodes C and F in Figure 23.1. If a leaf node gives an intersection then we need to render the enclosed geometry but with clipping on, nodes C and F in the figure.

If the scene is held in a hierarchical space subdivision, rather than a bounding volume hierarchy, then the test is slightly different. Let us take, for example, a binary tree such as a BSP tree or a KD-tree. Here each node subdivides the space into two convex, disjoint subspaces using a partitioning plane. For view volume culling, again we start traversing at the very top of the hierarchy. Once we establish that the overall subspace enclosing the scene is not entirely outside or entirely inside, we start the recursive descent. At each node we test the view volume against the partitioning plane. If the view volume lies entirely on one side, then we can safely ignore the subtree on the other side, for example the left children of H_1 and H_3 in Figure 23.2 are not traversed. If the plane intersects the view volume then we need to traverse both subtrees, as is the case with node H_4 in Figure 23.2.

An alternative method with a very different approach was proposed by Slater and Chrysanthou (1996). It is a stochastic approach dependent on temporal coherence, where objects have associated probabilities of being in the visible set, which are updated as the scene changes or the viewpoint moves.

View volume culling is comparatively straightforward to implement and is found on most rendering systems nowadays.

On average, at any given moment about half of the polygons within the view frustum will not contribute to the final image since they will be facing away from the viewer. Instead of using the techniques in Chapter 11 to test each one of them, back-face culling can also be done hierarchically in sub-linear time, as demonstrated by Kumar *et al.* (1996). In their paper concerned with hierarchical back-face computation, the model is partitioned at pre-processing into clusters based on the normals and physical proximity of the polygons, with large clusters represented hierarchically. Space is partitioned with respect to each of these clusters into three distinct regions. The first region is defined as the space from which all the cluster faces are front facing, *FrontRegion* (the intersection of the front half-spaces of all cluster polygons), the second one is where all cluster faces are back facing (*BackRegion*) and the third is the remaining space (*MixedRegion*). At run-time the algorithm tracks the viewpoint with respect to the regions of each cluster. For each cluster, if the viewpoint lies in its BackRegion (FrontRegion), all the polygons belonging to that cluster are back-facing (front-facing). Otherwise, it's a mixed region and we need to check the subclusters. Frame-to-frame coherence can be used to speed up things further.

Occlusion culling

This is by far the most complex and most interesting of the culling classes due to its global nature. It cannot be determined by considering the polygons individually, but rather involves examining the interrelations between them. From any given viewpoint, a large number of objects might be hidden from view behind geometry closer to the viewer. The task here is to quickly identify and reject objects that are completely hidden. Many occlusion culling algorithms exist in the literature; a full survey is beyond the scope of this section and the interested reader is referred to Cohen-Or *et al.* (2000).

Recently a number of culling methods have been presented that attempt to find a potentially visible set, not from a single point but from a finite region (Cohen-Or *et al.*, 1998; Durand *et al.*, 2000; Schaufler *et al.*, 2000). There can be several reasons why this is desirable. Since the result is valid for any viewpoint within that region, the same PVS can be reused and thus the cost of computing it is amortized over a number of frames. Other benefits are that the solution can be used for determining what geometry to load from disk, if the whole model cannot be held in memory, or what parts to stream down the line from a remote server when using this in an Internet application.

On the other hand, from-point algorithms tend to be simpler to code and faster to run. They also result in a smaller amount of geometry to be rendered because they compute only the relevant geometry for the specific viewpoint. But, of course, they have to be repeated every frame.

In this book we will not be considering the from-region visibility methods any further. We will look at some from-point methods. These can be further classified into object space (OS) and image space (IS) methods. For both OS and IS methods the scene is usually placed in a hierarchy of some sort, a bounding volume hierarchy or a space partitioning. And often some pre-processing in the form of identifying potential occluders is carried out.

Image space occlusion

Image space methods operate in the discrete resolution of the image, although there are exceptions. The realization here is that eventually what we want to produce is a discrete image and therefore finding the visible objects at the pixel level is sufficient.

Because of their discrete nature they are often simpler and with potentially lower computational complexity. They can make use of specialized graphics hardware for added speed and they can be more robust than object space methods. Also, approximate solutions with control on the error can be produced by some of these algorithms by classifying as occluded geometry parts which are visible through an insignificant pixel count. This invariably results in an increase in running speed.

The projections of many small and individually insignificant occluders can be accumulated on the image using standard graphics rasterizing hardware, to cover a significant part of the image which can then be used for culling. Another advantage of these methods is that the occluders do not have to be polyhedral; any object that can be rasterized can be used.

The outline of an image space method might look like this:

```
traverse the scene hierarchy front-to-back (top-down) and at each
node N do
  compare N against the view volume
  if not outside
    test N for occlusion
    if not occluded,
      if N is a leaf node
        render the enclosed objects
        augmenting the occlusion structures
      else
        recurse down children of N
```

This form is probably ideal because it means that as we process each object we compare it against the *total accumulated* occlusion to that point. However, the continuous update of the occlusion information can be very slow and that is why most algorithms employ a two-pass approach. In the first, they render the set of pre-selected occluders and create the occlusion information, while in the second they just traverse the hierarchy and cull/render without changing the occlusion information.

A typical way of testing a node for occlusion is to project the faces defining its boundary onto the image plane and test each one of them. If they are all hidden then the node is hidden.

One of the first image space methods presented is the *hierarchical z-buffer* (HZB) (Greene *et al.*, 1993), which can be seen as an extension of the z-buffer that we have already seen in Chapter 13. The initial idea closely follows the pseudocode above. The scene is arranged into an octree which is traversed front-to-back (although other hierarchical representations are also possible). As visible objects are scan-converted the *z-pyramid* is built incrementally. Each node is tested against the z-pyramid for occlusion before processing any further.

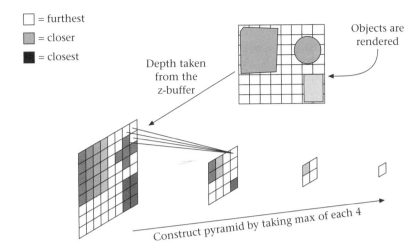

Figure 23.3
Hierarchical z-buffer:
the z-pyramid

The z-pyramid, which is the occlusion representation, is a layered buffer with a different resolution at each level. At the finest level it is just the content of the z-buffer, while coarser levels are created by halving the resolution in each dimension and each element holding the furthest z-value in the corresponding 2×2 window of the finer level below. The coarsest level is just one value corresponding to overall maximum z of the image. During scan-conversion of the primitives, if the contents of the z-buffer change then the new z-values are propagated up the pyramid to the coarser levels. A simple example can be seen in Figure 23.3.

To determine whether a node is visible, each of its faces is projected onto the image plane and tested hierarchically against the z-pyramid. Starting from the finest-level sample of the pyramid whose corresponding image region covers the screen-space bounding box of the face, the nearest z value of the projected face is compared with the value in the z-pyramid. If it is found to be further away then it is occluded, otherwise we recursively descend down to finer levels until its visibility can be determined.

To maintain the z-pyramid, every time an object is rendered, causing a change in the z-buffer, the change has to be propagated through to the coarser levels. However, this is not a practical approach since it requires continuous access to the graphics hardware and processing for the updates. A more realistic implementation is to use frame-to-frame coherence and fall back into a two-pass method (Greene *et al.*, 1993). At the start of each frame we first render the nodes that were visible in the previous frame. Then the z-buffer is read and the z-pyramid is constructed in one go. Finally the scene hierarchy is traversed using the z-pyramid for occlusion but without updating it.

The *hierarchical occlusion maps* (HOM) (Zhang *et al.*, 1997) is a later method, similar in principle to the HZB. However, here the occlusion problem is

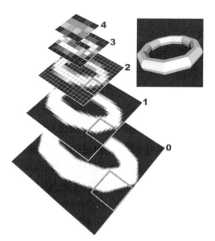

Figure 23.4
The hierarchy of
occlusion maps
Courtesy of Hansong Zhang,
PhD thesis, *Effective Occlusion
Culling for the Interactive
Display of Arbitrary Models*,
Department of Computer
Science, UNC-Chapel Hill,
1998

decomposed into two sub-problems. (1) A two-dimensional overlap test which determines whether the screen space projection of the potential occludee is completely enclosed by the accumulated projection of the occluders. The hierarchical occlusion maps are used for this. (2) A second test on the depth to determine whether or not the potential occludee is behind the occluders.

This is also is a two-pass method. In the first pass the occlusion map hierarchy and depth information is built from a set of "good" occluders, and then the scene hierarchy is traversed using the HOM for deciding on the visibility of each node.

An example of the occlusion map hierarchy can be seen in Figure 23.4. At the finest level it is just a bit map with 0 (black) denoting a transparent pixel and 1 (white) an opaque one, while higher levels store gray-scale values.

To build the HOM, a set of occluders is selected from the occluder database and rendered into the frame-buffer. At this point only occupancy information is required; therefore texturing, lighting, and z-buffering are all turned off. The occluders are rendered as pure white on a black background. The result is read from the buffer and forms the highest resolution in the occlusion map hierarchy. The coarser levels are created by averaging squares of 2×2 pixels to form a map which has half the resolution on each dimension. Texturing hardware can provide some acceleration of the averaging if the size of the map is large enough to warrant the setup cost of the hardware.

As we proceed to coarser levels the pixels are not just black or white (occluded or visible) but can be shades of gray. The intensity of a pixel at such a level shows the opacity of the corresponding region.

An object is tested for occlusion by first projecting its bounding box onto the screen and finding the level in the hierarchy where the pixels have approximately the same size as the extent of the projected box. If the box overlaps pixels of the HOM which are not opaque, it means that the box cannot be culled. If the pixels are opaque, that means the object is projected on a region

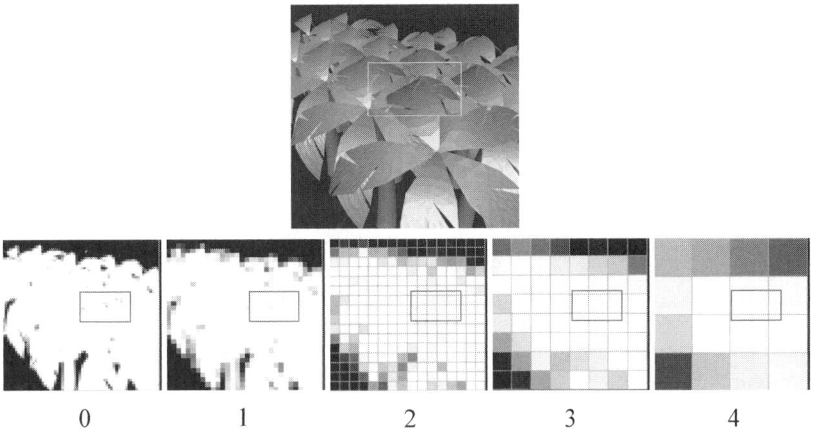

Figure 23.5
Hierarchical occlusion maps: approximate culling
Courtesy of Hansong Zhang, PhD thesis, *Effective Occlusion Culling for the Interactive Display of Arbitrary Models*, Department of Computer Science, UNC-Chapel Hill, 1998

of the image that is covered. In this case an extra depth test is needed to determine whether the object is behind the occluders.

In the paper (Zhang *et al.*, 1997) a number of methods are proposed for testing the depth of the objects against that of the occluders. The simplest one makes use of a plane placed behind all the occluders. This plane is parallel to the near clip plane and placed at the maximum z of all occluders. When an object passes the opacity test and its closest z-value is further than this plane, we can classify it as occluded. Although this is fast and simple, it can be over-conservative. An alternative method is what they called the *depth estimation buffer*. In this, the screen space is partitioned into a set of regions and a separate plane is used for each region of the partition. In this way a finer measure of the distances of the occluders is obtained and the number of false-visible is reduced.

One advantage of the HOM method compared to the HZB is that it also supports approximate visibility culling. Objects that are visible in only a few pixels through holes among the occluders can be ignored. This can easily be done by setting an *opacity threshold*, above which a pixel in the occlusion map is treated as fully opaque. This is demonstrated in Figure 23.5. The rectangle in the image corresponds to the projection of a bounding box of an object which we want to test for occlusion. If we look at the pixels it overlaps in map 4, we will see that they are almost opaque. They are not fully opaque, as we can see from map 0 which shows some small holes. However, if their opacity is above the threshold, we can classify the object as occluded and not render it or process it any further.

A number of current graphics cards provide functionality for performing basic image-based culling with hardware testing. A typical way of doing it is by adding a feedback mechanism in the hardware which is able to check if changes will be made to the z-buffer when scan-converting a primitive (Scott *et al.*, 1998). If the scene is stored in a hierarchy of bounding boxes, we can traverse the hierarchy top to bottom, performing this test on the sides of the box at each step. If the sides are all further away than what is already in the z-buffer, we can stop the traversal of that subtree, otherwise continue recursively.

Object space occlusion

Probably the simplest method for object space occlusion culling is to use shadow frusta of individual occluders. Hudson *et al.*, (1997) presented a method using this idea. Unlike the image space methods we have seen above, it does not aggregate the occlusion. Objects can be occluded by individual occluders only, which makes the method useful only in scenes that contain large convex polygons. On the positive side though, it does not rely on any special graphics hardware and with the right models it can be fast. Two other methods presented by Coorg and Teller (Coorg and Teller, 1996, 1997) use similar concepts and the second one also uses some occluder fusion. They provide some very interesting ideas well worth studying but here we will concentrate on the simpler shadow frusta method.

The culling is done hierarchically, therefore the scene needs to be stored in a spatial hierarchy. To do the culling we will need to have a set of good occluders for each frame. To make the run-time selection of the occluders faster we can pre-process the model and store for each region of space a set of potentially good occluders. These might be stored with the scene hierarchy, or just in a regular grid over the whole space. Then at run-time, a list of occluders is selected based on the viewpoint and reduced to only those within the view frustum.

From a given viewpoint, once we have the occluders, we can proceed with the culling. For each occluder we construct a *shadow frustum*. We saw the definition of a shadow frustum in Chapter 14; it is the same here. The shadow frustum defines the volume hidden from view behind the occluder; any object contained completely in it is not visible and can be ignored. We traverse the scene hierarchy from top to bottom and at each node N we do the following. Test N against the view volume; if it is outside then stop, otherwise test N against each of the shadow frusta in turn. If at any point it is found to be fully inside one of them then we stop and ignore the geometry held in N for this fame. If N intersects none of the frusta then we go ahead and render all the geometry in the volume N *with no more culling tests*. However, if N did partly overlap some of the frusta then we need to recurse and continue the traversal with the children of N.

For this method to work effectively it requires a fast node-to-frustum intersection calculation. By assuming that the spatial hierarchy is done using an axis aligned scheme, fast specialized tests can be devised. Details can be found in the paper (Hudson *et al.*, 1997). A basic (and slow) implementation can be done using the point-against-plane test that we saw earlier in this book (Chapter 8).

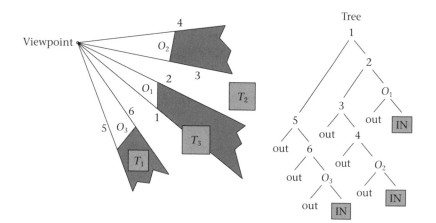

Figure 23.6
Hierarchical visibility
using occlusion trees

However, after having seen the SVBSP algorithm in Chapter 14 ("Shadow volume BSP trees" on page 304), the classification of the hierarchy nodes against each shadow frusta individually might seem non-optimal, to say the least. In fact it is very easy to apply the SVBSP tree ideas to the occlusion method above (Bittner *et al.*, 1998). Using the viewpoint as the "light source" we can construct an occlusion tree following the same procedure as in "Shadow volume BSP trees" on page 304. Figure 23.6 shows an example of an occlusion tree built from the three occluders O_1, O_2, O_3. The IN nodes denote occluded regions while OUT is visible.

Given the occlusion tree, the rest of the process is the same as before with the only difference being the way we classify a node of the scene hierarchy for occlusion. Instead of testing it against the individual frusta, we insert it into the occlusion tree. In Bittner *et al.* (1998) this was done by inserting each of the 6 polygonal sides of the node into the tree individually and tracing them down to the leaves. We saw in Chapter 11 how to insert a polygon into a BSP tree. A node is said to be fully visible (occluded) if all the fragments reach OUT (IN) regions. Otherwise the node is partly occluded and we need to test each child.

We can probably do better than inserting the sides of nodes individually. If the scene hierarchy is also in the form of a binary tree, we can use the BSP tree-merging algorithm of Naylor *et al.* (1990) and find the occlusion by performing an intersection operation between the occlusion tree and the scene tree (Chrysanthou, 2001).

Selecting good occluders

Finding the right occluders is an important part of any occlusion method but especially so with the object space ones. The solid angle subtended by a polygon is a good measure but it is slow to compute exactly. An approximation that is often used is the following (Coorg and Teller, 1996):

Figure 23.7
Occluder selection

$$\frac{(-(a \cdot N \cdot V))}{|V|^2}$$

where a is the area of the polygon, N is the polygon's normal vector, and V is the vector from the viewpoint to the center of the polygon (see Figure 23.7).

Architectural scenes

We will now look at architectural scenes as a separate case, not only because many of the common large models are such (buildings, cities) but also because they have dense and well-defined occlusions which make the development of fast algorithms easier. We have two types of architectural models, indoor and outdoor ones. We will look at algorithms for both cases.

The *cells and portals* method (Airey *et al.*, 1990; Teller and Séquin, 1991) is the classic occlusion method for use with indoor scenes. It works differently from the methods we have seen up to now because it doesn't trace the occluders to find what is hidden, but traces through portals (doors and other openings) to find what is visible.

During pre-processing, the model is first subdivided into convex cells using a BSP tree. The main opaque surfaces, such as the walls, are used for defining the partitions and thus the boundaries of the cells. Smaller detailed scene elements are considered "non-occluding" and are ignored at this step. Non-opaque portals, such as doors, are identified on cell boundaries, and used to form an adjacency graph connecting the cells of the subdivision (see example in Figure 23.8). The thick black lines are the walls which are used for partitioning

Figure 23.8
Cells and portals: the adjacency graph and stab tree

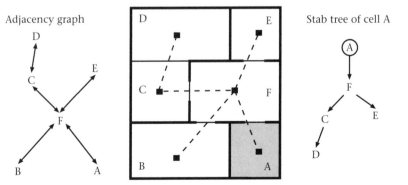

into cells and the light gray lines are the portals. On the left, the adjacency graph shows which cells are directly connected through the portals.

The *cell-to-cell* visibility is determined by testing if sightlines exist that connect any point in one cell to any point in another. Actually, it is clear that if a line exists from one cell to another, it has to go through a portal and thus we only need to determine if the portals are visible between them. For each cell, the adjacency graph is utilized to generate portal sequences which are then "stabbed" with the sightlines. For example, the tree on the right of Figure 23.8 shows the cells that are visible from cell A. The cells that are reached by the sightlines from a given view-cell contain the potentially visible set (PVS) for any given point in that cell.

During an interactive walkthrough the cell-to-cell visibility can be further dynamically culled using the view volume of the observer, producing a superset of the visible scene data, the *eye-to-cell* visibility. A cell is visible if all these are true: it is in the view volume, and all cells along the stab tree are in the view volume, and all portals along the stab tree are in the view volume, and a sightline within the view volume exists through portals, although we might decide to apply only some of these tests. The geometry contained in each visible cell is then passed down the graphics pipeline for rendering.

In the method above, the pre-processing required for building the cell-to-cell information can be quite extensive. Luebke and Georges (1995) presented another method for using cells and portals. The only pre-processing required is the generation of the cells and portals and building the adjacency graph. The rest is done at run-time.

Starting from the cell containing the viewpoint, first we render the geometry in that cell (with view volume culling) and then traverse through to the adjacent cells. For the traversal, the vertices of the portals are projected into image space. We compute the 2D axis aligned bounding box for them, called the cull box, which is a conservative approximation to the portals. Any object across a portal whose projection is outside the cull box is not visible. As we go from cell to cell we keep an aggregate cull box which is the intersection of the successive boxes. When this intersection is null we stop the traversal along that sequence. Otherwise we test the projections of the object bounding boxes against it to decide which ones to render. Figure 23.9 shows an example. On the left we see the cull boxes and their intersections. On the right we see an overview which also suggests that this method is equivalent to shrinking the shadow volume as we go through each portal. Mirrors can also be simulated with the same process.

A number of specialized methods exist for outdoor urban environments as well. What is special about outdoor urban environments is that we can consider the occluders to be 2.5 dimensional. That is, we can describe them using their footprint and height. And although we don't have the easily defined subdivision into cells connected with portals, we can use this attribute to create almost equally fast methods. An example is the *occluder shadows* of Wonka and Schmalstieg (1999).

Figure 23.9
Image space cells
and portals
Courtesy of David Luebke,
Chris Georges, and the
Department of Computer
Science, University
of North Carolina

Figure 23.10
Occluder shadows
for culling in urban
models
Courtesy of Peter Wonka,
Institute of Computer
Graphics, Vienna University
of Technology, Austria

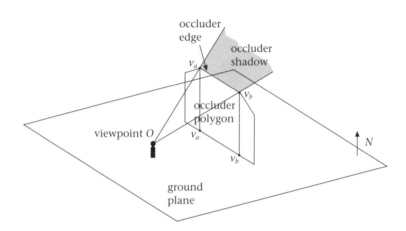

The scene is placed into a regular 2D grid coincident with the ground plane. Each cell holds the objects in the corresponding region. During runtime the occlusion information is constructed as follows. A set of occluders is selected; their *occluder shadows* are computed and rasterized, using the hardware graphics pipeline, into a depth buffer, the *cull map*. An occluder shadow is shown in Figure 23.10. A shadow plane is defined with its apex at the current viewpoint and going through the top edge of the occluder (v_a, v_b). The occluder shadow is the part of the shadow plane behind the occluder away from the viewpoint. For the rasterization of these planes, we set an orthogonal projection looking down from above the model, with the image plane parallel to the scene ground plane. The extent of the view volume and resolution of the image are also defined so that each pixel covers exactly one cell of the scene grid.

When the hardware rasterizes the occluder shadows, the values of the z-buffer give us the height of occlusion at each pixel and at the corresponding cell. To determine the visible objects we go through the cells of the 2D grid

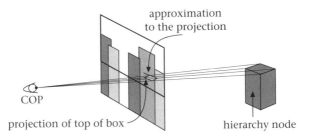

Figure 23.11
Occlusion map for
urban models

that are within the view volume and we test the height of each object against the z-value in the cull map. If the object has a smaller z then we can ignore it.

The algorithm as described above is not conservative since a pixel partially covered by an occluder shadow will be set as fully covered if it goes over the mid-point. To avoid these errors, in the paper the authors propose moving the edges of the occluder shadow inwards by a proportion of the pixel size. A correction is also applied to the z-direction.

Fallon and Chrysanthou (2001) presented another very simple to implement urban culling method, a simplified version of the occlusion maps. They do away with the map hierarchy, which might be costly to build. The occluders are rendered and the buffer is read, and then the scene hierarchy is traversed for occlusion. For each node, it is sufficient to project its top rim and test it for occlusion. If that is hidden then the rest of the node will also be hidden, since we assume that the occluders are 2.5D (see Figure 23.11). The occlusion of the top rim can be determined conservatively very quickly. It is approximated by a horizontal line placed at the highest y and the same x extent as the projection. If this line corresponds to covered pixels, the node is occluded.

23.3 Multi-resolution representations

Static level of detail

Level of detail (LOD) is a simple technique that reduces the detail of representation of objects that would appear far away from the viewer. The rationale is that there is no point rendering many polygons onto the screen if the resulting image would occupy only a few pixels. Thus a low detail version of the model is used whenever the viewpoint is far enough away that the difference in the rendered image between the two versions would be sufficiently small.

Figure 23.12 shows an object with two levels of detail. The object on the left in both pictures is a low detail version (1047 polygons) of the object on the right (69451 polygons). The middle object in both pictures is a level of detail switching between both versions. Note the small difference in images in the distant (lower) view.

In practice, several versions of a model might be used over a set of distance ranges, and optionally the last range might be left blank so that the object is

Figure 23.12
Level of detail example
Courtesy of Joao Oliveira,
Department of Computer
Science, UCL

not drawn if the viewpoint is more than a certain distance away. For example, consider an LOD object that has 3 representatives labelled A, B and C and the range set [15, 30, 40]. When the viewer is less than 15 units away child A is rendered. Child B is rendered when the viewpoint is between 15 and 30 units away. Child C is rendered when the viewpoint is between 30 and 40 units away, and nothing is rendered if the viewpoint is more than 40 units away.

One problem with simple LOD is that the transition from one model to another is often very noticeable since it takes place over a single frame. A technique that is offered in the IRIS Performer toolkit (Rohlf and Helman, 1994) is alpha transparency blending between two levels of detail. Instead of abruptly switching, both objects are drawn simultaneously during a transition range. The two views are blended using transparency, and the transparency is changed over a number of frames to hide the transition. The downside is that during the transition both versions of the object are drawn, and thus this transition should occur only infrequently else there is no overall benefit in using level of detail at all.

Alternatively, instead of switching between two disjoint geometry sets, we could morph the geometry from one representation to the other over a transition range. The progressive mesh technique in the following section exploits a variation of morphing.

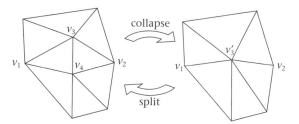

Figure 23.13
Vertex split method of
mesh refinement

A complementary problem to level of detail switching is the automatic creation of the actual levels of detail from the original high detail geometry. A crude technique often employed for the creation of very low detail representation is the replacement of each mesh with a bounding box or other simple bounding object. We introduce the general problem of mesh decimation as a process of generating lower levels of detail in a subsequent section.

Progressive meshes

The idea behind progressive meshes is very simple (Hoppe, 1996). Instead of switching between a small, fixed number of objects, we create a continuous deformation from high detail meshes to low detail meshes and back again by iteratively adding or removing edges from the mesh in a manner that is hopefully imperceptible to the viewer. The method assumes that the high detail object is composed of a triangle mesh. Edges are removed or added by repeated application of the operation, depicted in Figure 23.13.

When using this technique in a run-time system, we have to decide a target number of polygons for the mesh. We can then apply one or more collapses or splits to move from the current mesh to the target mesh. As with the static level of detail switching, we try to disguise the transformation by animating the change over a few frames. Consider the example in Figure 23.13. It is possible to animate the collapse, by first moving vertices v_3 and v_4 towards each other, and replacing them by v_3' only when they are within some tolerance. This appears to be smooth, as the two triangles $v_1 v_3 v_4$ and $v_3 v_2 v_4$ gradually diminish in size as the adjacent triangles expand.

A mesh is thus represented by a base mesh M_0 and a list of splits $vsplit_0$, $vsplit_1$, $vsplit_2 \ldots vsplit_{n-1}$. Each *vsplit* identifies the vertex to split (v_3' in the example), the final position of the original vertex (v_3 in the example), and the position for the inserted vertex (v_4 in the example).

Refinements can be applied individually, but in practice the level of detail can change quickly so Hoppe discusses how to combine several split animations in parallel. The problem with applying several *vsplit* operations simultaneously is that one vertex might be moved twice in nearby splits, so a simple animation does not suffice.

The complement of the progressive mesh technique is choosing the sequence of edge collapses that deform the original mesh into a lower detail mesh.

Mesh decimation

The problem we encounter is selecting which edges to collapse in order to make a decimated mesh appear close to the original. A naive solution would be simply to remove the shortest edges in order. This certainly gives a progressively simpler mesh but the results can look quite ragged.

The problem is that short edges are often found in areas of high detail, and thus they might be more important to the overall shape than large polygons elsewhere. As a generalization, mesh decimation should remove detail in large planar areas first, and consider local curvature of the surface when deciding which edges to remove (Garland and Heckbert, 1997).

A full treatment of this subject is beyond the scope of this book, but Figure 23.14 illustrates the point in question. The top row shows a wire-frame and a smooth rendering of a mesh with 69,451 triangles. On each of the next three rows, the left-hand pair are the meshes derived from the naive shortest edge removal and the right-hand pair are the meshes derived from consideration of local curvature. In the second row, both meshes contain 6,450 triangles. In the third row, both meshes contain 1,042 triangles. In the fourth row, both meshes contain 540 triangles. Note the greater loss of detail in the naive algorithm, especially around the ears.

Figure 23.14
Example mesh decimation
The original bunny model is courtesy of Stanford University Computer Graphics Laboratory. Mesh decimations provided by Joao Oliveira, Department of Computer Science, UCL. The algorithm used to construct these meshes is described in Oliveira and Buxton (2001)

Frame rate control

Level of detail and image-based techniques (considered in the next section) on their own do not provide guaranteed frame rates for virtual environments. First, they are only distance dependent, not view dependent, so it is difficult to select appropriate ranges for switching between levels of detail. However, there is a more serious problem, in that the ranges can only be optimized to match a frame rate for one particular machine configuration. If a faster machine is available then we will find the target frame rate exceeded and consequently would want to move the ranges out so that more detail could be encompassed.[1]

The general problem is that rendering time is a fixed commodity and we must strive to generate the best image we can by apportioning rendering time to the elements in the scene graph. Funkhouser and Séquin (1993) state the problem as follows.

Define an object tuple (O, L, R) to represent a scene object O, rendered at level of detail level L with rendering algorithm R. The rendering algorithm might employ, for example, flat shading or Gouraud shading or Phong shading or one of various types of lighting model which have different levels of complexity. For each tuple we can define *Cost* and *Benefit* heuristics, where *cost* is the rendering time required, and *benefit* is a measure of the contribution that tuple makes to the overall perception of the scene. The problem is then to

$$\text{maximize } \sum_{S} Benefit(O, L, R)$$

over all OLR triples potentially visible in the next frame (S)

$$\text{subject to } \sum_{S} Cost(O, L, R) \leq RenderingTime$$

The cost of rendering an object at a certain level depends on many factors, including the geometric complexity and the number of pixels rendered. Both of these can be expensive to estimate (sometimes more so than simply rendering the object!), so some rough estimate based on total vertices is often used. Benefit is even more complex. It depends upon the object size, accuracy of the level of detail, focus of the user, motion blur, and a hysteresis factor. The hysteresis is factored in to ensure that a level of detail does not change rapidly in situations on the borderline between two levels of detail. A rough estimate of benefit is simply projected screen size.

The progressive mesh approach is ideal for this situation, since it provides fine-tuning on the L factor – since it can vary between the full mesh representation and the lowest possible consistent polyhedral representation.

---

1. IRIS Performer has several techniques to alleviate this problem. This simplest is the capability to dynamically scale the level of detail ranges if the frame rate drops.

The optimization problem is solved by a heuristic – let *Value = Cost/Benefit*. Funkhouser used the idea of sorting *OLR* triples according to their value, and then increasing the *L* or *R* attribute at the high end of the list, and decreasing at the low end of the list, until the same object had been changed twice in opposite directions. This relies on frame-to-frame coherence, so that the list does not have to be repeatedly sorted. It is not a "correct" solution of the optimization problem, which is NP-complete.

23.4 Image-based rendering

In this section we briefly discuss the idea of image-based rendering (IBR). It is motivated by the observation that it is much faster to render a texture representing a complex object or scene than it is to render the scene itself starting from its original specification in a scene graph. In other words, if we can render one polygon with a texture representing a complex object, then this will be orders of magnitude faster than directly rendering the complex object. This is, after all, the general motivation for texture mapping (see "Texturing" on page 275) – for example, we would render an image (texture) of bricks on a wall, rather than try to individually render the wall from geometric descriptions of the bricks.

How can we make use of this to speed up rendering of a scene? Of course, in the extreme we could make a kind of texture of the whole scene, and just render that. This is fundamentally the approach of "Quicktime VR" pioneered by Apple Computers (Chen, 1995), where a set of digital images of a scene are stitched together to create a complete 3D surrounding environment. The user can view this scene from a number of preset vantage points, with image interpolation to synthesize new images from the existing set. We will see another example of this type of approach to computer graphics in the next section, and see also McMillan and Bishop (1995) who used cylindrical projections of the scene.

Here we are concerned with hybrid techniques that combine the standard (geometry-based) rendering pipeline with an efficient use of textures to save rendering time where possible. The idea is generally called *billboards* or *imposters*. An *imposter* is the name given to an image of an object that is used in the form of a texture map. A *dynamic imposter* is usually created at run-time by rendering an object, and using this rendering to create a texture on a transparent rectangular polygon. The idea is that because of the inherent coherence in consecutive frames in a moving viewpoint sequence, the same imposter can be reused for a number of frames until an error measure exceeds some threshold.

This idea was presented by Schaufler (1995) (see also Schaufler, 1996). Earlier, Maciel and Shirley (1995) studied a similar idea, but where the textures were precomputed and stored with the scene database. Schaufler's method computes the imposters at run-time, and once computed the same imposter can be reused for a series of frames while an error bound between the image

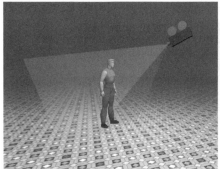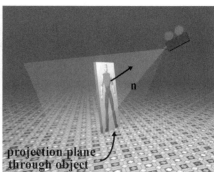

projection plane
through object

n

Figure 23.15
Creating an imposter
Courtesy of Franco Tecchia,
Department of Computer
Science, UCL

in the imposter and the image that would have been obtained from rendering the actual geometry remains below a threshold.

The process of creating an imposter for an object is shown in Figure 23.15. Let C be the center of the object, and n a vector from C toward the current COP. A projection plane (P) is constructed through C with n as its normal. The object is projected onto P, and the bounding extent of the object is also projected onto P. The smallest rectangle enclosing the projection of the bounding extent of the object is taken as the extent of the imposter image. This image is then created as a texture map on a rectangular polygon given by this extent. The polygon itself is marked as being transparent, so that it does not itself obscure objects that are behind it, but only the (opaque) texture formed by the projection does so. The idea is that the object is rendered only once (to form the imposter), and for viewpoints near the current COP this texture can be rendered instead of the object.

The textured polygon can be made transparent by use of the so-called alpha-channel that is available on modern graphics hardware. We have considered pixels to consist of RGB values. However, typically (and accessible, for example, through OpenGL) there is a further value called the A or alpha value. This is a value between 0.0 and 1.0 such that 1.0 means that the pixel color is opaque and therefore the corresponding RGB value should directly overwrite whatever is currently in the frame buffer. A value of 0.0 means that the pixel color is completely transparent, which means that anything "behind" (e.g., already in the frame-buffer) will be seen (so writing RGB with alpha = 0.0 has no effect). For values in the range 0.0 to 1.0, the new RGB value is linearly interpolated with the existing value in the frame-buffer: $(1 - \alpha)RGB_{old} + \alpha RGB$. Hence when creating the imposter, the original rectangular polygon should be set with all alpha values equal to 0.0. However, for those areas where the image is generated on the polygon the alpha values are set to 1.0. Note that this description is of the typical use of the alpha buffer, and OpenGL allows many other possibilities.

What resolution should the texture map be? Schaufler suggests that this should be proportional to the screen resolution scaled by the size of the object divided by the distance of the object from the COP. Hence, other things being equal, objects that are further away need lower resolution texture maps.

The rule used by Schaufler to decide whether to render the original object or the imposter of the object is based on the relative size of a texel seen from the viewpoint compared to the size of a pixel. If we let α_{texel} be the angle subtended by a texel, and α_{pixel} be the angle subtended by a pixel from the same viewpoint, then the imposter can be used while $\alpha_{texel} < \alpha_{pixel}$, since this condition indicates that the error involved in using the imposter is anyway less than can be displayed at the screen resolution.

When an imposter is displayed, its underlying polygon (i.e., the polygon on which the texture is mapped) is always rotated so that its normal points towards the COP. In this way the image always faces the viewer, and the process of texture mapping itself of course makes sure that the appropriate perspective is applied. However, of course there will come a moment when the viewpoint has changed so much compared to the original viewpoint at which an imposter was created that the imposter is no longer valid and should be re-created.

While the viewpoint remains in the same position, and only the direction of view changes, the projection of the object will be topologically the same (i.e., the same vertices are projected), and the same imposter can be used. However, if the viewpoint translates relative to its original position when the imposter was created then significant errors are introduced. There are two cases: the first is when the viewpoint translates along a plane parallel to the center plane of the object, and the second is when the viewpoint moves toward or away from the object. Schaufler provides an analysis of the maximum errors of these situations making use of the projection of points on the bounding box of the object. In the first case, if we take a diagonal from one corner of the bounding box to another, and imagine the viewpoint sliding along a path parallel to this, then points that might be projected coincidentally from one viewpoint will separate as the viewpoint moves. A maximum angle in the discrepancy between such points is defined, which if exceeded requires the generation of a new imposter. Similarly, if the viewpoint is moving, say, toward the object, on a vector normal to a side of the bounding box, then the same analysis will hold for extremal vertices of the bounding box: the angle between the original and new positions will be allowed to reach a maximum before a new imposter must be generated.

The above discussion has been couched in terms of an imposter for an object. Of course, the idea is that all complex polygonal objects should have associated imposters, and ideally most of the time the renderer will be rendering imposters rather than the geometry. However, this still has a problem: if there are tens of thousands of such objects, for example forming a backdrop to a scene, there is still both the memory and speed overhead in rendering such a large number of individual textures. It would be better somehow to be able to combine objects into clusters and form one overall imposter for each cluster. This was achieved by Shade et al. (1996). They noted that objects that are relatively distant require less frequent updates than those that are close. Hence it might be possible to cluster such distant objects, and create a single image as an imposter for the entire cluster. They achieved this with a hierarchical representation of the scene based on a BSP tree.

Briefly, there is a pre-processing stage where the environment is represented by a BSP tree, where the leaf nodes are convex regions of space each with an associated set of geometric primitives. A balanced tree is preferred. There are two traversals of this tree. In the first traversal each node is marked as being in one of three states. The first state is "culled," if it is outside the view frustum. The second state is "geometry," if the geometry of the node does not meet certain criteria (such as within a specified distance to the viewpoint, projected size above a certain threshhold). The third state is "image," if it is neither culled nor geometry. In this case an imposter is formed for rendering, rather than the geometry. This image imposter might already exist, if we computed it in a previous frame, but we need to make sure it is still valid from the current viewpoint. If the image does not exist or it is no longer valid then we compute it by rendering the subtrees of the current node, either as geometry or from existing caches if they are still valid.

The second traversal is in front-to-back order and we render each node as geometry or image depending on the classification from the previous traversal.

IBR techniques have generated an enormous amount of interest and research over the past few years (see, for example, Popescu *et al.*, 2000). Rendering images is fast, rendering complex geometry is (relatively) slow. The use of IBR is an excellent way to optimize rendering through the use of texturing hardware. Figure 23.16 (color plate) shows, for example, an urban crowd scene with tens of thousands of virtual people. This would be impossible to render in real-time on today's hardware without the use of IBR techniques. In some ways the interest in this approach is an admission of the fact that standard geometry-based rendering hardware is bound by the linear dependence on the number of polygons (triangles) to be rendered. IBR techniques significantly reduce this linear dependence – in the extreme, no matter how many polygons were in the original scene, it always takes the same time to render one image. Hence if the entire scene and all possible viewpoints within it could always be rendered as essentially a single image, then this completely breaks the linear dependency of rendering time on the number of triangles. We turn to such an extreme solution in the next section.

23.5 Light fields

Introduction

An image-based method that provides a kind of brute force solution of the radiance equation of Chapter 3 was introduced by Levoy and Hanrahan (1996) and also by Gortler *et al*. (1996). The radiance equation is a recursive expression

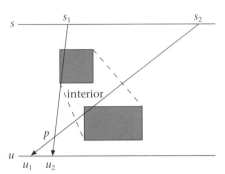

Figure 23.17
Parameterizing the space
of all rays in free-space

for radiance $L(p, \omega)$ where p is any surface point and ω is the set of all directions. Any specific p and ω together form a ray, hence we can think of $L(p, \omega)$ being defined over the set of all rays with origins at points on surfaces. Hence the domain of L is a five-dimensional ray space.

However, radiance is constant along a given direction in "free space," that is, where there are no discontinuities due to intersections with objects. Hence radiance is constant along each direction outside the convex hull of a scene. Figure 23.17 shows a simple 2D example. Consider the set of all rays with origin on line s which terminate on line u. All such rays intersecting the scene consisting of the two shaded boxes can be parameterized in 2D using (s, u). Suppose that a radiance value were (somehow) assigned to each such (s, u), i.e., that $L(s, u)$ was known. Now to form an image, we place an image plane and center of projection in the scene, and collect all those rays passing through the COP which intersect the image plane.

Clearly this parameterization is only valid for views outside the *convex hull* of the scene, for it is only for these rays that the radiance is constant. Views from anywhere in the interior would not be possible, since the radiance abruptly changes along such paths.

For example, suppose an image for a pin-hole camera were required from point p for the view "volume" within the arrowed lines. Then, by capturing the radiance from all the rays between the arrowed lines, such an image could be constructed.

In order to construct the complete set of rays (for the convex hull of the scene) four copies of the "light slab" defined by s and u would be needed – one as shown, another with the directions reversed, and two others with, for example, two vertical lines on either side of the scene. Nevertheless, the overall representation is still two-dimensional, albeit with four such two-dimensional representations.

Such a representation is called a *light field*. A *lumigraph* is the same idea, though with some additional information.

Staying with this two-dimensional example, and with the single "light slab" for s and u, the light field radiance would be a continuous function of s and u, $L(s, u)$. For computational purposes a discrete representation is required. The *two-line parameterization* is illustrated in Figure 23.18 (with a 2D analog). Grids are imposed on the s and u axes, and then all possible lines between each grid

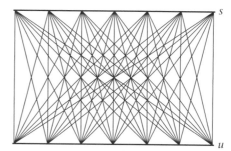

Figure 23.18
Discrete representation
of a light field (one light
slab)

point on one to each grid point on the other form the discrete representation
of the set of all such lines.

The radiance attached to each ray in the light field would be estimated by
choosing each grid point s_i on s as a center of projection with u as the image
plane (and a fixed interval of u as the view plane window). In this way, every
ray that intersects the convex hull of the scene would have an associated
radiance determined by the "rendering" of the image formed by the set of
perspective projections.

For 3D scenes the "two-line" parameterization is replaced by a *two-plane
parameterization* (2PP), the first parameterized by (s, t) and the second by (u, v).
The light field (in fact a subset of it) is then represented by $L(s, t, u, v)$, and
discretized by all possible lines between the two planes defined by a rectangular
grid imposed on each. The st plane is subdivided into squares with each vertex
forming a center of projection, with a rectangular subset of the uv plane as the
view plane window to form an associated image. Hence there is an image
associated with each grid point of the st plane, and a radiance associated with
each (s, t, u, v) combination representing lines that intersect the convex hull
of the scene. This describes how to form one light slab. In order to cover all
possible ray directions, six copies are needed – three orthogonal rotations, with
two directions in each case.

The light field, once constructed, can be used for synthesis of an image from
a virtual camera which does not correspond to the set of cameras on the st
planes. A new image can be formed by sampling the corresponding set of lines
through the viewpoint and in the required directions.

The light field approach was designed as a method of forming new views
from images of real scenes. Suppose digital photographs were taken, under
strict conditions, forming the set of viewpoints and directions associated with
the st planes. Such a set of images can clearly be used to construct a light field.
A virtual light field, that is, a light field for virtual scenes, can also be constructed by using some other rendering system in order to form the images.
The only possible advantage of this is where the rendering system includes
global illumination with a mixture of diffuse and specular surfaces. The light
field approach then provides, in principle, a means for real-time walkthrough
of a globally illuminated scene including glossy and specular reflectors – something which is still not possible in any other way.

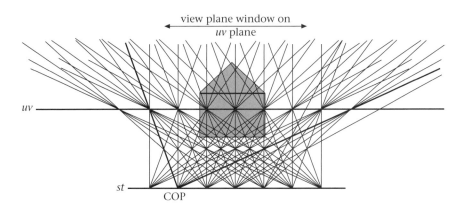

Figure 23.19
An image is created
for each point on the
st plane

In the next sections we consider some issues in more detail. We mainly consider one light slab parameterized by *st* and *uv*. The extensions to multiple light slabs are obvious.

Rendering: interpolation

Suppose that the *st* plane is discretized with an $M \times M$ grid, and the *uv* plane with $N \times N$. Then the light field will consist of M^2 perspective images, each of resolution N^2. This is illustrated in 2D in Figure 23.19; the *st* point marked COP will have an associated image with a view volume between the two thicker lines. All rays converging on this COP will therefore have an associated radiance determined by this image. The image might either have been formed by placing a digital camera in a real scene, or by rendering a virtual scene with the given COP and view volume. The COP is shifted to each point on the *st* plane in turn, thus completing the full light slab. The whole process must be repeated for each of five other light slabs forming the full light field in order to attain a complete ray coverage.

Once the light field has been created it may be used for rendering images from camera positions and orientations outside the convex hull of the scene. First we describe the basic way in which this is carried out.

Figure 23.20 shows the *st* and *uv* planes and a new camera position and orientation. Each ray through a pixel of the virtual camera will intersect the *st* and *uv* planes. For example, the ray *r* intersects the *st* plane at (s_0, t_0) and the *uv* plane at (u_0, v_0). Hence the pixel corresponding to that ray would be set with the value of $L(s_0, t_0, u_0, v_0)$. In other words, each primary ray generated from the camera is used to look up the nearest ray in the 4D space of rays corresponding to the light field.

This method can be implemented very efficiently using texture mapping. Figure 23.21 shows one grid point (s_i, t_j) on the *st* plane, and a square containing all the points on the plane that would be approximated by this particular grid point. Now the square projects to points *a*, *b*, *c*, *d* on the *uv* plane.

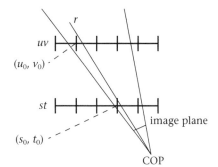

Figure 23.20
Synthesizing an image
for a new view

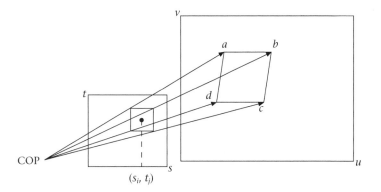

Figure 23.21
Using texture mapping

Corresponding to (s_i, t_j) there is an image on the *uv* plane. This image may be used as a texture to render the *st* square for (s_i, t_j), with texture coordinates given by *a, b, c, d*. In this approach, therefore, the square corresponding to each *st* grid point is rendered using as a texture map the image corresponding to that grid point. This involves finding the set of texture coordinates for each square, but since neighboring squares will share grid points the number of projections required is approximately the number of squares drawn. Of course, not all M^2 squares would be rendered, depending on the view volume of the camera.

In practice, this simplistic technique will lead to significant aliasing. An alternative scheme is to use quadrilinear interpolation. There are four nearest neighbors to the intersection point on the *st* plane, and four nearest neighbors on the *uv* plane, as shown in Figure 23.22. Consider first interpolation on *s* only, with all other parameters fixed. (EQ 23.1) shows an identity expression for *s* as a barycentric combination of s_0 and s_1.

$$s = \left(\frac{s_1 - s}{s_1 - s_0}\right)s_0 + \left(\frac{s - s_0}{s_1 - s_0}\right)s_1$$

or

$$s = \alpha_0 s_0 + \alpha_1 s_1$$

where $\alpha_0 + \alpha_1 = 1$

(EQ 23.1)

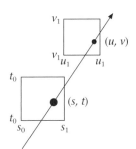

Figure 23.22
Quadrilinear interpolation

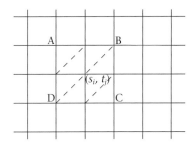

Figure 23.23
Support for the
quadrilinear basis

Quadrilinear interpolation makes the assumption that the L function is itself affine (of course it will not be so). Hence applying this to (EQ 23.1) we obtain:

$$L(s, t_0, u_0, v_0) = \left(\frac{s_1 - s}{s_1 - s_0}\right)L(s_0, t_0, u_0, v_0) + \left(\frac{s - s_0}{s_1 - s_0}\right)L(s_1, t_0, u_0, v_0)$$

$$= \alpha_0 L(s_0, t_0, u_0, v_0) + \alpha_1 L(s_1, t_0, u_0, v_0)$$

(EQ 23.2)

Repeating this argument for each of the parameters we obtain:

$$L(s, t, u, v) = \sum_{i=0}^{1}\sum_{j=0}^{1}\sum_{k=0}^{1}\sum_{l=0}^{1}\alpha_i\beta_j\gamma_k\delta_l L(s_i, t_j, u_k, v_l)$$

(EQ 23.3)

where each of the β_j, γ_k, δ_l are defined in the same way as α_i in (EQ 23.1), and correspond to t, u, and v respectively. Now, of course, all the interpolated s, t, u, v values can be easily found using a method similar to finding interpolated texture coordinates during the process of rendering the st squares and uv squares as polygons.

Gortler *et al.* (1996) show that this method cannot exactly be implemented using the texture mapping hardware. The support for the quadrilinear interpolation at (s_i, t_j) extends out to ABCD in Figure 23.23, and hence neighboring grid points will have overlapping supports. Consider the six triangles surrounding the grid point. Gortler *et al.* show that if each of these six triangles is rendered with texture mapping as before plus alpha blending, where $\alpha = 1$ at the grid point and $\alpha = 0$ at the other triangle vertices, then this is equivalent to linear interpolation on st and bilinear interpolation on uv. It is suggested that results are not visually distinguishable from full bilinear interpolation.

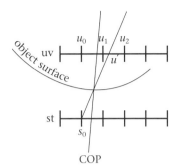

Figure 23.24
Depth correction

Gortler *et al*. (1996) show that keeping some geometric information together with the light field rays can lead to an improvement in radiance estimation. Figure 23.24 shows a viewing ray with origin at the COP intersecting an object surface. Now the nearest grid point on the *st* plane is shown as s_0, and normally u_0 and u_1 would be used for interpolation. However, it is clear that more accurate information can be obtained from the ray s_0 through u', and therefore the better interpolation would be between u_1 and u_2. Gortler *et al*. suggests storing a polygonal mesh approximating the scene geometry in order to allow for such depth corrections. This approach can result in less blurred images for the same *st* resolution, since a compensation is introduced for the errors involved in the interpolation. A further analysis concerned with speed-up to the rendering process, in particular trade-offs between quality and time, can be found in Sloan *et al*. (1997).

Representing light fields

The 2PP has obvious computational advantages, especially with respect to storage (rectangular images) and the use of rendering (especially texture) hardware for reconstruction. However, the representation does not provide a uniform distribution of rays in 4-space – in other words, if we think of any arbitrary ray in space, not all rays are equally likely to have the same degree of approximation of representation in the light field space. In practice, what this means is that the quality of the rendered image will be a function of the viewpoint and viewing direction. Viewpoints near the center of the *st* plane, and directions orthogonal to this plane, will result in better images than viewpoints off to one side with oblique viewing directions – simply because the number and distribution of rays will be different at such positions. A thorough analysis of the 2PP as a 4D space can be found in Gu *et al*. (1997).

Camahort and Fussel (1999) carried out a theoretical study of three alternative light field representations – the 2PP as above, a two-sphere representation (2SP), and a direction and point representation (DPP). These were considered by Camahort *et al*. (1998). The 2SP involves placing a bounding sphere around the scene, and partitioning the sphere into a uniform grid. Then all connections between all vertices on the sphere form the parameterization. The DPP similarly involves placing a sphere around the scene. Now choose a point uniformly at random on the surface of the sphere. This defines a vector from the origin through that point. Consider the plane orthogonal to that vector and through the center of the sphere, and bounded by the sphere (i.e., a disk at the origin of the sphere). Now choose a uniformly distributed set of points on the disk as the origin of rays in the same direction as the original vector. The collection of all such rays will form a uniformly distributed set of rays in ray space. Each ray is represented by its direction, and its intersection on the disk through the origin. A different two-sphere parameterization was introduced in Ihm *et al.* (1997) which puts a bounding sphere around the scene, and then a set of small spheres on the surface of the bounding spheres to represent directions. They also introduce an efficient wavelet compression scheme for this data structure.

Camahort and Fussel (1999) provide an in-depth analysis of these different schemes (as well as a thorough discussion of uniformity), and show that the direction and point approach results in less rendering bias, and corrections that are simple to apply.

Practical issues

There are a number of practical issues to consider. First, what is the ideal placement of the *st* and *uv* planes? Clearly *st* is outside of the scene, whereas *uv* should be through the center of the scene. Ideally the geometry of the scene should be as close as possible to the *uv* plane, so that the grid points are (very rough!) approximations to surface geometry. In practice, this means that light fields cannot adequately represent scenes of significant depth. A distribution of rays which is adequate for the representation of near surfaces will not be sufficient for the representation of far-away surfaces.

What resolutions should be used for M and N? The latter is more important since, as suggested, it determines the degree of approximation of scene geometry. The higher the resolution on the *uv* plane, the greater the accuracy of this representation. Hence in practice $N > M$, and values of $N = 256$ and $M = 32$ have been shown to be sufficient for images of size 256×256.

Assume that this resolution is used, then one light slab will require 2^{26} rays. Suppose each ray carries 3 bytes, then 192 MB is needed, and therefore over 1 GB for a full light field (6 light slabs). Remember that this will enable only static scene walkthrough and relatively low resolution images. Clearly a compression scheme is needed! Levoy and Hanrahan (1996) used vector quantization (Gersho and Gray, 1992). This is a compression scheme, where the data set is partitioned into clusters, each being represented by one vector found during a training phase. Each vector corresponds to a codebook which stores indices of the members of the cluster which it represents. Decoding is a very fast operation – especially useful in the context of rendering. Levoy and Hanrahan demonstrated compression ratios of more than 100:1 using this scheme.

Further developments

The original light field/lumigraph papers were published in 1996. Since then, a great deal of interest has been generated, and we briefly summarize some of the significant developments.

As mentioned earlier, one of the drawbacks of the light field scheme is that it is most appropriate for scenes without significant depth. Isaksen *et al.* (2000) discuss how to overcome this problem, in addition to supporting depth-of-field effects and showing how light fields can be used for the basis of auto-stereoscopic display systems. This latter development has also taken up in detail in Perlin *et al.* (2000).

The light field approach is clearly for static scene walkthrough rather than interaction with objects in the scene. Nevertheless, Seitz and Kutulakos (1998) allow some degree of interaction by showing how it is possible to edit one image of a scene and propagate the changes to all other images, maintaining overall consistency among all the images.

A surface light field is a light field consisting of rays emanating from surfaces – in principle, for any point on a surface, the set of all rays leaving that point with their associated radiances. Wood *et al.* (2000) show how to construct, edit, and display such light fields for real scenes. An important general contribution is to show how such compressed light fields may be directly rendered from the compressed representation.

The theory of light field representations was considered in Camahort and Fussel (1999) as discussed earlier. Chai *et al.* (2000) provide a thorough analysis of sampling requirements. This includes a minimum sampling curve which provides the relationship between scene complexity, output resolution, and the image sampling.

Summary

This section has introduced the idea of light fields as an image-based approach to providing a "solution" to the radiance equation. The LF approach is almost "brute force" for this purpose – it works with a discrete representation of all possible rays covering a scene, and then assigns radiance to those rays by image rendering. Based on a finite sample of images, which have been used to color rays, it was shown how images from new viewpoints can be constructed. There was some discussion of efficient rendering using the texture mapping hardware in the context of interpolation schemes. Alternative schemes for representing a uniform set of rays were considered, followed by a brief discussion of recent developments.

In this section we have concentrated on the basic ideas of LFs, without considering the source of the images from which they are constructed. The most widespread use of light fields is for virtual walkthroughs of real scenes. A stunning application of light fields in the area of cultural heritage is shown in plate P.3.

23.6 Full screen anti-aliasing

One of the fundamental problems with the real-time graphics pipeline is that scan-converting shapes to the screen or sampling a texture can result in aliasing. For example, in "Rasterization of line segments" on page 366, aliasing occurred when drawing line segments because a continuous shape was approximated by square pixels.

One way to combat this problem is by full screen anti-aliasing. This involves rendering the image several times from slightly different positions and then composing the result. This process is also called *super-sampling*, since it is analogous to rendering to a larger image and then down-sampling to provide the required image. If the screen is rendered N times there is a corresponding drop in frame rate by a factor of N for most renderers, but this technique is sometimes implemented in hardware with little or no time penalty. Each of the individual frames is rendered from a camera whose position is jittered from the original position by a factor of less than one pixel. Current graphics hardware aids the process of composition, by providing an *accumulation buffer* (Haeberli and Akeley, 1990). The accumulation buffer holds RGBA (where A is an alpha channel) color values, as do the color buffers. It is not possible to render directly to the accumulation buffer; it must be accessed through pixel region copying. The use of the accumulation buffer is illustrated by the following steps:

```
render screen from jittered position 0
load accumulation buffer with weighting 1.0/N
render screen from jitteredPosition 1
add to accumulation with weighting 1.0/N
render screen from jittered position 2
add to accumulation with weighting 1.0/N
...
render screen from jittered position n-1
add to accumulation with weighting 1.0/N
display completed accumulation buffer
```

After each screen is rendered it is added to the accumulation buffer with a weighting of 1.0/N. After N images have been accumulated, this accumulation buffer is then displayed to the screen. Figure 23.25 (color plate) shows an example of full screen anti-aliasing. The teapots on the left are a single frame rendering, and the teapots on the right are a rendering composed from eight jittered renderings.

In OpenGL the jittered camera rendering can be set up in the following manner, which is derived from an example in the "Red Book" (Woo *et al.*, 1999).

```
/* jitteredFrustum()
 * The first 6 arguments are identical to the glFrustum() call.
 * pixdx and pixdy are anti-alias jitter in pixels.
 */

void jitteredFrustum(GLdouble left, GLdouble right, GLdouble bottom,
   GLdouble top, GLdouble near, GLdouble far, GLdouble pixdx,
   GLdouble pixdy) {

   GLdouble xwsize, ywsize;
   GLdouble dx, dy;
   GLint viewport[4];

   glGetIntegerv (GL_VIEWPORT, viewport);

   xwsize = right - left;
   ywsize = top - bottom;

   dx = -(pixdx*xwsize/(GLdouble) viewport[2]);
   dy = -(pixdy*ywsize/(GLdouble) viewport[3]);

   glMatrixMode(GL_PROJECTION);
   glLoadIdentity();
   glFrustum (left + dx, right + dx, bottom + dy, top + dy, near,
   far);
   glMatrixMode(GL_MODELVIEW);
   glLoadIdentity();
}

/* jitteredPerspective()
 *
 * The first 4 arguments are identical to the gluPerspective() call.
 * pixdx and pixdy are anti-alias jitter in pixels.
 */

void jitteredPerspective(GLdouble fovy, GLdouble aspect,
   GLdouble near, GLdouble far, GLdouble pixdx, GLdouble pixdy){

GLdouble fov2,left,right,bottom,top;

   fov2 = ((fovy*PI_)/180.0)/2.0;

   top = near/(cos(fov2)/sin(fov2));
   bottom = -top;

   right = top * aspect;
   left = -right;

   jitteredFrustum (left, right, bottom, top, near, far, pixdx, pixdy);
}
```

The definition of these jittered cameras is very similar to the usual `glFrustrum` and `gluPerspective` functions (see "Creating 3D stereo views" on page 217). The following function demonstrates how these camera functions might be used in combination with the accumulation buffer. In this function `displayObjects` goes through the program data structures or scene graph to describe the actual scene.

```
#define ACSIZE8

void display(void)
{
  GLint viewport[4];
  int jitter;

  glGetIntegerv (GL_VIEWPORT, viewport);

  if (doAntialias) {
    glClear(GL_ACCUM_BUFFER_BIT);
    for (jitter = 0; jitter < ACSIZE; jitter++) {
      glClear(GL_COLOR_BUFFER_BIT | GL_DEPTH_BUFFER_BIT);
      jitteredPerspective (50.0,
        (GLdouble) viewport[2]/(GLdouble) viewport[3],
          1.0, 15.0, j8[jitter].x, j8[jitter].y);
      displayObjects ();
      glAccum(GL_ACCUM, 1.0/ACSIZE);
    }
    glAccum (GL_RETURN, 1.0);
  }
  else {
    glClear(GL_COLOR_BUFFER_BIT | GL_DEPTH_BUFFER_BIT);
    glMatrixMode(GL_PROJECTION);
    glLoadIdentity();
    gluPerspective(50.0,
      (GLdouble) viewport[2]/(GLdouble) viewport[3], 1.0, 15.0);
    glMatrixMode(GL_MODELVIEW);
    glLoadIdentity();
    displayObjects ();
  }
  glFlush();
  glutSwapBuffers();
}
```

23.7   VRML examples

Both static level of detail and billboards are supported in VRML97. The example in Figure 23.12 was described using the VRML given in Figure 23.26. The `Inline` node is a mechanism to include other files in the scene rather than having everything in one file. The file `bunny_high.wrl` contains the high detail object, `bunny_low.wrl` contains the low detail version. We also use the

```
#VRML V2.0 utf8

DirectionalLight
  intensity 0.8
{

Transform {
  translation 0.2 0 0
  children [
    DEF BUNNY1 Inline {
      Url "bunny_high.wrl"
    }
  ]
}

Transform {
  translation -0.2 0 0
  children [
    DEF BUNNY2 Inline {
      Url "bunny_low.wrl"
    }
  ]
}
```

```
Transform {
  translation 0 0 0
  children [
    LOD {
      range [20.0]
      level [
        USE BUNNY1,
        USE BUNNY2
      ]
    }
  ]
}
```

Figure 23.26
VRML97 level of detail example

```
#VRML V2.0 utf8
Transform {
  translation 0 0 0
  children [
    DEF MY_BOX Shape {
      appearance Appearance {
        texture ImageTexture {
          url ["default.jpg"]
        }
      }
      geometry Box {
        size 2 2 2
      }
    }
  ]
}

Transform {
  translation 3 0 0
  children [
    Billboard {
      axisOfRotation 0 1 0
      children [
        USE MY_BOX
      ]
    }
  ]
}

Transform {
  translation -3 0 0
  children [
    Billboard {
      axisOfRotation 0 0 0
      children [
        USE MY_BOX
      ]
    }
  ]
}
```

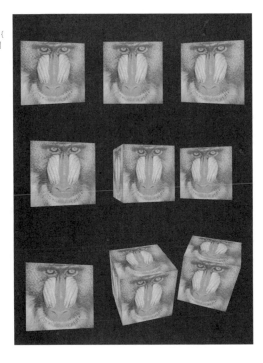

Figure 23.25
VRML97 billboard example

DEF/USE mechanism to share the static objects with the level of detail node. There is a single value in the range field of the *LOD* node, so at 20.0 from the viewpoint we switch from low to high detail or vice versa.

VRML97 also has billboard nodes. The axis about which to revolve is set with the axisOfRotation field. If the axis is specified as 0 0 0, then the object is viewpoint facing. That is, the local Z axis of the object points directly as the viewpoint, and the local Y axis is parallel to the VUV of the camera.

The example in Figure 23.27 shows two types of billboard, axis rotational and viewpoint facing. In each row of the figure, the left-hand box is a viewpoint-facing billboard, the center box is not a billboard, and the right-hand box is an axis rotational billboard. The first row of boxes shows the view from the starting position. In the second row, as the camera yaws (rotation about Y) both the left- and right-hand billboards look similar. In the third row the camera pitches as well (rotation about X) and the difference between viewpoint-facing and axis rotational billboards becomes clear.

(23.8) Summary

This chapter has surveyed some current techniques for real-time processing. We started with visibility culling, that is, a process designed to try to minimize the set of polygons ultimately sent for display to only those that are likely to be visible. Once objects are to be rendered, a second technique is to try to reduce their rendering time by adjusting their level of detail. Another method of reducing rendering time is to use imposters and billboards. The first are texture maps that hold images close to what would have been rendered with a direct rendering of the geometry. Clearly, rendering the texture map results in significant saving while it is still current (that is, represents the geometry to a good enough accuracy). Billboards are also texture maps that represent specific complex objects (such as trees) that turn to face the viewpoint as this dynamically changes through an interactive session. If these are done carefully enough, the participant in a VE with such billboards would not notice that in fact their geometry is "flat." We then considered a radically different approach to rendering based on the idea of light fields. Here the objective is to synthesize new views from a large set of existing images. A major advantage of light fields is that their rendering time is independent of the original scene geometry. Finally we considered a simple anti-aliasing technique illustrating the use of the underlying graphics hardware, accessed via OpenGL.

Appendix A
Introduction to VRML

A.1   Introduction

The Virtual Reality Modeling Language (VRML, 1997) is a standard that specifies a file format for the description of 3D scenes and a mechanism for describing animation, interaction, and simulation of those scenes. A VRML scene is typically displayed in a VRML browser such as Blaxxun's Contact which is a plug-in to an HTML browser (Blaxxun, HTTP). VRML was designed to be distributed across the World Wide Web and a VRML file can be embedded within a HTML document. A VRML file can be identified by a ".wrl" file name extension, and the corresponding MIME type is *model/vrml*.

Figure A.1 (color plate) shows a view of a reconstruction of the Lindos temple on the island of Rhodes (COVEN, HTTP) within Blaxxun's Contact VRML browser. The controls on the bottom of the screen allow the user to navigate about the scene and some of the objects within the scene are "active" in that they react to the user moving the cursor over them or clicking on them. Thus, unlike other 3D file formats such as VRML1.0 which only describe a static scene, a VRML97 scene evolves over time. We are using an over-the-shoulder view of our virtual avatar which is the blue humanoid in the middle of the picture (refer to "Simulation of body" on page 439).

In this appendix we give an overview of VRML in three stages. The first stage outlines the basics of the scene graph with a description of hierarchy, geometry, and appearance. The second stage discusses animation and the third stage discusses the interaction and scripting capabilities.

In addition, you will find additional discussion of some nodes among the other chapters where appropriate. In particular:

- materials in "Illumination in VRML97" on page 153;
- camera in "VRML97 examples" on page 160;
- geometry and transformations in "Using VRML97" on page 181;
- texturing in "VRML97 examples" on page 293;
- interaction and vehicles in "VRML examples" on page 462;
- LOD and billboards in "VRML examples" on page 522.

VRML as scene description

Nodes and fields

A VRML file contains a set of *Nodes* that describe the scene. Each node is defined with several *Fields*. For example, VRML has a Cone node that allows the author to describe a cone with four fields, bottomRadius, height, side, and bottom. The specification of the fields for Cone is shown below.

```
Cone {
   field SFFloat bottomRadius 1
   field SFFloat height       2
   field SFBool  side         TRUE
   field SFBool  bottom       TRUE
}
```

For each field there is a field *type* (in this case SFFloat or SFBool – floating point number or boolean), the field name, and the default value for the field. In specifying a cone, the role of bottomRadius and height should be obvious. The fields bottom and side specify whether the cone has a bottom or a side to the geometry. Setting bottom to FALSE, for example, makes the cone open at the wide end.

When a cone node is actually written in a VRML file, only the field name and the value are given, as in the following example:

```
Cone {
  height 5
  bottom FALSE
}
```

Here, because neither bottomRadius nor side was set, they assume their default values (1 and TRUE respectively).

Fields come in four flavors, plain field, eventIn, eventOut, and exposedField. We will return to the use of each of these in "VRML as animation description" on page 531 For the moment, it is sufficient to say that for description of static geometry only `fields` and `exposedFields` are necessary. There are also single-valued fields (denoted by the `SF` prefix) and multiple-valued fields (prefixed by `MF`). To add further complexity, the type of a field can be a single node or multiple nodes (`SFNode` or `MFNode` respectively). This will become clearer with the following examples.

Technicalities

Every VRML97 file starts "`#VRML V2.0 utf8`". The following piece of code gives a description of a sphere with a green material.

```
#VRML V2.0 utf8

  Transform {
    children [
    Shape {
      appearance Appearance {
        material Material {
          diffuseColor 0.1 0.7 0.2
        }
      }
      geometry Sphere {
        radius 2
      }
    }
  ]
}
```

A hash ("#") at the start of any line apart from the first indicates a comment that will be ignored by the VRML browser.

VRML97 was designed for use on the web so it is usually integrated into a web page. This is usually done using a plug-in, and the following piece of HTML code illustrates how the VRML is embedded onto the page. Note that the size of the rendering window, and thus the aspect ratio of the resulting camera view, is specified within the HTML, not the VRML.

```
<html>
  <head>
    <title>VRML - Example1</title>
  </head>

<body>
  <h1>VRML - Example1 </h1>
    <center>
      <embed src="example1.wrl" border=0 height="300" width="400">
    </center>
  </body>
</html>
```

Shapes and geometry

The basic components of a 3D scene are a set of *Shapes* that define the visible objects. Each `Shape` has a *geometry field* that contains a `Geometry` node and an *appearance field* that contains an `Appearance` node. The definition of a `Shape` node is as follows (note the field types):

```
Shape {
  exposedField SFNode appearance NULL
  exposedField SFNode geometry NULL
}
```

In the previous example, the geometry node was a sphere:

```
geometry Sphere {
  radius 2
}
```

and the appearance node included a material with a diffuse color:

```
appearance Appearance {
  material Material {
    diffuseColor 0.1 0.7 0.2
  }
}
```

The basic geometry nodes include `Box`, `Sphere`, `Cylinder`, `Cone`, and `Text`. Figure A.2 gives some basic examples that illustrate the principal fields in each of the corresponding nodes.

The most flexible geometry node, `IndexedFaceSet`, is described in "Using VRML97" on page 181.

An appearance node specifies the look of an object and it is comprised of potentially three fields: a `Material` node, a `Texture` node, and a `Texture-Transform` node.

The details of the `Material` node are covered in "Illumination in VRML97" on page 153. `Texture` and `TextureTransform` are covered in "VRML97 examples" on page 293.

Groups, transformations, and scene graphs

Once a set of objects has been created with geometry and appearance, they must be positioned within the scene. A `Transform` node is used for this purpose. The details of transformations are given in "Using VRML97" on page 181.

A useful tool in constructing scene graphs is the `Group` node. This provides a node in the scene graph which has no intrinsic properties. This gives it the same role as a transform node with an identity transformation. Groups are

```
Box {
   size 2.0 2.0 2.0
}

Sphere {
   radius 1.5
}

Cylinder {
   height 2.0
   radius 1.0
}

Cone {
   radius 1.3
   height 1.8
}

Text {
   string ["Hi!"]
   fontStyle FontStyle {
      family "TYPEWRITER"
      style "ITALIC"
   }
}
```

Figure A.2
Examples of the five basic geometry nodes

useful for identifying collections of objects that serve a particular role, and it is especially useful when elements of the scene graph are shared.

VRML97 supports sharing of nodes to reduce both the size of the files and the size of the eventual scene graph in memory. Any node in the scene graph can be designated as a sharable node with the DEF keyword. A sharable node can then be reused later with the USE keyword (for another example and a longer description of DEF and USE, see "Using VRML97" on page 181). Both DEF and USE can be nested and this allows very large models with repetitive elements to be stored in a compact manner. In the example in Figure A.3 the DEF ONE_BOX statement creates a simple textured box and labels that part of the scene graph for future reuse (see "VRML97 examples" on page 293 for a description of texture mapping in VRML97). When we USE the ONE_BOX we get a copy of those nodes at the current point in the scene graph. Note how we have wrapped these first two boxes in a Group node, and have given that pair the name PAIR_BOX. We then reuse PAIR_BOX to create a total of four boxes.

```
DEF PAIR_BOX Group {
  children [
    Transform {
      translation -2 0 0
        children [
        DEF ONE_BOX Shape {
          appearance Appearance {
            texture ImageTexture {
              url ["default.jpg"]
            }
          }
          geometry Box {
            size 2 2 2
          }
        }
      ]
    }
    Transform {
      translation 2 0 0
      children [
        USE ONE_BOX
      ]
    }
  ]
}

Transform {
  translation 0 2 0
    children [
      USE PAIR_BOX
    ]
}
```

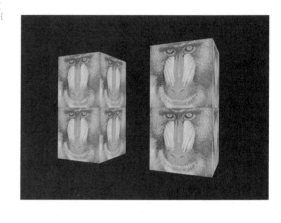

Figure A.3
Example of DEF/USE
and Group

Note that although any node can be DEFed, attention must be paid to places where that node can be USEed. VRML nodes are implicitly typed. If a field is of the general type SFNode or MFNode, there is a subtype implied by the situation of use. Thus only Material nodes can be used for the value of the material field of the Appearance node, and USEing a node that was attached to a Geometry node with the corresponding DEF would be illegal.

Lights

Light nodes provide illumination in the scene. Light interacts with the materials of objects in order to produce the final image that is seen within the VRML browser. Three types of light are supported: DirectionalLight, PointLight, and SpotLight. DirectionalLight specifies light rays that travel in parallel lines, for example sunlight. PointLight specifies light rays that originate from a specific point and illuminate in all directions. A SpotLight specifies light rays that originate from a point but only travel in certain directions with the possibility of specifying different intensities of light over the volume illuminated. The effect of SpotLight and PointLight attenuate over distance. Figure A.4 (color plate) shows an example of each light.

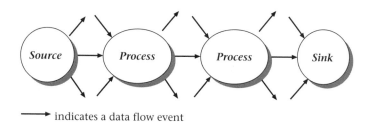

Figure A.5
Example of an abstract
data flow scheme

⟶ indicates a data flow event

A.3

VRML as animation description

One of the most important factors for VRML97's success on the web is its ability to define animated models. Simple animation can be specified with nodes and does not require the use of any scripting. A data flow model is used to describe the evolution of the animation over time.

Abstract data flow

An abstract view of data flow is shown in Figure A.5. A graph structure is built of nodes and arcs where nodes represent data processing and arcs represent the transfer of data from one node to another. Certain nodes constantly generate values at a steady rate. In a general model they might be clocks or real-world sensing devices such as a user-interface device. The data *events* that are generated are transferred to other nodes as specified by the arcs, where they are processed, and these nodes then might generate further data events. Eventually data is received at a node that propagates no further events. Data flow models are useful for describing systems where time-driven data processing is the most common operation. Some important properties are that a data event generated by a node might be sent to more than one destination. Similarly, a node might receive data events from several sources.

Fields revisited

Recall that nodes are made up of fields (which might be other nodes). Fields come in four flavors: `field`, `exposedField`, `eventOut`, `eventIn`. A plain `field` may only be set at initialization. `eventIns` are fields that can be set by the data flow. `eventOuts` are fields that can not be set, only read. `exposed-Fields` can be set at initialization and set and read at run-time.

We have already seen several types of field such as `SFBool` and `SFVec3f`. The complete list of types includes the following single-valued fields: `SFBool`,

SFVec2f, SFVec3f, SFRotation, SFFloat, SFNode, SFString, SFColor, SFTime, SFImage, and SFInt32, and the corresponding multi-valued fields: MFColor, MFFloat, MFInt32, MFNode, MFRotation, MFString, MFTime, MFVec2f, and MFVec3f.

The following examples illustrate the use of the different classes and types of field by looking at the node specification and determining which fields can be set and/or read and/or written at run-time.

```
Box {
  field SFVec3f size 2 2 2
}
```

The size of a box is a plain field so it can only be set at initialization time.

```
Shape {
  exposedField SFNode appearance NULL
  exposedField SFNode geometry NULL
}
```

Both the geometry and appearance of a Shape node are exposedField, so either can be set at initialization and either can be changed at run-time.

```
OrientationInterpolator {
  eventIn SFFloat set_fraction
  eventOut SFRotation value_changed
  exposedField MFFloat key []
  exposedField MFRotation keyValue []
}
```

The OrientationInterpolator node is discussed on the next page in "Animation, TimeSensors and Interpolators". It takes in a single float value between 0 and 1, and outputs a rotation value (SFRotation). The different flavors of the fields imply that the current float value can not be read, and that the current rotation value can not be set directly, but can only be read. Neither of these values has an initial value. The key and keyValue fields specify how float values map onto rotation values. Since these are exposed fields, they can be set at initialization time and changed and read at run-time.

Data flow and routes

In the abstract data flow model, data values flow from left to right. In VRML this corresponds to data flowing from an eventOut field or exposedField to an eventIn or exposedField. In order to make such connections we use a ROUTE statement.

ROUTE statements identify the node and field pairs to be connected. The nodes to connect are identified by the name they were given with DEF. See

"Groups, transformations and scene graphs" on page 528 for a description of the DEF/USE mechanism. In VRML, both fan-in and fan-out of routes are allowed. This implies, for example, that multiple routes might affect the appearance of a Shape, or that a particular OrientationInterpolator might drive the orientation of multiple Transform nodes. Each event in the data flow is time-stamped and data flow occurs "instantaneously" in that all events in the same cascade are given the same time stamp. Events are processed in time stamp order, so one cascade from a source completes before the next source fires. With the ROUTE mechanism, it is possible to create circular routes, but these are broken by not allowing the generation of an event on the data flow with the same time stamp and value as a previous event on that route.

Animation, TimeSensors, and Interpolators

The data flow mechanism is used to generate animation through the use of *TimeSensors* and *Interpolators*. We illustrate these through the example in Figure A.6 which gives some example code and a diagrammatic representation of the data flow for a rotating box.

In this example we see a basic use of the TimeSensor to generate a periodic value. The TimeSensor continuously (*loop TRUE*) generates fractional float values between 0 and 1. The value changes smoothly from 0 to 1 over 2 seconds (cycleInteral 2.0), after which it resets instantaneously to 0 and continues.

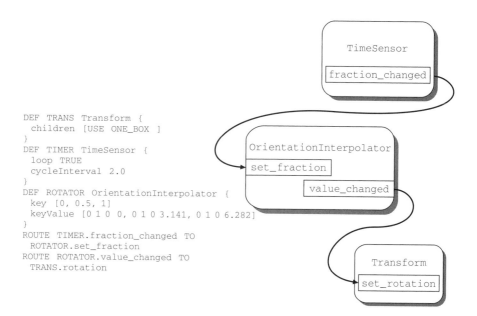

```
DEF TRANS Transform {
  children [USE ONE_BOX ]
}
DEF TIMER TimeSensor {
  loop TRUE
  cycleInterval 2.0
}
DEF ROTATOR OrientationInterpolator {
  key [0, 0.5, 1]
  keyValue [0 1 0 0, 0 1 0 3.141, 0 1 0 6.282]
}
ROUTE TIMER.fraction_changed TO
  ROTATOR.set_fraction
ROUTE ROTATOR.value_changed TO
  TRANS.rotation
```

Figure A.6
Rotating textured
cube example

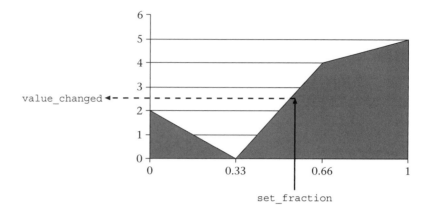

Figure A.7
Graph of key against
keyValue for the
ScalarInterpolator
example

The OrientationInterpolator, like all interpolators, takes in a value between 0 and 1. It generates an orientation which is then routed to a Transform node. The overall effect is to generate an object that rotates continuously.

TimeSensor is a complex node that can be used to generate continuous or single execution loops. The TimeSensor can be triggered by setting a start and end time for operation. A more complex example is given in the following section.

OrientationInterpolator is one of a set of interpolators that all operate in a similar manner. We illustrate the operation of interpolators by the simplest example, ScalarInterpolator, but the techniques also apply to the other interpolators, OrientationInterpolator, ColorInterpolator, CoordinateInterpolator, NormalInterpolator, and PositionInterpolator.

ScalarInterpolator is specified as follows:

```
ScalarInterpolator {
    eventIn SFFloat  set_fraction
    exposedField MFFloat  key []
    exposedField MFFloat  keyValue []
    eventOut SFFloat  value_changed
}
```

The exposedFields, key and keyValue contain the same number of elements[1] and they define a mapping from set_fraction to value_changed. For example

```
key [0, 0.33, 0.66, 1]
    keyValue [2.0, 0.0, 4.0, 5.0]
```

defines the mapping illustrated in the graph in Figure A.7.

---

1. For a node such as CoordinateInterpolator, each keyValue element is a set of coordinates so the total length of keyValue is a integer multiple of the length of key.

The `value_changed` is derived from a simple interpolation between the `keyValues` of the `key` that bound the `set_fraction` event. Obviously there must only be a single `keyValue` for each `key` and thus the `keys` are defined in monotonically increasing order.

A.4   VRML as interactive experience

Scripting

Sensors and interpolators alone are not sufficient to describe complex behaviors. VRML supports scripting of behaviors through the `Script` node. This allows the scene author to create a node with arbitrary fields that they can program to provide the required functionality.

Currently VRML97 supports two scripting languages: JavaScript and Java. Both languages have a similar application programming interface with three broad areas of functionality: data flow event handling, scene graph manipulation, and VRML browser interface.

The main purpose of a `Script` node is to provide complex data processing in cascades of data flow events. A `Script` node identifies a set of input fields to which it will respond when there are events on them. A data flow cascade that results in one of those input fields being set will cause a function to be called within the `Script`. The actual mechanism and name of script execution depends on the scripting language. In JavaScript, for example, the scene author creates a function with the same name as the input field. The `Script` node then performs some task on the input data and can optionally trigger a further event cascade by writing to an output field.

We illustrate the data flow processing behavior with the examples in Figures A.8 and A.9. Figure A.8 shows the outline of the VRML code for a cow model that can be rotated with a `SphereSensor`, and that emits a 'moo' when it is turned upside down and righted again. Figure A.9 shows the corresponding routes between the nodes.

Not only do `Script` nodes provide general data flow processing capabilities, they can also create and delete nodes in the scene graph, and create and delete `ROUTE`s between nodes. Finally, there is also a small set of functionality available to scripts to control and query the browser itself. Capabilities include forcing a new scene to be loaded or querying the current frame rate. For further discussion of these capabilities and more detail on scripting in general, the reader is referred to a more in-depth tutorial on VRML97 (e.g., Carey and Bell, 1997).

```
#VRML V2.0 utf8

Group {
   children [
      DEF ROT SphereSensor {
      }
      ,
      DEF TRANS Transform {
         translation 0 0 0
         children [
            Inline {
               url "cow-model.wrl"
            },
            Sound {
            source DEF
               MOO_SOUND
                  AudioClip {
                     url "moo.wav"
                  }
            }
         ]
      }
   ]
}

ROUTE ROT.rotation_changed
   TO TRANS.set_rotation
```

```
DEF MOOER Script  {
   eventIn SFRotation set_rotation
   eventOut SFTime mooTime

   field SFBool last_updir TRUE
   field SFBool first TRUE
   field SFBool lastup TRUE
   url "javascript:

function set_rotation(value, timestamp){
   updir = value.multVec(new SFVec3f(0,1,0));
   up = (updir.y > 0.0);
   if (first) {
      lastup = up;
      first = false;
   } else {
      if ((!lastup) && up) {
         mooTime = timestamp;
      }
      lastup = up;
   }
}
"
}

ROUTE TRANS.rotation_changed
   TO MOOER.set_rotation
ROUTE MOOER.mooTime TO MOO_SOUND.startTime
```

Figure A.8
VRML code for the cow example

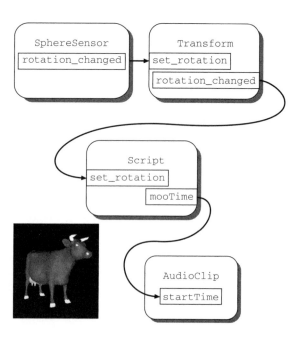

Figure A.9
Data flow for the
cow example

A.5 ## Summary

This appendix has given an overview of VRML that is sufficient to enable the reader to understand and experiment with the VRML examples in this book. We have not covered many of the multimedia aspects of VRML such as movie textures and spatialized audio, nor have we delved very deeply into the scripting aspects of VRML. We have also not touched upon the interesting and powerful PROTO mechanism which allows new node types to be defined.

Further examples may be seen at many sites on the web. A good starting point is the Web3D Consortium's page `http://www.web3d.org`.

References

Airey, J.M., Rohlf, J.H., and Brooks, Jr., F.P. (1990). Towards image realism with interactive update rates in complex virtual building environments, *Computer Graphics* (1990 Symposium on Interactive 3D Graphics), 24(2), 41–50.

Amanatides, J. (1984) Ray tracing with cones, *Computer Graphics (ACM SIG-GRAPH) Annual Conference Series*, 18, 129–135. Addison-Wesley.

Amanatides, J. (1987) A fast voxel traversal algorithm for ray tracing, *Proc. Eurographics 87*, pp. 3–10.

Andreev, R.D. (1989) Algorithm for clipping arbitrary polygons, *Computer Graphics Forum*, 8(3), 183–91.

Appel, A. (1968) Some techniques for shading machine renderings of solids, *Proc. AFIPS JSCC 1968*, 32, 37–45.

Arvo, J. and Kirk, D. (1987) Fast ray tracing by ray classification, *Computer Graphics (ACM SIGGRAPH) Annual Conference Series*, 21(4), 55–64. Addison-Wesley.

Arvo, J. and Kirk, D. (1990) Particle transport and image synthesis, *Computer Graphics (ACM SIGGRAPH) Annual Conference Series*, 24(4), 63–66. Addison-Wesley.

Ascension, MotionStar (http://www.ascension-tech.com/)

Aserinsky, E. and Kleitman, N. (1953) Regularly occurring periods of eye motility, and concomitant phenomena, during sleep, *Science*, 118, 273–74.

Atherton, P.R., Weiler, K., and Greenberg, D. (1978) Polygon shadow generation, *Computer Graphics (ACM SIGGRAPH) Annual Conference Series*, (12), 275–81. Addison-Wesley.

Azuma, R.T. (1997) A survey of augmented reality, *Presence: Teleoperators and Virtual Environments*, 6(4).

Badler, N.I., Hollick, M., and Granieri, J. (1993) Real-time control of a virtual human using minimal sensors, *Presence: Teleoperators and Virtual Environments*, 2(1), 82–6.

Barfield, W. and Hendrix, C. (1995) The effect of update rate on the sense of presence within virtual environments, *Virtual Reality: The Journal of the Virtual Reality Society*, 1(1), 3–16.

Bartels, R.H., Beatty, J.C., and Barsky, B.A. (1987) *An Introduction to Splines for Use in Computer Graphics and Geometric Modeling*, Morgan Kaufmann Publishers, Inc., Los Altos, California.

Baum, D.R., Mann, S., Smith, K.P., and Winget, J.M. (1991) Making radiosity usable: Automatic preprocessing and meshing techniques for the generation of accurate radiosity solutions. In T.W. Sederberg (ed.), *ACM Computer Graphics*, vol. 25, 51–60.

Baumgart, B.G. (1974) Geometric modeling for computer vision. AIM-249, STA–CS-74-463, CS Dept, Stanford U.

Baumgart, B.G. (1975) A polyhedron representation for computer vision, IFIPS.

Bentley, J.L. (1975) Multidimensional binary search trees used for associative searching, *Communications of the ACM*, 18, 509–17.

Bergeron, P. (1986) A general version of Crow's shadow volumes, *IEEE CG&A*, 6(9), 17–28.

Bernardini, F., Klosowski, J.T., and El-Sana, J. (2000) Directional discretized occluders for accelerated occlusion culling, *Computer Graphics Forum*, 19(3).

Bier, E.A. (1990) Snap-dragging in three dimensions, *Proceedings of the 1990 Symposium on Interactive 3D Graphics*, in *Computer Graphics*, 24(2), 193–204.

Bishop, G. and Weimer, D.M. (1986) Fast Phong shading, *Computer Graphics (ACM SIGGRAPH) Annual Conference Series*, 20(4), 103–6. Addison-Wesley.

Bittner, J., Havran, V., and Slavik, P. (1998) Hierarchical visibility culling with occlusion trees. *Proceedings of Computer Graphics International '98*, pp. 207–19.

Blaxxun, http://www.blaxxun.com

Blinn, J.F. (1978) Simulation of wrinkled surfaces, *Computer Graphics (ACM SIGGRAPH) Annual Conference Series*, 12(3), 286–92. Addison-Wesley.

Blinn, J.F. (1988) Jim Blinn's corner: Me and my (fake) shadow, *IEEE Computer*, January, *Graphics and Applications*, 8(1), 82–6.

Blinn, J.F. (1991) A trip down the graphics pipeline – line clipping, *IEEE CG&A*, January, 11(1) 98–105.

Blinn, J.F. and Newell, M.E. (1976) Texture and reflection in computer generated images, *Communications of the ACM*, 19(10), October, 542–47.

Blinn, J.F. and Newell, M.E. (1978) Clipping using homogeneous coordinates, *Computer Graphics (ACM SIGGRAPH) Annual Conference Series*, 12, 245–51. Addison-Wesley.

Bouknight, W.J. (1970) A procedure for generation of three-dimensional half-toned computer graphics presentations, *Communications of the ACM*, 13(9), September, 527–36.

Bouknight, W.J. and Kelley, K. (1970) An algorithm for producing half-tone computer graphics presentations with shadows and movable light sources, *AFIPS Conf. Proc. 36*, 1–10.

Boulic, R., Rezzonico, S., and Thalmann, D. (1996) Multi finger manipulation of virtual objects, *Proc. of ACM Symposium on Virtual Reality Software and Technology VRST'96*, Hong-Kong, July.

Bresenham, J.E. (1965) Algorithm for computer control of digital plotter, *IBM System Journal*, 4(1), 25–30.

Bresenham, J.E. (1977) A linear algorithm for incremental digital display of circular arcs, *Communications of the ACM*, 20(2), 100–6.

Brooks, F.P. Jr (1986) Walkthrough – a dynamic graphics system for buildings, *Proc. 1986 ACM Workshop on Interactive 3D Graphics*, Chapel Hill, NC, October, pp. 9–21.

Brookshire Conner, D., Snibber, S.S., Herndon, K.P., Robbins, D.C., Zeleznik, R.C., and van Dam, A. (1992) Three-dimensional widgets, *Proc. 1992 Symposium on Interactive 3D Graphics*, in *Computer Graphics*, 25(2), pp. 183–88.

Brotman, L.S. and Badler, N.I. (1984) Generating soft shadows with a depth buffer algorithm, *IEEE Computer Graphics & Applications*, 4(10), 71–81.

Bruce, V. and Green, P.R. (1990) *Visual Perception*, 2nd edn, Lawrence Erlbaum Associates, East Sussex UK, ISBN 0-86377-146-7, reprinted in 1992.

Bui-Tong, Phong (1975) Illumination for computer-generated pictures, *Communications of the ACM*, 18(6), 311–17.

Buxton, W. (1986) There's more to interaction than meets the eye: some issues in manual input. In D.A. Norman and S.W. Draper, (eds) *User Centered System Design: Net Perspectives on Human-Computer Interaction*. Lawrence Erlbaum Associates, Hillsdale, New Jersey, pp. 319–37.

Camahort, E. and Fussell, D. (1999) A geometric study of light field representations. Technical Report TR-99-35, Department Of Computer Science, University of Texas at Austin.

Camahort, E., Lerios, A., and Fussell, D. (1998) Uniformly sampled light fields, *Rendering Techniques '98*, 117–30.

Campbell, A.T. (1991) Modelling global diffuse illumination for image synthesis. PhD Thesis, Department of Computer Science, University of Texas at Austin, December.

Campbell, A.T. and Fussell, D.S. (1990) Adaptive mesh generation for global illumination, *ACM Computer Graphics*, 24(4), 155–64.

Campbell, III, A.T. and Fussell, D.S. (1991) An analytic approach to illumination with area light sources. Technical Report R-91-25, Department of Computer Sciences, University of Texas at Austin.

Carey, R. and Bell, G. (1997) *The Annotated VRML97 Reference*, Addison Wesley Longman, Inc.

Carlbom, I. and Paciorek, J. (1978) Planar geometric projections and viewing transformations, *Computing Surveys*, 10(4), 465–502.

Catmull, E. (1974) A subdivision algorithm for computer display of curved surfaces. PhD Thesis, Report UTEC-CSc-74-133, Computer Science Department, University of Utah, Salt Lake City, UT.

Chai, J.-X., Tong, X., Chan, S.-C., and Shum, H.-Y. (2000) Plenoptic sampling, *Computer Graphics (ACM SIGGRAPH) Annual Conference Series*, 307–318. Addison-Wesley.

Chan, K.C. and Tan, S.T. (1988) Hierarchical structure to Winged Edge structure: a conversion algorithm, *The Visual Computer*, 4, 133–41.

Chapman, J., Calvert, T.W., and Dill, J. (1991) Spatio-temporal coherence in ray tracing, *Graphics Interface '91*, 101–108.

Chen, E. (1990) Incremental radiosity: an extension of progressive radiosity to an interactive image synthesis system, *Computer Graphics (ACM SIGGRAPH) Annual Conference Series*, 24(4), 135–44. Addison-Wesley.

Chen, M., Mountford, S.J., and Sellen, A. (1988) A study in interactive 3D rotation using 2D control devices, *Computer Graphics (ACM SIGGRAPH) Annual Conference Series*, August, 121–9, Addison-Wesley.

Chen, S.E. (1995) Quicktime VR – an image-based approach to virtual environment navigation, *Computer Graphics (ACM SIGGRAPH), Annual Conference Series*, 29–38. Addison-Wesley.

Chen, H. and Wang, W. (1996) The feudal priority algorithm on hidden-surface removal, *Computer Graphics (ACM SIGGRAPH) Annual Conference Series*, 55–64. Addison-Wesley.

Chen, S. and Williams, L. (1993) View interpolation for image synthesis. In *Computer Graphics (ACM SIGGRAPH) Annual Conference Series*, 279–288. Addison-Wesley.

Chen, S.E., Rushmeier, H.E., Miller, G., and Turner, D. (1991) A progressive multi-pass method for global illumination, *Computer Graphics (ACM SIGGRAPH) Annual Conference Series*, 25(4), 165–74. Addison-Wesley.

Chin, N. and Feiner, S. (1989) Near real-time shadow generation using BSP trees, *Computer Graphics*, 23(3), 99–106.

Chin, N. and Feiner, S. (1992) Fast object-precision shadow generation for area light sources using BSP trees. In *ACM Computer Graphics (Symp. on Interactive 3D Graphics)*, pp. 21–30.

Chrysanthou, Y. (1996) Shadow computation for 3D interaction and animation. PhD thesis, Queen Mary and Westfield College, University of London.

Chrysanthou, Y. (2001) Occlusion culling using tree collapsing. UCL Department of Computer Science, Research Note.

Chrysanthou, Y. and Slater, M. (1992) Dynamic changes to scenes represented as BSP trees. In A. Kilgour and L. Kjelldahl (eds) *Eurographics 92*, September, Blackwells, pp. 321–32.

Chrysanthou, Y. and Slater, M. (1995) Shadow volume BSP trees for fast computation of shadows in dynamic scenes, *Proc. ACM Symposium on Interactive 3D Graphics*, 45–50.

Chrysanthou, Y. and Slater, M. (1997) Incremental updates to scenes illuminated by area light sources. In J. Dorsey and Ph. Slusallek (eds) *Rendering Techniques '97*, pp. 103–14. Springer Computer Science.

Clark, J.H. (1976) Hierarchical geometric models for visible surface algorithms, *Communications of the ACM*, 19(10), 547–54.

Claussen, U. (1989) On reducing the phong shading method. In W. Hansmann, F.R.A. Hopgood and W. Strasser (eds) *Eurographics 89*, pp. 333–44 (North-Holland).

Cleary, J.G. and Wyvill, G. (1988) Analysis of an algorithm for fast ray tracing using uniform space subdivision, *The Visual Computer*, 4, 65–83.

Cohen, M.F. and Greenberg, D.P. (1985) The hemi-cube: a radiosity solution for complex environments, *Computer Graphics (ACM SIGGRAPH) Annual Conference Series*, 19(3), 31–40. Addison-Wesley.

Cohen, M.F., Greenberg, D.P., Immel, D.S., and Brock, P.J. (1986) An efficient radiosity approach for realistic image synthesis, *IEEE Computer Graphics and Applications*, 6(3), 26–35.

Cohen, M.F., Shenchang, Ec., Wallace, J.R., and Greenberg, D.P. (1988) A progressive refinement approach to fast radiosity image generation, *Computer Graphics (ACM SIGGRAPH) Annual Conference Series*, 22(4), 75–84. Addison-Wesley.

Cohen-Or, D., Fibich, G., Halperin, D., and Zadicario, E. (1998) Conservative visibility and strong occlusion for viewspace partitioning of densely occluded scenes, *Computer Graphics Forum*, 17(3), 243–54.

Cohen-Or, D., Chrysanthou, Y., Silva, C., and Drettakis, G. (2000) Visibility, problems, techniques and applications. *Computer Graphics (ACM SIGGRAPH) Annual Conference Series*, course notes. Addison-Wesley.

Cook, R.L., Porter, T., and Carpenter, L. (1984) Distributed ray tracing, *Computer Graphics (ACM SIGGRAPH) Annual Conference Series*, 18, 137–45. Addison-Wesley.

Coorg, S. and Teller, S. (1996) Temporally coherent conservative visibility. In *Proc. 12th Annu. ACM Sympos. Comput. Geom.*, pp. 78–87.

Coorg, S. and Teller, S. (April 1997) Real-time occlusion culling for models with large occluders. In *1997 Symposium on Interactive 3D Graphics*, pp. 83–90.

COVEN, The Collaborative Virtual Environment project, http://coven.lancs.ac.uk

Coxeter, H.S.M. (1973) *Regular Polytopes*, Dover Publications, New York.

Crocker, G.A. (1984) Invisibility coherence for faster scan-line hidden surface algorithms, *Computer Graphics (ACM SIGGRAPH) Annual Conference Series*, 18(3), 95–102. Addison-Wesley.

Crow, F. (1977) Shadow algorithms for computer graphics, *Computer Graphics (ACM SIGGRAPH) Annual Conference Series*, 11(2), 242–7. Addison-Wesley.

Cruz-Neira, C., Sandin, D.J., DeFanti, T.A., Kenyon, R.V., and Hart, J.C. (1992) The CAVE: audio visual experience automatic virtual environment, *Communications of the ACM*, 36(5), June, 65–72, ACM Press.

Cruz-Neira, C., Sandin, D.J., and DeFanti, T.A. (1993) Surround-screen projection-based virtual reality: the design and implementation of the CAVE, *Computer Graphics (ACM SIGGRAPH) Annual Conference Series*, 135–42. Addison-Wesley.

Cyrus, M. and Beck, J. (1978) Generalised two- and three-dimensional clipping, *Computers and Graphics*, 3(1), 23–8.

Darken, R.P., Cockayne, W.R., and Carmein, D. (1997) The omni-directional treadmill, a locomotion device for virtual worlds, *Proceedings of UIST '97*, Banff, Canada, October 14–17, 1997, pp. 213–221, ACM Press.

Darken, R.P., Allard, T., and Achille, L.B. (1999) Spatial orientation and wayfinding in large-scale virtual spaces II: guest editors' introduction to the special issue, *Presence: Teleoperators and Virtual Environments*, 8(6), iii–vi.

de Berg, M., van Kreveld, M., Overmars, M., and Schwarzkopf, O. (1997) *Computational Geometry: Algorithms and Applications*, Springer-Verlag, Berlin, Heidelberg, New York, ISBN 3-540-61270-X.

de Casteljau, P. (1986) *Shape Mathematics and CAD*, Kogan Page Ltd, London.

Dippe, M. and Swensen, J. (1984) An adaptive subdivision algorithm and parallel architecture for realistic image *Synthesis, Computer Graphics (SIGGRAPH)*, 18(3), 149–58.

Dorr, M. (1990) A new approach to parametric line clipping, *Computers and Graphics*, 14(3/4), 449–64.

Draper, J.V., Kaber, D.B., and Usher, J.M. (1998) Telepresence, *Human Factors*, 40(3), 354–75.

Drettakis, G. (1994) Structured sampling and reconstruction of illumination for image synthesis. PhD thesis, Department of Computer Science, University of Toronto.

Drettakis, G. and Fiume, E. (1994) A fast shadow algorithm for area light sources using backprojection, *Computer Graphics (ACM SIGGRAPH) Annual Conference Series*, 223–30. Addison-Wesley.

Durand, F., Drettakis, G., Thollot, J., and Puech, C. (2000) Conservative visibility preprocessing using extended projections, *Computer Graphics (ACM SIGGRAPH) Annual Conference Series*, 239–48. Addison-Wesley.

Duvanenko, V.J., Robbins, W.E., and Gyurcsik, R.S. (1990) Improving line segment clipping, *Dr Dobb's Journal of Software Tools*, 15(7), July, 36, 38, 40, 42, 44–5, 98, 100.

Edwards, B. (1999) *The New: Drawing on the Right Side of the Brain*, Jeremy P. Tarcher/Putnam, New York.

Ellis, S.R. (1991) Nature and origin of virtual environments: a bibliographic essay, *Computing Systems in Engineering*, 2(4), 321–47.

Ellis, S.R. (ed.) (1993) *Pictorial Communication in Virtual and Real Environments*, 2nd edn, Taylor and Francis Ltd, London, ISBN 0-74840-0082-6.

Ellis, S.R., Young, M.J., Adelstein, B.D., and Ehrlich, S.M. (1999) Discrimination of changes in latency during head movement. In *Proceedings of HCI '99*, Munich, pp. 1129–33.

Ellis, S.R., Adelstein, B.D., and Young, M.J. (2000) Studies and management of latency in virtual environments. In *Proc. 3rd International Conference on Human and Computer*, Aizu Uinversity, pp. 291–300.

Fakespace Inc., Pinch Glove (http://www.fakespace.com/products/pinch.html)

Fallon, N. and Chrysanthou, Y. (2001) Image space occlusion for urban scenes. UCL Department of Computer Science Research Note.

Farin, G.E. (1992) From conics to NURBS: a tutorial and survey, *IEEE CG&A*, September, 78–86.

Farin, G.E. (1996) *Curves and Surfaces for Computer-Aided Geometric Design: A Practical Guide* (4th edn) (Computer Science and Scientific Computing Series), Academic Press; ISBN: 0122490541.

Feynman, R.F., Leighton, R.B., and Sands, M. (1977) *The Feynmann Lectures on Physics*, Addison-Wesley Publishing Company, Reading, Mass. (sixth printing), ISBN 0-201-02116-1-P.

Foley, J.D., Wallace, V.L., and Chan, P. (1984) The human factors of computer graphics interaction techniques, *IEEE Computer Graphics and Applications*, November, 13–48.

Foley, J.D., van Dam, A., Feiner, S.K., and Hughes, J.F. (1990) *Computer Graphics: Principles and Practice*, 2nd edn, Addison-Wesley Publishing Company.

Freud, S. (1983) *The Interpretation of Dreams*, Avon; ISBN: 0380010003.

Fuchs, H., Kedem, Z.M., and Naylor, B.F. (1980) On visible surface generation by a priori tree structures, *Computer Graphics (ACM SIGGRAPH) Annual Conference Series*, 14(3), 124–33. Addion-Wesley.

Fuchs, H., Abram, G.D., and Grant, E.D. (1983) Near real-time shaded display of rigid objects, *Computer Graphics (ACM SIGGRAPH) Annual Conference Series*, 17(3), 65–72. Addison-Wesley.

Fujimoto, A., Tanaka, T., and Iwata, K. (1986) ARTS: Accelerated Ray-Tracing System, *IEEE CG&A*, 6(4), 16–26.

Fung, K.Y., Nicholl, T.M., and Dewdney, A.K. (1992) A run-length slice line drawing algorithm without division operations, *Eurographics 92, Computer Graphics Forum*, 11(3), Conference Issue, eds A. Kilgour and L. Kjelldahl, 267–277.

Funkhouser, T.A., and Séquin, C.H. (1993) Adaptive display algorithm for interactive frame rates during visualisation of complex virtual environments, Proceedings of SIGGRAPH '93. In *Computer Graphics (ACM SIGGRAPH) Annual Conference Series, 1993*, 247–254. Addison-Wesley.

Garland, M. and Heckbert, P.S. (1997) Surface simplification using quadric error metrics, *Computer Graphics (ACM SIGGRAPH) Annual Conference Series*, 209–216. Addison-Wesley.

Gatenby, N. (1995) Incorporating hierarchical radiosity into discontinuity meshing radiosity. PhD thesis, University of Manchester, Manchester, UK.

Gersho, A., and Gray, R. (1992) *Vector Quantization And Signal Compression*, Kluwer Academic Publishers.

Gibson, J.J. (1986) *The Ecological Approach to Visual Perception*, Lawrence Erlbaum Associations, Publishers, New Jersey.

Gibson, S. and Hubbold, R.J. (1997) Perceptually-driven radiosity, *Computer Graphics Forum*, 16(2), 129–40.

Gigus, Z. and Malik, J. (1990) Computing the aspect graph for the line drawings of polyhedral objects. *IEEE Trans. on Pattern Analysis and Machine Intelligence*, 12(2), 113–33.

Gigus, Z., Canny, J., and Seidel, R. (1991) Efficiently computing and representing aspect graphs of polyhedral objects. *IEEE Trans. on Pattern Analysis and Machine Intelligence*, 13(6), 542–51.

Glassner, A.S. (1984) Space subdivision for fast ray tracing, *IEEE Computer Graphics and Applications*, 4(10), 15–22.

Glassner, A.S. (ed.) (1989) *An Introduction to Ray Tracing*, Academic Press, San Diego, CA. ISBN 0-12-286160-4.

Glassner, A.S. (1995) *Principles of Digital Image Synthesis*, Vols 1–2, Morgan Kaufmann Publishers, San Francisco, California, ISBN 1-55860-276-3.

Goldman, R.N. (1990) Blossoming and knot insertion algorithms for B-spline curves, *Computer Aided Geometric Design*, 7, 69–81.

Goldsmith, J. and Salmon, J. (1987) Automatic creation of object hierarchy for ray tracing, *IEEE CG&A*, 7(5), 14–20.

Gomes, J. and Velho, L. (1997) *Image Processing for Computer Graphics*, Springer-Verlag, New York, ISBN 0-387-94854-6.

Goral, C., Torrance, K.E., and Greenberg, D. (1984) Modeling the interaction of light between diffuse surfaces, *Computer Graphics (ACM SIGGRAPH) Annual Conference Series*, 18(3), 213–22. Addison-Wesley.

Gordon, D. and Chen, S. (1991) Front-to-back display of BSP trees, *IEEE CG&A*, 11(5), 79–85.

Gortler, S., Grzeszczuk, R., Szeliski, R., and Cohen, M. (1996) The Lumigraph, *Computer Graphics (ACM SIGGRAPH) Annual Conference Series*, 43–52.

Gouraud, H. (1971) Continuous shading of curved surfaces, *IEEE Trans. on Computers*, C(20)–6, 623–629.

Greene, N., Kass, M., and Miller, G. (1993) Hierarchical Z-buffer visibility, *Computer Graphics (ACM SIGGRAPH) Annual Conference Series*, 20, 231–8. Addison-Wesley.

Gregory, R.L. (1998a) *Mirrors in Mind*, Penguin Books, London.

Gregory, R.L. (1998b) *Eye and Brain: The Psychology of Seeing*, 5th edn, Oxford University Press, ISBN 0 19 852412 9.

Gu, X., Gortler, S., and Cohen, M. (1997) Polyhedral geometry and the two-plane parameterization, *Eighth Eurographics Workshop on Rendering*, pp. 1–12.

Haeberli, P. and Akeley, K. (1990) The accumulation buffer: Hardware support for high-quality rendering. *Proc. Computer Graphics (ACM SIGGRAPH) Annual Conference Series*, 24(4), 309–18. Addison-Wesley.

Haines, E.A. and Greenberg, D.P. (1986) The Light Buffer: a shadow testing accelerator, *IEEE CG&A*, 6(9), 6–16.

Haines, E. and Wallace, J. (1991) Shaft culling for efficient ray-traced radiosity. In *Proc. Second Eurographics Workshop on Rendering* (Barceloha, Spain, May 1991), Eurographics, Springer Verlag. Also published in SIGGRAPH 91 course notes: Frontiers of Rendering.

Hall, R. (1989) *Illumination and Color in Computer Generated Imagery*, Springer-Verlag, New York, ISBN 3-540-06774-5.

Hall, R. (1999) Comparing spectral color computation methods, *IEEE Computer Graphics & Applications*, 19(4), July/August, 36–45.

H-Anim (1999), Humanoid Animation Specfcation, Version 1.1, http://ece.uwaterloo.ca/~h-anim/spec1.1/

Hanrahan, P., Saltzman, D., and Aupperle, L. (1991) A rapid hierarchical radiosity algorithm, *Computer Graphics (ACM SIGGRAPH) Annual Conference Series*, 25(4), 197–206. Addison-Wesley.

Hardt, S. and Teller, S. (1996) High-fidelity radiosity rendering at interactive rates, in *Proc. 7th Eurographics Rendering Workshop*, June, pp. 71–80.

Havran, V. and Bittner, J. (2000) LCTS: Ray shooting using longest common traversal sequences, *Computer Graphics Forum*, 19(3), 59–70 (Proceedings of EG 2000, Interlaken, Switzerland).

Hedley, D. (1998) Discontinuity meshing for complex environments. PhD thesis, Department of Computer Science, University of Bristol, August.

Heckbert, P.S. (1984) The mathematics of quadric surface rendering and SOID. 3-D Technical Memo No. 4, Three Dimensional Animation Systems Group, Computer Graphics Lab, New York Institute of Technology.

Heckbert, P.S. (1986) A survey of texture mapping, *IEEE CG&A*, 6(11), 56–67.

Heckbert, P.S. (1990) Adaptive radiosity textures for bidirectional ray tracing, *Computer Graphics (ACM SIGGRAPH) Annual Conference Series*, 24, 145–54. Addison-Wesley.

Heckbert, P. (1991) Simulating global illumination using adaptive meshing. PhD thesis, CS Division (EECS), University of California, Berkeley.

Heckbert, P. (1992a) Radiosity in flatland, Eurographics 1992, *Computer Graphics Forum*, 11(3), 181–92.

Heckbert, P. (1992b) Discontinuity meshing for radiosity, Third Eurographics Workshop on Rendering, Bristol, UK, May pp. 203–26.

Heidmann, T. (1991) Real shadows in real time, *IRIS Universe* (18), 28–31.

Held, R.M. and Durlach, N.I. (1992) Telepresence, *Presence: Teleoperators and Virtual Environments*, 1(1), 109–12.

Herf, M. and Heckbert, P. (1996) Fast soft shadows. In Technical Sketches, *Computer Graphics (ACM SIGGRAPH) Annual Conference Series*, p. 145. Addison-Wesley.

Hodges, L.F. and MacAllister, D.F. (1993) Computing stereo views, in D.F. McAllister (ed.) *Stereo Computer Graphics and Other True 3D Technologies*, Princeton University Press, New Jersey, ISBN 0-691-08741-5.

Hoggar, S.G. (1992) *Mathematics for Computer Graphics*, Cambridge University Press, ISBN 0521 375746.

Hoppe, H. (1996) Progressive meshes. In *Computer Graphics (ACM SIGGRAPH) Annual Conference Series*, pp. 99–108. Addison-Wesley.

Hudson, T., Manocha, D., Cohen, J., Lin, M., Hoff, K., and Zhang, H. (1997). Accelerated occlusion culling using shadow frusta. In *Proc. 13th International Annual Symposium on Computational Geometry (SCG–97)*, pp. 1–10, ACM Press, New York.

Hutchins, E.L., Hollan, J.D., and Norman, D.A. (1986) Direct manipulation interfaces. In D.A. Norman and S.W. Draper (eds) *User Centered System Design: New Perspectives on Human-Computer Interaction*, Lawrence Erlbaum Associates, Hillsdale, NJ, pp. 87–214.

Ihm, I., Park, S., and Lee, R.K. (1997) Rendering Of Spherical Light Fields, *Proc. Pacific Graphics 97*.

Immel, D.S., Cohen, M.F., and Greenberg, D.P. (1986) A radiosity method for non-diffuse environments, *Computer Graphics (ACM SIGGRAPH) Annual Conference Series*, 20(4), 133–42. Addison-Wesley.

Intersense, Intersense IS-900 (http://www.isense.com/)

Isaksen, A., McMillan, L., and Gortler, S.J. (2000) Dynamically reparameterized lightfields, *Computer Graphics (ACM SIGGRAPH) Annual Conference Series*, pp. 297–306. Addison-Wesley.

James, A. and Day, A.M. (1998) The priority face determination tree for hidden surface removal, *Computer Graphics Forum*, 17(1), 55–71.

Jansen, F. (1986) Data structures for ray tracing, in L. Kessener, F. Peters and M. van Lierop (eds) *Data Structures for Raster Graphics, Eurographics Seminar*, NY, Springer-Verlag, 57–73.

Jenkins, F.A. and White, H.E. (1981) *Fundamentals of Optics*, International Edition, McGraw-Hill, ISBN 0-07-085346-0.

Jensen, H.W. (1996) Global illumination using photon maps, *Rendering Techniques '96, Proc. 7th Eurographics Workshop on Rendering*, pp. 21–30.

Jensen, H.W. and Christensen, N.J. (1995) Photon maps in bidirectional Monte Carlo ray tracing of complex objects, *Computers & Graphics*, 19(2), 215–24.

Jensen, H.W. and Christensen, P.H. (1998) Efficient simulation of light transport in scenes with participating media using photon maps, *Computer Graphics (ACM SIGGRAPH) Annual Conference Series*, pp. 311–20. Addison-Wesley.

Kajiya, J.T. (1986) The rendering equation, *Computer Graphics (ACM SIGGRAPH) Annual Conference Series*, 20(4), 143–50. Addison-Wesley.

Kalawsky, R.S. (1993) *The Science of Virtual Reality and Virtual Environments*, Addison-Wesley.

Kaplan, M.R. (1985) Space-tracing, a constant time ray tracer, *Computer Graphics (ACM SIGGRAPH) Annual Conference Series*, State of the Art in Image Synthesis notes. Addison-Wesley.

Kaplan, M.R. (1987) The use of spatial coherence, in David F. Rogers and Rac A. Earnshaw (eds), *Ray Tracing Techniques for Computer Graphics*, Springer-Verlag, pp. 184–193.

Kaufman, A.E. (1996) Volume synthesis, in *Discrete Geometry for Computer Imagery*, 6th International Workshop, DGCI'06, Lyon, France, Proceedings, eds S. Miguet, A. Montanvert, S. Ubeda, Springer.

Kay, T.L. and Kajiya, J.T. (1986) Ray tracing complex scenes, *Computer Graphics (ACM SIGGRAPH) Annual Conference Series*, 20(4), 269–78. Addison-Wesley.

Keating, B. and Max, N. (1999) Shadow penumbras for complex objects by depth-dependent filtering of multi-layer depth images. In *Rendering Techniques '99 (Proc. of Eurographics Rendering Workshop)*, pp. 197–212, June. Springer Wein, Eurographics.

Kuipers, J.B. (1999) *Quaternians and Rotation Sequences*, Princeton University Press, New Jersey, ISBN 0-691-05872-5.

Kumar, S., Manocha, D., Garrett, W., and Lin, M. (1996) Hierarchical backface computation, *Eurographics Rendering Workshop*, pp. 235–44, Eurographics Springer Wein.

LaBerg, S. (1985) *Lucid Dreaming*, Ballantine Books, NY.

Lee, E.T.Y. (1989) A note on blossoming, *Computer Aided Geometric Design*, (6), 359–62.

Leibovic, K.N. (ed.) (1990) *Science of Vision*, Springer-Verlag, New York, ISBN 0-387-97270-6.

Levoy, M. and Hanrahan, P. (1996) Light field rendering, *Computer Graphics (ACM SIGGRAPH) Annual Conference Series*, 31–42. Addison-Wesley.

Liang, Y.-D. and Barsky, B.A. (1984) A new concept and method for line clipping, *ACM Transactions on Graphics*, 3(1), 1–22.

Liang, Y.-D. and B.A. Barsky (1990) An improved parametric line clipping algorithm, in E.F. Deprettere (ed.), *Algorithms and Parallel VLSI Architectures*, Elsevier Science Publishers, Amsterdam. Conference held 10–16 June 1990 in Pont-à-Mousson, France.

Lischinski, D., Tampieri, F., and Greenberg, D. (1992) Discontinuity meshing for accurate radiosity, *IEEE Computer Graphics and Applications*, 12(6), 25–39.

Loscos, C. and Drettakis, G. (1997) Interactive high-quality soft shadows in scenes with moving objects, in *Proc. Eurographics '97, Computer Graphics Forum (Conference Issue)*, 17(3), 219–230.

Luebke, D. and Georges, C. (1995) Portals and mirrors: Simple, fast evaluation of potentially visible sets. In P. Hanrahan and J. Winget (eds), *1995 Symposium on Interactive 3D Graphics*, pp. 105–6, ACM SIGGRAPH.

Maciel, P.W.C. and Shirley, P. (1995) Visual navigation of large environments using textured clusters, Symposium on Interactive 3D Techniques, *Proc. 1995 symposium on Interactive 3D graphics*, April 9–12, Monterey, CA, USA, pp. 95–102.

Mackinlay, J., Card, S.K., and Robertson, G.G. (1990) A semantic analysis of the design space of input devices, *Human–Computer Interaction*, Vol. 5, pp. 145–90, Lawrence Erlbaum Associates.

McAllister, D.F. (1993) *Stereo Computer Graphics and Other True 3d Technologies*, Princeton University Press.

McCool, M.D. (2000) Shadow volume reconstruction from depth maps, *ACM Transactions on Graphics*, 19(1), 1–26.

McMillan, L. and Bishop, G. (1995) Plenoptic modeling: an image-based rendering system, *Computer Graphics (ACM SIGGRAPH) Annual Conference Series*, Los Angeles, CA, August 6–11, 39–46.

Melzer, J.E. and Moffitt, K. (1996) *Head-Mounted Displays: Designing for the User*, McGraw-Hill.

Meyer, K., Applewhite, H.L., and Biocca, F.A. (1992) A survey of position trackers, *Presence: Teleoperators and Virtual Environments*, 1(2), 173–200.

Mine, M., Brooks, F.P. Jr, and Séquin, C. (1997) Moving objects in space: exploiting proprioception in virtual environment interaction, *Computer Graphics (ACM SIGGRAPH) Annual Conference Series*, Los Angeles, CA, ACM Press, 19–26. Addison-Wesley.

Minsky, M. (1980) Telepresence, *Omni*, June, 45–51.

Möller, T. (1997) A fast triangle–triangle intersection test, *Journal of Graphics Tools*, 2(2), 25–30.

Mortenson, M.E. (1985) *Geometric Modeling*, John Wiley & Sons.

Muller, H. and Winckler, J. (1992) Distributed image synthesis with breadth-first ray tracing and the ray-z-buffer, data structures and efficient algorithms. Final Report on the DFG Special Initiative, in B. Monien and T. Ottmann (eds), *Lecture Notes in Computer Science*, 594, 124–47, Springer-Verlag.

Nakamaru, K. and Ohno, Y. (1997) Breadth-first ray tracing utilizing uniform spatial subdivision, *IEEE Transactions on Visualization and Computer Graphics*, 3(4), 316–28.

Naylor, B. (1990) SCULPT: an interactive solid modeling tool, *Graphics Interface 90*, Morgan-Kaufmann Publishers, pp. 138–55.

Naylor, B.F. (1992) Partitioning tree image representation and generation from 3D geometric models. In *Proc. Graphics Interface '92*, pp. 201–12, Canadian Information Processing Society.

Naylor, B.F. (1993) Constructing good partitioning trees, in *Proc. Graphics Interface '93*, pp. 181–91.

Naylor, B., Amantides, J., and Thibault, W. (1990) Merging BSP trees yields polyhedral set operations, *Computer Graphics (ACM SIGGRAPH) Annual Conference Series*, 24(4), 115–24. Addison-Wesley.

Neider, J., Davis, T., and Woo, M. (1993) *OpenGL Programming Guide: The Official Guide to Learning OpenGL, Release 1*, Addison-Wesley Publishing Company.

Newell, M.E., Newell, R.G., and Sancha, T.L. (1972) A solution to the hidden surface problem, *Proc. ACM National Conference*, pp. 443–50, ACM.

Newman, W.M. and Sproull, R.F. (1979) *Principles of Interactive Computer Graphics*, 2nd edn, McGraw-Hill.

Nicholl, R.A. and Nicholl, T.N. (1990) Performing geometric transformations by program transformation, *ACM Transactions on Graphics*, 9(1), 28–40.

Nicholl, T.M., Lee, D.T., and Nicholl, R.A. (1987) An efficient new algorithm for 2-D line clipping: its development and analysis, *Computer Graphics (ACM SIGGRAPH) Annual Conference Series*, 21(4), 253–62. Addison-Wesley.

Nielsen, G.M. and Olsen, D.R. Jr (1986) Direct manipulation for 3D objects using 2D locator devices, *Proc. 1986 Workshop on Interactive 3D Graphics*, Chapel Hill, NC, USA, October 23–24, pp. 175–82, ACM Press.

Nishita, T. and Nakamae, E. (1983) Half-tone representation of 3-D objects illuminated by area sources or polyhedron sources, *Proc. COMPSAC 83: The IEEE Computer Society's Seventh Internat. Computer Software and Applications Conf.*, pp. 237–42, IEEE.

Ohta, M. and Maekawa, M. (1987) Ray coherence theorem and constant time ray tracing algorithm, *Computer Graphics 1987* (Proc. CG International '87), pp. 303–314, Springer Verlag.

Oliveira, J. and Buxton, B. (2001) Lightweight virtual humans, *Proc. EUROGRAPHICS-UK 2001*, University College London, March.

OpenGL Achitecture Review Board (1992) *OpenGL Reference Manuel: The Official Reference Document for OpenGL, Release 1*, Addison-Wesley Publishing Company.

Paterson, M.S. and Yao, F.F. (1989) Binary partitions with applications to hidden surface removal and solid modeling, in *Proc. 5th Annual ACM Symposium on Computational Geometry*, pp. 23–32, ACM.

Paterson, M.S. and Yao, F.F. (1990) Optimal binary space partitions for orthogonal objects, *Discrete Computational Geometry*, (5), 485–503.

Perlin, K., Paxia, S., and Kollin, J.S. (2000) An autostereoscopic display, *Computer Graphics (ACM SIGGRAPH) Annual Conference Series*, 319–326. Addison-Wesley.

Pertaub, D.-P., Slater, M., and Barker, C. (2001) An experiment on public speaking anxiety in response to three different types of virtual audience, *Presence: Teleoperators and Virtual Environments*, MIT Press, in press.

Phillips, C.B., Badler, N.I., and Granieri, J. (1992) Automatic viewing control for 3D direct manipulation, Proc. 1992 Symposium on Interactive 3D Graphics, in *Computer Graphics*, 25(2), 71–4.

Pineda, J. (1988) A parallel algorithm for polygon rasterization, *Computer Graphics*, 22(4), 17–20.

Pitteway, M.L.V. (1967) Algorithm for drawing ellipses or hyperbolae with a digital plotter, *Computer Journal*, 10(3), 282–289.

Polhemus Inc. 3SPACE Fastrak and 3BALL (http://www.polhemus.com/)

Popescu, V., Eyles, J., Lastra, A., Steinhurst, J., England, N. and Nyland, L. (2000) The WarpEngine: an architecture for the post-polygonal age, *Computer Graphics (ACM SIGGRAPH) Annual Conference Series*, 433–42. Addison-Wesley.

Preparata, F.P. and Shamos, M.I. (1985) *Computational Geometry: An Introduction*, Texts and Monographs in Computer Science, Springer, New York.

Puerta, A.M. (1989) The power of shadows: shadow stereopsis, *Journal of the Optical Society of America*, 6, 309–11.

Ramshaw, L. (1987a) Blossoming: a connect the dots approach to splines, Digital Systems Research Center, 130 Lytton Avenue, Palo Alto, California 94301.

Ramshaw, L. (1987b) Beziers and B-splines as multiaffine maps, *Theoretical Foundations of Computer Graphics and CAD, Proc. NATO International Advanced Study Institute*, ed. R.A. Earnshaw, pp. 757–76, Springer-Verlag.

Ramshaw, L. (1989) Blossoms are polar forms, *Computer Aided Geometric Design*, 6, 323–358.

Rappaport, A. (1991a) An efficient algorithm for line and polygon clipping, *The Visual Computer*, 7(1), 19–28.

Rappaport, A. (1991b) Rendering curves and surfaces with hybrid subdivision and forward differencing, *ACM Transactions on Graphics*, 10(4), October, 323–341.

Reeves, W.T., Salesin, D.H., and Cook, R.L. (1987) Rendering antialiased shadows with depth maps, *Computer Graphics (ACM SIGGRAPH) Annual Conference Series*, 21, 283–91. Addison-Wesley.

Robinett, W. and Holloway, R. (1992) Implementation of flying, scaling and grabbing in virtual worlds, *Proc. 1992 Symposium on Interactive 3D Graphics*, March 29–April 1, Cambridge, MA, ACM, pp. 189–192.

Robinett, W. and Rolland, J.P. (1992) A computational model for the stereoscopic optic of a head-mounted display, *Presence: Teleoperators and Virtual Environments*, 1(1), 45–62.

Rokne, J.G. and Rao, Y. (1992) Double-step incremental linear interpolation, *ACM Transactions on Graphics*, 11(2), 183–92.

Rokne, J.G. and Wyvill, B. (1990) Fast line scan-conversion, *ACM Transactions on Graphics*, 9(4), 376–88.

Rohlf, J. and Helman, J. (1994) IRIS Performer: a high performance multiprocessing toolkit for real-time 3D graphics, *Computer Graphics (ACM SIGGRAPH) Annual Conference Series*, 381–394. Addison-Wesley.

Roth, S.D. (1982) Ray casting for modeling solids, *Computer Graphics and Image Processing*, 18, 109–44.

Rothbaum, B.O., Hodges, L.F., Kooper, R., Opdyke, D., Williford, J., and North, M.M. (1995) Effectiveness of computer-generated (virtual reality) graded exposure in the treatment of acrophobia, *American Journal of Psychiatry*, 152, 626–8.

Sacks, O.W. (1998) *The Man Who Mistook His Wife for a Hat: And Other Clinical Tales*, Touchstone Books, ISBN: 0684853949.

Sadagic, A. and Slater, M. (2000) Dynamic polygon visibility ordering for head-slaved viewing in virtual environments, *Computer Graphics Forum*, 19(2), 111–22.

Salesin, D. and Stofi, J. (1990) Rendering CSG models with a ZZ-Buffer, *Computer Graphics*, 24(4), 67–76.

Samet, H. (1990) *The Design and Analysis of Spatial Data Structures*, Addison-Wesley, Reading, MA.

Schaufler, G. (1995) Dynamically generated impostors, in D.W. Fellner (ed.) *GI Workshop: Modeling – Virtual Worlds – Distributed Graphics*, infix Verlag, November, 129–35.

Schaufler, G. (1996) Exploiting frame to frame coherence in a virtual reality system, *VRAIS '96*, Santa Clara, California, April 1996, pp. 95–102.

Schaufler, G., Dorsey, J., Decoret, X., and Sillion, F.X. (2000) Conservative volumetric visibility with occluder fusion, *Computer Graphics (ACM SIGGRAPH) Annual Conference Series*, pp. 229–38. Addison-Wesley, ISBN 1-58113-208-5.

Schumacker, R., Brand, B., Gilliland, M., and Sharp, W. (1969) Study for applying computer-generated images to visual simulation. Technical Report AFHRL-TR-69-14, NTIS AD700375, U.S. Air Force Human Resources Lab., Air Force Systems Command, Brooks AFB, TX.

Scott, N., Olsen, D. and Gannet, E. (1998) An Overview of the VISUALIZE fx Graphics Accelerator Hardware, *The Hewlett-Packard Journal*, May, 28–34.

Segal, M., Korobkin, C., Van Widenfelt, R., Foran, J., and Haeberli, P. (1992) Fast shadow and lighting effects using texture mapping, *Computer Graphics (ACM SIGGRAPH) Annual Conference Series*, 26(2), 249–52. Addison-Wesley.

Seidel, H.-P. (1989) A new multiaffine approach to B-splines, *Computer Aided Geometric Design*, 6, 23–32.

Seitz, S. and Kutulakos, K. (1998) Plenoptic image editing, in *Proc. Sixth Int. Conf. on Computer Vision*, pp. 17–24.

Shade, J., Lischinski, D., Salesin, D.H., DeRose, T. and Snyder, J. (1996) Hierarchical image caching for accelerated walkthroughs of complex environments, *Computer Graphics (ACM SIGGRAPH) Annual Conference Series*, 75–82. Addison-Wesley.

Shi, K.K., Edwards J.A., and Cooper D.C. (1990) An efficient line clipping algorithm, *Computers and Graphics*, 14(2), 297–301.

Shirley, P. (2000) *Realistic Ray Tracing*, A.K. Peters Ltd, ISBN: 1568811101.

Shirley, P., Wade, B., Zareski, D., Hubbard, P., Walter, B., and Greenberg, D.P. (1995) Global illumination via density estimation, *Proc. Sixth Eurographics Workshop on Rendering*, June, pp. 187–99.

Shue-Ling Lien, Shantz, M., and Pratt, V. (1987) Adaptive forward differencing for rendering curves and surfaces, *Computer Graphics*, 21(4), 111–17.

Singhal, S. and Zyda, M. (1999) *Networked Virtual Environments: Design and Implementation*, Addison-Wesley Publishing Co., ISBN: 0201325578.

Skala, V. (1989) Algorithms for 2D line clipping, *New Advances in Computer Graphics, Proc. of CG International 89*, pp. 121–8, eds R.A. Earnshaw and B. Wyvill, Springer-Verlag, Tokyo, Japan.

Slater, M. (1992a) A comparison of three shadow volume algorithms, *The Visual Computer*, 9(1), 25–38.

Slater, M. (1992b) Tracing a ray through uniformly subdivided n-dimensional space, *The Visual Computer*, 9(1), 39–46.

Slater, M. and Barsky, B. (1994) 2D line and polygon clipping based on space subdivision, *The Visual Computer*, 10(7), 407–22.

Slater, M. and Chrysanthou, Y. (1996) View volume culling using a probabilistic cashing scheme, in S. Wilbur and M. Bergamasco (eds), *Proceedings of Framework for Immersive Virtual Environments (FIVE)*, ACM Symposium on Virtual Reality Software and Technology, ACM Press.

Slater, M. and Steed, A. (2000) A virtual presence counter, *Presence: Teleoperators and Virtual Environments*, 9(5), 413–34.

Slater, M. and Usoh, M. (1994) Body centered interaction in immersive virtual environments, in M. Magnenat-Thalman and D. Thalman (eds), *Virtual Reality and Arti-ficial Life*, John Wiley.

Slater, M. and Wilbur, S. (1997) A Framework for Immersive Virtual Environments (FIVE): speculations on the role of presence in virtual environments, *Presence: Teleoperators and Virtual Environments*, 6(6), 603–16.

Sloan, P.-P., Cohen, M.F., and Gortler, S.J. (1997) Time critical lumigraph rendering, *ACM Symposium on Interactive 3D Graphics*, pp. 17–23, ACM SIGGRAPH.

Sobkow, M.S., Pospilsil, P., and Yang, Y.-H. (1987) A fast two-dimensional line clipping algorithm via line encoding, *Computers and Graphics*, 11(4), 459–67.

Soler, C. and Sillion, F.X. (1998) Fast calculation of soft shadow textures using convolution, *Computer Graphics (ACM SIGGRAPH) Annual Conference Series*, 321–32.

Sony, Glasstron (http://www.sony.com)

Stark, L.W. (1995) How virtual reality works: The illusions of vision in "real" and virtual environments, *SPIE Proceedings: Symposium on Electronic Imaging: Science and Technology*, Feb. 5–10, San Jose, California.

Stark, L.W. and Choi, Y.S. (1996) Experimental metaphysics: the scanpath as an epistemological mechanism, in W.H. Zangemeister, H.S. Stiehl and C. Freksa (eds), *Visual Attention and Cognition*, Elsevier Science, B.V., Ch. 2.

Stark, L.W., Privitera, C.M., Yang, H., Azzariti, M., Ho, Y.F., Blackmon, T., and Chernyak, D. (2001) *Representation of Human Vision in the Brain: How Does Human Perception Recognise Images? Journal of Electronic Imaging (Special Issue on Human Vision)*, 10(1), 123–51.

Steed, A.J., Slater, M., Sadagic, A., Tromp, J., and Bullock, A. (1999) Leadership and collaboration in virtual environments, *IEEE Virtual Reality*, Houston, March, IEEE Computer Society, ISBN 0-7695-0093-5, pp. 112–15.

Stewart, A.J. and Ghali, S. (1994) Fast computation of shadow boundaries using spatial coherence and backprojections. In A. Glassner (ed.) *Computer Graphics (ACM SIGGRAPH) Annual Conference Series*, pp. 231–38. Addison-Wesley.

Stiles, W.S. and Burch, J.M. (1955) Interim report to the Commission Internationale de l'Éclairage Zurich, 1955, on the National Physical Laboratory's investigation of colour-matching (1955) with an appendix by W.S. Stiles and J.M. Burch. *Optica Acta*, 2, 168–81.

Stiles, W.S. and Burch, J.M. (1959) NPL colour-matching investigation: Final report. *Optica Acta*, 6, 1–26.

Stiles, R., Tewari, S., and Mehta, M. (1997) Adapting VMRL2.0 for Immersive User, *Proc. VRML97 Symposium*, February 24–28, Monterey, CA, ACM SIGGRAPH.

Stockman, A. and Sharpe, L.T. (2000) Spectral sensitivities of the middle- and long-wavelength sensitive cones derived from measurements in observers of known genotype, *Vision Research*, 40, 1711–37.

Sutherland, I.E. (1963) Sketchpad: a man–machine graphical communication system, *Proc. pring Joint Computer Conference*, Spartan Books, Baltimore.

Sutherland, I.E. (1965) A head-mounted three-dimensional display, *AFIPS Conference Proceedings*, Vol. 33, Part I, 1968, pp. 757–64.

Sutherland, I.E. and Hodgman, G.W. (1974) Reentrant polygon clipping, *Communications of the ACM*, 17(1), 32–42.

Sutherland, I.E., Sproull, R.F., and Schumacher, R.A. (1974) A characterization of ten hidden-surface algorithms, *ACM Computing Surveys*, 6(1), 1–55.

Tampieri, F. (1993) Discontinuity meshing for radiosity image synthesis. Ph.D. thesis, Cornell University, Ithaca, NY.

Tecchia, F. and Chrysanthou, Y. (2000) Real-time rendering of densely populated urban environments, Eurographics Rendering Workshop 2000, Brno, Czech Republic, pp. 83–8, Eurographics.

Teller, S.J. and Séquin, C.H. (1991) Visibility preprocessing for interactive walkthroughs, *Computer Graphics (ACM SIGGRAPH) Annual Conference Series*, 25(4), 61–9. Addison-Wesley.

Teller, S.J. (1992) Computing the antipenumbra of an area light source. In E.E. Catmull (ed.) *ACM Computer Graphics*, vol. 26, pp. 139–48.

Teller, S., Bala, K., and Dorsey, J. (1996) Conservative radiance interpolants for ray tracing, *Rendering Techniques '96, Proceedings of the Eurographics Workshop* in Porto, Portugal, June 17–19, X. Pueyo and P. Schroder (eds), Springer, pp. 257–68.

Thomas, F. and Johnston, O. (1981) *Disney Animation: The Illusion of Life*, Aberville Press Publishers, New York.

Thibault, W.C., and Naylor, B.F. (1987) Set operations on polyhedra using binary space partition trees, *Computer Graphics (ACM SIGGRAPH) Annual Conference Series*, 21(4), 153–62. Addison-Wesley.

Tilove, R.B. (1981) Line/polygon classification: a study of the complexity of geometrical classication, *IEEE Computer Graphics and Applications*, April, 75–86.

Torres, E. (1990) Optimization of the binary space partition algorithm (BSP) for the visualization of dynamic scenes, C.E. Vandoni and D.A. Duce (eds), *Eurographics 90*, Elsevier Science Publishers B.V., North-Holland, pp. 507–18.

Usoh, M., Arthur, K., Whitton, M., Bastos, R., Steed, A.J., Slater, M., and Brooks, F. (1999) Walking > Walking-in-Place > Flying, in *Virtual Environments, Computer Graphics (ACM SIGGRAPH) Annual Conference Series*, 359–364. Addison-Wesley.

Usoh, M., Catena, E., Arman, S., and Slater, M. (2000) Presence questionnaires in reality, *Presence: Teleoperators and Virtual Environments*, 497–503.

VRML (1997) ISO/IEC (1997) ISO/IEC 14772 Virtual Reality Modeling Language (VRML97).

Wald, I., Slusallek, P. and Benthin, C. (2001) Interactive Distributed Ray Tracing of Highly Complex Models, Rendering Techniques 2001 *Proceedings of the 12th Eurographics Workshop on Rendering*, eds S.J. Gortler and K. Kyszkowski, London 25–27 June 2001, 274–85.

Wallace, J.R., Cohen, M.F., and Greenberg, D.P. (1987) A two-pass solution to the rendering equation: a synthesis of ray tracing and radiosity methods, *Computer Graphics (ACM SIGGRAPH) Annual Conference Series*, pp. 311–20. Addison-Wesley.

Wallace, J.R., Elmquist, K.A., and Haines, E. (1989) A ray tracing algorithm for progressive radiosity, *Computer Graphics (ACM SIGGRAPH) Annual Conference Series*, 23(3), 315–23. Addison-Wesley.

Walter, B., Hubbard, P.M., Shirley, P., and Greenberg, D.P. (1997) Global illumination using local linear density estimation, *ACM Transactions on Graphics*, 16(3), 217–59.

Ward, G.J., Rubinstein, F.M., and Clear, R.D. (1988) A ray tracing solution for diffuse interreflection, *Proc. 15th annual conference on Computer graphics*, ACM, August 1–5, Atlanta, GA, USA, pp. 85–92.

Ward, G.J. and Heckbert, P.S. (1992) Irradiance gradients, in A. Chalmers and D. Paddon (eds), *Third EUROGRAPHICS Workshop on Rendering*, Bristol, pp. 85–98.

Ward-Larson, G. and Shakespeare, R. (1997) *Rendering with Radiance: The Art and Science of Lighting Visualization*, Morgan Kaufmann Publishers, San Francisco, CA, ISBN-1-55860-499-5.

Ware, C. and Arthur, K. *et al.* (1993) Fish tank virtual reality, *Proc. Inter-CHI 93 Conference on Human Factors in Computing Systems*, pp. 37–42.

Ware, C. and Jessome, D.R. (1988) Using the bat: a six-dimensional mouse for object placement, *IEEE Computer Graphics and Applications*, November, 8, 65–70.

Ware, C. and Osborne, S. (1990) Exploration and virtual camera control in virtual three dimensional environments. *Proc. 1990 ACM Symposium on Interactive 3D Graphics*, ACM Press.

Ware, C. and Slipp, L. (1991) Using velocity control to navigate 3D graphical interfaces: a comparison of three interfaces, *Proc. Human Factors Society 35th Annual Meeting*, San Francisco, September, pp. 300–4. Human Factors Society.

Warnock, J.E. (1969) A hidden-surface algorithm for computer generated half-tone pictures. University of Utah Computer Science Department, TR 4–15, NTIS AD-753 671.

Watkins, G.S. (1970) A real-time visible surface algorithm. PhD Thesis, University of Utah Computer Science Department Technical Report, UTEC-CSC-7-101.

Watt, A.H. and Watt, M. (1992) *Advanced Animation and Rendering Techniques: Theory and Practice*, Addison-Wesley Publishing Co., ISBN: 0201544121.

Weiler, K. (1980) Polygon comparison using a graph representation, *Computer Graphics (ACM SIGGRAPH) Annual Conference Series*, 14(4), 10–18. Addison-Wesley.

Weiler, K. and Atherton, P. (1977) Hidden surface removal using polygon area sorting, *Computer Graphics (ACM SIGGRAPH) Annual Conference Series*, 11(2), 214–22. Addison-Wesley.

Welch, G., Bishop, G., Vicci, L., Brumback, S., Keller, K., and Colucci, D. (2001) High-performance wide-area optical tracking – the HiBall tracking system, *Presence: Teleoperators and Virtual Environments*, 10(1), in press.

Wenzel, E.M. (1992) Localization in virtual acoustic displays, *Presence: Teleoperators and Virtual Environments*, 1(1), 80–102.

Wernecke, J. (1994) *The Inventor Mentor: Programming Object-Oriented 3d Graphics with Open Inventor*, Addison Wesley.

Whitted, T. (1980) An improved illumination model for shaded display, *Communications of the ACM*, 23(6), 343–9.

Williams, L. (1978) Casting curved shadows on curved surfaces, *Computer Graphics*, 12, 270–4.

Witmer, B.G. and Singer, M.J. (1998) Measuring presence in virtual environments: a presence questionnaire, *Presence: Teleoperators and Virtual Environments*, 7(3), 225–40.

Wonka, P. and Schmalstieg, D. (1999) Occluder shadows for fast walkthroughs of urban environments. In H.-P. Seidel and S. Coquillart (eds) *Computer Graphics Forum*, vol. 18, Eurographics Association and Blackwell Publishers Ltd, pp. C51–C60.

Woo, A., Poulin, P., and Fourier, A. (1990) A survey of shadow algorithms, *IEEE CG&A*, 10(6), 13–31.

Woo, M., Neider, J., Davis, T., and Shreiner, D. (1999) *OpenGL Programming Guide*, 3rd edn, Addison-Wesley.

Wood, D.N., Azuma, D.I, Aldinger, K., Curless, B., Duchamp, T., Salesin, D.H., and Stuetzle, W. (2000) Surface light fields for 3D photography, *Computer Graphics (ACM SIGGRAPH) Annual Conference Series*, 287–96. Addison-Wesley.

Worrall, A., Willis, C., and Paddon, D. (1995) Dynamic discontinuities for radiosity. In *Edugraphics + Compugraphics Proceedings*, pp. 367–75, P.O. Box 4076, Massama, 2745 Queluz, Portugal, December.

Worrall, A., Hedley, D., and Paddon, D. (1998) Interactive animation of soft shadows, in *Proc. Computer Animation 1998*, IEEE Computer Society, June, pp. 88–94.

Wylie, C., Romney, G.W., Evans, D.C., and Erdahl, A.C. (1967) *Halftone Perspective Drawings by Computer*, FJCC 67, Thompson Books, Washington DC, pp. 49–58.

Yagel, R., Cohen, D., and Kaufman, A. (1992) Discrete ray tracing, *IEEE Computer Graphics and Applications*, 12(5), 19–28.

Zhang, H., Manocha, D., Hudson, T., and Hoff III, K.E. (1997) Visibility culling using hierarchical occlusion maps, in T. Whitted (ed.), *Computer Graphics (ACM SIGGRAPH) Annual Conference Series*, pp. 77–88, Addison-Wesley.

Zimmerman, T.G., Lanier, J., Blanchard, C., Bryson, S. and Harvill, Y. (1987) A hand gesture interface device, *Proc. CHI+GI'87*, pp. 189–92, ACM Press.

Index